VOICES
of ANCIENT
PHILOSOPHY

VOICES OF ANCIENT PHILOSOPHY

An Introductory Reader

Julia Annas

University of Arizona

New York   Oxford

OXFORD UNIVERSITY PRESS

2001

Oxford University Press

Oxford   New York
Athens   Auckland   Bangkok   Bogotá   Buenos Aires   Calcutta
Cape Town   Chennai   Dar es Salaam   Delhi   Florence   Hong Kong   Istanbul
Karachi   Kuala Lumpur   Madrid   Melbourne   Mexico City   Mumbai
Nairobi   Paris   São Paulo   Singapore   Taipei   Tokyo   Toronto   Warsaw

and associated companies in
Berlin   Ibadan

Copyright © 2001 by Oxford University Press, Inc.

Published by Oxford University Press, Inc.
198 Madison Avenue, New York, New York, 10016
http://www.oup-usa.org

Oxford is a registered trademark of Oxford University Press

Library of Congress Cataloging-in-Publication Data
Voices of ancient philosophy : an introductory reader / [edited by] Julia Annas.
    p. cm.
  ISBN 0-19-512694-7 (alk. paper) — ISBN 0-19-512695-5 (pbk. : alk. paper)
  1. Philosophy, Ancient. I. Annas, Julia.
  B162.9.V65 2000
  180—dc21

                                                              00-020531

Printing (last digit): 10 9 8 7 6 5 4 3 2 1

Printed in the United States of America
on acid-free paper.

Contents

List of Boxed Material

Preface

It may seem presumptuous to produce a book of readings for teaching ancient philosophy at an introductory level, when I have not used such books myself. My excuse is that none of the available books gave a selection that reflected the nature of ancient philosophy as I wanted to get it across. Over the years, I have tried, like most of my colleagues, a variety of ways of teaching such courses, and this book is the result of my efforts. As the Introduction makes clear, it has no pretensions to being comprehensive; the idea is to present teachers with a range of readings that will enable them to vary their syllabi but still introduce students to central philosophers and issues in the huge ancient tradition. If the book has any success, I hope that feedback and criticisms can improve it. Its differences from traditional collections of readings are obvious, and teachers who are used to these collections may easily find much to criticize, but I hope they will also find much that is stimulating and interesting.

I am grateful to Robert Miller, of Oxford University Press USA, for his encouragement in this project, which, of course, turned out to take far longer than I had envisaged. I am also grateful to Elissa Morris for help with permissions. Above all, I am grateful to the students who responded to the material presented here and helped me learn how to teach it over the years.

As ever, my biggest debt is to my husband, David Owen, and to our daughter Laura Owen.

Introduction

This introduction to ancient philosophy brings the reader into ancient debates about a number of problems, rather than taking him or her through a selection of the works of some great ancient thinkers in chronological order. This book does not impose a single narrative on the teacher and student, not just because we are now suspicious of these narratives, but mainly because a single authoritative narrative, particularly one that takes the student past a selection of Great Thinkers, is false to the spirit of ancient philosophy itself. Philosophy in the ancient world was typically characterized by discussion and debate, and by an awareness of alternative points of view on matters of importance. Throughout its long history, from the emergence of grand speculations in the sixth century B.C. to the end of the professional teaching schools of philosophy under the Christian Roman emperors, ancient philosophy is characterized by argument—argument in the sense of reasoned disagreement and sometimes also in the sense of contentious opposition. Philosophers in organized philosophical schools taught a variety of theories; ordinary people, then as now, were aware that philosophical issues were disputed and that on any issue they would find a more or less developed discussion.

Some readers may prefer the greater security that comes from proceeding in an orderly chronological way; some may miss being able to study a single philosopher in depth, bringing together views on different topics and being able to set them in a historical and social background. In an introductory course, however, the amount of historical background that can be provided is not great anyway. Furthermore, it is now easier than ever before to go on to read more of the works of particular philosophers. I have provided brief suggestions for further reading in the major areas of ancient philosophy, to help the reader who would like to read more Plato, more Epicurus, more about major thinkers and debates.

Following ancient dicussions can kindle intellectual excitement that is missing if ancient philosophy is presented in terms of a few Great Thinkers. If we read Plato's *Republic,* we find that Plato opposes social-contract theories of the state by means of his example of the Ring of Gyges. But we don't so often find out that Epicurus later rejected the Ring of Gyges argument and put forward his own social contract theory that was meant to withstand Plato's kind of objection. We may learn about Plato's theory of Forms as though it were an obvious, standard kind of ancient metaphysical theory—not noticing the many different kinds of objection it produced. If we find in the *Republic* that Plato thinks that experts are entitled to rule, we may miss the fact that this idea is argued for not in the *Republic*, but in Plato's later dialogue the *Statesman*, and that Aristotle responds to these arguments in his *Politics*. Plato's argument that Protagoras' relativism undermines itself is similar in form to Epicurus' argument that the determinist undermines himself. Too exclusive a focus on Plato and Aristotle and on their major works can isolate their ideas from the continuing ancient debates they were part of and that continued after them.

Indeed, if we focus primarily on Plato and Aristotle, we may miss some ancient philosophical debates completely, such as the issue of fate, freedom, and determinism. We may think that their views were more dominant in ancient philosophy than they were—for many centuries Stoic and Epicurean positions were as important, or even more important, for most people. And if we focus only on those philosophers who have been singled out as Great Thinkers, we will miss the contributions made by others—the ancient medical writers, satirists, Jewish and Christian writers with a philosophical education, historians, and others. We will also miss connections that may light up issues for us— as, for example, in this book I put together two responses to the idea that God may know what we are going to do, so that our future is already fixed—one pagan and one Christian.

This book obviously reflects my own views on what topics are interesting and my views on what topics are best for an introduction to ancient philosophy. (Aristotle's views on form and substance in the central books of his *Metaphysics*, for example, are important for any deep understanding of his thought, but I remain convinced that they are too difficult to be part of a good introduction to ancient philosophy; the same goes for some other important views.) Teachers will find many familiar "golden oldies" here, though perhaps not in a familiar context. Some texts are likely always to be central to any reasonable introduction to ancient philosophy. I hope that teachers may find that a new context for these and other texts brings or keeps them alive and that students find themselves involved in the issues and motivated to pursue them further.

Obviously, these selections have no claim to be exhaustive or to cover all the major issues in ancient philosophy. By providing six sections, I hope to have enabled teachers to make different selections in different semesters and to develop their own interests. The comments on the texts are intended to help the reader without being too directive; a commentary that is too coercive is not helpful to students and is likely to be resented by teachers who disagree with it. This aim has been difficult to fulfill, and I expect that students and teachers may sometimes find that the commentary is too sparse or too full; I hope that they will bear in mind the aim of engaging readers, both students and teachers, in the ongoing discussions of ancient philosophy.

If the effect of the book is kaleidoscopic, I think that is appropriate. Ancient philosophy has a long and varied history and takes many forms. We find questions discussed in a diversity of styles and from a variety of perspectives. There are many traditions to follow up and many interesting philosophers to read further in. If this book conveys a fraction of the interest and joy I have got from studying the varieties of ancient philosophy, it will have done well.

To orient the user of the book, I have provided a short chronological outline of the main currents of ancient philosophy, a time line, and a list of references to the pages where particular philosophers are introduced.

Chronological Sketch of Ancient Philosophy

Sixth and Fifth Centuries B.C.: The Pre-Socratics

Ancient philosophy in the classical world is traditionally held to have begun in the sixth century B.C., in Ionia, the coastal and island cities of Asia Minor, which had been settled by Greeks. The philosophers of this period are called "Pre-Socratics," implying that a new period of Greek philosophy begins with Socrates. They do not form a unified movement.

The earliest philosophers produced large and ambitious schemes explaining the cosmos and various natural happenings within it. The first are Thales, Anaximander, and Anaximenes, all from Miletus. Heraclitus of Ephesus' interests moved to attempts to understand the self and reason by means of an obscure and aphoristic style. In the Greek cities of southern Italy, Pythagoras of Samos began another tradition, one emphasizing mysticism, authority, and discipleship. The nature of early Pythagoreanism is much disputed.

Xenophanes of Elea, in southern Italy, introduced the theme of skepticism. He was followed by Parmenides of Elea. Parmenides' argument against the idea that not-being can be spoken or thought of proved influential. His strange metaphysical conclusions were defended by Melissus of Samos, and Zeno of Elea argued against common sense in indirect defense of Parmenides.

Three fifth-century philosophers developed ambitious theories of natural explanation that took account of Parmenides by sharply distinguishing between what we find out by experience and what we reach by thought. Empedocles of Acragas produced the first version of the idea that there are four elements or basic kinds of things that make up everything. Anaxagoras of Clazomenae held a complex and difficult theory of the constituents of matter. Democritus of Abdera (following the shadowy figure of Leucippus) held the first version of a theory of atomism. (Democritus outlived Socrates and so is a Pre-Socratic only in the sense of belonging to a tradition most of whose members lived before Socrates.)

In the second half of the fifth century, there developed a type of intellectual called a sophist, a person who traveled around various cities and taught a variety of skills for fees. Some of the sophists' interests and skills were philosophical, but more prominent were skills in arguing and public speaking, valuable for political life. The best-known sophists were Protagoras of Abdera, Gorgias of

Leontini, Hippias of Elis, Antiphon of Athens, and Prodicus of Cos. While Protagoras was famous for his relativism, the other sophists do not seem to have been relativists. Most of what we know about them comes from Plato's hostile and satirical portrayals of them.

Socrates

Socrates of Athens was a charismatic figure who devoted his life to philosophy in a new way by asking questions and demanding that people explain what they were supposed to be experts in. Although he seems to have held positive views, he wrote nothing, and after his death he was claimed as a figurehead by a variety of "Socratic schools." Aristippus of Cyrene, one of his pupils, founded a form of hedonism. Another, Antisthenes, taught a very ascetic philosophy and was later regarded as a forerunner of Cynicism. The school of Euclides of Megara, which focused on logic, developed his interest in argument. Later, Stoics, Cynics, and Academic Skeptics all looked back to Socrates as a founding figure. However, Socrates' most influential pupil, both as a philosopher himself and as a portrayer of Socrates, was Plato.

Fourth Century B.C.: Plato and Aristotle

Plato of Athens founded the Academy, the first philosophical school, where he taught and discussed; his most famous pupil was Aristotle of Stagira. Plato wrote a large number of dialogues, in many of which Socrates is the major figure. Some depict Socrates arguing against other people, others set out positive views, and some discuss positions and problems raised by other philosophers. Plato's literary skill has always made him the most famous and accessible ancient philosopher.

Aristotle's published works are lost; we have his lecture and research notes, edited some time after his death. After twenty years in Plato's Academy, Aristotle lived in Asia Minor and was tutor to Alexander the Great (his father was physician to the kings of Macedonia). He then returned to Athens and set up his own philosophical school, the Lyceum. The Academy and the Lyceum both continued until the first century B.C.

Hellenistic Philosophy

Traditionally, the "Hellenistic period" went from 323 (the death of Alexander the Great) to 31 B.C. (the battle of Actium, which marked the emergence of Augustus as the first Roman emperor). During this period, several new philosophical movements emerged.

Epicurus of Athens founded his "Garden" school of philosophy, which spread to many other cities.

The Stoics founded a new school of philosophy named after the Painted Porch in the Athenian Agora, or marketplace. Zeno of Citium, the founder, was followed by Cleanthes of Assos and the more influential Chrysippus of Soli. Divergent trends in early Stoicism were led by Ariston of Chios and Herillus of Carthage. In the second century Panaetius and Posidonius produced more accessible and eclectic versions of Stoicism, particularly for a Roman audience.

Diogenes of Sinope became the founding figure (along with the earlier Antisthenes) of Cynicism, a philosophical movement whose followers called themselves dogs (*kunes*), seeing themselves as shameless and living outside society's norms and conventions. The Cynics wrote little and functioned outside the philosophical mainstream, living as street preachers, often on the street.

Pyrrho of Elis, who had gone with Alexander the Great to India, became the founding figure of Greek skepticism. Like Socrates, he wrote nothing, and although he had a few pupils, he left no organized school.

Plato's Academy turned to skepticism under Arcesilaus of Pitane in the late third century. Carneades, in the second century, was the most famous head of the skeptical Academy. The Academic Skeptics debated continually with the Stoics, until later Academics took over much of the Stoic framework for debate. In the first century, the Academy's last head, Philo of Larissa, tried to sustain a compromise view, until the Academy came to an end as a school because Athens was caught in a destructive war. One member, Antiochus of Ascalon, broke away to found a new positive philosophy based on combining ideas from Plato, Aristotle, and the Stoics. Another, Aenesidemus, broke away to return to a more radical form of skepticism, which he named after Pyrrho.

The Roman Period: First Century B.C. to Second Century A.D.

Philosophy flourished in this period, in a more dispersed way since Athens had declined as an intellectual center, and other centers grew, especially in Alexandria, Rome, and cities in the eastern Mediterranean.

Epicureanism and Stoicism continued as schools of philosophy. Plato's own Academy had come to an end, and although some individuals styled themselves Academics, interest in Plato changed to a study of his positive doctrines. The philosophers who studied these doctrines are generally called "Middle Platonists." Interest in Pythagoras' ideas led to a movement called "Neopythagoreanism." Aristotle's school came to an end, but the edition of his lecture and research works by Andronicus gave rise to a long and vigorous tradition of teaching and commenting on them.

In this period active philosophy was lively and varied. Writers discussed and criticized the various schools' ideas, and some tried to combine ideas from different schools in forms of "eclecticism."

Late Antiquity

Plotinus marked a shift to a new form of revived Platonism, which became the dominant philosophy, and the one that eventually was to influence Christianity the most. As Christianity became the official religion of the Roman Empire and the Empire divided into its western and eastern parts, Platonism became the dominant worldview, and other philosophies were less serious competitors. By the time the Emperor Justinian closed the schools of philosophy in Athens in A.D. 529, Neoplatonism was the only pagan philosophy with any vigor. In the western Empire, as philosophical writers like Augustine wrote in Latin with decreasing knowledge of Greek philosophy, philosophical ideas other than those that had survived in Christianity faded from view. But knowledge and study of major philosophers continued in the Eastern Empire, to be retransmitted to the West centuries later.

TIME LINE

600 B.C.	550 B.C.	500 B.C.	450 B.C.	400 B.C.	350 B.C.	300 B.C.	250 B.C.	200 B.C.
	Thales	Parmenides	Socrates	Diogenes of Sinope			Chrysippus	Arcesilaus
	Xenophanes	Zeno of Elea	Aristippus	(The Cynic)			Archimedes	Carneades
	Anaximander	Heraclitus	Democritus	Aristotle				
	Anaximenes	Empedocles	Antisthenes	Theophrastus				
	Pythagoras	Anaxagoras	Plato	Pyrrho				
				Epicurus				
				Zeno of Citium				

150 B.C.	100 B.C.	50 B.C.	A.D. 1	A.D. 50	A.D. 100	A.D. 150	A.D. 200	A.D. 250
	Antiochus			Seneca		Sextus Empiricus	Plotinus	
	Cicero			Epictetus				

A.D. 300	A.D. 350	A.D. 400	A.D. 450	A.D. 500	A.D. 550
	Augustine				

SECTION ONE

FATE AND FREEDOM

Homer *Iliad* 16, 512–548
Lucian *Zeus Answers a Few Awkward Questions*

A. PRAISE, BLAME, AND RESPONSIBILITY FOR OUR ACTIONS

Aristotle *Nicomachean Ethics* III, 5
The Stoics on Fate
Alexander of Aphrodisias *On Fate* 22
The Stoics on Moral Responsibility
Cicero *On Fate* 40–43
Aulus Gellius *Attic Nights* 7.2, 6–13
Alexander of Aphrodisias *On Fate* 11–14
Epicurus *On Nature* 34, 26–30
Diogenes of Oenoanda *Epicurean Inscription* fragment 54, II–III
Lucretius *On the Nature of Things* 2, 251–293

B. RESPONSIBILITY FOR THE LIVES WE LEAD

Plato *Republic* 10 (the Myth of Er)
Alcinous *Handbook of Platonism* 26

C. DIVINE FOREKNOWLEDGE OF THE FUTURE

Alexander of Aphrodisias *On Fate* 30–31
Boethius *The Consolation of Philosophy* 5

D. IS THE FUTURE FIXED?

Aristotle *On Interpretation* 9
Diodorus Cronus *The Master Argument* (Epictetus, *Discourses*
        II.19, 1–5)
The Stoics on Possiblity and Necessity
Cicero *On Fate* 12–15
Alexander of Aphrodisias *On Fate* 10

HOMER

The Greeks credited their two most famous epic poems, the *Iliad* and the *Odyssey*, to a single poet called Homer, about whom various traditions developed, such as that he was blind. Modern scholars date the composition of the two poems to roughly the eighth century B.C. Both poems deal with episodes in the Trojan War, the *Iliad* with the anger of Achilles and the *Odyssey* with the efforts of Odysseus to return home after the sack of Troy. The poems are different in tone, reflecting the difference between the unyielding warrior Achilles, concerned, above all, with his honor, and Odysseus the survivor, who relies on cunning and adapts himself to circumstances.

The epics were basic to Greek educational and intellectual tradition and formed an important part of education. From early on, philosophers criticized the poems' values and attacked their role in giving certain ideals to the young. These confrontations attest to the poems' continued influence within Greek culture. The philosophers Xenophanes, Heracleitus, and Plato all attacked Homer, mostly for what they saw as his immoral depiction of the gods. Aristotle studied the poems more objectively, in the *Poetics,* his work of literary criticism. Some later philosophers, such as the Stoics and the later Platonists, interpreted Homer allegorically and thus avoided having to take a confrontational approach.

Iliad 16, 512–548

HOMER

And Zeus the son of Cronus with Cronus' twisting ways,
filling with pity now to see the two great fighters,
said to Hera, his sister and his wife, "My cruel fate . . .
my Sarpedon, the man I love the most, my own son—
doomed to die at the hands of Menoetius' son Patroclus.
My heart is torn in two as I try to weigh all this.
Shall I pluck him up, now, while he's still alive
and set him down in the rich green land of Lycia,
far from the war at Troy and all its tears?
Or beat him down at Patroclus' hands at last?"

But Queen Hera, her eyes wide, protested strongly:
"Dread majesty, son of Cronus—what are you saying?

A man, a mere mortal, his doom sealed long ago?
You'd set him free from all the pains of death?
Do as you please, Zeus . . .
but none of the deathless gods will ever praise you.
And I tell you this—take it to heart, I urge you—
If you send Sarpedon home, living still, beware!
Then surely some other god will want to sweep
his own son clear of the heavy fighting too.
Look down. Many who battle round King Priam's
mighty walls are sons of the deathless gods—
you will inspire lethal anger in them all.
                                                No,
dear as he is to you, and your heart grieves for him,
leave Sarpedon there to die in the brutal onslaught,
beaten down at the hands of Menoetius' son Patroclus.
But once his soul and the life force have left him,
send Death to carry him home, send soothing Sleep,
all the way till they reach the broad land of Lycia.
There his brothers and countrymen will bury the prince
with full royal rites, with mounded tomb and pillar.
These are the solemn honors owed the dead."
                                                So the pressed
and Zeus the father of men and gods complied at once.
But he showered tears of blood that drenched the earth,
showers in praise of him, his own dear son,
the man Patroclus was just about to kill
on Troy's fertile soil, far from his fatherland.

COMMENTS

Zeus, king of the gods, feels sorrow at the impending death of his son by a mortal woman and wonders whether to interfere with the course of fate, but in the end merely expresses his own grief at what will happen.

The gods accept that there is such a thing as fate—what is bound to happen independently of them. Sarpedon, being mortal, is bound to die some day—and, being a lesser warrior than his opponent, is bound to die now. Why, though, is this now, before the fight, *inevitable*? If Zeus knows the future, does that mean that the future is already fixed, that Zeus knows it because he is a god and that if our knowledge were more extensive, we could know it, too? And what does Zeus have in mind when he suggests that he might try to interfere with the course of fate? Both he and Hera seem to think that interfering with fate is *possible*, although the results would be disastrous.

Homer is a poet, not a philosopher, so we don't expect him to try to solve or even to follow through the questions that are raised by this passage. But later Greek philosophers did follow up the thoughts that surface here.

The scene from Homer is here illustrated by a vase painter, Euphronios, at the end of the sixth century B.C. Sarpedon is shown as young and beardless, highlighting the pathos of his death. The figure between Sleep and Death is Hermes, the god of journeys. He is not mentioned in Homer, but the artist puts him in to underline the fact of Sarpedon's journey from life to the land of the dead. (Attic red-figure calyx-krater signed by Euphronios, 515–510 B.C. The Metropolitan Museum of Art, Bequest of Joseph H. Durkee, Gift of Darius Ogden Mills, and Gift of C. Ruxton Love, by Exchange, 1972. [1972.11.10].)

Is there such a thing as fate—the way the world has to be? Obviously, there are some regularities—all humans have to die some time. But do particular events have to occur the way they do? If so, is it now inevitable that some future event, such as the death of a warrior in battle, will occur? Is it something that the gods could know, even if we can't?

LUCIAN

Lucian of Samosata, in Syria (about A.D. 120–180) lived at a time when Greek culture had spread over much of the Roman Empire and had become dominant in its eastern part. By this time, Greek culture had nearly a thousand-year history and had evolved a canon of "classical" authors and a "classical" way of writing.

As a Syrian, Lucian's native language was not Greek, but he mastered Greek language and culture and became a highly successful writer in a number of genres—essays, dialogues, and public speeches. As a non-Greek, he is especially conscious of the tradition of Greek culture over which he has more mastery than most Greeks, but he is detached from it in a way that enables him to write in a comic and satirical way about many canonical topics. In many ways Lucian can be compared to a modern "postcolonial" writer like Salman Rushdie. He is writing in the language of the people who colonized his own culture and doing so in a way that brilliantly illuminates Greek culture to the Greeks themselves.

Zeus Answers a Few Awkward Questions
Lucian

Zeus Catechized

CYNISCUS   But, Zeus, I for my part won't annoy you that way by asking for wealth or gold or dominion, which are, it seems, very desirable to most people, but not very easy for you to give; at any rate I notice that you generally turn a deaf ear to their prayers. I should like to have you grant me only a single wish, and a very simple one.

ZEUS   What is it, Cyniscus? You shall not be disappointed, especially if your request is reasonable, as you say it is.

CYNISCUS   Answer me a question; it isn't hard.

ZEUS   Your prayer is indeed trivial and easy to fulfil; so ask what you will.

CYNISCUS   It is this, Zeus: you certainly have read the poems of Homer and Hesiod: tell me, then, is what they have sung about Destiny and the Fates true, that whatever they spin for each of us at his birth is inevitable?

Reprinted by permission of the publishers and the Loeb Classical Library from *Lucian*, Volume II, translated by A. M. Harmon, Cambridge, Mass.: Harvard University Press, 1915.

ZEUS   It is really quite true. There is nothing which the Fates do not dispose; on the contrary, everything that comes to pass is controlled by their spindle and has its outcome spun for it in each instance from the very beginning, and it cannot come to pass differently.

CYNISCUS   Then when this same Homer in another part of his poem says: "Take care lest ere your fated hour you go to house in Hell" and that sort of thing, of course we are to assume that he is talking nonsense?

ZEUS   Certainly, for nothing can come to pass outside the control of the Fates, nor beyond the thread they spin.

CYNISCUS   Well, we'll assume this to be so. But answer me another question. There are only three of the Fates, are there not—Clotho, Lachesis, I believe, and Atropos?

ZEUS   Quite so.

CYNISCUS   Well then, how about Destiny and Fortune? They are also very much talked of. Who are they, and what power has each of them? Equal power with the Fates, or even somewhat more than they? I hear everyone saying that there is nothing more powerful than Fortune and Destiny.

ZEUS   It is not permitted you to know everything, Cyniscus. But why did you ask me that question about the Fates?

CYNISCUS   Just tell me something else first, Zeus. Are you gods under their rule too, and must you needs be attached to their thread?

ZEUS   We must, Cyniscus. But what made you smile?

CYNISCUS   I happened to think of those lines of Homer in which he described you making your speech in the assembly of the gods, at the time when you threatened them that you would hang the universe upon a cord of gold. You said, you know, that you would let the cord down from Heaven, and that the other gods, if they liked, might hang on it and try to pull you down, but would not succeed, while you, whenever you chose, could easily draw them all up, "and the earth and the sea along with them." At that time it seemed to me that your power was wonderful, and I shuddered as I heard the lines; but I see now that in reality you yourself with your cord and your threats hang by a slender thread, as you admit. In fact, I think that Clotho would have a better right to boast, inasmuch as she holds you, even you, dangling from her spindle as fishermen hold fish dangling from a rod.

ZEUS   I don't know what you are driving at with these questions.

CYNISCUS   This, Zeus—and I beg you by the Fates and by Destiny not to hear me with exasperation or anger when I speak the truth boldly. If all this is so, and the Fates rule everything, and nobody can ever change anything that they have once decreed, why do we men sacrifice to you gods and make you great offerings of cattle, praying to receive blessings from you? I really don't see what benefit we can derive from this precaution, if it is impossible for us through our prayers either to get what is bad averted or to secure any blessing whatever by the gift of the gods.

ZEUS   I know where you get these clever questions—from the cursed sophists, who say that we do not even exert any providence on behalf of men. At any rate they ask questions like yours out of impiety, and dissuade the rest from sacrificing and praying on the ground that it is silly; for we, they say, not only pay no heed to what goes on among you, but have no power at all over affairs on earth. But they shall be sorry for talking in that way.

CYNISCUS   I swear by the spindle of Clotho, Zeus, they did not put me up to ask you this, but our talk itself as it went on led somehow or other to the conclusion that sacrifices are superfluous. But if you have no objection I will question you briefly once more. Do not hesitate to answer, and take care that your answer is not so weak.

ZEUS   Ask, if you have time for such nonsense.

CYNISCUS   You say that all things come about through the Fates?

ZEUS   Yes, I do.

CYNISCUS   And is it possible for you to change them, to unspin them?

ZEUS   Not by any means.

CYNISCUS   Then do you want me to draw the conclusion or is it patent even without my putting it into words?

ZEUS   It is patent, of course; but those who sacrifice do not do so for gain, driving a sort of bargain, forsooth, and as it were buying blessings from us; they do so simply to honour what is superior to themselves.

CYNISCUS   Even that is enough, if you yourself admit that sacrifices are not offered for any useful purpose, but by reason of the generosity of men, who honour what is superior. And yet, if one of your sophists were here, he would ask you wherein you allege the gods to be superior, when really they are fellow-slaves with men, and subject to the same mistresses, the Fates. For their immortality will not suffice to make them seem better, since that feature certainly is far worse, because men are set free by death at least, if by nothing else, while with you gods the thing goes on to infinity and your slavery is eternal, being controlled by a long thread.

ZEUS   But, Cyniscus, this eternity and infinity is blissful for us, and we live in complete happiness.

CYNISCUS   Not all of you, Zeus; circumstances are different with you as with us, and there is great confusion in them. You yourself are happy, for you are king and can draw up the earth and the sea by letting down a well-rope, so to speak, but Hephaestus is a cripple who works for his living, a blacksmith by trade, and Prometheus was actually crucified once upon a time. And why should I mention your father (Cronus), who is still shackled in Tartarus? This does not seem to me altogether blissful; on the contrary, some few of you are probably favoured by Fate and Fortune, while others are the reverse. I say nothing of the fact that you are carried off by pirates even as we are, and plundered by temple-robbers, and from very rich become very poor in a second; and many have even been melted down before now, being of gold or silver; but of course they were fated for this.

ZEUS   See here, your talk is getting insulting, Cyniscus, and you will perhaps regret it some day.

CYNISCUS   Be chary of your threats, Zeus, for you know that nothing can happen to me which Fate has not decreed before you. I see that even the temple-robbers I mentioned are not punished, but most of them escape you; it was not fated, I suppose, that they should be caught!

ZEUS   Didn't I say you were one of those fellows that abolish Providence in debate?

CYNISCUS   You are very much afraid of them, Zeus, I don't know why. At any rate, you think that everything I say is one of their tricks. I should like to ask you, though—for from whom can I learn the truth except from you?—what this Providence of yours is, a Fate or a goddess, as it were, superior to the Fates, ruling even over them?

ZEUS   I have already told you that it is not permitted you to know everything. At first you said that you would ask me only one question, but you keep chopping all this logic with me, and I see that in your eyes the chief object of this talk is to show that we exert no providence at all in human affairs.

CYNISCUS   That is none of my doing: you yourself said not long ago that it was the Fates who brought everything to pass. But perhaps you repent of it and take back what you said, and you gods lay claim to the oversight, thrusting the Fates aside?

ZEUS   By no means, but Fate does it all through us.

CYNISCUS   I understand; you allege that you are servants and assistants of the Fates. But even at that, the providence would be theirs, and you are only their instruments and tools, as it were.

ZEUS   What do you mean?

CYNISCUS   You are in the same case, I suppose, as the adze and the drill of the carpenter, which help him somewhat in his craft, and yet no one would say that they are the craftsman or that the ship is the work of the adze or the drill, but of the shipwright. Well, in like manner it is Destiny who does all the building and you at most are only drills and adzes of the Fates, and I believe men ought to sacrifice to Destiny and ask their blessings from her instead of going to you and exalting you with processions and sacrifices. But no: even if they honoured Destiny they would not be doing so to any purpose, for I don't suppose it is possible even for the Fates themselves to alter or reverse any of their original decrees about each man.

ZEUS   Then you leave nothing for us, and we are gods to no purpose, not contributing any providence to the world and not deserving our sacrifices, like drills or adzes in very truth? Indeed, it seems to me that you scorn me with reason, because although, as you see, I have a thunderbolt clenched in my hand, I am letting you say all this against us.

CYNISCUS   Strike, Zeus, if it is fated that I am really to be struck by lightning, and I won't blame you for the stroke but Clotho, who inflicts the injury through you; for even the thunderbolt itself, I should say, would not be the cause of the injury. There is another question, however, which I will put to you and to Destiny, and you can answer for her. You have put me in mind of it by your threat. Why in the world is it that, letting off the temple-robbers and pirates and so many who are insolent and violent and forsworn, you repeatedly blast an oak or a stone or the mast of a harmless ship, and now and then an honest and pious wayfarer? Why are you silent, Zeus? Isn't it permitted me to know this, either?

ZEUS   No, Cyniscus. You are a meddler, and I can't conceive where you got together all this stuff that you bring me.

CYNISCUS   Then I am not to put my other question to you and to Providence and Destiny, why in the world is it that honest Phocion and Aristides before him died in so great poverty and want, while Callias and Alcibiades, a lawless pair of lads, were all exceeding rich; and again, why is it that Socrates was given over to the Eleven instead of Meletus, not to speak to you in detail of the present state of affairs, when the wicked and the selfish are happy and the good are driven about from pillar to post, caught in the pinch of poverty and disease and other ills without number?

ZEUS   Why, don't you know, Cyniscus, what punishments await the wicked when life is over, and in what happiness the good abide?

CYNISCUS   Do you talk to me of Hades and of Tityus and Tantalus and their like? For my part, when I die I shall find out for certain whether there is really any such thing, but for the present I prefer to live out my time in happiness, however short it may be, and then have my liver torn by sixteen vultures after my death, rather than go as thirsty as Tantalus here on earth and do my drinking in the Isles of the Blest, lying at my ease among the heroes in the Elysian Fields.

ZEUS   What's that you say? Don't you believe that there are any punishments and rewards, and a court where each man's life is scrutinized!

CYNISCUS   I hear that somebody named Minos, a Cretan, acts as judge in such matters down below. And please answer me a question on his behalf, for he is your son, they say.

ZEUS   What have you to ask *him*, Cyniscus?

CYNISCUS   Whom does he punish principally?

ZEUS   The wicked, of course, such as murderers and temple-robbers.

CYNISCUS   And whom does he send to join the heroes?

ZEUS   Those who were good and pious and lived virtuously.

CYNISCUS   Why is that, Zeus?

ZEUS   Because the latter deserve reward and the former punishment.

CYNISCUS   But if a man should do a dreadful thing unintentionally, would he think it right to punish him like the others?

ZEUS   Not by any means.

CYNISCUS   I suppose, then, if a man did something good unintentionally, he would not think fit to reward him, either?

ZEUS   Certainly not!

CYNISCUS   Then, Zeus, he ought not to reward or punish anyone.

ZEUS   Why not?

CYNISCUS   Because we men do nothing of our own accord, but only at the behest of some inevitable necessity, if what you previously admitted is true, that Fate is the cause of everything. If a man slay, it is she who slays, and if he rob temples, he only does it under orders. Therefore if Minos were to judge justly, he would punish Destiny instead of Sisyphus and Fate instead of Tantalus, for what wrong did they do in obeying orders?

ZEUS   It isn't proper to answer you any longer when you ask such questions. You are an impudent fellow and a sophist, and I shall go away and leave you now.

CYNISCUS   I wanted to ask you just this one question, where the Fates live and how they go into such minute detail in attending to so much business, when there are only three of them. There is much labour and little good-fortune in the life they live, I think, with all the cares they have, and Destiny, it would appear, was not too gracious when they themselves were born. At any rate if I were given a chance to choose, I would not exchange my life for theirs, but should prefer to be still poorer all my days rather than sit and twirl a spindle freighted with so many events, watching each carefully. But if it is not easy for you to answer me these questions, Zeus, I shall content myself with the answers you have given, for they are full enough to throw light on the doctrine of Destiny and Providence. The rest, perhaps, I was not fated to hear!

COMMENTS

By Lucian's time, questions about fate and the gods had been extensively discussed. Homer's Zeus is now confronted with the idea that fate causes everything and proves unable to defend the traditional roles of the gods (himself included) in the face of this idea. He fails to defend any alternative to the conclusion that the gods are no use; they are in the same boat as humans. Two issues turn out to be important.

1. If the gods can't do anything about the way things have to be, then why do we bother with them? The traditional Zeus that we see here obviously doesn't deserve our respect.

2. Fate is worrying in our attitude toward humans, for the actions we do are among the particular events that come about inevitably because of fate. But then how are we responsible for doing them? And if we are not responsible for doing them, can we be fairly praised and blamed for them or rewarded and punished? This is the problem about fate that is the most urgent to most people.

Lucian just raises the question in an amusing way. He is mainly concerned to point out that there is an internal conflict in a culture that accepts both traditional accounts of the gods, such as Homer's, and the view that fate is the cause of everything. However, many ancient philosophers discussed the question of whether we are responsible for our actions and so can be fairly rewarded or punished for them.

A. Praise, Blame, and Responsibility for Our Actions

One question raised by worry about fate is whether we are responsible for our actions and the effects of those actions, such as the development of our character. Our usual practices of praise and blame seem unfair and unreasonable if we are not responsible for what we do.

ARISTOTLE

Aristotle (384–322 B.C.) came from Stagira (a small town in northern Greece). His father was court physician to the kings of Macedonia, and at one point later in life Aristotle was appointed tutor to the young Alexander the Great. At the age of seventeen Aristotle entered Plato's school, the Academy, and remained there, as a pupil and teacher, for twenty years. After Plato's death, he left Athens and spent the next decade in Asia Minor and Macedonia, but then returned to Athens and set up his own philosophical school, the Peripatos, or Lyceum.

Aristotle is a problem-centered philosopher; he begins from problems that arise either from our everyday ways of regarding things or from the work of previous philosophers. He is a systematic thinker in that he develops a number of philosophical concepts, such as *form, matter, substance,* and *nature,* which he uses to approach problems in a variety of areas. However, he is not primarily a system builder; his interest lies in working through the arguments on both sides of a problem, and often it is difficult to locate, in a discussion, what his own view of a problem is. (The works of Aristotle that we possess are his lecture and research notes, which explains why so much of it consists of working through problems, rather than driving at solutions. His published works, which are lost, were probably more single-minded in presenting Aristotle's own views.)

Aristotle had much wider interests than most philosophers and produced bodies of work on an amazing variety of topics. He was the first to formalize logic; he produced, in science, both theoretical work on basic concepts and large amounts of empirical research, pioneering the study of biology. He wrote on cosmology, psychology, ethics, politics, rhetoric, political history, and literary criticism, as well as difficult theoretical works later called "metaphysics."

Aristotle is one of the most influential Greek philosophers, but in an unfortunate way and largely because of historical accident. His works came to prominence in the early Middle Ages in Western Europe at a time when they had little philosophical competition, and Aristotle became "the philosopher" for a great deal of the Christian, Jewish, and Islamic medieval philosophical traditions. Intensive study of his works resulted in the view that Aristotelianism formed a large dogmatic system containing views on everything, one that could be adapted to the needs of monotheistic religions. This dogmatic form of Aristotelianism became a block to original thought, and philosophers from the Early Modern period onward have tended to associate Aristotle with reactionary dogma. When reading Aristotle, it is important to remember that in the ancient world Aristotle was read as a contributor to philosophical discussion, rather than as a source of dogma.

Nicomachean Ethics III, 5

ARISTOTLE

The end, then, being what we wish for, the means what we deliberate about and choose, actions concerning means must be according to choice and voluntary. Now the exercise of the virtues is concerned with means. Therefore virtue also is in our own power, and so too vice. For where it is in our power to act it is also in our power not to act, and vice versa; so that, if to act, where this is noble, is in our power, not to act, which will be base, will also be in our power, and if not to act, where this is noble, is in our power, to act, which will be base, will also be in our power. Now if it is in our power to do noble or base acts, and likewise in our power not to do them, and this was what being good or bad meant, then it is in our power to be virtuous or vicious.

The saying that "no one is voluntarily wicked nor involuntarily happy" seems to be partly false and partly true; for no one is involuntarily happy, but wickedness *is* voluntary. Or else we shall have to dispute what has just been said, at any rate, and deny that man is a moving principle or begetter of his actions, as of children. But if these facts are evident and we cannot refer actions to moving principles other than those in ourselves, the acts whose moving principles are in us must themselves also be in our power and voluntary.

Witness seems to be borne to this both by individuals in their private capacity and by legislators themselves; for these punish and take vengeance on those who do wicked acts (unless they have acted under compulsion or as a result of ignorance for which they are not themselves responsible), while they honour those who do noble acts, as though they meant to encourage the latter and deter the former. But no one is encouraged to do the things that are neither in our power nor voluntary; it is assumed that there is no gain in being persuaded not to be hot or in pain or hungry or the like, since we shall experience these feel-

From Aristotle, *Nicomachean Ethics*, translated by W. D. Ross, revised by J. L. Ackrill and J. O. Urmson (Oxford: Oxford University Press, 1980). Reprinted with the permission of Oxford University Press.

ings none the less. Indeed, we punish a man for his very ignorance, if he is thought responsible for the ignorance, as when penalties are doubled in the case of drunkenness; for the moving principle is in the man himself, since he had the power of not getting drunk and his getting drunk was the cause of his ignorance. And we punish those who are ignorant of anything in the laws that they ought to know and that is not difficult, and so too in the case of anything else that they are thought to be ignorant of through carelessness; we assume that it is in their power not to be ignorant, since they have the power of taking care.

But perhaps a man is the kind of man not to take care. Still they are themselves by their slack lives responsible for becoming men of that kind, and men are themselves responsible for being unjust or self-indulgent, in that they cheat or spend their time in drinking-bouts and the like; for it is activities exercised on particular objects that make the corresponding character. This is plain from the case of people training for any contest or action; they practise the activity the whole time. Now not to know that it is from the exercise of activities on particular objects that states of character are produced is the mark of a thoroughly senseless person. Again, it is irrational to suppose that a man who acts unjustly does not wish to be unjust or a man who acts self-indulgently to be self-indulgent. But if *without* being ignorant a man does the things which will make him unjust, he will be unjust voluntarily. Yet it does not follow that if he wishes he will cease to be unjust and will be just. For neither does the man who is ill become well on those terms. We may suppose a case in which he is ill voluntarily, through living incontinently and disobeying his doctors. In that case it was *then* open to him not to be ill, but not now, when he has thrown away his chance, just as when you have let a stone go it is too late to recover it; but yet it was in your power to throw it, since the moving principle was in you. So, too, to the unjust and to the self-indulgent man it was open at the beginning not to become men of this kind, and so they are unjust and self-indulgent voluntarily; but now that they have become so it is not possible for them not to be so. . . .

. . . Now someone may say that all men aim at the apparent good, but have no control over the appearance, but the end appears to each man in a form answering to his character. We reply that if each man is somehow responsible for his state of character, he will also be himself somehow responsible for the appearance; but if not, no one is responsible for his own evildoing, but everyone does evil acts through ignorance of the end, thinking that by these he will get what is best, and the aiming at the end is not self-chosen but one must be born with an eye, as it were by which to judge rightly and choose what is truly good, and he is well endowed by nature who is well endowed with this. For it is what is greatest and most noble, and what we cannot get or learn from another, but must have just such as it was when given us at birth, and to be well and nobly endowed with this will be perfect and true excellence of natural endowment. If this is true, then, how will virtue be more voluntary than vice? To both men alike, the good and the bad, the end appears and is fixed by nature or however it may be, and it is by referring everything else to this that men do whatever they do.

Whether, then, it is not by nature that the end appears to each man such as it does appear, but something also depends on him, or the end is natural but because the good man adopts the means voluntarily virtue is voluntary, vice also will be none the less voluntary; for in the case of the bad man there is equally present that which depends on himself in his actions even if not in his end. If, then, as is asserted, the virtues are voluntary (for we are ourselves somehow part-causes of our states of character, and it is by being persons of a certain kind that we set the end to be so and so), the vices also will be voluntary; for the same is true of them.

COMMENTS

Aristotle here claims that we are responsible for being people of one kind, rather than another (brave or cowardly, for example), because we are responsible for doing brave or cowardly actions, as a result of which we get ourselves to become either brave or cowardly. As a result of consistently acting in certain ways, we develop the corresponding character, and then it is no longer open to us to act differently. Still, Aristotle holds, the coward is responsible for acting in a cowardly way, for he is responsible for making himself into a coward.

Philosophers sometimes object that Aristotle is being unfair, since we do not have control over our early upbringing and education, and it may be that somebody became cowardly as a result of bad early training. If so, is it fair to blame him now for acting in a cowardly way? Aristotle would consider this a weak objection, since early training and education, though they have an effect, do not take away the ability we all have, when we grow up, to think about our education and formation and to endorse it or not.

Aristotle considers an objection from someone who insists that he is not responsible for his bad actions because he cannot help seeing things in such a way that, for example, it is the cowardly action that appears to be what he should do; he is that way by nature. Aristotle's response to this objection is interesting. If this were so, he says, then the person wouldn't be responsible for acting well either; all our actions would be brought about by our nature in a way that would deprive us of any responsibility for performing them.

Clearly, Aristotle thinks that this idea is absurd; he does not take seriously the idea that *all* our actions may be brought about in a way that leaves us not responsible for them. For him, this idea puts a stop to argument.

Aristotle was aware of the idea of fate as we find it in Homer, for example. But clearly, he does not regard it as answering to any serious philosophical position. For him, it is a rock-bottom fact that we are responsible for our actions, and thus morally acountable for them, and for some consequences of this responsibility, such as the characters that we develop.

Just this rock-bottom fact is what we find thrown into doubt by philosophers after Aristotle.

STOICISM

Stoicism is a philosophical school founded by Zeno of Citium, who came to Athens in 313 B.C. and began to teach in the Stoa Poikile, or Painted Porch (a colonnade with paintings). Zeno had several pupils, including Cleanthes, Ariston, and Herillus, whose thinking developed in different directions. The school was saved from petering out by Chrysippus of Soli, who restated Zeno's position and strengthened it by extensive argument; it was said that if there had been no Chrysippus, there would have been no Stoa. Later Stoics did introduce some modifications of the approach, which will be noted as they come up.

Stoic methodology is what is now called holistic; all the parts are mutually supportive, and there is no single foundation. Philosophy is divided into three parts: logic (including theory of knowledge and philosophy of language), physics (including metaphysics), and ethics. Each of these parts is developed separately, but ultimately the entire system can be seen to fit together as a unified whole.

The Stoics were known for saying uncompromising and outrageous things, such as that emotions are always wrong and only the virtuous are happy. In isolation these statements have shock value, but by the time they are understood in the complete argumentative context, they generally can be seen to be more reasonable than they appear in isolation. Stoicism often initially strikes students as a collection of strange and sometimes unattractive ideas, but the more the ideas are studied separately and together, the more one appreciates their depth and complexity.

The Stoics on Fate

1.   The Stoics call fate a chain of causes, that is, an ordering and connection that is inevitable. (Aetius, 1.28.4)

2.   What I call fate is what the Greeks call *heimarmenē,* that is, an ordering and series of causes, since it is cause linked to cause that produces a thing from itself. And this is everlasting truth, flowing from all eternity. Given this, nothing has happened that was not going to happen, and similarly nothing is going to happen without its causes being contained by nature, causes bringing that very thing about. Hence it can be understood that we are talking about the fate not of superstition but of natural science, the eternal cause of things—the reason why the past happened, why the present is happening, why the future will happen. (Cicero, *On Divination* 1, 125–126)

On Fate 22

ALEXANDER OF APHRODISIAS

Well then, they say that this universe, which is one and contains in itself all that exists, and is organised by a Nature which is alive, rational and intelligent, possesses the organisation | of the things that are, which is eternal and progresses 192.1 according to a certain sequence and order; the things which come to be first are causes for those after them, and in this way all things are bound together with one another. Nothing comes to be in the universe in such a way that there is not something else which follows it with no alternative and is attached to it as to a cause; nor, on the other hand, can any of the things | which come to be subse- 5 quently be disconnected from the things which have come to be previously, so as not to follow some one of them as if bound to it. But everything which has come to be is followed by something else which of necessity depends on it as a cause, and everything which comes to be has something preceding it to which it is connected as a cause. For nothing either is or comes to be in the universe without a cause, because there is nothing | of the things in it that is separated 10 and disconnected from all the things that have preceded. For the universe would be torn apart and divided and not remain single for ever, organised according to a single order and organisation, if any causeless motion were introduced; and it would be introduced, if all the things that are and come to be did not have causes which have come to be beforehand [and] which they follow of necessity. And they say that for something to come to be without a cause | is 15 similar to, and as impossible as, the coming to be of something from what is not. The organisation of the whole, which is like this, goes on from infinity to infinity evidently and unceasingly.

There is a certain difference among the causes, in expounding which they speak of a swarm of causes, some initiating, some contributory, some sustaining, some constitutive, and so on (for [our] need is not | at all to prolong the 20 argument by bringing in everything they say, but to show the point of their opinion concerning fate).—There are, then, several sorts of cause, and they say that it is equally true of all of them that it is impossible that, when all the circumstances surrounding both the cause and that for which it is a cause are the same, the matter should sometimes *not* turn out in a particular way and sometimes should. For if this | happens there will be some motion without a cause. 25

Fate itself, Nature, and the reason according to which the whole is organised, they assert to be God; it is present in all that is and comes to be, and in this way employs the individual nature of every thing for the organisation of the whole. And such, | to put it briefly, is the opinion they lay down concerning 193.1 fate.

Extract from *Alexander of Aphrodisias, On Fate* by R. W. Sharples. Used by permission of Cornell University Press and Gerald Duckworth & Co. Ltd.

COMMENTS

The Stoics think that the everyday notion of fate does answer to something that philosophers can give an account of: what they call a sequence of *causes*. For them, a cause *does* something, brings something about. They hold that everything that happens has a cause, since they think of the world as a unity, in which there are no stray uncaused events.

This amounts to a position like modern forms of determinism: Everything that happens has a cause, and so all events are part of a causal chain. Hence we can see why the Stoics thought of this view as a philosophical understanding of fate. Fate is the way things have to happen, and things have to happen the way they do because they are part of a sequence of causes.

We should remember, though, that the Stoics' reasons for being determinists are different from those of modern philosophers, who are often impressed by scientific success in discovering causes for many happenings and infer that there are causes to be discovered scientifically for every happening. The Stoics, on the other hand, were not particularly impressed by science; they held that everything has a cause on the basis of the metaphysical claim that the world has a unity like that of a living thing. In the ancient world, it was common to think of the universe as an organic unity.

Given their acceptance of determinism, how do the Stoics face the problem of moral responsibility?

The Stoics on Moral Responsibility
On Fate 40–43
Cicero

Those men of old, to whom it seemed that everything came about by fate, said that assentings were brought about by force and necessity. Those however who disagreed with them freed assentings from fate, and said that if fate applied to assentings it would be impossible for necessity to be removed from them. They argued as follows: "if all things come about by fate, all things come about by an antecedent cause; and if impulses do, so too do those things which follow on impulse; and therefore so too do assentings. But if the cause of impulse is not located in us, impulse itself too is not in our power; and if this is so, neither do those things which are brought about by impulse depend on us. So neither

From *Cicero, On Fate and Boethius, Consolation of Philosophy*, translated by R. Sharples (Warminster, England: Aris & Phillips, 1991).

assentings nor actions are in our power; and from this it follows that neither praise nor blame nor honours nor punishments are just." But since this is wrong, they think that the conclusion can persuasively be drawn that it is not the case that all things that come about do so by fate.

But Chrysippus, since he both disapproved of necessity and wanted nothing to come about without causes laid down beforehand, distinguished types of causes so that he could both escape necessity and retain fate. "For," he said, "some causes are perfect and primary, others auxiliary and proximate; and for this reason, when we say that everything comes about by fate through antecedent causes, we do not want this to be understood as "through perfect and primary causes," but as "through auxiliary and proximate causes." And so he meets the argument, which I set out a short while ago, as follows. If all things come about by fate (he says), it does indeed follow that all things come about by causes that precede them, but these are not perfect and primary causes, rather auxiliary and proximate ones. And [even] if these themselves are not in our power, it does not follow that impulse too is not in our power. This *would* follow, if we said that all things come about through perfect and primary causes, so that, since those causes are not in our power, impulse too would not be in our power.

For this reason, those who introduce fate in such a way that they add necessity to it will have to accept that conclusion, but against those who are not going to speak of antecedent causes that are perfect or primary it will have no force. For as for the statement that assentings come about through causes laid down beforehand, (Chrysippus) thinks that he can easily explain this. For although assenting could not occur unless aroused by a sense-impression, nevertheless, since it has this sense-impression as proximate and not as primary cause, it may be explained, as Chrysippus would have it, in the way that we described some time ago; not indeed that the assenting could occur without being aroused by any external force—for it is necessary that assenting should be caused by a sense-impression—but he goes back to his cylinder and spinning-top; these cannot begin to move unless pushed, but, when this has happened, he thinks that for the rest it is by their own nature that the cylinder rolls and the top moves in a curve. "As therefore," he says, "he who pushes a cylinder gives it the beginning of its motion, but does not give it the power of rolling; so a sense-impression when it strikes will, it is true, impress and as it were stamp its appearance on the mind, but assenting will be in our power, and, in the same way as was said in the case of the cylinder, it is pushed from outside but for the rest moves by its own force and nature. If something were to occur without an antecedent cause, it would not be true that everything occurred by fate; if however it seems likely that everything which happens is preceded by a cause, what reason can be adduced for not admitting that everything occurs by fate?—provided only that it is understood what is the distinction and difference among causes."

Attic Nights 7.2, 6–13
AULUS GELLIUS

6 | Against this Chrysippus brought many acute and subtle arguments; but the sense of almost everything which he wrote on that topic is of the following sort.
7 | Although it is the case," he said, "that all things are constrained and bound together by fate through a certain necessary and primary principle, yet the way in which the natures of our minds themselves are subject to fate depends on
8 their own individual quality. | For if they have been fashioned through nature originally in a healthy and expedient way, they pass on all that force, which assails them from outside through fate, in a more placid and pliant manner. If however they are harsh and ignorant and uncultured, and not sustained by any supports from good practices, then even if they are pressed on by little or no necessity from an adverse fate, through their own perversity and voluntary
9 impulse they hurl themselves into constant crimes and errors. | And that this very thing should come about in this way is a result of that natural and neces-
10 sary sequence which is called fate. | For it is as it were a fated consequence of their type itself, that bad natures should not lack crimes and errors.
11 | Then he employs an illustration of approximately this point which is certainly not lacking in relevance or wit. "It is," he says, "just as if you throw a cylindrical stone across a region of ground which is sloping and steep; you were the cause and beginning of headlong fall for it, but soon it rolls headlong, not because *you* are now bringing that about, but because that is how its fashion and the capacity for rolling in its shape are. Just so the order and rule and necessity of fate sets types and beginnings of causes in motion, but the impulses of our minds and deliberations, and our actions themselves, are governed by each per-
12 son's own will and by the natures of our minds." | Then he introduces the following words, which are in agreement with what I have said:

> And this is why it has also been said by the Pythagoreans, "You shall know that men suffer woes that they choose themselves," since harm comes to them on their own account in each case, when they themselves go wrong and come to harm in accordance with their impulse and in accordance with their own thought and disposition.

13 | For these reasons he says that one should not endure or listen to people who are wicked or idle, and both harmful and bold, who when they are convicted of guilt and wrong-doing, have recourse to the necessity of fate as if to some sanctuary in a temple, and say that the worst things they have done should be attributed not to their own rashness but to fate.

From *Cicero, On Fate and Boethius, Consolation of Philosophy,* translated by R. Sharples (Warminster, England: Aris & Phillips, 1991).

COMMENTS

Chrysippus tries to show that the fact that everything is fated to occur, since every event is part of the sequence of causes, is compatible with recognizing that we are morally responsible for what we do, and thus he provides the first philosophical defense of *compatibilism*.

Our actions, according to the Stoics, are brought about by "acts of assent." That is, we act as a result of assenting to the thought that we should perform the action. Every action is brought about by an assent, though, of course, most of our actions are not brought about by *conscious* acts of assent.

Our actions, and the acts of assent that lead to them, are, of course, fated, that is, part of a sequence of causes. But it turns out that there are different kinds of causes, and our actions are brought about by causes that, although they are fated, leave our actions "in our power" and thus something we are morally responsible for. Causes can be either "complete and primary" or "auxiliary and proximate." The first sort are causes in that they are the causes of something's acting in one way rather than in another. The shape of a cylinder is a "complete cause" of its rolling as it does when pushed. An "auxiliary and proximate" cause is the cause of something beginning to act; the push is a proximate cause of the cylinder's rolling, since it triggers the motion. But it does not determine what form the motion takes; the shape of the cylinder does that.

At first this does not look like an intuitive way of distinguishing kinds of causes. But Chrysippus is concerned to show that fate is compatible with some things being in our control, or up to us. Hence he analyzes what happens when I act. The situation in which I am makes an impression on me, and this impression triggers in me an assent to some action or other. For example, I encounter someone who needs help; the person's plight produces in me an impression of someone needing to be helped, and I act. I won't act without being triggered by an impression, and the impression is a proximate cause that brings it about that I act and so, in a sense, brings about my action. But the impression brings it about *that I act;* it doesn't bring about *what I do.* What, then, does bring about what I do? I do, or more strictly my nature and character bring it about. For I could either help the person or walk on by, and which I do is up to me, not to the impression. My nature and character is thus the complete cause of what I do, in the way that the cylinder's shape is the complete cause of its rolling the way it does and not in the way that a top does. Neither the cylinder nor the top will roll without a push, but the push produces very different results with the cylinder and with the top because of differences in them.

Thus what I do is not brought about by fate in the sense of being a simple product of the way things impinge on me. Although everything that happens is part of fate, this does not erase the distinction between what comes about through events that are external to me (the impression) and what comes about through me. My action is not just a result of some event impinging on me, and thus going through me, as it were; it depends on *me,* and thus what I do depends on the way I am and have developed as a result of past actions.

Chrysippus does not deny that what I do is part of fate; what he is concerned to establish is that fate does not make what I do simply a part of a causal chain no different from those that do not involve humans. We can if we like say that what I do is fated, as long as we realize that this does not force us to deny that what I do is up to me or in my control, in just the way we previously thought—that is, it depends on the kind of person I am.

The distinction between complete and proximate causes is not limited to human action, as we can see from the examples of the cylinder and cone. It simply enables us to see how accepting that everything is part of fate does not force us to take a different view of ourselves and how our actions depend on us.

Compatibilist views try to show how determinism does not take away our view of ourselves as agents, whose actions are up to us. Does Chrysippus succeed? Does his account allow us all that we need to regard ourselves as morally responsible for our actions and thus as appropriately to be praised or blamed?

ALEXANDER OF APHRODISIAS

Alexander, from Aphrodisias in Asia Minor, was a professional philosopher who was, at some time between A.D. 198 and 209, appointed by the Emperors Septimius Severus and Caracalla to a publicly funded chair of Aristotelian philosophy, perhaps at Athens. Not an original philosopher, he devoted his energies to writing commentaries on Aristotle's works, to arguing against views hostile to Aristotle, and to restating Aristotle's positions in a form in which they could be protected from objections raised to them after Aristotle's death.

Alexander's position was quite like that of modern philosophy professors, and the way he writes is similar, too.

On Fate 11–14
ALEXANDER OF APHRODISIAS

178.8   Moreover the consequence, | if all the things that come to be follow on some
         causes that have been laid down beforehand and are definite and exist before-
   10   hand, is that men | deliberate in vain about the things that they have to do. And
         if deliberating were in vain, man would have the power of deliberation in vain.

Extract from *Alexander of Aphrodisias, On Fate* by R. W. Sharples. Used by permission of Cornell University Press and Gerald Duckworth & Co. Ltd.

(And yet, if nature does nothing of what is primary in vain, and man's being a living creature with the power of deliberation is a primary product of nature (and not something that [merely] accompanies and happens along with the primary products), the conclusion would be drawn that men do | not have the 15 power of deliberation in vain.)

That deliberating is in vain if everything comes to be of necessity can easily be realised by those who know the use of deliberating. It is agreed by everyone that man has this advantage from nature over the other living creatures, that he does not follow appearances in the same way as them, but has reason from her as a judge of | the appearances that impinge on him concerning certain things 20 as deserving to be chosen. Using this, if, when they are examined, the things that appeared *are* indeed as they initially appeared, he assents to the appearance and so goes in pursuit of them; but if they appear different or something else [appears] more deserving to be chosen, he chooses that, leaving behind what initially appeared to him as deserving of choice. At any rate [there are] many things [which], having seemed different to us in their first appearances [from what they appeared to us subsequently], no longer | remained as in our previ- 25 ous notion when reason put them to the test; and so, though they would have been done as far as concerned the appearance of them, on account of [our] deliberating about them they were not done—we being in control of the deliberating and of the choice of the things that resulted from the deliberation.

It is, at any rate, for this reason that we do not deliberate about the eternal things or about the things which are agreed to come to be of necessity—because | no advantage would come to us from deliberating about them. And neither 30 do we deliberate about the things which do not come to be of necessity but depend on some other people, because there is not any advantage to us from deliberation about these things either. Nor yet do we deliberate about the things which were able to be done by us but are past, because | no advantage comes 179.1 to us by deliberation about these things either. But we deliberate only about the things which are both done by us and future, clearly on the grounds that we will gain something from this [deliberating] for the choice and doing of them.

For if we do not deliberate in those matters in which no advantage comes to us from deliberating | beyond the fact of having deliberated itself, it is clear 5 that, in those matters where we *do* deliberate, we deliberate about them [because] we will gain some advantage from deliberating besides the fact of having deliberated. For the fact of having deliberated itself, at any rate, is a consequence enjoyed also by those who deliberate about the other things of which we have spoken earlier.

What then is the advantage from deliberation? That we, having power over the choice of the things that are to be done, choose and do what | we would not 10 have done if we had not deliberated, because we would have done something else on account of yielding to the impression that impinged [on us; we choose and do] the former rather than the latter when it has appeared through reason to be more deserving of choice. And this will happen if we do not do everything compulsorily. But if we should do everything we do through some causes laid

down beforehand, so as to have no power to do this particular thing or not, but
15 [only] to do precisely | each of the things that we do, in the same way as the fire
that heats and the stone that is carried downwards and the cylinder that rolls
down the slope—what advantage comes to us, as far as action is concerned,
from deliberating about what will be done? For [on this view] it is necessary for
us, even after deliberating, to do what we would have done if we had not delib-
20 erated, so that no advantage comes to us | from the deliberating beyond the fact
of having deliberated itself. But in fact, [although] we could do this even in the
case of those things that do not depend on us, we declined to do it on the
grounds that it was useless. So [on our opponents' hypothesis] deliberating will
be useless even in those cases in which we use it on the grounds that it provides
something useful to us.

From this it followed that nature's gift to us of having the power of deliberation is in vain; and if to this there were added the view held by these men them-
25 selves | and in common by nearly all philosophers, that nothing is brought
about by nature in vain, that [premiss] would be refuted from which it followed
180.1 that our having the power of deliberation was in vain. | But this followed on
our not having such power over the things done by us as to be able to do their
opposites.

180.3   Deliberating is done away with according to them, as has been shown, and
so clearly is what depends on us. For this is what all those who are not defend-
5 ing some | position accept as depending on us—that over which we have con-
trol both to do it and not to do it, not following some causes which surround us
from outside or giving in to them [and following] in the way in which they lead
us. And choice, the peculiar activity of man, is concerned with the same things;
for choice is the impulse with desire towards what has been preferred as a result
of deliberation. And for this reason choice does not apply to the things | that
10 come to be necessarily, nor to those that do so not necessarily but not through
us, nor even in the case of all the things that do so through us; but in the case of
those things that come to be through us over which we have control both to do
and not to do them.

For the person who deliberates about something either (i) deliberates about
whether he should do it or not, or (ii) he enquires earnestly by what means he
15 might attain some good; | and if in his enquiry he comes upon something
impossible, he leaves that aside, and similarly he leaves aside the things that are
possible but do not depend on him, but persists in his enquiry concerning the
proposed [end], until he comes upon something of which he is persuaded he
himself has the power; and after this he ceases from deliberating, since he has
brought back the enquiry to that which is the principle of actions [i.e. himself],
20 and begins on the action | leading to what is proposed. But his enquiry [in case
(ii)] too is carried out on the assumption that he has the power also to do the
opposite things [to what he in fact does]. For concerning each of the things that
fall under the deliberation the deliberator's enquiry is "whether this or its opposite should be done by me"—even if he says that all things come to be in accordance with fate.

For the truth [displayed] in the things that are to be done refutes the erroneous opinions concerning them; and how it is not absurd to say | that this mis- 25 take [sc. of supposing that they *do* have the power to do the opposite] is one that all men in common have made by nature? For we assume that we have this power in actions, that we can choose the opposite, and not that everything which we choose has causes laid down beforehand, on account of which it is not possible for us not to choose it; this is sufficiently shown also by the regret that often occurs in relation to what has been chosen. For it is on the grounds that it was possible | for us also not to have chosen and not to have done this that we 30 feel regret and blame ourselves for our neglect of deliberation. But also, when we see others | not judging well about the things that they have to do, we 181.1 reproach them too as going wrong, and we think that these people should make use of advisers—on the grounds that it depends on us to call in advisers for ourselves or not and to do, on account of the presence of such people, other things too and not those | which we [in fact] do.   5

It is clear even in itself that "what depends on us" is applied to those things over which we have the power of also choosing the opposite things; [but] this is also adequately called to mind by what has been said.

This being what [that which depends on us] is like, | they do not even begin 181.7 to try to show that this is preserved according to those who say that all things come to be in accordance with fate (for they know that they will be attempting the impossible); but, as in the case of luck they substitute another meaning for the term | "luck" and try to mislead their hearers into thinking that they them- 10 selves, too, preserve the coming-to-be of some things from luck—so they do also in the case of what depends on us. For, doing away with men's possession of the power of choosing and doing opposites, they say that what depends on us is what comes about through us.

| For since, they say, the natures of the things that are and come to be are 15 various and different (for those of animate and inanimate things are not the same, nor even, again, are those of all animate things the same; for the differences in species of the things that are show the differences in their natures), and the things that are brought about by each thing come about in accordance with its proper nature—those by a stone in accordance with that of | a stone, those 20 by fire in accordance with that of fire and those by a living creature in accordance with that of a living creature—nothing of the things which are brought about by each thing in accordance with its proper nature, they say, can be otherwise, but each of the things brought about by them comes about compulsorily, in accordance not with the necessity that results from force but [with that] resulting from its being impossible for that which has a nature of that sort to be moved at that time in some other way and not in this, | when the circumstances 25 are such as could not possibly not have been present to it. For it is not possible for the stone, if it is released from some height, not to be carried downwards, if nothing hinders. Because it has weight in itself, and this is the natural cause of such a motion, whenever the external causes which contribute to the natural movement of the stone are also present, | of necessity the stone is moved in the 30

182.1 way in which it is its nature to be moved; and certainly it is of necessity | that
those causes are present to it on account of which it is then moved. Not only can
it not fail to be moved when these [causes] are present, but it is moved then of
necessity, and such movement is brought about by fate through the stone. And
the same account [applies] in the case of other things, too. And as it is in the case

5 of inanimate | things, so it is also, they say, in that of living creatures. For there
is a certain movement that is in accordance with nature for living creatures too,
and this is movement in accordance with impulse; for every living creature that
moves qua living creature is moved in a movement according to impulse
brought about by fate through the creature.

These things being so, and fate bringing about movements and activities in

10 the world, some | through earth, if it so happens, some through air, some
through fire, some through something else, and some also being brought about
through living creatures (and such are the movements in accordance with
impulse), they say that those brought about by fate through the living creatures
"depend on" the living creatures—coming about in a similar way, as far as
necessity is concerned, to all the others; because for these too [i.e. the living crea-

15 tures] the external causes must of necessity be present | then, so that of neces-
sity they perform the movement which is from themselves and in accordance
with impulse in some such way. But because [the movements of living crea-
tures] come about through impulse and assent, [the others] in some cases on
account of weight, in others on account of heat, in others in accordance with
some other cause, [for this reason] they say that this [movement] depends on the
living creatures, but not that each of the others depends, in one case on the

20 stone, in another on the fire.—And such, to state it briefly, is | their opinion
about what depends on us.

182.20   It is possible to see whether, | saying these things, they preserve the com-
mon conceptions of all men about what depends on us. For those who ask them
how it is possible for what depends on us to be preserved if all things are in
accordance with fate do not ask this putting forward only the *name* of what
depends on us, but also that thing which it signifies, that which is in our own

25 power. | For it is on account of their conviction that this is what that which
depends on us is like that they censure those who say that all things come to be
of necessity. These ought straight away to have said that it was not preserved,
and to have sought for and presented the reasons for its not being preserved; but
since they saw that this was something altogether paradoxical and that many of
their doctrines would suffer the same as what depends on us, they showed that

30 [what depends on us] was in accord with the doctrine of fate, thinking | that by
misleading their hearers through the ambiguity they would escape the absurdities that follow for those who say that nothing depends on us.

But when they say these things, first of all one might reasonably ask them

183.1 why, when different things are brought about | through different things by fate,
and fate acts through the proper nature of each of the things that are, they do not
apply "what depends on them" to any of the other things, but only to living

creatures. For the reasons why they say that the things that come about through the living creatures depend on the living creatures can be asserted also in the case of each | of the other things. For since the things that come about through 5 the living creature would not come about if the living creature had not exercised impulse, but they come about through the living creature's assenting and exercising impulse and do not come about if it does not assent—for this reason they say that these things depend on the living creature. They will be brought about by it of necessity (for it is not possible [that they should come about] in another way); but they think that they depend on the living creature because they cannot come about through | anything else, or through it in any other way.   10

But this can be asserted also concerning each of the other things. For what comes about through the fire could neither come about through anything else, nor through the fire in any other way than through its heating; so that, since the things that come about through the fire could not come about in any other way than if the fire heats, and will come about if the fire heats | but not if it does not, 15 these things would depend on the fire. And it will be possible to say the same in the case of each of the other things. What need is there to make a long story of it when what is said is obvious? [We] do not begrudge [their use] of *names*; but it is their thinking that they are according more to living creatures in the things that come about through them than to the other things too through which something comes about, when they are preserving nothing more for them than the *name* | of what depends on them—this is what is blameworthy, because they 20 themselves are deceived through the *name* being common [to their position and ours], or because they choose to deceive others.

And in addition to this one might wonder at them over this point, why on earth they say that what depends on us is [to be found] in impulse and assent (for which reason they preserve it in all living creatures alike). For what depends on us is not [to be found] in [creatures'] yielding of their own accord | to an 25 appearance when it impinges on them and exercising impulse towards what has appeared, but this perhaps is what constitutes and indicates the voluntary. But the voluntary and what depends on us are not indeed the same thing. For it is what comes about from an assent that is not enforced that is voluntary; but it is what comes about with an assent that is in accordance with reason and judgement that depends on us. And for this reason, if something depends on us it is | also voluntary, but not everything that is voluntary depends on us. For the 30 irrational living creatures too, which act in accordance with the impulse and assent in them, act voluntarily; but it is peculiar to man that something of the things that are brought about by him depends on him. For this is what his being rational is, having in himself reason which is a judge and discoverer of the appearances that impinge and generally of the things that are and are not | to 184.1 be done. And for this reason the other living creatures, which yield to appearances alone, have the causes of their assents and of their impulses to actions in accordance with these; but man has reason as a judge of the appearances which impinge on him from outside concerning things that are to be done, and using

5 this he examines each of them, | not only as to whether it *appears* of the kind it
appears [to be] but whether it also *is* [of the kind it appears to be]. And if he finds
in his reasoned enquiry that its reality is different from the appearance, he does
not concede to it because it *appears* of a certain kind, but resists it because it *is* not
also of that kind. In this way, at least, he often refrains from things that appear
10 pleasant, although he has a desire for them, because his reason is not | in accord
with what appears; and similarly he passes over some things that seem advantageous, since this is the judgement of reason [i.e. that he should pass over
them].

   If what depends on us is [to be found] in rational assent, which comes about
through deliberating, and they say that it is [to be found] in assent and impulse,
because it also comes about irrationally, it is clear from what they say that they
15 consider it in too lazy a fashion, since they do not say either what | it is or in
what it comes to be. For to be rational is nothing other than to be a beginning of
actions. For as the being of different things is [to be found] in different things,
that of a living creature in being a living creature with impulse, that of fire in
being hot and a thing with the power to heat, and that of other things in other
things, so that of man is [to be found] in being rational, which is equivalent to
having in oneself a principle (beginning) of both choosing something and not;
20 and both are the same thing, so that the person who | does away with this does
away with man.

   But they seem to have passed over reason and to locate what depends on us
in impulse because, if they say that it is [to be found] in deliberation, their
sophistical argument no longer goes forward. For in the case of impulse they are
able to say that what comes about in accordance with impulse depends on the
living creatures, because it is not possible for [the living creatures] to do the
things that come about through them without impulse; but if what depends on
25 us | were [to be found] in deliberation, then it would no longer follow for them
that the things that come about through man cannot come about in any other
way. For [although] man has the power of deliberating, he does not do all the
things that come about through him by deliberating. For we do not do all the
things that we do after deliberating, but often, when the right moment for doing
the things that need doing does not allow time for deliberating, we do some
30 things | also without having deliberated; and often on account of laziness or
some other cause. But if some things come about when we have deliberated and
some also when we have not, there is no longer any room to say that the things
185.1 that come about through deliberating | depend on man because nothing can
come about through him in any other way.

   So, if we do some things after deliberating and some not after deliberating,
no longer do the things that come to be through us come about simply in the
way that the things [do] that come about through [the other] living creatures or
through fire or through the two heavy bodies [i.e. earth and water]. And if we
5 have from | nature the power of doing something after deliberating, it is clear
that we would also have the power of doing something else through having
deliberated, and not [doing], with no alternative, what [we would have done]
even if we had not deliberated. For [otherwise] we would deliberate in vain.

COMMENTS

Alexander argues, in defense of Aristotle's position, that Stoic determinism cannot do justice to our view of ourselves as agents. If it does not genuinely depend on us what actions we perform, then deliberation is a sham; we *think* that we are deciding what to do, but, in fact, we shall act in a certain definite way whatever we think. Furthermore, if determinism is true, there is no sense in which what I do depends on me that is not also true of inanimate things (which we do not hold morally responsible for what they do).

Alexander develops a positive view, which Aristotle did not, of what it is for our actions to be genuinely dependent on us. For me to be morally responsible for what I do, it must be up to me whether I do the action or not in a strong sense—it must be possible for me to do that action and also possible for me to do a different, even opposed action. Alexander accepts the determinists' view that events that are brought about by causes are brought about in such a way that they could not turn out differently. However, he thinks that human decisions, and hence human actions, are an exception to this view—he gives an *indeterminist* account of human action. My action does not genuinely depend on me unless it is not determined by previous causes, so that I can either perform it or not.

If my action is not brought about by prior causes, then there is nothing to bring it about; why does it occur at all? Alexander's response to this is that what brings about the action is the *agent,* so that my actions are causally explicable without being determined by prior events. Thus, he shares the Stoic view that a cause must be an active cause that brings something about.

Alexander thus defends a *libertarian* account of human action; human actions are brought about by the agent in a way that forms an exception to the way in which events are normally brought about in chains of causation.

Alexander's account raises (at least) two interesting issues. Is he right that this kind of account is implied by our everyday assumption that our actions depend on us? And is he right that his account is in the spirit of Aristotle's?

EPICURUS

Epicurus of Athens (341–270 B.C.) founded a philosophical school in Athens (about 307 B.C.) in a house with a garden, which came to symbolize the spirit of the retired and quiet community of friends that he recommended.

Epicurus' philosophy breaks notably with many trends in ancient philosophy (and Epicurus underlined this fact by claiming to have no teachers and by writing in a jarring and inelegant way). He defends a form of hedonism, the claim that happiness, our end in life, is to be found in pleasure. He accepts atomism, the view that matter is ultimately composed of atomic units, and mechanism, the view that the world is the result of the fortuitous combination of atoms and displays no purpose or rational design. He holds that knowledge is built up empirically, as a result of our repeated encounters with experience. Some form of these views can be found in thinkers prior to Epicurus, but he is the first to put forward a systematic account that embraces all of them and that thus forms a position that contrasts strongly on nearly every issue with the positions of Plato, Aristotle, and the Stoics. Partly because of this, Epicurus' views have been welcomed by philosophers from the Early Modern period on who saw in him someone with more "modern" views than other ancient thinkers.

Epicurus wrote extensively on philosophical topics. Most of his work has been lost, but we do have his three summaries of parts of his philosophy and a collection of sayings. These have come down to us in a book called *Lives of the Philosophers* by Diogenes Laertius. We also have accounts of his philosophy from other ancient writers, works by other ancient Epicureans, and fragments of Epicurean books carbonized when a country house at Herculaneum was buried under lava when the volcano Vesuvius erupted in A.D. 79. These include fragments from Epicurus' major work *On Nature.*

Epicurus strongly denies that there is such a thing as fate, as fate is conceived of by philosophers—that is, he rejects determinism. (He thinks of the popular notion of fate, in Homer, for example, as muddled and harmful.) He rejects determinism on grounds that are different from Alexander's, and it is interesting to compare them. But like Alexander, he takes himself to be rejecting determinism in the name of our everyday confidence that some things, including our actions, depend on us.

It is not easy to be sure just what Epicurus' grounds are for denying determinism. The problem is that he puts forward two different lines of argument, and we have to work out how they are related.

First, we find an argument from Epicurus' work *On Nature,* book 34.

On Nature 34, 26–30
Epicurus

From the beginning we have seeds directing us, some toward some things, others toward others, others toward both—in every case, seeds, which may be many or few, of actions, thoughts, and dispositions. Thus it depends on us at first absolutely what becomes of what is already a development, whether of one or another kind, and the things that, of necessity, flow in from the environment through the pores depend on us when they come about at some time and depend on our beliefs that come from ourselves. . . .

People advise, combat, and reform one another, as having the cause in themselves and not only in the original constitutions and in the necessity of what environs us and enters into us spontaneously.

For if someone were to attribute to advising and being advised themselves the spontaneous necessity of whatever is present to himself at any time, he will never, I'm afraid, understand it in this way. . . .

[Suppose he were to continue] praising and blaming. But if he were to do this, he would be leaving alone the very behavior that creates the preconception of causing in our own case. . . .

For such an argument refutes itself and never can establish that everything is such as the things that are said to happen according to necessity. Rather, he combats a person on this very point as though it were because of himself that the person were being silly. And even if he goes on ad infinitum saying that the person is doing *that* according to necessity, always from arguments, he is failing to reason in that he ascribes to himself the cause of having reasoned correctly and to his opponent the cause of having reasoned incorrectly. Unless he ceased attributing what he does to himself, rather than to necessity, he would not [be consistent].

[But on the other hand] if in using the word *necessity* of what is said to come about through ourselves he is only changing a word, and will not be able to show that in calling what comes about through ourselves responsible, we have formed a preconception with rotten features [it will make no real difference]. . . . If he cannot prove this, and has nothing to help him, no impulse to avert us from the actions of which, when we perform them, we say that the cause is through us ourselves; if he is just using the name of blank necessity for all the things we are committed to doing, saying that their cause is through us ourselves—then he is only changing the word. He will not be revising any of our behavior, as sometimes happens when a person who discerns the kind of thing that comes about of necessity is accustomed to dissuading people who attempt to do something contrary to force. Our minds will search to find out how to think about an action that is done in a way as a result of us ourselves but is one we do not desire to do; for he cannot avoid saying what kind of thing is according to necessity. . . . But unless someone forces this through or lays out what he is refuting or putting forward, it is only an utterance that is changed, as I keep on saying.

The thinkers who from the start gave a satisfactory account of causes [Democritus the atomist], thinkers not only much greater than their predecessors but also many times greater than their successors [Plato and Aristotle], failed to notice their own selves, although in many matters they had produced great improvements, in order to hold necessity and spontaneity responsible for everything. Indeed, the argument teaching this broke down, and Democritus failed to notice that in his actions he was running up against his own position. If a kind of forgetfulness of his own position had not come on him where his actions were concerned, he would have been continually upsetting himself; insofar as the position was dominant, he would have fallen into the greatest misfortunes, and insofar as it was not dominant, he would be filled with conflict because of the tension between his behavior and his position.

COMMENTS

This is an "overturning" argument, claiming that the person holding a position is *thereby,* in holding it, undermining herself. What is meant is not contradicting yourself but *pragmatic self-refutation;* what the person claims is undermined *by her claiming it.* If I *prove* to you that there is no such thing as proof, then what I prove (that there is no such thing as proof) is undermined by my proving it. Epicurus holds that the same is true of the determinist, who thinks that all actions are movements of atoms and so "necessitated," but also puts forward this view, argues for it, thinks that Epicurus is wrong, and so on. For all these activities make sense only if determinism is not true. Thus the opponent's engaging in these activities undermines his claim, showing it to be untenable.

How forceful is this kind of overturning argument? It doesn't claim to show that the opponent's position is *false;* rather, it shows that it isn't tenable for the opponent to hold it.

Epicurus assumes that the opponent is a *reductive* determinist, someone who thinks that if events are brought about by prior causes they cannot also turn out to be human actions that depend on us. (So the "fate of the philosophers" that he is talking about can't be that of the Stoics, who think that fate is compatible with our actions being up to us.)

We also find another argument, appealing to Epicurus' physical account of the world, according to which it is made up of atoms that come together in empty space or void. Worlds like ours are formed when atoms collide, and as a result of such collisions, objects begin to hang together in ever more large and solid clumps. How, though, do atoms collide? The theory, as Epicurus accepts it, has all atoms falling through space at the same speed; how do collisions ever occur? Epicurus, in a move that he hails as original, holds that the atoms "swerve" slightly in a way that allows for atomic collisions to occur. He also holds that this "swerve" accounts in some way for human freedom of action.

Epicurean Inscription FRAGMENT 54, II–III
DIOGENES OF OENOANDA

How, if prophecy has been eliminated, will there be any other indication of fate? If someone makes use of Democritus' argument, asserting that there is no free motion among the atoms because of their collision with one another and that hence it appears that everything is moved in a way that has been necessitated, we shall say to him, "Don't you know, whoever you are, that there *is* a free kind of motion among the atoms, which Democritus did not discover but which Epicurus brought to light, a swerving motion, as he shows from things that are evident?" The main point is this: If fate is credited, then all advice and blame is done away with, and not even the wicked [will be blamed].

LUCRETIUS

Titus Lucretius Carus was a Roman poet and Epicurean, who lived from roughly the 90s to the 50s B.C. About his life we know almost nothing reliable; Cicero refers to him once in a letter. His poem *The Nature of Things*, written in Latin hexameter meter, consists of six books on various aspects of Epicureanism and appears to be unfinished. Lucretius' purpose is ethical, indeed evangelical; he wishes to convert people from the unhappiness of their conventional lives to the happy life they will have if they accept the message of Epicurus. But unfortunately, the poem mostly covers the least original and interesting part of the theory—the scientific atomism that Epicurus adapted from the earlier atomist Democritus. However, Lucretius does contain some interesting material and on some issues is our best or only source for Epicureanism. As a work of Latin literature, the poem is great, and a prose translation barely indicates the power of the poetry.

On the Nature of Things 2, 251–293

LUCRETIUS

Again, if all motion is always connected and a new motion arises out of the old one in a fixed order, and if it is not the case that the atoms by swerving make a beginning of motion that could break the decrees of fate, to stop cause following cause from infinity—if this is so, then whence comes this free impulse in living things? Whence, I ask, comes this impulse torn from the fates, through which we proceed in whatever direction each of us is led by pleasure, and swerve our motions not at fixed times or in fixed places, but where our mind itself takes us? It is beyond doubt that each person's impulse gives the beginning to these things and that it is from this that motions spread through their limbs.

Besides, don't you see that when at a moment the starting gates are thrown open, the eager force of the horses can still not burst forward as suddenly as their mind itself wishes? All the mass of matter must be stirred up throughout the entire body, so that stirred up through the limbs it may strive together to follow the mind's effort. Thus you can see that the beginning of motion is created from the heart and proceeds first from the mind's impulse and only then is spread further through the entire body and limbs.

Nor is it the same when we go forward impelled by a blow from the great strength and great coercion of another person. Then it is obvious that all the matter of the entire body goes forward and is hurried against our will until our impulse has reined it back through the limbs. Do you see, therefore, that although external force propels many and often forces them to go forward against their will and to be hurried headlong, still there is in our breast something capable of fighting against this and resisting it? When this decides, too, the mass of matter is at times compelled to be turned back throughout the limbs and body, and, although thrown forward, to be reined back and settle down.

So, you must admit that there is the same thing in the atoms also: There is another cause for their motions besides collisions and weight, from which this power is born in us (since we see that nothing can come into being from nothing). Weight prevents everything coming about by collisions, by a kind of external force. But that the mind itself should not have internal necessity in all actions and be as it were conquered and forced to suffer and be acted on—that is brought about by the tiny swerve of the atoms at no fixed place and no fixed time.

COMMENTS

It is clear that the Epicureans thought that swerves explained how we are agents whose actions depend on us. But how? Is the idea that actions are free because there is a swerve immediately preceding in the causal chain? But swerves happen at random, and if they precipitated action, then our actions would be random.

Scholars have explored a number of ways in which the swerve could have the role of explaining how it is that our actions depend on us, so that we are morally responsible for them.

Perhaps swerves are frequent, so that there will always be one around before actions are performed? But swerves are everywhere; if there are frequent swerves in the atomic makeup of trees and stones as well, their presence in humans can hardly explain human action.

Perhaps swerves are frequent everywhere, but only have certain sorts of effect in human souls? Thus we are freely acting and morally responsible agents because we have a distinctive physical makeup, within which atomic swerves can produce an active and morally responsible character. This suggestion, however, does not fit the Lucretius passage that actually describes the swerve.

Perhaps swerves are not *causes* of action at all. Maybe Epicurus is assuming that we deliberate and decide in a way that depends on us and allows for us to be morally responsible, and swerves explain what it is about our physical makeup that allows us to put our decisions into effect. On this view, what is important about swerves is that they provide a mechanism whereby action that depends on us can come about. If this is the case, though, we still face the previously stated difficulty: Swerves occur everywhere, not just in human beings, so there must be something distinctive about human beings that allows swerves to provide a mechanism for morally responsible human action. But there already is something distinctive about human beings; any physical theory has to allow for the fact that humans deliberate and make choices in a way that stones and trees don't. So why do we *also* need swerves?

In the present state of our knowledge of Epicurus' position, the role of the swerve remains a puzzle.

Which do you think is the best role for the swerve?

How does the role of swerves fit (or not) with the argument that determinism is self-undermining, and so is an untenable position?

B. Responsibility for the Lives We Lead

Here we find Plato giving expression to a common thought—that we are responsible for the moral quality of the lives we lead—and we see this thought brought into connection with determinism.

PLATO

Plato of Athens (427–347 B.C.) came from a prominent family with connections on both the democratic and the oligarchic sides of the civil war that erupted after Athens' defeat by Sparta in the long Peloponnesian War. Plato took no active part in politics; he founded a philosophical school, the Academy, in his own city and devoted his life to teaching and writing. Otherwise, we know almost nothing about his life.

Plato rejected the usual form of philosophical writing in his day, the treatise, and instead wrote dialogues in which philosophical questions are discussed and sometimes philosophical positions are put forward. In most of these dialogues, Plato uses the figure of Socrates to display what he takes to be the intellectual activity of the philosopher. There was a real person, Socrates of Athens (469–399 B.C.; see p. 131), an Athenian who devoted his life to the activity of philosophical discussion but wrote nothing. Socrates was executed on a vague charge of "corrupting the youth" by the restored democracy in 399, and for Plato and many others thereafter, he served as a figure of the person who devotes his life unconditionally to philosophy and is prepared to die for it.

Plato's works are diverse. Although Plato presents Socrates as a prominent figure in most of his works, no consistent picture is produced, since Plato's ideas of what philosophy is vary so much among the different dialogues. So different comments will be presented for different selections from Plato.

Here we have an imaginative myth (*mythos* means "story" in Greek), which presents in a narrative form an idea that has been argued philosophically in the dialogue. Plato is insistent, earlier in the work, that stories like this are merely a pointer to the true way of thinking, and we should not be literal minded in interpreting it.

The *Republic* is about the question, Is it better for us to be virtuous even if we suffer for it or to devote our lives to getting the conventional good things of life by being wicked, if necessary? The myth, showing the virtuous being rewarded and the wicked punished in the afterlife, is an imaginative way of saying that virtue is its own reward in this life, and wickedness its own punishment.

Plato then uses the myth to raise a question that he never discusses in a more straightforward way: Is it fair for people to be rewarded and punished for the lives they have led? Some people live in circumstances that are so bad that they don't seem to have much room to choose how to live their lives. And many people seem to make the choices that they do on the basis of habit or the influence of their surroundings or what other people think. Are we, then, really responsible for the kind of life we lead?

Plato's answer is yes: It is up to us to decide how to live, and even though we are constrained by factors, such as wealth or its absence, and by the habits we form, we are still responsible for choosing or endorsing the kind of life we lead and cannot evade being judged for it. Although much in our lives is due to the power of "Necessity," we still have enough control over our own lives to make ourselves happy or unhappy by being the kind of person we are.

Republic 10 (THE MYTH OF ER)
PLATO

"Endurance will be my theme, however—that of brave Er the son of Armenius, who was a Pamphylian by birth. Once upon a time, he was killed in battle, and by the time the corpses were collected, ten days later, they had all putrefied except his, which was still in good shape. He was taken home and, twelve days after his death, just as his funeral was about to start and he was lying on the pyre, he came back to life. Then he told people what he'd seen in the other world.

"He said that his soul left his body and went on a journey, with lots of other souls as his companions. They came to an awesome place, where they found two openings next to each other in the earth, and two others directly opposite them up in the sky. There were judges sitting between the openings who made their assessment and then told the moral ones to take the right-hand route which went up and through the sky, and gave them tokens to wear on their fronts to show what behaviour they'd been assessed for, but told the immoral ones to take the left-hand, downward route. These people also had tokens, but on their backs, to show all their past deeds. When Er approached, however, the judges said that he had to report back to mankind about what goes on there, and they told him to listen and observe everything that happened in the place.

From where he was, he could see souls leaving, once they'd been judged, by one or the other of the two openings in the sky and in the earth, and he noticed how the other two openings were used too: one was for certain souls, caked in grime and dust, to arise out of the earth, while the other was for other, clean souls to come down out of the sky. They arrived periodically, and he gained the impression that it had taken a long journey for them to get there; they were grateful to turn aside into the meadow and find a place to settle down. The scene resembled a festival. Old acquaintances greeted one another; those who'd come

From Plato, *Republic*, translated by Robin Waterfield (Oxford: Oxford University Press, 1993). Reprinted with the permission of Oxford University Press.

out of the earth asked those from the heavens what had happened to them there, and were asked the same question in return. The tales of the one group were accompanied by groans and tears, as they recalled all the awful things they'd 615a experienced and seen in the course of their underworld journey (which takes a thousand years), while the souls from heaven had only wonderful experiences and incredibly beautiful sights to recount.

"It would take ages to tell you a substantial proportion of their tales, Glaucon, but here's a brief outline of what Er said. Each individual had been punished—for every single crime he'd ever committed, and for every person he'd ever wronged—ten times, which is to say once every hundred years (assuming that the span of human life is a hundred years), to ensure that the penalty he b paid was ten times worse than the crime. Take people who had caused a great many deaths, by betraying a country or an army, and people who had enslaved others or been responsible for inflicting misery in some other way: for every single person they had hurt, they received back ten times the amount of pain. Conversely, the same principle applied to the rewards people received for their good deeds, their morality and justice. Things are different, however, for those who c die at birth or shortly afterwards, but what he told me about them isn't worth mentioning. However, he did tell a story about the even greater rewards and penalties for observance and nonobservance of the proper behaviour towards gods and one's parents, and for murder with one's own hand.

"He said that he overheard someone asking someone else where Ardiaeus the Great was. (A thousand years earlier, this Ardiaeus had been the dictator of a certain city-state in Pamphylia, and is said to have committed a great many abominable crimes, including killing his aged father and his elder brother.) The d person who'd been asked the question replied, 'He's not here, and he never will be. One of the terrible sights we saw was when we were near the exit. At last, after all we'd been through, we were about to come up from underground, when we suddenly caught sight of Ardiaeus. There were others with him, the vast majority of whom had been dictators, while the rest had committed awful nonpolitical crimes. They were under the impression that they were on the point e of leaving, but the exit refused to take them. Whenever anyone whose wickedness couldn't be redeemed tried to go up, or anyone who hadn't been punished enough, it made bellowing sounds. Fierce, fiery-looking men were standing there,' he went on, 'and they could make sense of the sounds. These men simply grabbed hold of some of the criminals and took them away, but they placed fetters on Ardiaeus' wrists, ankles, and neck, and others got the same treatment; 616a then they threw their prisoners to the ground and flayed them, and finally dragged them away along the roadside, tearing them to pieces on the thorny shrubs. They told any passers-by that they were taking them away to hurl them into Tartarus, and explained why as well.'

"He added that of all the various terrors they experienced there, the worst was the fear they each felt that, as they started their ascent, they'd encounter the bellowing sound, and that there was nothing more gratifying than hearing no sound and making the ascent.

"So much for Er's description of the penalties and punishments, and the
b equivalent rewards. They spent seven days in the meadow, and on the eighth
day they had to leave and go elsewhere. On the fourth day after that they
reached a place from where they could see a straight shaft of light stretching
from on high through the heavens and the earth; the light was like a pillar, and
it was just like a rainbow in colour, except that it was brighter and clearer. It took
another day's travelling to reach the light, and when they got there they were at
the mid-point of the light and they could see, stretching away out of the heav-
c ens, the extremities of the bonds of the heavens (for this light binds the heavens
together, and as the girth that underpins a trireme holds a trireme together, so
this light holds the whole rotation together), while stretching down from the
extremities was the spindle of Necessity, which causes the circular motion of all
the separate rotations.

. . . "Now, although the rotation of the spindle as a whole was uniform, nevertheless within the motion of the whole the seven inner circles moved, at regu-
lar speeds, in orbits which ran counter to the direction of the whole. The seven
inner circles varied in speed: the eighth was the fastest; then second fastest were,
b all at once, the seventh, sixth, and fifth; the third fastest seemed to them (Er said)
to be the fourth, which was in retrograde motion; the fourth fastest was the
third, and the fifth fastest was the second. The spindle was turning in the lap of
Lady Necessity. Each of the spindle's circles acted as the vehicle for a Siren. Each
Siren, as she stood on one of the circles, sounded a single note, and all eight
notes together made a single harmonious sound.

c   "Three other women were also sitting on thrones which were evenly spaced
around the spindle. They were the Fates, the daughters of Necessity, robed in
white, with garlands on their heads; they were Lachesis, Clotho, and Atropos,
accompanying the Sirens' song, with Lachesis singing of the past, Clotho of the
present, and Atropos of the future. Clotho periodically laid her right hand on
the outer circle of the spindle and helped to turn it; Atropos did the same with
her left hand to the inner circles; and Lachesis alternately helped the outer cir-
d cle and the inner circles on their way with one hand after the other.

"As soon as the souls arrived, they had to approach Lachesis. An intermediary arranged them in rows and then, once he'd taken from Lachesis' lap lottery tokens and sample lives, stepped up on to a high rostrum and said, 'Hear
the words of Lady Lachesis, daughter of Necessity. You souls condemned to
impermanence, the cycle of birth followed by death is beginning again for you.
e No deity will be assigned to you: you will pick your own deities. The order of
gaining tokens decides the order of choosing lives, which will be irrevocably
yours. Goodness makes its own rules: each of you will be good to the extent that
you value it. Responsibility lies with the chooser, not with God.'

"After this announcement, he threw the tokens into the crowd, and everybody (except Er, who wasn't allowed to) picked up the token that fell beside
him. Each soul's position in the lottery was clear once he'd picked up his token.
618a Next, the intermediary placed on the ground in front of them the sample lives,
of which there were far more than there were souls in the crowd; every single

kind of human and animal life was included among the samples. For instance, there were dictatorships (some lifelong, others collapsing before their time and ending in poverty, exile, and begging), and also male and female versions of lives of fame for one's physique, good looks, and general strength and athleticism, or for one's lineage and the excellence of one's ancestors; and there were b lives which lacked these distinctions as well. Temperament wasn't included, however, since that inevitably varies according to the life chosen; but otherwise there was every possible combination of qualities with one another and with factors like wealth, poverty, sickness, and health, in extreme or moderate amounts.

"Now, it looks as though this is an absolutely critical point for a person, my dear Glaucon. And that is why every single one of us has to give his undivided attention—to the detriment of all other areas of study—to trying to track down c and discover whether there is anyone he can discover and unearth anywhere who can give him the competence and knowledge to distinguish a good life from a bad one, and to choose the better life from among all the possibilities that surround him at any given moment. He has to weigh up all the things we've been talking about, so as to know what bearing they have, in combination and in isolation, on living a good life. What are the good or bad results of mixing good looks with poverty or with wealth, in conjunction with such-and-such a d mental condition? What are the effects of the various combinations of innate and acquired characteristics such as high and low birth, involvement and lack of involvement in politics, physical strength and frailty, cleverness and stupidity, and so on? He has to be able to take into consideration the nature of the mind and so make a rational choice, from among all the alternatives, between a better and a worse life. He has to be in a position to think of a life which leads his mind towards a state of increasing immorality as worse, and consider one which leads e in the opposite direction as better. There's no other factor he'll regard as important: we've already seen that this is the cardinal decision anyone has to make, whether he does so during his lifetime or after he's died. By the time he reaches Hades, then, this belief must be absolutely unassailable in him, so that there too 619a he can resist the lure of afflictions such as wealth, and won't be trapped into dictatorship or any other activity which would cause him to commit a number of foul crimes, and to suffer even worse torments himself. Instead, he must know how to choose a life which occupies the middle ground, and how to avoid either extreme, as much as possible, in this world and throughout the next. For this is how a person guarantees happiness for himself.   b

"Anyway, according to the report the messenger from the other world delivered on the occasion I'm talking about, the intermediary continued: 'Even the last to come forward will find an acceptable life, not a pernicious one, if he chooses wisely and exerts himself during his lifetime. The first to choose should take care, and the last need not despair.'

"Er said that no sooner had the intermediary fallen silent than the person whose turn was first stepped up and chose the most powerful dictatorship available. His stupidity and greed made him choose this life without inspecting

it thoroughly and in sufficient detail, so he didn't notice that it included the fate
c of eating his own children and committing other horrible crimes. When he took
the time to examine his choice, he beat his breast and wept, but he didn't com-
ply with the intermediary's earlier words, because he didn't hold himself
responsible for his afflictions; instead he blamed fortune, the gods, and anything
rather than himself. He was one of those who had come out of the heavens, since
he'd spent his previous life in a well-regulated community, and so had been
good to a certain extent, even though it was habituation rather than philosophy
d that had made him so. In fact, those who had come from the heavens fell into
this trap more or less as often as the others, since they hadn't learnt how to cope
with difficult situations, whereas the majority of those who had come out of the
earth didn't rush into their decisions, because they knew about suffering from
their own experiences as well as from observing others. That was one of the
main reasons—another being the unpredictability of the lottery—that most of
the souls met with a reversal, from good to bad or vice versa. The point is this:
if during his lifetime in this world a person practises philosophy with integrity,
e and if it so happens, as a result of the lottery, that he's not one of the last to
choose, then the report brought back from that other world makes it plausible
to expect not only that he'd be happy here, but also that he'd travel from here to
there and back again on the smooth roads of the heavens, rather than on rough
underground trails.

    "It was well worth seeing, Er said, how particular souls chose their lives; the
620a sight was by turns sad, amusing, and astonishing. Their choice was invariably
dictated by conditioning gained in their former incarnation. For instance, he
said he saw the soul which had once belonged to Orpheus choose the life of a
swan; because women had killed him, he hated everything female, and wanted
to avoid a female incarnation. He saw Thamyras choose a nightingale's life,
while a swan and other songbirds opted for change and chose to live as human
b beings. The soul which was twentieth in line picked the life of a lion; it was Ajax
the son of Telamon, and he didn't want a human incarnation because he was
unable to forget the decision that had been made about the armour. The next
soul was that of Agamemnon: again, his sufferings had embittered him against
humanity, and he chose instead to be reborn as an eagle. About halfway
through, it was the turn of Atalanta's soul, and she caught sight of a male athlete's life: when she noticed how well rewarded it was, she couldn't walk on by,
and she took it. After Atalanta, Er saw the soul of Epeius the son of Panopeus
c becoming a craftswoman; and later, towards the end, he saw the soul of Ther-
sites the funny man taking on a monkey's form. As the luck of the lottery had it,
Odysseus' soul was the very last to come forward and choose. The memory of
all the hardship he had previously endured had caused his ambition to subside,
so he walked around for a long time, looking for a life as a nonpolitical private
d citizen. At last he found one lying somewhere, disregarded by everyone else.
When he saw it, he happily took it, saying that he'd have done exactly the same
even if he'd been the first to choose. And the same kind of thorough exchange
and shuffling of roles occurred in the case of animals, too, as they became men
or other animals—wild ones if they'd been immoral, tame ones otherwise.

"When the souls had all finished choosing their lives, they approached Lachesis in the order the lottery had assigned them. She gave each of them the personal deity they'd selected, to accompany them throughout their lives, as e their guardians and to fulfil the choices they had made. Each deity first led its soul to Clotho, to pass under her hand and under the revolving orbit of the spindle, and so to ratify the destity the soul had chosen in the lottery. Then, once a connection had been made with her, the deity led the soul to Atropos and her spinning, to make the web woven by Clotho fixed and unalterable. Afterwards, the soul set a fixed course for Lady Necessity's throne and passed under it; once it was on the other side, and when everyone else had joined it there, they all 621a travelled through terrible, stifling heat (since no trees or plants grew in that place) to the Plain of Oblivion. Since the day was now drawing to a close, they camped there by the River of Neglect, whose waters no vessel can contain.

"Now, they were all required to drink a certain amount of water, but some were too stupid to look after themselves properly and drank more than the required amount. As each person drank, he forgot everything. They lay down to sleep, and in the middle of the night there was thunder and an earthquake. All b of a sudden, they were lifted up from where they were, and they darted like shooting stars away in various directions for rebirth. As for Er, although he hadn't been allowed to drink any of the water he had no idea what direction he took, or how he got back to his body, but he suddenly opened his eyes and found that it was early in the morning and that he was lying on the funeral pyre."

ALCINOUS

Alcinous is the author of a *Handbook of Platonism,* which has come down to us; this is all we know about him. The handbook belongs to a philosophical movement (not a unified school or tradition) known as "Middle Platonism," and its date could be from the first century B.C to the second century A.D. Middle Platonism is in the middle between Plato's own school, the Academy, which came to an end in the first century B.C., and Neoplatonism, which began with Plotinus at the end of the second century A.D. Authors like Alcinous did something that neither Plato nor anyone else had done; they produced accounts of Plato's views, extracting them from various dialogues. They did so in terms of the philosophical movements that they had been educated in, just as authors of books on Plato do today. We aren't sure of the intended audience for these works; in some ways they are like modern textbooks, but they are more like books for the teacher than for the students.

Handbook of Platonism 26

ALCINOUS

179   1. On the subject of fate, Plato's views are roughly as follows. All things, he
says, are within the sphere of fate, but not all things are fated. Fate, in fact, has
the status of a law. It does not say, as it were, that such and such a person will
5 do this, and that such and such another will suffer that, for that would result in
an infinity of possibilities, since the number of people who come into being is
infinite, and the things that happen to them are also infinite; and then the concept of what is in our power would go out of the window, and so would praise
and blame, and everything like that. But fate consists rather in the fact that if a
10 soul chooses a given type of life and performs such-and-such actions, such-and-
such consequences will follow for it.

         2. The soul, therefore, owns no master, and it is in its power to act or not,
and it is not compelled to this, but the consequences of the action will be fulfilled
in accordance with fate. For example, from the fact that Paris will steal away
Helen, this being a voluntary action of his, there will follow that the Greeks will
15 go to war about Helen. This is, after all, how Apollo put it to Laius: "If you beget
a son, that offspring will kill you" (Euripides, *Ph.* 19). Here, in the oracle, Laius
and his begetting a son are taken as premises, and the consequence is fated.

20   3. The nature of the possible falls somehow between the true and the false,
and being by nature undetermined it becomes the sphere of operation of our
free will. Whatever results from a choice on our part, on the other hand, will be
either true or false. That which is potentially is different from what is said to be
25 in a realized state or in actuality. Potentiality, after all, indicates a certain apti-
tude in something which does not yet possess the corresponding realized state;
as, for instance, a boy will be said to be potentially a scholar, or a flautist, or a
carpenter, but only then will be "in the state" of being one or two of these, when
30 he learns and acquires one of these skills. He will possess them in actuality, on
the other hand, when he acts on the basis of that state which he has attained. The
possible, however, is none of these, but remains indefinite, and takes on truth or
falsity in consequence of the inclination in either direction of our free will.

COMMENTS

Here we can compare a philosophical idea expressed in an imaginative form with
the "normalized" form it takes in a professional philosophical discussion. According
to Alcinous, Plato accepts the notion of fate in that he allows that although human

From *Alcinous: The Handbook of Platonism*, translated and edited by J. Dillon (Oxford:
Oxford University Press, 1963). Reprinted with the permission of Oxford University
Press.

choices are free, they take place within a framework of laws that express necessary connections. It is these laws that are what we mean by fate. Insofar, then, as our actions fall under these laws, certain consequences are fated to follow. But it does not follow that everything we do, we have been fated to do.

Alcinous' examples of fate, however, are of connections between kinds of human action themselves. If you steal a king's wife, for example, the king is bound to retaliate. We may wonder whether this is really a good example of what people intuitively mean by fate, since the connection does not seem to be necessary; there could be exceptions. Furthermore, Paris' action of stealing away Helen is said to be free, and so not fated, but the action that follows from it (Menelaus' revenge) is fated. But doesn't the action of stealing Helen fall under some generalizations (about handsome guests seducing hostesses, and so on)?

Alcinous also puts forward a Platonic answer to a question raised only later (discussed in section 1.D). When I still have the choice to do an action or not, it is possible that I will do it, and, he continues, it is not true that I will do it or true that I will not do it and so false that I will do it. He accepts the idea that for there to be a genuinely open choice as to whether I will do it or not, it cannot already be true that I will do it or false that I will do it (and so true that I will not do it). The reasoning behind this idea is explored further in section 1.D.

C. Divine Foreknowledge of the Future

The traditional gods of Greek religion could be either identified with the workings of fate or regarded as its instruments. But even if the gods can't interfere with fate, they can at least foretell what will happen—one of the functions of ancient gods and divine figures was various forms of predicting the future. However, doesn't even the ability to foretell what will happen threaten the freedom of the person whose action is predicted? Here we find two answers, one of them influential in the Christian tradition.

On Fate 30–31
ALEXANDER OF APHRODISIAS

To say that it is reasonable that the gods should have foreknowledge of the things that will be, because it is absurd to say that they fail to know anything of the things that will be, and, assuming this, to try to establish by means of it that all things | come to be of necessity and in accordance with fate—[this] is neither true nor reasonable. For if the nature of the things admits of this, there is non- 200.12

15

Extract from *Alexander of Aphrodisias On Fate* by R. W. Sharples. Used by permission of Cornell University Press and Gerald Duckworth & Co. Ltd.

one for whom it would be more reasonable to know the things that are going to
be than [it would be] for the gods [to do so]; but when [the nature of the things]
is not able to admit of such prediction and foreknowledge, it is no longer reasonable even for the gods to know anything that is impossible. For the things

20 that are impossible in their own nature | preserve the same nature even where
the gods are concerned. For it is impossible even for the gods either to make the
diagonal commensurable with the side [of a square], or twice two five, or any of
the things that have happened not to have happened. Nor do they even want to
[do so] in the first place in the case of things that are impossible in this way [i.e.
in their own nature]; for the difficulty is present in the very statement of them.
And it is similarly impossible for them, in the case of that which has in its proper

25 nature the possibility | of both coming to be and not, to have foreknowledge
that at all events it *will* be or that at all events it *will not* be. For if foreknowledge
about these things before they [occur] does away with what is contingent in
them, it is clear that, if this were to be preserved, foreknowledge concerning
them would be impossible.

　　And that this is so according to [the determinists] too is clear from their
assuming that the gods have foreknowledge of the things that are going to be

30 and establishing by means of this | that they come to be of necessity, on the
grounds that, if they did *not* come to be in this way, [the gods] would not have
foreknowledge of them. But if even according to them necessity follows on the
gods' foreknowledge and prediction, [then], if necessity were *not* present in the

201.1 things that come to be, not even according to | them would the gods have fore-
knowledge of the things that are going to be. So they too themselves preserve
the same lack of power for the gods—if indeed one should say that it is through
lack of power and weakness that it comes about that one is unable to do things
that are impossible. They do not indeed ascribe greater power to the divine

5 through [the power of] prediction, but, on account of their | assuming [that the
gods have this power] they introduce the view of things [that they do], saying
things that are in no way consistent and harmonious with the things that come
to be and are evident.

　　For by applying this [argument] it will be possible to show that all the things
that are impossible are possible, since it is not reasonable that the gods should
fail to know them. For someone could assume that it is absurd that the gods

10 should not know the measure of the infinite, | and, laying this down, go on to
suppose that it is possible to know the measure of the infinite, and that, if this is
so, it is possible for there to be a certain definite measure of the infinite; for if it
were not [possible], not even the gods would have known the measure of it.

　　But since to have foreknowledge of the things that are going to be is to have
cognizance of them *as being such as they are* (for having foreknowledge is differ-

15 ent from bringing about), it is clear | that he who has foreknowledge of things
that are contingent will have foreknowledge of them *as such*. For it is not foreknowledge to say that what is contingent will be in the manner of [what] will be
necessarily. So the gods too would have foreknowledge of the things that are
contingent *as contingent*, and necessity will not at all follow on this on account

of foreknowledge of *this* sort. And it is in this way that we actually listen to those who make predictions. For those who make predictions along with advising someone | to choose and do what he should, do not speak about the things they 20 predict as things that will be of necessity.

And in general, if [i] they say that *all* things are possible for the gods, and even impossible things will be possible for them, it will not indeed be shown through their foreknowledge concerning the things that are going to be that all the things that come to be do so of necessity. But if [ii] they concede that the things that are impossible are so also for the gods, they | should first show that 25 this sort of foreknowledge [i.e., the sort that they assert—as opposed to fore-knowledge of the contingent as contingent] is possible, and *then* attribute it to the gods. For it is neither evident nor in agreement with the things that [actu-ally] come to be that it is this sort of foreknowledge concerning the things that are going to be that the gods exercise.

We therefore do not do away either with prophecy or with the gods' fore-knowledge by saying that they make predictions about things in accordance with | the way the things naturally are; but neither do we take away from men the 201.30 usefulness of prophecy, which comes about through someone's being able actu-ally to take precautions against something, when he would not have done so if the god had not advised him. But those who sing the praises of prophecy | 202.1 and say that it is preserved only by their own account, and use it as a proof that all things come to be in accordance with fate, not only say nothing that is true but in addition have the effrontery, what is more, to say things about the gods that are absurd and altogether alien from them. For how are the things that they say about these matters not | absurd? Certain people raise the difficulty 5 against them why indeed, if all the things that come to be do so of necessity, the prophecies that come from the gods resemble pieces of advice, as if those who had heard them could both take precautions against something and do some-thing on account of what they had heard. Moreover, [the objectors] bring for-ward the oracle given to Laius, in which Pythian [Apollo] says to him, concern-ing the fact that he ought not to beget children, | "If you beget a child, the one 10 who is born will slay you, and all your house will wade in blood" [Euripides *Phoenissae* 19–20]. But, as their writings proclaim, [the determinists] do not say that [Apollo] prophesied in this way because he did not know that [Laius] would not obey (for he knew this above all). Rather, [they say] that if he had not made any such prophecy, none of the things that came about in the | tragic 15 reversal concerning Laius and Oedipus would have done so. For neither would Laius have exposed the son that was born to him in the way that he did, nor would the child have been taken up by the herdsman and given for adoption to the Corinthian Polybus, and, when he grew up and met Laius on the road, slain him without recognising him or being recognised. For if he had been brought up as a son in his parents' house, | he would never have failed to recognise them, 20 and so killed one of them and married the other. So, in order that [the occurrence of] all these things should be preserved and the drama of fate fulfilled, the god gave Laius the impression through the oracle that he could take precautions

against what was said; and when he had become drunk and begotten a child, he
exposed the child that had been born in order to destroy it; and it was this expo-
25 sure | that became the cause of the unholy stories.

Well, if someone says these things, how does he either preserve prophecy,
or teach pious conceptions concerning the gods, or show that prophecy has any
203.1 usefulness? For prophecy is thought to be prediction | of the things that are
going to happen, but they make Apollo the author of the things he predicts. For
that which would not have happened thus if the god had not prophesied in this
way (and he prophesied in this way for this very reason, that the things that
came about concerning them should come about)—how is this not the deed of
him who prophesied, rather than revelation of the things that were going to be?
5 But even if the gods | must have some advantage over the other prophets, so
that they assist the things that are going to be, it is reasonable that they should
contribute to the coming about of what is good (for the poets constantly sing this
about the gods, that they are "givers of good things"). Yet according to what [the
determinists] say, at least, Apollo does not contribute to anything good for
Laius, but strives and does all he can with a view to his house escaping nothing
10 | of [all] that is most unholy and impious. Who, when he heard these things,
would not say that the absence of [divine] providence asserted by the followers
of Epicurus was more pious than this sort of providential care?

And how is it consistent both to say that fate is god and employs the things
that are and come to be in the universe for the preservation both of the universe
15 itself and of the ordering of the things within it, and [also] | to say such things
about it as that it employs even Apollo as an accomplice in the most unholy
deeds on account of its eagerness that they [should happen]? What will they say
fate preserves by its employment of the killing of a father by his son and the
unholy marriage of a mother and her son and the birth of children who are also
the brothers of their father? What [aspect] of the organisation of the universe is
20 it reasonable [to suppose] has its preservation from these things, | so that even
Apollo should fear that any of them might be left undone? If they had not come
about, would it have hindered the dwelling of men in cities and according to
laws? Or the preservation of the elements of the universe? Or the orderly and
eternal revolution of the heavenly bodies? Or which of the things out of which
the universe comes to be constituted and organised in accordance with reason?
25 It is clear that, if again they hear | any other story from one of the tragic poets
whose concern is fictions of this sort—either some woman who through jealousy plotted against someone else's children but slew her own, or some unfortunate old Thyestes eating the flesh of his own children when some Atreus his
brother has put such a meal before him—they believe such stories as things that
30 happened, and establish | fate and providence through them, as if making it
204.1 their business | to do away with what they want to establish through the very
[arguments that they use to] establish it. And yet it would be far better and more
sensible to do away with their assumptions on account of the absurdity of their
consequences, [rather] than to defend such absurdities on account of the
assumptions. But they both find it easy to believe in the most absurd things, and

do not | shrink from stating explanations of how their coming about is in accor- 5
dance with reason.

COMMENTS

Alexander assumes traditional Greek polytheism, the view that there are many gods, with different areas of concern. (Like most philosophers after Plato, however, he also accepts that these gods are good and therefore that many of the traditional unedifying stories about them are false.) Boethius, being a Christian, is a monotheist, who holds that there is one God, who is all-powerful (omnipotent) and benevolent to humanity. Ask yourself which of their answers you find more compelling. How does this relate to your own view of God?

Alexander holds that I am free to act or not on a particular occasion and that until the choice is made, it is not determinately true that I will act or that I will not. Thus, there is no truth about what I will do in the future for the gods to know now. The gods, then, cannot have foreknowledge of what I will do in the future. Alexander realizes that this is a serious limitation on the gods and argues that this is unobjectionable; even the gods can't do the impossible.

But Alexander wants to preserve the traditional role of the gods in giving oracles. Can he really do so? If you go to an oracle, say, of Apollo (the prophetic god), you want to be told not just that you will do something, but *what* you will do—and in Alexander's account, Apollo doesn't know what you will do until you do it. This leaves a role for oracles in giving advice, telling you the kind of thing you should do—often the way oracles were regarded.

Alexander, however, also argues against a determinist's account of the gods' prophecies, using (like Alcinous) the example of Laius, who was told by Apollo that if he fathered a son by his wife, he would be killed by him. Laius avoided sex with his wife, Jocasta, but one night got drunk and fathered a son. When the baby was born, he was exposed on a mountain to evade the oracle, but was rescued, given the name Oedipus, and brought up elsewhere. Eventually he killed Laius, not knowing him to be his father, and married Jocasta. This example forms the background of Sophocles' play *Oedipus the King*.

According to Alexander, a determinist has to hold that Apollo's oracle is actually the cause that brings about Laius' action and hence is responsible for it. But for the oracle, Laius would have behaved differently, and the subsequent history would have been different. But this view is objectionable. First, the oracle, in this account, was not what it appeared to be, a piece of advice; Apollo knew perfectly well what would happen, including the role of his own oracle. So oracles, even when they appear to give advice, are, in fact, manipulative ways in which the gods enter the causal chain. Second, this view makes the gods accomplices in horrible events.

Thus, according to Alexander, if you want to avoid an objectionable view of the gods, you have to hold that they do not know now what you will do in the future (though they know that you will do something). Could a determinist believe in prophecy and avoid the consequences that Alexander lands him with?

BOETHIUS

Anicius Manlius Severinus Boethius (c. A.D. 480–524/6) belongs to the period when the western Roman empire had been taken over by the invading Goths and is often considered to belong to "early medieval," rather than ancient, philosophy; but he can equally well be considered to belong to either period; the chronological lines we draw are often arbitrary.

Boethius belonged to the Roman aristocracy and held high political office under Theodoric the Ostrogoth, head of the western Roman empire. The Goths, who had conquered parts of the Roman empire, did not try to replace the elaborate Roman system of government and administration, and Boethius and two of his sons held the ancient high office of consul. Eventually, because of political and religious intrigues Boethius fell from power; after lengthy imprisonment, he was tortured and executed.

Boethius translated and wrote commentaries on Aristotle's logical works (part of a projected translation of and commentary on the complete works of Plato and Aristotle). He also wrote theological treatises. All these works were influential in the Middle Ages, but Boethius' most famous work was the *Consolation of Philosophy*, written in prison. In a mixture of prose and verse, Boethius presents himself as consoled and enlightened by Lady Philosophy. Boethius was a Christian, but the *Consolation* does not contain overtly religious elements; it is a work in which philosophical reflection is what answers Boethius' deepest difficulties.

The Consolation of Philosophy 5

BOETHIUS

3 "There seems to be a considerable contradiction and inconsistency," I said,
4 "between God's foreknowing all things and the existence of any free will. If God foresees all things and cannot be in any way mistaken, then what Providence
5 has foreseen will happen must inevitably come to pass. So if God has prior knowledge from eternity not only of men's actions but also of their plans and wishes, there will be no freedom of will; for the only action and any sort of intention which can possibly exist in the future will be foreknown by divine Provi-
6 dence, which cannot be misled. If such actions and aspirations can be forcibly diverted in some direction other than was foreseen, certain foreknowledge of the future will no longer exist, but instead there will be vacillating opinion; and I regard it as sacrilege to believe this of God.

From Boethius, *The Consolation of Philosophy*, translated by P. G. Walsh (Oxford: Oxford University Press, 1999). Reprinted with the permission of Oxford University Press.

"I do not subscribe to the argument by which some believe that they can dis- 7
entangle this knotty problem. What they suggest is that Providence's fore- 8
knowledge of a future event is not the cause of its happening, but that it is the
other way round. Since something is about to happen, this cannot be hidden
from divine Providence, and in this sense, they claim, the element of necessity
is reversed. Their argument is that things foreseen do not therefore happen by 9
necessity, but that things which will happen are necessarily foreseen. The
assumption here is that we are toiling over the problem of which is the cause of
which: is foreknowledge the cause of the necessity of future events, or is the
necessity of future events the cause of Providence? In fact, however, we are
struggling to show that whatever the sequence of causes, the outcome of things
foreknown is necessary, even if such foreknowledge does not appear to impose
an inevitable outcome upon future events.

"Take the case of a person who is seated. The belief which hazards that he 10
is seated must necessarily be true; and conversely, if the belief that a certain person is seated is true, then he must be seated. In each of the two formulations
some necessity is present: in the one that it is true, and in the other that he is 11
seated. But the individual is not seated because the belief that he is seated is 12
true; rather, the belief is true because the person was already seated. Thus,
though the reason for its being true emerges from the fact that he was seated, 13
there is a necessity which both statements share. Clearly the argument about 14
Providence and the future is similar; for even if things are foreseen because they
are about to happen, and they do not in fact happen because they are foreseen,
nevertheless necessity lies either in that future events are foreseen by God, or
that things foreseen happen because they are foreseen. This alone is sufficient to
eliminate the freedom of the will.

"And besides, how topsy-turvy is the suggestion that the outcome of events 15
in time is the cause of eternal foreknowledge! What distinction is there between 16
thinking that God has foresight of future events because they are about to happen, and believing that things which have occurred at some earlier time are the
cause of that highest Providence? A further point: when I know that something 17
exists, it is necessary that it exists, and likewise when I know that something will
happen, it is necessary that it will happen. The conclusion therefore is that the
outcome of something foreknown cannot be avoided. Finally, if a person 18
believes that something is other than it is, not only is that not knowledge, but it
is a mistaken assumption far removed from the truth of knowledge. So if some- 19
thing is about to happen in such a way that its outcome is not certain and
necessary, how can it possibly be foreknown that it will occur? True knowledge 20
is not compounded with untruth, and likewise what is grasped by knowledge
cannot be other than what is grasped; for the reason why knowledge embraces 21
no falsehood is because everything must be as knowledge understands it
to be.

"So what is the solution? How, I wonder, can God know beforehand that 22
these uncertainties will come to pass? If he thinks that things which possibly 23
may not happen will necessarily occur, he is mistaken—and this is sacrilegious

24 both to contemplate and to utter. But if he decrees that the future is as it really
is, in other words realizes that future events equally may or may not happen,
what sort of foreknowledge is that, since it constitutes nothing definite or
25 unchanging? How does this differ from that absurd prophecy of Tiresias

> Each utterance of mine will come to pass—or not!

26 Again, how does divine Providence rise above mere human opinion, if like
human beings she assesses as uncertain those things whose outcome *is* uncer-
27 tain? But if no such uncertainty can reside in that most unerring source of all
things, then what God assuredly knows will happen is guaranteed to come
28 about. What follows from this is that there is no freedom for human plans and
actions, since the divine mind foresees all of them without straying into error;
he confines and restricts them to a single outcome.
29   "Once this is admitted, the extent of the decline in human fortunes becomes
30 evident. Rewards or punishments offered to good or wicked men are pointless,
for they have not been won by any free and voluntary impulse of their minds.
31 What is now considered utterly just—punishments for the wicked and rewards
for the good—will be seen to be the greatest injustice imaginable, because they
have been impelled to commit good or evil not by their own will, but by the
32 unchanging necessity of what will be. So neither vices nor virtues will exist at
all; instead all the deserts of people are mingled and undifferentiated in the
melting-pot. Moreover—and nothing more heinous than this can be imagined—
since the entire ordering of human affairs derives from Providence, and no discretion is granted to our human intentions, our vices as well are to be ascribed
to the author of all things good.
33   "So there is no point in hoping to obtain, or in praying to avert, anything,
for what is the individual to pray to obtain or to avoid when all that we long for
34 is set fast in an interlinked chain that cannot be set aside? Thus the one and only
transaction made between men and God, namely our hopes and prayers for
deliverance, will be abolished, if indeed by payment of a proper humility we
deserve the priceless recompense of divine grace. This is the only way in which
men are seen to be able to converse with God, and to be united by this means of
supplication to that unapproachable Light, even before obtaining what they ask
35 for. But if we accept that the course of the future is fixed by necessity, and such
approaches to God are considered ineffectual, what means will remain by which
we can join and attach ourselves to that highest source of all that is?"

1 Then Philosophy said: "This is a long-standing argument about Providence.
Marcus Tullius, when he put paid to divination, had a lively discussion of it, and
you yourself have investigated it for quite a time, but up to now not one of you
2 philosophers has explained it with the necessary care or incisiveness. The reason for the cloud that envelops you is that the process of human reasoning cannot attain to the simplicity of divine foreknowledge. If that simplicity could
3 somehow be grasped, it is certain that no ambiguity would remain. I shall later

try to clarify and explain it, once I have dealt with the problems that trouble you."

"The reason for this error is that all men believe that the totality of their 24 knowledge is obtained solely from the impact and nature of things known. But 25 the reality is wholly different: all that becomes known is apprehended not by this impact, but rather by the capability of those who grasp it. Let me make this clear 26 with a brief example. The roundness of the same physical object is identified in one way by the eyes, but in another by the touch, for the eyes remain at a distance, and at one and the same moment they observe the whole by means of light-rays which they project, while the touch clings closely to the sphere, and as it circles round its perimeter, it apprehends its roundness bit by bit.

"In the case of man, the senses, the imagination, the reason and the under- 27 standing all regard him in different ways. The organs of sense examine his shape 28 in the matter that lies before them. The imagination visualizes his shape independently of the matter. The reason too rises higher, and surveys the appearance 29 of each individual in the light of the universal to which all belong. The eye of the 30 understanding rises still higher, and transcending the boundaries of the created world, it gazes on the simple Form with the unsullied sight of the mind. Your 31 most concentrated thought should be directed on this, for the higher power of the understanding embraces the lower, but the lower in no way rises to the higher. For the senses cannot be exercised at all outside matter; the imagination 32 does not behold universals; the reason cannot grasp the simple Form. But the understanding looks down, so to say, from above. It visualizes the Form, and distinguishes all that lies beneath it, but in such a way that it apprehends the Form itself, which could not be known to any of the other faculties; for it recognizes the 33 universal as the reason does, and the shape which the imagination sees, and the matter which the senses grasp, but without deploying the reason or imagination or senses. Rather, by that single appraisal of the mind it regards all these things, so to say, as Form. Likewise the reason, when it observes some universal, does 34 not deploy the imagination or the senses, but grasps what is apparent to the imagination and the senses; for the reason defines the universal which it has con- 35 ceived like this: 'Man is a two-footed rational animal.' Though this is a universal 36 concept, everyone knows that the object is open to the imagination and the senses, but the reason ponders it not by the imagination or the senses, but by visualizing it rationally. The imagination too, though it takes its starting-point of 37 sighting and fashioning shapes from the senses, even in the absence of the senses surveys all that is accessible to them by the criterion not of sensation but by that of the imagination. So do you see how in the acquisition of knowledge all these 38 elements deploy their own powers rather than those of the objects perceived? 39 And this is how it should be, for since every judgement emerges as the act of one who judges, it is inevitable that each performs its work by its own power rather than by that of another."

"It is possible that when men perceive material objects, those external proper- 1 ties strike the organs of sense, and the effect on the body precedes the exertion

of the active mind; and that effect stirs the mind to activity within itself, arousing the forms previously quiescent within. On the other hand, I suggest, if in the perception of material objects the mind is not stamped by that experience, but assesses by its own power the effect sustained by the body, how much more do those things which are freed from all bodily sensations promote the activity of their minds, refraining in their discernment from paying heed to external
2 objects! By this process many modes of cognition accrue to various beings of dif-
3 ferent types. Sensation alone, unaccompanied by all other modes of knowledge, is possessed by creatures without movement, like molluscs and others which are nurtured while clinging to rocks. Imagination is the property of mobile animals, which at that level already appear to have some instinct of what to avoid
4 and what to seek. But reason is unique to the human race, just as understanding belongs solely to the divine. Hence this last means of apprehending is superior to the rest, for by its own nature it recognizes not only the object proper to it, but also all that is accessible to other means of knowledge.
5   "Suppose, then, that sensation and imagination were at odds with reason-
6 ing, claiming that the universal, which reason claims to perceive, is non-existent, on the grounds that what can be grasped by the senses or by the imagination cannot be universal. On this view either the judgement of the reason is valid, and nothing can be grasped by the senses; or alternatively, since the senses and the imagination are well aware that numerous things are perceptible to them, the notion held by the reason, that the individual object which can be
7 grasped by the senses is a sort of universal, is without foundation. Reason might rejoin that in fact she beholds things perceptible to the senses and imagination by virtue of their universality, whereas they cannot aspire to knowledge of universality because their awareness cannot pass beyond bodily shapes; and moreover, that where knowledge of objects is concerned, assent should be lent to the judgement that is more consistent and perfect. Surely in a dispute of this kind we who have the faculty of reasoning as well as those of imagination and sensation should prefer to approve reason's cause?
8   "Similarly the human reason believes that the divine understanding observes the future only in the way she herself knows it. What you claim is this:
9 if certain things do not seem to have an outcome fixed and necessary, it cannot
10 be known beforehand that they will certainly occur. Therefore there is no foreknowledge of these things; and even if we were to believe that there *is* foreknowledge of them, there will be nothing which does not happen of necessity.
11 Well then, if we could possess the judgement exercised by the divine mind in the same way as we partake of reason, just as we have decreed that the imagination and the senses ought to yield to the reason, so we would regard it as most just
12 that the human reason should defer to the divine mind. So if we can, let us raise ourselves to the peak of that highest understanding, for there the reason will look upon what she cannot of herself observe: that is, how even things which have no certain outcome are witnessed by an unerring and precise foreknowledge, a foreknowledge which is not mere opinion, but rather the simplicity of highest knowledge confined by no bounds."

"So since, as we made clear a moment ago, all that is known is known not 1
through its own nature but through the nature of those who apprehend it, let us
now, in so far as divine law allows, examine what is the nature of the divine
being, so that we may likewise come to know what his knowledge is.

"It is the common view of all who live by reason that God is eternal. So we 2
must ponder what eternity is, for this will clarify for us his divine nature and his 3
knowledge alike. Eternity, then, is the total and perfect possession of life with- 4
out end, a state which becomes clearer if compared with the world of time; for
whatever lives in time lives in the here and now, and advances from past to 5
future. Nothing situated in time can at the one moment grasp the entire duration of its life. It does not as yet apprehend the morrow, and it has already relin-
quished its yesterday; and even in your life of today, you humans live for no
more than that fleeting and transient moment. So anything subject to a status 6
within time, even if it has had no beginning and never ceases to exist, and even
if its life extends without limit in time, as Aristotle argued is the case with the
world, is not yet such as can be rightly accounted eternal; for it does not grasp 7
and embrace at the one moment the whole extent of its life, even if that life is
without end. It does not yet possess the future, and it no longer owns time past. 8
So what does rightly claim the title of eternal is that which grasps and possesses
simultaneously the entire fullness of life without end; no part of the future is
lacking to it, and no part of the past has escaped it. It must always appear to
itself as in the present, and as governing itself; the unending course of fleeting
time it must possess as the here and now.

"Therefore, since every judgement which is made comprehends the things 15
lying before it according to its own nature, and since God's status is abidingly
eternal and in the present, his knowledge too transcends all movement in time.
It abides in the simplicity of its present, embraces the boundless extent of past
and future, and by virtue of its simple comprehension, it ponders all things as if
they were being enacted in the present. Hence your judgement will be more cor- 16
rect should you seek to envisage the foresight by which God discerns all things
not as a sort of foreknowledge of the future, but as knowledge of the unceas-
ingly present moment. For this reason it is better to term it *providentia* ('looking 17
forward spatially') rather than *praevidentia* ('looking forward in time'), for it is
not set far apart from the lowliest things, and it gazes out on everything as from
one of the world's lofty peaks.

"Why, then, do you demand that things surveyed by the divine light be nec- 18
essary, when even men do not pronounce as necessary the things they see? 19
Surely, when you observe things before you, your seeing them does not impose
any necessity on them?"

"Of course not."

"But if it is appropriate to compare the divine present with the human, then 20
just as you men see certain things in this temporal present of yours, so God sees
all things in his eternal present. Hence this divine foreknowledge does not
change the nature and character of things; God sees them as present before his 21
eyes as they will emerge at some time in the future. Nor does he make confused 22

judgements about things; with a single mental glance he distinguishes those future events which will occur by necessity from those which will not. Consider this parallel. When you observe at the one time a man walking on the earth and the sun rising in the sky, even though you see them simultaneously, you distin-

23 guish them, and you judge the first movement to be voluntary, and the second to be necessary. So it is the same with the divine vision, as it looks out on the whole world; it certainly does not dislocate the nature of those things which for God are

24 in the present, but which in their temporal aspect are in the future. So when God knows that something is about to take place, something which he is well aware need not come to pass, this is not an opinion but knowledge which rests on truth.

25   "At this point you may say that what God sees will happen must inevitably happen, and that what must inevitably happen, happens of necessity. If you tie me down on this term necessity, I shall concede that this is a concept most sub-stantially true, but one which scarcely anyone other than the student of theol-

26 ogy has grasped. For my response will be that a future happening which is nec-essary when viewed by divine knowledge seems to be wholly free and

27 unqualified when considered in its own nature. In fact there are two kinds of necessity. One is simple; for example, it is necessary that all men are mortal. The other is conditional; for example, a man must be walking if you are aware that

28 he is walking. What a person knows cannot be other than as it is known; but this conditional necessity is far from involving with it that other simple kind.

29 For conditional necessity is shaped not by a thing's particular nature, but by the condition appended to it. When a person voluntarily takes a walk, no necessity impels him to move forward, though it is necessary for him to move forward the

30 moment he walks. Likewise, then, if Providence sees something in the present, that thing necessarily exists, even though of its nature it incorporates no such

31 necessity. But God sees in the present the future events which proceed from free choice. So these things become necessary as related to God's observation of them, through the condition of his divine knowledge; but considered in them-

32 selves they do not forfeit the total freedom of their nature. So the future events which God foreknows will all undoubtedly come to pass, but some of them pro-ceed from free choice. Though these do take place, their occurrence does not mean that they surrender their own true nature, which would have allowed the possibility of their not happening before they took place.

33   "What difference, then, does it make that those things are not necessary, when the condition of God's knowledge will in all ways result in the equivalent

34 of necessity? Observe the difference in the instances which I adduced a moment ago, the sun rising and the man walking; while these actions take place, they cannot not take place, but in the first example, before it actually happened, it was necessary for it to do so, whereas in the second it was certainly not. Like-

35 wise those events which God sees in the present will undoubtedly come to be, but some will result from their innate necessity, and others at the discretion of

36 those who perform them. So we were by no means wrong in stating that these things are necessary from the aspect of divine knowledge, but considered in themselves they are free from the bonds of necessity, just as all things accessible

to the senses are universals from the aspect of the reason, but particulars considered in themselves.

"You will respond that if it lies in my power to change my course of action, 37 I will deprive Providence of her role when I happen to change an act which she foreknows. My response will be that you can indeed divert your course of 38 action, but the truth of Providence observes in the present your ability to do this, and whether you are doing it, or in what direction you are changing it. So you cannot evade the divine foreknowledge, just as you cannot escape the gaze of a person's eye which observes you at this moment, even though you vary your actions by use of your free will.

"So your question then will be: will the arrangements which I make cause a 39 change in God's knowledge, so that when my intention switches from one thing to another, his knowledge too seems to vacillate? By no means, for God's gaze 40 anticipates everything that is to happen, and draws it back and recalls it to his own knowing in the present. There is no vacillation such as you imagine, with his foreknowledge changing this way and that; rather, with a single glance it anticipates and embraces the changes which you make, while itself remaining 41 unchanged. God derives this understanding and vision in the present not from the outcome of future events, but from his own simplicity. This also offers the 42 solution to your earlier objection, that it is unworthy to suggest that our future actions are the cause of God's knowledge; for it is the force of that knowledge, 43 embracing all things in its awareness in the present, which itself imposes a limit on all things, and owes nothing to events which occur later.

"Since this is the case, man's freedom of will remains intact, and the laws 44 which prescribe rewards and punishments for acts of will which are free of all necessity are not unjust. Moreover, God continually observes with foreknowl- 45 edge all things from on high, and his eternal vision, which is ever in the present, accords with the future nature of our actions, and dispenses rewards to the good and punishments to the wicked. The hopes which we rest in God, and the 46 prayers addressed to him, are not in vain; when they are righteous, they cannot 47 be ineffectual. So avoid vices, cultivate the virtues, raise your minds to righteous hopes, pour out your humble prayers to heaven. As long as you refuse to 48 play the hypocrite, a great necessity to behave honourably is imposed on you, for your deeds are observed by the judge who sees all things."

COMMENTS

Boethius begins by vividly depicting the way in which divine foreknowledge of what we will do appears threatening to us. Moreover, this feeling of threat does not depend on the thought that God's foreknowledge *causes* its object. We tend to think of God's knowledge on the analogy of our knowledge. If I know now what you are going to do tomorrow, then it is threatening, for it implies that what you are going to do is already determined. But God's knowledge is entirely different from ours because God's nature is different from ours and relates to time in a different way.

What makes kinds of knowledge different is the nature of the knowing subject, not the nature of the object. Boethius illustrates this from the difference between sensing something and thinking of it. Our way of knowing is different from God's in a similar way. God is an eternal being, which implies that his existence is not something that goes on through time, as ours does. For God, all time is present without any succession of past, present, and future, and so for God things do not happen before or after other things. For God, things happen in what is sometimes called the "eternal present." So strictly God does not have *fore*knowledge of what I will do; his knowledge encompasses everything that I have done, do, and will do, but for God these are not items that are strung out through time, and thus God does not know what I will do *before* I do it; therefore, his knowledge is not threatening, since it does not imply that what I will do is necessitated.

Boethius' solution depends on our accepting two things: (1) God's existence stands in a radically different relation to time than ours does and (2) God is still aware of things in time, particularly human actions. These are difficult notions and have given rise to controversy. However, it is interesting to note that Boethius takes the path of claiming that we and God have radically different perspectives on what happens in time, rather than allowing, as does Alexander, that we and the gods have a similar perspective. Clearly, Boethius and Alexander have different notions of what has to be true of God, or the gods.

D. Is the Future Fixed?

One more technical and sophisticated worry that arises from the idea of fate is this: If it is already fated that something will happen, then it is already true that it *will* happen; but then how can it not happen? The future seems to be already fixed.

On Interpretation 9
ARISTOTLE

Chapter 9

With regard to what is and what has been it is necessary for the affirmation or the negation to be true or false. And with universals taken universally it is always necessary for one to be true and the other false, and with particulars too, as we have said; but with universals not spoken of universally it is not necessary. But with particulars that are going to be it is different.

For if every affirmation or negation is true or false it is necessary for every-thing either to be the case or not to be the case. For if one person says that some-thing will be and another denies this same thing, it is clearly necessary for one of them to be saying what is true—if every affirmation is true or false; for both will not be the case together under such circumstances. For if it is true to say that it is white or is not white, it is necessary for it to be white or not white; and if it is white or is not white, then it was true to say or deny this. If it is not the case it is false, if it is false it is not the case. So it is necessary for the affirmation or the negation to be true. It follows that nothing either is or is happening, or will be or will not be, by chance or as chance has it, but everything of necessity and not as chance has it (since either he who says or he who denies is saying what is true). For otherwise it might equally well happen or not happen, since what is as chance has it is no more thus than not thus, nor will it be.

Again, if it is white now it was true to say earlier that it would be white; so that it was always true to say of anything that has happened that it would be so. But if it was always true to say that it was so, or would be so, it could not not be so, or not be going to be so. But if something cannot not happen it is impossible for it not to happen; and if it is impossible for something not to happen it is nec-essary for it to happen. Everything that will be, therefore, happens necessarily. So nothing will come about as chance has it or by chance; for if by chance, not of necessity.

Nor, however, can we say that neither is true—that it neither will be nor will not be so. For, firstly, though the affirmation is false the negation is not true, and though the negation is false the affirmation, on this view, is not true. Moreover, if it is true to say that something is white and large, both have to hold of it, and if true that they will hold tomorrow, they will have to hold tomorrow; and if it neither will be nor will not be the case tomorrow; then there is no "as chance has it." Take a sea-battle: it would *have* neither to happen nor not to happen.

These and others like them are the absurdities that follow if it is necessary, for every affirmation and negation either about universals spoken of universally or about particulars, that one of the opposites be true and the other false, and that nothing of what happens is as chance has it, but everything is and happens of necessity. So there would be no need to deliberate or to take trouble (thinking that if we do this, this will happen, but if we do not, it will not). For there is noth-ing to prevent someone's having said ten thousand years beforehand that this would be the case, and another's having denied it; so that whichever of the two was true to say then, will be the case of necessity. Nor, of course, does it make any difference whether any people made the contradictory statements or not. For clearly this is how the actual things are even if someone did not affirm it and another deny it. For it is not because of the affirming or denying that it will be or will not be the case, nor is it a question of ten thousand years beforehand rather than any other time. Hence, if in the whole of time the state of things was such that one or the other was true, it was necessary for this to happen, and for the state of things always to be such that everything that happens happens of necessity. For what anyone has truly said would be the case cannot not happen; and of what happens it was always true to say that it would be the case.

But what if this is impossible? For we see that what will be has an origin both in deliberation and in action, and that, in general, in things that are not always actual there is the possibility of being and of not being; here both possibilities are open, both being and not being, and, consequently, both coming to be and not coming to be. Many things are obviously like this. For example, it is possible for this cloak to be cut up, and yet it will not be cut up but will wear out first. But equally, its not being cut up is also possible, for it would not be the case that it wore out first unless its not being cut up were possible. So it is the same with all other events that are spoken of in terms of this kind of possibility. Clearly, therefore, not everything is, or happens of necessity: some things happen as chance has it, and of the affirmation and the negation neither is true rather than the other; with other things it is one rather than the other and as a rule, but still it is possible for the other to happen instead.

What is, necessarily is, when it is; and what is not, necessarily is not, when it is not. But not everything that is, necessarily is; and not everything that is not, necessarily is not. For to say that everything that is, is of necessity, when it is, is not the same as saying unconditionally that it is of necessity. Similarly with what is not. And the same account holds for contradictories: everything necessarily is or is not, and will be or will not be; but one cannot divide and say that one or the other is necessary. I mean, for example: it is necessary for there to be or not to be a sea-battle tomorrow; but it is not necessary for a sea-battle to take place tomorrow, nor for one not to take place—though it is necessary for one to take place or not to take place. So, since statements are true according to how the actual things are, it is clear that wherever these are such as to allow of contraries as chance has it, the same necessarily holds for the contradictories also. This happens with things that are not always so or are not always not so. With these it is necessary for one or the other of the contradictories to be true or false—not, however, this one or that one, but as chance has it; or for one to be true *rather* than the other, yet not *already* true or false.

Clearly, then, it is not necessary that of every affirmation and opposite negation one should be true and the other false. For what holds for things that are does not hold for things that are not but may possibly be or not be; with these it is as we have said.

COMMENTS

The issues in this and the other readings in section 1.D concern what is called "logical determinism," which is a less intuitive and more sophisticated worry about fate than those we have looked at so far.

Chapter 9 of *On Interpretation* became influential as the first sustained philosophical discussion of the problem of logical determinism. The chapter is typical of Aristotle; he is keen on understanding the full ramifications of the problem, but is less than clear as to what his own answer to it is.

The problem arises from the assumption that every "affirmation or negation"— every statement that something is or is not the case—must have a truth value, that is, must be either true or false. As Aristotle points out, this assumption raises a problem with statements about the future, in particular statements about individual things or events, such as his example, "There will be a sea-battle tomorrow." We are normally in no position to say now whether it is true that there is going to be a sea-battle tomorrow, but the question is not whether or not we can say it, but whether the statement *is* true. Now, if it is true that there will be a sea-battle tomorrow, then it always was true that there will be a sea-battle tomorrow. But then how could there fail to *be* a sea-battle tomorrow? Similarly, if it is false that there will be a sea-battle tomorrow, nothing anyone can do will bring it about that there will be one. Thus, starting from the reasonable-looking assumption that every statement is true or false, we seem to be forced to the conclusion that whatever we will do is already fixed.

Aristotle confronts this line of thought with an equally reasonable one that conflicts with it. We all deliberate, work out what to do, and then do it as a result of our deliberations. This idea presupposes that it is up to us to do or not to do these actions and, in turn, presupposes that the future is not fixed; if it were, deliberation would be useless, since nothing we do would change what is going to happen anyway.

Aristotle does not doubt that our deep belief that deliberation does make a difference is better founded than the philosophical worries that lead to logical determinism. It is not, however, clear what form Aristotle's solution takes. Two lines of thought seem to be present in the final part of the chapter:

1. Particular statements about the future are not true or false until the relevant fact occurs. This is to accept that if every statement is true or false, logical determinism follows, but to deny that every statement is true or false. Yet Aristotle appears to hold that it is true that "Either there will be a sea-battle or there won't be," and it would be strange for this to be true but for it not to be true that there will be a sea-battle and not to be true that there will not be a sea-battle.

2. Particular statements about the future are true or false, like other statements, but they are not "necessary." That is, their truth does not have the implication, as it does with true statements about the present and past, that the state of affairs making the statement true is already fixed. Thus, we can state that one or other of the two possibilities (there will be a sea-battle or there won't be a sea-battle) is true, but we cannot definitely claim that there will be a sea-battle or that there won't. (Note that this is a different sense of "necessary" from the one usual in modern philosophical discussions, in which what is necessary is a *connection* between two statements or between two states of affairs.)

Each of these lines of thought raises some problems. Also, they are clearly *different* lines of thought—Aristotle can't consistently hold both. Is Aristotle then in a muddle? It is possible, but it is also possible that the passage as we have it shows him in the process of working out an answer that never achieved a satisfactory final form. Aristotle is a problem-centered philosopher, and we often find him working on difficult problems and trying out various lines of thought without working out a complete and satisfactory answer. We should remember that the texts we have from Aristotle are not published works; they are his lecture and research notes. They tell us how far he got with a problem.

DIODORUS CRONUS

Diodorus, from Iasos in Asia Minor, lived in the late fourth and early third centuries B.C. Apparently, he inherited the unflattering nickname Cronus (roughly meaning Old Idiot) from his teacher Apollonius; we have no idea why. Diodorus was a Dialectical Philosopher, belonging to a school whose focus was logic and analytical argument, with no apparent interest in ethics or other forms of practical philosophy.

All we know of Diodorus' philosophical activity centers on three topics. First, Diodorus argued against the existence of continuous motion, in favor of the view that motion takes the form of instantaneous displacements. Second, he gave an account of truth conditions for conditionals ("if . . . then" statements) in terms of its never being the case that a sound conditional begins with a truth and leads to a falsehood. (This is a contribution to a debate about conditionals in the Hellenistic period that, in spite of its technical nature, became quite famous.) Finally, Diodorus was known for the Master Argument, presented here.

EPICTETUS

Epictetus of Hierapolis in Phrygia (c. A.D. 50–130), a Stoic philosopher, was born a slave, and for a time was one of the slaves of the Emperor Nero's freedman Epaphroditus. He was a student of a Stoic philosopher, Musonius Rufus, some of whose writings have come down to us, who held some notably egalitarian views, such as that women should receive the same kind of education as men. Later in life, Epictetus was freed and set up a philosophical school in Nicopolis in Epirus. Epictetus was a charismatic teacher and attracted many pupils. Like Socrates, he wrote nothing; however, one of his pupils, a historian called Arrian, wrote notes of Epictetus' lectures and teaching. We have four books of his conversations and lectures and a short handbook (the *Encheiridion*) that contains extracts and summaries of his views on major points.

Epictetus concentrated on Stoicism as a view to be lived by, and his focus is on practical ethics. He does not much discuss the theoretical structure of Stoic philosophy. His teachings, however, rely on this structure, and sometimes, as with the Master Argument, he is our source for aspects of Stoicism for which other sources let us down.

The Master Argument (EPICTETUS,
DISCOURSES II.19, 1–5)
DIODORUS CRONUS

The Master Argument seems to have been posed on this basis. The following three items are in mutual conflict with one another: (a) Everything past that is true is necessary, (b) Something impossible does not follow from something possible, (c) Something is possible that neither is nor will be true.

Diodorus discerned this conflict and used the convincingness of the first two to establish that nothing is possible that neither is nor will be true. Still, someone might keep the two, that there is something possible that neither is nor will be true and that something impossible does not follow from something possible, and then deny that every past truth is necessary. Cleanthes and his followers seem to have done this, and Antipater largely supported this. But others keep two others, that something is possible that neither is nor will be true and that every past truth is necessary, and hold that something impossible does follow from something possible. There is no way of holding all three because of their mutual conflict. If someone asks *me*, then, "Which of them do you keep?" I shall answer him that I don't know, but that I have acquired this information: Diodorus kept the first two, Panthoides (I think) and Cleanthes the second and third, and Chrysippus and his followers the first and third.

COMMENTS

Our knowledge of the Master Argument comes from this passage, which gives us the bare structure, but nothing about what motivated the argument, which comes to an extreme and counterintuitive conclusion.

Diodorus puts forward three propositions, which form an *inconsistent triad*—they cannot all be true together. You must reject one on the basis of holding the other two to be true. The argument itself simply presents you with this situation; it doesn't indicate *which* of the propositions you should reject. As you can see, various logicians and philosophers made different choices. Here we are concerned with Diodorus' own choice: He held the first two to be true and rejected the third.

The first proposition, "Every past truth is necessary," encapsulates the thought we have seen at work already in Aristotle's discussion. If it true that something happened, then it cannot be the case that it didn't happen. The second proposition, "Something impossible does not follow from something possible" at first seems to be a truism. How can something that cannot be the case follow from what can be the case? But the force it has here comes from the way it can be used to transfer the necessity of the past to the future, contrary to what we *may* intuitively think.

Take the third proposition, "There is something possible which neither is nor will be true." This is a commonsense kind of assumption; we think all the time that something *could have* happened, even though it isn't happening and we may have reason to think that it won't. (Aristotle gives an example: This cloak will not be cut up, but will wear out first; but we think that it could have been cut up.) However, if it will not be cut up, then it is true that it will not be cut up. But if this is true, then it always was true that it will not be cut up. Thus it is necessary that it not be cut up; there is no way that it can be cut up, since it always was true that it will not be cut up. Thus we find that the third proposition is false: we have to reject the idea that something is possible even though it is not the case and will not be the case. We are forced to the strange conclusion that only what is or will be the case is possible.

What makes this conclusion so strange, of course, is that we use the notion of possibility to do precisely what the conclusion of the argument rules out, namely, to talk about things and events that *won't* be the case, but *could* or *might* be. If Diodorus is right, then a lot of our ways of talking about things are wrong. Our everyday notion of the possible, as opposed to and more expansive than what actually happens, turns out not to apply to anything. Hence the Master Argument is shocking to us in the way that many technical philosophical results are; our first reaction is to think that we cannot accept the conclusion, so that there must be something wrong with the argument. However, it is not so easy to find just what is wrong with the argument.

We do not know enough about Diodorus to determine whether he accepted any of the resolutions of the Master Argument or wanted it to provoke people into thinking about matters that they normally took for granted.

The Stoics on Possibility and Necessity

Further, some propositions are possible and others impossible. And some are necessary and others nonnecessary. Possible is what admits of being true, and external factors do not prevent it from being true—for example, "Diocles is alive." Impossible is what does not admit of being true [or does admit of being true but is prevented by external factors from being true]—for example, "The earth flies." Necessary is what is true and does not admit of being false or does admit of being false but is prevented by external factors from being false—for example, "Virtue is beneficial." Nonnecessary is what is true but is such as to be false and is not prevented by external factors from being false—for example, "Dion is walking around." (Diogenes Laertius, *Lives of the Philosophers* 7,75)

CICERO

Marcus Tullius Cicero (106–43 B.C.) was a prominent politician in the late Roman Republic. He is also one of our best and most intelligent sources for the philosophy of his time.

Cicero had a thorough philosophical education and a good grasp of the major schools and debates of the day. Temperamentally, he was attracted to the Academic Skeptics, who did not put forward philosophical positions of their own, but argued against those of others. Cicero was attracted to argument, rather than to conviction, and as a famous arguer in the law courts, he was also attracted to the idea that truth emerges from the confrontation of opposing views.

As a Roman politician, Cicero did not think of philosophy as a worthy full-time occupation. Only toward the end of his life, after the ascendancy of Julius Caesar had left Cicero no scope for public action, did he compose philosophical works, aiming to produce the first comprehensive treatment of philosophical topics in Latin (Greek had been regarded as the language for philosophy). The series was cut short by his return to politics after the death of Caesar and eventually his own assassination. Cicero was aiming to educate his Roman audience in Greek philosophy and to familiarize them with the method of philosophical debate; the works generally take the form of dialogues, in which Cicero and other people defend or attack the major philosophical positions on a given issue.

For Cicero what matters is not so much that he should himself have and defend a view about fate as that he should understand the various philosophical options and the arguments for and against them.

On Fate 12–15
CICERO

Let us suppose, then, that the observations of the astrologers are like this: "If anyone has been born with the Dogstar rising," for example, "that man will not die at sea." Take care, Chrysippus, that you do not desert your own cause, over which there is a great struggle between you and the powerful dialectician Diodorus. For if the conditional "If anyone has been born with the Dogstar rising, he will not die at sea" is true, then so too is "If Fabius has been born with the Dogstar rising, Fabius will not die at sea." So these things are incompatible,

---

From *Cicero, On Fate and Boethius, Consolidation of Philosophy*, translated by R. Sharples (Warminster, England: Aris & Phillips, 1991).

namely that Fabius has been born with the Dogstar rising and that Fabius will die at sea; and since it is supposed as certain in the case of Fabius that he *has* been born with the Dogstar rising, these things also are incompatible, namely that Fabius exists and that he will die at sea. So the following conjunction, too, is a combination of things that are incompatible: "Fabius exists, and Fabius will die at sea." Put forward in this way, this cannot actually happen. So "Fabius will die at sea" belongs to the class of what cannot happen. Therefore everything which is said to be false in the future cannot happen.

But this, Chrysippus, is what you least want, and there is a great dispute about this very point between you and Diodorus. For he says that only what either is true or will be true can happen, and he says that whatever is going to happen must necessarily happen, and that whatever will not happen cannot happen. *You* say that things that will not happen, too, *can* happen, for example that this precious stone should be broken can happen, even if this is never going to happen, and that it was not necessary for Cypselus to rule in Corinth although this had been declared by the oracle of Apollo a thousand years before. But if you accept those divine predictions, you will have false statements about future events in such cases, with the result that it will be impossible for those things to happen, for example if it were said that Scipio will not capture Carthage. And if a true statement were made about the future and that thing were going to happen in that way, you would have to say that it is necessary. But all this is the view of Diodorus, which is opposed to you. For if this is a true conditional, "If you were born with the Dogstar rising, you will not die at sea," and the first clause in the conditional, "You were born with the Dogstar rising," is necessary—for all true statements about past things are necessary, in the view of Chrysippus who disagrees with his teacher Cleanthes, because they are unchangeable and cannot be turned from true to false—well then, if the first clause in the conditional is necessary, what follows becomes necessary as well. True, Chrysippus does not think this applies in every case; but nevertheless, if there is a cause in nature for Fabius not dying at sea, Fabius *cannot* die at sea.

At this point Chrysippus, becoming agitated, hopes that the astrologers and the other diviners can be foiled, and that they will not make use of conditionals but rather of conjunctions, so that they will not declare their observations as follows, "If someone was born with the Dogstar rising, that man will not die at sea," but rather will speak as follows, "It is not the case both that someone was born with the Dogstar rising and that that man will die at sea." What amusing presumption! So that he shall not himself fall into Diodorus' position, he instructs the astrologers how they ought to express their observations.

COMMENTS

The Stoics were causal determinists, holding that everything that happens is part of the chain of causes that is fate. Nonetheless, they claimed that Diodorus was wrong to hold that only what happens is possible. That is, they wanted to retain something like our everyday notion of the possible—what can or could happen though it does not—but within a system of causal determinism.

We know from the first passage that they defined the possible as what is true and is "not prevented" from happening by "external" factors. The second passage gives us the example of a jewel that *can* be broken, being fragile, though it will be broken only if there are specific external factors. (A jewel seems an odd example; what may be meant is a fragile cup made out of some precious stone.)

It is easy to see why we might want to defend this commonsense idea against Diodorus, but on what basis does Chrysippus hold that although it is causally determined that the precious stone will be broken or not, it is still possible for it to be broken, though it will not be broken? Here we lack Chrysippus' own arguments, and most of our information comes from people who strongly disagree with him.

In the Cicero passage, the opponent argues that Chrysippus' position is internally self-contradictory, since he wants to retain the everyday notion of possibility yet also accept that we can sometimes foretell the future by "divination." The Stoics maintained that divination, the skill of foretelling the future by signs (like birds' flights and omens), had a defensible basis, since they thought that future events could be predicted and regarded contemporary practices as crude versions of something that could be done more accurately.

Chrysippus thus has to accept the truth of "If Fabius was born at the rising of the Dog Star, Fabius will not die at sea." But we are supposing that Fabius was, in fact, born at the rising of the Dog Star. This is true about the past, and thus necessary, in the sense that we are concerned with: Nothing can make it false. If the conditional (the "if . . . then" statement) is true and the antecedent ("Fabius was born at the rising of the Dog Star") is true, then the consequent ("Fabius will not die at sea") is true. Is it, however, necessary—that is, is it such that it could not be false? Chrysippus wants to say no, for it is *possible* that Fabius will die at sea, even if he won't.

Chrysippus gets out of the difficulty by holding that this kind of claim about the future should not be put in the form of conditionals at all, but in the form of negated conjunctions—that is, the form "Not both: Fabius was born at the rising of the Dog Star and Fabius will die at sea." Why should this make any difference? For a Stoic, a conditional implies that there is a connection between the antecedent and the consequent such that denying the consequent conflicts with the antecedent. That is, there is a kind of necessary connection between Fabius being born at the rising of the Dog Star and Fabius not dying at sea. Not everybody would agree that a conditional implies so strong a claim, and we know that some other philosophers thought that a conditional was equivalent to a negated conjunction, where all that is excluded is the situation in which the antecedent is true and the consequent false. Thus, Chrysippus thinks that even though a past truth is connected to a future truth in such a way that the first can't be true and the second is false, and even though the past truth is necessary in the sense of being fixed—it could not be otherwise—the future truth is not necessary, and there is a sense in which it could be otherwise. If they could be linked in a true conditional, then the necessity of the past would transfer to the future; but they needn't be linked in that way, even if they are connected in a way that enables us to make a true prediction.

Whether this response works depends on the view you take of what the conditions are for the truth of a conditional. In the ancient world, this was a matter of great controversy (the poet Callimachus says that even the birds on the rooftops of Alexandria cawed answers to this question), and it is still controversial today.

This argument against Chrysippus is, as philosophical arguments often are in ancient philosophy, an ad hominem one: It claims that Chrysippus has a problem internal to his own position. Other objections can be raised. What sorts of possibility can a determinist allow? Would Chrysippus' problem be solved just by distinguishing logical possibility from causal possibility? Look back at the Master Argument and Chrysippus' response to it. Is it the best way of disarming that argument?

On Fate 10

ALEXANDER OF APHRODISIAS

176.14 [Consider the following argument]: | "The possible and contingent is not done
   15 away with if all things | come to be according to fate, on these grounds. [i] It is
        possible for that to come to be which is not prevented from coming to be by any-
        thing, even if it does not come to be. [ii] The opposites of the things that come to
        be in accordance with fate have not been prevented from coming to be (for
        which reason they are still possible even though they do not come to be). [iii]
        That they have not been prevented from coming to be is shown by the fact that
        the things that prevent them are unknown to us, although there certainly *are*
   20 some." (For | the causes of the coming to be of the opposites of these things in
        accordance with fate are also the causes of these things' *not* coming to be, if, as
        they say, it is impossible for opposites to come to be in the same circumstances.
        However, because certain things that exist are not known to us, for this reason
        they say that the coming to be [of the opposites of the things that are in accor-
        dance with fate] is not prevented.)—Well, how is saying this not the action of
   25 those who jest in arguments where jesting is not what is needed? | For our igno-
        rance makes no difference to the existence or non-existence of the facts. It is
        clear, when people speak like this, that the possible will according to them exist
        in virtue of our [degree of] knowledge. For those things will not be possible, for
177.1 those who can know their causes (and these would be | the prophets), that *are*
        possible for those who know that they have been prevented but do not know by
        what they are prevented.

        Preserving the nature of the possible in the way we have described, they say
        that even the things that come to be in accordance with fate, although they come
        to be unalterably, do not come to be of necessity, for this reason, that it is possi-
    5 ble | for their opposite too to come to be—possible in the sense described

Extract from *Alexander of Aphrodisias On Fate* by R. W. Sharples. Used by permission of Cornell University Press and Gerald Duckworth & Co. Ltd.

above. But these are, as I have said, the arguments of those who jest rather than of those who are supporting a position.

COMMENTS

Alexander is quite rude about the Stoics' attempt to reject Diodorus and hang on to our ordinary notion of possibility, given that they are determinists. But is the position he is criticizing so harshly really the one that the Stoics hold?

Alexander says that the Stoics support their view that some things are possible because they are not prevented from coming about by external factors, by the claim that we are ignorant of these external factors. We hold that the precious cup is breakable, for example, because we are unaware of any factors that will guarantee either its breaking or its not breaking. (If we were to discover that the material was unbreakable, we would revise our view.) Alexander points out that whether or not something *is* possible is not the same as whether or not we *know* that it is. If we don't know, that might just show an inadequacy in us, rather than constituting an important fact about the world.

This seems right; if Alexander's criticism is fair, then the Stoics were simply confused between the metaphysical issue (is something possible or not?) and the issue of knowledge (are we in a position to say whether something is the case or not?). But is Alexander being fair? Perhaps we can suggest that the Stoics didn't claim that our ignorance *constitutes* the absence of external factors, but that it indicates or *shows* that external factors are absent. (If we aren't aware of any external factors, it indicates that there aren't any around and thus that the possibility is still open.) If this is so, do the Stoics have a better view than Alexander makes out?

A. EXPLANATION OF INNER CONFLICT

Plato *Republic* 4, 436a–444a
Plato *Republic* 9, 588b–590d
Plato *Phaedrus* 253d–254e

B. WHAT IS AN EMOTION?

Aristotle *Rhetoric* II, part of 1, 2, 5, 8
Aristotle *Nicomachean Ethics* II, 1, parts of 2 and 3; IV, 5
The Early Stoics on the Emotions
Seneca *On Anger* I, 7–9, 12–14, 17–18; II, 1–4, 6–10, 28

C. A TEST CASE

Euripides *Medea* 1021–1080
Epictetus *Discourses* I, 28, 1–9; II, 17, 17–25
Galen *On the Doctrines of Hippocrates and Plato* III, 3, 13–24

D. REASON, THE EMOTIONS, AND FAITH

The Fourth Book of Maccabees selections

A. Explanation of Inner Conflict

In these passages, Plato produces the first systematic attempt to explain the phenomenon of inner psychological conflict in terms of a theory that there are distinct "parts" to the person's soul. (Here and elsewhere, talk of the "soul" is just a way of referring to psychological complexity and does not import spiritual or religious ideas.)

PLATO

The *Republic* and *Phaedrus* are long dialogues in which Plato discusses the soul, claiming that a person's psychological unity is the result of some kind of accommodation between different "parts"—kinds of motivation—within the person, whose distinctness is shown in cases of inner conflict. In the *Republic*, this is part of a larger ethical argument as to how we should live; in the *Phaedrus*, it is part of a discussion of different kinds of love and different kinds of literature. The analysis of the soul's parts, however, is similar in the different dialogues and clearly interested Plato in its own right.

Plato is the first philosopher to pay attention to psychological phenomena in a systematic way. The idea that the soul has three parts appears in these two dialogues and in Plato's account of the physical universe, the *Timaeus*, where it is given a physical interpretation and the parts are located in different areas of the human body. These passages are among the most famous in ancient philosophical writing for their imaginative treatment of a challenging idea.

For more on Plato, see pp. 35 and 235.

Republic 4, 436a–444a
PLATO

"But here's a hard one: is there just a single thing which we use for doing everything, or are there three and we use different things for different tasks? Do we learn with one of our aspects, get worked up with another, and with a third desire the pleasures of eating, sex, and so on, or do we use the whole of our

From Plato, *Republic*, translated by Robin Waterfield (Oxford: Oxford University Press, 1993). Reprinted with the permission of Oxford University Press.

b   mind for every task we actually get going on? These questions won't be easy to
    answer satisfactorily."

        "I agree," he said.

        "Well, let's approach an answer by trying to see whether these aspects are
    the same as one another or are different."

        "How?"

        "It's clear that the same one thing cannot simultaneously either act or be
    acted on in opposite ways in the same respect and in the same context. And con-
    sequently, if we find this happening in the case of these aspects of ourselves,
c   we'll know that there are more than one of them."

        "All right."

        "What about this, then?"

        "What?"

        "Is it possible for the same thing to be simultaneously at rest and in motion
    in the same respect?" I asked.

        "Of course not."

        "Let's take a closer look before agreeing, otherwise we'll start arguing later.
    My assumption is that if someone claims that a person who is standing still, but
    moving his hands and head, is the same person simultaneously being still and
    moving, we won't approve of this way of putting it, as opposed to saying that
d   one part of him is still, and another part of him is moving. Yes?"

        "Yes."

        "So even if the advocate of the claim were to get even more subtle and
    ingeniously maintain that when a top is spinning round with its peg fixed in
    place, then this is definitely a case of something simultaneously being still and
    moving as a whole, or that the same goes for anything else which spins round
    on one spot, we wouldn't accept this assertion. We'll say that in this situation
e   these objects are not still and moving in the same respects. We'll point out that
    they include an axis and a circumference, and that they may be still in respect of
    their axes (in the sense that they're not tipping over at all), but they have circu-
    lar motion in respect of their circumferences; and we'll add that when one of
    these objects tips its upright to the right or left or front or back while simulta-
    neously spinning round, then it has no stillness in any respect."

        "Yes, that's right," he said.

        "No assertion of this kind will put us off, then, or make us in the slightest
437a inclined to believe that the same thing could ever simultaneously be acted on or
    exist or act in opposite ways in the same respect and in the same context."

        "I won't be put off, anyway," he said.

        "That's as may be," I said. "But let's not feel compelled to have all the bother
    of going through every single one of these arguments and proving them false.
    Let's assume that we're right and carry on, with the understanding that if we
    ever turn out to have been mistaken, all the conclusions we draw on the basis of
    this assumption will be invalidated."

        "Yes, that's what we'd better do," he said.

"Wouldn't you count assent and dissent," I asked, "seeking and avoidance, b and liking and disliking, as all pairs of opposites? It'll make no difference whether you think of them as ways of acting or of being acted on."

"Yes, they're opposites," he answered.

"What about thirst and hunger and the desires generally," I went on, "and what about wishing and wanting? Wouldn't you say that all these things belong somewhere among the sets we've just mentioned? For example, won't you describe the mind of anyone who is in a state of desire as seeking to fulfil his c desires, or as liking whatever the desired object is? Or again, to the extent that it wants to get hold of something, don't you think it is internally assenting to this thing, as if in response to a question, and is longing for it to happen?"

"Yes, I do."

"And what about the states of antipathy, reluctance, or unwillingness? Won't we put these states in the opposite category, which includes dislike and aversion?"

"Of course." d

"Under these circumstances, then, won't we say that there is a category which consists of the desires, and that the most conspicuous desires are the ones called thirst and hunger?"

"Yes," he said.

"And the one is desire for drink, the other desire for food?"

"Yes."

"Now, is thirst, in itself, the mental desire for anything more than the object we mentioned? For example, is thirst thirst for a hot drink or a cold one, a lot of drink or a little, or in short for any particular kind of drink at all? Doesn't it take heat in addition to thirst to give it the extra feature of being desire for something e cold, and cold to make it desire for something hot? Doesn't it take a thirst which has been aggravated into becoming strong to produce the desire for a lot of drink, and doesn't it take a weak thirst to produce the desire for a little drink? The actual state of being thirsty, however, cannot possibly be desire for anything other than its natural object, which is just drink; and the same goes for hunger and food."

"Yes," he said. "Each desire is for its natural object only, and the desire for an object of this or that type is a result of some addition."

"It should be quite impossible, then," I said, "for anyone to catch us 438a unawares and rattle us with the claim that no one desires drink, but a good drink, and no one desires food, but good food. Everyone desires good, they say, so if thirst is a desire, it must be desire for a good drink or whatever; and so on for the other desires."

"There might seem to be some plausibility to the claim," he remarked.

"But there are only two categories of things whose nature it is to be relative," I said. "The first category consists, in my opinion, of things which have particular qualities and whose correlates have particular qualities; the second category consists of things which are just what they are and whose correlates are b just what they are."

"I don't understand," he said.

"Don't you realize," I said, "that anything which is greater is greater than something?"

"Yes."

"Than something smaller?"

"Yes."

"Whereas anything which is a lot greater is relative to something which is a lot smaller. Agreed?"

"Yes."

"And anything which was once greater (or will be) is relative to something which was once smaller (or will be), isn't it?"

"Of course," he said.

c   "And the same goes for more in relation to less, and double in relation to half (and all similar numerical relations); also for heavier in relation to lighter, quicker in relation to slower, and moreover hot in relation to cold, and so on and so forth, don't you think?"

"Yes."

"And what about the branches of knowledge? Isn't it the same story? Knowledge in itself is knowledge of information in itself (or whatever you choose to call the object of knowledge), but a particular branch of knowledge,
d   knowledge qualified, is knowledge of a particular qualified kind of thing. Here's an example: when the knowledge of making houses was developed, didn't it differ from the rest of the branches of knowledge and consequently gain its own name, building?"

"Of course."

"And didn't it do so by virtue of the fact that it is a particular kind of knowledge, a kind which none of the other branches of knowledge is?"

"Yes."

"And wasn't it when its object came into being as a particular kind of thing that it too came into being as a particular kind of knowledge? And doesn't the same go for all the other branches of expertise and knowledge?"

"Yes, it does."

"I wonder if you've grasped my meaning now," I said. "You should think of this as the point I was trying to make before, when I said that there are two categories of things whose nature it is to be relative: some are only themselves and are related to objects which are only themselves; others have particular qualities and are related to objects with particular qualities. I don't mean to imply that
e   their quality is the same as the quality of their objects—that knowledge of health and illness is itself healthy and ill, and knowledge of evil and good is itself evil and good. I mean that when knowledge occurs whose object is not the unqualified object of knowledge, but an object with a particular quality (say, health and illness), then the consequence is that the knowledge itself also acquires a particular quality, and this is why it is no longer called just plain knowledge: the qualification is added, and it is called medical knowledge."

"I do understand," he said, "and I agree as well."

"As for thirst, then," I said, "don't you think it finds its essential place 439a among relative things? And what it essentially is, of course, is thirst . . ."

". . . for drink," he said. "Yes, I agree."

"So for drink of a particular kind there is also thirst of a particular kind; but thirst in itself is not thirst for a lot of drink or a little drink, or a beneficial drink or a harmful drink, or in short for drink of any particular kind. Thirst in itself is essentially just thirst for drink in itself."

"Absolutely."

"When someone is thirsty, then, the only thing—in so far as he is thirsty— that his mind wants is to drink. This is what it longs for and strives for."   b

"Clearly."

"So imagine an occasion when something is making it resist the pull of its thirst: isn't this bound to be a different part of it from the thirsty part, which is impelling it towards drink as if it were an animal? I mean, we've already agreed that the same one thing cannot thanks to the same part of itself simultaneously have opposite effects in the same context."

"No, it can't."

"As an analogy, it isn't in my opinion right to say that an archer's hands are simultaneously pushing the bow away and pulling it closer. Strictly, one hand is pushing it away and the other is pulling it close."

"I quite agree," he said.   c

"Now, do we know of cases where thirsty people are unwilling to drink?"

"Certainly," he said. "It's a common occurrence."

"What could be the explanation for these cases?" I asked. "Don't we have to say that their mind contains a part which is telling them to drink, and a part which is telling them not to drink, and that this is a different part and overcomes the part which is telling them to drink?"

"I think so," he said.

"And those occasions when thirst and so on are countermanded occur thanks to rationality, whereas the pulls and impulses occur thanks to afflictions and diseased states, don't they?"   d

"I suppose so."

"So it wouldn't be irrational of us to expect that these are two separate parts," I said, "one of which we can describe as rational, and the other as irrational and desirous. The first is responsible for the mind's capacity to think rationally, and the second—which is an ally of certain satisfactions and pleasures—for its capacity to feel lust, hunger, and thirst, and in general to be stirred by desire."

"No, it wouldn't be irrational," he said. "This would be a perfectly reason- e able view for us to hold."

"Let's have these, then," I said, "as two distinct aspects of our minds. What about the passionate part, however, which is responsible for the mind's capacity for passion? Is it a third part, or might it be interchangeable with one of the other two?"

"I suppose it might be the same as the desirous part," he said.

"But there's a story I once heard which seems to me to be reliable," I said, "about how Leontius the son of Aglaeon was coming up from the Piraeus, outside the North Wall but close to it, when he saw some corpses with the public executioner standing near by. On the one hand, he experienced the desire to see them, but at the same time he felt disgust and averted his gaze. For a while, he struggled and kept his hands over his eyes, but finally he was overcome by the
440a desire; he opened his eyes wide, ran up to the corpses, and said, 'There you are, you wretches! What a lovely sight! I hope you feel satisfied!'"

"Yes, I've heard the story too," he said.

"Now, what it suggests," I said, "is that it's possible for anger to be at odds with the desires, as if they were different things."

"Yes, it does," he agreed.

"And that's far from being an isolated case, isn't it?" I asked. "It's not at all
b uncommon to find a person's desires compelling him to go against his reason, and to see him cursing himself and venting his passion on the source of the compulsion within him. It's as if there were two warring factions, with passion fighting on the side of reason. But I'm sure you wouldn't claim that you had ever, in yourself or in anyone else, met a case of passion siding with the desires against the rational mind, when the rational mind prohibits resistance."

"No, I certainly haven't," he said.

c   "And what about when you feel you're in the wrong?" I asked. "If someone who in your opinion has a right to do so retaliates by inflicting on you hunger and cold and so on, then isn't it the case that, in proportion to your goodness of character, you are incapable of getting angry at this treatment and your passion, as I say, has no inclination to get worked up against him?"

"True," he said.

"But suppose you feel you're being wronged. Under these circumstances, your passion boils and rages, and fights for what you regard as right. Then hunger, cold, and other sufferings make you stand firm and conquer them, and
d only success or death can stop it fighting the good fight, unless it is recalled by your rational mind and calmed down, as a dog is by a shepherd."

"That's a very good simile," he said. "And in fact the part we've got the auxiliaries to play in our community is just like that of dogs, with their masters being the rulers, who are, as it were, the shepherds of the community."

"Yes, you've got it," I said. "That's exactly what I mean. But there's something else here too, and I wonder if you've noticed it as well."

e   "What is it?"

"That we're getting the opposite impression of the passionate part from what we did before. Previously, we were thinking that it was an aspect of the desirous part, but now that seems to be way off the mark, and we're saying that when there's mental conflict, it is far more likely to fight alongside reason."

"Absolutely," he said.

"Is it different from the rational part, then, or is it a version of it, in which case there are two, not three, mental categories—the rational and the desirous? Or will the analogy with the community hold good? Three classes constituted the
441a community—the one which works for a living, the auxiliaries, and the policy-

makers—so is there in the mind as well a third part, the passionate part, which is an auxiliary of the rational part, unless it is corrupted by bad upbringing?"

"It must be a third part," he said.

"Yes," I said, "*if* we find that it's as distinct from the rational part as it is from the desirous part."

"But that's easy," he said. "Just look at children. It's evident that from the moment of their birth they have a copious supply of passion, but I'm not convinced that some of them ever acquire reason, and it takes quite a time for most b of them to do so."

"Yes, you've certainly put that well," I said. "And animals provide further evidence of the truth of what you're saying. Moreover, we can adduce the passage from Homer we quoted earlier: "He struck his breast and spoke sternly to his heart." Clearly, Homer here has one distinct part rebuking another distinct part—the part which has thought rationally about what is better and worse c rebuking the part whose passion is irrationally becoming aroused."

"You're absolutely right," he said.

"It's not been easy," I said, "but we've made it to the other shore: we've reached the reasonable conclusion that the constituent categories of a community and of any individual's mind are identical in nature and number."

"Yes, they are."

"Isn't it bound to follow that the manner and cause of a community's and an individual's wisdom are identical?"

"Naturally."

"And that the manner and cause of a community's and an individual's d courage are identical, and that the same goes for every other factor which contributes in both cases towards goodness?"

"Inevitably."

"So no doubt, Glaucon, we'll also be claiming that human morality is the same in kind as a community's morality."

"Yes, that's absolutely inevitable too."

"We can't have forgotten, however, that a community's morality consists in each of its three constituent classes doing its own job."

"No, I'm sure we haven't," he said.

"So we should impress upon our minds the idea that the same goes for human beings as well. Where each of the constituent parts of an individual does its own job, the individual will be moral and will do *his* own job."   e

"Yes, we certainly should do that," he said.

"Since the rational part is wise and looks out for the whole of the mind, isn't it right for it to rule, and for the passionate part to be its subordinate and its ally?"

"Yes."

"Now—to repeat—isn't it the combination of culture and exercise which will make them attuned to each other? The two combined provide fine discussions and studies to stretch and educate the rational part, and music and rhythm to relax, calm, and soothe the passionate part."   442a

"Absolutely."

"And once these two parts have received this education and have been trained and conditioned in their true work, then they are to be put in charge of the desirous part, which is the major constituent of an individual's mind and is naturally insatiably greedy for things. So they have to watch over it and make sure that it doesn't get so saturated with physical pleasures (as they are called)

b that in its bloated and strengthened state it stops doing its own job, and tries to dominate and rule over things which it is not equipped by its hereditary status to rule over, and so plunges the whole of everyone's life into chaos."

"Yes, indeed," he said.

"Moreover, these two are perfect for guarding the entire mind and the body against external enemies, aren't they?" I asked. "The rational part will do the planning, and the passionate part the fighting. The passionate part will obey the ruling part and employ its courage to carry out the plans."

"True."

"I imagine, then, that it is the passionate part of a person which we are tak-

c ing into consideration when we describe him as courageous: we're saying that neither pain nor pleasure stops his passionate part retaining the pronouncements of reason about what is and is not to be feared."

"That's right," he agreed.

"And the part we take into consideration when we call him wise is that little part—his internal ruler, which made these pronouncements—which knows what is advantageous for each of the three parts and for their joint unity."

"Yes."

"And don't we call him self-disciplined when there's concord and attunement between these same parts—that is, when the ruler and its two subjects

d unanimously agree on the necessity of the rational part being the ruler and when they don't rebel against it?"

"Yes, that's exactly what self-discipline is, in both a community and an individual," he said.

"And we're not changing our minds about the manner and cause of morality."

"Absolutely not."

"Well," I said, "have we blunted the edge of our notion of morality in any way? Do we have any grounds for thinking that our conclusions about its nature in a community don't apply in this context?"

"I don't think so," he replied.

"If there's still any doubt in our minds," I said, "we can eradicate it com-

e pletely by checking our conclusion against everyday cases."

"What cases?"

"Take this community of ours and a person who resembles it by virtue of both his nature and his upbringing, and suppose, for instance, we had to state whether, in our opinion, a person of this type would steal money which had been deposited with him. Is it conceivable to you that anyone would think our

443a man capable of this, rather than any other type of person?"

"No one could think that," he said.

"And he could have nothing to do with temple-robbery, theft, and betrayal either of his personal friends or, on a public scale, of his country, could he?"

"No, he couldn't."

"Moreover, nothing could induce him to break an oath or any other kind of agreement."

"No, nothing."

"And he's the last person you'd expect to find committing adultery, neglecting his parents, and failing to worship the gods."

"Yes, of course," he said.

"And isn't the reason for all of this the fact that each of his constituent parts b does its own job as ruler or subject."

"Yes, that's the only reason."

"Do you need to look any further for morality, then? Don't you think it can only be the capacity we've come up with, which enables both people and communities to be like this?"

"I for one certainly don't need to look any further," he said.

"Our dream has finally come true, then. We said we had a vague impression that we had probably—with the help of some god—stumbled across the origin c and some kind of outline of morality right at the start of our foundation of the community."

"Absolutely."

"It turns out, then, Glaucon—and this is why it was so useful—that the idea that a person who has been equipped by nature to be a shoemaker or a joiner or whatever should make shoes or do joinery or whatever was a dreamt image of morality."

"So it seems."

"And we've found that in real life morality is the same kind of property, apparently, though not in the field of external activities. Its sphere is a person's inner activity: it is really a matter of oneself and the parts of oneself. Once he has d stopped his mental constituents doing any job which is not their own or intruding on one another's work; once he has set his own house in order, which is what he really should be concerned with; once he is his own ruler, and is well regulated, and has internal concord; once he has treated the three factors as if they were literally the three defining notes of an octave—low, high, and middle—and has created a harmony out of them and however many notes there may be in between; once he has bound all the factors together and made him- e self a perfect unity instead of a plurality, self-disciplined and internally attuned: then and only then does he act—if he acts—to acquire property or look after his body or play a role in government or do some private business. In the course of this activity, it is conduct which preserves and promotes this inner condition of his that he regards as moral and describes as fine, and it is the knowledge which oversees this conduct that he regards as wisdom; however, it is any conduct which disperses this condition that he regards as immoral, and the thinking 444a which oversees this conduct that he regards as stupidity."

"You're absolutely right, Socrates," he said.

Republic 9, 588b–590d
PLATO

b "All right," I said. "At this point in the argument, let's remind ourselves of the original assertion which started us off on our journey here. Wasn't it someone saying that immorality was rewarding if you were a consummate criminal who gave an impression of morality? Wasn't that the assertion?"

"Yes, it was."

"Well, now that we've decided what effect moral and immoral conduct have," I said, "we can engage him in conversation."

"What shall we say?" he asked.

"Let's construct a theoretical model of the mind, to help him see what kind of idea he's come up with."

c "What sort of model?" he asked.

"Something along the lines of those creatures who throng the ancient myths," I said, "like the Chimera, Scylla, Cerberus, and so on, whose form is a composite of the features of more than one creature."

"Yes, that's how they're described," he said.

"Make a model, then, of a creature with a single—if varied and many-headed—form, arrayed all around with the heads of both wild and tame animals, and possessing the ability to change over to a different set of heads and to generate all these new bits from its own body."

d "That would take some skilful modelling," he remarked, "but since words are a more plastic material than wax and so on, you may consider the model constructed."

"A lion and a man are the next two models to make, then. The first of the models, however, is to be by far the largest, and the second the second largest."

"That's an easier job," he said. "It's done."

"Now join the three of them together until they become one, as it were."

"All right," he said.

"And for the final coat, give them the external appearance of a single entity. Make them look like a person, so that anyone incapable of seeing what's inside,

e who can see only the external husk, will see a single creature, a human being."

"It's done," he said.

"Now, we'd better respond to the idea that this person gains from doing wrong, and loses from doing right, by pointing out to its proponent that this is tantamount to saying that we're rewarded if we indulge and strengthen the

589a many-sided beast and the lion with all its aspects, but starve and weaken the man, until he's subject to the whims of the others, and can't promote familiarity and compatibility between the other two, but lets them bite each other, fight, and try to eat each other."

From Plato, *Republic*, translated by Robin Waterfield (Oxford: Oxford University Press, 1993). Reprinted with the permission of Oxford University Press.

"Yes, that's undoubtedly what a supporter of immorality would have to say," he agreed.

"So the alternative position, that morality is profitable, is equivalent to saying that our words and behaviour should be designed to maximize the control the inner man has within us, and should enable him to secure the help of the leo- b nine quality and then tend to the many-headed beast as a farmer tends to his crops—by nurturing and cultivating its tame aspects, and by stopping the wild ones growing. Then he can ensure that they're all compatible with one another, and with himself, and can look after them all equally, without favouritism."

"Yes, that's exactly what a supporter of morality has to say," he agreed.

"Whichever way you look at it, then, a supporter of morality is telling the truth, and a supporter of immorality is wrong. Whether your criterion is pleas- c ure, reputation, or benefit, a supporter of morality is right, and a critic of morality is unreliable and doesn't know what he's talking about."

"I quite agree: he doesn't in the slightest," he said.

"But he doesn't mean to make a mistake, so let's be gentle with him. Here's a question we can ask him, to try to win him over: 'My friend, don't you think that this is also what accounts for conventional standards of what is and is not acceptable? Things are acceptable when they subject the bestial aspects of our nature to the human—or it might be more accurate to say the divine—part of d ourselves, but they're objectionable when they cause the oppression of our tame side under the savage side.' Will he agree, do you think?"

"Well, I'll be recommending him to," he answered.

"So what follows from this argument? Can there be any profit in the immoral acquisition of money, if this entails the enslavement of the best part of oneself to the worst part? The point is, if there's no profit in someone selling his e son or daughter into slavery—slavery under savage and evil men—for even a great deal of money, then what happens if he cruelly enslaves the most divine part of himself to the vilest, most godless part? Isn't unhappiness the result? Isn't the deadly business he's being paid for far more terrible than what Eriphyle did when she accepted the necklace as the price for her husband's death?" 590a

"Yes, by a long way," Glaucon said. "I mean, I'll answer on behalf of our supporter of immorality."

"Now, do you think the reason for the traditional condemnation of licentiousness is the same—because it allows that fiend, that huge and many-faceted creature, greater freedom than it should have?"

"Obviously," he said.

"And aren't obstinacy and bad temper considered bad because they distend b and invigorate our leonine, serpentine side to a disproportionate extent?"

"Yes."

"Whereas a spoilt, soft way of life is considered bad because it makes this part of us so slack and loose that it's incapable of facing hardship?"

"Of course."

"And why are lack of independence and autonomy despised? Isn't it still to do with the passionate part, because we have to subordinate it to the unruly beast and, from our earliest years, get the lion used to being insulted and to becoming a monkey instead of a lion—and all for the sake of money and to satisfy our greed?"

c   "Yes."

"What about mundane, manual labour? Why do you think it has a bad name? Isn't it precisely because there's an inherent weakness in the truly good part of the person which makes him incapable of controlling his internal beasts, so that all he does is pander to them, and all he can learn is their whims?"

"I suppose that's right," he said.

"The question is, how can a person in this condition become subject to the kind of rulership which is available to a truly good person? By being the slave,

d we suggest, of a truly good person, whose divine element rules within him. But we're not suggesting, as Thrasymachus did about subjects, that his status as a subject should do him harm; we're saying that subjection to the principle of divine intelligence is to everyone's advantage. It's best if this principle is part of a person's own nature, but if it isn't, it can be imposed from outside, to foster as much unanimity and compatibility between us as might be possible when we're all governed by the same principle."

"You're right," he said.

Phaedrus 253d–254e
PLATO

Now let us stay with the threefold division of each soul we made at the beginning of our story: two forms in the shape of horses and one like a charioteer. Of the horses, one, we said, is good and the other not; but we did not describe the goodness of the good horse and the badness of the bad one, and we must do that now. The one on the nobler side is upright in form and clean limbed, with a high neck and commanding nose; he is white in color, with dark eyes. He is a lover of honor accompanied by self-restraint and a sense of shame and is a companion of true glory. He needs no whip—the charioteer guides him by command and word alone. The other one is crooked and massive, badly put together, with a thick, short neck and snub nose; he is dark-colored, with bloodshot gray eyes. He is a companion of excess and showing off. He is shaggy round the ears and deaf, scarcely yielding to the whip along with the goad.

Well, when the charioteer sees the vision of his beloved, at the sight he suffused his entire soul with warmth and is filled with tingling and the pricks of desire. Of the horses, the one that is obedient to the charioteer is controlled, then as always, by its sense of shame and holds itself back from leaping on the beloved boy; but the other one no longer heeds the charioteer's goad or whip, but prances violently forward and, causing all sorts of trouble to its yoke-fellow and the charioteer, compels them to approach the boy and make mention of the delights of sex. At first they both resist in displeasure, thinking that it is dreadful and forbidden things that they are being compelled to do; but finally, when there is no end to the trouble, they follow its lead, giving in and agreeing to do what it demands.

Now they come up to him and see the face of the beloved, like flashing lightning. When the charioteer sees it, his memory is taken back to the nature of beauty, and he sees it again established on a sacred pedestal together with self-restraint. At the sight he falls backward with a feeling of fear and reverence and is compelled at the same time to pull back the reins so strongly that both horses are forced down on their haunches, one willingly because it makes no resistance, but the insolent one most unwillingly.

They go farther back, and one horse feels shame and dread and drenches the entire soul with sweat, while the other, as soon as it recovers from the pain it felt from the bit and from its fall, no sooner gets its breath than it bursts into angry insults, covering the charioteer and its yoke-fellow with abuse for deserting their position and their agreement in a cowardly and unmanly way. Again it forces them unwillingly to go forward and barely yields to them when they beg it to put things off till later. When the time agreed on comes round, it reminds them when they are pretending to have forgotten; struggling, neighing, and dragging, it forces them again to approach the beloved boy with the same proposition, and when they are near, it bites on the bit and drags shamelessly, head bent and tail stretched out. But the charioteer is affected the same way as before, only more so; he falls back as if from the race-barrier, and wrenching back the bit even more strongly from the teeth of the insolent horse, he bloodies its evil-speaking tongue and jaws, forces its legs and haunches to the ground, and delivers it over to pains.

When the bad horse has frequently suffered this, it stops its insolence. It is humbled and now follows the charioteer's foresight, and when it sees the beautiful boy, it dies with fright. So now the lover's soul follows the boy in reverence and awe.

COMMENTS

The *Republic* argument is designed to show that each of us contains three distinct sources of motivation ("parts" of the soul). First, Plato distinguishes reason from desires by the point that desire goes only for its own immediate gratification, whereas reason understands the viewpoint of the whole person overall. Hence it is reason that prevents us from giving in to an immediate desire to drink, for example, if it will be bad for us in the future. The third part is not so clearly distinguished from the other two. Like the desires, it goes for the object of impulse without regard to the person's overall good. But unlike the desires, Plato regards it as educable to support reason, by aspiring to an ideal given by reason but not fully understood. Emotions like anger belong with this part; Plato regards them as able to absorb what reason demands and to motivate the person accordingly.

How does this model of the three-part soul affect the way we think of the person as a whole and her behavior? How can the interaction of parts of the soul result in action of the person as a whole? We can see two ways in which Plato thinks of the parts' interrelations. Sometimes he thinks of them as communicating in a rational way, described in terms of using a kind of language; they agree about their different roles or settle disagreements. An integrated life is achieved when the motivations other than reason come to be educated by it so that they do not motivate the person in a way that reason does not endorse.

Sometimes, however, Plato thinks of the parts other than reason as lacking anything like rational communication, and they are portrayed as subhuman, imagined in the shape of animals. In the *Phaedrus,* the charioteer (reason) is a human trying to control a biddable horse (the emotions) and an unbiddable and refractory horse (desire, especially sexual desire). In the *Republic,* the person is thought of as containing a little person trying to control a repulsive shape-changing beast (desire) with the help of a lion (the emotions). These pictures imply that we should identify with reason, for that is what is human in us, and that an ordered life is possible only if reason controls the other parts, which are, in themselves, subhuman, by force and repression if necessary.

These are different pictures of our psychology. Plato employs them both and does not seem to think that he has to choose between them. Are they, in fact, incompatible?

What do you make of Plato's insistence that there is a third part of the soul as well as reason and desire? It implies that the emotions, for example, are like reason in that they are not just immediate urges for gratification, like desires, and they are like desires in that they do not, like reason, grasp the importance of the overall good of the whole person, but can go for a lesser good that can undermine the overall good. Is this a plausible account?

In the *Republic,* Plato calls this the "passionate" part (translators sometimes call it the "spirited" part; the Greek is *thumos,* which can mean anger). In so doing, and in his examples, he is focusing on the aggressive, rather than the gentle, emotions. A division of the soul that gave more weight to emotions like caring and pity might give a different picture of this part. However, we shall see that anger is the focus of much ancient discussion of the emotions. The ancients thought it particularly important to understand aggressive emotions, such as anger, because of their impact on other people and their potential for social disruption.

Do you agree with the way in which, in the *Phaedrus* passage, sexual attraction is treated as a refractory and apparently uneducable desire? Look at the way the charioteer treats the refractory horse. Is this a good imaginative description of the kind of situation Plato is talking about?

B. What Is an Emotion?

Aristotle and the Stoics both produce philosophical accounts of emotion, which turn out to have conflicting implications, showing that everyday beliefs about emotions leave open the possibility of mutually incompatible theories.

ARISTOTLE

Aristotle's *Rhetoric* takes seriously the techniques of persuasion, which in the ancient world were those of public speaking. The person employing rhetoric is aiming to persuade the audience, rather than to get them to believe what is true. Nonetheless, Aristotle claims that this endeavor is worthy of philosophical attention. It is not random, but organized in a way that repays study, and it is related to the philosopher's search for truth, since, he claims, humans tend overall to find truth more persuasive than error. (If we could be so easily manipulated as to find error as persuasive as truth, we would be grievously ill adapted to the world.)

Aristotle's discussion of the emotions has been particularly admired for its acute observation. The orator is concerned not with truth but with what works to persuade people. But to do this he must be right about their emotions and what the emotions involve; to rouse them rather than annoy them or to make them feel fear rather than indifference, he has to be right about what anger and fear are and what produces, sustains and diminishes them.

Aristotle's *Nicomachean Ethics* is a collection of his lectures on ethics, put together by an editor some time after his death. For some reason now lost, it was named after Aristotle's son Nicomachus. Although it is often regarded as Aristotle's definitive work on ethics, it is not a modern book, written to an overall plan; there are different treatments of the same topic in different parts, and we have no reason to think that the order of the parts is Aristotle's. Some of the parts are particularly brilliant and memorable treatments of happiness and virtue.

For more on Aristotle, see p. 12.

Rhetoric II, PART OF 1, 2, 5, 8

ARISTOTLE

The emotions are all those feelings that so change men as to affect their judgements, and that are also attended by pain or pleasure. Such are anger, pity, fear and the like, with their opposites. We must arrange what we have to say about each of them under three heads. Take, for instance, the emotion of anger: here we must discover what the state of mind of angry people is, who the people are with whom they usually get angry, and on what grounds they get angry with them. It is not enough to know one or even two of these points; unless we know all three, we shall be unable to arouse anger in anyone. The same is true of the other emotions. So just as earlier in this work we drew up a list of propositions, 30 let us now proceed in the same way to analyse the subject before us.

2. Anger may be defined as a desire accompanied by pain, for a conspicuous revenge for a conspicuous slight at the hands of men who have no call to slight oneself or one's friends. If this is a proper definition of anger, it must always be felt towards some particular individual, e.g. Cleon, and not man in 1378ᵇ1 general. It must be felt because the other has done or intended to do something to him or one of his friends. It must always be attended by a certain pleasure— that which arises from the expectation of revenge. For it is pleasant to think that 5 you will attain what you aim at, and nobody aims at what he thinks he cannot attain. Hence it has been well said about wrath,

> Sweeter it is by far than the honeycomb dripping with sweetness,
> And spreads through the hearts of men.

It is also attended by a certain pleasure because the thoughts dwell upon the act of vengeance, and the images then called up cause pleasure, like the images called up in dreams.
10   Now slighting is the actively entertained opinion of something as obviously of no importance. We think bad things, as well as good ones, have serious importance; and we think the same of anything that tends to produce such things, while those which have little or no such tendency we consider unimportant. There are three kinds of slighting—contempt, spite, and insolence. 15 Contempt is one kind of slighting: you feel contempt for what you consider unimportant, and it is just such things that you slight. Spite is another kind; it is a thwarting another man's wishes, not to get something yourself but to prevent his getting it. The slight arises just from the fact that you do not aim at something for yourself: clearly you do not think that he can do you harm, for then 20 you would be afraid of him instead of slighting him, nor yet that he can do you any good worth mentioning, for then you would be anxious to make friends with him. Insolence is also a form of slighting, since it consists in doing and saying things that cause shame to the victim, not in order that anything may happen 25 pen to yourself, or because anything has happened to yourself, but simply for the pleasure involved. (Retaliation is not insolence, but vengeance.) The cause of the pleasure thus enjoyed by the insolent man is that he thinks himself greatly superior to others when ill-treating them. That is why youths and rich men are insolent; they think themselves superior when they show insolence. One sort of 30 insolence is to rob people of the honour due to them; you certainly slight them thus; for it is the unimportant, for good or evil, that has no honour paid to it. So Achilles says in anger:

> He hath taken my prize for himself and hath done me dishonour,

and

> Like an alien honoured by none,

meaning that this is why he is angry. A man expects to be specially respected by
his inferiors in birth, in capacity, in goodness, and generally in anything in which   1379ª1
he is much their superior: as where money is concerned a wealthy man looks for
respect from a poor man; where speaking is concerned, the man with a turn for
oratory looks for respect from one who cannot speak; the ruler demands the
respect of the ruled, and the man who thinks he ought to be a ruler demands the
respect of the man whom he thinks he ought to be ruling. Hence it has been said

> Great is the wrath of kings, whose father is Zeus almighty,

and   5

> Yea, but his rancour abideth long afterward also,

their great resentment being due to their great superiority. Then again a man
looks for respect from those who he thinks owe him good treatment, and these
are the people whom he has treated or is treating well, or means or has meant to
treat well, either himself, or through his friends, or through others at his request.

It will be plain by now, from what has been said, in what frame of mind,
with what persons, and on what grounds people grow angry. The frame of mind   10
is that in which any pain is being felt. In that condition, a man is always aiming
at something. Whether, then, another man opposes him either directly in any
way, as by preventing him from drinking when he is thirsty, or indirectly;
whether someone works against him, or fails to work with him, or otherwise
vexes him while he is in this mood, he is equally angry in all these cases. [Hence   15
people who are afflicted by sickness or poverty or love or thirst or any other
unsatisfied desires are prone to anger and easily roused: especially against those
who slight their present distress.] Thus a sick man is angered by disregard of his
illness, a poor man by disregard of his poverty, a man waging war by disregard   20
of the war he is waging, a lover by disregard of his love, and so in other cases
too. Each man is predisposed, by the emotion now controlling him, to his own
particular anger. Further, we are angered if we happen to be expecting a contrary result; for a quite unexpected evil is specially painful, just as the quite
unexpected fulfilment of our wishes is specially pleasant. Hence it is plain what
seasons, times, conditions, and periods of life tend to stir men easily to anger,   25
and where and when this will happen; and it is plain that the more we are under
these conditions the more easily we are stirred.

These, then, are the frames of mind in which men are easily stirred to anger.
The persons with whom we get angry are those who laugh, mock, or jeer at us,
for such conduct is insolent. Also those who inflict injuries upon us that are   30
marks of insolence. These injuries must be such as are neither retaliatory nor

profitable to the doers; for then they will be felt to be due to insolence. Also those who speak ill of us, and show contempt for us, in connexion with the things we ourselves most care about: thus those who are eager to win fame as philosophers get angry with those who show contempt for their philosophy; those who pride themselves upon their appearance get angry with those who show contempt for their appearance; and so on in other cases. We feel particularly angry on this account if we suspect that we are in fact, or that people think we are, lacking completely or to any effective extent in the qualities in question. For when we are convinced that we excel in the qualities for which we are jeered at, we can ignore the jeering. Again, we are angrier with our friends than with other people, since we feel that our friends ought to treat us well and not badly. We are angry with those who have usually treated us with honour or regard, if a change comes and they behave to us otherwise; for we think that they feel contempt for us, or they would still be behaving as they did before. And with those who do not return our kindnesses or fail to return them adequately, and with those who oppose us though they are our inferiors; for all such persons seem to feel contempt for us—those who oppose us seem to think us inferior to themselves, and those who do not return our kindnesses seem to think that those kindnesses were conferred by inferiors. And we feel particularly angry with men of no account at all, if they slight us. For we have supposed that anger caused by the slight is felt towards people who are not justified in slighting us, and our inferiors are not thus justified. Again, we feel angry with friends if they do not speak well of us or treat us well; and still more, if they do the contrary; or if they do not perceive our needs, which is why Plexippus is angry with Meleager in Antiphon's play; for this want of perception shows that they are slighting us—we do not fail to perceive the needs of those for whom we care. Again, we are angry with those who rejoice at our misfortunes or simply keep cheerful in the midst of our misfortunes, since this shows that they either hate us or are slighting us. Also with those who are indifferent to the pain they give us: this is why we get angry with bringers of bad news. And with those who listen to stories about us or keep on looking at our weaknesses; this seems like either slighting us or hating us; for those who love us share in all our distresses and it must distress anyone to keep on looking at his own weaknesses. Further, with those who slight us before five classes of people: namely, our rivals, those whom we admire, those whom we wish to admire us, those for whom we feel reverence, those who feel reverence for us: if anyone slights us before such persons, we feel particularly angry. Again, we feel angry with those who slight us in connexion with what we are as honourable men bound to champion—our parents, children, wives, or subjects. And with those who do not return a favour, since such a slight is unjustifiable. Also with those who reply with humorous levity when we are speaking seriously, for such behaviour indicates contempt. And with those who treat us less well than they treat everybody else; it is another mark of contempt that they should think we do not deserve what everyone else deserves. Forgetfulness, too, causes anger, as when our own names are forgotten, trifling as this may be; since forgetfulness is felt to be another sign that we are being slighted; it is due to negligence, and to neglect us is to slight us.

The persons with whom we feel anger, the frame of mind in which we feel it, and the reasons why we feel it, have now all been set forth. Clearly the orator will have to speak so as to bring his hearers into a frame of mind that will dispose them to anger, and to represent his adversaries as open to such charges and possessed of such qualities as do make people angry.

5. Next, we show the things and persons of which, and the states of mind in which, we feel afraid. Fear may be defined as a pain or disturbance due to imagining some destructive or painful evil in the future. For there are some evils, e.g. wickedness or stupidity, the prospect of which does not frighten us: only such as amount to great pains or losses do. And even these only if they appear not remote but so near as to be imminent: we do not fear things that are 25 a very long way off; for instance, we all know we shall die, but we are not troubled thereby, because death is not close at hand. From this definition it will follow that fear is caused by whatever we feel has great power of destroying us, or of harming us in ways that tend to cause us great pain. Hence the very indica- 30 tions of such things are terrible, making us feel that the terrible thing itself is close at hand; and this—the approach of what is terrible—is danger. Such indications are the enmity and anger of people who have power to do something to us; for it is plain that they have the will to do it, and so they are on the point of doing it. Also injustice in possession of power; for it is the unjust man's choice that makes him unjust. Also outraged excellence in possession of power; for it is 1382ᵇ1 plain that, when outraged, it always chooses to retaliate, and now it has the power to do so. Also fear felt by those who have the power to do something to us, since such persons are sure to be ready to do it. And since most men tend to be bad—slaves to greed, and cowards in danger—it is, as a rule, a terrible thing 5 to be at another man's mercy; and therefore, if we have done anything horrible, those in the secret terrify us with the thought that they may betray or desert us. And those who can do us wrong are terrible to us when we are liable to be wronged; for as a rule men do wrong to others whenever they have the power to do it. And those who have been wronged, or believe themselves to be 10 wronged, are terrible; for they are always looking out for their opportunity. Also those who have done people wrong, if they possess power, since they stand in fear of retaliation: we have already said that wickedness possessing power is terrible. Again, our rivals for a thing cause us fear when we cannot both have it at once; for we are always at war with such men. We also fear those who are to be feared by stronger people than ourselves: if they can hurt those stronger peo- 15 ple, still more can they hurt us; and, for the same reason, we fear those whom those stronger people are actually afraid of. Also those who have destroyed people stronger than we are. Also those who are attacking people weaker than we are: either they are already formidable, or they will be so when they have thus grown stronger. Of those we have wronged, and of our enemies or rivals, it is 20 not the passionate and outspoken whom we have to fear, but the quiet, dissembling, unscrupulous; since we never know when they are upon us, we can never be sure they are at a safe distance. All terrible things are more terrible if they give us no chance of retrieving a blunder—either no chance at all, or only one that depends on our enemies and not ourselves. Those things are also worse which 25

we cannot, or cannot easily, help. Speaking generally, anything causes us to feel fear that when it happens to, or threatens, others causes us to feel pity.

The above are, roughly, the chief things that are terrible and are feared. Let us now describe the conditions under which we ourselves feel fear. If fear is asso-
30 ciated with the expectation that something destructive will happen to us, plainly nobody will be afraid who believes nothing can happen to him; we shall not fear things that we believe cannot happen to us, nor people who we believe cannot inflict them upon us; nor shall we be afraid at times when we think ourselves safe from them. It follows therefore that fear is felt by those who believe something to be likely to happen to them, at the hands of particular persons, in a particular
1383ª1 form, and at a particular time. People do not believe this when they are, or think they are, in the midst of great prosperity, and are in consequence insolent, con-temptuous, and reckless—the kind of character produced by wealth, physical strength, abundance of friends, power; nor yet when they feel they have experi-
5 enced every kind of horror already and have grown callous about the future, like men who are being flogged to death—if they are to feel the anguish of uncer-tainty, there must be some faint expectation of escape. This appears from the fact that fear sets us thinking what can be done, which of course nobody does when things are hopeless. Consequently, when it is advisable that the audience should be frightened, the orator must make them feel that they really are in danger of something, pointing out that it has happened to others who were stronger than
10 they are, and is happening, or has happened, to people like themselves, at the hands of unexpected people, in an unexpected form, and at an unexpected time.

Having now seen the nature of fear, and of the things that cause it, and the various states of mind in which it is felt, we can also see what confidence is,
15 about what things we feel it, and under what conditions. It is the opposite of fear, and what causes it is the opposite of what causes fear; it is, therefore, the imaginative expectation of the nearness of what keeps us safe and the absence or remoteness of what is terrible: it may be due either to the near presence of
20 what inspires confidence or to the absence of what causes alarm. We feel it if we can take steps—many, or important, or both—to cure or prevent trouble; if we have neither wronged others nor been wronged by them; if we have either no rivals at all or no strong ones; if our rivals who are strong are our friends or have treated us well or been treated well by us; or if those whose interest is the same as ours are the more numerous party, or the stronger, or both.
25 As for our own state of mind, we feel confidence if we believe we have often succeeded and never suffered reverses, or have often met danger and escaped it safely. For there are two reasons why human beings face danger calmly: they may have no experience of it, or they may have means to deal with it: thus when
30 in danger at sea people may feel confident about what will happen either because they have no experience of bad weather, or because their experience gives them the means of dealing with it. We also feel confident whenever there is nothing to terrify other people like ourselves, or people weaker than our-selves, or people than whom we believe ourselves to be stronger—and we believe this if we have conquered them, or conquered others who are as strong as they are, or stronger. Also if we believe ourselves superior to our rivals in the

number and importance of the advantages that make men formidable—plenty
of money, men, friends, land, military equipment (of all, or the most important, 1383ᵇ1
kinds). Also if we have wronged no one, or not many, or not those of whom we
are afraid. And when we are being wronged; [[and generally, if our relations 5
with the gods are satisfactory, as will be shown especially by signs and oracles]]
for anger makes us confident and, anger is excited by our knowledge that we are
not the wrongers but the wronged, and that the divine power is always supposed to be on the side of the wronged. Also when, at the outset of an enterprise,
we believe that we cannot fail, or that we shall succeed. So much for the causes 10
of fear and confidence.

8. So much for kindness and unkindness. Let us now consider pity, asking
ourselves what things excite pity, and for what persons, and in what states of our
mind pity is felt. Pity may be defined as a feeling of pain at an apparent evil,
destructive or painful, which befalls one who does not deserve it, and which we
might expect to befall ourselves or some friend of ours, and moreover to befall
us soon. For if we are to feel pity we must obviously be capable of supposing that
some evil may happen to us or some friend of ours, and moreover some such evil
as is stated in our definition or is more or less of that kind. It is therefore not felt
by those completely ruined, who suppose that no further evil can befall them, 20
since the worst has befallen them already; nor by those who imagine themselves
immensely fortunate—their feeling is rather insolence, for when they think they
possess all the good things of life, it is clear that the impossibility of evil befalling
them will be included, this being one of the good things in question. Those who
think evil *may* befall them are such as have already had it befall them and have
safely escaped from it; elderly men, owing to their good sense and their experi- 25
ence; weak men, especially men inclined to cowardice; and also educated people, since these can take long views. Also those who have parents living, or children, or wives; for these are our own, and the evils mentioned above may easily
befall them. And those who are neither moved by any courageous emotion such 30
as anger or confidence (these emotions take no account of the future), nor by a
disposition to insolence (insolent men, too, take no account of the possibility that
something evil will happen to them), nor yet by great fear (panic-stricken people
do not feel pity, because they are taken up with what is happening to themselves);
only those feel pity who are between these two extremes. In order to feel pity we
must also believe in the goodness of at least some people; if you think nobody 1386ᵃ1
good, you will believe that everybody deserves evil fortune. And, generally, we
feel pity whenever we are in the condition of remembering that similar misfortunes have happened to us or ours, or expecting them to happen in future.

So much for the mental conditions under which we feel pity. What we pity
is stated clearly in the definition. All unpleasant and painful things excite pity, 5
and all destructive things; and all such evils as are due to chance, if they are serious. The painful and destructive evils are: death in its various forms, bodily
injuries and afflictions, old age, diseases, lack of food. The evils due to chance
are: friendlessness, scarcity of friends (it is a pitiful thing to be torn away from 10
friends and companions), deformity, weakness, mutilation; evil coming from a
source from which good ought to have come; and the frequent repetition of such

misfortunes. Also the coming of good when the worst has happened: e.g. the
15 arrival of the Great King's gifts for Diopeithes after his death. Also that either no
good should have befallen a man at all, or that he should not be able to enjoy it
when it has.

The grounds, then, on which we feel pity are these or like these. The people
we pity are: those whom we know, if only they are not very closely related to
us—in that case we feel about them as if we were in danger ourselves. For this
20 reason Amasis did not weep, they say, at the sight of his son being led to death,
but did weep when he saw his friend begging: the latter sight was pitiful, the
former terrible, and the terrible is different from the pitiful; it tends to cast out
pity, and often helps to produce the opposite of pity. For we no longer feel pity
25 when the danger is near ourselves. Also we pity those who are like us in age,
character, disposition, social standing, or birth; for in all these cases it appears
more likely that the same misfortune may befall us also. Here too we have to
remember the general principle that what we fear for ourselves excites our pity
when it happens to others. Further, since it is when the sufferings of others are
close to us that they excite our pity (we cannot remember what disasters happened a hundred centuries ago, nor look forward to what will happen a hun-
30 dred centuries hereafter, and therefore feel little pity, if any, for such things): it
follows that those who heighten the effect of their words with suitable gestures,
tones, appearance, and dramatic action generally, are especially successful in
exciting pity: they thus put the disasters before our eyes, and make them seem
1386^{b}1 close to us, just coming or just past. Anything that has just happened, or is going
to happen soon, is particularly piteous: so too therefore are the signs of suffering—the garments and the like of those who have already suffered; the words
and the like of those actually suffering—of those, for instance, who are on the
5 point of death. For all this, because it seems close, tends to produce pity. Most
piteous of all is it when, in such times of trial, the victims are persons of noble
character, for their suffering is undeserved and it is set before our eyes.

Nicomachean Ethics II, 1, PARTS OF 2 AND 3; IV, 5
ARISTOTLE

Virtue, then, being of two kinds, intellectual and moral, intellectual virtue in the
main owes both its birth and its growth to teaching (for which reason it requires
experience and time), while moral virtue comes about as a result of habit,
whence also its name is one that is formed by a slight variation from the word
habit. From this it is also plain that none of the moral virtues arises in us by
nature; for nothing that exists by nature can form a habit contrary to its nature.
For instance the stone which by nature moves downwards cannot be habituated

From Aristotle, *Nicomachean Ethics*, translated by W. D. Ross, revised by J. L. Ackrill and
J. O. Urmson (Oxford: Oxford University Press, 1980). Reprinted with the permission of
Oxford University Press.

to move upwards, not even if one tries to train it by throwing it up ten thousand times; nor can fire be habituated to move downwards, nor can anything else that by nature behaves in one way be trained to behave in another. Neither by nature, then, nor contrary to nature do the virtues arise in us; rather we are adapted by nature to receive them, and are made perfect by habit.

Again, of all the things that come to us by nature we first acquire the potentiality and later exhibit the activity (this is plain in the case of the senses; for it was not by often seeing or often hearing that we got these senses, but on the contrary we had them before we used them, and did not come to have them by using them); but the virtues we get by first exercising them, as also happens in the case of the arts as well. For the things we have to learn before we can do them, we learn by doing them, e.g. men become builders by building and lyre-players by playing the lyre; so too we become just by doing just acts, temperate by doing temperate acts, brave by doing brave acts.

This is confirmed by what happens in states; for legislators make the citizens good by forming habits in them, and this is the wish of every legislator, and those who do not effect it miss their mark, and it is in this that a good constitution differs from a bad one.

Again, it is from the same causes and by the same means that every virtue is both produced and destroyed, and similarly every art; for it is from playing the lyre that both good and bad lyre-players are produced. And the corresponding statement is true of builders and of all the rest; men will be good or bad builders as a result of building well or badly. For if this were not so, there would have been no need of a teacher, but all men would have been born good or bad at their craft. This, then, is the case with the virtues also; by doing the acts that we do in our transactions with other men we become just or unjust, and by doing the acts that we do in the presence of danger, and by being habituated to feel fear or confidence, we become brave or cowardly. The same is true of appetites and feelings of anger; some men become temperate and good-tempered, others self-indulgent and irascible, by behaving in one way or the other in the appropriate circumstances. Thus, in one word, states of character arise out of like activities. This is why the activities we exhibit must be of a certain kind; it is because the states of character correspond to the differences between these. It makes no small difference, then, whether we form habits of one kind or of another from our very youth; it makes a very great difference, or rather *all* the difference.

First, then, let us consider this, that it is the nature of such things to be destroyed by defect and excess, as we see in the case of strength and of health (for to gain light on things imperceptible we must use the evidence of sensible things); exercise either excessive or defective destroys the strength, and similarly drink or food which is above or below a certain amount destroys the health, while that which is proportionate both produces and increases and preserves it. So too is it, then, in the case of temperance and courage and the other virtues. For the man who flies from and fears everything and does not stand his ground against anything becomes a coward, and the man who fears nothing at all but goes to meet every danger becomes rash; and similarly the man who indulges in every pleasure and abstains from none becomes self-indulgent, while the man who shuns every pleasure, as boors do, becomes in a way insensible; temperance and courage, then, are destroyed by excess and defect, and preserved by the mean.

But not only are the sources and causes of their origination and growth the same as those of their destruction, but also the sphere of their actualization will be the same; for this is also true of the things which are more evident to sense, e.g. of strength; it is produced by taking much food and undergoing much exertion, and it is the strong man that will be most able to do these things. So too is it with the virtues; by abstaining from pleasures we become temperate, and it is when we have become so that we are most able to abstain from them; and similarly too in the case of courage; for by being habituated to despise things that are fearful and to stand our ground against them we become brave, and it is when we have become so that we shall be most able to stand our ground against them.

We must take as a sign of states of character the pleasure or pain that supervenes upon acts; for the man who abstains from bodily pleasures and delights in this very fact is temperate, while the man who is annoyed at it is self-indulgent, and he who stands his ground against things that are terrible and delights in this or at least is not pained is brave, while the man who is pained is a coward. For moral excellence is concerned with pleasures and pains; it is on account of the pleasure that we do bad things, and on account of the pain that we abstain from noble ones. Hence we ought to have been brought up in a particular way from our very youth, as Plato says, so as both to delight in and to be pained by the things that we ought; this is the right education.

Again, if the virtues are concerned with actions and passions, and every passion and every action is accompanied by pleasure and pain, for this reason also virtue will be concerned with pleasures and pains. This is indicated also by the fact that punishment is inflicted by these means; for it is a kind of cure, and it is the nature of cures to be effected by contraries.

Good temper is a mean with respect to anger; the middle state being unnamed, and the extremes almost without a name as well, we place good temper in the middle position, though it inclines towards the deficiency, which is without a name. The excess might be called a sort of "irascibility." For the passion is anger, while its causes are many and diverse.

The man who is angry at the right things and with the right people, and, further, as he ought, when he ought, and as long as he ought, is praised. This will be the good-tempered man, then, since good temper is praised. For the good-tempered man tends to be unperturbed and not to be led by passion, but to be angry in the manner, at the things, and for the length of time, that the rule dictates; but he is thought to err rather in the direction of deficiency; for the good-tempered man is not revengeful, but rather tends to make allowances.

The deficiency, whether it is a sort of "unirascibility" or whatever it is, is blamed. For those who are not angry at the things they should be angry at are thought to be fools, and so are those who are not angry in the right way, at the right time, or with the right persons; for such a man is thought not to feel things nor to be pained by them, and, since he does not get angry, he is thought unlikely to defend himself; and to endure being insulted and put up with insult to one's friends is slavish.

The excess can be manifested in all the points that have been named (for one can be angry with the wrong persons, at the wrong things, more than is right, too quickly, or too long); yet *all* are not found in the same person. Indeed they could not; for evil destroys even itself, and if it is complete becomes unbearable. Now *hot-tempered* people get angry quickly and with the wrong persons and at the wrong things and more than is right, but their anger ceases quickly—which is the best point about them. This happens to them because they do not restrain their anger but retaliate openly owing to their quickness of temper, and then their anger ceases. By reason of excess *choleric* people are quick-tempered and ready to be angry with everything and on every occasion; whence their name. *Sulky* people are hard to appease, and retain their anger long; for they repress their passion. But it ceases when they retaliate; for revenge relieves them of their anger, producing in them pleasure instead of pain. If this does not happen they retain their burden; for owing to its not being obvious no one even reasons with them, and to digest one's anger in oneself takes time. Such people are most troublesome to themselves and to their dearest friends. We call *bad-tempered* those who are angry at the wrong things, more than is right, and longer, and cannot be appeased until they inflict vengeance or punishment.

To good temper we oppose the excess rather than the defect; for not only is it commoner (since revenge is the more human), but bad-tempered people are worse to live with.

What we have said in our earlier treatment of the subject is plain also from what we are now saying; viz. that it is not easy to define how, with whom, at what, and how long one should be angry, and at what point right action ceases and wrong begins. For the man who strays a little from the path, either towards the more or towards the less, is not blamed; since sometimes we praise those who exhibit the deficiency, and call them good-tempered, and sometimes we call angry people manly, as being capable of ruling. How far, therefore, and how a man must stray before he becomes blameworthy, it is not easy to state in words; for the decision depends on the particular facts and on perception. But so much at least is plain, that the middle state is praiseworthy—that in virtue of which we are angry with the right people, at the right things, in the right way, and so on, while the excesses and defects are blameworthy—slightly so if they are present in a low degree, more if in a higher degree, and very much if in a high degree. Evidently, then, we must cling to the middle state.—Enough of the states relative to anger.

COMMENTS

In the *Rhetoric,* Aristotle brings out the role of belief in emotion. Having certain beliefs is essential to having particular emotions; you can't, for example, feel anger at a person if you do not think that he has slighted you in some way. This belief is not just a cause or necessary condition of the emotion; it is part of what the emotion is, and so a correct specification of the beliefs is essential to a correct account of the emotion. Emotions can stand in the way of rational reflection, but for Aristotle this does not mean that they belong to a part of the soul that is subrational. Emotions involve their own beliefs and sometimes quite complex reasonings. These beliefs are, however, based on an immediate and hence partial view of the situation (for example, pity is defined as a feeling of pain at an *apparent* evil), and more rational reflection may modify the beliefs and so dispel or calm down the emotion.

Aristotle begins with anger, prominent in all ancient accounts of emotion; he associates it with feeling slighted and with contexts of competition and awareness of status and entitlements. Are these contexts central to anger? Are there cases of anger that we would have trouble fitting into Aristotle's analysis? This question raises the issue that different cultures understand and express emotions differently. Some aspects of anger are "socially constructed"; they depend on beliefs that are important in one culture, but may be unimportant in others. Where this is the case, the emotion in question will be expressed in different ways and may play a different role. An analysis like Aristotle's, which lays weight on the role of beliefs in emotions, is particularly useful for pointing up such differences.

Fear and pity are central to Aristotle's analysis of the effect of tragic drama in the *Poetics,* his work on poetry and drama. These emotions are relevant to tragedy because in these plays the events—murder, incest, defeat in war—are the kinds of things we fear happening to us, and because we feel that the people suffering these events in the play are like us, we pity them. Aristotle thinks that tragic drama achieves in some way a catharsis of these emotions, but unfortunately it is not clear what this is, other than some kind of clarification or purifying.

In the *Ethics,* Aristotle's account of the development of virtue gives an important role to the emotions. You develop a virtue, such as courage, rather as you learn a skill. You begin by copying what experts do and eventually master what has to be done, becoming an expert yourself. With skills, however, all that matters is being able to produce the expert result; with virtue, you need not only to do the right action, but to do it in the right way—roughly, for the right reason and without having to battle contrary motivation. For Aristotle, a virtue is a settled state of character not only to act rightly but to have the right motivation. Doing the right thing, but having to overcome desires not to do it, shows that you are merely "self-controlled"; the virtuous person does the right thing gladly, with pleasure. What this shows is that becoming virtuous requires a training of the emotions as well as of the intelligence. If the emotions were thought of as subrational forces, this process could merely be one of repression, but since Aristotle thinks that emotions involve beliefs as part of what they are, we can see that he thinks of them as educable and trainable.

Aristotle holds that virtue "lies in a mean" and aims at a mean between two extremes. That is, virtue is always getting things right (in action and in the way you feel) where you could go wrong either through doing and feeling too much, or through doing and feeling too little. Regarding anger, Aristotle analyzes the virtue of "good temper" as aiming at the mean intermediate between the bad extremes of being too prone to anger and being not prone enough to anger. The virtuous person will get angry "at the right things and with the right people, and, further, as he ought, when he ought, and as long as he ought." Is this a good analysis of anger? Aristotle includes different ways of being too prone to anger or too slow to be angry. Do they all fit the model of excess, deficiency, and the mean between them?

The Early Stoics on Emotions

1. They say that what moves an impulse is nothing but an impulsory appearance of what is then and there appropriate, and that impulse is in general a movement of the soul toward something. The species of impulse, they say, is observed to be that which comes about in the rational animals and that in the nonrational ones; but these have no [distinct] names; for desire is not rational impulse, but a species of rational impulse. As for rational impulse, it would properly be defined by saying that it is a movement of the mind toward something involved in acting; and to this is opposed counterimpulse, a kind of movement [of the mind away from something in acting]. (Arius Didymus in Stobaeus, *Eclogae* II, 86–87)

2. They say that all the impulses are assents, but that the practical ones contain the motive element. Actually, assents are to one thing, and impulses toward another; assents are to statements of a kind, and impulses are toward predicates, those that are somehow contained in the statements to which they assent. . . .

An emotion (*pathos*), they say, is an impulse that is excessive and disobedient to reason, which is dictating: or an [irrational] movement in the soul contrary to nature (all emotions belong in the soul's ruling part); so that every upset is an emotion, and again every emotion is an upset. Emotion being of such a kind, we must suppose that some are primary and lead the way, while others have their reference to these. Primary in the genus are these four: desire, fear, pain, and pleasure. Desire and fear take the lead, desire being directed toward apparent good and fear directed toward apparent evil. Pleasure and pain supervene on these, pleasure when we get what we were desiring or escape what we were fearing, and pain when we fail to get what we were desiring or happen on what we were fearing. With all the soul's emotions, since they call them beliefs, the belief is understood as a weak supposition. (Arius, 88–89)

3. First, one must keep in mind that the rational animal is by nature such as to follow reason and to act with reason as his guide. But often he moves in another way toward some things and away from some things in disobedience to reason when he is pushed too much. Both definitions refer to this movement: The unnatural motion arises irrationally in this way and also the excess in the impulses. For this irrationality must be understood as disobedient to reason and rejecting it, and with reference to this motion, we say in ordinary usage that some persons are pushed and moved irrationally without reason and judgment.

For when we use these expressions, it is not as if a person is carried away by error. . . .

When a man walks in accordance with an impulse, the motion of his legs is not excessive but is in some way commensurate with the impulse, so that he may stop when he wishes or change his pace. But when persons run in accordance with an impulse, this sort of thing no longer happens. The movement of the legs exceeds the impulse, so that they are carried away and do not obediently change their pace [as they did before] the moment they set out to do so. I think that something similar to these [movements of the legs] happens also in impulses because of an excess beyond the rational measure, so that when a man exercises the impulse he is not obedient to reason, and whereas the excess in running is termed contrary to the impulse, the excess in impulse is termed contrary to reason. (Galen, *The Doctrines of Hippocrates and Plato* IV, 2, 10–12, 15–17)

4. They say that the emotion is not distinct from reason and that there is no dispute or civil war between two things, but a turning of one and the same reason to both sides, which we do not notice because of its suddenness and speed; for we do not grasp that it is the nature of the same aspect of the soul to feel desire and to change one's mind, to feel anger and feel fear, to be carried toward what is shameful by pleasure and to be carried back again and get a hold of itself. (Plutarch, *On Moral Virtue* 446 ff)

COMMENTS

For the Stoics, any action, in humans or in animals, is brought about by an impulse (*horme*), which is a response to something in the environment that strikes the agent as requiring a response (technically, this is an "impulsory appearance"). Humans are distinguished from animals, however, in their possession of reason, and this informs everything they do. Reason is the "craftsman of impulse," so in a human, every impulse, that is, every response to our environment, is rational in the sense of involving reason in some way, although, of course, not every impulse is rational in the sense of involving *good* reasoning.

All our impulses can be represented as articulated in language (for the Stoics, the ability to communicate in language is the most important characteristic of reason). Hence, in the second passage, we find an articulation of the logical form of the beliefs, which, for the Stoics, are implied in every human impulse. (The details of this point are controversial and disputed by scholars.) This does not, of course, imply that every time we act on an impulse, we utter language or go through statements in our heads. In any case, when a human acts in accordance with an impulse, there is a belief that can, in principle, be represented in language and that has a particular logical form.

Emotions are a kind of impulse—that is, a kind of response we make to the world when it seems to us to require a reaction on our part. What distinguishes them is that an impulse is always an *excessive* impulse, one that, while rational in the sense in which all human impulses are rational, is also disobedient to reason in the sense of *good* reason.

In the ancient world this idea was frequently ridiculed and misunderstood. A sympathetic interpretation needs to bear two points in mind.

1. Emotions are often said to be beliefs or opinions. This is because for the Stoics, they are impulses, and any human impulse involves a belief that can, in principle, be articulated in language. They are not just like the belief that it is raining because they are also irrational—that is, motivations that run contrary to what the person judges to be good reasoning and hence are experienced as upsetting or blocking factors in the person. Although the Stoics stress the intellectual side of emotions more, their analysis on this point is not different from Aristotle's.

2. For the Stoics, all of a human soul is rational; we have no motivations that lack belief and reason altogether. Their model of human action is different from Plato's and Aristotle's. For the Stoics, the person always acts as a whole; different motivations are not to be thought of as coming from different parts of the soul. When a person feels conflicted between two courses of action, she does not have two different things inside her that are battling for control; rather, the person as whole is oscillating between two different evaluations of the situation. Chrysippus describes the person overcome by emotion not as someone who is internally conflicted, but as someone who as a whole is out of control, just like a walker who starts running and then finds it hard to stop and to control what she is doing.

The Stoics, with their model of a unitary soul, stress that we are just as responsible for what we do when in the grip of anger as we are for what we do in a calm and considered way. We cannot say that we were "overwhelmed" by emotion or think of reason as our real self that was overcome by some other force. In the Stoics' view, the whole self is integrated in its reactions, and we express and identify ourselves and our commitments in the entirety of our affective responses, not just in good reasoning.

But why are all emotions bad? A later Stoic, Seneca, gives us more illumination.

SENECA

Lucius Annaeus Seneca (c. 1 B.C.–A.D. 65), Stoic philosopher, was born in Cordoba, Spain, but studied in Rome and made headway as a writer and orator. In 41 he was banished by the emperor Claudius for adultery with Julia Livilla, Claudius' niece. Political motives now unclear to us may have been behind the charge. In 49 Seneca was recalled by Agrippina, another of Claudius' nieces and now his wife, and was made tutor to her twelve-year-old son, the future emperor Nero. Seneca tutored Nero in rhetoric and became an adviser to and restraining influence on Nero in the early years of his reign. As Nero came increasingly under the influence of people who flattered his sense of self-

importance, Seneca's influence weakened, and in 62 he withdrew from public life. In 65 Nero suspected Seneca of being implicated in a conspiracy
against him that included the poet Lucan, Seneca's nephew; Seneca duly committed suicide.

Seneca wrote prose treatises on philosophical subjects and a large number of literary letters, as well as tragic dramas in verse. His style is highly rhetorical, always pointed, and forceful, forcing the reader to think about the issues.
Seneca is less good at sustaining a continuous argument, and his philosophical
works are often untidy in overall structure, although particular pieces of argument are brilliantly clear. He is always conscious of writing for an educated
general audience, not an audience of professional philosophers, and thus his
writing can lack rigor and clarity; but it gives a vivid sense of Stoicism as a set
of beliefs to be lived by and the demands that this makes. From antiquity on,
there has been a debate as to whether Seneca's own life, that of a very rich
man deeply involved in politics, compromises his stance as a Stoic philosopher.
Certainly, Seneca never claims to be a model of Stoic virtue himself, but he
does give us a feeling of what it is like to try to live up to a rigorous and
demanding theory.

On Anger I, 7–9, 12–14, 17–18; II, 1–4, 6–10, 28
SENECA

Book 1

1. Can it really be that anger, although it is not natural, should be adopted
because it has often proved useful? "It rouses and spurs on the mind. Without
it, courage can achieve nothing magnificent in war—without the flame of anger
beneath, to goad men on to meet danger with boldness." Some, accordingly,
think it best to moderate anger, not to remove it. They would confine it to a
wholesome limit by drawing off any excess, while retaining what is essential for
unenfeebled action, for unsapped force and vigour of spirit. <Well>, in the first
place, it is easier to exclude the forces of ruin than to govern them, to deny them
admission than to moderate them afterwards. For once they have established
possession, they prove to be more powerful than their governor, refusing to be
cut back or reduced. Moreover, reason itself, entrusted with the reins, is only
powerful so long as it remains isolated from the affections. Mixed and contaminated with them, it cannot contain what it could previously have dislodged.
Once the intellect has been stirred up and shaken out, it becomes the servant of

From *Seneca: Moral and Political Essays*, translated by John Procopé and edited by John
M. Cooper (Cambridge University Press, 1995). Reprinted with the permission of
Cambridge University Press.

the force which impels it. Some things at the start are in our power; thereafter they sweep us on with a force of their own and allow no turning back. Bodies in free fall have no control over themselves. They cannot delay or resist the downward course. Any deliberation and second thoughts are cut short by the peremptory force of gravity. They cannot help completing a trajectory which they need not have begun. In the same way, the mind, if it throws itself into anger, love and other affections, is not allowed to restrain the impulse. It is bound to be swept along and driven to the bottom by its own weight and by the natural downward tendency of any failing.

It is best to beat back at once the first irritations, to resist the very germs of anger and take care not to succumb. Once it has begun to carry us off course, the return to safety is difficult. Reason amounts to nothing, once the affection has been installed and we have voluntarily given it some legal standing. From then on, it will do what it wants, not what you allow it. The enemy, I say, must be stopped at the very frontier; when he has invaded and rushed on the city gates, there is no "limit" which his captives can make him accept. It is not the case that the mind stands apart, spying out its affections from without, to prevent their going too far—the mind itself turns into affection. It cannot, accordingly, reinstate that useful and wholesome force which it has betrayed and weakened. As I said, it is not the case that they dwell apart, in isolation from one another. Reason and affection are the mind's transformations for better or for worse. How then can reason, under the oppressive domination of its failings, rise again, if it has already given way to anger? How can it free itself from the chaos, if the admixture of baser ingredients has prevailed? "But some people," it may be said, "control their anger." So as to do nothing that anger dictates—or some of it? If nothing, there is clearly no need, when it comes to doing things, of the anger which you recommend as somehow more forceful than reason. Now my next question: is anger stronger than reason—or weaker? If stronger, how can reason put a limit on it? It is only the feebler, normally, who submit. If anger is weaker, reason can do without it. It is sufficient by itself for getting things done and has no need for a weaker ally. "But some people stay true to themselves and control themselves in their anger." When? As their anger evaporates and departs of its own accord, not at its boiling-point—it is too strong then. "Well, is it not sometimes true that, even in anger, people release the objects of their hatred unharmed and untouched? Do they not refrain from harming them?" They do. But when? When affection has driven back affection, when fear or lust has obtained its demand. Quiet has ensued, thanks not to reason, but to an evil, untrustworthy armistice between the affections.

Again, there is nothing useful in anger. It does not whet the mind for deeds of war. Virtue needs no vice to assist it; it suffices for itself. Whenever impetus is necessary, it does not break out in anger; it rises to action aroused and relaxed to the extent that it thinks necessary, in just the same way that the range of a missile shot from a catapult is under the control of the operator. "Anger," says Aristotle, "is needful; no fight can be won without it, without its filling the mind and kindling enthusiasm there; it must be treated, however, not as a commander but as one of the rank and file." That is false. If it listens to reason and follows where led, it is no longer anger, the hallmark of which is wilful disobedience. But if it rebels against orders to stay still and follows its own ferocious fancy, it is as useless a subordinate in the soul as a soldier who ignores the signal for retreat. So if it accepts a limit, it needs some other name, having ceased to be anger, which I understand to be something unbridled and ungoverned. If it does not, it is ruinous and not to be counted as an assistant. Either it is not anger at all, or it is useless. Anyone who exacts punishment not through greed for the punishment itself, but because he should, does not count as angry. A good soldier is one who knows how to obey orders and carry out decisions. The affections are no less evil as subordinates than they are as commanders.

2. "Tell me then, is the good man not angry if he sees his father slain and his mother ravished?" No, he will not be angry. He will punish and protect. Why should not filial devotion, even without anger, be enough of a stimulus? You could argue in the same way: "Tell me then, if he sees his father or son undergoing surgery, will the good man not weep or faint?" We see this happening to women whenever they are struck by the slightest suggestion of danger. The good man will do his duty, undismayed and undaunted; and he will do what is worthy of a good man without doing anything unworthy of a *man.* "My father is about to be killed—I will defend him; he has been killed—I will avenge him; not because I am pained, but because I should." "Good men are angry at wrongs done to their friends." When you say this, Theophrastus, you cast odium on braver teachings. You turn from the judge to the gallery. Since everyone is angry when something like that happens to his friends, you think that men will judge what they do to be what ought to be done. Nearly everyone holds emotions to be justified which he acknowledges in himself. But they behave in the same way if the hot drinks are not served properly, if a piece of glassware is broken, if a shoe has mud on it. The motive for such anger is not devotion, but weakness, just as it is with children who bewail the loss of their parents—exactly as they bewail the loss of their toys. Anger for one's friends is the mark of a weak mind, not a devoted one. What is fine and honourable is to go forth in defence of parents, children, friends and fellow-citizens, under the guidance of duty itself, in the exercise of will, judgment and foresight—and not through some raving impulse. No affection is keener to punish than anger is. For that very reason, it is ill fitted for punishing. Headlong and mindless like almost every burning desire, it gets in the way of what it rushes to do. So neither in peace nor in war has it ever been any good. In fact it makes peace resemble war. Under arms, it forgets that "Mars is impartial" and falls into the power of others, having no power over itself.

Again, failings should not be pressed into service on the grounds that they sometimes achieve something. Fevers, too, alleviate some kinds of ill health. But that does not mean that it would not be better to be without them altogether— it is a hateful sort of remedy that leaves one owing one's health to disease. In the same way, anger may sometimes have proved unexpectedly beneficial—like poison, a fall, or a shipwreck. But that does not make it wholesome. Lives, after all, have often been saved by deadly objects.

Again, things worth having are the better and more desirable the more of them there is. If justice is a good thing, no one will say that it is better with a bit taken off. If courage is a good, no one will want it partly diminished. Therefore, in the case of anger too, the more, the better. Who would refuse an addition of anything that is good? But the augmentation of anger is not of positive use. Nor, therefore, is its existence. There is no good that becomes bad by increment.

"Anger is of use," it may be said, "because it makes men keener to fight." On that principle, drunkenness too would be useful—it makes men reckless and bold; many have proved better at arms when worse for drink. On the same principle, you could say that lunacy and madness are necessary for strength—frenzy often makes men stronger. Tell me, have there not been times when fear has, paradoxically, made for boldness and dread of death has aroused even the most indolent to battle? But anger, drunkenness, fear and other such conditions are vile, unsteady incitements. What they provide is not the equipment for courage—virtue has no need for vices—but merely a slight uplift for souls otherwise slothful or cowardly. No one is braver for being angry, save he who would not have been brave without anger. It comes not as an aid to courage, but as a replacement for it.

And what about this? If anger were a good, it would go with the highest degree of moral perfection. But those most prone to anger are children, the old and the sick. Anything weak is naturally inclined to complain.

"A good man," says Theophrastus, "cannot help being angry at bad people." On that principle, the better a man is, the more prone he will be to anger. Are you sure that he will not, on the contrary, be the calmer and free from affections, someone who hates no one? What has he, in truth, to hate about wrong-doers? Error is what has driven them to their sort of misdeeds. But there is no reason for a man of understanding to hate those who have gone astray. If there were, he would hate himself. He should consider how often he himself has not behaved well, how often his own actions have required forgiveness—his anger will extend to himself. No fair judge will reach a different verdict on his own case than on another's. No one, I say, will be found who can acquit himself; anyone who declares himself innocent has his eyes on the witness-box, not on his own conscience. How much humaner it is to show a mild, paternal spirit, not harrying those who do wrong, but calling them back! Those who stray in the fields, through ignorance of the way, are better brought back to the right path than chased out altogether.

3. Aristotle says that some emotions, if well used, serve as arms. That would be true if, like weapons of war, they could be picked up and put down at will. But these arms which Aristotle would give to virtue go to war by themselves, without awaiting the hand of the warrior. They possess us; they are not our possessions. We have no need for other weapons; it is enough that nature has equipped us with reason. What she has given us is firm, enduring, accommodating, with no double edge to be turned on its owner. Reason by itself is enough not merely for foresight but for action. Indeed, what could be stupider than for reason to seek protection in bad temper, for something that is stable,

trustworthy and sound to seek protection in something unsteady, untrustworthy and sick? And what of the fact that for action too, the one area with some
apparent need for the services of bad temper, reason by itself is far stronger?
Having judged that something should be done, it sticks to its judgment. It will
find nothing better than itself into which it might change. So it stands by its decisions once they are made. Anger is often driven back by pity. For it has no solid
strength. An empty swelling with a violent onset, like winds which rise from the
earth and, begotten in river and marsh, are strong without staying-power, it
begins with a mighty impulse, and then fails exhausted before its time. Having
pondered nothing save cruelty and new kinds of punishment, it shows itself,
when the time has come to punish, broken and weak. Affections collapse
quickly; reason remains constant. Moreover, even where anger has persisted,
we sometimes find that, if there are several who deserve to die, it stops the
killing after the first two or three. Its first blows are the fierce ones. In the same
way, it is when the serpent first crawls out of its den that its venom is harmful;
drained by repeated use, its fangs are innocuous. Hence equal crimes receive
unequal punishment, and one who has committed less often receives more,
being exposed to fresher wrath. Anger is altogether inconsistent. Sometimes it
goes further than it should, sometimes it stops short. It indulges itself, judges
capriciously, refuses to listen, leaves no room for defence, clings to what it has
seized and will not have its judgment, even a wrong judgment, taken from it.

Reason gives time to either side, and then demands a further adjournment
to give itself room to tease out the truth: anger is in a hurry. Reason wishes to
pass a fair judgment: anger wishes the judgment which it has already passed to
seem fair. Reason considers nothing save the matter at issue; anger is roused by
irrelevant trifles. An overconfident look, a voice too loud, speech too bold, a
manner too refined, a rather too ostentatious show of support, popularity with
the public—all serve to exasperate it. For hatred of the lawyer it often damns the
accused. Even if the truth is put before its eyes, it fondly defends its error. Refusing to be proved wrong, it sees obstinacy, even in what is ill begun, as more honourable than a change of mind.

Book II

4. Our question is whether anger starts with a decision or with an impulse,
that is, whether it is set in motion of its own accord—or in the same way as most
inner events which occur with our full knowledge. Our discussion must plunge
into these topics so that it can rise again to loftier ones. In the organization of our
bodies too, the bones, muscles and joints, which underpin the whole and give it
vitality, though not at all attractive, come first. They are followed by the com-
ponents on which beauty in appearance and looks depends. After all this, comes
what most seizes the eye; when the body is at last complete, the complexion is
finally applied.

Anger is undoubtedly set in motion by an impression received of a wrong.
But does it follow immediately on the impression itself and break out without

any involvement of the mind? Or is some assent by the mind required for it to be set in motion? Our view is that it undertakes nothing on its own, but only with the mind's approval. To receive an impression of wrong done to one, to lust for retribution, to put together the two propositions that the damage ought not to have been done and that punishment ought to be inflicted, is not the work of a mere involuntary impulse. That would be a simple process. What we have here is a complex with several constituents—realization, indignation, condemnation, retribution. These cannot occur without assent by the mind to whatever has struck it.

"What is the point," you ask, "of this question?" That we may know what anger is, since it will never, if it comes to birth against our will, yield to reason. Involuntary movements can be neither overcome nor avoided. Take the way that we shiver when cold water is sprinkled on us, or recoil at the touch of some things. Take the way that bad news makes our hair stand on end and indecent language brings on a blush. Take the vertigo that follows the sight of a precipice. None of these is in our power; no amount of reasoning can induce them not to happen. But anger *is* put to flight by precept. For it is a voluntary fault of the mind, and not one of those which occur through some quirk of the human condition and can therefore happen to the very wisest of men, even though they include that first mental jolt which affects us when we think ourselves wronged. This steals upon us even while we are watching a performance on stage or reading of things that happened long ago. We are sometimes incited by singing, by a quickened tempo, by the martial sound of trumpets. Our minds are moved by a gruesome painting, by the grim sight of the justest punishment. That is why we join in laughing with those who laugh, why a crowd of mourners depresses us, why we boil over at conflicts which have nothing to do with us. But these are not cases of anger, any more than it is grief which makes us frown at the sight of a shipwreck on stage or fear that runs through the reader's mind as Hannibal blockades the walls after the battle of Cannae. No, all these are motions of minds with no positive wish to be in motion. They are not affections, but the preliminaries, the prelude to affections. So it is that in time of peace a military man in civilian clothes pricks up his ears at the sound of a trumpet, that camp horses rear at the clattering of arms.

None of these fortuitous mental impulses deserves to be called an "emotion." They are something suffered, so to speak, not something done by the mind. Emotion is not a matter of being moved by impressions received, but of surrendering oneself to them and following up the chance movement. If anyone thinks that pallor, falling tears, sexual excitement or deep sighing, a sudden glint in the eyes or something similar are an indication of emotion or evidence for a mental state, he is wrong; he fails to see that these are just bodily agitations. Thus it is that even the bravest man often turns pale as he puts on his armour, that the knees of even the fiercest soldier tremble a little as the signal is given for battle, that a great general's heart is in his mouth before the lines have charged against one another, that the most eloquent orator goes numb at the fingers as he prepares to speak. Anger, however, must not only be set in motion: it has to break out, since it is an impulse. But impulse never occurs without the mind's assent, nor is it possible to act for retribution and punishment unbeknown to the mind. Suppose that someone thinks himself harmed and wishes to exact retribution, that something dissuades him and he promptly calms down—this I do not call "anger," since it is a motion of the mind obedient to reason. Anger is a motion which outleaps reason and drags it along. So the first mental agitation induced by the impression of wrong done is no more anger than is the impression itself. The impulse that follows, which not only registers but confirms the impression, is what counts as anger, the agitation of a mind proceeding by its own deliberate decision to exact retribution. Nor can there be any doubt that, as fear implies flight, anger implies attack. Do you really think, then, that anything can be sought or shunned without the mind's assent?

If you want to know how the emotions begin, grow or get carried away, the first movement is involuntary, a preparation, as it were, for emotion, a kind of threat. The next is voluntary but not insistent—I may, for example, think it right for me to wreak vengeance because I have been harmed or for him to be punished because he has committed a crime. The third really is out of control; wanting retribution not just "if it is right" but at all costs, it has completely overcome the reason. The first is a mental jolt which we cannot escape through reason, just as we cannot escape those physical reactions which I mentioned—the urge to yawn when some one else yawns, or blinking when fingers are flicked at the eye. These cannot be overcome by reason, though habituation and constant attention may perhaps lessen them. The other sort of movement, generated by decision, can be eliminated by decision.

5. "Virtue that looks with favour upon things that are honourable ought likewise to look with anger upon things shameful." Do you mean to say that virtue should be both base and great? But that is what is being said by one who would have it exalted and abased, in as much as joy at right action is glorious and splendid, while anger at another's transgression is sordid and narrow-minded. Nor will virtue ever allow itself to imitate vice in the act of suppressing it. Anger itself it holds to deserve chastisement, being not one bit better, and often still worse, than the misdeeds which arouse it. Rejoicing and joy are the natural property of virtue; to be angry accords no more with the dignity of virtue than does grief. Sorrow is the companion of irascibility; all anger reverts to it, either remorseful or rebuffed. Again, if the wise man's nature is to be angry at transgressions, he will be angrier the greater they are, and he will be angry often. It follows that the wise man will not only lose his temper on occasion; he will be habitually bad-tempered. But if we believe that there is no room in his mind for great or frequent anger, why should we not make him free of this affection altogether? For there can be no limit to his anger, if it is to tally with each man's action. Either he will be unfair, if he is equally angry at unequal misdeeds, or he will be very irascible indeed, if he flares up as often as crimes are committed that merit his anger.

It would be scandalous—could anything be more so?—for the wise man's state of mind to depend on the wickedness of others. Is Socrates to lose his power to come home with the same expression on his face as when he left it? Yet, if the wise man has a duty to be angry at shameful deeds, to be provoked and depressed by crime, nothing will be more troubled than the wise man. His entire life will be spent in bad temper and grief. At every moment he will see something to disapprove of. Every time that he leaves his house, he will have to step through criminals, grasping, spendthrift, shameless—and prospering as a result. Everywhere that his eyes turn they will find some ground for indignation. His powers will fail him if he forces himself to anger as often as anger is due. All those thousands rushing to the forum at day-break—how vile their law-suits are, how much viler their advocates! One brings an action against the verdicts of his father—he would have done better not to deserve them. Another proceeds against his mother. A third arrives to denounce a crime of which he is the more obvious culprit. A judge is selected to condemn what he himself has committed; and the gallery, corrupted by good pleading, sides with the bad.

Why go into details? When you see the forum crammed, the enclosures thronged with an entire population, when you see the Circus with the mass of the people on show, you can be sure of this, that there are as many vices here as men. You will see people here out of military dress but still at war with each other. One man is brought for a paltry gain to ruin someone else; no one makes a profit except by wronging another; they hate the prosperous, they despise the unfortunate; they feel oppressed by their betters, and are themselves oppressive to their inferiors. Goaded by diverse appetites, they would sacrifice everything for some trivial pleasure or plunder. Life is the same here as in a school of gladiators—living together means fighting together. A gathering of wild animals is what you have here, were it not that animals are calm among themselves and refrain from biting their own kind, while these people glut themselves with tearing one another apart. Nor is this their only difference from dumb beasts. Animals grow tame to those who nurture them; human frenzy feeds on those who feed it.

The wise man will never cease to be angry, if once he starts.

You will do better to hold, instead, that no one should be angry at error. Surely no one would be angry with people who stumble in the dark or whose deafness stops them from hearing an order. Or with children who fail to see what they should be doing and turn their attention to games and the silly jokes of those their own age. Or with the sick, the old, the weary. This too is one of the misfortunes of our mortal condition: darkness of mind, the inevitability of error—and, still more, the love of error. To avoid anger with individuals, you must forgive the whole group, you must pardon the human race. If you are angry with young and old for their wrongdoing, be angry with infants, too: they are going to do wrong. No one is angry with children who are too young to know the difference between things. But being human is more of an excuse, and a juster excuse, than being a child. For this was what we were born to be—animals prone to ailments of the mind no less than of the body, not exactly stupid or slow, but given to misusing our shrewdness, each an example of vice to the other. Anyone who has followed his predecessors down the wrong path has surely the excuse of having gone astray on a public highway. A general applies severity to individuals: when the whole army has deserted, he can only show clemency. What rids the wise man of anger? The sheer multitude of wrongdoers. He knows that it is unfair and unsafe to be angry at failings shared by all.

6. If we wish our judgment to be fair in all things, we must start from the conviction that no one of us is faultless. For here is where indignation most arises—"I haven't done anything wrong!," "I haven't done a thing!" On the contrary, you won't *admit* anything! We grow indignant at any rebuke or punishment, while at that very moment doing the wrong of adding insolence and obstinacy to our misdeeds. Who can claim himself innocent in the eyes of every law? Suppose he can—to be good in the sense of being law-abiding is a very narrow form of innocence. So much wider are the principles of moral duty than those of law, so many the demands of piety, humanity, justice and good faith, none of them things in the statute-book. But even under that very restricted definition we cannot establish our innocence. We have done some things; others we have planned, or wanted or felt inclined to do. In some cases, our innocence has simply been through lack of success.

This thought should make us more reasonable towards wrongdoers, ready to accept reproach, free of anger, at any rate, towards good men—who would not arouse our anger, if even good people can?—and above all towards the gods. It is not by any fault of theirs, but through the law of our mortal condition, that anything untoward happens to us. "But disease and pain intrude upon us!" Some things just have to be endured if your lot is live in a crumbling house. Suppose, then, that someone speaks ill of you—think whether you did not do so to him, think of how many people *you* speak ill of. We should think, I maintain, of some not as doing us wrong but as paying us back, of others as acting on our behalf, or as acting under compulsion, or in ignorance; we should think that even those who wrong us knowingly and deliberately are not out for the wrong itself when they wrong us. A person may have slipped into it through delight in his own wit; or he may have done something, not to disoblige us, but because he could not get what he wanted without first having rebuffed us. Besides, flattery is often offensive in its fawning. Anyone who calls to mind how often he himself has come under false suspicion, how many services on his part have chanced to look like injustice, how many people he has hated and then begun to love, can avoid immediate anger, especially if he says quietly to himself at every vexation "I too have done this myself."

But where can you find such a reasonable judge? The very same man who fancies everyone's wife, and finds justification enough for an affair in the mere fact that she belongs to another, will not have his own wife looked at; the keenest to insist on trust will be given to breaking it; the persecutor of lies is himself a perjuror; the vexatious litigant cannot bear to have a case brought against himself; and the chastity of servants is guarded from temptation by a master with no regard for his own. Other people's faults are before our eyes, our own lie over our shoulders. That is why the ungodly hour of a son's dinner-party is berated by a father who is worse than the son, why no allowance is made for other people's self-indulgence by a man with no restraint on his own, why a murderer meets with wrath from a tyrant and theft with punishment from a temple-robber. Many of mankind, indeed, are angry not with the sin, but the sinner. A look at ourselves will make us more forbearing, if we start to consider: "Surely we too have done something like this? Surely we have made this sort of mistake. Is it in our interest to damn it?"

COMMENTS

For the Stoics, all emotions are faulty, and we should get rid of them. For the Stoics, only virtue is good, while other things have a different kind of value, and hence all emotions are faulty because they involve a misguided belief that things other than virtue—honor, money, health, and so on—are good. The virtuous person, they think, will be without emotion—*apathes*. This does not mean that she will be affectless; it means that her motivation will not conflict with her considered views about value. (The Stoics have a different word—*eupatheiai* or "good feelings"—for the state of the virtuous person's feelings.) Properly understood, the Stoics think, emotions hinder virtue and the good life, and our usual fairly favorable view of them rests on serious misconceptions.

Even if you do not accept Stoic ethical theory, you can take the point that emotions tend to pull us away from our considered view of what is valuable. Seneca is writing for a general audience and aims to make the Stoic position as plausible as he can, since he is aware that the bare position, especially if stated in academic terms, appears counterintuitive and unattractive. (At times he appeals to his audience's beliefs even when a Stoic would ultimately reject them—for example, when he appeals to the idea that resisting emotion is manly and giving in to it is typically female.)

Contrary to Aristotle, Seneca claims, in the first and third extracts, that anger cannot be limited to a mean that avoids extremes. Once you give in to it, there is no safe way of controlling the way you act, since anger is essentially an unstable and untrustworthy motivation. Aristotle is thus wrong to think that the virtuous way of dealing with anger is to develop a right way of feeling it and a correct way of channeling it into action. Anger is not a part of you that reason can control; to let yourself become angry is to let your reason become corrupted into evaluating the situation wrongly. Hence anger should be eliminated, not controlled and trained. Seneca tries to show that this conclusion is actually truer than Aristotle's to what we really think about anger when we put our minds to the matter. Do you agree? This is an issue on which it is not as obvious as it first appears what we really think about anger and other emotions.

In the second extract, Seneca undercuts the opposition by showing how anger is not required as a motivation. We may think that we need anger to fuel a reaction to some dreadful action. But, says Seneca, our moral outrage is sufficient to get us to do what is needed. Moreover, if we are angry, we are liable to go beyond what is morally required, to overreact and go morally wrong ourselves.

In the first of the Book II extracts, Seneca gets us to rethink our deep-seated conviction that we cannot help getting angry. There *are* phenomena, he admits, that are not under our control; we can't help the way we react to some happenings. But this is not really anger, which involves a commitment to an evaluation of what happened; it is in our power, if we think about it, to commit ourselves, or not, to it. Once we accept this point, then we can see that what we thought of as an emotional state forced on us by events is actually a product of the way we choose to think about and evaluate what is happening to us.

The two final extracts illustrate, in different ways, another aspect of the Stoic theory of the emotions, one shared by some other philosophers. People who think of themselves as being in the grip of emotions are misguided and, as such, should not be opposed and attacked, but helped. In much ancient philosophy, there is a *therapeutic* strand, which represents philosophy as a cure for problems of the soul in a way similar to that in which medicine cures the body. Seneca urges us not to feel anger at the one thing that might seem to warrant it—moral badness. If we allow ourselves to get worked up at crime and moral evil, he warns, our lives will be unlivable, since there is so much of it around. Rather than let ourselves be driven neurotic by trying to oppose moral evil, we should try to cure it if we can. Seneca thinks that we should not look away from the evil in the world, and we should react to it in as moral a way as we can. But anger is never an appropriate or helpful reaction to it. Furthermore, the final extract emphasizes the idea that the best thing we can do is to concentrate on ourselves and our own tendency to find fault. Only when we have thought honestly about our own shortcomings will we be in shape to judge those of others.

C. A Test Case

One of the most famous plays in the ancient world, Euripides' *Medea,* led to a dispute among philosophers as to how Medea's inner conflict should be understood.

EURIPIDES

Euripides of Athens (c. 485–406 B.C.) was the latest of the three writers of tragic drama to become canonical in the ancient world (the others being Aeschylus and Sophocles). Eighteen of his ninety plays survive. There are many passages in the plays in which characters argue points, often of contemporary intellectual concern. Some scholars have taken these passages to be expressions of intellectual attitudes, statements of or responses to philosophical arguments. However, Euripides does not use his plays to present a systematic set of his own ideas; rather, he uses intellectual ideas at different points to develop a character or to create theatrical effects, and we do not know what his own ideas were.

The present passage from his play *Medea* became famous, as we shall see, among philosophers, who gave different philosophical explanations of it, but it would be wrong to think that Euripides himself is using a speech at a dramatic point of the play to offer the audience a philosophical idea of his own. Like some other passages in his plays, it stimulated philosophical discussion, but is not itself a piece of philosophy.

Medea 1021–1080
EURIPIDES

(Medea speaking) Oh, children, children, you have a city and home, and, once you've left me in my misery, you will live here, forever motherless. But I shall go into exile in another land before having the pleasure of seeing you happy, before seeing your bridal baths and wives and laying out your marriage-beds and holding the wedding-torches.—Oh, my misery stems from my hard-heartedness!—It was for nothing, children, that I brought you up, for nothing that I suffered and was torn with agony, bearing the sharp pains of childbirth. Once, sadly for me, I had many hopes for you, that you would look after me in my old age and wrap me up carefully with your own hands after my death, something that human beings long for. But now that sweet hope has died. Without you I shall lead a life that is bitter and painful for me. You will no longer see your mother with your dear eyes, moving off to another form of life.

Ah, Ah! Why do you gaze at me with your eyes, children? Why do you smile your last smile? Oh, what shall I do? My courage has gone, women, now that I've seen the shining eyes of the children. I couldn't do it. Goodbye to my former plans! I'll take my children from this land. Why should I, in harming them to give their father pain, make myself suffer twice as much? I cannot. Goodbye plans!

But what is happening to me? Do I want to make myself ridiculous, letting my enemies go unpunished? I must go through with this. What a coward I am—even to admit soft words into my mind! Go into the house, children. If there is anyone who should not be present at my sacrifice, that will be up to them. I shall not weaken my hand.

Ah, Ah! Don't, my heart, don't you do this! Leave them alone, wretched heart, spare the children! Living there with me they will give you joy.

By the avenging furies down in Hades, I swear I'll never leave these children for my enemies to insult and torture! They must certainly die; and since they must, then I who gave birth to them shall kill them. In any case, the thing's done now and she will not escape: yes, the coronet is on her head and the royal bride is wearing the dress and dying, I'm sure of that.

But, now that I'm to go on the saddest of roads, and to send them on a sadder one still, I want to speak to the children. Give me, children, give me your right hand for your mother to hold. Oh hand and mouth that are dearest to me, and the fine body and face of children! Be happy, both of you—but there. Your life here has been taken away by your father. Oh, sweet embrace, oh soft skin and the sweetest breath of children! Go away, go away! I can no longer look at you but I am overcome by troubles.

I know that what I am about to do is bad, but anger is master of my plans, which is the source of the greatest troubles for humankind.

COMMENTS

Medea is a figure of Greek myth, with several clusters of stories round her. Euripides' play deals with Medea's relationship with Jason, who sailed in the ship *Argo* to Colchis in the far north to find the Golden Fleece. The king of Colchis, Aeetes, refused Jason's request for the Fleece, but his daughter Medea fell in love with Jason and helped him, by her magic skills, to perform the tasks the king set him. Returning to Greece with the Fleece and Medea, Jason was driven from his own kingdom after Medea used her magic to kill his uncle. In the play Jason, Medea, and their two sons have ended up in Corinth, living on the hospitality of King Creon. To mend his fortunes, Jason has left his family and intends to marry the king's daughter. Medea responds passionately to this betrayal. She kills the king and his daughter by poison, and to punish Jason, kills their sons. This act puts her beyond the bounds of the human; in the last scene she appears in the role of a divine being, carried off to safety in the chariot of her grandfather the Sun, leaving behind Jason condemned to a life in which he has lost everything.

Mythical stories could take various forms. Euripides' play, which made a strong impact, fixed Medea as the killer of her children (not true of all previous versions of the story). Euripides plays down Medea's character as a foreigner with magic skills and presents her story as that of a wronged woman, whom the Chorus of Greek women see as one of themselves. The horrific outcome develops from an ordinary situation, that of a husband seeking present advantage by abandoning a loyal wife who has made sacrifices for him.

This is the scene where Medea, who had resolved to kill her children, finds her intent weakening when she sees them. She goes through a series of fluctuations, which she sees as moving between reason and her pride and resentment at Jason's abandonment. She kills the children, much as it devastates her to do so, because nothing less than this will punish Jason for what he has done.

At the end of the speech Medea utters words that became famous and controversial. She knows how evil the action is that she has resolved to do, but she says that anger is master of her plans. What is meant by "master of" (*kreissōn*)? It could mean that Medea is aware of two conflicting forces within herself, passion and reasoned resolve, and finds that passion is the stronger force. Or it could mean that passion is

The story of Medea had a continuing fascination in the ancient world. This wall painting is from Pompeii, a Roman city destroyed by volcanic ash when the volcano Vesuvius erupted in A.D. 79, but is probably a copy of an older original. It illustrates the scene in Euripides' play quite closely, though it is not a depiction of actors (in the ancient theater actors wore stylized costume and masks) but an interpretation of Medea's situation. (Wall painting from the House of the Dioscuri, Pompeii Naples, National Archaeological Museum. Alinari/Art Resource, New York.)

directing her resolves, that she has committed herself to her passionate anger and pride.

This ambiguity can't be reproduced in English, and translators (and actors) have to decide for themselves what reading to give it. As we shall see, two philosophically different interpretations of Medea's state develop these two ways of interpreting the line and of reading the entire speech.

Discourses I, 28, 1–9; II, 17, 17–25

EPICTETUS

1. What is the reason of our assenting to anything?—Its appearing to be so.—Therefore, assenting to what appears not to be so is impossible.—Why?— Because the nature of the mind is just this, to agree to things that are true, to be unsatisfied with things that are false, and to suspend judgment about things that are unclear. What is the proof of this?—Have the experience now, if you can, that it is night.—It's not possible.—Don't have the experience now that it is day.—It's not possible. Have the experience that the stars are even in number, or don't have it.—It's not possible.—So, whenever someone assents to something false, be assured that he did not want to assent to something false, for "every soul is unwilling to be deprived of the truth," as Plato says; the false thing appeared to him to be true.

Well, with actions what do we have corresponding to the true and the false there? Appropriate and inappropriate actions, advantage and disadvantage, what is proper for me and proper for you, and the like.—Can't someone, then, think that something is to his advantage, but not choose it?—No, he can't.

—But what about Medea, who says, "I know that what I am about to do is bad, but anger is master of my plans"?

—It's precisely this, gratifying her anger and being revenged on her husband, that she thinks more advantageous than saving her children.—Yes, but she's deceived.—Then show her clearly that she is deceived, and she won't do it. But as long as you don't show her, what else can she follow but what appears to her to be so? Nothing. Why then are you angry with her, because the poor woman has gone astray in what matters most and has become a viper instead of a human? If anything, why not rather pity her? Why do we not pity people who have become blinded and lamed in what matters most in the way we pity the blind and the lame?

2. Right now, do you not want what is possible, and possible for you in particular? What stands in your way, then? Why are you troubled? Right now, are you not trying to escape what is necessary? Why, then, do you fall into difficulties? Why are you unfortunate? Why is it that when you want something, it doesn't come about, but it does come about when you don't want it? This is the greatest proof of trouble and unhappiness: I want something, and it doesn't come about—and what is more wretched than I am? I don't want something, and it does come about—and what is more wretched than I am?

Medea, for example, could not endure this and so ended by killing her children. In this respect, at least, she acted from a great spirit—for she had the right impression of what it is not to get what one wants. "Well then," she says, "I shall be revenged on the man who wronged and insulted me. But what shall I gain from his being reduced to such a state? How can it come about? I will kill our children. Yet I shall be punishing myself, too. But what do I care?" This is the outburst of a soul of great force. For she did not know where the power lies to do what we want—that this is not to be got from outside ourselves or by changing and rearranging things. Stop wanting your husband, and nothing you want will fail to come about. Stop wanting him to live with you at any cost, stop wanting to stay in Corinth—in general, stop wanting anything but what god wants. Who will stop you, who will compel you? Nobody, any more than they could stop or compel Zeus.

When you have such a leader and want and desire along with him, why are you still afraid of failing? Commit your desire and aversion to riches and poverty—you will fail and will fall into what you want to avoid. Commit them to health—you will fall into misfortune, as you will if you commit them to political offices, honors, your native country, your friends, your children, and, in general, to anything not an object of moral choice. But commit them to Zeus and the other gods, hand them over to them, let them do the steering, let your desire and aversion be ranged on their side—and how can you be troubled any more?

COMMENTS

From the start, the Stoics discussed Euripides' Medea, as we can see from the work of later Stoics like Epictetus. Medea is oscillating between two resolves; first she decides one way and then the other, depending on how much weight she gives to her passionate resentment or her calmer judgment. (Look back at the Plutarch passage on p. 98.) Medea's lucidity about her position makes her a good example of the Stoic unitary model of the soul: People are responsible for what they do when led by emotion just as much as for what they do when led by calm and correct judgment. Medea does not think of herself as overwhelmed by a force that is not her real self; she identifies completely with the course she resolves on, painful though it is for her.

In the first passage, Epictetus stresses that we don't act in accordance with beliefs that we recognize to be false or perverse; hence Medea is not being swept away on a tide of passion against her view of what is good, but is acting for the best, although she is deeply misguided about what is best. We should sympathize with her, rather than feel angry; she acted in accordance with what she most valued (and this was hardly trivial). If you criticize Medea, then you are committed to showing her why she was wrong to do what she did. Until you do so, the appropriate attitude is that of sympathy for the misguided. (Compare the Seneca passage.)

Epictetus also emphasizes that it is always possible to change our view of our situation and so to act differently. Medea did not have to revenge herself on Jason; she could have decided to stop thinking that revenge was the most important thing. She did not do so because she did not try hard enough to accept what had happened and to adjust to it. (This is what Epictetus means by accepting the will of Zeus.) Accepting what has happened produces a realistic view of the situation, which is blocked by emotion that traps Medea into a wrong view of what her options are.

GALEN

Galen (A.D. 129–c. 200) of Pergamum was a physician who rose from being physician to the school of gladiators at Pergamum to being personal physician to the emperor Marcus Aurelius. He wrote at enormous length on a vast range of medical and philosophical subjects; by historical accident he became the major medical authority in the Middle Ages and beyond in Western Europe. In medicine he defended the views of the much earlier "Hippocrates" (a collection of mostly fifth-century B.C. writings), including a theory of the four "humors." He defended the view in one of his writings that "the best doctor should be a philosopher" and brings theoretical and philosophical considerations into discussions of medical topics. The present passage is taken from a long work, *On the Doctrines of Hippocrates and Plato,* in which medical theories are mixed up with a discussion of Platonic and Stoic views on the unity of the soul and the nature of emotion. Galen is an unattractive writer, pompous and self-important, who is constantly using philosophy to impress the reader, but whose philosophical grasp is often uncertain, and who has strong prejudices that get in the way of his understanding theories other than the one he favors.

On the Doctrines of Hippocrates and Plato III, 3, 13–24
GALEN

Odysseus [in Homer] seeing the maidservants misbehaving was dragged forcibly toward punishing them by his anger, but was held back by reason, which explained that this would be untimely. . . .

Plato, I consider, recalls this passage of Homer most opportunely in the fourth book of the *Republic.* But it is most inopportune of Chrysippus to cite it, and even more so is his citation of the passage that Euripides has Medea speak when reason was warring with anger in her soul. She knew that she was performing an impious and terrible action in setting her hand to the murder of her children, and for this reason was hesitant, put it off, and did not do at once the deed she had had the impulse to do. But then again anger, like a disobedient horse that has got the better of the charioteer, dragged her by force toward the children—and back again reason pulled her and led her away, and then again anger pulled against this, and then again reason.

So as she is repeatedly driven back and forth between the two of them, when she has conceded to anger, then at that point Euripides has her say, "I know that what I am about to do is bad, but anger is master of my plans." She understands, indeed, the magnitude of the evils that she intends to do because she is taught by reason, but she says that anger is stronger than it and that for this reason she is led forcibly by it toward the action. She is the opposite of Odysseus, who held back his anger by reason. Euripides has put forward his Medea as an example of barbarians and other uncivilized people, in whom anger is stronger than reason. With Greeks and civilized people, such as Homer represents Odysseus as being, reason is stronger than anger.

Often reason is stronger than the spirited part of the soul to such an extent that there is never any conflict between them: The one rules and the other is ruled. This happens with people who have reached the goal of philosophy. Often, however, anger is so much stronger than reason that it rules and completely governs; this is observable in barbarians and children who are spirited by nature, in several wild animals, and in humans who are animal-like. Sometimes neither is sufficiently strong to pull the other over right away; they oppose each other and fight it out, and eventually one of them wins—reason in Odysseus, anger in Medea—since they are two parts of the soul (or, if not parts, at least powers of a sort).

But Chrysippus, who does not think that they are parts of the soul or even irrational powers separate from the rational, still does not hesitate to recall the words of Odysseus and Medea, words that obviously refute his opinion. How can anyone argue with people like this, who pay no attention to what is patently evident (as I have already shown repeatedly) and who bring up things that refute their doctrines as though they were evidence *for* them?

COMMENTS

Galen thinks that Medea is an obvious *counterexample* to the Stoic view; why can't the Stoics just *see* that Medea refutes their theory? He thinks that the idea of distinct parts of the soul, which battle with each other until one wins by superior force, is built into commonsense ways of understanding talk of psychological conflict.

Is Galen moving too fast here? Or is there something to the thought that it is more natural for us, when we talk of reason and emotion conflicting, to think in terms of distinct sources of motivation than to think of the whole person oscillating between different courses?

Galen's language is also meant to recall the picture of the soul as a chariot and horses in Plato's *Phaedrus* (see pp. 82–83). Is he correct in thinking that Plato is committed to this description of Medea? Note that in the *Phaedrus* passage, the bad horse is desire, while here, Galen takes it to be Medea's pride and anger (which in Plato would be the good horse). Clearly, later thinkers in sympathy with Plato's picture of internal conflict simplified it so that the mind is divided into two, rather than three, parts.

As Galen interprets Plato, the soul's parts do not mutually agree or disagree; rather, reason dominates and represses the other elements. In keeping with this view, he sees the parts other than reason as subhuman and entirely irrational. People who are led by these elements he sees as irrational, and he is unable to identify with what motivates them. Note how unsympathetic he is to Medea and how he distances himself from women and foreigners, who are too different from himself for him to identify with them.

Galen thinks that anger is an overwhelming force. Is his attitude that it is characteristic of animals and of people whom we see as alien and foreign to us a natural result of thinking of reason and emotion as distinct parts of the soul? Does it spring from the picture of our soul as having parts that are human and parts that are less than human? Or is it just Galen's personal prejudice?

D. Reason, the Emotions, and Faith

A narrative of martyrdom brings out the point that a life in which reason is in control of the emotions could be seen, in the ancient world, as not merely compatible with a commitment to religious faith, but also as the best foundation for it.

THE FOURTH BOOK OF MACCABEES

This work, by an unknown Jewish author, dates from the first century A.D., before the destruction of the Temple in A.D. 70. In it, the author recounts a much earlier persecution of Jews by the Hellenistic king Antiochus Epiphanes (c. 168 B.C.). These earlier events are recorded in the Books of Maccabees (part of the Apocrypha, books written in Greek attached to the Hebrew scriptures) and the present work, originally titled "The Sovereignty of Reason," was at some point added on as the fourth book. The author makes major historical mistakes, and his interest is clearly not historical; he recounts earlier martyrdoms for Judaism to encourage his community in their faith.

From the first century A.D. onward, "martyrdom narratives" evolved as a genre. The present narrative of Jewish martyrdom was influential among Christian writers, and the tombs of these martyrs were honored at Antioch by Christians as well as Jews. These narratives have some features that make them difficult for modern taste. Events are presented in a stylized and rhetorical way, and the individuals appear as types, which tends to detach a modern audience. An ancient audience, moreover, found the highly rhetorical prose moving; a modern account would use a different style.

One feature of this narrative is also found in many Christian martyr stories: The protagonist who emerges as the most heroic is a woman. Martyr stories stress the way that powerful regimes and their values can be resisted, and women, who tended to lack power and influence, provide the most dramatic example of this resistance. In this story, the mother's triumph over emotion is the more remarkable since in the ancient world, as in many societies, women were commonly thought of as more prone to emotion and less able to resist it than men.

This story centers on the Jews' refusal to eat forbidden food. What is at stake here is not just the eating of pork, but idolatry. In Greek cities citizens shared in feasts of meat from animals killed after they were sacrificed to the gods at pagan festivals (the main occasions when meat was eaten). This was seen by many Greeks as a normal part of belonging to the community. But for Jews (and Christians), this meat had been "offered to idols" and therefore to join in eating it amounted to idolatry. In the story, what Antiochus demands as an ordinary part of civic life is seen by the Jews as requiring something contrary to a basic tenet of their religion because it amounts to colluding in the worship of the pagan gods. The Greeks had difficulty understanding this attitude, since they did not see religions as mutually exclusive, and Jews (and later Christians) were seen as irrationally stubborn in refusing to accept pagan practices. Antiochus' persecution of Jews for their practices was most unusual among rulers in the pagan world, but in cities where there were large populations of Greeks and Jews, such as Alexandria, there was often tension between the communities on issues on which ordinary Greek civic life clashed with traditional Jewish observance.

The Fourth Book of Maccabees SELECTIONS

1 The subject that I am about to discuss is most philosophical, that is, whether devout reason is sovereign over the emotions. So it is right for me to advise you to pay earnest attention to philosophy. [2]For the subject is essential to everyone who is seeking knowledge, and in addition it includes the praise of the highest virtue—I mean, of course, rational judgment. [3]If, then, it is evident that reason rules over those emotions that hinder self-control, namely, gluttony and lust, [4]it is also clear that it masters the emotions that hinder one from justice, such as malice, and those that stand in the way of courage, namely anger, fear, and pain. [5]Some might perhaps ask, "If reason rules the emotions, why is it not sovereign over forgetfulness and ignorance?" Their attempt at argument is ridiculous! [6]For reason does not rule its own emotions, but those that are opposed to justice, courage, and self-control; and it is not for the purpose of destroying them, but so that one may not give way to them.

This striking figure is a depiction of Moses with the scroll of the Jewish Law. It comes from a series of paintings in the third-century A.D. synagogue at Dura Europus in Asia Minor. In the ancient world, Jews did not always take the Second Commandment, forbidding graven images, to forbid all representational art. Two-dimensional paintings, unlike statues, could not be confused with objects of a cult. In this synagogue, entire walls are painted with Jewish symbols and important stories from Jewish history. (Painting of Moses from Dura Europus, Syria, third century A.D. National Museum, Damascus. Yale University Art Gallery, Dura-Europus Collection.)

7 I could prove to you from many and various examples that reason is dominant over the emotions, 8but I can demonstrate it best from the noble bravery of those who died for the sake of virtue, Eleazar and the seven brothers and their mother. 9All of these, by despising sufferings that bring death, demonstrated that reason controls the emotions. 10On this anniversary it is fitting for me to praise for their virtues those who, with their mother, died for the sake of nobility and goodness, but I would also call them blessed for the honor in which they are held. 11All people, even their torturers, marveled at their courage and endurance, and they became the cause of the downfall of tyranny over their nation. By their endurance they conquered the tyrant, and thus their native land was purified through them. 12I shall shortly have an opportunity to speak of this; but, as my custom is, I shall begin by stating my main principle, and then I shall turn to their story, giving glory to the all-wise God.

13 Our inquiry, accordingly, is whether reason is sovereign over the emotions. 14We shall decide just what reason is and what emotion is, how many kinds of emotions there are, and whether reason rules over all these. 15Now reason is the mind that with sound logic prefers the life of wisdom. 16Wisdom, next, is the knowledge of divine and human matters and the causes of these. 17This, in turn, is education in the law, by which we learn divine matters reverently and human affairs to our advantage. 18Now the kinds of wisdom are rational judgment, justice, courage, and self-control. 19Rational judgment is supreme over all of these, since by means of it reason rules over the emotions. 20The two most comprehensive types of the emotions are pleasure and pain: and each of these is by nature concerned with both body and soul. 21The emotions of both pleasure and pain have many consequences. 22Thus desire precedes pleasure and delight follows it. 23Fear precedes pain and sorrow comes after. 24Anger, as a person will see by reflecting on this experience, is an emotion embracing pleasure and pain. 25In pleasure there exists even a malevolent tendency, which is the most complex of all the emotions. 26In the soul it is boastfulness, covetousness, thirst for honor, rivalry, and malice; 27in the body, indiscriminate eating, gluttony, and solitary gormandizing.

28 Just as pleasure and pain are two plants growing from the body and the soul, so there are many offshoots of these plants, 29each of which the master cultivator, reason, weeds and prunes and ties up and waters and thoroughly irrigates, and so tames the jungle of habits and emotions. 30For reason is the guide of the virtues, but over the emotions it is sovereign.

Observe now, first of all, that rational judgment is sovereign over the emotions by virtue of the restraining power of self-control. 31Self-control, then, is dominance over the desires. 32Some desires are mental, others are physical, and reason obviously rules over both. 33Otherwise, how is it that when we are attracted to forbidden foods we abstain from the pleasure to be had from them? Is it not because reason is able to rule over appetites? I for one think so. 34Therefore when we crave seafood and fowl and animals and all sorts of foods that are forbidden to us by the law, we abstain because of domination by reason. 35For the emotions of the appetites are restained, checked by the temperate mind, and all the impulses of the body are bridled by reason.

2 And why is it amazing that the desires of the mind for the enjoyment of beauty are rendered powerless? [2]It is for this reason, certainly, that the temperate Joseph is praised, because by mental effort he overcame sexual desire. [3]For when he was young and in his prime for intercourse, by his reason he nuilified the frenzy of the passions. [4]Not only is reason proved to rule over the frenzied urge of sexual desire, but also over every desire. [5]Thus the law says, "You shall not covet your neighbor's wife or anything that is your neighbor's." [6]In fact, since the law has told us not to covet, I could prove to you all the more that reason is able to control desires.

Just so it is with the emotions that hinder one from justice. [7]Otherwise how could it be that someone who is habitually a solitary gormandizer, a glutton, or even a drunkard can learn a better way, unless reason is clearly lord of the emotions? [8]Thus, as soon as one adopts a way of life in accordance with the law, even though a lover of money, one is forced to act contrary to natural ways and to lend without interest to the needy and to cancel the debt when the seventh year arrives. [9]If one is greedy, one is ruled by the law through reason so that one neither gleans the harvest nor gathers the last grapes from the vineyard.

In all other matters we can recognize that reason rules the emotions. [10]For the law prevails even over affection for parents, so that virtue is not abandoned for their sakes. [11]It is superior to love for one's wife, so that one rebukes her when she breaks the law. [12]It takes precedence over love for children, so that one punishes them for misdeeds. [13]It is sovereign over the relationship of friends, so that one rebukes friends when they act wickedly. [14]Do not consider it paradoxical when reason, through the law, can prevail even over enmity. The fruit trees of the enemy are not cut down, but one preserves the property of enemies from marauders and helps raise up what has fallen.

15 It is evident that reason rules even the more violent emotions: lust for power, vainglory, boasting, arrogance, and malice. [16]For the temperate mind repels all these malicious emotions, just as it repels anger—for it is sovereign over even this. [17]When Moses was angry with Dathan and Abiram, he did nothing against them in anger, but controlled his anger by reason. [18]For, as I have said, the temperate mind is able to get the better of the emotions, to correct some, and to render others powerless. [19]Why else did Jacob, our most wise father, censure the households of Simeon and Levi for their irrational slaughter of the entire tribe of the Shechemites, saying, "Cursed be their anger"? [20]For if reason could not control anger, he would not have spoken thus. [21]Now when God fashioned human beings, he planted in them emotions and inclinations, [22]but at the same time he enthroned the mind among the senses as a sacred governor over them all. [23]To the mind he gave the law; and one who lives subject to this will rule a kingdom that is temperate, just, good, and courageous.

24 How is it then, one might say, that if reason is master of the emotions, it does not control forgetfulness

3 and ignorance? [1]But this argument is entirely ridiculous; for it is evident that reason rules not over its own emotions, but over those of the body. [2]No one of us can eradicate that kind of desire, but reason can provide a way for us not to be enslaved by desire. [3]No one of us can eradicate anger from the mind, but reason can help to deal with anger. [4]No one of us can eradicate malice, but reason can fight at our side so that we are not overcome by malice. [5]For reason does not uproot the emotions but is their antagonist.

15 When King Seleucus died, his son Antiochus Epiphanes succeeded to the throne, an arrogant and terrible man, [16]who removed Onias from the priesthood and appointed Onias's brother Jason as high priest. [17]Jason agreed that if the office were conferred on him he would pay the king three thousand six hundred sixty talents annually. [18]So the king appointed him high priest and ruler of the nation. [19]Jason changed the nation's way of life and altered its form of government in complete violation of the law, [20]so that not only was a gymnasium constructed at the very citadel of our native land, but also the temple service was abolished. [21]The divine justice was angered by these acts and caused Antiochus himself to make war on them. [22]For when he was warring against Ptolemy in Egypt, he heard that a rumor of his death had spread and that the people of Jerusalem had rejoiced greatly. He speedily marched against them, [23]and after he had plundered them he issued a decree that if any of them were found observing the ancestral law they should die. [24]When, by means of his decrees, he had not been able in any way to put an end to the people's observance of the law, but saw that all his threats and punishments were being disregarded [25]—even to the extent that women, because they had circumcised their sons, were thrown headlong from heights along with their infants, though they had known beforehand that they would suffer this—[26]when, I say, his decrees were despised by the people, he himself tried through torture to compel everyone in the nation to eat defiling foods and to renounce Judaism.

5 The tyrant Antiochus, sitting in state with his counselors on a certain high place, and with his armed soldiers standing around him, [2]ordered the guards to seize each and every Hebrew and to compel them to eat pork and food sacrificed to idols. [3]If any were not willing to eat defiling food, they were to be broken on the wheel and killed. [4]When many persons had been rounded up, one man, Eleazar by name, leader of the flock, was brought before the king. He was a man of priestly family, learned in the law, advanced in age, and known to many in the tyrant's court because of his philosophy.

5 When Antiochus saw him he said, [6]"Before I begin to torture you, old man, I would advise you to save yourself by eating pork, [7]for I respect your age and your gray hairs. Although you have had them for so long a time, it does not seem to me that you are a philosopher when you observe the religion of the Jews. [8]When nature has granted it to us, why should you abhor eating the very excellent meat of this animal? [9]It is senseless not to enjoy delicious things that are not shameful, and wrong to spurn the gifts of nature. [10] It seems to me that you will do something even more senseless if, by holding a vain opinion concerning the truth, you continue to despise me to your own hurt. [11]Will you not awaken from your foolish philosophy, dispel your futile reasonings, adopt a mind appropriate to your years, philosophize according to the truth of what is beneficial, [12]and have compassion on your old age by honoring my humane advice? [13]For consider this: if there is some power watching over this religion of yours, it will excuse you from any transgression that arises out of compulsion."

14 When the tyrant urged him in this fashion to eat meat unlawfully, Eleazar asked to have a word. [15]When he had received permission to speak, he began to address the people as follows: [16]"We, O Antiochus, who have been persuaded to govern our lives by the divine law, think that there is no compulsion more powerful than our obedience to the law. [17]Therefore we consider that we should not transgress it in any respect. [18]Even if, as you suppose, our law were not truly divine and we had wrongly held it to be divine, not even so would it be right for us to invalidate our reputation for piety. [19]Therefore do not suppose that it would be a petty sin if we were to eat defiling food; [20]to transgress the law in matters either small or great is of equal seriousness, [21]for in either case the law is equally despised. [22]You scoff at our philosophy as though living by it were irrational, [23]but it teaches us self-control, so that we master all pleasures and desires, and it also trains us in courage, so that we endure any suffering willingly; [24]it instructs us in justice, so that in all our dealings we act impartially, and it teaches us piety, so that with proper reverence we worship the only living God.

25 "Therefore we do not eat defiling food; for since we believe that the law was established by God, we know that in the nature of things the Creator of the world in giving us the law has shown sympathy toward us. [26]He has permitted us to eat what will be most suitable for our lives, but he has forbidden us to eat meats that would be contrary to this. [27]It would be tyrannical for you to compel us not only to transgress the law, but also to eat in such a way that you may deride us for eating defiling foods, which are most hateful to us. [28]But you shall have no such occasion to laugh at me, [29]nor will I transgress the sacred oaths of my ancestors concerning the keeping of the law, [30]not even if you gouge out my eyes and burn my entrails. [31]I am not so old and cowardly as not to be young in reason on behalf of piety. [32]Therefore get your torture wheels ready and fan the fire more vehemently! [33]I do not so pity my old age as to break the ancestral law by my own act. [34]I will not play false to you, O law that trained me, nor will I renounce you, beloved self-control. [35]I will not put you to shame, philosophical reason, nor will I reject you, honored priesthood and knowledge of the law. [36]You, O king, shall not defile the honorable mouth of my old age, nor my long life lived lawfully. [37]My ancestors will receive me as pure, as one who does not fear your violence even to death. [38]You may tyrannize the ungodly, but you shall not dominate my religious principles, either by words or through deeds."

6 When Eleazar in this manner had made eloquent response to the exhortations of the tyrant, the guards who were standing by dragged him violently to the instruments of torture. [2]First they stripped the old man, though he remained adorned with the gracefulness of his piety. [3]After they had tied his arms on each side they flogged him, [4]while a herald who faced him cried out, "Obey the king's commands!" [5]But the courageous and noble man, like a true Eleazar, was unmoved, as though being tortured in a dream; [6]yet while the old man's eyes were raised to heaven, his flesh was being torn by scourges, his blood flowing, and his sides were being cut to pieces. [7]Although he fell to the ground because his body could not endure the agonies, he kept his reason upright and unswerving. [8]One of the cruel guards rushed at him and began to kick him in the side to make him get up again after he fell. [9]But he bore the pains and scorned the punishment and endured the tortures. [10]Like a noble athlete the old man, while being beaten, was victorious over his torturers; [11]in fact, with his face bathed in sweat, and gasping heavily for breath, he amazed even his torturers by his courageous spirit.

[12] At that point, partly out of pity for his old age, [13]partly out of sympathy from their acquaintance with him, partly out of admiration for his endurance, some of the king's retinue came to him and said, [14]"Eleazar, why are you so irrationally destroying yourself through these evil things? [15]We will set before you some cooked meat; save yourself by pretending to eat pork."

[16] But Eleazar, as though more bitterly tormented by this counsel, cried out: [17]"Never may we, the children of Abraham, think so basely that out of cowardice we feign a role unbecoming to us! [18]For it would be irrational if having lived in accordance with truth up to old age and having maintained in accordance with law the reputation of such a life, we should now change our course [19]and ourselves become a pattern of impiety to the young by setting them an example in the eating of defiling food. [20]It would be shameful if we should survive for a little while and during that time be a laughingstock to all for our cowardice, [21]and be despised by the tyrant as unmanly by not contending even to death for our divine law. [22]Therefore, O children of Abraham, die nobly for your religion! [23]And you, guards of the tyrant, why do you delay?"

[24] When they saw that he was so courageous in the face of the afflictions, and that he had not been changed by their compassion, the guards brought him to the fire. [25]There they burned him with maliciously contrived instruments, threw him down, and poured stinking liquids into his nostrils. [26]When he was now burned to his very bones and about to expire, he lifted up his eyes to God and said, [27]"You know, O God, that though I might have saved myself, I am dying in burning torments for the sake of the law. [28]Be merciful to your people, and let our punishment suffice for them. [29]Make my blood their purification, and take my life in exchange for theirs." [30]After he said this, the holy man died nobly in his tortures; even in the tortures of death he resisted, by virtue of reason, for the sake of the law.

[31] Admittedly, then, devout reason is sovereign over the emotions. [32]For if the emotions had prevailed over reason, we would have testified to their domination. [33]But now that reason has conquered the emotions, we properly attribute to it the power to govern. [34]It is right for us to acknowledge the dominance of reason when it masters even external agonies. It would be ridiculous to deny it. [35]I have proved not only that reason has mastered agonies, but also that it masters pleasures and in no respect yields to them.

7 For like a most skillful pilot, the reason of our father Eleazar steered the ship of religion over the sea of the emotions, [2]and though buffeted by the stormings

of the tyrant and overwhelmed by the mighty waves of tortures, [3]in no way did he turn the rudder of religion until he sailed into the haven of immortal victory.

16 If, therefore, because of piety an aged man despised tortures even to death, most certainly devout reason is governor of the emotions. [17]Some perhaps might say, "Not all have full command of their emotions, because not all have prudent reason." [18]But as many as attend to religion with a whole heart, these alone are able to control the passions of the flesh, [19]since they believe that they, like our patriarchs Abraham and Isaac and Jacob, do not die to God, but live to God. [20]No contradiction therefore arises when some persons appear to be dominated by their emotions because of the weakness of their reason. [21]What person who lives as a philosopher by the whole rule of philosophy, and trusts in God, [22]and knows that it is blessed to endure any suffering for the sake of virtue, would not be able to overcome the emotions through godliness? [23]For only the wise and courageous are masters of their emotions.

8 For this is why even the very young, by following a philosophy in accordance with devout reason, have prevailed over the most painful instruments of torture. [2]For when the tyrant was conspicuously defeated in his first attempt, being unable to compel an aged man to eat defiling foods, then in violent rage he commanded that others of the Hebrew captives be brought, and that any who ate defiling food would be freed after eating, but if any were to refuse, they would be tortured even more cruelly.

3 When the tyrant had given these orders, seven brothers—handsome, modest, noble, and accomplished in every way—were brought before him along with their aged mother. [4]When the tyrant saw them, grouped about their mother as though a chorus, he was pleased with them. And struck by their appearance and nobility, he smiled at them, and summoned them nearer and said, [5]"Young men, with favorable feelings I admire each and every one of you, and greatly respect the beauty and the number of such brothers. Not only do I advise you not to display the same madness as that of the old man who has just been tortured, but I also exhort you to yield to me and enjoy my friendship. [6]Just as I am able to punish those who disobey my orders, so I can be a benefactor to those who obey me. [7]Trust me, then, and you will have positions of authority in my government if you will renounce the ancestral tradition of your national life. [8]Enjoy your youth by adopting the Greek way of life and by changing your manner of living. [9]But if by disobedience you rouse my anger, you will compel me to destroy each and every one of you with dreadful punishments through tortures. [10]Therefore take pity on yourselves. Even I, your enemy, have compassion for your youth and handsome appearance. [11]Will you not consider this, that if you disobey, nothing remains for you but to die on the rack?"

12 When he had said these things, he ordered the instruments of torture to be brought forward so as to persuade them out of fear to eat the defiling food.

15 But when they had heard the inducements and saw the dreadful devices, not only were they not afraid, but they also opposed the tyrant with their own philosophy, and by their right reasoning nullified his tyranny. [16]Let us consider, on the other hand, what arguments might have been used if some of them had been cowardly and unmanly. Would they not have been the following? [17]"O wretches that we are and so senseless! Since the king has summoned and exhorted us to accept kind treatment if we obey him,[18] why do we take pleasure in vain resolves and venture upon a disobedience that brings death? [19]O men and brothers, should we not fear the instruments of torture and consider the threats of torments, and give up this vain opinion and this arrogance that threatens to destroy us? [20]Let us take pity on our youth and have compassion on our mother's age; [21]and let us seriously consider that if we disobey we are dead! [22]Also, divine justice will excuse us for fearing the king when we are under compulsion. [23]Why do we banish ourselves from this most pleasant life and deprive ourselves of this delightful world? [24]Let us not struggle against compulsion or take hollow pride in being put to the rack. [25]Not even the law itself would arbitrarily put us to death for fearing the instruments of torture. [26]Why does such contentiousness excite us and such a fatal stubbornness please us, when we can live in peace if we obey the king?"

27 But the youths, though about to be tortured, neither said any of these things nor even seriously considered them. [28]For they were contemptuous of the emotions and sovereign over agonies.

13 Since, then, the seven brothers despised sufferings even unto death, everyone must concede that devout reason is sovereign over the emotions. [2]For if they had been slaves to their emotions and had eaten defiling food, we would say that they had been conquered by these emotions. [3]But in fact it was not so. Instead, by reason, which is praised before God, they prevailed over their emotions. [4]The supremacy of the mind over these cannot be overlooked, for the brothers mastered both emotions and pains. [5]How then can one fail to confess the sovereignty of right reason over emotion in those who were not turned back by fiery agonies? [6]For just as towers jutting out over harbors hold back the threatening waves and make it calm for those who sail into the inner basin, [7]so the seven-towered right reason of the youths, by fortifying the harbor of religion, conquered the tempest of the emotions.

11 Do not consider it amazing that reason had full command over these men in their tortures, since the mind of woman despised even more diverse agonies, [12]for the mother of the seven young men bore up under the rackings of each one of her children.

24 Although she witnessed the destruction of seven children and the ingenious and various rackings, this noble mother disregarded all these because of faith in God. [25]For as in the council chamber of her own soul she saw mighty advocates—nature, family, parental love, and the rackings of her children— [26]this mother held two ballots, one bearing death and the other deliverance for her children. [27]She did not approve the deliverance that would preserve the seven sons for a short time, [28]but as the daughter of God-fearing Abraham she remembered his fortitude.

29 O mother of the nation, vindicator of the law and champion of religion, who carried away the prize of the contest in your heart! [30]O more noble than males in steadfastness, and more courageous than men in endurance! [31]Just as

Noah's ark, carrying the world in the universal flood, stoutly endured the waves, [32]so you, O guardian of the law, overwhelmed from every side by the flood of your emotions and the violent winds, the torture of your sons, endured nobly and withstood the wintry storms that assail religion.

16 If, then, a woman, advanced in years and mother of seven sons, endured seeing her children tortured to death, it must be admitted that devout reason is sovereign over the emotions. [2]Thus I have demonstrated not only that men have ruled over the emotions, but also that a woman has despised the fiercest tortures. [3]The lions surrounding Daniel were not so savage, nor was the raging fiery furnace of Mishael so intensely hot, as was her innate parental love, inflamed as she saw her seven sons tortured in such varied ways. [4]But the mother quenched so many and such great emotions by devout reason.

COMMENTS

The Jewish author of this work has obviously been educated in Greek philosophy and has read many of the authors in this part. Although influenced by some other writers, his own view is Platonic; like Galen, he interprets the relation between reason and the other parts as domination, rather than agreement, and simplifies Plato's three parts of the soul to two. He follows Plato in holding that the life in which reason rules is the life of virtue, which takes the form of wise judgment, justice, courage, and self-control.

This Platonic scheme is interpreted in a specifically Jewish way; the virtuous person's wisdom consists in following the Jewish Law. (Hence the virtues are illustrated by examples from Scripture.) Because the observant Jewish life is a specific form of the life of virtue, and the life of virtue is the life in which reason is in control, the author argues that the martyrdoms of Jews who died rather than go against the Law support his thesis that reason can control and rule the passions.

The idea that the life that is rationally committed to virtue is worth dying for in the face of temptations to abandon it was familiar in the ancient world in nonreligious versions. The author argues, through the confrontation of Eleazar and the king, that the observant Jewish life is such a life, despite what seemed to pagans the arbitrary nature of some Jewish observances. Judaism is referred to as a "philosophy," since following the Law orders and unifies the lives of those who do it in a rationally defensible way. Compare the extract from Plato's *Gorgias* in section 5 and the attitudes of Socrates and the martyrs here in the face of the argument that it is foolish to accept pain and death rather than abandon the life of virtue that results from reason's rule in the soul.

Is this role of religion different from the one you think it has? Do you think of reason as *opposed* to religious faith? If so, what do you think this shows about your conceptions of reason and of religious faith?

SECTION THREE

KNOWLEDGE, BELIEF, AND SKEPTICISM

A. KNOWLEDGE AND EXPERTISE

Plato *Laches* 189d–201c

B. KNOWLEDGE AND TRUE BELIEF

Plato *Meno* 80a–86d, 96b–99e
Plato *Theaetetus* 200d–201c

C. RELATIVISM

Plato *Theaetetus* 166e–172b, 177c–179b

D. THE STRUCTURE OF A SYSTEM OF KNOWLEDGE

Plato *Republic* 475b–484a, 507b–511e, 514a–518d,
    523a–525b, 531c–535a
Aristotle *Posterior Analytics* I, 1–3; II, 19
Aristotle *Metaphysics* I, 1–3; II, 1
Aristotle *Parts of Animals* I, 5

E. KNOWLEDGE FROM EXPERIENCE

Epicurus on Knowledge
The Stoics on Knowledge

F. SKEPTICISM

Plato *Theaetetus* 148c–151d
Sextus Empiricus *Outlines of Pyrrhonism* I, 1–30, 100–117; III 1–12

A. Knowledge and Expertise

In ancient philosophy, we find, not a single issue that is regarded as "the problem of knowledge," but, rather, a whole cluster of issues and concerns with knowledge. Some of these issues turn out to be similar to issues in modern epistemology (theory of knowledge). Some, on the other hand, are, at first glance, different from modern concerns. Among these different concerns is the idea, which is important to Plato, that a good example of knowledge is to be found in someone who is an expert in a particular field. In Plato's "Socratic" dialogues (short, lively dramatic dialogues in which Socrates plays a mainly negative role), Socrates undermines the claims of various self-styled experts to have knowledge of the kind they think they have. What is at issue here is knowledge of an entire field, as opposed to knowledge of particular facts.

SOCRATES

Socrates of Athens (469–399 B.C.) was arguably the most influential philosophical figure in the ancient world and became so without writing anything. Nothing in this book comes directly from Socrates, but Socrates is a powerful influence on many of the texts in it.

Socrates' father was a stonemason and his mother a midwife. Socrates began his adult life fairly well off, since he served as a heavy-armed soldier, which required substantial means, but by the end of his life he was poor, presumably because of his neglect of practical matters in favor of philosophy. His wife's name, Xanthippe, suggests that she came from an aristocratic family; tradition represented her as a nag and Socrates as a put-upon husband, but we have no way of knowing whether any of this is true.

Socrates was tried on a charge of introducing new deities and corrupting the youth in 399 B.C.; he was found guilty and executed. The trial and execution may have been partly due to political prejudice against some of Socrates' friends and to general anti-intellectualism. Athenian courts allowed vague and prejudicial charges and were easy to influence by rhetoric and pandering to prejudices.

Socrates rapidly became seen as an ideal figure of the philosopher, as someone who devotes his life to philosophy and is prepared to die in its cause. The accounts of Socrates' defense at his trial vary widely, but all stress what was seen as his arrogance in standing by his life and values and refusing to compromise or apologize for them, even when his life was at stake.

What did Socrates take philosophy to be? Because he wrote nothing himself, he soon became a figure who could be seen in different ways by different people, several of whom wrote, after his death, works in which he is the main character. Of this "Socratic literature," we have fragments by many authors and much by Xenophon, a soldier and politician, and by Plato, an important philosopher in his own right. The accounts from these sources clash in several ways, and we have little hope of recovering what Socrates "really" thought. Later, philosophers, such as Aristotle, the Stoics, and the Academic Skeptics, all produced their own accounts of Socrates, which are also diverse. Right from the start, Socrates was seen as the ideal philosopher, and most philosophical movements, whatever their own ideas, wanted him as a figurehead and ascribed their ideas to him. (The exception is the Epicureans, who thought that Epicurus was the only worthwhile philosopher and ridiculed Socrates.)

What really sets Socrates apart from other philosophers is his identification of philosophy with the activity of arguing and debate, rather than with the production of authoritative ideas. Socrates argued with anybody who was willing; he did philosophy in the marketplace, rather than in a secluded philosophical school. Presenting Socrates as arguing in a dialogue appeared the most suitable way of recording his activity as a philosopher. We do not know how precise Socrates' own view of argument was, but what was seen as most characteristic of him was the practice of *ad hominem* argument, that is, arguing on the basis of what the other person holds (asking the person to support it, showing the person that there is a problem with it), rather than arguing for his own views.

In some of Plato's dialogues, although it is clear that Socrates has views of his own, he does not argue for them, but limits himself to examining problems with other people's views. In other dialogues, Plato has Socrates put forward positive views of various kinds, sometimes bold and definite, but he always retains the dialogue form, which ensures that the reader is distanced from Socrates and does not take his view to be presented authoritatively. Plato's dialogues are varied, and he takes Socrates to represent different kinds of philosophy in different dialogues, but he always retains the dialogue form, presumably to retain what he sees as the most important fact about Socrates: He never put forward views authoritatively, seeing himself as a searcher and arguer, not as someone with philosophical knowledge.

Laches 189d–201c
PLATO

SOCRATES   Well, Nicias and Laches, we must be persuaded by Lysimachus and Melisias. Perhaps it's no bad thing to ask ourselves what we just undertook to consider, namely, who our teachers in this sort of education have been, or
e   whom we've made better. But I suppose the following kind of inquiry bears on the same issue and is perhaps more nearly fundamental: if we happen to know of anything whatever that, being present to something, makes that to

From *Dialogues of Plato 3*, by R. E. Allen (New Haven, Conn.: Yale University Press, 1996). Reprinted with the permission of Yale University Press.

which it is present better, and if in addition we are able to make it come to be present to that thing, it is clear that we know the thing about which we might become advisors as to how one might best and most easily possess it. Perhaps you don't understand what I mean, and you'll learn more easily this way. If we know that sight, when present to eyes, makes that to which 190a it is present better, and if in addition we're able to make it come to be present to eyes, clearly we know what sight itself is, about which we may become counselors as to how one might best and most easily possess it. For if we don't know this very thing—what sight is, or what hearing is—we'd scarcely be worth mentioning as counselors and doctors of eyes or ears, and of how one might best possess hearing or sight.

LACHES   True, Socrates.   b

SOCRATES   Then, Laches, these two friends now summon us to counsel over how virtue may come to be present to their sons and so make them better in soul?

LACHES   Yes, they do.

SOCRATES   Does this then first require knowing what virtue is? For surely if we didn't at all know what virtue happens to be, how could we become counselors for anyone as to how he might best possess it?

LACHES   In no way at all, it seems to me, Socrates.   c

SOCRATES   So we claim, Laches, to know what it is.

LACHES   Yes, certainly.

SOCRATES   Then we could tell, presumably, what it is that we know?

LACHES   Of course.

SOCRATES   Then let's not inquire straightaway about the whole of virtue, dear friend, for perhaps it's too big a job. Let's first look at some part to see if we have adequate knowledge. The inquiry will likely be easier for us.

LACHES   Why, let's do as you wish, Socrates.   d

SOCRATES   Then which of the parts of virtue should we choose? Isn't it clear it's that to which learning to fight in armor is thought to be relevant? Most people surely think it relevant to courage, do they not?

LACHES   Yes indeed, very much so.

SOCRATES   Then let us first try to say what courage is, Laches. After that, we'll consider how it might come to be present in these young men, insofar as it can come to be present from practice and study. But try to tell what I ask: e What is courage?

LACHES   Why really, Socrates, it's not hard to say: if someone is willing to stay in ranks and ward off the enemy and not flee, rest assured he is courageous.

SOCRATES   Excellent, Laches. But perhaps I'm at fault for not speaking clearly: you didn't answer the question I meant to ask, but a different one.

LACHES   How do you mean, Socrates?

SOCRATES   I'll tell you, if I can. This man you mention is courageous if he 191a remains in ranks and fights the enemy.

LACHES   So I claim, at any rate.

SOCRATES   I do too. On the other hand, what about the man who fights the enemy while fleeing rather than remaining?

LACHES   How fleeing?

SOCRATES   As the Scythians are said to fight no less while fleeing than while attacking. And Homer surely praises the horses of Aeneas, "how they
b   understood their plain, and how to traverse it in rapid pursuit and withdrawal." And he lauded Aeneas himself for this, for his knowledge of fear, and said he was "author of fright."

LACHES   Yes, and properly, Socrates, because he was talking about chariots, and you're talking about the tactics of Scythian horsemen. Cavalry fights that way, but Greek heavy infantry as I described.

c SOCRATES   Except perhaps Spartan infantry, Laches. For they say that the Spartans at Plataea, when they met troops using wicker shields, refused to stand and fight but fled, and when the Persians broke ranks, the Spartans turned to fight like cavalry and so won the battle.

LACHES   True.

SOCRATES   This then is what I meant just now, that I was at fault for your not
d   answering properly because I didn't ask properly: for I wished to learn from you about those who are courageous not only in the heavy infantry, but also in the cavalry and every other form of warfare; and not only about those courageous in war but in perils at sea, and all who are courageous in disease and poverty and politics; and still again, those who are not only courageous against pains or fears, but also skilled to fight against desires or pleasures, both standing fast and turning to run away—for surely some people are also courageous in these sorts of things, Laches.

e LACHES   Very much so.

SOCRATES   Then they're all courageous, but some are possessed of courage in the midst of pleasures, others in the midst of pains or desires or fears. And others, I suppose, are possessed of cowardice in these same things.

LACHES   Of course.

SOCRATES   What is each of these two? That's what I was asking. Try again, then, to say, first, of courage: what is it which is the same in all these? Or don't you fully yet understand what I mean?

LACHES   Not quite.

192a SOCRATES   I mean this. Suppose I were to ask what quickness is, as we find it in running and lyre playing and talking and learning and many other things; we pretty well have it in anything worth mentioning in the actions of hands or legs, mouth and voice, or intelligence. Don't you agree?

LACHES   Of course.

b SOCRATES   Well, suppose someone asked me, "Socrates, what do you say it is which in all things you name quickness?" I'd tell him that I call quickness a power of getting a lot done in a little time, both in speech and in a race, and in everything else.

LACHES   And you're surely correct.

SOCRATES   Try then also to speak this way about courage, Laches. What power is it which, being the same in pleasure and pain and all the things we just now were mentioning, is then called courage?

LACHES   Well, it seems to me that it's a kind of perseverance of soul, if one must say what its nature is through all cases.

SOCRATES   Of course one must, at least if we're to answer the question among c ourselves. It appears to me, though, that not every perseverance appears to you to be courage. My evidence is this: I know pretty well, Laches, that you believe courage is a very noble thing.

LACHES   Be assured that it is among the most noble.

SOCRATES   Now, perseverance accompanied by wisdom is noble and good?

LACHES   Of course.

SOCRATES   But what if it's accompanied by folly? In that case, isn't it on the con- d trary harmful and injurious?

LACHES   Yes.

SOCRATES   Then will you say this sort of thing is at all noble, if it's injurious and harmful?

LACHES   No, at least not rightly, Socrates.

SOCRATES   So you won't agree that this kind of perseverance is courage, since it's not noble, but courage is a noble thing.

LACHES   True.

SOCRATES   So wise perseverance, according to your account, would be courage.

LACHES   It seems so.

SOCRATES   Let's see, then. Wise in respect to what? Everything, large and e small? For example, if someone perseveres in spending money wisely, knowing that by spending he'll get more, would you call that courageous?

LACHES   Certainly not.

SOCRATES   But, for example, if someone is a doctor, and his son or someone else is taken with inflammation of the lungs and begs him to give food or drink, and he doesn't give in but perseveres in refusing?

LACHES   That's not it either.   193a

SOCRATES   But take a man who perseveres in war and is willing to fight on a wise calculation, knowing that others will come to his aid, and suppose that he fights fewer and inferior men compared to those on his side, and still fur- ther that he has a stronger position. Would you say that the man who per- severes with this sort of wisdom and preparation is more courageous than the man willing to remain and persevere in the opposing camp?

LACHES   No, the man in the opposing camp is more courageous, it seems to me, b Socrates.

SOCRATES   Yet surely his perseverance is less wise than that of the other.

LACHES   True.

SOCRATES   So you'll say that the man with knowledge of horsemanship who perseveres in a cavalry fight is less courageous than the man without that knowledge.

LACHES   It seems so to me.

SOCRATES   And the man who perseveres with skill in using the sling or the bow, c or any other such art.

LACHES   Of course.

SOCRATES   And anyone willing to go down into wells and dive, and to persevere in this work without being skilled at it, or some other work of the same sort, you'll say is more courageous than those skilled in it.

LACHES   What else can one say, Socrates?

SOCRATES   Nothing, if one supposes it's so.

LACHES   But I surely do suppose it.

SOCRATES   Moreover, Laches, people of this sort run risks and persevere more foolishly than those who do the same thing with an art?

LACHES   It appears so.

d SOCRATES   Didn't foolish boldness and perseverance appear to us before to be shameful and harmful?

LACHES   To be sure.

SOCRATES   But courage, it was agreed, is something noble.

LACHES   Yes.

SOCRATES   But now, on the contrary, we're saying that this shameful thing—namely, foolish perseverance—is courage.

LACHES   We seem to be.

SOCRATES   Then do you think we're right?

LACHES   No, Socrates, I certainly don't.

e SOCRATES   So by your account, Laches, you and I are not tuned in the Dorian mode: our deeds are not in concord with our words. In deeds, it seems, one might say we have a share of courage, but not I think in words, if he now heard us conversing.

LACHES   Very true.

SOCRATES   Well then, does it seem noble for us to be so situated?

LACHES   Not at all.

SOCRATES   Well, do you wish us to be persuaded at least to this extent by what we're claiming?

LACHES   To what extent? And by what claim?

194a SOCRATES   The claim that bids us persevere. If you wish, let's stand our ground and persevere in the inquiry, so that courage herself won't laugh at us for not seeking her courageously, if perhaps perseverance is often courage after all.

LACHES   I'm not ready to give up, Socrates. And yet I'm not accustomed to such arguments. But a certain love of victory over these questions has taken hold
b   of me, and I'm truly angry that I'm so unable to say what I mean. For I do think I have a concept of what courage is; I don't know how it just slipped away from me, so that I can't capture it in a statement and say what it is.

SOCRATES   Well, my friend, the good hunter must follow the trail and not give up.

LACHES   To be sure.

SOCRATES   Do you wish us then to call on Nicias here to join the hunt? He may be more resourceful than we are.

LACHES   Yes, why not.

c SOCRATES   Come then, Nicias, and if you can, rescue friends storm-tossed and perplexed in argument. You see how perplexed we are. If you state what

you believe courage is, you'll release us from perplexity and yourself establish in speech what you conceive.

NICIAS   Well, Socrates, I've been thinking for some time that you're not defining courage well because you don't use what I've already heard you say so
well.

SOCRATES   How so, Nicias?

NICIAS   I've often heard you say that each of us is good in things in which he is   d
wise, bad in those of which he is ignorant.

SOCRATES   Why, that's certainly true, Nicias.

NICIAS   Then since the courageous man is good, it's clear he's wise.

SOCRATES   Hear that, Laches?

LACHES   Yes, and I don't at all understand what he means.

SOCRATES   I think I do. I think he means courage is a kind of wisdom.

LACHES   What kind of wisdom, Socrates?

SOCRATES   Why don't you ask him?   e

LACHES   Very well, I will.

SOCRATES   Come then, Nicias, tell him what kind of wisdom courage is, by
your account. Not, surely, the kind involved in flute playing

NICIAS   Not at all.

SOCRATES   Nor again lyre playing.

NICIAS   Of course not.

SOCRATES   Then what is this knowledge, or of what?

LACHES   A good question, Socrates. Let him say what he claims it is.

NICIAS   I say it's this, Laches: knowledge of what things to fear and what to be   195a
confident about, both in war and everything else.

LACHES   How absurdly he talks, Socrates.

SOCRATES   What do you have in view in saying this, Laches?

LACHES   Why, that wisdom is surely separate from courage.

SOCRATES   Nicias denies that.

LACHES   Yes, he does. He also babbles.

SOCRATES   Then let's instruct him, not abuse him.

NICIAS   No, Socrates, I think Laches wants to show I'm also saying nothing,
because he just appeared that way himself.

LACHES   Yes, Nicias, and I'll try to prove it. Because you really are saying noth-   b
ing. Take doctors, for example. Don't they know what things to fear in diseases? Or do you think the courageous know? Or do you call doctors
courageous?

NICIAS   Not at al.

LACHES   No, nor farmers either, I dare say. And yet they surely know what
things to fear in farming. And all other craftsmen know what to fear and
what to be confident about in their own arts. But they aren't any the more
courageous for it.

SOCRATES   What do you think Laches is saying, Nicias? He certainly appears to   c
be talking sense.

NICIAS   Sense, yes. Truth, no.

SOCRATES   How so?

NICIAS   Because he thinks doctors know something about sick people beyond being able to tell what's healthy and diseased. But surely that's only as much as they know. Whether it's more to be feared for someone to be healthy rather than sick—do you believe doctors know that, Laches? Don't you think it's better for many people not to rise than to get up from their ill-ness? Tell me this: do you claim that in each case it's better to survive and not for many preferable to be dead?

d LACHES   I suppose that's so.

NICIAS   Then do you think the same things are to be feared by those better off dead and those better off alive?

LACHES   No, I don't.

NICIAS   But do you give it to the doctors to know this, or to any other craftsman except him who knows what things to fear and not to fear, whom I call courageous?

SOCRATES   Do you understand clearly what he's saying, Laches?

e LACHES   I do. He calls seers courageous. For who else will know for whom it is better to live than to be dead? Well, Nicias, do you agree you're a seer, or that you're neither a seer nor courageous?

NICIAS   What's this? It's for a seer, you think, to know what things to fear and what to be confident about?

LACHES   Of course. Who else?

196a NICIAS   Much rather the man I mean, dear friend. Because the seer needs only to know the signs of things to come, whether there will be death for some-one or disease or loss of money, or victory or defeat in war or any other con-test. But which of these it is better for someone to suffer or not suffer—why is that for a seer to judge more than anyone else?

LACHES   I don't understand what he means to say, Socrates: he makes clear that he doesn't mean a seer or a doctor or anyone else is courageous, unless he means it's some god. Well, it appears to me that Nicias is unwilling gener-

b   ously to agree that he's saying nothing, but twists back and forth to hide his own perplexity. And yet, you and I just now could have twisted that way too, if we wished not to seem to contradict ourselves. If this were a law court, there'd be some point in it; but as it is, in a meeting of this sort, why decorate oneself in vain with empty words?

c SOCRATES   I think there's no reason at all, Laches. But let's see whether Nicias doesn't suppose he's saying something after all, and not just talking for the sake of talk. Let's inquire of him more clearly what he means, and if he appears to be saying something, we'll agree, but if not, we'll instruct him.

LACHES   Well, if you want to inquire, Socrates, do so. I think I've perhaps found out enough.

SOCRATES   Why, nothing prevents me: the inquiry will be common to us both.

LACHES   Of course.

d SOCRATES   Tell me then, Nicias—or rather, tell us, for Laches and I share the argument. You claim that courage is knowledge of things to fear and be con-fident about?

NICIAS   I do.

SOCRATES   But to know this doesn't belong to every man, when neither a doctor nor a seer will know it or be courageous, unless he has this very knowledge in addition. Didn't you say that?

NICIAS   Yes, I did.

SOCRATES   So as the proverb has it, this really isn't something "any pig would know," nor would a pig be courageous.

NICIAS   No, I think not.

SOCRATES   Clearly then, Nicias, you don't believe that even the Crommyonian e
sow was courageous. I don't say this in jest, but because I think one who says this must either deny courage to any wild beast or agree that a wild beast is so wise as to know what few men know because it's difficult to understand, and claim a lion or panther or some wild boar knows these things. (*Socrates turns to Laches*) But one who claims courage to be what you do must assume that a lion, a stag, a bull, and an ape are naturally alike relative to courage.

LACHES   By the gods, you do speak well, Socrates. Answer this truly for us, 197a
Nicias. Do you claim that these wild animals, which we all agree are courageous, are wiser than we are, or do you dare oppose everybody and deny that they're courageous?

NICIAS   No, Laches, I don't call wild beasts courageous, or anything else which out of lack of understanding is fearless and foolish and unafraid of what is to be feared. Do you suppose I also call all children courageous, who fear b
nothing through lack of understanding? On the contrary, I think fearlessness and courage are not the same. Of courage and forethought, I think, very few have a share. But of boldness and daring and fearlessness accompanied by lack of forethought, quite a few have a share—men, women and children, and wild beasts. What you and most people call courage, then, I call boldness: what is wise concerning the things of which I speak, I call courageous.

LACHES   Look at how well he thinks he embellishes himself by his argument, c
Socrates; he tries to rob those whom everyone agrees are courageous of the honor.

NICIAS   But not you, Laches, so cheer up. For I say you're wise, and Lamachus too, since you're both courageous, and many other Athenians as well.

LACHES   I won't reply as I might, so that you won't claim I'm truly an Aexonian.

SOCRATES   No, don't say anything, Laches. Actually, I don't think you're aware d
that he's received this wisdom from Damon, a friend of ours, and that Damon associates a great deal with Prodicus, who is supposed to be the best among the sophists in making distinctions among names of this sort.

LACHES   Actually, Socrates, it befits a sophist to be clever in such subtleties, rather than a man whom the city thinks worthy to preside over her.

SOCRATES   Surely it befits a man presiding over the greatest matters to have a e
share of the greatest wisdom, my friend. It seems to me that Nicias deserves to be examined as to what he has in view in assigning this name "courage."

LACHES   Then examine him yourself, Socrates.

SOCRATES   I intend to, my friend. But don't at all suppose I'm releasing you from your partnership in the argument. Pay attention and join in considering what is said.

LACHES   Very well, if it seems I should.

SOCRATES   Of course it does. But you, Nicias, start again from the beginning: you know that we began our discussion by considering courage as a part of virtue?

198a NICIAS   Of course.

SOCRATES   Then again, you answered that it is a part, but that there are also other parts, which all together are called virtue?

NICIAS   Of course.

SOCRATES   Then do you also say what I do? I call temperance and justice and certain others of that sort parts, in addition to courage. Don't you too?

b NICIAS   Certainly.

SOCRATES   Hold it right there, for we agree on this. But let's inquire about what things to fear and what to be confident about, so that you don't think they're one thing and we another. Now, we'll tell you what we believe: if you don't agree, you'll instruct us. We believe that what produces fear is fearful, but what does not produce fear is something to be confident about. Fear is produced not by past or present evils but by expected evils: for fear is expectation of evil to come. Doesn't that seem so to you too, Laches?

c LACHES   Yes, very much so, Socrates.

SOCRATES   Then hear our claim, Nicias. We say that evils to come are to be feared, but things to come which are not evil, or are good, one may be confident about. Do you agree?

NICIAS   In this, yes.

SOCRATES   And you call knowledge of these things courage?

NICIAS   Exactly.

SOCRATES   Then let us inquire whether you concur with us about a third thing.

d NICIAS   What's that?

SOCRATES   Socrates I'll tell you. It seems to me and to Laches here that, in respect to the various kinds of knowledge, there isn't one knowledge of the past, another of the present, another of what may and will be best in future: they're the same. Take health, for example: at all times there is no other knowledge of health than medicine, which, since it is one, observes what is

e   and has been and will come to be in future. So similarly again farming, concerning things which grow from the soil. And no doubt you would yourselves testify that in warfare generalship best exercises forethought specifically about what will happen in future; nor does it suppose it ought to serve but rather to rule prophecy, the seer's art, because it better knows what happens and what will happen in war. And the law so orders: the seer doesn't rule the general but the general the seer. Shall we say this, Laches?

199a LACHES   We shall.

SOCRATES   Then do you agree with us, Nicias, that the same knowledge understands the same things, future, present, and past?

NICIAS   I do: it seems true to me, Socrates.

SOCRATES   Now, my friend, courage is knowledge of what things to fear and
what to be confident about, you say?

NICIAS   Yes.   b

SOCRATES   But it was agreed that things to fear and things to be confident about
are, respectively, future evils and future goods.

NICIAS   Of course.

SOCRATES   But the same knowledge is of the same things, both of things to
come and generally.

NICIAS   True.

SOCRATES   So courage is not only knowledge of things to fear and to be confident about. For it understands not only future goods and evils, but those of
the present and those of the past and things generally, as the other kinds of
knowledge do.

NICIAS   Yes, so it seems.   c

SOCRATES   So your answer covered scarcely a third part of courage for us,
Nicias; and yet we were asking what courage is as a whole. But as it is, it
seems, by your account courage is not only knowledge of things to fear and
be confident about but, as your present account has it, courage would pretty
nearly be knowledge about all goods and evils and everything generally. Do
you accept that revision, Nicias?

NICIAS   I think so, Socrates.   d

SOCRATES   Then, my friend, do you think that a courageous man would lack
anything of virtue, since he would know all good things, and in general
how they are and will be and have been, and evil things in like manner? Do
you think he'd lack temperance, or justice and holiness, when to him alone
it pertains to guard carefully against what is to be feared and what is not
concerning both gods and men, and to provide good things for himself by
knowing how to behave correctly toward them?

NICIAS   I think there's something in what you say, Socrates.   e

SOCRATES   So what you're now talking about, Nicias, would not be a part of
virtue, but virtue as a whole.

NICIAS   It seems so.

SOCRATES   And yet, we were saying that courage is one part of virtue.

NICIAS   Yes.

SOCRATES   But that doesn't appear to be what we're saying now.

NICIAS   It seems not.

SOCRATES   And so, Nicias, we haven't found out what courage is.

NICIAS   We don't appear to.

LACHES   Really, my dear Nicias, I thought you'd find it, since you disdained my
answer to Socrates. I had high hope indeed that you'd discover it by the wis-   200a
dom you got from Damon.

NICIAS   Fine, Laches. You think it's at this point of no importance that you yourself were shown just now to know nothing about courage, but if I too am
revealed as another such, you look to that. It makes no difference at this
point, it seems, that you along with me know nothing of what a man who   b
thinks he amounts to something ought to have knowledge of. Well, you

seem to me to do a very human thing: you don't look at all at yourself but at others. I think I've spoken suitably about the things we just now were discussing, and if anything has not been adequately said, I'll correct it later with the help of Damon—whom you apparently think it proper to laugh at, and this without ever having laid eyes on Damon—and with the help of others. And when I confirm the matter for myself, I'll instruct you too and not begrudge it: for you seem to me to be in very great need of learning.

c LACHES   That's because you're wise, Nicias. Nevertheless, I advise Lysimachus here and Melisias to dismiss you and me on the subject of educating the lads but, as I said to begin with, not to let go of Socrates here. If my sons were of an age, I'd do the same thing.

d NICIAS   On that I too agree. If Socrates is willing to care for the youngsters, I'd seek no one else. Indeed, I'd gladly entrust Niceratus to him, if Socrates were willing; but when I mention something about it to him, he keeps recommending others to me but refuses himself. But see if Socrates will pay more heed to you, Lysimachus.

LYSIMACHUS   Yes, Nicias, it's surely only right. Indeed, I'd do many things for him that I'd refuse to most others. What say you, then, Socrates? Will you pay heed and share our eagerness that the youngsters become as good as possible?

e SOCRATES   It would be fearful indeed, Lysimachus, if I refused to share in eagerness for anyone to become as good as possible. Now, if in the present discussion I appeared to know, but these two here did not, it would be right to summon me specifically to this task. But as it is, all of us were equally in 201a perplexity. How then choose any of us? Better then choose none. Since this is so, consider whether my advice is worthwhile. For I say, gentlemen—just among ourselves—that all of us jointly should first seek the best possible teacher for ourselves—for we need him—and afterward for the young men, sparing neither expense nor aught else. I do not advise that we allow ourselves to be as we now are. And if any of us is laughed at because at our age we think it right to go to school, I think we should quote Homer, who said, "Shame, for a man in need, is not a good quality." So if anyone says anything, let's dismiss it; we'll be jointly concerned for our own selves and for the young men.

b LYSIMACHUS   What you say pleases me, Socrates. By as much as I'm the eldest, I'll in that degree most eagerly learn with the young. But please do this for me: you must come to my house at dawn tomorrow, so that we may take counsel about these very things. But for now, now let's end our meeting.

SOCRATES   Why, I'll do it gladly, Lysimachus. I'll come to your house tomorrow, if god is willing.

COMMENTS

When you are asked what you know, you are probably likely to think of obvious facts, but you may also reflect that you know French, the clarinet, basketball, or some other skill. Plato's Socrates is looking for knowledge, and he goes about it by first investigating what goes wrong when people who are supposed to have knowledge turn out to lack it; his examples are people who are supposed to be expert in some skill.

Some experts simply have a skill without being able to say much about it. Socrates demands that the expert be able to articulate his knowledge, particularly by being able to "give an account" of the subject of his expertise. Thus in the *Laches*, two generals, Laches and Nicias, are supposed by everyone to be experts about courage, but they fail Socrates' demand that they be able to give a consistent account of courage and defend it in argument. Their failure to do so raises several points.

Is Socrates making too intellectual a demand? Does an expert lack knowledge if she fails to be able to defend an account of what it is she thinks she is expert in?

Socrates himself does not claim to be an expert in anything, and he often says that he has no knowledge (expert knowledge, that is; he admits to knowing ordinary matters of fact). How can he show that someone else is not an expert in a field when he is not an expert either? What does this show about his methods of arguing?

Socrates assumes that if you have expert knowledge, you can articulate and express it in a way that conveys it to others—that is, it is teachable. Do you think that expert knowledge is teachable? Do you think that there are kinds of knowledge that are not teachable? If so, what relation is there between these kinds of knowledge and expert knowledge?

B. Knowledge and True Belief

An issue that arises in some of Plato's most famous passages is the relation of knowledge to true belief. The two seem to be different, but wherein does the difference lie? These passages explore more than one suggestion.

Meno 80a–86d, 96b–99e
PLATO

MENO   Socrates, before I as much as made your acquaintance I had heard that 80 you are simply perplexed yourself and that you make others perplexed as well; and now, as it seems to me, you are bewitching me with magic and altogether putting a spell on me, so that I am completely at a loss. And you seem to me, if I may actually make a joke, to be altogether most like, both in 5 appearance and in other respects, to that flat sea-fish, the electric ray. For this causes whoever at any time comes close to it and comes into contact

From Plato, *Meno* translated by R. W. Sharples (Warminster, England: Aris and Phillips, 1985).

b

5

with it to be numb; and I think you too have now done something like this to me. For I am truly numbed both in my mind and in my speech, and I have no answer to give you. And yet I have on countless occasions said a great deal about excellence to many people, and very well too, at least as I thought; but now I can't even say at all what it is. I think you make a right decision in not travelling abroad from here or living abroad; for if you did such things as a foreigner in another city, you might well be arrested as a wizard.

SOCRATES   You are very naughty, Meno, and you almost fooled me.

MENO   How, exactly, Socrates?

c SOCRATES   I know why you produced a comparison for me.

MENO   Why, do you think?

SOCRATES   So that I could produce one for you in return. I know this about all handsome people, that they enjoy being compared to things; it is in their interest, as the comparisons for handsome people are themselves handsome. But I am not going to compare you to anything in return. As for me, if the electric ray is itself numb and it is in this way that it causes others too to be numb, then I am like it; but otherwise not. For it is not that, having an abundance of answers myself, I cause others to be at a loss; rather, I am most definitely at a loss myself, and it is in this way that I cause others to be at a loss as well. And now, as far as excellence is concerned, *I* don't know what it is; you perhaps knew before you came into contact with me, but now you are like someone who doesn't know. All the same, I want to consider it with you and to join with you in searching for whatever it is.

5 MENO   And how are you going to search for this, Socrates, when you don't have the faintest idea what it is? Which of the things that you don't know will you suppose that it is, when you are searching for it? And even if you *do* come across it, how are you going to know that this is the thing you didn't know?

e SOCRATES   I see what you're getting at, Meno. Do you see what a contentious argument you're conjuring up, that it isn't possible for a man to search either for what he knows or for what he doesn't know? For he wouldn't search for what he knows—for he knows it, and there is no need to search for something like that; nor for what he doesn't know, for he doesn't even know what he's going to search for.

81 MENO   Well, doesn't this argument appear to you to be a good one, Socrates?

SOCRATES   No.

MENO   Can you say in what way?

5 SOCRATES   Yes, I can. I have heard both men and women who are wise concerning divine matters—

MENO   Saying what saying?

SOCRATES   One that is true, as it seems to me, and fine.

MENO   What is this, and who are those who say it?

10 SOCRATES   Those who say it are those of both priests and priestesses who have

d

5

made it their concern to be able to give an account of their practices; and it b
is also said by Pindar and by many others of the poets, as many as are
divinely inspired. *What* they say is as follows; but consider whether they
seem to you to speak the truth. They say that the soul of man is immortal,
and at one time ends a life—what people call dying—and at another is born 5
again, but never perishes; and that for this reason one must live one's entire
life in the most pious way possible. For, of those from whom

Persephone accepts the requital for her ancient
Grief, in the ninth year she restores their soul
Back again to the sun above,   10
And from these grow lordly kings   c
And men who are swift in strength and great
In wisdom; and for the rest of time people call them holy heroes.

So, since the soul is immortal and has been born many times, and has seen 5
both the things here on earth and those in the underworld and all things,
there is nothing that it has not learned. So there is nothing surprising in its
being possible for it to recollect things concerning both excellence and other
matters, seeing that it knew them before also. For since all nature is akin, and d
the soul has learned all things, nothing prevents it, if it has recollected one
thing—what men call "learning"—from discovering all other things, if one
is courageous and does not weary of the search. For the whole of searching
and learning is recollection. So one should not be persuaded by that con- 5
tentious argument; for it would make us lazy, and is pleasant to hear for
those men who are soft, but this one makes men active and ready to search. e
Trusting that it is true, I am willing to search with you for what excellence is.

MENO   Yes, Socrates. But what do you mean by this, that we do not learn, but
     what we call learning is recollection? Can you teach me how this is so?   5

SOCRATES   I said just now, Meno, that you are naughty; and now you are ask-
     ing if I can teach you, although I say that it is not teaching, but rather recol- 82
     lection—so that I might at once be shown to be contradicting myself.

MENO   No, indeed, Socrates, I didn't speak with this in mind, but from force 5
     of habit; but if you can in any way show me that it is as you say, show
     me.

SOCRATES   Well, it isn't easy, but I'm willing to try for your sake. Call here for b
     me one of your many attendants here, whichever you like, so that I can per-
     form the demonstration on him for you.

MENO   Certainly. Come here!

SOCRATES   Is he a Greek, at any rate, and does he speak Greek?

MENO   Yes, indeed; he's home-bred.   5

SOCRATES   Then pay attention as to which seems to you to be true of him, either
     that he is recollecting or that he is learning from me.

MENO   Yes, I will.

10 SOCRATES   Tell me then, boy, are you aware that a square figure is like this? [*Socrates draws the square ABCD*]

c   BOY: Yes, I am.—SOCRATES: So a square figure is one that has all these lines [*AB, BC, CD, DA*] equal, being four in number?—BOY: Certainly.—SOCRATES: And doesn't it also have these here across the middle (*EG, FH*) equal?—BOY:
5   Yes.—SOCRATES: Well, could there be both a larger figure of this sort, and a smaller one?—BOY: Certainly.—SOCRATES: Then, if this side were two feet and this side were two feet, how many square feet would the whole be? Look at it this way; if it was two feet in this direction, but only one in this,
d   wouldn't the figure be one times two square feet?—BOY: Yes.—SOCRATES: But since it's two feet in this direction as well, isn't it twice two?—BOY:—
5   Yes.—SOCRATES: So it's twice two square feet?—BOY: Yes.—SOCRATES: Then how many are twice two square feet? Work it out and tell me.—BOY: Four, Socrates.—SOCRATES: Well, could there be another figure twice the size of this one, but like it, having all its lines equal just like this one?—BOY: Yes.—
e   SOCRATES: How many square feet will it be?—BOY: Eight.—SOCRATES: Come on then, try and tell me how long each line in that one will be. For in this one it's two feet; what in that one which is twice the size?—BOY: Well, it's clear, Socrates, that it will be double.

5 SOCRATES   Do you see, Meno, that I'm not teaching him anything, but every-thing is a question? And now this boy thinks that he knows what the line is like that will produce the figure of eight square feet; or don't you think he does?

MENO   Yes.

SOCRATES   Well, does he know?

MENO   Certainly not.

10 SOCRATES   But he *thinks* it will be produced by the line that's twice as long?

MENO   Yes.

SOCRATES   Well, observe him recollecting in sequence, as one ought to recollect.

Now, you tell *me*. You say that the figure twice the size is produced by the line that is twice as long? I mean like this, not long in this way and short in that, but let it be equal in all directions like this one (*ABCD*), but twice the size of this, that is eight square feet. Consider whether you still think that it will be produced by the line that is twice as long.—BOY: Yes, I do.—SOCRATES: Well, isn't this line (*AJ*) twice this (*AB*), if we add a second line of the same length (*BJ*) from here (*B*)?—BOY: Certainly.—SOCRATES: And this, you say, will produce the figure of eight square feet, if there are four lines of this length?—BOY: Yes.—SOCRATES: Well, let's draw four equal lines, starting from it (*AJ, JL, LN, NA*). Wouldn't this (*AJLN*) be what you say is the figure of eight square feet?—BOY: Certainly.—SOCRATES: Then in it there are these four figures (*ABCD, BJKC, CKLM, DCNM*), each of which is equal to this four-square-foot one (*ABCD*)?—BOY: Yes.—SOCRATES: Then how big is it? Isn't it four times as big?—BOY: Yes, of course.—SOCRATES: Then is four times as big double?—BOY: Good heavens, no.—SOCRATES: Then what multiple is it?—BOY: Quadruple.—SOCRATES: Then the double side, boy, produces not a double but a quadruple figure.—BOY: You are right.—SOCRATES: For a figure of four times four square feet is a figure of sixteen square feet. Isn't it?—BOY: Yes.—SOCRATES: But what line produces a figure of eight square feet? This one produces one four times the size, doesn't it?—BOY: I agree.—And this quarter here (*ABCD*) is produced by this half here (*AB*)?—BOY: Yes.—SOCRATES: Well then: isn't the eight-square-foot figure double this one (*ABCD*) but half this one (*AJLN*)?—BOY: Yes.—SOCRATES: Won't it be produced by a line that is greater than one this long (*AB*) but by one that is less long than this one here (*AJ*)? Or isn't that so?—BOY: Yes, I think so.—SOCRATES: Good; what you think is what you should give as an answer. Tell me then; wasn't this one (*AB*) two feet, and this one (*AJ*) four?—BOY: Yes.—SOCRATES: Then the line that produces the eight-square-foot figure must be greater than this two-foot one, but less than the four-foot one.—BOY: It must.—SOCRATES: Then try and tell me how long you say it is.—BOY: Three feet.—SOCRATES: Then, if indeed it's going to be three feet, shall we take half of this line (AB) in addition and make it three feet? For there are two here (*AB*) and one here (*BP*). And from here in the same way there are two here (*AD*) and one here (*DR*); and this (*APQR*) is the figure you speak of.—BOY: Yes.—SOCRATES: Then if it's three feet this way and three feet this way, the whole figure comes out as three times three square feet?—BOY: It appears so.—SOCRATES: And how many are three times three square feet?—BOY: Nine.—SOCRATES: But the figure twice the size had to be how many square feet?—BOY: Eight.—SOCRATES: So we haven't yet got the eight-square-foot figure from the three-foot line, either.—BOY: No, indeed.—SOCRATES: But from what line, then? Try and tell us exactly; and if you don't want to work out a number for it, at least point out from what line.—BOY: But indeed, Socrates, I don't know.

SOCRATES   Do you see, Meno, what point this boy has now reached on the path of recollection? For at first he didn't *know* what is the side of the eight-square-foot figure, just as he doesn't yet know now either; but even so he *thought* that he knew then, and answered confidently supposing that he

b knew, and didn't think that he was perplexed; *now* he realises that he *is* now at a loss, and just as he doesn't in fact know, so also he doesn't even *think* he knows.

MENO   You are right.

SOCRATES   Then isn't he now in a better state with regard to the thing he didn't

5 know?

MENO   Yes this too seems so to me.

SOCRATES   So in causing him to be at a loss and to be numb, as the electric ray does, surely we haven't done him any harm?

MENO   No, I don't think so.

10 SOCRATES   Indeed, we have done something useful, as it seems, for his finding out how the matter is; for now he might actually enquire into it gladly, as he doesn't know it, whereas then he thought that he could easily speak well to

c many people and on many occasions about the figure twice the size, saying that it must have a side twice the length.

MENO   It seems so.

SOCRATES   Then do you think he would have tried to enquire into or learn what

5 he *thought* he knew, though he didn't, before he was plunged into perplexity, realising that he didn't know, and felt the need for knowledge?

MENO   I don't think so, Socrates.

SOCRATES   Then he has benefited by being numbed?

10 MENO   Yes, I think so.

SOCRATES   Well, observe what he will after all discover, starting from this per-

d plexity, by enquiring with me, with me just asking and not teaching him; watch to see if you find me teaching and instructing him at any point, rather than asking him his opinions.

Now, you tell me (*Socrates starts drawing a new diagram*): isn't this (*ABCD*) our figure of four square feet? Do you follow?

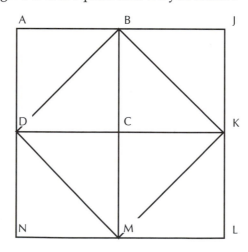

BOY   Yes.—SOCRATES: And we could add this other one here (*BJKC*), equal to 5
it?—BOY: Yes.—SOCRATES: And this third one (*DCMN*), equal to each of
them?—BOY: Yes.—SOCRATES: Then we could fill up this one in the corner
(*CKLM*) in addition?—BOY: Certainly.—SOCRATES: Then won't there be
these four equal figures?—BOY: Yes.—SOCRATES: Well then, how many times e
this one (*ABCD*) is this whole one (*AJLN*)?—BOY: Four times.—SOCRATES:
But we needed it to be double; or don't you remember?—BOY: Certainly. 85
SOCRATES: Well, is there a line here from corner to corner (*BD*), cutting each
of these figures in two?—BOY: Yes.—SOCRATES: Then these four lines (*BD,
BK, DM, KM*) are equal, surrounding this figure (*BKMD*)?—BOY: Yes, they
are.—SOCRATES: Consider then. How big is this figure (*BKMD*)?—BOY: I
don't know.—SOCRATES: Hasn't each line cut off the inside half of each of 5
these four figures? Or not?—BOY: Yes, it has.—SOCRATES: Then how many
figures of this size (*BCD*) are there in this (*BKMD*)?—BOY: Four.—SOCRATES:
And how many in this (*ABCD*)?—BOY: Two.—SOCRATES: And what is four
in relation to two?—BOY: Double.—SOCRATES: Then how many square feet
is this one (*BKMD*)?—BOY: Eight.—SOCRATES:—From what line have we got b
it?—BOY: From this one (*BD*).—SOCRATES: From the line that stretches from
one corner of the four-square-foot figure to the other?—BOY: Yes.—
SOCRATES: The experts call this the diagonal; so if this is named the diagonal, then it is the diagonal, as you say, Meno's boy, that will give the double 5
figure.—BOY: Yes, certainly, Socrates.

SOCRATES   What do you think, Meno? Is there any opinion that this boy
answered that isn't his own?

MENO   No, they're his own.   c

SOCRATES   And yet he didn't know the answer, as we said a little while ago.

MENO   You're right.

SOCRATES   But these opinions were in him, weren't they?

MENO   Yes.   5

SOCRATES   So the person, who doesn't have knowledge about whatever it may
be he doesn't know, has in him true opinions about what he doesn't know?

MENO   It appears so.

SOCRATES   Well, now these opinions have been newly aroused in this boy as if
in a dream; but if someone asks him these same things many times and in 10
many ways, you can be sure that in the end he will come to have exact
knowledge of these things as well as anyone else does.   d

MENO   It seems so.

SOCRATES   Then he will come to have knowledge without having been taught
by anyone, but only having been asked questions, and having recovered
this knowledge from himself?

MENO   Yes.   5

SOCRATES   And isn't recovering knowledge oneself, in oneself, recollecting?

MENO   Certainly.

SOCRATES   Then didn't this boy either acquire at some time the knowledge
which he now has, or else always possess it?   10

MENO   Yes.

SOCRATES   Well, if he always possessed it, he was always knowledgeable; and if he acquired it at some time, at any rate he won't have acquired it in this
e   present life. Or has anyone taught this boy geometry? For he will do the same where every part of geometry is concerned, and all other subjects too. Is there then anyone who has taught this boy everything? You ought to know, I suppose, especially as he was born and brought up in your
5   household.

MENO   No, I do indeed know that no-one ever taught him.

SOCRATES   But does he have these opinions, or not?

MENO   Necessarily so, it appears, Socrates.

86 SOCRATES   But if it isn't by having acquired them in this present life, isn't this now clear, that at some other time he possessed them and had already learned them then?

MENO   It appears so.

SOCRATES   Then isn't this the time when he wasn't a human being?

5 MENO   Yes.

SOCRATES   Well, if both in whatever time he is a human being and in whatever time he is not a human being there are going to be true opinions in him, which become knowledge when they have been awoken by questioning, won't his soul for the whole of time be in a state of having learned? For it's
10   clear that for the whole of time he either *is*, or *is not*, a human being.

MENO   It appears so.

b SOCRATES   Then if the truth about the things that are is always present in our soul, won't the soul be immortal, so that you must confidently try to search for and to recollect what you don't happen to know now—that is, what you don't happen to remember?

5 MENO   I think you are right, Socrates, but I don't know how.

SOCRATES   And *I* think I'm right too, Meno. As far as the other points are concerned, I wouldn't altogether take a stand on the argument; but that we will be better and more manly and less idle if we think one should search for
c   what one doesn't know than if we thought that it isn't possible to discover what we don't know and that we don't need to search for it—*this* is something that I would certainly fight for to the end, if I could, both in word and in deed.

MENO   Well, I think you're right about *this*, Socrates.

5 SOCRATES   Then, since we agree that one should search for what one doesn't know, would you like us to attempt to search together for what excellence is?

MENO   Certainly. But, Socrates, I would most like to consider and hear from
10   you what I asked first of all, whether one should make the attempt assum-
d   ing that it can be taught, or that it is something that men possess by nature, or that they possess it in what way?

SOCRATES   Then if neither the sophists nor the accomplished gentlemen themselves are teachers of the subject, is it clear that no-one else will be?

MENO   I don't think anyone else will be.

SOCRATES   But if there aren't teachers, there won't be pupils either?   c

MENO   I think it is as you say.

SOCRATES   But we have agreed that a thing of which there are neither teachers
   or pupils is not teachable?

MENO   Yes, we have.   5

SOCRATES   Then teachers of excellence are nowhere to be seen?

MENO   That is so.

SOCRATES   And if there are no teachers, there are no pupils either?

MENO   It appears so.

SOCRATES   Then excellence won't be teachable?   10

MENO   It doesn't look like it, if our considerations have been correct. And so I d
   really wonder, Socrates, whether there aren't any good men at all, or, if there
   are, in what manner those who come to be good do so.

SOCRATES   It looks, Meno, as if you and I are not very good, and you were not 5
   adequately trained by Gorgias nor I by Prodicus. So we should above all
   look to ourselves, and enquire after someone who will make us better in
   some way at least. I say this considering how, in our recent enquiry, we
   absurdly failed to realise that it is *not* only when knowledge guides them e
   that men conduct their affairs rightly and well; and it is in this way, no
   doubt, that recognition is also escaping us of the way in which the men who
   are good come to be so.   5

MENO   How do you mean, Socrates?

SOCRATES   Like this. That good men must be beneficial was something which
   we rightly agreed couldn't be otherwise. Wasn't it?   97

MENO   Yes.

SOCRATES   And that they will be beneficial if they guide us aright in our
   affairs—this too I suppose we were right to agree?

MENO   Yes.   5

SOCRATES   But that it is not possible to guide aright if one is not wise—concerning *this* we are like those who have *not* agreed aright.

MENO   How do you mean?

SOCRATES   I'll tell you. If someone, knowing the road to Larisa or anywhere else
   you like, went there and guided others, wouldn't he guide them aright and 10
   well?

MENO   Certainly.

SOCRATES   But what if someone had the right opinion as to which is the road, b
   though he had never gone there and had no *knowledge* of it? Wouldn't this
   man too guide people aright?

MENO   Certainly.

SOCRATES   And, I suppose, as long as he has a right opinion about the matters 5
   about which the other man has knowledge, then, even though he thinks
   what is true but does not have wisdom, he will be no worse a guide than the
   man who has wisdom about the matter in question.

MENO   No, not at all.

SOCRATES   So, then, true opinion is no worse a guide to right action than wisdom; and this is what we left out just now in considering what sort of thing
excellence was, when we said that wisdom alone guides men in right action,
whereas there was also, it seems, true opinion.

MENO   It seems so.

SOCRATES   So right opinion is no less beneficial than knowledge.

MENO   Except in this much, Socrates, that the person who had knowledge
would always get the answer right, while the one who had right opinion
would sometimes get it right and sometimes not.

SOCRATES   What are you saying? Wouldn't the person who always had right
opinion always get the answer right, as long as he had right opinion?

MENO   That does seem necessary to me; and so I wonder, Socrates, why knowledge is much more valuable than right opinion, and why one of them is different from the other.

SOCRATES   Well, do you know why you wonder about this, or shall I tell you?

MENO   By all means tell me.

SOCRATES   It's because you haven't directed your attention to the statues of
Daedalus; but perhaps you don't have them in your country.

MENO   Why do you say this?

SOCRATES   Because these too, if they haven't been tied down, run away like
fugitives, but if they are tied down, they stay in their places.

MENO   So?

SOCRATES   It isn't worth a high price to acquire one of his works untied, just as
with a slave who runs away, for it doesn't stay put; but it's worth a great
deal to acquire one that is tied down, for the works are very fine. Why do I
say this? With reference to true opinions. For true opinions too are a very
fine thing as long as they stay in their place, and produce all sorts of good
things; but they are not willing to stay in their place for a long time, but run
away out of a man's soul, so they are not worth very much, until someone
ties them down by working out the explanation. This, my friend Meno, is
recollection, as we have agreed in what we said before. When they are tied
down, they first of all become pieces of knowledge, and then permanent;
and it is for this reason that knowledge is more valuable than right opinion,
and it is by being tied down that knowledge differs from right opinion.

MENO   Yes, indeed, Socrates, it seems to be something like that.

SOCRATES   And yet I too speak as one not having knowledge, but making a conjecture; however, that right opinion is different from knowledge, this I *don't*
think is conjecture on my part, but if there is anything I would say I know—
and there are few things of which I would say this—I would count this too
as one of the things that I know.

MENO   And you are quite right in what you say, Socrates.

SOCRATES   Well then, isn't this right, that when true opinion directs, it brings
every action to completion in just as good a way as knowledge does?

MENO   I think you are right in this, too.

SOCRATES   Then right opinion is not at all inferior to knowledge, nor will it be c
     less beneficial where actions are concerned, nor is the man who has right
     opinion of less benefit than the man who has knowledge.

MENO   That is so.

SOCRATES   And we have agreed that the good man brings benefit.   5

MENO   Yes.

SOCRATES   Then men will be good and bring benefit to their cities, if they do, not
     only on account of knowledge but also on account of right opinion; and nei- 10
     ther of these is something that men possess naturally, neither knowledge nor d
     true opinion—or do you think that either of them is possessed naturally?

MENO   No.

SOCRATES   Then, since they are not possessed naturally, neither will good men 5
     be good by nature.

MENO   No, indeed.

SOCRATES   Then since they aren't good by nature, we considered after that
     whether this was something that could be taught.

MENO   Yes.   10

SOCRATES   And it seemed that it could be taught, if excellence is wisdom?

MENO   Yes.

SOCRATES   And that if it was teachable, it would be wisdom?

MENO   Certainly.

SOCRATES   And that it would be teachable if there were teachers of it, but not if e
     there weren't?

MENO   Yes.

SOCRATES   But we have agreed that there *aren't* teachers of it?

MENO   That is so.   5

SOCRATES   Then we've agreed both that it can't be taught and that it isn't wis-
     dom?

MENO   Certainly.

SOCRATES   But we agree that it is good?

MENO   Yes.   10

SOCRATES   And that what guides rightly is beneficial and good?

MENO   Certainly.

SOCRATES   And that these things alone, being two in number, guide aright— 99
     true opinion and knowledge? If a man possesses these he guides things
     aright; the things that come about aright as the result of some chance don't
     do so by human guidance, but the things in which a man guides aright are
     guided by these two things, true opinion and knowledge.   5

MENO   It seems so to me.

SOCRATES   Then, since this isn't something that is teachable, we can't say any
     longer that excellence comes about through knowledge?

MENO   It appears not.

SOCRATES   So, of the two things that are good and beneficial, one has been b
     acquitted, and it can't be *knowledge* that directs us in political action.

MENO   It seems not.

5 SOCRATES　Then it is not by any wisdom, nor by being wise, that such men as Themistocles and those whom Anytus here just mentioned guided their cities; and *this* is also why they aren't able to make others like themselves, because it's not on account of knowledge that they are like that.

10 MENO　It seems to be as you say, Socrates.

SOCRATES　Then, if it's not by knowledge, we are left with the alternative that it
c comes about by true opinion; it is by using *this* that politicians guide their cities aright, though they are no different as far as *wisdom* is concerned to soothsayers and inspired prophets. For these too say many true things in a
5 state of divine possession, but they don't know about any of the things they say.

MENO　It looks as if it is like that.

SOCRATES　Then, Meno, isn't it right to call these men "inspired" who, though having no knowledge, nevertheless achieve many great successes in what they do and say?

10 MENO　Certainly.

d SOCRATES　We would be right both to apply the term "inspired" to the sooth-sayers and prophets we mentioned just now, and to all poets; *and* to say that politicians are not the least divinely inspired and possessed of these, being
5 inspired and possessed by god, when they achieve success in speaking of many great matters while knowing nothing about what they say.

MENO　Certainly.

SOCRATES　And women, I suppose, Meno, call good men "divine"; and when
e the Spartans praise some good man they say "He's a divine man."

MENO　And it appears that they're right in what they say, Socrates.

Theaetetus 200d–201c

PLATO

5 SOCRATES　Well then, let's start again from the beginning: what should one say knowledge is? Because we're presumably not going to give up yet.

THEAETETUS　No, not unless you do.

SOCRATES　Tell me, then, what can we say it is with the least risk of contradict-ing ourselves?

e THEAETETUS　What we were trying before, Socrates; because I haven't got any-thing else to suggest.

SOCRATES　And what was that?

THEAETETUS　That true judgement is knowledge. Making a true judgement is,
5 at any rate, something free of mistakes, and everything that results from it is admirable and good.

From Plato, *Theaetetus*, translated and edited by J. McDowell (Oxford: Oxford University Press, 1973). Reprinted with the permission of Oxford University Press.

SOCRATES   Well, Theaetetus, the man who was leading the way across the river
said, apparently. "It will show for itself." The same goes for this: if we go on
and search into it, perhaps the very thing we're looking for will come to   201
light at our feet, but if we stay put, nothing will come clear to us.

THEAETETUS   Yes, you're right; let's go on and look into it.

SOCRATES   Well, this point doesn't take much looking: because there's a whole   5
art which shows you that that isn't what knowledge is.

THEAETETUS   How do you mean? What art?

SOCRATES   The art of those who are greatest of all in point of wisdom: people
call them speech-makers and litigants. Because those people, you see, persuade others by means of their art, not teaching them, but making them
judge whatever they want them to judge. Or do you think there are people   10
who are so clever as teachers that, in the short time allowed by the clock,   b
they can teach the truth, about what happened, to people who weren't there
when some others were being robbed of money or otherwise violently
treated?

THEAETETUS   No, I don't think so at all. What they can do is persuade.

SOCRATES   And you say persuading is making someone judge something?   5

THEAETETUS   Of course.

SOCRATES   So when jurymen have been persuaded, in accordance with justice,
about things which it's possible to know only if one has seen them and not
otherwise, then, in deciding those matters by hearsay, and getting hold of a   c
true judgement, they have decided without knowledge; though what they
have been persuaded of is correct, given that they have reached a good verdict. Is that right?

THEAETETUS   Absolutely.

SOCRATES   But if true judgement and knowledge were the same thing, then   5
even the best of jurymen would never make correct judgements without
knowledge; and, as things are, it seems that the two are different.

COMMENTS

The first passage is a famous one that has influenced a number of philosophers, not
just in the ancient world but also in the early modern period, such as Leibniz.
Socrates solves the sophistical "Paradox of Inquiry" (it is pointless to inquire, whether
you know what you are inquiring for or not) by showing that it is possible first to
come to have true beliefs about something and then to proceed to knowledge of it.
Socrates guides a boy who knows no geometry through a simple proof, so that he
first comes to see that his suggestion must be wrong and then that Socrates' suggestion must be right. He has true beliefs; if he were to go over the proof and others,
Socrates says, he would become able to do this from his own resources without relying on Socrates or anyone else, and then he would have knowledge. (It is not an
objection, as some have supposed, that Socrates asks the boy leading questions. He
has precisely picked someone who could not work the right answer out for himself

and needs initial guidance. The passage shows that he can come first to follow Socrates in working out the right answer and then come to understand the answer for himself.) In the later passage, Socrates says that it is "giving an account of the reason why" that ties down true beliefs and turns them into knowledge, and it is this that the boy has to be able to do on his own account before he can truly be said to have knowledge.

Socrates also says that this process is "recollection"—recovering knowledge that you already had. For the boy to come to understand the proof is for him—his soul, that is—to recollect what it knew before his present life. Is Socrates' account of true belief and knowledge dependent on this idea of the soul's preexistence? Or is this idea merely a metaphorical and poetic expression of an idea that can be separated from it?

The later passage of the *Meno* talks of the knowledge–true belief distinction in relation to the road to Larisa (Meno's hometown). Can the difference between true belief and knowledge come to the same thing here as in the geometry passage? The person who has been to Larisa knows for himself, but what is there in this case to "giving an account of the reason why"? Has Plato clearly made up his mind as to what kind of thing can be the object of knowledge?

The passage from the *Theaetetus* introduces another distinction between knowledge and true belief—the latter can be produced by rhetoric and quick techniques of mere persuasion, whereas knowledge requires sound and relevant argument, which may take a great deal of time. Notice, though, that this contrast implies that were they given enough time and proper argument, the jury might come to have knowledge, but Socrates goes on to imply that, even so, they could not know about the crime if they were not eyewitnesses. Is Plato in confusion, implying both that knowledge is conveyable and that it is not? Is there a conflict between the idea that knowledge is teachable and the idea that knowledge is something that each person must come to an understanding of for herself? How do the ideas about teaching in the *Meno* apply to this passage?

C. Relativism

One issue that arises when we ask about knowledge is whether we can have knowledge of objective facts, about which we can disagree and about which some people can be right and others wrong, or whether there is, in fact, no real disagreement, or right and wrong, since in fact we make claims that are not objective, but are relative to our own situation and are not in competition with claims that are relative to other people's situations. This basic idea of relativism can come in several versions, depending on what it is that our claims are taken to be relative to and whether it applies to all, or only some, of the areas in which we ordinarily talk of having knowledge. In the ancient world there was one famous relativist, Protagoras, whose ideas Plato went to some lengths to refute.

PROTAGORAS

Protagoras of Abdera (c. 485–415 B.C.) was the first person to become well known as a "sophist," meaning a traveling intellectual who visited various cities, setting up as a teacher of various topics, including rhetoric and public speaking. Protagoras was famous and successful and was followed by others, many of whom are portrayed, along with Protagoras himself, by Plato. Plato was hostile to the sophists, whom he regarded as pompous, mercenary, and intellectually confused, and since most of our evidence about them comes from him, it is always uncertain whether we have got a fair picture.

Protagoras was famous, or notorious, for two of his positions, which we know only in the barest outline. On the subject of the gods, he seems to have been agnostic; he is said to have held that, "As for the gods, I am unable to know either that they are or that they are not, or what their appearance is like. For there are many things that get in the way of knowledge: the obscurity of the matter and the shortness of human life" (fragment DK B 4). There are stories that Protagoras was banished from Athens and that his books were burned; these stories may be later inventions, but may also indicate that his views were controversial at the time.

The most famous of Protagoras' positions is relativism. Unfortunately, the only passage we have from him on this is indeterminate: "A human being is the measure of all things—of things that are, that they are, and of things that are not, that they are not" (fragment 1). We do not know exactly what Protagoras meant by "measure" here. Moreover, "the things that are" can cover both the existence of things and their being one way rather than another.

Plato's discussion of Protagoras' relativism in the *Theaetetus* is the best explication of the idea that we have. Plato understands Protagoras to mean that things just are the way they appear to an individual to be and identifies this idea with the theory that all there is to knowledge is perception. On this view, there is no genuine disagreement between people as to the way things are, since what appears to be disagreement about the way things are simply comes down to different reports on the way things appear to different people. Relativism, that is, defuses disagreement. All we actually do is report on the way that things appear to us to be, and since I can't be wrong about the way things appear to me, and you can't be wrong about the way things appear to you, we are not really disagreeing about anything if I say, for example, that the wind is hot and you say that it is cold. All there is, is the fact that it appears hot to me and cold to you.

Theaetetus 166e–172b, 177c–179b

PLATO

SOCRATES (putting forward Protagoras' position): I do say that the truth is as I've written: each of us is the measure of the things which are and the things which are not. Nevertheless, there's an immense difference between one man and another in just this respect: the things which are and appear to one
5   man are different from those which are and appear to another. As for wisdom or a wise man, I'm nowhere near saying there's no such thing: on the contrary, I do apply the word "wise," to precisely this sort of person: anyone who can effect a change in one of us, to whom bad things appear and are, and make good things both appear and be for him. Here again, don't chase after
e   what I've said on the basis of how it's expressed; but let me tell you still more clearly what I mean. Remember the sort of thing you were saying before: to a sick man what he eats appears, and is, bitter, whereas to a healthy man it is, and appears, the opposite. Now what must be done isn't to make either of
167   them wiser, because that isn't even possible: nor is it to accuse the sick one of being ignorant because he makes the sort of judgments he does, and call the healthy one wise because he makes judgements of a different sort. What must be done is to effect a change in one direction; because one of the two
5   conditions is better. In education, too, in the same way, a change must be effected from one of two conditions to the better one; but whereas a doctor makes the change with drugs, a sophist does it with things he says.

It's not that anyone ever makes someone whose judgments are false come, later on, to judge what's true: after all, it isn't possible to have in one's judgements the things which are not, or anything other than what one's
b   experiencing, which is always true. What does happen, I think, is this: when, because of a harmful condition in his mind, someone has in his judgements things which are akin to that condition, then by means of a beneficial condition one makes him have in his judgements things of that same sort—appearances which some people, because of ignorance, call true; but I call them better than the first sort, but not at all truer.

5   And as for the wise. Socrates, I'm nowhere near calling them frogs. On the contrary, where bodies are concerned, I say it's doctors who are the wise,
e   and where plants are concerned, gardeners—because I claim that they, too, whenever any of their plants are sick, instil perceptions that are beneficial and healthy, and true too, into them, instead of harmful ones. My claim is, too, that wise and good politicians make beneficial things, instead of harmful ones, seem to their states to be just. If any sort of thing seems just and
5   admirable to any state, then it actually is just and admirable for it, as long as that state accepts it; but a wise man makes beneficial things be and seem just and admirable to them, instead of any harmful things which used to be so for them. And according to the same principle the sophist is wise, too, in

From Plato, *Theaetetus*, translated and edited by J. McDowell (Oxford: Oxford University Press, 1973). Reprinted with the permission of Oxford University Press.

that he can educate his pupils in that way: and he deserves a lot of money d
from those he has educated.

Thus it's true, both that some people are wiser than others, and that no
one judges what's false; and you have to put up with being a measure
whether you like it or not, because that doctrine of mine is saved on these
grounds.

If you can go back to the beginning and dispute it, do so. Set out your 5
objections in a speech; or, if you like, do it by asking questions, because
there's no need to avoid that method either: in fact, if one has any intelligence, one ought to pursue it more than any other. But whatever you do, e
don't be unjust in your questioning. It's quite unreasonable that someone
who professes to be concerned about virtue should spend his time doing
nothing but behaving unjustly in arguments. Behaving unjustly, in this sort
of pursuit, is what one is doing when one fails to keep separate the time one
spends in controversy and the time one spends in dialectic. In controversy 5
one may joke, and trip people up as much as one can; but in dialectic one
should be serious, and help up the person one is talking to, showing up to 168
him only those of his mistakes where his tripping up was his own fault or
due to the company he used to keep. If you behave like that, the people who
spend their time with you will blame themselves, not you, for their confusion and difficulties; they'll run after you and like you, but they'll hate 5
themselves and seek refuge from themselves in philosophy, so as to become
different people and get rid of those they used to be. But if you do the opposite, like most people, you'll find the opposite will happen, and instead of
making philosophers of those who associate with you, you'll make them b
turn out to hate the whole business of philosophy when they get older.

So if you'll listen to me, then, as was said earlier, you'll sit down with
me, not in a spirit of ill will or contentiousness, but with a friendly attitude,
and genuinely look into what we mean when we declare that everything
changes, and that what seems to any private person or state actually is for 5
that person or state. And you'll go on from there to investigate whether
knowledge and perception are the same or different: but not as you did just
now, arguing from the habitual use of expressions and words, which most c
people exploit by dragging them around just anyhow, so as to cause one
another all sorts of difficulties.

Well, Theodorus, that's the beginnings of an attempt to support your
friend. It's the best I can do—a feeble effort from my feeble resources. If he'd 5
been alive himself, he'd have supported his own doctrines on a much
grander scale.

THEODORUS   You're joking, Socrates. You've supported him very powerfully.

SOCRATES   It's good of you to say so.

Now tell me: I take it you noticed how, when Protagoras was speaking
just now, he told us off for addressing our arguments to a child, and argu- d
ing like controversialists against what he said, on the basis of the boy's fear?
He labelled that a sort of frivolity: and he spoke solemnly about his measure of all things, and told us to be serious about his theory.

THEODORUS   Yes, of course I noticed. Socrates.   5

SOCRATES   And you say we must do as he tells us?

THEODORUS   Definitely.

SOCRATES   Well, you see that all the people here are children, apart from you.

e   So if we're to do as Protagoras tells us, it's you and I who must give his the-
       ory serious treatment by questioning and answering each other about it.
       That way, at least he won't have this charge to bring against us: that we
       examined his theory by way of a childish diversion with some boys.

5 THEODORUS   But look here, wouldn't Theaetetus be better at following an
       inquiry into a theory than a good many men with long beards?

SOCRATES   But no better than you. Theodorus. So stop thinking I'm under

169   every obligation to defend your dead friend, whereas you're not under any.
       Come on: come with me a little way: just until we know whether it's you
       who ought to be the measure about diagrams, or whether everyone is as
       self-sufficient as you are in astronomy and the other subjects you have a rep-

5   utation for excelling in.

THEODORUS   It isn't easy to avoid saying something when one's sitting with
       you, Socrates. I was talking nonsense just now, when I claimed that you'd
       let me keep my clothes on and not make me take them off, like the Spartans.

b   You seem to me to incline more in the direction of Sciron. The Spartans tell
       one either to take one's clothes off or to go away, but you seem to me to act
       a part more like that of Antaeus: you don't let go of anyone who comes up
       to you until you've forced him to take his clothes off and wrestle with you
       in an argument.

5 SOCRATES   You've found an excellent comparison for what's wrong with me.
       Theodorus. But I've got more endurance than Sciron or Antaeus. Countless
       times already a Heracles or a Theseus, dauntless in arguing, has met me and

c   given me a good thrashing, but that doesn't make me give up: such a terri-
       ble passion for exercise about these matters has infected me. So you, too,
       mustn't grudge me the chance of benefiting both of us, if you have a bout
       with me.

5 THEODORUS   I won't protest any longer: lead on, wherever you like. Whatever
       happens, one has to endure the thread of destiny which, about these mat-
       ters, you spin for one, and submit to being tested. But I shan't be able to put
       myself at your disposal any further than the point which you proposed.

SOCRATES   Well, even that far will do. And please watch out that we don't pro-

d   duce some childishly frivolous form of argument without noticing it, and
       have someone telling us off for that again.

THEODORUS   I'll try as hard as I can.

SOCRATES   Very well then, let's take up the argument at the same point as

5   before. Let's see if we were right or wrong to be dissatisfied, when we criti-
       cized the theory on the ground that it made everyone self-sufficient in point
       of wisdom. We had Protagoras concede that some people are superior to
       others on the question of what's better or worse, and that it's those people
       who are wise. Isn't that so?

THEODORUS   Yes.

SOCRATES Now if he'd been here and made the admission himself, instead 10
of our conceding it on his behalf in the course of supporting him, there e
wouldn't have been any need to take it up again and put it on a firm foot-
ing. But as things are, someone might perhaps rule that we haven't the
authority to make admissions on his behalf. So it would be better to come to
a clearer agreement about precisely that point; because it makes a great deal 5
of difference whether it's so or not.

THEODORUS That's true.

SOCRATES Well then, let's get that agreement in the quickest possible way, not
through others but from Protagoras' own words.

THEODORUS How?   170

SOCRATES Like this. He says, doesn't he, that what seems to anyone actually is
for the person to whom it seems?

THEODORUS Yes.   5

SOCRATES Well now, Protagoras, we, too, are talking about the judgements of
a man, or rather of all men, when we say that there isn't anyone who doesn't
believe that he's wiser than others in some respects, whereas others are
wiser than him in other respects. In the greatest of dangers, when people are 10
in trouble on campaigns, or in diseases, or at sea, they treat the leading men
in each sphere like gods, expecting them to be their saviours, because b
they're superior precisely in respect of knowledge. The whole of human life
is surely full of people looking for teachers and leaders for themselves and
other living things, and for what they do; and on the other hand, of people
who think themselves capable of teaching and capable of leading. Now 5
what can we say, in all these cases, except that men themselves believe that
there is wisdom and ignorance in them?

THEODORUS Nothing else.

SOCRATES And they believe that wisdom is true thinking and that ignorance is
false judgement?

THEODORUS Of course.   c

SOCRATES Well then, how are we to deal with your theory, Protagoras? Should
we say that people always judge things which are true? Or that they sometimes judge things which are true and sometimes things which are false?
Because from both alternatives it follows, I think, that they don't always
judge things which are true, but judge both truths and falsehoods. Ask 5
yourself, Theodorus, whether you, or any of Protagoras' followers, would
be willing to contend that no one person ever believes of another that he's
stupid and makes false judgements.

THEODORUS No, that's incredible. Socrates.

SOCRATES Still, that's what the theory that a man is the measure of all things is d
inevitably driven to.

THEODORUS How?

SOCRATES When you've decided something by yourself, and express a judgement about it to me, let's grant that, as Protagoras' theory has it, that's true 5
for you. But what about the rest of us? Is it impossible for us to get to make

decisions about your decision? Or do we always decide that your judgements are true? Isn't it rather the case that on every occasion there are countless people who make judgements opposed to yours and contend against
you, in the belief that what you decide and think is false?

e THEODORUS   Good heavens, yes, Socrates, countless thousands, as Homer puts
it: they give me all the trouble in the world.

SOCRATES   Well now, do you want us to say that what you judge on those occa-
5   sions is true for you but false for those countless people?

THEODORUS   It looks as if we must, at any rate as far as the theory is concerned.

SOCRATES   And what about Protagoras himself? Isn't it necessarily the case
that, if he didn't himself think a man is the measure, and if the masses don't
either, as in fact they don't, then that *Truth* which he wrote wasn't the truth

171   for anyone? Whereas if he did think so himself, but the masses don't share
his view, then, in the first place, it's more the case that it isn't the truth than
that it is: more in the proportion by which those to whom it doesn't seem to
be outnumber those to whom it does.

THEODORUS   Yes, that must be so, if it's to depend on each individual judge-
5   ment whether it is or isn't.

SOCRATES   And, secondly, it involves this very subtle implication. Protagoras
agrees that everyone has in his judgements the things which are. In doing
that, he's surely conceding that the opinion of those who make opposing
judgements about his own opinion—that is, their opinion that what he
thinks is false—is true.

10 THEODORUS   Certainly.

b SOCRATES   So if he admits that their opinion is true—that is, the opinion of
those who believe that what he thinks is false—he would seem to be conceding that his own opinion is false?

THEODORUS   He must be.

SOCRATES   But the others don't concede that what they think is false?

5 THEODORUS   No.

SOCRATES   And Protagoras, again, admits that that judgement of theirs is true,
too, according to what he has written.

THEODORUS   Evidently.

SOCRATES   So his theory will be disputed by everyone, beginning with Pro-
10   tagoras himself; or rather, Protagoras himself will agree that it's wrong.

c   When he concedes that someone who contradicts him is making a true
judgement, he will himself be conceding that a dog, or an ordinary man,
isn't the measure of so much as one thing that he hasn't come to know. Isn't
that so?

THEODORUS   Yes.

5 SOCRATES   Well then, since it's disputed by everyone, it would seem that Protagoras' *Truth* isn't true for anyone: not for anyone else, and not for Protagoras himself.

THEODORUS   We're running my friend too hard, Socrates.

10 SOCRATES   But it isn't clear that we're running past where we ought. Of course

he's older than we are, so it's likely that he's wiser. If he suddenly popped d
up out of the ground here, from the neck up, he'd very probably convict me
of talking a great deal of nonsense, and you of agreeing to it, and then he'd
duck down again and rush off. But we have to make do with ourselves as
we are, I think, and always say what seems to us to be the case. Let's do that 5
now. Shouldn't we say that anyone whatever will admit at least this: some
people are wiser than others, some more ignorant?

THEODORUS   Yes, I think we should.

SOCRATES   And also that the theory stands up best in the version in which we e
sketched it while we were supporting Protagoras? It goes like this. Most
things actually are, for each person, the way they seem to him, for instance
hot, dry, sweet, or anything of that sort. But if there are any questions on
which it will concede that one person is superior to another, it will be about 5
what's healthy and unhealthy. It would be prepared to say that not every
creature—woman, child, or indeed animal—knows what's healthy for itself
and is capable of curing itself. On the contrary, here, if anywhere, one person is superior to another. Is that right?

THEODORUS   Yes, I think so.

SOCRATES   And about matters that concern the state, too—things which are 172
admirable or dishonourable, just or unjust, in conformity with religion or
not—it will hold that whatever sort of thing any state thinks to be, and lays
down as, lawful for itself actually is, in strict truth, lawful for it, and that on
those questions no individual is at all wiser than any other, and no state is 5
at all wiser than any other. But again, when it's a matter of a state's laying
down what's advantageous or disadvantageous for it, it will admit that
here, if anywhere, one adviser is superior to another, and the judgement of
one state is superior in point of truth to the different judgement of another. b
It wouldn't have the face to say that whatever a state thinks to be, and
lays down as, advantageous to itself will, whatever happens, actually be
advantageous to it. But in that other sphere I was speaking of—in the case
of what's just or unjust, in conformity with religion or not—they're prepared to insist that none of them has by nature a being of its own: on the 5
contrary, what seems to a community is in fact true at the time when it
seems so and for as long as it seems so. At any rate those who don't altogether assert Protagoras' theory carry on their philosophy on some such
lines as these.

SOCRATES   Very well then. We'd reached roughly this point in our argument: 5
we were saying that those who speak of being as moving, and who say that
what seems to anyone at any time actually is for the person to whom it
seems, are prepared to insist on that doctrine in most cases, and in particular on the question of what's just: whatever things a state decides to be, and d
lays down as, just, in fact are just, whatever happens, for the state which
lays them down, so long as they remain laid down. But on the question of
what's good, no one would be brave enough to have the face to contend that
whatever a state thinks to be, and lays down as, useful for itself actually is

5 useful so long as it's laid down: not unless he's talking about the word. But
that would surely be to make fun of what we're saying, wouldn't it?

THEODORUS Yes, it certainly would.

e SOCRATES Well, let's suppose he's not talking about the word, but thinking of
the thing to which it's applied.

THEODORUS Yes.

SOCRATES But whatever word it applies to it, that's surely what a state aims at
5 when it legislates, and it lays down all its laws, to the best of its ability and
judgement, as being most useful for itself. Or does a state have something
else in view when it legislates?

178 THEODORUS Certainly not.

SOCRATES Now does each one always hit the target, or do they also miss on
many occasions?

THEODORUS I think they also miss.

5 SOCRATES Well now, we'd be still more likely to get everyone to agree to that
same point, if we began by asking about the whole class in which what's useful belongs. What's useful is surely something to do with the future. Because
when we legislate, we lay down the laws for the time to come, in the belief
10 that they're going to be useful; and we may rightly call that "future."

b THEODORUS Certainly.

SOCRATES Come on, then, let's put this question to Protagoras, or anyone else
who says the same as he does. Protagoras, you and your followers say that
5 a man is the measure of all things which are white, heavy, light, or anything
of that sort; because he has in himself the authority for deciding about
them, and when he thinks they're the way he experiences them, he thinks
things which are true for him and things which are for him. Isn't that so?

THEODORUS Yes.

SOCRATES But, Protagoras (we'll say), what about the things which are going
c to be, in the future? Does he have in himself the authority for deciding about
them, too? If someone thinks there's going to be a thing of some kind, does
that thing actually come into being for the person who thought so? Take
heat, for instance. Suppose a layman thinks he's going to catch a fever and
5 there's going to be that degree of heat, whereas someone else, a doctor,
thinks not. Which one's judgement should we say the future will turn out
to accord with? Or should we say it will be in accordance with the judgements of both: for the doctor he'll come to be neither hot nor feverish,
whereas for himself he'll come to be both?

THEODORUS No, that would be absurd.

d SOCRATES And when it's a question of the future dryness or sweetness of wine,
I should think it's the judgement of a vine-grower, not that of a musician,
that's authoritative.

THEODORUS Of course.

SOCRATES Again, suppose it's a question of what's going to be in tune or out
5 of tune. An athletic trainer's judgement wouldn't be better than a musician's about what's going to seem, later on, to be in tune, even to the trainer
himself.

THEODORUS   Certainly not.

SOCRATES   And if someone who has no skill at cooking is going to be given a
   dinner, then while the banquet is being prepared, his verdict about the
   pleasure there's going to be is less authoritative than the chef's. Let's not 10
   make any contentions, at this stage in the argument, about what already is, e
   or has come to be, sweet for anyone. But about what's going to seem, and
   be, for anyone in the future, is everyone best at deciding for himself? Or
   would you, Protagoras, be a better judge than any ordinary person, at any 5
   rate in anticipating what's going to be convincing to any of us in speeches
   meant for lawcourts?

THEODORUS   Yes, Socrates, that was certainly a point on which he used to give
   firm assurances that he was better than anyone else.

SOCRATES   Good heavens, yes. Otherwise nobody would have paid a great deal
   of money to have discussions with him: not if he'd persuaded those who 179
   associated with him that about the future, too, there's no prophet or anyone
   else who can decide better than one can for oneself.

THEODORUS   That's quite true.

SOCRATES   Well now, legislation, too, and what's useful, have to do with the 5
   future, and everyone would agree that when a state legislates, it's inevitable
   that it should often fail to hit on what's most useful?

THEODORUS   Certainly.

SOCRATES   So we'll be giving fair measure if we tell your teacher he's bound to 10
   admit that one person is wiser than another, and that it's that sort of person b
   who's a measure; whereas someone with no knowledge, like me, is in no
   way bound to be a measure, though our argument just now, on Protagoras'
   behalf, was trying to force me to be such a thing whether I liked it or not.   5

COMMENTS

Relativism was most prominently defended in the ancient world by Protagoras. But
not only are his actual works lost, it also seems that what he said was not extensive
or clear. In this passage, Plato first brings up some objections to Protagoras' ideas that
are not very strong, so that the answers to them serve to bring out clearly what relativism amounts to (whatever Protagoras himself said), and then brings up what he
takes to be strong objections to the position. (You might like to ask yourself, after
working through the arguments, whether you think that Plato's presentation of relativism is too influenced by the fact that he thinks it is false. Could you present relativism more effectively?)

   Plato identifies relativism with the thesis that "knowledge is perception." At first,
it may seem that this is too narrow a way to understand a thesis that is meant to apply
to values, for example, as well as to properties that we perceive by the senses. But
"perception" should not be understood too narrowly. What Plato is after is the idea
that when you have knowledge, you are authoritative and can't be wrong; for the
relativist, this means that what you have knowledge about can be only what is given
in your experience. There is no need to interpret experience narrowly, and Plato
assumes that relativism is supposed to apply to a wide variety of cases.

Two of Plato's arguments at 169e ff are worth particular attention:

1. The "self-undermining" argument at 171a ff. Compare this to Epicurus' argument against the determinists in section 1.A. Plato claims that relativism is not a thesis that can seriously be put forward and defended without undermining its own claim. Does the argument work? Has Plato been consistent in his characterization of relativism here?

2. The argument involving the present and the future (178b ff). This is one way of bringing out the point that relativism has a problem accounting for expertise—cases in which we do uncontroversially think that one person's judgment is more authoritative than those of others. Remember that for Plato (cf section 3.A), expertise is a prominent example of undisputed knowledge. Notice that the passage contains quite a few references to Protagoras' own claim to expertise (and thus to making money).

The passage omitted here, in which Socrates develops a view of objective value without reference to Protagoras, was famous in the ancient world as giving Plato's view of how we should best live. You can find it in section 5.D.

D. The Structure of a System of Knowledge

In both Plato and Aristotle, we find sketches of the form that would be taken by a systematic structured area of knowledge. Although there are large differences between them, they both agree that to have knowledge requires being able to fit particular claims to knowledge into larger structured wholes and to see their significance within the structure. Both examine the question of the foundations of knowledge, and both contribute to what we call the idea of a *science*.

Republic 475b–484d, 507b–511e, 514c–518d, 523a–525b, 531c–535d
PLATO

"So tell me where you stand on this question. If in our opinion someone desires something, are we to say that he desires that type of thing as a whole, or only some aspects of it?"
"The whole of it," he replied.

From Plato, *Republic*, translated by Robin Waterfield (Oxford: Oxford University Press, 1993). Reprinted with the permission of Oxford University Press.

"So the same goes for a philosopher too: we're to say that what he desires is the whole of knowledge, not just some aspects of it. True?"

"True."

"If someone fusses about his lessons, then, especially when he's still young c and without rational understanding of what is and isn't good for him, we can't describe him as a lover of knowledge, a philosopher, just as we can't describe someone who is fussing about his food as hungry, as desiring food, and don't call him a gourmand, but a poor eater."

"Yes, it would be wrong to call him anything else."

"On the other hand, if someone is glad to sample every subject and eagerly sets about his lessons with an insatiable appetite, then we'd be perfectly justified in calling him a philosopher, don't you think?"

"Then a motley crowd of people will be philosophers," Glaucon said. "For d instance, sightseers all do what they do because they enjoy learning, I suppose; and it would be very odd to count theatre-goers as philosophers, when they'd never go of their own accord to hear a lecture or spend time over anything like that, but they rush around the festivals of Dionysus to hear every theatrical troupe, as if they were getting paid for the use of their ears, and never miss a single festival, whether it's being held in town or out of town. Are we to describe all these people and the disciples of other amusements as philosophers? And e what about students of trivial branches of expertise?"

"No," I replied, "they're not philosophers, but they resemble philosophers."

"Who are the true philosophers you have in mind?" he asked.

"Sightseers of the truth," I answered.

"That must be right, but what exactly does it mean?" he asked.

"It wouldn't be easy to explain to anyone else," I said. "But you'll grant me this, surely."

"What?"

"Since beautiful is the opposite of ugly, they are two things."

"Of course." 476a

"In so far as they are two, each of them is single?"

"Yes."

"And the same principle applies to moral and immoral, good and bad, and everything of any type: in itself, each of them is single, but each of them has a plurality of manifestations because they appear all over the place, as they become associated with actions and bodies and one another."

"You're right," he said.

"Well,"I continued, "this is what enables me to distinguish the sightseers (to borrow your term) and the ones who want to acquire some expertise or other and the men of action from the people in question, the ones who are philoso- b phers in the true sense of the term."

"What do you mean?" he asked.

"Theatre-goers and sightseers are devoted to beautiful sounds and colours and shapes, and to works of art which consist of these elements, but their minds are constitutionally incapable of seeing and devoting themselves to beauty itself."

"Yes, that's certainly right," he said.

"However, people with the ability to approach beauty itself and see beauty as it actually is are bound to be few and far between, aren't they?"

c   "Definitely."

"So does someone whose horizon is limited to beautiful things, with no conception of beauty itself, and who is incapable of following guidance as to how to gain knowledge of beauty itself, strike you as living in a dream-world or in the real world? Look at it this way. Isn't dreaming precisely the state, whether one is asleep or awake, of taking something to be the real thing, when it is actually only a likeness?"

"Yes, that's what I'd say dreaming is," he said.

"And what about someone who does the opposite—who does think that
d there is such a thing as beauty itself, and has the ability to see it as well as the things which partake in it, and never gets them muddled up? Do you think he's living in the real world or in a dream-world?"

"Definitely in the real world," he said.

"So wouldn't we be right to describe the difference between their mental states by saying that while this person has knowledge, the other one has beliefs?"

"Yes."

"Now, suppose this other person—the one we're saying has beliefs, not knowledge—were to get cross with us and query the truth of our assertions.
e Will we be able to calm him down and gently convince him of our point of view, while keeping him in the dark about the poor state of his health?"

"We really ought to," he said.

"All right, but what shall we say to him, do you think? Perhaps this is what we should ask him. We'll tell him that we don't resent any knowledge he might have—indeed, we'd be delighted to see that he does know something—and then we'll say, 'But can you tell us, please, whether someone with knowledge knows something or nothing?' You'd better answer my questions for him."

"My answer will be that he knows something," he said.

"Something real or something unreal?"

477a   "Real. How could something unreal be known?"

"We could look at the matter from more angles, but we're happy enough with the idea that something completely real is completely accessible to knowledge, and something utterly unreal is entirely inaccessible to knowledge. Yes?"

"Perfectly happy."

"All right. But if something is in a state of both reality and unreality, then it falls between that which is perfectly real and that which is utterly unreal, doesn't it?"

"Yes."

"So since the field of knowledge is reality, and since it must be incomprehension whose field is unreality, then we need to find out if there is in fact something which falls between incomprehension and knowledge, whose field is this b intermediate, don't we?"

"Yes."

"Now, we acknowledge the existence of belief, don't we?"

"Of course."

"Is it a different faculty from knowledge, or is it the same?"

"Different."

"Every faculty has its own distinctive abilities, so belief and knowledge must have different domains."

"Yes."

"Now, since the natural field of knowledge is reality—its function is to know reality as reality . . . Actually, I think there's something else we need to get clear about first."

"What?"

"Shall we count as a distinct class of things the faculties which give human c beings and all other creatures their abilities? By 'faculties' I mean things like sight and hearing. Do you understand the type of thing I have in mind?"

"Yes, I do," he said.

"Let me tell you something that strikes me about them. I can't distinguish one faculty from another the way I commonly distinguish other things, by looking at their colours or shapes or anything like that, because faculties don't have any of those sorts of qualities for me to look at. The only aspect of a faculty I can look at is its field, its effect. This is what enables me to identify each of them as d a particular faculty. Where I find a single domain and a single effect, I say there is a single faculty; and I distinguish faculties which have different fields and different effects. What about you? What do you do?"

"The same as you," he said.

"Let's go back to where we were before, then, Glaucon," I said. "Do you think that knowledge is a faculty, or does it belong in your opinion to some other class?"

"I think it belongs to that class," he said, "and is the most powerful of all the faculties."

"And shall we classify belief as a faculty, or what?" e

"As a faculty," he said. "Belief is precisely that which enables us to entertain beliefs."

"Not long ago, however, you agreed that knowledge and belief were different."

"Of course," he said. "One is infallible and the other is fallible, so anyone with any sense would keep them separate."

"Good," I said. "There can be no doubt of our position: knowledge and belief are different." 478a

"Yes."

"Since they're different faculties, then, they have different natural fields, don't they?"

"Necessarily."

"The field of knowledge is reality, isn't it? Its function is to know the reality of anything real?"

"Yes."

"And the function of belief, we're saying, is to entertain beliefs?"

"Yes."

"Does it entertain beliefs about the same thing which knowledge knows? Will what is accessible to knowledge and what is accessible to belief be identical? Or is that out of the question?"

"It's ruled out by what we've already agreed," he said. "If different faculties
b naturally have different fields, and if both knowledge and belief are faculties, and different faculties too, as we said, then it follows that it is impossible for what is accessible to knowledge and what is accessible to belief to be identical."

"So if it is reality that is accessible to knowledge, then it is something else, not reality, that is accessible to belief, isn't it?"

"Yes."

"Does it entertain beliefs about what is unreal? Or is it also impossible for that to happen? Think about this: isn't it the case that someone who is entertaining a belief is bringing his believing mind to bear on something? I mean, is it possible to have a belief, and to be believing nothing?"

"That's impossible."

"In fact, someone who has a belief has some single thing in mind, doesn't he?"

"Yes."

"But the most accurate way to refer to something unreal would be to say
c that it is nothing, not that it is a single thing, wouldn't it?"

"Yes."

"Didn't we find ourselves forced to relate incomprehension to unreality and knowledge to reality?"

"That's right," he said.

"So the field of belief is neither reality nor unreality?"

"No."

"Belief can't be incomprehension or knowledge, then?"

"So it seems."

"Well, does it lie beyond their limits? Does it shed more light than knowledge or spread more obscurity than incomprehension?"

"It does neither."

"Alternatively, does belief strike you as more opaque than knowledge and more lucid than incomprehension?"

"Considerably more," he said.
d   "It lies within their limits?"

"Yes."

"Then belief must fall between them."

"Absolutely."

"Now, didn't we say earlier that something which is simultaneously real and unreal (were such a thing to be shown to exist) would fall between the perfectly real and the wholly unreal, and wouldn't be the field of either knowledge or incomprehension, but of an intermediate (again, if such a thing were shown to exist) between incomprehension and knowledge?"

"Right."

"And now we've found that what we call belief is such an intermediate, haven't we?"

"We have."

"So the only thing left for us to discover, apparently, is whether there's any- e thing which partakes of both reality and unreality, and cannot be said to be perfectly real or perfectly unreal. If we were to come across such a thing, we'd be fully justified in describing it as the field of belief, on the principle that extremes belong together, and so do intermediates. Do you agree?"

"Yes."

"Let's return, on this basis, to the give and take of conversation with that 479a fine fellow who doesn't acknowledge the existence of beauty itself or think that beauty itself has any permanent and unvarying character but takes the plurality of beautiful things as his norm—that sightseer who can't under any circumstances abide the notion that beauty, morality, and so on are each a single entity. What we'll say to him is, 'My friend, is there one beautiful thing, in this welter of beautiful things, which won't turn out to be ugly? Is there one moral deed which won't turn out to be immoral? Is there one just act which won't turn out to be unjust?'"

"No, there isn't," he said. "It's inevitable for these things to turn out to be b both beautiful and ugly, in a sense, and the same goes for all the other qualities you mentioned in your question."

"And there are doubles galore—but they turn out to be halves just as much as doubles, don't they?"

"Yes."

"And do things which are large, small, light, and heavy deserve these attributes any more than they deserve the opposite attributes?"

"No, each of them is bound to have both qualities," he said.

"So isn't it the case, then, that any member of a plurality no more *is* whatever it is said to be than it *is not* whatever it is said to be?"

"This is like those *double entendres* one hears at parties," he said, "or the rid- c dle children tell about the eunuch and his hitting a bat—they make a riddle by asking what he hit it with and what it was on—in the sense that the members of the plurality are also ambiguous: it is impossible to form a stable conception of any of them as either being what it is, or not being what it is, or being both, or being neither."

"How are you going to cope with them, then?" I asked. "Can you find a better place to locate them than between real being and unreality? I mean, they can't turn out to be more opaque and unreal than unreality, or more lucid and d real than reality."

"True," he said.

"So there we are. We've discovered that the welter of things which the masses conventionally regard as beautiful and so on mill around somewhere between unreality and perfect reality."

"Yes, we have."

"But we have a prior agreement that were such a thing to turn up, we'd have to call it the field of belief, not of knowledge, since the realm which occupies some uncertain intermediate point must be accessible to the intermediate faculty."

"Yes, we do."

e   "What shall we say about those spectators, then, who can see a plurality of beautiful things, but not beauty itself, and who are incapable of following if someone else tries to lead them to it, and who can see many moral actions, but not morality itself, and so on? That they only ever entertain beliefs, and do not *know* any of the things they believe?"

"That's what we have to say," he said.

"As for those who can see each of these things in itself, in its permanent and unvarying nature, we'll say they have knowledge and are not merely entertaining beliefs, won't we?"

"Again, we have to."

"And won't our position be that they're devoted to and love the domain of
480a   knowledge, as opposed to the others, who are devoted to and love the domain of belief? I mean, surely we haven't forgotten our claim that these others love and are spectators of beautiful sounds and colours and so on, but can't abide the idea that there is such a thing as beauty itself?"

"No, we haven't forgotten."

"They won't think us nasty if we refer to them as 'lovers of belief' rather than as philosophers, who love knowledge, will they? Are they going to get very cross with us if we say that now?"

"Not if they listen to me," he replied. "It's not right to get angry at the truth."

"But the term 'believers' is inappropriate for those who are devoted to everything that is real: they should be called philosophers, shouldn't they?"

"Absolutely."

484a   "It's taken a long and thorough discussion, Glaucon," I said, "and it's not been easy, but we've now demonstrated the difference between philosophers and non-philosophers."

507b   "As we talk," I said, "we mention and differentiate between a lot of beautiful things and a lot of good things and so on."

"Yes, we do."

"And we also talk about beauty itself, goodness itself and so on. All the things we refer to as a plurality on those occasions we also conversely count as belonging to a single class by virtue of the fact that they have a single particular character, and we say that the x itself is 'what really is.'"

"True."

"And we say that the first lot is visible rather than intelligible, whereas characters are intelligible rather than visible."

"Absolutely."

c   "With what aspect of ourselves do we see the things we see?"

"With our sight," he replied.

"And we use hearing for the things we hear, and so on for all the other senses and the things we perceive. Yes?"

"Of course."

"Well, have you ever stopped to consider," I asked, "how generous the creator of the senses was when he created the domain of seeing and being seen?"

"No, not really," he said.

"Look at it this way. Are hearing and sound deficient? Do they need an extra something to make the one hear and the other be heard—some third thing with- d out which hearing won't hear and sound won't be heard?"

"No," he answered.

"And in my opinion," I went on, "the same goes for many other domains, if not all: they don't need anything like this. Or can you point to one that does?"

"*I* can't," he said.

"But do you realize that sight and the visible realm are deficient?"

"How?"

"Even if a person's eyes are capable of sight, and he's trying to use it, and what he's trying to look at is coloured, the sight will see nothing and the colours will remain unseen, surely, unless there is also present an extra third thing e which is made specifically for this purpose."

"What is this thing you're getting at?" he asked.

"It's what we call light," I said.

"You're right," he said.

"So if light has value, then because it links the sense of sight and the ability to be seen, it is far and away the most valuable link there is." 508a

"Well, it certainly does have value," he said.

"Which of the heavenly gods would you say is responsible for this? Whose light makes it possible for our sight to see and for the things we see to be seen?"

"My reply will be no different from what yours or anyone else's would be," he said. "I mean, you're obviously expecting the answer, 'the sun.'"

"Now, there are certain conclusions to be drawn from comparing sight to this god."

"What?"

"Sight and the sun aren't to be identified: neither the sense itself nor its loca- b tion—which we call the eye—is the same as the sun."

"True."

"Nevertheless, there's no sense-organ which more closely resembles the sun, in my opinion, than the eye."

"The resemblance is striking."

"Moreover, the eye's ability to see has been bestowed upon it and chan- nelled into it, as it were, by the sun."

"Yes."

"So the sun is not to be identified with sight, but is responsible for sight and is itself within the visible realm. Right?"

"Yes," he said.

"The sun is the child of goodness I was talking about, then," I said. "It is a
c counterpart to its father, goodness. As goodness stands in the intelligible realm
to intelligence and the things we know, so in the visible realm the sun stands to
sight and the things we see."

"I don't understand," he said. "I need more detail, please."

"As you know," I explained, "when our eyes are directed towards things
whose colours are no longer bathed in daylight, but in artificial light instead,
then they're less effective and seem to be virtually blind, as if they didn't even
have the potential for seeing clearly."

"Certainly," he said.

d   "But when they're directed towards things which are lit up by the sun, then
they see clearly and obviously do have that potential."

"Of course."

"Well, here's how you can think about the mind as well. When its object is
something which is lit up by truth and reality, then it has—and obviously has—
intelligent awareness and knowledge. However, when its object is permeated
with darkness (that is, when its object is something which is subject to generation
and decay), then it has beliefs and is less effective, because its beliefs chop and
change, and under these circumstances it comes across as devoid of intelligence."

"Yes, it does."

e   "Well, what I'm saying is that it's goodness which gives the things we know
their truth and makes it possible for people to have knowledge. It is responsible
for knowledge and truth, and you should think of it as being within the intelligible realm, but you shouldn't identify it with knowledge and truth, otherwise
509a you'll be wrong: for all their value, it is even more valuable. In the other realm,
it is right to regard light and sight as resembling the sun, but not to identify
either of them with the sun; so in this realm it is right to regard knowledge and
truth as resembling goodness, but not to identify either of them with goodness,
which should be rated even more highly."

"You're talking about something of inestimable value," he said, "if it's not
only the source of knowledge and truth, but is also more valuable than them. I
mean, you certainly don't seem to be identifying it with pleasure!"

"How could you even think it?" I exclaimed. "But we can take our analogy
even further."

b   "How?"

"I think you'll agree that the ability to be seen is not the only gift the sun
gives to the things we see. It is also the source of their generation, growth, and
nourishment, although it isn't actually the process of generation."

"Of course it isn't."

"And it isn't only the known-ness of the things we know which is conferred
upon them by goodness, but also their reality and their being, although goodness isn't actually the state of being, but surpasses being in majesty and might:"

c   "It's way beyond human comprehension, all right," was Glaucon's quite
amusing comment.

"It's your fault for forcing me to express my views on the subject," I replied.

"Yes, and please don't stop," he said. "If you've left anything out of your explanation of the simile of the sun, then the least you could do is continue with it."

"There are plenty of omissions, in fact," I said.

"Don't leave any gaps," he said, "however small."

"I think I'll have to leave a lot out," I said, "but I'll try to make it as complete as I can at the moment."

"All right," he said.

"So bear in mind the two things we've been talking about," I said, "one of d which rules over the intelligible realm and its inhabitants, while the other rules over the visible realm—I won't say over the heavens in case you think I'm playing clever word-games. Anyway, do you understand this distinction between visible things and intelligible things?"

"Yes."

"Well, picture them as a line cut into two unequal sections and, following the same proportion, subdivide both the section of the visible realm and that of the intelligible realm. Now you can compare the sections in terms of clarity and unclarity. The first section in the visible realm consists of likenesses, by which I e mean a number of things: shadows, reflections (on the surface of water or on 501a anything else which is inherently compact, smooth, and bright), and so on. Do you see what I'm getting at?"

"I do."

"And you should count the other section of the visible realm as consisting of the things whose likenesses are found in the first section: all the flora and fauna there are in the world, and every kind of artefact too."

"All right."

"I wonder whether you'd agree," I said, "that truth and lack of truth have been the criteria for distinguishing these sections, and that the image stands to the original as the realm of beliefs stands to the realm of knowledge?"

"Yes," he said, "I certainly agree."   b

"Now have a look at how to subdivide the section which belongs to the intelligible realm."

"How?"

"Like this. If the mind wants to explore the first subdivision, it can do so only by using those former originals as likenesses and by taking things for granted on its journey, which leads it to an end-point, rather than to a starting-point. If it wants to explore the second subdivision, however, it takes things for granted in order to travel to a starting-point where nothing needs to be taken for granted, and it has no involvement with likenesses, as before, but makes its approach by means of types alone, in and of themselves."

"I don't quite understand what you're saying," he said.

"You will if I repeat it," I said, "because this preamble will make it easier to c understand. I'm sure you're aware that practitioners of geometry, arithmetic,

and so on take for granted things like numerical oddness and evenness, the geo-
metrical figures, the three kinds of angle, and any other things of that sort which
are relevant to a given subject. They act as if they know about these things, treat
them as basic, and don't feel any further need to explain them either to themselves or to anyone else, on the grounds that there is nothing unclear about
d them. They make them the starting-points for their subsequent investigations,
which end after a coherent chain of reasoning at the point they'd set out to reach
in their research."

"Yes, I'm certainly well aware of this," he said.

"So you must also be aware that in the course of their discussions they make
use of visible forms, despite the fact that they're not interested in visible forms
as such, but in the things of which the visible forms are likenesses: that is, their
discussions are concerned with what it is to be a square, and with what it is to
be a diagonal (and so on), rather than with the diagonal (and so on) which
e occurs in their diagrams. They treat their models and diagrams as likenesses,
when these things have likenesses themselves, in fact (that is, shadows and
reflections on water); but they're actually trying to see squares and so on in
511a themselves, which only thought can see."

"You're right," he said.

"So it was objects of this type that I was describing as belonging to the intelligible realm, with the rider that the mind can explore them only by taking
things for granted, and that its goal is not a starting-point, because it is incapable
of changing direction and rising above the things it is taking for granted. And I
went on to say that it used as likenesses those very things which are themselves
the originals of a lower order of likenesses, and that relative to the likenesses,
the originals command respect and admiration for their distinctness."

b   "I see," he said. "You're talking about the objects of geometry and related
occupations."

"Now, can you see what I mean by the second subdivision of the intelligible realm? It is what reason grasps by itself, thanks to its ability to practise
dialectic. When it takes things for granted, it doesn't treat them as starting-
points, but as basic in the strict sense—as platforms and rungs, for example.
These serve it until it reaches a point where nothing needs to be taken for
granted, and which is the starting-point for everything. Once it has grasped this
starting-point, it turns around and by a process of depending on the things
which depend from the starting-point, it descends to an end-point. It makes
c absolutely no use of anything perceptible by the senses: it aims for types by
means of types alone, in and of themselves, and it ends its journey with types."

"I don't quite understand," he said. "I mean, you're talking about crucial
matters here, I think. I do understand, however, that you want to mark off that
part of the real and intelligible realm which is before the eyes of anyone who
knows how to practise dialectic as more clear than the other part, which is
before the eyes of practitioners of the various branches of expertise, as we call
them. The latter make the things they take for granted their starting-points, and
although they inevitably use thought, not the senses, to observe what they

observe, yet because of their failure to ascend to a starting-point—because their d
enquiries rely on taking things for granted—you're saying that they don't
understand these things, even though they are intelligible, when related to a
starting-point. I take you to be describing what geometers and so on do as thinking rather than knowing, on the grounds that thinking is the intermediate state
between believing and knowing."

"There's nothing wrong with your understanding," I said. "And you
should appreciate that there are four states of mind, one for each of the four sections. There's knowledge for the highest section and thought for the second one;
and you'd better assign confidence to the third one and conjecture to the final e
one. You can make an orderly progression out of them, and you should regard
them as possessing as much clarity as their objects possess truth."

"I see," he said. "That's fine with me: I'll order them in the way you suggest."

"Next," I said, "here's a situation which you can use as an analogy for the 514a
human condition—for our education or lack of it. Imagine people living in a
cavernous cell down under the ground; at the far end of the cave, a long way off,
there's an entrance open to the outside world. They've been there since childhood, with their legs and necks tied up in a way which keeps them in one place b
and allows them to look only straight ahead, but not to turn their heads. There's
firelight burning a long way further up the cave behind them, and up the slope
between the fire and the prisoners there's a road, beside which you should
imagine a low wall has been built—like the partition which conjurors place
between themselves and their audience and above which they show their
tricks."

"All right," he said.

"Imagine also that there are people on the other side of this wall who are
carrying all sorts of artefacts. These artefacts, human statuettes, and animal c
models carved in stone and wood and all kinds of materials stick out over the 515a
wall; and as you'd expect, some of the people talk as they carry these objects
along, while others are silent."

"This is a strange picture you're painting," he said, "with strange prisoners."

"They're no different from us," I said. "I mean, in the first place, do you
think they'd see anything of themselves and one another except the shadows
cast by the fire on to the cave wall directly opposite them?"

"Of course not," he said. "They're forced to spend their lives without moving their heads."
                                                                                 b
"And what about the objects which were being carried along? Won't they
only see their shadows as well?"

"Naturally."

"Now, suppose they were able to talk to one another: don't you think they'd
assume that their words applied to what they saw passing by in front of them?"

"They couldn't think otherwise."

"And what if sound echoed off the prison wall opposite them? When any of
the passers-by spoke, don't you think they'd be bound to assume that the sound
came from a passing shadow?"

"I'm absolutely certain of it," he said.

c   "All in all, then," I said, "the shadows of artefacts would constitute the only reality people in this situation would recognize."

"That's absolutely inevitable," he agreed.

"What do you think would happen, then," I asked, "if they were set free from their bonds and cured of their inanity? What would it be like if they found that happening to them? Imagine that one of them has been set free and is suddenly made to stand up, to turn his head and walk, and to look towards the firelight. It hurts him to do all this and he's too dazzled to be capable of making out

d the objects whose shadows he'd formerly been looking at. And suppose someone tells him that what he's been seeing all this time has no substance, and that he's now closer to reality and is seeing more accurately, because of the greater reality of the things in front of his eyes—what do you imagine his reaction would be? And what do you think he'd say if he were shown any of the passing objects and had to respond to being asked what it was? Don't you think he'd be bewildered and would think that there was more reality in what he'd been seeing before than in what he was being shown now?"

"Far more," he said.

e   "And if he were forced to look at the actual firelight, don't you think it would hurt his eyes? Don't you think he'd turn away and run back to the things he could make out, and would take the truth of the matter to be that these things are clearer than what he was being shown?"

"Yes," he agreed.

"And imagine him being dragged forcibly away from there up the rough, steep slope," I went on, "without being released until he's been pulled out into

516a the sunlight. Wouldn't this treatment cause him pain and distress? And once he's reached the sunlight, he wouldn't be able to see a single one of the things which are currently taken to be real, would he, because his eyes would be overwhelmed by the sun's beams?"

"No, he wouldn't," he answered, "not straight away."

"He wouldn't be able to see things up on the surface of the earth, I suppose, until he'd got used to his situation. At first, it would be shadows that he could most easily make out, then he'd move on to the reflections of people and so on in water, and later he'd be able to see the actual things themselves. Next, he'd feast his eyes on the heavenly bodies and the heavens themselves, which would

b be easier at night: he'd look at the light of the stars and the moon, rather than at the sun and sunlight during the daytime."

"Of course."

"And at last, I imagine, he'd be able to discern and feast his eyes on the sun—not the displaced image of the sun in water or elsewhere, but the sun on its own, in its proper place."

"Yes, he'd inevitably come to that," he said.

"After that, he'd start to think about the sun and he'd deduce that it is the source of the seasons and the yearly cycle, that the whole of the visible realm is

c its domain, and that in a sense everything which he and his peers used to see is its responsibility."

"Yes, that would obviously be the next point he'd come to," he agreed.

"Now, if he recalled the cell where he'd originally lived and what passed for knowledge there and his former fellow prisoners, don't you think he'd feel happy about his own altered circumstances, and sorry for them?"

"Definitely."

"Suppose that the prisoners used to assign prestige and credit to one another, in the sense that they rewarded speed at recognizing the shadows as they passed, and the ability to remember which ones normally come earlier and later and at the same time as which other ones, and expertise at using this as a d basis for guessing which ones would arrive next. Do you think our former prisoner would covet these honours and would envy the people who had status and power there, or would he much prefer, as Homer describes it, 'being a slave labouring for someone else—someone without property,' and would put up with anything at all, in fact, rather than share their beliefs and their life?"

"Yes, I think he'd go through anything rather than live that way," he said.   e

"Here's something else I'd like your opinion about," I said. "If he went back underground and sat down again in the same spot, wouldn't the sudden transition from the sunlight mean that his eyes would be overwhelmed by darkness?"

"Certainly," he replied.

"Now, the process of adjustment would be quite long this time, and suppose that before his eyes had settled down and while he wasn't seeing well, he 517a had once again to compete against those same old prisoners at identifying those shadows. Wouldn't he make a fool of himself? Wouldn't they say that he'd come back from his upward journey with his eyes ruined, and that it wasn't even worth trying to go up there? And wouldn't they—if they could—grab hold of anyone who tried to set them free and take them up there and kill him?"

"They certainly would," he said.

"Well, my dear Glaucon," I said, "you should apply this allegory, as a b whole, to what we were talking about before. The region which is accessible to sight should be equated with the prison cell, and the firelight there with the light of the sun. And if you think of the upward journey and the sight of things up on the surface of the earth as the mind's ascent to the intelligible realm, you won't be wrong—at least, I don't think you'd be wrong, and it's my impression that you want to hear. Only God knows if it's actually true, however. Anyway, it's my opinion that the last thing to be seen—and it isn't easy to see either—in the realm of knowledge is goodness; and the sight of the character of goodness c leads one to deduce that it is responsible for everything that is right and fine, whatever the circumstances, and that in the visible realm it is the progenitor of light and of the source of light, and in the intelligible realm it is the source and provider of truth and knowledge. And I also think that the sight of it is a prerequisite for intelligent conduct either of one's own private affairs or of public business."

"I couldn't agree more," he said.

"All right, then," I said, "I wonder if you also agree with me in not finding it strange that people who've travelled there don't want to engage in human business: there's nowhere else their minds would ever rather be than in the d upper region—which is hardly surprising, if our allegory has got this aspect right as well."

"No, it's not surprising," he agreed.

"Well, what about this?" I asked. "Imagine someone returning to the human world and all its misery after contemplating the divine realm. Do you think it's surprising if he seems awkward and ridiculous while he's still not seeing well, before he's had time to adjust to the darkness of his situation, and he's forced into a contest (in a lawcourt or wherever) about the shadows of morality or the

e statuettes which cast the shadows, and into a competition whose terms are the conceptions of morality held by people who have never seen morality itself?"

"No, that's not surprising in the slightest," he said.

518a   "In fact anyone with any sense," I said, "would remember that the eyes can become confused in two different ways, as a result of two different sets of circumstances: it can happen in the transition from light to darkness, and also in the transition from darkness to light. If he took the same facts into consideration when he also noticed someone's mind in such a state of confusion that it was incapable of making anything out, his reaction wouldn't be unthinking ridicule. Instead, he'd try to find out whether this person's mind was returning from a mode of existence which involves greater lucidity and had been blinded by the unfamiliar darkness, or whether it was moving from relative ignorance to relative lucidity and had been overwhelmed and dazzled by the increased brightness. Once he'd distinguished between the two conditions and modes of exis-

b tence, he'd congratulate anyone he found in the second state, and feel sorry for anyone in the first state. If he did choose to laugh at someone in the second state, his amusement would be less absurd than when laughter is directed at someone returning from the light above."

"Yes," he said, "you're making a lot of sense."

"Now, if this is true," I said, "we must bear in mind that education is not capable of doing what some people promise. They claim to introduce knowl-

c edge into a mind which doesn't have it, as if they were introducing sight into eyes which are blind."

"Yes, they do," he said.

"An implication of what we're saying at the moment, however," I pointed out, "is that the capacity for knowledge is present in everyone's mind. If you can imagine an eye that can turn from darkness to brightness only if the body as a whole turns, then our organ of understanding is like that. Its orientation has to be accompanied by turning the mind as a whole away from the world of becoming, until it becomes capable of bearing the sight of real being and reality at its

d most bright, which we're saying is goodness. Yes?"

"Yes."

"That's what education should be," I said, "the art of orientation. Educators should devise the simplest and most effective methods of turning minds around. It shouldn't be the art of implanting sight in the organ, but should proceed on the understanding that the organ already has the capacity, but is improperly aligned and isn't facing the right way."

"I'll try to clarify my point of view," I said. "In my mind, I distinguish 523a between things which are and things which are not attractive in the way we're talking about. I'll try to get you to appreciate the distinction as well, and then you can tell me whether or not you agree, so that we can be better placed to see how accurate my hunch is."

"Yes, do explain," he said.

"All right," I said. "I'm sure you'll see what I mean if I say that at the level of the senses, some things don't encourage the intellect to explore further, b because the situation can be adequately assessed by the relevant sense, while other things can't help provoking an enquiring attitude, because sense-percep-tion fails to produce a sound result."

"You're obviously talking about distant impressions and illusory paint-ings," he said.

"No, you haven't quite got my point," I said.

"What are you talking about, then?"

"In order to count as thought-provoking, in my opinion," I explained, "they c have to produce contradictory sense-impressions at the same time; otherwise, they aren't thought-provoking. The impression sense-perception has to give of an object is that it is no more X than the opposite of X, however close or far away it is when you encounter it. An example will help you understand what I'm get-ting at. Here are three fingers, we'd say, the little finger, the second one and the middle one."

"Yes," he said.

"And please assume that I'm talking about seeing them from close range. Now, here's what I want you to think about."

"What?"

"Well, each of them equally gives the impression of being a finger. There's no difference between them in this respect, and it doesn't matter whether the d finger that's being looked at is in the middle or on either end, pale or dark, thick or thin, and so on and so forth. It's almost inconceivable that anyone's mind would feel impelled in any of these circumstances to think and try to come up with an answer to the question what a finger is, since sight has given the mind no grounds for supposing that the finger is at the same time the opposite of a finger."

"That's right," he agreed.

"So it makes sense to say that this situation doesn't provoke or arouse thought," I said.   e

"Agreed."

"What about the bigness or smallness of the fingers, however? Is what sight sees adequate in this case? Does it make no difference to it whether or not the finger it's looking at is in the middle or on either end? And doesn't the same go for touch and the fingers' thickness and thinness or hardness and softness? And the other senses also give inadequate impressions in this kind of situation, don't they? I mean, here's how each sense works: the main point is that the sense into 524a whose domain hardness falls is inevitably also the sense into whose domain softness falls; and the message it passes on to the mind is that, in its perception, the same thing is both hard and soft. True?"

"True," he said.

"So isn't what happens in these situations that the mind inevitably feels puzzled about what this sense means by hardness, since it's saying that the same thing is soft as well? And when the sense that perceives weight reports that something heavy is light and that something light is heavy, isn't the mind bound to wonder what lightness and heaviness are?"

b   "Yes," he said, "because the messages it's receiving are strange and demand clarification."

"It makes sense to suppose, then," I went on, "that these are the circumstances in which the chief thing the mind does is summon up calculation and thought to help it examine whether in any given case it's being informed about one object or two objects."

"Of course."

"And if there turn out to be two objects, then each of them is single and they're different from each other, aren't they?"

"Yes."

"If each of them is single, then, and it takes two of them to make two, then
c it'll think about them as two separate objects. I mean, if they were inseparable, it wouldn't be thinking about two objects: it would be thinking about one object."

"Right."

"However, in our current example sight sees both big and small as a kind of mixture, not as separate from each other. Yes?"

"Yes."

"And in order to clarify the situation, the intellect is forced in its turn to look at big and small as distinct entities, not mixed together, which is the opposite of what sight does."

"True."

"And this, in outline, is why it occurs to us to ask what in fact bigness and smallness really are, isn't it?"

"Absolutely."

"And that's how we come to distinguish what we call the intelligible realm from the visible realm."

d   "You're quite right," he said.

"So that's what I was getting at just now, when I was saying that some things are thought-provoking, and some things aren't. I define as thought-provoking the things which impinge upon our sense-perception along with their opposites, whereas I describe things which don't do that as incapable of arousing thought."

"I understand now," he said, "and I agree."

"All right, then. Which of these two categories do you think number— which is to say, oneness—belongs to?"

"I don't know," he answered.

"Well, you can work it out from what we've already said," I replied. "If one-ness is adequately seen (or grasped by any other sense) for what it is, then it e
doesn't have any power to attract towards reality—as a finger doesn't, we were
saying. However, if it's never seen without its opposite simultaneously being
seen, so that the impression it gives is no more of oneness than of the opposite,
then evaluation becomes imperative and the mind has no choice but to be puzzled: it sets its thought-processes in motion, and casts about for an answer to the
question what oneness itself actually is. And if this is what happens, then one- 525a
ness is one of those subjects which guide and turn people towards the contem-
plation of reality."

"But that's exactly what seeing oneness does, in fact," he said. "We see the
same thing simultaneously as one and as infinitely many."

"And if oneness is like that," I said, "then number as a whole is as well."

"Naturally."

"Now, calculation and arithmetic are entirely concerned with number."

"Certainly."

"And they clearly guide one towards truth."   b

"Yes, they're exceptionally good at that."

"Then arithmetic is one of the subjects we're after, apparently. A man of war
can't do without it, because he deploys troops, and a philosopher can't do without it, because he has to extricate himself from the world of becoming and make
reality his field of operation, or else he'll never be able to reason and calculate."

"What I'd say," I continued, "is that engaging in all the subjects we've been d
discussing has some relevance to our purposes, and all that effort isn't wasted,
if the work takes one to the common ground of affinity between the subjects,
and enables one to work out how they are all related to one another; otherwise
it's a waste of time."

"I suspect you're right," he said. "But you're talking about an awful lot of
hard work, Socrates."

"What?" I asked. "The prelude is hard, you say? Don't you realize that this
is all just the prelude to the main theme, which is the important subject? I mean,
you surely don't think that being accomplished in these subjects makes one
good at dialectic."   e

"No, certainly not," he answered, "although it does happen sometimes—
very occasionally—in my experience."

"But don't you think the inability to explain anything, and to understand
explanations, rules out the possibility of knowing any of the things we're saying are important?" I asked.

"Yes, I agree with you on this too," he replied.

"And isn't this exactly the theme which dialectic develops, Glaucon?" I 523a
asked. "It may be an intelligible theme, but sight can be said to reflect it, when,
as we were saying, it sets about looking at actual creatures, at the heavenly bodies themselves, and finally at the sun itself. Just as, in this case, a person ends up
at the supreme point of the visible realm, so the summit of the intelligible realm
is reached when, by means of dialectic and without relying on anything per-

b   ceptible, a person perseveres in using rational argument to approach the true reality of things until he has grasped with his intellect the reality of goodness itself."

"Absolutely," he said.

"And this is the journey a practitioner of dialectic makes, wouldn't you say?"

"Of course."

"And the prisoners' release from their bonds," I went on, "their reorientation away from shadows and towards figurines and firelight, their ascent out from under the ground into sunlight, their lingering inability to look in the upper world at creatures and plants and the light of the sun, rather than gazing

c   at reflections in water and at shadows (shadows, that is, of real things, not the shadows of figurines cast by a light which, relative to the sun, is of the same order as the figurines)—just as, in this case, the most lucid part of the body is taken up to see the most lucid part of the material, visible realm, so the whole business of studying the areas of expertise we've been discussing has the ability

d   to guide the best part of the mind upwards until it sees the best part of reality."

"I'm happy with that," he said, "despite the fact that acceptance and rejection both seem to me to be problematic, from different points of view. However, we shouldn't let this be just a one-off discussion today, but should often return to the issue. So let's assume that our ideas are correct, and get on with discussing the actual main theme in as much detail as we did the prelude. So please tell us

e   the ins and outs of the ability to do dialectic, and how many different types of it there are, and what methods it employs, since they'd presumably be the means of approaching that place which, once reached, is travellers' rest and journey's end."

533a   "You won't be able to follow me there, my dear Glaucon," I said, "which is a pity, because there'd be no shortage of determination from me, and what you'd see there wouldn't be an image of what we're talking about: you'd see the truth itself—or that's what I think, anyway. I may be right, and I may be wrong—that's not for us to insist on at the moment; but we can state with confidence that there'd be something of the kind to be seen, don't you think?"

"Of course."

"And what about the idea that dialectic alone can elucidate these matters, to someone with experience in the subjects we've discussed, and that otherwise it's impossible?"

"Yes, we should state that confidently too," he said.

b   "Anyway, what is indisputable in what we're saying," I said, "is that dialectic is the only field of enquiry which sets out methodically to grasp the reality of any and every thing. All the other areas of expertise, on the other hand, are either concerned with fulfilling people's beliefs and desires, or are directed towards generation and manufacture or looking after things while they're being generated and manufactured. Even any that are left—geometry and so on, which we were saying do grasp reality to some extent—are evidently dreaming

c   about reality. There's no chance of their having a conscious glimpse of reality as long as they refuse to disturb the things they take for granted and remain incapable of explaining them. For if your starting-point is unknown, and your end-point and intermediate stages are woven together out of unknown material, there may be coherence, but knowledge is completely out of the question."

"Yes, it is," he agreed.

"So dialectic is the only field of enquiry," I went on, "whose quest for certainty causes it to uproot the things it takes for granted in the course of its journey, which takes it towards an actual starting-point. When the mind's eye is lit- d
erally buried deep in mud far from home, dialectic gently extracts it and guides it upwards, and for this reorientation it draws on the assistance of those areas of expertise we discussed. It's true that we've often called them branches of knowledge in the past, but that's only a habit and they really need a different word, which implies a higher degree of clarity than belief has, and a higher degree of opacity than knowledge has. Earlier, we used the term 'thought.' But I don't suppose we'll quarrel about terminology when we're faced with matters as e
important as the ones we're looking into at the moment."

"No, we won't," he said, "just so long as whatever term is used expresses the state of mental clarity."

"So the terms we used earlier will do," I said. "We'll call the first section knowledge, the second thought, the third confidence, and the fourth conjecture; 534a
and the first pair constitute intellect (which is concerned with real being), the second pair belief (which is concerned with becoming). As being stands to becoming, so intellect stands to belief; and as intellect stands to belief, so knowledge stands to confidence and thought to conjecture. However, we'd better pass over the proportionate relations between the objects of intellect and belief, Glaucon, and the twofold division of each of the two realms—the domain of belief and the domain of intellect—if we want to avoid getting entangled in an argument which would be many times as long as the ones our discussion has already thrown up."

"Well, I agree with everything else you've said, in so far as I can follow it," b
he said.

"And don't you think that the ability to understand what it is to be any given thing, when someone else explains it, is indicative of a dialectician? And wouldn't you say that, in so far as anyone who lacks this ability is incapable of explaining anything to himself or to anyone else either, then he doesn't know anything?"

"Of course I would," he answered.

"The same principle applies to goodness, then, as well. If someone is incapable of arguing for the separation and distinction of the character of goodness from everything else, and cannot, so to speak, fight all the objections one by one c
and refute them (responding to them resolutely by referring to the reality of things, rather than to people's beliefs), and can't see it all through to the end without his position suffering a fall—if you find someone to be in this state, you'll deny that he has knowledge of goodness itself or, in general, of anything good at all. Instead, if he does somehow manage to make contact with a reflection of

goodness, you'll claim that the contact is due to belief, not knowledge. He dreams his current life away in a state of semi-consciousness, you'll say, and he'll never

d   wake up here: he'll go to Hades, the place of total sleep, first. Agreed?"

"Yes, definitely," he said. "I'll certainly be making all of these claims."

"Now, suppose your theoretical upbringing and education of your younger generation were to become a reality. I imagine you'd deny them power and crucial responsibility in the community if they were as irrational as surds."

"Yes, I would," he said.

"Will you include in your legislation, then, the ruling that a major part of the education they engage in must be the subject which will enable them to acquire particular expertise at the give and take of discussion?"

"I will," he replied, "if you join me."

e   "Don't you think," I asked, "that dialectic occupies the highest position and forms, as it were, the copestone of the curriculum? And that, if so, there's no subject which ought to occupy a higher position, and therefore it completes our educational programme?"

535a   "Yes, I agree," he answered.

COMMENTS

In the central books of the *Republic*, Plato develops a new account of knowledge, the one for which he is best known. It has several striking and controversial features:

1. In the first passage, Socrates undertakes to show that reflection on knowledge and what it requires leads us to see that its objects are not the objects of ordinary experience but objects that it takes intellectual effort to understand. Ordinary things that are beautiful, or double, allegedly suffer from systematic deficiencies from the intellectual point of view, and the person who uses her mind is led to see that what we know must be more intellectually satisfactory items. Plato characterizes these items as reality, which the intellectually active person wakes up to. He also calls them "forms" (here "types") and refers to them by an idiom that sounds odd in English: "the beautiful itself." How far is Plato entitled to represent this conclusion as the outcome of a debate with somebody who, as a "sightseer" with confidence in everyday experience, has no metaphysical commitments?

2. Notice that the argument assumes that the object or field of knowledge must be distinct from the object or field of true belief. This is a different approach to the relationship of knowledge and true belief from what we find in other works by Plato (see section 3.B). What are Plato's grounds for looking at the matter in the way that he does here?

3. What is the argument for the supposed intellectual deficiency of the objects of ordinary experience? Notice that the argument seems to be limited to terms with opposites—beautiful/ugly, double/half, and so on. Could the argument be extended to terms without opposites? (Compare these passages to the passages from the *Phaedo* and *Parmenides* in section 4.)

4. The argument relies on the idea that ordinary objects of experience fail to *be* in some way in which the satisfactory intellectual objects of knowledge succeed. The Greek verb *to be* (*einai*) is used in a way that does not distinguish between *being something* (for example, being beautiful) and *being* (which we render as "exists" or regard as a distinct sense of the verb). Would the argument still go through if we distinguish these two uses of the verb *to be?*

The passages of Sun, Line, and Cave gives us an imaginative picture of what Plato takes knowledge to be; he then gives us some pointers to a more rigorous way of understanding them. For Plato, metaphor and imaginative picturing are the lowest intellectual stage; we have to go on to rigorous argument before we are entitled to claim knowledge. So Plato is conscious that what he is offering to us is no more than the beginnings of an account of knowledge that could itself amount to knowledge. Still, on some points he is clearly confident that he is broadly right:

a. Knowledge here requires intellectual reflection and argument in a way that rejects our ordinary reliance on everyday experience. Plato is clearly impressed by the example of mathematics and thinks that the knowledge achieved by a philosophical thinking, here called dialectic, will be like mathematics in having a clear structure, traced out by proof, and in achieving results that can be regarded with confidence as being true, though produced independently of our everyday experience. Is this a convincing picture of what philosophy does? If mathematics is not a good model for philosphical thinking, what is?

b. For Plato, all knowledge springs from, and is in some way dependent on, the Good. Even mathematical and abstract philosophical thinking culminate in an understanding of the nature of the Good. Are you inclined to find it more natural to regard some kinds of knowledge, like mathematical knowledge, as being "value-free," while considering others to be concerned with value? If so, what is the basis of this?

c. Plato's Cave analogy represents our actual state with respect to knowledge as being a limited and degraded one. Is he too pessimistic about ordinary people's claims to knowledge? Is he too optimistic about what, ideally, knowledge should be?

Posterior Analytics I, 1–3; II, 19
ARISTOTLE

1. All teaching and all intellectual learning come about from already existing knowledge. This is evident if we consider it in every case; for the mathe- 71^a1

matical sciences are acquired in this fashion, and so is each of the other arts. And
5   similarly too with arguments—both deductive and inductive arguments proceed in this way; for both produce their teaching through what we are already
aware of, the former getting their premises as from men who grasp them, the
latter proving the universal through the particular's being clear. (And rhetorical
10 arguments too persuade in the same way; for they do so either through examples, which is induction, or through enthymemes, which is deduction.)

It is necessary to be already aware of things in two ways: of some things it is
necessary to believe already that they are, of some one must grasp what the thing
said is, and of others both—e.g. of the fact that everything is either affirmed or
15 denied truly, one must believe that it is; of the triangle, that it signifies *this*; and
of the unit both (both what it signifies and that it is). For each of these is not
equally clear to us.

But you can become familiar by being familiar earlier with some things but
getting knowledge of the others at the very same time—i.e. of whatever happens to be under the universal of which you have knowledge. For that every tri-
20 angle has angles equal to two right angles was already known; but that there is
a triangle in the semicircle here became familiar at the same time as the induction. (For in some cases learning occurs in this way, and the last term does not
become familiar through the middle—in cases dealing with what are in fact particulars and not said of any underlying subject.)
25   Before the induction, or before getting a deduction, you should perhaps be
said to understand in a way—but in another way not. For if you did not know
if it is *simpliciter*, how did you know that it has two right angles *simpliciter*? But
it is clear that you understand it in *this* sense—that you understand it universally—but you do not understand it *simpliciter*. (Otherwise the puzzle in the
30 *Meno* will result; for you will learn either nothing or what you know.)

For one should not argue in the way in which some people attempt to solve
it: Do you or don't you know of every pair that it is even? And when you said
Yes, they brought forward some pair of which you did not think that it was, nor
therefore that it was even. For they solve it by denying that people know of
70ᵇ1 every pair that it is even, but only of anything of which they know that it is a
pair.—Yet they know it of that which they have the demonstration about and
which they got their premises about; and they got them not about everything
of which they know that it is a triangle or that it is a number, but of every number and triangle *simpliciter*. For no proposition of such a type is assumed (that
5   *what you know to be a number* . . . or *what you know to be rectilineal* . . .), but they are
assumed as holding of every case.

But nothing, I think, prevents one from in a sense understanding and in a
sense being ignorant of what one is learning; for what is absurd is not that you
should know in some sense what you are learning, but that you should know it
in *this* sense, i.e. in the way and sense in which you are learning it.

2. We think we understand a thing *simpliciter* (and not in the sophistic fash-
10 ion accidentally) whenever we think we are aware both that the explanation
because of which the object is is its explanation, and that it is not possible for this

to be otherwise. It is clear, then, that to understand is something of this sort; for both those who do not understand and those who do understand—the former think they are themselves in such a state, and those who do understand actually 15 are. Hence that of which there is understanding *simpliciter* cannot be otherwise.

Now whether there is also another type of understanding we shall say later; but we say now that we do know through demonstration. By demonstration I mean a scientific deduction; and by scientific I mean one in virtue of which, by having it, we understand something.

If, then, understanding is as we posited, it is necessary for demonstrative 20 understanding in particular to depend on things which are true and primitive and immediate and more familiar than and prior to and explanatory of the conclusion (for in this way the principles will also be appropriate to what is being proved). For there will be deduction even without these conditions, but there will not be demonstration; for it will not produce understanding.

Now they must be true because one cannot understand what is not the 25 case—e.g. that the diagonal is commensurate. And they must depend on what is primitive and non-demonstrable because otherwise you will not understand if you do not have a demonstration of them; for to understand that of which there is a demonstration non-accidentally is to have a demonstration. They must be both explanatory and more familiar and prior—explanatory because we only 30 understand when we know the explanation; and prior, if they are explanatory, and we are already aware of them not only in the sense of grasping them but also of knowing that they are.

Things are prior and more familiar in two ways; for it is not the same to be prior by nature and prior in relation to us, nor to be more familiar and more 72ª1 familiar to us. I call prior and more familiar in relation to us what is nearer to perception, prior and more familiar *simpliciter* what is further away. What is most universal is furthest away, and the particulars are nearest; and these are 5 opposite to each other.

Depending on things that are primitive is depending on appropriate principles; for I call the same thing primitive and a principle. A principle of a demonstration is an immediate proposition, and an immediate proposition is one to which there is no other prior. A proposition is the one part of a contradiction, one thing said of one; it is dialectical if it assumes indifferently either part, 10 demonstrative if it determinately assumes the one that is true. [A statement is either part of a contradiction.] A contradiction is an opposition of which of itself excludes any intermediate; and the part of a contradiction saying something *of* something is an affirmation, the one saying something *from* something is a denial.

An immediate deductive principle I call a posit if one cannot prove it but it 15 is not necessary for anyone who is to learn anything to grasp it; and one which it is necessary for anyone who is going to learn anything whatever to grasp, I call an axiom (for there are some such things); for we are accustomed to use this name especially of such things. A posit which assumes either of the parts of a contradiction—i.e., I mean, that something is or that something is not—I call a 20 supposition; one without this, a definition. For a definition is a posit (for the arithmetician posits that a unit is what is quantitatively indivisible) but not a supposition (for what a unit is and that a unit is are not the same).

25   Since one should both be convinced of and know the object by having a deduction of the sort we call a demonstration, and since this is the case when *these* things on which the deduction depends are the case, it is necessary not only to be already aware of the primitives (either all or some of them) but actually to be better aware of them. For a thing always belongs better to that thing because
30 of which it belongs—e.g. that because of which we love is better loved. Hence if we know and are convinced because of the primitives, we both know and are convinced of them better, since it is because of them that we know and are convinced of what is posterior.

It is not possible to be better convinced than one is of what one knows, of what one in fact neither knows nor is more happily disposed toward than if one in fact knew. But this will result if someone who is convinced because of a
35 demonstration is not already aware of the primitives, for it is necessary to be better convinced of the principles (either all or some of them) than of the conclusion.

Anyone who is going to have understanding through demonstration must not only be familiar with the principles and better convinced of them than of
72ᵇ1 what is being proved, but also there must be no other thing more convincing to him or more familiar among the opposites of the principles on which a deduction of the contrary error may depend—if anyone who understands *simpliciter* must be unpersuadable.

5   3. Now some think that because one must understand the primitives there is no understanding at all; others that there is, but that there are demonstrations of everything. Neither of these views is either true or necessary.

For the one party, supposing that one cannot understand in another way, claim that we are led back *ad infinitum on* the grounds that we would not understand what is posterior because of what is prior if there are no primitives; and
10 they argue correctly, for it is impossible to go through infinitely many things. And if it comes to a stop and there are principles, they say that these are unknowable since there is no *demonstration* of them, which alone they say is understanding; but if one cannot know the primitives, neither can what depends on them be understood *simpliciter* or properly, but only on the supposition that they are the case.

15   The other party agrees about understanding; for it, they say, occurs only through demonstration. But they argue that nothing prevents there being demonstration of everything; for it is possible for the demonstration to come about in a circle and reciprocally.

But *we* say that neither is all understanding demonstrative, but in the case
20 of the immediates it is non-demonstrable—and that this is necessary is evident; for if it is necessary to understand the things which are prior and on which the demonstration depends, and it comes to a stop at some time, it is necessary for these immediates to be non-demonstrable. So as to that we argue thus; and we

also say that there is not only understanding but also some principle of understanding by which we become familiar with the definitions.

And that it is impossible to demonstrate *simpliciter* in a circle is clear, if 25 demonstration must depend on what is prior and more familiar; for it is impossible for the same things at the same time to be prior and posterior to the same things—unless one is so in another way (i.e. one in relation to us, the other *simpliciter*), which induction makes familiar. But if so, knowing *simpliciter* will not 30 have been properly defined, but will be twofold. Or is the other demonstration not demonstration *simpliciter* in that it comes from about what is more familiar *to us*?

There results for those who say that demonstration is circular not only what has just been described, but also that they say nothing other than that this is the case if this is the case—and it is easy to prove everything in this way. It is clear 35 that this results if we posit three terms. (For it makes no difference to say that it bends back through many terms or through few, or through few or two.) For whenever if *A* is the case, of necessity *B* is, and if this then *C*, then if *A* is the case *C* will be the case. Thus given that if *A* is the case it is necessary that *B* is, and if this is that *A* is (for that is what being circular is)—let *A* be *C*: so to say that if *B* 73ª1 is the case *A* is, is to say that *C* is, and this implies that if *A* is the case *C* is. But *C* is the same as *A*. Hence it results that those who assert that demonstration is circular say nothing but that if *A* is the case *A* is the case. And it is easy to prove 5 everything in this way.

19. Now as for deduction and demonstration, it is evident both what each 15 is and how it comes about—and at the same time this goes for demonstrative understanding too (for that is the same thing). But as for the principles—how they become familiar and what is the state that becomes familiar with them— that will be clear from what follows, when we have first set down the puzzles.

Now, we have said earlier that it is not possible to understand through 20 demonstration if we are not aware of the primitive, immediate, principles. But as to knowledge of the immediates, one might puzzle both whether it is the same or not the same—whether there is understanding of each, or rather understanding of the one and some other kind of thing of the other—and also whether the states are not present in us but come about in us, or whether they are pres- 25 ent in us but escape notice.

Well, if we have them, it is absurd; for it results that we have pieces of knowledge more precise than demonstration and yet this escapes notice. But if we get them without having them earlier, how might we become familiar with them and learn them from no pre-existing knowledge? For that is impossible, as we said in the case of demonstration too. It is evidently impossible, then, both for us 30 to have them and for them to come about in us when we are ignorant and have no such state at all. Necessarily, therefore, we have some capacity, but do not have one of a type which will be more valuable than these in respect of precision.

And *this* evidently belongs to all animals; for they have a connate discrimi- 35 natory capacity, which is called perception. And if perception is present in them,

in some animals retention of the percept comes about, but in others it does not come about. Now for those in which it does not come about, there is no knowledge outside perceiving (either none at all, or none with regard to that of which there is no retention); but for some perceivers, it is possible to grasp it in their
100ª1 minds. And when many such things come about, then a difference comes about, so that some come to have an account from the retention of such things, and others do not.

So from perception there comes memory, as we call it, and from memory
5 (when it occurs often in connection with the same thing), experience; for memories that are many in number from a single experience. And from experience, or from the whole universal that has come to rest in the soul (the one apart from the many, whatever is one and the same in all those things), there comes a principle of skill and of understanding—of skill if it deals with how things come about, of understanding if it deals with what is the case.
10   Thus the states neither belong in us in a determinate form, nor come about from other states that are more cognitive; but they come about from perception—as in a battle when a rout occurs, if one man makes a stand another does and then another, until a position of strength is reached. And the soul is such as to be capable of undergoing this.
15   What we have just said but not said clearly, let us say again: when one of the undifferentiated things makes a stand, there is a primitive universal in the mind (for though one perceives the particular, perception is of the universal—e.g. of
100ᵇ1 man but not of Callias the man); again a stand is made in these, until what has no parts and is universal stands—e.g., *such and such* an animal stands, until animal does, and in this a stand is made in the same way. Thus it is clear that it is necessary for us to become familiar with the primitives by induction; for per-
5 ception too instils the universal in this way.

Since of the intellectual states by which we grasp truth some are always true and some admit falsehood (e.g. opinion and reasoning—whereas understanding and comprehension are always true), and no kind other than comprehension is more precise than understanding, and the principles of demonstrations
10 are more familiar, and all understanding involves an account—there will not be understanding of the principles; and since it is not possible for anything to be truer than understanding, except comprehension, there will be comprehension of the principles—both if we inquire from these facts and because demonstration is not a principle of demonstration so that understanding is not a principle of understanding either—so if we have no other true kind apart from under-
15 standing, comprehension will be the principle of understanding. And the principle will be of the principle, and understanding as a whole will be similarly related to the whole object.

Metaphysics I, 1–3; II, 1

ARISTOTLE

1. All men by nature desire to know. An indication of this is the delight we
take in our senses; for even apart from their usefulness they are loved for themselves; and above all others the sense of sight. For not only with a view to action,   980ª25
but even when we are not going to do anything, we prefer sight to almost everything else. The reason is that this, most of all the senses, makes us know and
brings to light many differences between things.

By nature animals are born with the faculty of sensation, and from sensation
memory is produced in some of them, though not in others. And therefore the
former are more intelligent and apt at learning than those which cannot remember; those which are incapable of hearing sounds are intelligent though they
cannot be taught, e.g. the bee, and any other race of animals that may be like it;
and those which besides memory have this sense of hearing, can be taught.   980ᵇ25

The animals other than man live by appearances and memories, and have
but little of connected experience; but the human race lives also by art and reasonings. And from memory experience is produced in men; for many memories
of the same thing produce finally the capacity for a single experience. Experi-   981ª1
ence seems to be very similar to science and art, but really science and art come
to men *through* experience; for "experience made art," as Polus says, "but inex-   5
perience luck." And art arises, when from many notions gained by experience
one universal judgement about similar objects is produced. For to have a judgement that when Callias was ill of this disease this did him good, and similarly
in the case of Socrates and in many individual cases, is a matter of experience;
but to judge that it has done good to all persons of a certain constitution, marked   10
off in one class, when they were ill of this disease, e.g. to phlegmatic or bilious
people when burning with fever,—this is a matter of art.

With a view to action experience seems in no respect inferior to art, and we
even see men of experience succeeding more than those who have theory without experience. The reason is that experience is knowledge of individuals, art of   15
universals, and actions and productions are all concerned with the individual;
for the physician does not cure a man, except in an incidental way, but Callias
or Socrates or some other called by some such individual name, who happens   20
to be a man. If, then, a man has theory without experience, and knows the universal but does not know the individual included in this, he will often fail to
cure; for it is the individual that is to be cured. But yet we think that *knowledge*
and *understanding* belong to art rather than to experience, and we suppose   25
artists to be wiser than men of experience (which implies that wisdom depends

in all cases rather on knowledge); and this because the former know the cause,
but the latter do not. For men of experience know that the thing is so, but do not
30 know why, while the others know the "why" and the cause. Hence we think that
the master-workers in each craft are more honourable and know in a truer sense
981ᵇ1 and are wiser than the manual workers, because they know the causes of the
things that are done (we think the manual workers are like certain lifeless things
which act indeed, but act without knowing what they do, as fire burns,—but
while the lifeless things perform each of their functions by a natural tendency,
the labourers perform them through habit); thus we view them as being wiser
5 not in virtue of being able to act, but of having the theory for themselves and
knowing the causes. And in general it is a sign of the man who knows, that he
can teach, and therefore we think art more truly knowledge than experience is;
for artists can teach, and men of mere experience cannot.
10   Again, we do not regard any of the senses as wisdom; yet surely these give
the most authoritative knowledge of particulars. But they do not tell us the
"why" of anything—e.g. why fire is hot; they only say that it is hot.
        At first he who invented any art that went beyond the common perceptions
15 of man was naturally admired by men, not only because there was something
useful in the inventions, but because he was thought wise and superior to the
rest. But as more arts were invented, and some were directed to the necessities
of life, others to its recreation, the inventors of the latter were always regarded
20 as wiser than the inventors of the former, because their branches of knowledge
did not aim at utility. Hence when all such inventions were already established,
the sciences which do not aim at giving pleasure or at the necessities of life were
discovered, and first in the places where men first began to have leisure. This is
why the mathematical arts were founded in Egypt; for there the priestly caste
was allowed to be at leisure.
25   We have said in the *Ethics* what the difference is between art and science and
the other kindred faculties; but the point of our present discussion is this, that
all men suppose what is called wisdom to deal with the first causes and the prin-
30 ciples of things. This is why, as has been said before, the man of experience is
thought to be wiser than the possessors of any perception whatever, the artist
wiser than the men of experience, the master-worker than the mechanic, and the
theoretical kinds of knowledge to be more of the nature of wisdom than the pro-
982ª1 ductive. Clearly then wisdom is knowledge about certain causes and principles.

        2. Since we are seeking this knowledge, we must inquire of what kind are
5 the causes and the principles, the knowledge of which is wisdom. If we were to
take the notions we have about the wise man, this might perhaps make the
answer more evident. We suppose first, then, that the wise man knows all
things, as far as possible, although he has not knowledge of each of them indi-
10 vidually; secondly, that he who can learn things that are difficult, and not easy
for man to know, is wise (sense-perception is common to all, and therefore easy
and no mark of wisdom); again, he who is more exact and more capable of
teaching the causes is wiser, in every branch of knowledge; and of the sciences,

also, that which is desirable on its own account and for the sake of knowing it is 15
more of the nature of wisdom than that which is desirable on account of its
results, and the superior science is more of the nature of wisdom than the ancillary; for the wise man must not be ordered but must order, and he must not obey
another, but the less wise must obey *him*.

Such and so many are the notions, then, which we have about wisdom and 20
the wise. Now of these characteristics that of knowing all things must belong to
him who has in the highest degree universal knowledge; for he knows in a sense
all the subordinate objects. And these things, the most universal, are on the
whole the hardest for men to know; for they are furthest from the senses. And 25
the most exact of the sciences are those which deal most with first principles; for
those which involve fewer principles are more exact than those which involve
additional principles, e.g. arithmetic than geometry. But the science which
investigates causes is also more capable of reaching, for the people who teach
are those who tell the causes of each thing. And understanding and knowledge 30
pursued for their own sake are found most in the knowledge of that which is
most knowable; for he who chooses to know for the sake of knowing will choose
most readily that which is most truly knowledge, and such is the knowledge of 982^{b}1
that which is most knowable; and the first principles and the causes are most
knowable; for by reason of these, and from these, all other things are known, but
these are not known by means of the things subordinate to them. And the sci- 5
ence which knows to what end each thing must be done is the most authoritative of the sciences, and more authoritative than any ancillary science; and this
end is the good in each class, and in general the supreme good in the whole of
nature. Judged by all the tests we have mentioned, then, the name in question
falls to the same science; this must be a science that investigates the first principles and causes; for the good, i.e. that for the sake of which, is one of the causes. 10

That it is not a science of production is clear even from the history of the earliest philosophers. For it is owing to their wonder that men both now begin and
at first began to philosophize; they wondered originally at the obvious difficulties, then advanced little by little and stated difficulties about the greater mat- 15
ters, e.g. about the phenomena of the moon and those of the sun and the stars,
and about the genesis of the universe. And a man who is puzzled and wonders
thinks himself ignorant (whence even the lover of myth is in a sense a lover of
wisdom, for myth is composed of wonders); therefore since they philosophized 20
in order to escape from ignorance, evidently they were pursuing science in
order to know, and not for any utilitarian end. And this is confirmed by the facts;
for it was when almost all the necessities of life and the things that make for
comfort and recreation were present, that such knowledge began to be sought. 25
Evidently then we do not seek it for the sake of any other advantage; but as the
man is free, we say, who exists for himself and not for another, so we pursue this
as the only free science, for it alone exists for itself.

Hence the possession of it might be justly regarded as beyond human
power; for in many ways human nature is in bondage, so that according to 30

Simonides "God alone can have this privilege," and it is unfitting that man should not be content to seek the knowledge that is suited to him. If, then, there 983ª1 is something in what the poets say, and jealousy is natural to the divine power, it would probably occur in this case above all, and all who excelled in this knowledge would be unfortunate. But the divine power cannot be jealous (indeed, according to the proverb, "bards tell many a lie"), nor should any science be thought more honourable than one of this sort. For the most divine sci- 5 ence is also most honourable; and this science alone is, in two ways, most divine. For the science which it would be most meet for God to have is a divine science, and so is any science that deals with divine objects; and this science alone has both these qualities; for God is thought to be among the causes of all things and to be a first principle, and such a science either God alone can have, or God 10 above all others. All the sciences, indeed, are more necessary than this, but none is better.

Yet the acquisition of it must in a sense end in something which is the opposite of our original inquiries. For all men begin, as we said, by wondering that 15 the matter is so (as in the case of automatic marionettes or the solstices or the incommensurability of the diagonal of a square with the side; for it seems wonderful to all men who have not yet perceived the explanation that there is a thing which cannot be measured even by the smallest unit). But we must end in the contrary and, according to the proverb, the better state, as is the case in these 20 instances when men learn the cause; for there is nothing which would surprise a geometer so much as if the diagonal turned out to be commensurable.

We have stated, then, what is the nature of the science we are searching for, and what is the mark which our search and our whole investigation must reach.

3. Evidently we have to acquire knowledge of the original causes (for we 25 say we know each thing only when we think we recognize its first cause), and causes are spoken of in four senses. In one of these we mean the substance, i.e. the essence (for the "why" is referred finally to the formula, and the ultimate 30 "why" is a cause and principle); in another the matter or substratum, in a third the source of the change, and in a fourth the cause opposed to this, that for the sake of which and the good (for this is the end of all generation and change). We 983b1 have studied these causes sufficiently in our work on nature, but yet let us call to our aid those who have attacked the investigation of being and philosophized about reality before us. For obviously they too speak of certain principles and causes; to go over their views, then, will be of profit to the present inquiry, for 5 we shall either find another kind of cause, or be more convinced of the correctness of those which we now maintain.

1. The investigation of the truth is in one way hard, in another easy. An indication of this is found in the fact that no one is able to attain the truth adequately, while, on the other hand, no one fails entirely, but every one says something true about the nature of things, and while individually they contribute little or nothing to the truth, by the union of all a considerable amount is amassed. Therefore, 5 since the truth seems to be like the proverbial door, which no one can fail to hit,

in this way it is easy, but the fact that we can have a whole truth and not the particular part we aim at shows the difficulty of it.

Perhaps, as difficulties are of two kinds, the cause of the present difficulty is not in the facts but in us. For as the eyes of bats are to the blaze of day, so is the reason in our soul to the things which are by nature most evident of all.

It is just that we should be grateful, not only to those whose opinions we may share, but also to those who have expressed more superficial views; for these also contributed something, by developing before us the powers of thought. It is true that if there had been no Timotheus we should have been without much of our lyric poetry; but if there had been no Phrynis there would have been no Timotheus. The same holds good of those who have expressed views about the truth; for from the better thinkers we have inherited certain opinions, while the others have been responsible for the appearance of the better thinkers.

It is right also that philosophy should be called knowledge of the truth. For the end of theoretical knowledge is truth, while that of practical knowledge is action (for even if they consider how things are, practical men do not study what is eternal but what stands in some relation at some time). Now we do not know a truth without its cause; and a thing has a quality in a higher degree than other things if in virtue of it the similar quality belongs to the other things (e.g. fire is the hottest of things; for it is the cause of the heat of all other things); so that that which causes derivative truths to be true is most true. Therefore the principles of eternal things must be always most true; for they are not merely sometimes true, nor is there any cause of their being, but they themselves are the cause of the being of other things, so that as each thing is in respect of being, so is it in respect of truth.

Parts of Animals I, 5

ARISTOTLE

5. Of substances constituted by nature some are ungenerated, imperishable, and eternal, while others are subject to generation and decay. The former are excellent and divine, but less accessible to knowledge. The evidence that might throw light on them, and on the problems which we long to solve respecting them, is furnished but scantily by sensation; whereas respecting perishable plants and animals we have abundant information, living as we do in their midst, and ample data may be collected concerning all their various kinds, if only we are willing to take sufficient pains. Both departments, however, have their special charm. The scanty conceptions to which we can attain of celestial

things give us, from their excellence, more pleasure than all our knowledge of
the world in which we live; just as a half glimpse of persons that we love is more
645ᵃ1 delightful than an accurate view of other things, whatever their number and
dimensions. On the other hand, in certitude and in completeness our knowledge of terrestrial things has the advantage. Moreover, their greater nearness
and affinity to us balances somewhat the loftier interest of the heavenly things
that are the objects of the higher philosophy. Having already treated of the celes-
5 tial world, as far as our conjectures could reach, we proceed to treat of animals,
without omitting, to the best of our ability, any member of the kingdom, however ignoble. For if some have no graces to charm the sense, yet nature, which
fashioned them, gives amazing pleasure in their study to all who can trace
10 links of causation, and are inclined to philosophy. Indeed, it would be strange
if mimic representations of them were attractive, because they disclose the
mimetic skill of the painter or sculptor, and the original realities themselves
15 were not more interesting, to all at any rate who have eyes to discern the causes.
We therefore must not recoil with childish aversion from the examination of the
humbler animals. Every realm of nature is marvellous: and as Heraclitus, when
the strangers who came to visit him found him warming himself at the furnace
20 in the kitchen and hesitated to go in, is reported to have bidden them not to be
afraid to enter, as even in that kitchen divinities were present, so we should venture on the study of every kind of animal without distaste; for each and all will
reveal to us something natural and something beautiful. Absence of haphazard
and conduciveness of everything to an end are to be found in nature's works in
the highest degree, and the end for which those works are put together and pro-
25 duced is a form of the beautiful.

　　　If any person thinks the examination of the rest of the animal kingdom an
unworthy task, he must hold in like disesteem the study of man. For no one can
look at the elements of the human frame—blood, flesh, bones, vessels, and the
30 like—without much repugnance. Moreover, when any one of the parts or struc-
tures, be it which it may, is under discussion, it must not be supposed that it is
its material composition to which attention is being directed or which is the
object of the discussion, but rather the total form. Similarly, the true object of
architecture is not bricks, mortar, or timber, but the house; and so the principal
object of natural philosophy is not the material elements, but their composition,
645ᵇ1 and the totality of the substance, independently of which they have no existence.

　　　The course of exposition must be first to state the essential attributes common to whole groups of animals, and then to attempt to give their explanation.
Many groups, as already noticed, present common attributes, that is to say, in
5 some cases absolutely identical—feet, feathers, scales, and the like; while in
other groups the affections and organs are analogous. For instance, some groups
have lungs, others have no lung, but an organ analogous to a lung in its place;
10 some have blood, others have no blood, but a fluid analogous to blood, and with
the same office. To treat of the common attributes separately in connexion with
each individual group would involve, as already suggested, useless iteration.
For many groups have common attributes. So much for this topic.

As every instrument and every bodily member is for the sake of something, 15
viz. some action, so the whole body must evidently be for the sake of some complex action. Thus the saw is made for sawing, for sawing is a function, and not
sawing for the saw. Similarly, the body too must somehow or other be made for
the soul, and each part of it for some subordinate function, to which it is 20
adapted.

We have, then, first to describe the common functions, and those which
belong to a genus or to a species. By "common" I mean those which belong to all
animals; by "to a genus," those of animals whose differences from one another
we see to be matters of degree—Bird is a genus. Man is a species, and so is every- 25
thing not differentiated into subordinate groups. In the first case the common
attributes may be called analogous, in the second generic, in the third specific.

When a function is ancillary to another, a like relation manifestly obtains
between the organs which discharge these functions; and similarly, if one function is prior to and the end of another, their respective organs will stand to each 30
other in the same relation. Thirdly, there are functions which are the necessary
consequences of others.

Instances of what I mean by functions and affections are Reproduction,
Growth, Copulation, Waking, Sleep, Locomotion, and other similar animal
actions. Instances of what I mean by parts are Nose, Eye, Face, and other so- 646^{a}1
called members; and similarly for the rest. So much for the method to be pursued. Let us now try to set forth the causes of all these things, both common and
special, and in so doing let us follow that order of exposition which conforms,
as we have indicated, to the order of nature.

COMMENTS

One striking difference between Aristotle and Plato is that Aristotle is less concerned
with the achievement of the individual knower. You can see from the *Metaphysics*
passages that Aristotle regards knowledge as a collective achievement, built up
cumulatively by means of the contributions made by present thinkers to the productions of past thinkers. Because he thinks this, Aristotle himself tends to start from
the contributions of past thinkers to a given topic, and he gives weight to common
sense and widely shared opinions that are *endoxa* or "reputable"—held by an overwhelming majority or defended by established thinkers. Aristotle sees philosophy
and what we call science as a continuous development from everyday thinking, not
a reaction against it, as Plato does. Aristotle's own conclusions are also a good deal
more conservative than are Plato's and nearer to common sense.

Whereas Plato sees knowledge as a single organized structure, focusing on the
Good, Aristotle stresses differences among different branches of knowledge and
insists that astronomy, say, is distinct from biology not only in its field but in its methods and procedures. In many ways, Aristotle's interest in knowledge is like the modern concern with science and the sciences. Again unlike Plato, Aristotle does not
think that a field like biology, which is about empirical matters, is of less value or
interest than a more abstract and mathematical field like astronomy.

We can see from the *Posterior Analytics* passage, however, that Aristotle shares with Plato the concern that a branch of knowledge should be firmly structured and begin from a starting point that is not taken for granted. In these chapters, Aristotle develops what is called a *foundationalist* approach to knowledge. Within any science or branch of knowledge, the truths that are its concern are either the first principles of the science or derived from them. Aristotle's arguments here are driven by the opening idea that new knowledge must be based on knowledge that we already have. As a result Aristotle's picture of a science is restrictive. We must *prove* other results from the first principles (Aristotle himself was the first to formalize proof and give a rigorous account of it), and the principles must be true, primitive, immediate, more familiar than the conclusion, prior to it, and explanatory of it. (Here Aristotle joins Plato in the idea that it is "giving an account of the reason why" that is crucial to turning true beliefs into knowledge.) Two problems with this account are particularly prominent:

1. How can we have knowledge of the first principles? If knowledge requires proof or demonstration, then a demand to prove the first principles will lead to infinite regress. Aristotle is unwilling to allow infinite regress, or to allow circular proof (in which all the parts of a science would hang together without any being foundational), or to allow that we don't know the first principles. His solution, that we know them in a different way, is filled out to some extent by the final chapter of book II, in which Aristotle explains how we come to have "comprehension" of the principles. Is Aristotle's solution the right one?

2. In the Middle Ages and later, this model of a science was rejected because it seems to be an absurd model for scientific *discovery,* suggesting that we should do science by proving results from principles without going out and looking at things. But Aristotle's own enormous scientific research took the form of empirical discovery, and Aristotle was an amazingly energetic researcher. The model for a science here is an ideal presentation of the results of discovery in a way that will enable us to understand them. For Aristotle, discoveries have to be organized theoretically before they give us knowledge. He does not think that individual discoveries add to our knowledge until we can make sense of them within a theoretical structure in which they can be traced to first principles. Is he right in this belief?

E. Knowledge from Experience

Both Plato and Aristotle concentrate on the knowledge we have that requires abstract thinking and reflection. Philosophers after Aristotle, particularly the Epicureans and Stoics, focus on the ways in which knowledge can be built up from the experiences that we get through our senses and build outward from this more cautiously than Aristotle does.

Epicurus on Knowledge

1. First, Herodotus, we must have grasped what underlies our utterances, so that we may be able to judge the objects of belief or inquiry or puzzlement, by referring them to these, and so that we may avoid either demonstrating things ad infinitum, with everything going unjudged, or our having utterances that are empty. It is necessary that the first concept corresponding to each utterance be seen, and not require demonstration, if we are to have something to which to refer the object of inquiry or puzzlement or belief. Then, we must observe everything in accordance with our perceptions, and in general in accordance with our present focusings whether of the mind or of any other of our faculties that provide a standard, and also in accordance with the feelings that we have, so as to have something with which to argue with signs to what still awaits evidence and what is unclear. (Epicurus, *Letter to Herodotus* 37–38)

2. By preconception they mean a sort of apprehension or correct belief or concept or universal thought stored up, that is, a memory of what has often appeared externally to us, e.g., "That kind of thing is a human"; for as soon as "human" is said, at once the form of it is thought of in accordance with the preconception, the senses leading the way. Thus for every word what primarily underlies it is clear; and we would not have inquired about the object of our inquiry, unless we had first recognized it—e.g., The thing standing over there is a horse or a cow. For we must at some point recognize according to the preconception the shape of horse and cow; nor would we have named anything unless we had first learned its form according to the preconception. Preconceptions, therefore, are clear. The object of belief depends on something prior which is clear, to which we refer when we speak—for example, "How do we know whether this is a human?" (Diogenes Laertius, *Lives of the Philosophers* X, 33)

3. If you throw out any perception absolutely and fail to distinguish on the one hand what is believed with respect to what still awaits evidence and on the other what is already present with respect to perception, the feelings and every focusing of the mind on appearances—if you do this then you will confuse the other perceptions also with foolish belief, so as to throw out any standard. And if you firmly accept in your concepts involving belief everything that still awaits evidence, as well as what has not yet [got] confirmation, you will not escape falsity, so that you will have removed all dispute and all judging of what is correct and what is not. (Epicurus, *Principal Doctrine* 24)

4. If you fight with all perceptions, you will have nothing to refer to in order to judge any of them that you say are wrong. (Epicurus, *Principal Doctrine* 23)

5. Epicurus says that all perception is irrational and cannot take on any memory. For it is not moved by itself, nor, when moved by something else, is it able to add or subtract anything. Nor is there anything that can refute perceptions. One perception cannot refute another similar in its origin, because of their equal weight; one perception cannot refute another dissimilar in its origin, since

they do not judge the same things; nor can reason, since all reason depends on perceptions; nor can one refute another, since we pay heed to them all. (Diogenes Laertius, *Lives of the Philosophers* X, 31)

6. Epicurus says that there are two things correlated with each other, the appearance and the belief, and that of these the appearance (which he calls the evident) is always true. . . . But some are deceived by the difference between the appearances which seem to strike them from the same perceived object—for example an object of sight—given which the object appears to have different colors or different shapes or to be altered in some other way. For they supposed that when appearances differ and conflict like this one must be true and the opposing one false.

But this is naive, and typical of people who do not see the nature of things. To rest our argument on objects of sight, it is not the entire solid body which is seen, but the body's color. Of the color, some is on the actual solid body (as with things seen close up and from a moderate distance) while some is outside the solid body and exists in the spaces in between (as with things seen from a great distance). This color in the spaces in between is altered, and takes on a shape of its own, producing an appearance which is just like the way it truly is.

Just as what we hear is not the sound inside the bronze instrument which is struck, or the sound in the mouth of a person shouting, but the sound which impinges on our perception, and just as nobody says that the person who hears a faint sound from a distance is mishearing just because when he goes nearer he takes in the same sound louder—in the same way I would not say that sight is mistaken because from a distance it sees the tower as small and round, but larger and square from close to. Rather, it is telling the truth, because when the perceived object appears to it small and of such a shape, it really *is* small and of such a shape, as the edges of the images are rubbed off by their passage through the air, and when again it appears big and of another shape, again likewise it *is* big and of another shape. However, it is not the same thing which is both of these. For it is left for distorted belief to think that the object given in appearance close to and the object observed from a distance are one and the same thing. It is the special function of perception to grasp only what is present and moves it, such as color—not to discern that the object here is one thing, and the object over there another.

So for these reasons all perceptions are true. But beliefs are not all true; they allow of a difference. Some of them are true and some false, since they are judgments of ours on our appearances, and we judge some things correctly, and others badly, either by adding something and attaching it to the appearances, or by subtracting something from them—in either case falsifying the irrational perception.

According to Epicurus, then, some beliefs are true and some false. True are those that are confirmed and not disconfirmed by what is evident; false are those that are disconfirmed and not confirmed by what is evident.

Confirmation is an apprehension through what is evident that the thing believed is such as it was believed to be. E.g., when Plato is approaching from a distance, I guess and believe, given the distance, that it is Plato. When he has come nearer, there is further testimony that it is Plato, the distance having been removed, and it is confirmed through what is evident itself.

Nondisconfirmation is when the unclear item which is supposed and believed follows from the apparent. E.g., Epicurus says that void, which is an unclear item, exists, and justifies this through something evident, motion. For if there were no void there ought not to be motion either, since the moving body would have no place into which to shift, everything being full and solid. So that, since motion does exist, what is apparent does not disconfirm the unclear object of belief.

Disconfirmation is something that conflicts with nondisconfirmation, since it is the elimination of the apparent by the unclear item which is supposed. E.g., the Stoics say that void does not exist, making a claim that is unclear. When this is supposed, the apparent (I mean motion) ought to be eliminated along with it; for if void does not exist then necessarily no motion comes about, in the way we have already indicated.

Likewise, nonconfirmation is opposed to confirmation; for it is the impact through something evident that what is believed is not such as it was believed to be. E.g., when someone is approaching from far off we guess, given the distance, that it is Plato, but when the distance is removed we recognize through what is evident that it is not Plato. This is what nonconfirmation is like; what was believed was not confirmed by what is apparent.

Hence confirmation and nondisconfirmation are the criterion of something's being true, while nonconfirmation and disconfirmation are the criterion of something's being false. Of everything the base and foundation is what is evident. (Sextus Empiricus, *Adversus Mathematicos* 7, 206–216)

COMMENTS

Epicurus attacks Aristotle's position in the *Posterior Analytics*. He agrees that new knowledge must come from knowledge we already have; otherwise we get an infinite regress, or else make statements that are "empty" or meaningless. (He takes the option of circular reasoning to be ruled out.) Like Aristotle, he thinks that knowledge must begin with items that are known in a different way from the way in which we know the items we get from them. But he differs from Aristotle in two fundamental ways that mark out his theory as *empiricist*.

First, he rejects Aristotle's notion of logical proof; he regards formal logic as a waste of time and disagrees with the claim that we need to prove items of knowledge from other items. He thinks that we build knowledge out from what is already known, relying as much as we can on experience at every step. If we know something "evident," we proceed by asking what is "confirmed" or "disconfirmed" by the evident. Later Epicureans developed a sophisticated theory of "signs," which is similar in spirit to some modern theories of induction.

Second, Aristotle's items of knowledge that serve as a foundation for the rest are

During the "classical" period, statues of philosophers, such as Plato and Aristotle, do not aim to reveal anything about the nature of their philosophy, but in the Hellenistic period, depictions of philosophers clearly try to indicate important points about the nature of what they held. Here Epicurus is presented in a strikingly different way from Chrysippus, the second founder of Stoicism. Epicurus is shown as an authoritative figure. His tranquil pose and expression indicate that his philosophy is one in which the final end is tranquillity and freedom from disturbance. Chrysippus is shown, by contrast, as somewhat ungainly and scruffy, hunched over in argument with the viewer. He is marking points of debate on his fingers, urging the viewer to see Stoicism as a philosophy of (initially unattractive) debate and argument, rather than the reception of the master's wisdom.

Statue of Epicurus, Capitoline Museum, Rome. Reprinted by permission of the Capitoline Museum—Photograph Archives, Piazza del Campidoglio, 00186, Rome

Statue of Chrysippus, Munich, Museum für Abgüße klassischer Bildwerke.

basic principles of a science, which are highly theoretical and probably the last things to be discovered. Knowledge for Epicurus is attained much more simply, in our experience, and the items basic for it are the product of our encounters with the world as we learn language. The foundations for knowledge are simply the clear grasps we have when we apply a concept entirely on the basis of experience without interference from beliefs, which might be false. Epicurus calls these grasps preconceptions (*prolepsis*).

Epicurus holds that we can, in principle, get a grasp of what we experience directly, unmediated by beliefs, and then subsequently build on it. Hence he holds that "all perception is true." Apparent conflicts in perception are explained by the idea that falsity is always the result of an added belief; the perception itself is always true. Does this thesis reduce the extent of perception too much? How can Epicurus distinguish between ordinary and deviant cases of perception?

The Stoics on Knowledge

1. The Stoics like to start with the theory of appearance and perception, since the criterion by which the truth of things is recognized is in the genus appearance, and since the theory of assent, and that of apprehension and thinking, which precede the rest, cannot be put together without appearance. For the appearance leads the way, and then the articulating thinking which is present brings out in words what the effect is on it of the appearance. (Diogenes Laertius, *Lives of the Philosophers* VII 49)

2. Zeno located that apprehension I mentioned between knowledge and ignorance, and counted it as neither a good nor a bad thing, but said that it alone should be trusted. (Cicero, *Varro* 42)

3. Knowledge is apprehension which is safe and unchangeable by argument. Alternatively: knowledge is a system made up of apprehensions of this kind, such as the reasoned knowledge of particulars which exists in the good person. Or again: a state receptive of appearances, which is unchangeable by argument, which they say consists in a certain tension and capacity. (Arius Didymus, in Stobaeus, *Eclogae* II, 73.14–74.3)

4. You say that nobody but the wise person knows anything—and this Zeno used to demonstrate by a gesture. He would hold out his hand with outstretched fingers, and say, "An appearance is like this"; then he closed the fingers a bit and said, "Assent is like this"; then he squeezed them right together, making a fist, and said that that was apprehension—it was from this example that he even gave the thing its name of *katalepsis*, which had not existed before. But then he brought across his left hand and squeezed the other fist tightly and firmly: knowledge, he would say, was like that, and nobody was in possession of it but the wise person. (Cicero, *Lucullus* 144)

5. [The Stoic-Skeptic debate, from the viewpoint of an Academic Skeptic:]
Doubtless Arcesilaus (the Skeptic) asked Zeno (the Stoic) what would happen if the wise person could not apprehend anything, but also would not, con-

sistently with being a wise person, form a mere belief. Zeno, I suppose, replied that the wise person would not have to have any mere beliefs, since there were things that could be apprehended. What would that be? An appearance, I suppose. What sort of appearance? Zeno then defined it as follows: an appearance impressed and sealed and reproduced from what is the case, in accordance with the way it is. Arcesilaus then asked whether this would still be the same if there were a true appearance just like a false one. Here Zeno was sharp enough to see that, if an appearance from what is the case could be of the same sort as one from what is not, there would be no appearance that could be apprehended. It was correct, Arcesilaus agreed, to add this to the definition, since neither a false appearance nor a true one could be apprehended if a true one could be just like a false one. But he put pressure on the controversial points in order to show that there is no appearance from something true which is such that there could not be an appearance from something false which is exactly like it.

        This is the one debate that has lasted right up to the present time. . . .

There are four theses to prove that there is nothing that can be known, apprehended or grasped, which is what this discussion is all about. The first is that there is such a thing as a false appearance. The second is that this cannot be apprehended. The third is that of appearances between which there is no difference it cannot be the case that some of them are apprehended and others not. The fourth is that there is no true appearance arising from perception which does not have put alongside it another appearance which is no different from it, but which cannot be apprehended. Of these four theses, everyone admits the second and third. The first is rejected by Epicurus, but you Stoics, with whom we are arguing, allow that one too. The whole battle is about the fourth. Suppose someone was looking at one of the Servilii twins, Publius, and thought he was looking at the other, Quintus; what was impressed on him was an appearance that could not be apprehended, because there was no mark by which the true was distinguished from the false. . . . You say that in the nature of things there is no such close resemblance. You show fight, but your opponent is easygoing. By all means let us admit that there isn't such a thing. But there can certainly *appear* to be, and therefore it deceives the senses, and if one such resemblance has slipped in, it has rendered everything subject to doubt. For with the removal of that criterion by which things should be judged, even if the person you are looking at is indeed the person he appears to you to be, still you will not make your judgment by means of that mark that you say you should have—namely, a mark such that there could not be one of the same kind which is false. (Cicero, *Lucullus* 77–78, 83–85)

COMMENTS

The Stoics are, like Epicurus, empiricists. However, they do not share his view that we can isolate an aspect of experience that is prior to any beliefs about it. Rather, they think that every experience, in humans, involves our having a belief of some kind, which can, in principle, be expressed in a statement that we commit ourselves to or "assent" to. Every "appearance"—every event of things appearing to us in any way—thus involves a belief. We can expect that our beliefs will tend to be confused and unclear, but some of the beliefs we acquire in perception can be relied upon. These are beliefs which amount to "apprehension" (a new term coined by the Stoics). An apprehension comes about when you assent to an apprehensive appearance (the terminology here sounds rather absurd to us, but the Stoics were not afraid of absurd coinages).

Apprehension does not amount to knowledge, since the Stoics think, along with Plato and Aristotle, that knowledge demands being able to defend your position with solid argument (represented in Zeno's analogy as one hand enclosing the other). However, apprehension is something that we might well be prepared to call knowledge, since on a particular occasion, if you have an apprehension of something, this is not just a belief: You can't be wrong, and this is something often taken to be a mark of knowledge. We can regard the Stoics as being the first to separate out what we would call different aspects of knowledge: the state when on a particular occasion you can't be wrong and the state when you can support an entire position by argument.

The longest passage represents the Stoics as reacting to criticism by the Academics (members of Plato's Academy in the period when it was a skeptical school). The skeptical Academics took an opponent's views and tried to derive contradictions or absurdities from them. They persistently tried to show that the Stoic account of apprehension allowed for the construction of a counterexample: two cases otherwise indistinguishable except that one is an apprehension and the other is not. The Stoics have to deny that such cases are possible; is this plausible?

This debate raises an important issue. Do the Stoics think that apprehension includes the person's being aware of having a perception that couldn't be wrong? Or do they mean that the person does, in fact, have a perception that couldn't be wrong, though the person may not be aware of this? See how strong you think the objections are to either way of taking it. You will probably find that one makes the Stoic theory look vulnerable, while the other makes the Skeptical objection look weak.

F. Skepticism

In the ancient world, skepticism is not a position about knowledge in particular, but involves a refusal to commit oneself to belief as well. Ancient skepticism, in both its forms, is a wide and deep concern with our grounds for holding any belief.

SKEPTICS

In the ancient world two distinct philosophical schools developed forms of skepticism, both different from what is now often defined as philosophical skepticism.

In Greek, "skeptic" comes from the word meaning "to inquire," and the skeptic is seen as the person who persists in inquiring, rather than resting content with holding a definite philosophical doctrine. Someone who goes on inquiring about an issue without building up a position of her own typically proceeds by arguing against the positions put forward by other people, and so skeptical argument typically is *ad hominem*—that is, aimed at positions held by others, showing that there is something wrong with them in a way that does not depend on having a position of one's own.

Two people serve as figureheads for skeptical philosophers, both of them people who devoted their lives to philosophical argument, without writing anything or developing their own philosophical positions.

One of these is Socrates, who served as a figurehead for many philosophical schools and is best known as the main speaker in Plato's dialogues. In the third century B.C., Arcesilaus, the head of Plato's school, the Academy, changed the school's activity from a concern with positive doctrine to a concern with arguing against the positions of others, representing this change as a return to Socrates' practice. From then until its end in the first century B.C., Plato's Academy was known as a training ground for skeptical argument—destroying the positions of others in a way not depending on having a position of your own. (Opinions differed as to whether the skeptical Academics had positions at all; if they did, they kept them out of the way they argued.) Moreover, the skeptical Academics thought that Plato, not just Socrates, thought that this was the best way of doing philosophy. In support of this belief, they pointed to the passage in the *Theaetetus* in which Plato has Socrates compare himself to a midwife, who brings others to birth without being pregnant herself.

The other "founding figure" of ancient skepticism is Pyrrho of Elis (c. 360–270 B.C.), who is said to have accompanied Alexander the Great on his conquest of north India. Pyrrho was remembered because of verse and prose written by his follower Timon, but he founded no school. Pyrrho served as a figure of the ideal wise person who achieves tranquillity and indifference to matters that leave other people hotly divided. Our evidence provides, at best, indications of the arguments he used to achieve this state.

Before the end of the skeptical Academy, there appears to have been a split within it, and one of its dissatisfied members, Aenesidemus, left to found a more radical trend in skepticism, called Pyrrhonism in honor of the long-dead Pyrrho. Our major representative of Pyrrhonian skepticism is Sextus Empiricus, a physician and philosopher who wrote an outline of skepticism and its arguments, as well as a longer work, some time probably in the second century A.D. Sextus systematically collects arguments for and against given posi-

> tions, offering them to us in the hope that appreciating their force will leave us to suspend judgment on these matters and so, he claims, tranquil.
>
> Both forms of ancient skepticism appeal to an ideal founding figure who wrote nothing but engaged in philosophical argument, and they urge us to do the same.

Theaetetus 148c–151d

PLATO

SOCRATES   And what about knowledge? Do you think it's a small matter to seek it out, as I was saying just now—not one of those tasks which are arduous in every way?

THEAETETUS   Good heavens, no: I think it's really one of the most arduous of tasks.

SOCRATES   Well then, don't lose heart about yourself, and accept that there was something in what Theodorus said. Always do your best in every way; and d as for knowledge, do your best to get hold of an account of what, exactly, it really is.

THEAETETUS   If doing my best can make it happen, Socrates, it will come clear.

SOCRATES   Come on, then—because you've just sketched out the way beauti- 5 fully—try to imitate your answer about the powers. Just as you collected them, many as they are, in one class, try, in the same way, to find one account by which to speak of the many kinds of knowledge.

THEAETETUS   But I assure you, Socrates, I've often set myself to think about it, e when I've heard reports of your questions. But I can't convince myself that I have anything adequate to say on my own account; and I haven't been able to hear anyone else saying the sort of thing you're asking for. On the other 5 hand, I can't stop worrying about it either.

SOCRATES   Yes, you're suffering the pains of labour, Theaetetus; it's because you're not barren but pregnant.

THEAETETUS   I don't know, Socrates; I'm only telling you what I've experienced.

SOCRATES   Do you mean to tell me you haven't heard that I'm the son of a fine 149 strapping midwife called Phaenarete?

THEAETETUS   Yes, I'd heard that.

SOCRATES   And have you also heard that I practise the same art?

THEAETETUS   No, I certainly haven't.   5

SOCRATES   Well, you can be sure I do. But you mustn't give me away to everybody else. You see, I've kept it secret that I have this art. It's one thing peo-

From Plato, *Theaetetus*, translated and edited by J. McDowell (Oxford: Oxford University Press, 1973). Reprinted with the permission of Oxford University Press.

ple don't say about me, because they don't know it. What they do say is that
10   I'm very odd, and that I make people feel difficulties. Have you heard that
       too?

b THEAETETUS   Yes.

SOCRATES   Shall I tell you the reason?

THEAETETUS   Yes, please.

5 SOCRATES   Well, call to mind how things are in general with midwives, and
       you'll find it easier to understand what I mean. No doubt you know that
       none of them attends other women while she's still conceiving and bearing
       children herself. It's those who are past being able to give birth who do it.

THEAETETUS   Certainly.

10 SOCRATES   They say it's Artemis who's responsible for that, because, being
c   childless herself, she's the patron of childbirth. She didn't grant the gift of
       midwifery to barren women, because human nature is too weak to acquire
       skill in matters of which it has no experience. But she did assign it to those
       who are unable to bear children because of their age, in honour of their like-
       ness to herself.

THEAETETUS   That's plausible.

5 SOCRATES   And isn't it both plausible and inevitable that midwives should be
       better than everyone else at recognizing women who are pregnant and
       women who aren't?

THEAETETUS   Certainly.

d SOCRATES   Moreover, by giving drugs and singing incantations, midwives can
       bring on the pains of labour, and make them milder if they want to? And
       they can make women who are having a difficult labour give birth? And if
       they see fit to cause a miscarriage when the embryo is young, they do so?

THEAETETUS   Yes.

5 SOCRATES   And have you also observed this characteristic of theirs: they're the
       cleverest of match-makers, in that there are no gaps in their wisdom as
       regards knowing which sort of woman should consort with which sort of
       man in order to produce the best possible children?

THEAETETUS   No, I didn't know that at all.

10 SOCRATES   Well, you can be sure that they pride themselves more on that than
e   on cutting the umbilical cord. After all, consider the art which has to do with
       the care and harvesting of the fruits of the earth, and the one which has to
       do with knowing which sort of plant and seed should be put into which sort
       of earth. Do you think they're the same or different?

5 THEAETETUS   The same.

SOCRATES   And with a woman, do you think there's one art for this latter sort
       of thing and another for the harvest?

THEAETETUS   No, that isn't plausible.

150 SOCRATES   No. But because of the wrong and unskilled way of bringing a man
       and a woman together which has the name of procuring, midwives, con-
       cerned as they are about their dignity, avoid even match-making, since

they're afraid that because of the latter activity they may fall foul of the former charge. Whereas in fact it's surely real midwives, and they alone, who 5
are the appropriate people to make matches correctly.

THEAETETUS   Evidently.

SOCRATES   Well now, that's the extent of the part midwives play; but it's smaller
than mine. Because it isn't the habit of women to give birth sometimes to imi- b
tations and sometimes to genuine children, with the difference not easy to
detect. If it were, the greatest and most admirable task of midwives would be
to distinguish what's true and what isn't: don't you think so?

THEAETETUS   Yes.   5

SOCRATES   Well, my art of midwifery has, in general, the same characteristics as
theirs, but it's different in that I attend men, not women, and in that I watch
over minds in childbirth, not bodies. And the greatest thing in my art is this: c
to be able to test, by every means, whether it's an imitation and a falsehood
that the young man's intellect is giving birth to, or something genuine and
true. Because I have, in common with midwives, the following characteristic: I'm unproductive of wisdom, and there's truth in the criticism which
many people have made of me before now, to the effect that I question oth- 5
ers but don't make any pronouncements about anything myself, because I
have no wisdom in me. The reason for it is this: God compels me to be a
midwife, but has prevented me from giving birth. So I'm not at all wise d
myself, and there hasn't been any discovery of that kind born to me as the
offspring of my mind. But not so with those who associate with me. At first
some of them seem quite incapable of learning; but, as our association
advances, all those to whom God grants it make progress to an extraordi- 5
nary extent—so it seems not only to them but to everyone else as well. And
it's clear that they do so, not because they have ever learnt anything from
me, but because they have themselves discovered many admirable things in
themselves, and given birth to them.

Still, for the delivery it's God, and I myself, who are responsible. That's e
clear from the following point. There have been many people before now
who didn't know all this, and held themselves responsible while thinking
nothing of me: and, either of their own accord or because they have been
persuaded by others, they have gone away sooner than they should have.
And once they have gone away, they have miscarried the rest of their off- 5
spring because of the bad company they kept; and they have lost the ones
which had been delivered by me, through rearing them badly, having set
more store by falsehoods and imitations than by what's true. In the end they
have come to seem incapable of learning, both to themselves and to everybody else. One of them was Aristeides, the son of Lysimachus, and there 151
have been a good many others. When they come back, begging for association with me and going to extraordinary lengths to get it, the supernatural
sign that comes to me stops me associating with some of them, but with oth- 5
ers it lets me, and those ones make progress again.

There's another experience which the people who associate with me have in common with women in childbirth: they feel pain, and they're full of difficulties, night and day—far more so than the women. And my art can bring on that pain, and end it.

Well then, that's how it is with them. But there are some people, Theaetetus, who somehow don't seem to me to be pregnant. Once I know that they have no need of me, I'm kind enough to arrange matches for them, and, with God's help, I guess quite adequately whose intercourse they'd benefit from. I've given away several of them to Prodicus, and several to other wise and gifted gentlemen.

Now here's why I've told you all this at such length: I suspect you're suffering pain—as indeed you think yourself—because you're pregnant with something inside you. So put yourself in my hands, bearing in mind that I'm a midwife's son and an expert in midwifery myself, and do your best to answer whatever I ask you as well as you can. And if, when I inspect the things you say, I take one of them to be an imitation, not something true, and so ease it out and throw it away, you mustn't be angry with me, as women in their first childbirth would be about their children. There have been many people before now who have been so disposed towards me as to be ready literally to bite me, when I was taking some piece of silliness away from them. They don't realize that I do it out of goodwill; they're a long way from knowing that no god bears ill will to men, and that I don't do anything of that kind out of ill will: it simply isn't right for me to acquiesce in a falsehood and obscure a truth.

COMMENTS

Here Plato has Socrates compare what he does as a philosopher to his mother's activity of helping to bring children to birth. It is remarkable that Plato should represent the central task of philosophy in terms of giving birth, which is what women do. In Plato's time and later, until the Hellenistic schools of Epicurus and the Stoics, philosophy was something only men did—in part, because schools of philosophy originated as informal discussion groups in the men-only gymnasiums. In the *Republic*, Plato himself endorses the idea that, in ideal circumstances, women could be philosophers, and there are stories that two women were members of his school.

Midwives help others give birth without being pregnant themselves. Socrates here describes what he does as though all he does is help others to formulate ideas that they have and to examine them when they have been clearly stated. Because he stresses his own barrenness so much, this passage was a key text in the ancient world for the tradition that Plato's work followed Socrates in being skeptical—that is, in thinking of philosophy as inquiring and examining the ideas of others, rather than producing and defending ideas of one's own. In the twentieth century, Plato has not often been read this way. We tend to read dialogues, such as the *Republic*, and think of Plato as putting forward his own ideas, hoping that we will accept them.

In the ancient world, though, this passage was held to show that Plato had no positive beliefs of his own.

The passage can be taken in a weaker way, though. Just as midwives may once have given birth before helping others, so Socrates (and, by implication, Plato) may have ideas of his own and just keep them separate from examining the ideas of others. This would explain why in some dialogues we find Socrates arguing against the ideas of other people and in others, putting forward positive ideas of his own. Plato's point may be that his own ideas are not to be read as though they were authoritative, something for a pupil to learn; they should be examined by the reader in the way that Socrates examines the ideas of other people.

Outlines of Pyrrhonism I, 1–30, 100–117; III, 1–12
SEXTUS EMPIRICUS

i. The Most Fundamental Difference among Philosophies

| When people are investigating any subject, the likely result is either a discov- 1 ery, or a denial of discovery and a confession of inapprehensibility, or else a continuation of the investigation. | This, no doubt, is why in the case of philosoph- 2 ical investigations, too, some have said that they have discovered the truth, some have asserted that it cannot be apprehended, and others are still investigating.

| Those who are called Dogmatists in the proper sense of the word think 3 that they have discovered the truth—for example, the schools of Aristotle and Epicurus and the Stoics, and some others. The schools of Clitomachus and Carneades, and other Academics, have asserted that things cannot be apprehended. And the Sceptics are still investigating. | Hence the most fundamental 4 kinds of philosophy are reasonably thought to be three: the Dogmatic, the Academic, and the Sceptical. The former two it will be appropriate for others to describe: in the present work we shall discuss in outline the Sceptical persuasion. By way of preface let us say that on none of the matters to be discussed do we affirm that things certainly are just as we say they are: rather, we report descriptively on each item according to how it appears to us at the time.

ii. The Accounts Constitutive of Scepticism

| The Sceptical philosophy contains both a general and a specific account. In the 5 general account we set out the distinctive character of Scepticism, saying what

From *Sextus Empiricus: Outlines of Scepticism*, translated by Julia Annas and Jonathan Barnes (New York: Cambridge University Press, 1994). Reprinted with the permission of Cambridge University Press.

the concept of it is, what are its principles and what its arguments, what is its standard and what its aim, what are the modes of suspension of judgement, how we understand sceptical assertions, and what distinguishes Scepticism
6 from neighbouring philosophies. | The specific account is the one in which we argue against each of the parts of what they call philosophy.

Let us first deal with the general account, beginning our sketch with the names given to the Sceptical persuasion.

iii. The Nomenclature of Scepticism

7 | The Sceptical persuasion, then, is also called Investigative, from its activity in investigating and inquiring; Suspensive, from the feeling that comes about in the inquirer after the investigation; Aporetic, either (as some say) from the fact that it puzzles over and investigates everything, or else from its being at a loss whether to assent or deny; and Pyrrhonian, from the fact that Pyrrho appears to us to have attached himself to Scepticism more systematically and conspicuously than anyone before him.

iv. What Is Scepticism?

8 | Scepticism is an ability to set out oppositions among things which appear and are thought of in any way at all, an ability by which, because of the equipollence in the opposed objects and accounts, we come first to suspension of judgement and afterwards to tranquillity.
9 | We call it an ability not in any fancy sense, but simply in the sense of "to be able to." Things which appear we take in the present context to be objects of perception, which is why we contrast them with objects of thought. "In any way at all" can be taken either with "an ability" (to show that we are to understand the word "ability" in its straightforward sense, as we said), or else with "to set out oppositions among the things which appear and are thought of": we say "in any way at all" because we set up oppositions in a variety of ways—opposing what appears to what appears, what is thought of to what is thought of, and crosswise, so as to include all the oppositions. Or else we take the phrase with "the things which appear and are thought of," to show that we are not to investigate how what appears appears or how what is thought of is thought of, but are simply to take them for granted.
10 | By "opposed accounts" we do not necessarily have in mind affirmation and negation, but take the phrase simply in the sense of "conflicting accounts." By "equipollence" we mean equality with regard to being convincing or unconvincing: none of the conflicting accounts takes precedence over any other as being more convincing. Suspension of judgement is a standstill of the intellect, owing to which we neither reject nor posit anything. Tranquillity is freedom

from disturbance or calmness of soul. We shall suggest in the chapter on the aim
of scepticism how tranquillity accompanies suspension of judgement.

v. The Sceptic

| The Pyrrhonian philosopher has been implicitly defined in our account of the 11
concept of the Sceptical persuasion: a Pyrrhonian is someone who possesses this
ability.

vi. The Principles of Scepticism

| The causal principle of scepticism we say is the hope of becoming tranquil. 12
Men of talent, troubled by the anomaly in things and puzzled as to which of them
they should rather assent to, came to investigate what in things is true and what
false, thinking that by deciding these issues they would become tranquil.

The chief constitutive principle of scepticism is the claim that to every
account an equal account is opposed; for it is from this, we think, that we come
to hold no beliefs.

vii. Do Sceptics Hold Beliefs?

| When we say that Sceptics do not hold beliefs, we do not take "belief" in the 13
sense in which some say, quite generally, that belief is acquiescing in something;
for Sceptics assent to the feelings forced upon them by appearances—for example, they would not say, when heated or chilled, "I think I am not heated (or:
chilled)." Rather, we say that they do not hold beliefs in the sense in which some
say that belief is assent to some unclear object of investigation in the sciences;
for Pyrrhonists do not assent to anything unclear.

| Not even in uttering the Sceptical phrases about unclear matters—for 14
example, "In no way more," or "I determine nothing," or one of the other
phrases which we shall later discuss—do they hold beliefs. For if you hold
beliefs, then you posit as real the things you are said to hold beliefs about; but
Sceptics posit these phrases not as necessarily being real. For they suppose that,
just as the phrase "Everything is false" says that it too, along with everything
else, is false (and similarly for "Nothing is true"), so also "In no way more" says
that it too, along with everything else, is no more so than not so, and hence it
cancels itself along with everything else. And we say the same of the other Scep-
tical phrases. | Thus, if people who hold beliefs posit as real the things they 15
hold beliefs about, while Sceptics utter their own phrases in such a way that
they are implicitly cancelled by themselves, then they cannot be said to hold
beliefs in uttering them.

But the main point is this: in uttering these phrases they say what is apparent to themselves and report their own feelings without holding opinions, affirming nothing about external objects.

viii. Do Sceptics Belong to a School?

16 | We take the same attitude to the question: Do Sceptics belong to a school? If you say that a school involves adherence to a number of beliefs which cohere both with one another and with what is apparent, and if you say that belief is assent to something unclear, then we shall say that Sceptics do not belong to any
17 school. | But if you count as a school a persuasion which, to all appearances, coheres with some account, the account showing how it is possible to live correctly (where "correctly" is taken not only with reference to virtue, but more loosely, and extends to the ability to suspend judgement)—in that case we say that Sceptics do belong to a school. For we coherently follow, to all appearances, an account which shows us a life in conformity with traditional customs and the law and persuasions and our own feelings.

ix. Do Sceptics Study Natural Science?

18 | We say something similar again when investigating the question of whether Sceptics should study natural science. We do not study natural science in order to make assertions with firm conviction about any of the matters on which scientific beliefs are held. But we do touch on natural science in order to be able to oppose to every account an equal account, and for the sake of tranquillity. This is also the spirit in which we approach the logical and ethical parts of what they call philosophy.

x. Do Sceptics Reject What Is Apparent?

19 | Those who say that the Sceptics reject what is apparent have not, I think, listened to what we say. As we said before, we do not overturn anything which leads us, without our willing it, to assent in accordance with a passive appearance—and these things are precisely what is apparent. When we investigate whether existing things are such as they appear, we grant that they appear, and what we investigate is not what is apparent but what is said about what is
20 apparent—and this is different from investigating what is apparent itself. | For example, it appears to us that honey sweetens (we concede this inasmuch as we are sweetened in a perceptual way); but whether (as far as the argument goes) it is actually sweet is something we investigate—and this is not what is apparent but something said about what is apparent.

And if we do propound arguments directly against what is apparent, it is not because we want to reject what is apparent that we set them out, but rather to display the rashness of the Dogmatists; for if reasoning is such a deceiver that it all but snatches even what is apparent from under our very eyes, surely we should keep watch on it in unclear matters, to avoid being led into rashness by following it?

xi. The Standard of Scepticism

| That we attend to what is apparent is clear from what we say about the stan- 21
dard of the Sceptical persuasion. "Standard" has two senses: there are standards adopted to provide conviction about the reality or unreality of something (we shall talk about these standards when we turn to attack them); and there are standards of action, attending to which in everyday life we perform some actions and not others—and it is these standards which are our present subject.
| We say, then, that the standard of the Sceptical persuasion is what is 22
apparent, implicitly meaning by this the appearances; for they depend on pas-sive and unwilled feelings and are not objects of investigation. (Hence no-one, presumably, will raise a controversy over whether an existing thing appears this way or that; rather, they investigate whether it is such as it appears.)
| Thus, attending to what is apparent, we live in accordance with everyday 23
observances, without holding opinions—for we are not able to be utterly inac-tive. These everyday observances seem to be fourfold, and to consist in guid-ance by nature, necessitation by feelings, handing down of laws and customs, and teaching of kinds of expertise. | By nature's guidance we are naturally 24
capable of perceiving and thinking. By the necessitation of feelings, hunger conducts us to food and thirst to drink. By the handing down of customs and laws, we accept, from an everyday point of view, that piety is good and impiety bad. By teaching of kinds of expertise we are not inactive in those which we accept.
And we say all this without holding any opinions.

xii. What Is the Aim of Scepticism?

| It will be apposite to consider next the aim of the Sceptical persuasion. Now 25
an aim is that for the sake of which everything is done or considered, while it is not itself done or considered for the sake of anything else. Or: an aim is the final object of desire. Up to now we say the aim of the Sceptic is tranquillity in mat-ters of opinion and moderation of feeling in matters forced upon us. | For Scep- 26
tics began to do philosophy in order to decide among appearances and to appre-hend which are true and which false, so as to become tranquil; but they came upon equipollent dispute, and being unable to decide this they suspended

judgement. And when they suspended judgement, tranquillity in matters of opinion followed fortuitously.

27 | For those who hold the opinion that things are good or bad by nature are perpetually troubled. When they lack what they believe to be good, they take themselves to be persecuted by natural evils and they pursue what (so they think) is good. And when they have acquired these things, they experience more troubles; for they are elated beyond reason and measure, and in fear of change

28 they do anything so as not to lose what they believe to be good. | But those who make no determination about what is good and bad by nature neither avoid nor pursue anything with intensity; and hence they are tranquil.

A story told of the painter Apelles applies to the Sceptics. They say that he was painting a horse and wanted to represent in his picture the lather on the horse's mouth; but he was so unsuccessful that he gave up, took the sponge on which he had been wiping off the colours from his brush, and flung it at the picture. And when it hit the picture, it produced a representation of the horse's

29 lather. | Now the Sceptics were hoping to acquire tranquillity by deciding the anomalies in what appears and is thought of, and being unable to do this they suspended judgement. But when they suspended judgement, tranquillity followed as it were fortuitously, as a shadow follows a body.

We do not, however, take Sceptics to be undisturbed in every way—we say that they are disturbed by things which are forced upon them; for we agree that

30 at times they shiver and are thirsty and have other feelings of this kind. | But in these cases ordinary people are afflicted by two sets of circumstances: by the feelings themselves, and no less by believing that these circumstances are bad by nature. Sceptics, who shed the additional opinion that each of these things is bad in its nature, come off more moderately even in these cases.

This, then, is why we say that the aim of Sceptics is tranquillity in matters of opinion and moderation of feeling in matters forced upon us. (Some eminent Sceptics have added as a further aim suspension of judgement in investigations.)

The Fourth Mode

100 | In order to end up with suspension of judgement even if we rest the argument on any single sense or actually leave the senses aside, we also adopt the fourth mode of suspension. This is the mode which gets its name from circumstances, where by "circumstances" we mean conditions. It is observed, we say, in natural or unnatural states, in waking or sleeping, depending on age, on moving or being at rest, on hating or loving, on being in need or sated, on being drunk or sober, on anterior conditions, on being confident or fearful, on being in distress or in a state of enjoyment.

101 | For example, objects produce dissimilar impressions on us depending on our being in a natural or an unnatural state, since people who are delirious or divinely possessed believe that they hear spirits, while we do not; and similarly they often say that they grasp an exhalation of storax or frankincense or the

like, and many other things, while we do not perceive them. The same water seems to be boiling when poured on to inflamed places, but to us to be luke-warm. The same cloak appears orange to people with a blood-suffusion in the eye, but not to me; and the same honey appears sweet to me, but bitter to people with jaundice.

| If anyone says that it is the mixing of certain humours which produces 102 inappropriate appearances from existing objects in people who are in an unnatural state, we should say that, since healthy people too have mixed humours, it is possible that these humours make the external existing objects appear different to the healthy, while they are by nature the way they appear to those who are said to be in an unnatural state. | For to grant one lot of humours but not 103 the other the power of changing external objects has an air of fiction. Again, just as healthy people are in a state natural for the healthy but unnatural for the sick, so the sick are in a state unnatural for the healthy but natural for the sick, so that they too are in a state which is, relatively speaking, natural, and they too should be found convincing.

| Different appearances come about depending on sleeping or waking. 104 When we are awake we view things differently from the way we do when we are asleep, and when asleep differently from the way we do when awake; so the existence or non-existence of the objects becomes not absolute but relative—relative to being asleep or awake. It is likely, then, that when asleep we will see things which are unreal in waking life, not unreal once and for all. For they exist in sleep, just as the contents of waking life exist even though they do not exist in sleep.

| Appearances differ depending on age. The same air seems cold to old 105 men but mild to the young, the same colour appears faint to the elderly but intense to the young, and similarly the same sound seems to the former dim but to the latter clearly audible. | Those who differ in age are also affected dissimi- 106 larly depending on their choices and avoidances. Children, for example, are serious about balls and hoops, while the young choose other things, and old men yet others. From this it is concluded that different appearances come about from the same existing objects depending on differences in age too.

| Objects appear dissimilar depending on moving or being at rest. Things 107 which we see as still when we are stationary seem to us to move when we sail past them. | Depending on loving and hating: some people have an excessive 108 revulsion against pork, while others consume it with great pleasure. Menander said:

How foul he appears even in his looks
since he has become like this! What an animal!
Doing no wrong actually makes us beautiful.

And many men who have ugly girl-friends think them most attractive. | 109 Depending on being hungry or sated: the same food seems most pleasant to people who are hungry but unpleasant to the sated. Depending on being drunk or

sober: things which we think shameful when sober do not appear shameful to us
110 when we are drunk. | Depending on anterior conditions: the same wine appears
sour to people who have just eaten dates or figs, but it seems to be sweet to people who have consumed nuts or chickpeas. And the bathhouse vestibule warms
people entering from outside but chills people leaving if they spend any time
111 there. | Depending on being afraid or confident: the same object seems fearful
and dreadful to the coward but not so at all to someone bolder. Depending on
being in distress or in a state of enjoyment: the same objects are annoying to people in distress and pleasant to people who are enjoying themselves.
112 | Since, therefore, there are so many anomalies depending on conditions,
and since at different times people come to be in different conditions, it is no
doubt easy to say what each existing object appears to be like to each person, but
not to say what it *is* like, since the anomalies are in fact undecidable.
     For anyone who decides them is either in some of these conditions or in
absolutely no condition at all. But to say that he is in no condition whatsoever
(i.e. neither healthy nor sick, neither moving nor at rest, of no particular age, and
free from the other conditions) is perfectly incongruous. But if he is in some con-
113 dition as he judges the appearances, he will be a part of the dispute. | And
again, he will not be an unbiassed judge of external existing objects because he
will have been contaminated by the conditions he is in. So a waking person cannot compare the appearances of sleepers with those of people who are awake,
or a healthy person those of the sick with those of the healthy; for we assent to
what is present and affects us in the present rather than to what is not present.
114 | And there is another reason why the anomalies among the appearances
are undecidable. Anyone who prefers one appearance to another and one circumstance to another does so either without making a judgement and without
proof or making a judgement and offering a proof. But he can do so neither
without these (for he will be unconvincing) nor yet with them. For if he judges
115 the appearances he will certainly judge them by means of a standard. | Now he
will say of this standard either that it is true or that it is false. If false, he will be
unconvincing. But if he says that it is true, then he will say that the standard is
true either without proof or with proof. If without proof he will be unconvincing. But if with proof, he will certainly need the proof to be true—otherwise he
will be unconvincing. Then when he says that the proof which he adopts to
make the standard convincing is true, will he do so after judging it or without
116 judging it? | If he has not judged it he will be unconvincing. But if he has judged
it, then clearly he will say that he has judged it by means of a standard—but we
shall demand a proof of that standard, and then a standard for that proof. For a
proof always requires a standard in order to be confirmed, and a standard
always requires a proof in order to be shown to be true. A proof cannot be sound
if there is no standard there already, nor can a standard be true if a proof has not
117 already been made convincing. | In this way standards and proofs fall into the
reciprocal mode, by which both of them are found to be unconvincing: each
waits to be made convincing by the other, and so each is as unconvincing as the
other.

If, then, one cannot prefer one appearance to another either without a proof and a standard or with them, the different appearances which come about depending on different conditions will be undecidable. Hence so far as this mode too goes suspension of judgement about external existing objects is introduced.

Arguments about the Gods

i. The Part Concerned with Physics

Our essay will keep the same character as we approach the part concerned with physics: we shall not argue against each of the things they say on this—rather, we shall try to shake the more general of them in which the others are encompassed. Let us begin with the account of first principles.

ii. Active Principles

Since it is agreed by most thinkers that of the principles some are material and others active, we shall begin our account with the active principles; for they say that these are in fact principles in a stricter sense than the material principles are.

iii. God

| Since the majority have asserted that god is a most active cause, let us first 2 consider god, remarking by way of preface that, following ordinary life without opinions, we say that there are gods and we are pious towards the gods and say that they are provident: it is against the rashness of the Dogmatists that we make the following points.

We ought to form a conception of the substance of the things we conceive, e.g. whether they are bodies or incorporeal. Also of their form—no-one could conceive of a horse unless he had previously learned the form of a horse. Further, what is conceived of ought to be conceived of somewhere.

| Now, since some of the Dogmatists say that god is a body, others that he 3 is incorporeal, some that he is anthropomorphic, others not, some in space, others not—and of those who say that he is in space, some say that he is within the universe, others that he is outside it—how shall we be able to acquire a conception of god if we possess neither an agreed substance for him nor a form nor a place in which he is? Let them first agree and form a consensus that god is of such-and-such a kind; and only then, having given us an outline account, let them require us to form a concept of god. As long as they remain in undecidable dispute, we have no agreement from them as to what we should think. | But, 4 they say, conceive of something indestructible and blessed, and hold that to be god. This is silly: just as, if you do not know Dio, you cannot think of his attributes as attributes of Dio, so, since we do not know the substance of god, we shall not be able to learn and to conceive of his attributes. | Moreover, let them tell 5 us what it is to be blessed—whether it is to act in accordance with virtue and to

provide for the things subordinated to you, or rather to be inactive and take no trouble to yourself and cause none to others. They have had an undecidable dispute about this too, thus making blessedness—and therefore god—inconceivable by us.

6 | Even granting that god is indeed conceivable, it is necessary to suspend judgement about whether gods exist or not, so far as the Dogmatists are concerned. For it is not clear that gods exist: if the gods made an impression on us in themselves, the Dogmatists would be in agreement as to what they are and of what form and where; but the undecidable dispute has made it seem to us that the gods are unclear and in need of proof.

7 | Now anyone who tries to prove that there are gods, does so either by way of something clear or else by way of something unclear. Certainly not by way of something clear; for if what proves that there are gods were clear, then since what is proved is thought of in relation to what proves and is therefore also apprehended together with it, as we have established, it will also be clear that there are gods, this being apprehended together with what proves it, which itself is clear. But it is not clear, as we have suggested; therefore it is not proved

8 by way of something clear. | Nor yet by way of something unclear. For the unclear item which is to prove that there are gods is in need of proof: if it is said to be proved by way of something clear, it will no longer be unclear but clear. Therefore the unclear item which is to prove that there are gods is not proved by way of something clear. Nor yet by way of something unclear: anyone who says this will fall into an infinite regress, since we shall always demand a proof of the unclear item brought forward to prove the point at issue.

9   The existence of gods, therefore, cannot be proved from anything else. | But if it is neither clear in itself nor proved by something else, then it will be inapprehensible whether or not there are gods.

Again, there is this to be said. Anyone who says that there are gods says either that they provide for the things in the universe or that they do not—and that if they provide, then either for all things or for some. But if they provided for all things, there would be nothing bad and evil in the universe; but they say that everything is full of evil. Therefore the gods will not be said to provide for every-

10 thing. | But if they provide for some things, why do they provide for these and not for those? Either they both want to and can provide for all, or they want to but cannot, or they can but do not want to, or they neither want to nor can. If they both wanted to and could, then they would provide for all; but they do not provide for all, for the reason I have just given; therefore it is not the case that they both want to and can provide for all. If they want to but cannot, they are weaker than the cause in virtue of which they cannot provide for the things for which they do not provide; |

11 they do not provide; | but it is contrary to the concept of god that a god should be weaker than anything. If they can provide for all but do not want to, they will be thought to be malign. If they neither want to nor can, they are both malign and weak—and only the impious would say this about the gods.

The gods, therefore, do not provide for the things in the universe. But if they have providence for nothing and have no function and no effect, we will not be able to say how it is apprehended that there are gods, since it is neither apparent in itself nor apprehended by way of any effects. For this reason too, then, it is inapprehensible whether there are gods.

| From this we deduce that those who firmly state that there are gods are 12 no doubt bound to be impious: if they say that the gods provide for everything, they will say that they are a cause of evil; and if they say that they provide for some things or even for none at all, they will be bound to say either that the gods are malign or that they are weak—and anyone who says this is clearly impious.

COMMENTS

Sextus presents skepticism as a general attitude of persisting in inquiring and arguing, rather than putting forward views of one's own, either positive or negative, both of which he calls forms of dogmatism. Skeptics are like everyone else—they inquire to discover truths and achieve knowledge. But the skeptic finds out what the dogmatist ignores: If you inquire rigorously, you find that there is as much to be said against the position you are considering as for it. There is "equipollence"—we are rationally drawn as much against it as for it. When this happens, the result is that we suspend judgment about the matter; we find ourselves unable to commit for or against it. And this, according to Sextus, turns out to give us what we were looking for: the tranquillity and respose from further searching that we thought we would get from finding the truth.

If we suspend judgment, we cease to have a belief on the matter. But we are not left with nothing or a mental blank; we are left with what Sextus calls an appearance, best understood as the content of the original belief, but now held in a way that is detached, rather than committed to its truth. Sextus thinks that far from disabling us for everyday life, this result endorses everyday life and frees us only from pretensions and illusions.

Sextus sometimes talks as though the skeptic lives without any beliefs. Is he committed to this idea or only to the view that the skeptic will be without beliefs when the matters are obscure and lead to inquiry? Sextus defines skepticism as an attitude of inquiry, but says that the skeptic's goal is tranquillity. Would you expect these two to lead to the same result?

Note that Sextus presents skepticism as a full-blown philosophy, with a goal, standard, method, and so on. Is this consistent with the view that a skeptic will suspend beliefs at any rate about controversial matters?

Sextus was writing at a time when skeptical argument had become organized. There are the "Ten Modes" (of which the fourth is given here) that are general skeptical patterns of argument to lead the reader to feel the force of conflicting appearances in a variety of cases. There are also skeptical arguments ordered in a way corresponding to all the parts of philosophy that were regularly taught. The topic of the gods is a part of physics or study of the world. Here Sextus is, as usual, aiming to bring us to equipollence, in which the considerations on each side are equally balanced. To do so, we need arguments against the existence of the gods. Where are the arguments *for* this? Sextus assumes that we don't need *arguments* for this; it is part of everyday life to engage in religious practice and pious ritual. We need argument to shift the authority of everyday assumptions. Is this different from the approach you would expect to a belief in the existence of God or the gods?

SECTION FOUR

METAPHYSICAL QUESTIONS

A. REALITY AND PARADOX

Parmenides *The Way of Truth* fragments 1–8
Zeno of Elea *Arguments against Motion*

B. PLATO'S FORMS: FOR AND AGAINST

Plato *Phaedo* 73c–76e
Plato *Phaedo* 78c–79a
Plato *Symposium* 209e–212a
Plato *Republic* 596a–597e
Plato *Parmenides* 128e–135c
Diogenes of Sinope *Lives of the Philosophers* VI, 53
The Stoics on Plato's Forms
Aristotle *On Forms*

C. CAUSE AND EXPLANATION

Hippocratic Writings *The Sacred Disease* selections
Plato *Phaedo* 96a–101e
Aristotle *On Coming-to-Be and Passing-Away* II, 9
Aristotle *Physics* II, 3, 7–9
Plutarch *Life of Pericles* 6
The Epicureans against Teleology

D. TIME

Aristotle *Physics* IV, 10–11, 14
The Stoics on Time
Augustine *Confessions* XI, selections

A. Reality and Paradox

Ancient Greek philosophy is often marked by awareness of the powers of reason and argument and the fact that these can sometimes be used in a way that arouses deep intellectual disquiet about things we take for granted and think that we understand. Parmenides and Zeno are the first thinkers who face us abruptly with these alarming powers.

PARMENIDES

Parmenides of Elea, in southern Italy (c. 515–c. 450 B.C.), produced a philosophical poem containing an astonishing argument, apparently impossible to refute, but with a conclusion impossible to accept. With Parmenides' *Way of Truth*, philosophy was faced for the first time with deep questions about its own method; the work shows that intellectual argument can lead, apparently unstoppably, to conclusions that are completely at variance with what we believe on the basis of our experience. After Parmenides, philosophers had to cope with the point that reasoning and experience may be in conflict. Parmenides' poem uses the poetic convention that the content of his work was given to him by a goddess; otherwise it lacks poetic qualities. Presumably, in a society where people standardly learned works by heart, rather than relied on written texts, Parmenides chose to write in verse, with its standard meter, so that the audience would remember his difficult argument correctly.

The Way of Truth FRAGMENTS 1–8
PARMENIDES

Fragment 1

The mares that carry me, as far as impulse might reach,
Were taking me, when they brought and placed me upon the much-speak-
ing route

From *Parmenides of Elea*, translated by David Gallop (Toronto: University of Toronto Press, 1984).

Of the goddess, that carries everywhere unscathed the man who knows;
Thereon was I carried, for thereon the much-guided mares were carrying me,
Straining to pull the chariot, and maidens were leading the way.
The axle, glowing in its naves, gave forth the shrill sound of a pipe,
(For it was urged on by two rounded
Wheels at either end), even while maidens, Daughters of the Sun, were has-
          tening
To escort me, after leaving the House of Night for the light,
Having pushed back with their hands the veils from their heads.

There are the gates of the paths of Night and Day,
And a lintel and a threshold of stone surround them,
And the aetherial gates themselves are filled with great doors;
And for these Justice, much-avenging, holds the keys of retribution.
Coaxing her with gentle words, the maidens
Did cunningly persuade her that she should push back the bolted bar for
          them
Swiftly from the gates; and these made of the doors
A gaping gap as they were opened wide,
Swinging in turn in their sockets the brazen posts
Fitted with rivets and pins; straight through them at that point
Did the maidens drive the chariot and mares along the broad way.

And the goddess received me kindly, and took my right hand with her
          hand,
And uttered speech and thus addressed me:
"Youth attended by immortal charioteers,
Who come to our House with mares that carry you,
Welcome; for it is no ill fortune that sent you forth to travel
This route (for it lies far indeed from the beaten track of men),
But right and justice. And it is right that you should learn all things,
Both the steadfast heart of persuasive truth,
And the beliefs of mortals, in which there is no true trust.
But nevertheless you shall learn these things as well, how the things which
          seem
Had to have genuine existence, permeating all things completely."

Fragment 2

Come, I shall tell you, and do you listen and convey the story,
What routes of inquiry alone there are for thinking:
The one—that [it] is, and that [it] cannot not be,
Is the path of Persuasion (for it attends upon truth);
The other—that [it] is not and that [it] needs must not be,
That I point out to you to be a path wholly unlearnable,

For you could not know what-is-not (for that is not feasible),
Nor could you point it out.

Fragment 3

. . . because the same thing is there for thinking and for being.

Fragment 4

Look upon things which, though far off, are yet firmly present to the mind;
For you shall not cut off what-is from holding fast to what-is,
For it neither disperses itself in every way everywhere in order,
Nor gathers itself together.

Fragment 5

And it is all one to me
Where I am to begin; for I shall return there again.

Fragment 6

It must be that what is there for speaking and thinking of *is;* for [it] is there
    to be,
Whereas nothing is not; that is what I bid you consider,
For <I restrain> you from that first route of inquiry,
And then also from this one, on which mortals knowing nothing
Wander, two-headed; for helplessness in their
Breasts guides their distracted mind; and they are carried
Deaf and blind alike, dazed, uncritical tribes,
By whom being and not-being have been thought both the same
And not the same; and the path of all is backward-turning.

Fragment 7

For never shall this prevail, that things that are not *are;*
But do you restrain your thought from this route of inquiry,
Nor let habit force you, along this route of much-experience,
To ply an aimless eye and ringing ear
And tongue; but judge by reasoning the very contentious disproof
That has been uttered by me.

Fragment 8

A single story of a route still·
Is left: that [*it*] *is;* on this [route] there are signs
Very numerous: that what-is is ungenerated and imperishable;
Whole, single-limbed, steadfast, and complete;
Nor was [it] once, nor will [it] be, since [it] is, now, all together,
One, continuous; for what coming-to-be of it will you seek?
In what way, whence, did [it] grow? Neither from what-is-not shall I allow
You to say or think; for it is not to be said or thought
That [*it*] *is not.* And what need could have impelled it to grow
Later or sooner, if it began from nothing?
Thus [it] must either be completely or not at all.

Nor will the strength of trust ever allow anything to come-to-be from what-is
Besides it; therefore neither [its] coming-to-be
Nor [its] perishing has Justice allowed, relaxing her shackles,
But she holds [it] fast; the decision about these matters depends on this:
Is [*it*] *or is* [*it*] *not?* but it has been decided, as is necessary,
To let go the one as unthinkable, unnameable (for it is no true
Route), but to allow the other, so that it is, and is true.
And how could what-is be in the future; and how could [it] come-to-be?
For if [it] came-to-be, [it] is not, nor [is it] if at some time [it] is going to be.
Thus, coming-to-be is extinguished and perishing not to be heard of.
Nor is [it] divisible, since [it] all alike *is;*
Nor is [it] somewhat more here, which would keep it from holding together,
Nor is [it] somewhat less, but [it] is all full of what-is.
Therefore [it] is all continuous; for what-is is in contact with what-is.
Moreover, changeless in the limits of great chains
[It] is un-beginning and unceasing, since coming-to-be and perishing
Have been driven far off, and true trust has thrust them out.
Remaining the same and in the same, [it] lies by itself
And remains thus firmly in place; for strong Necessity
Holds [it] fast in the chains of a limit, which fences it about.
Wherefore it is not right for what-is to be incomplete;
For [it] is not lacking; but if [it] were, [it] would lack everything.

The same thing is for thinking and [is] that there is thought;
For not without what-is, on which [it] depends, having been declared,
Will you find thinking; for nothing else <either> is or will be
Besides what-is, since it was just this that Fate did shackle
To be whole and changeless; wherefore it has been named all things
That mortals have established, trusting them to be true,
To come-to-be and to perish, to be and not to be,
And to shift place and to exchange bright colour.

Since, then, there is a furthest limit, [it] is completed,
From every direction like the bulk of a well-rounded sphere,
Everywhere from the centre equally matched; for [it] must not be any larger
Or any smaller here or there;
For neither is there what-is-not, which could stop it from reaching
[Its] like; nor is there a way in which what-is could be
More here and less there, since [it] all inviolably *is*;
For equal to itself from every direction, [it] lies uniformly within limits.
Here I stop my trustworthy speech to you and thought
About truth; from here onwards learn mortal beliefs,
Listening to the deceitful ordering of my words;
For they established two forms in their minds for naming,
Of which it is not right to name one—wherein they have gone astray—
And they distinguished opposites in body and established signs
Apart from one another: here, on the one hand, aetherial fire of flame,
Which is gentle, very light, everywhere the same as itself,
But not the same as the other; but on the other hand, that one too by itself
In contrast, dark night, a dense and heavy body;
All this arrangement I proclaim to you as plausible;
Thus no opinion of mortals shall ever overtake you.

COMMENTS

Parmenides' *Way of Truth* presses the consequences of thinking rigorously about our thought and its conditions and reaches strange metaphysical conclusions by forcing us to think through arguments. But notice that it is presented as revealed to Parmenides by a goddess. Divine revelation is seen as being the same thing as rigorously using your own reason, not as something in competition with it. When you think really hard about something, the insight that results is seen in terms of a gift from the gods.

Parmenides' actual argument makes use of a notion of *being* which is unfamiliar to us, in part because the Greek verb *to be* does not correspond exactly with ours. The argument begins from considering two options that are available for thinking or knowing: (1) that it is and that it is not possible for it not to be and (2) that it is not and that it is necessary for it not to be. But option 2 cannot be known or thought of—it is unavailable for thought. So we have to take option 1—as long, that is, as we are thinking rigorously and are not just following "mortal opinions" that we pick up from those around us without thinking them through. Here we find that everyday beliefs are misleading, the result of not thinking about what we are saying, so that we should not be surprised to find that rigorous philosophical thinking conflicts with ordinary beliefs.

What, though, is the option we should take? What is the subject, "it"? What is it for it to be and for it not to be possible for it not to be? Interpretation of Parmenides is disputed. One plausible account is that Parmenides is talking of any subject of speech or thought. If we can talk or think of something, it must *be*, or it would not be there to be talked or thought about. Parmenides follows through the thought that this excludes all sorts of things that we normally assume to be possible—its changing, moving, or varying in a number of ways. The problem is to see what notion of *being* is at work here. Is Parmenides saying that if we talk or think of something, it must exist? Or that it must be what we say or think it is? Or both of these? Parmenides is aware that we normally say that things *are* and regard this as compatible with things changing or varying. What notion of *being* is it that excludes this?

ZENO OF ELEA

Zeno of Elea (c.490–c.420 B.C.) was a pupil of Parmenides. According to Plato, he replied to critics of Parmenides, who objected to the completely counterintuitive conclusions of his poem, by showing that commonsense things that they took for granted led, in fact, to conclusions that were just as absurd and repugnant to common sense. He wrote a book with a large number of arguments; among the few that survive, the most famous are his arguments against motion, preserved by Aristotle. Obviously, motion exists, in that things, including ourselves, move. Zeno tries to show that the concept of motion is, in fact, incoherent—in which case, we are obviously in some kind of intellectual problem.

Unintellectual people can always dismiss Zeno's arguments as frivolous, given that there is no way that we can accept their conclusions. There are ancient stories about people who "refuted" Zeno's arguments against motion by getting up and walking out! The power of these arguments lies in the way that they force us to argue to render our commonsense views intellectually defensible, and Zeno was later seen as the founder of a concern with argument that would eventually lead to Aristotle's discovery of logic.

Arguments against Motion
Zeno of Elea

5   Zeno's reasoning, however, is fallacious, when he says that if everything when it occupies an equal space is at rest, and if that which is in locomotion is always in a now, the flying arrow is therefore motionless. This is false; for time is not composed of indivisible nows any more than any other magnitude is composed of indivisibles.

10   Zeno's arguments about motion, which cause so much trouble to those who try to answer them, are four in number. The first asserts the non-existence of motion on the ground that that which is in locomotion must arrive at the halfway stage before it arrives at the goal. This we have discussed above.

The second is the so-called Achilles, and it amounts to this, that in a race the quickest runner can never overtake the slowest, since the pursuer must first 15 reach the point whence the pursued started, so that the slower must always hold a lead. This argument is the same in principle as that which depends on bisection, though it differs from it in that the spaces with which we have successively to deal are not divided into halves. The result of the argument is that the slower 20 is not overtaken; but it proceeds along the same lines as the bisection-argument (for in both a division of the space in a certain way leads to the result that the goal is not reached, though the Achilles goes further in that it affirms that even the runner most famed for his speed must fail in his pursuit of the slowest), so 25 that the solution too must be the same. And the claim that that which holds a lead is never overtaken is false: it is not overtaken while it holds a lead; but it is overtaken nevertheless if it is granted that it traverses the finite distance. These then are two of his arguments.

The third is that already given above, to the effect that the flying arrow is 30 at rest, which result follows from the assumption that time is composed of moments: if this assumption is not granted, the conclusion will not follow.

The fourth argument is that concerning equal bodies which move alongside equal bodies in the stadium from opposite directions—the ones from the end of the stadium, the others from the middle—at equal speeds, in which he thinks it follows that half the time is equal to its double. The fallacy consists in requiring 240ª1 that a body travelling at an equal speed travels for an equal time past a moving body and a body of the same size at rest. That is false. E.g. let the stationary equal bodies be AA; let BB be those starting from the middle of the A's (equal in 5 number and in magnitude to them); and let CC be those starting from the end (equal in number and magnitude to them, and equal in speed to the B's). Now it follows that the first B and the first C are at the end at the same time, as they are moving past one another. And it follows that the C has passed all the A's and 10 the B half; so that the time is half, for each of the two is alongside each for an equal time. And at the same time it follows that the first B has passed all the C's. For at the same time the first B and the first C will be at opposite ends, being an equal time alongside each of the B's as alongside each of the A's, as he says, 15 because both are an equal time alongside the A's. That is the argument, and it rests on the stated falsity.

COMMENTS

Zeno's arguments against motion were preserved for us by Aristotle, who has his own views as to what they are about. There is continued dispute among scholars as to Zeno's own intentions. It is plausible, however, that all Zeno's arguments are aimed at showing that everyday beliefs, which presuppose that there is change and movement, can be shown to lead to intellectual difficulty and paradox and that the point of this was to provide an indirect defence of Parmenides, who had demonstrated that rigorous thinking led to conclusions at odds with everyday beliefs. Zeno's arguments thus show that we are not entitled to reject arguments like Parmenides' on the basis of everyday beliefs, which are in trouble, too. If we refuse to accept this view, we have to show what is wrong with the argument.

The "dichotomy" or stadium and the "Achilles" arguments are, as Aristotle points out, variants of the same idea. The stadium argument shows that the runner can never start, and the Achilles argument shows that he can never finish. (Later the argument was made more colorful by having Achilles unable to overtake a tortoise.) In both cases, the argument rests on the point that the runner has to complete an infinite series of moves in a finite time. Aristotle thinks that this rests on a mistake about infinity. Where do you think the mistake is?

The Flying Arrow that is shown to be stationary rests on the idea that since the arrow is moving over a period and at any point in that period we can say that *now* the arrow is not in motion, the arrow cannot be moving during the period; hence it doesn't move. Aristotle locates the mistake in thinking that the period is made up of nows, that is, of the instants at which we say that *now* the arrow is not moving. Aristotle develops this idea in his own account of time (in section 4.D). But even if we don't accept Aristotle's own account of time, there must be something wrong with the argument; what is it?

The Moving Rows argument is controversial, and the text is problematic. A generally accepted interpretation is that row A moves past both row B, which is stationary, and row C, which is moving in the other direction; hence the first A passes one B, but two Cs. So it will have taken a period and half that period. Why is this problematic? Is Zeno assuming that it always takes the same amount of time for one block to pass another block? Why? One tradition of interpretation takes it that the argument makes sense if we suppose that the As, Bs, and Cs are supposed to be *atomic* units of some kind and that the argument indicates problems with the idea of atomic movement—that is, movement in an atomic period. Although this would make sense of the argument, it would also alter its status, since a belief in atoms and atomic movement is scarcely an ordinary belief that Zeno is targeting as having paradoxical implications. It is a pity that we do not know more about the original context of these arguments.

B. Plato's Forms: For and Against

Plato is probably the best-known ancient philosopher, and he is most famous for his "Theory of Forms," which has been celebrated and ridiculed since antiquity as the very model of a bold metaphysical theory. But what are Forms? Once we look at Plato's own works, we can see that this is not an easy question to answer. Moreover, not only were Forms subject to criticism in the ancient world, one of the most powerful critics was Plato himself.

PLATO

Plato's works are all in the form of dialogues, in which he does not appear. Plato takes advantage of the way in which this makes ideas more accessible, but there is a further, philosophical, reason. He always avoids writing from authority in his own person, since it is important to him that the reader think about ideas for herself rather than accept them on the writer's authority. Only if you think about an idea for yourself does it become yours, something you understand. Taking in ideas from someone else passively does not lead to understanding.

In most of his dialogues, the main figure is Socrates, who is, for Plato, the figure of the ideal philosopher. Many of the shorter and more attractive dialogues show Socrates in conversation with someone who confidently puts forward a big idea or a bold claim, usually about his own expertise. Socrates undermines this claim by asking questions that show that the person does not understand what he confidently makes claims about, since he cannot adequately defend it, and problems and inconsistencies are shown up, to which no answer is offered. However, in some dialogues, Socrates has a different role, that of putting forward positive ideas for discussion, sometimes, as in the *Republic,* at length. And in the *Parmenides,* it is a young Socrates who confidently puts forward a big idea, that of Forms, which figure in many dialogues, and is shown, by his inability to sustain questioning about it, not to understand it. Here, Socrates is on the receiving end of what he is normally shown doing to others.

The role of the questioner is given to Parmenides, presumably as a mark of Plato's respect for the older philosopher. In some other dialogues, Socrates merely introduces the main speaker, a Visitor from Elea, Parmenides' hometown. Sometimes Plato feels that it is inappropriate for Socrates to be the main speaker, but he never gives up the dialogue form, which leaves the author detached from the claims that the speakers make.

Phaedo 73c–76e

PLATO

"I'll put it this way. We agree, I take it, that if anyone is to be reminded of a thing,   c
he must have known that thing at some time previously."

"Certainly."

"Then do we also agree on this point: that whenever knowledge comes to be present in this sort of way, it is recollection? I mean in some such way as this: 5

From Plato, *Phaedo,* translated by David Gallop (Oxford: Oxford University Press, 1993). Reprinted with the permission of Oxford University Press.

if someone, on seeing a thing, or hearing it, or getting any other sense-perception of it, not only recognizes that thing, but also thinks of something else, which
is the object not of the same knowledge but of another, don't we then rightly say
b that he's been 'reminded' of the object of which he has got the thought?"

"What do you mean?"

"Take the following examples: knowledge of a person, surely, is other than
that of a lyre?"

"Of course."

5   "Well now, you know what happens to lovers, whenever they see a lyre or
cloak or anything else their loves are accustomed to use: they recognize the lyre,
and they get in their mind, don't they, the form of the boy whose lyre it is? And
10 that is recollection. Likewise, someone seeing Simmias is often reminded of
Cebes and there'd surely be countless other such cases."

"Countless indeed!" said Simmias.

e   "Then is something of that sort a kind of recollection? More especially,
though, whenever it happens to someone in connection with things he's since
forgotten, through lapse of time or inattention?"

"Certainly."

5   "Again now, is it possible, on seeing a horse depicted or a lyre depicted, to
be reminded of a person; and on seeing Simmias depicted, to be reminded of
Cebes?"

"Certainly."

10   "And also, on seeing Simmias depicted, to be reminded of Simmias himself?"

74   "Yes, that's possible."

"In all those cases, then, doesn't it turn out that there is recollection from
similar things, but also from dissimilar things?"

"It does."

5   "But whenever one is reminded of something from similar things, mustn't
one experience something further: mustn't one think whether or not the thing is
lacking at all, in its similarity, in relation to what one is reminded of?"

"One must."

10   "Then consider whether this is the case. We say, don't we, that there is something that is equal—I don't mean a log to a log, or a stone to a stone, or anything
else of that sort, but some further thing beyond all those, the equal itself: are we
to say that it is a reality or not?"

b   "We most certainly are to say that it is," said Simmias; "unquestionably!"

"And do we know it, know what it is?"

"Certainly."

"Where did we get the knowledge of it? Wasn't it from the things we were
5 just mentioning: on seeing logs or stones or other equal things, wasn't it from
those that we thought of that object, it being different from them? Or doesn't it
seem different to you? Look at it this way: aren't equal stones and logs, the very
same ones, sometimes evidently equal to one, but not to another."

"Yes, certainly."   10

"But now, were the equals themselves ever, in your view, evidently unequal, c
or equality inequality?"

"Never yet, Socrates."

"Then those equals, and the equal itself, are not the same."   5

"By no means, Socrates, in my view."

"But still, it is from those equals, different as they are from that equal, that
you have thought of and got the knowledge of it?"

"That's perfectly true."   10

"It being either similar to them or dissimilar?"

"Certainly."

"Anyway, it makes no difference; so long as on seeing one thing, one does, d
from that sight, think of another, whether it be similar or dissimilar, that must
be recollection."

"Certainly."

"Well now, with regard to the instances in the logs, and, in general, the 5
equals we mentioned just now, are we affected in some way as this: do they
seem to us to be equal in the same way as is the thing itself, that which it is? Do
they fall short of it at all in being like the equal, or not?"

"Very far short of it."

"Then whenever anyone, on seeing a thing, thinks to himself, 'this thing 10
that I now see seeks to be like another reality, but falls short, and cannot be like e
that object: it is inferior,' do we agree that the man who thinks that must previously have known the object he says it resembles but falls short of?"

"He must."   5

"Now then, have we ourselves been affected in just that way, or not, with
regard to the equals and the equal itself?"

"Indeed we have."

"Then we must previously have known the equal, before that time when we
first, on seeing the equals, thought that all of them were striving to be like the 75
equal but fell short of it."

"That is so."

"Yet we also agree on this: we haven't derived the thought of it, nor could 5
we do so, from anywhere but seeing or touching or some other of the senses—
I'm counting all those as the same."

"Yes, they are the same, Socrates, for what the argument seeks to show."   10

"But of course it is from one's sense-perceptions that one must think that all b
sensible items are striving for that thing which equal is, yet are inferior to it; or
how shall we put it?"

"Like that."

"Then it must, surely, have been before we began to see and hear and use 5
the other senses that we got knowledge of the equal itself, of what it is, if we
were going to refer the equals from our sense-perceptions to it, supposing that
all things are doing their best to be like it, but are inferior to it."

"That must follow from what's been said before, Socrates."

10   "Now we were seeing and hearing, and were possessed of our other senses, weren't we, just as soon as we were born?"

"Certainly."

c   "But we must, we're saying, have got our knowledge of the equal before those?"

"Yes."

5   "Then it seems that we must have got it before we were born."

"It seems so."

"Now if, having got it before birth, we were born in possession of it, did we
10 know, both before birth and as soon as we were born, not only the equal, the larger and the smaller, but everything of that sort? Because our present argu-
d   ment concerns the beautiful itself, and the good itself, and just and holy, no less than the equal; in fact, as I say, it concerns everything on which we set this seal,
5   'that which it is,' in the questions we ask and in the answers we give. And so we must have got pieces of knowledge of all those things before birth."

"That is so."

"Moreover, if having got them, we did not on each occasion forget them, we must always be born knowing, and must continue to know throughout life:
10 because this is knowing—to possess knowledge one has got of something, and not to have lost it; or isn't loss of knowledge what we mean by 'forgetting,' Sim-mias?"

e   "Certainly it is, Socrates."

"But on the other hand, I suppose that if, having got them before birth, we lost them on being born, and later on, using the senses about the things in ques-tion, we regain those pieces of knowledge that we possessed at some former
5   time, in that case wouldn't what we call 'learning' be the regaining of knowl-edge belonging to us? And in saying that that was being reminded, shouldn't we be speaking correctly?"

"Certainly."

76   "Yes, because it did seem possible, on sensing an object, whether by seeing or hearing or getting some other sense-perception of it, to think from that of some other thing one had forgotten—either a thing to which the object, though dissimilar to it, was related, or else something to which it was similar; so, as I
5   say, one of two things is true: either all of us were born knowing those objects, and we know them throughout life; or those we speak of as 'learning' are sim-ply being reminded later on, and learning would be recollection."

"That's quite true, Socrates."

"Then which do you choose, Simmias? That we are born knowing, or that
b   we are later reminded of the things we'd gained knowledge of before?"

"At the moment, Socrates, I can't make a choice."

"Well, can you make one on the following point, and what do you think
5   about it? If a man knows things, can he give an account of what he knows or not?"

"Of course he can, Socrates."

"And do you think everyone can give an account of those objects we were discussing just now?"

"I only wish they could," said Simmias, "but I'm afraid that, on the contrary, 10 this time tomorrow there may no longer be any human being who can do so properly."

"You don't then, Simmias, think that everyone knows those objects?" c

"By no means."

"Are they, then, reminded of what they once learned?"

"They must be." 5

"When did our souls get the knowledge of those objects? Not, at any rate, since we were born as human beings."

"Indeed not."

"Earlier, then."

"Yes." 10

"Then our souls did exist earlier, Simmias, before entering human form, apart from bodies; and they possessed wisdom."

"Unless maybe, Socrates, we get those pieces of knowledge at the very moment of birth; that time still remains." 15

"Very well, my friend; but then at what other time, may I ask, do we lose d them? We aren't born with them, as we agreed just now. Do we then lose them at the very time at which we get them? Or have you any other time to suggest?"

"None at all, Socrates. I didn't realize I was talking nonsense." 5

"Then is our position as follows, Simmias? If the objects we're always harping on exist, a beautiful, and a good, and all such reality, and if we refer all the things from our sense-perceptions to that reality, finding again what was formerly ours and if we compare these things with that, then just as surely as those objects exist, so also must our souls exist before we are born. On the other hand, if they don't exist, this argument will have gone for nothing. Is this the position? Is it equally necessary that those objects exist, and that our souls existed before birth, and if the former don't exist, then neither did the latter?"

Phaedo 78c–79a

PLATO

"Then is it true that what has been put together and is naturally composite is c liable to undergo this, to break up at the point at which it was put together; whereas if there be anything non-composite, it alone is liable, if anything is, to escape this?"

From Plato, *Phaedo*, translated by David Gallop (Oxford: Oxford University Press, 1993). Reprinted with the permission of Oxford University Press.

5   "That's what I think," said Cebes.

"Well now, aren't the things that are constant and unvarying most likely to be the non-composite, whereas things that vary and are never constant are likely to be composite?"

"I think so."

10   "Then let's go back to those entities to which we turned in our earlier argu-
d   ment. Is the reality itself, whose being we give an account of in asking and answering questions, unvarying and constant, or does it vary? Does the equal
5   itself, the beautiful itself, that which each thing itself is, the real, ever admit of any change whatever? Or does that which each of them is, being uniform alone by itself, remain unvarying and constant, and never admit of any kind of alter- ation in any way or respect whatever?"

"It must be unvarying and constant, Socrates," said Cebes.

10   "But what about the many beautiful things, such as human beings or horses
e   or cloaks or anything else at all of that kind? Or equals, or all things that bear the same name as those objects? Are they constant, or are they just the opposite of those others, and practically never constant at all, either in relation to them- selves or to one another?"

5   "That is their condition," said Cebes; "they are never unvarying."

79   "Now these things you could actually touch and see and sense with the other senses, couldn't you, whereas those that are constant you could lay hold of only by reasoning of the intellect; aren't such things, rather, invisible and not seen?"

5   "What you say is perfectly true."

"Then would you like us to posit two kinds of beings, the one kind seen, the other invisible?"

"Let's posit them."

10   "And the invisible is always constant, whereas the seen is never constant?"

"Let's posit that too."

b   "Well, but we ourselves are part body and part soul, aren't we?"

"We are."

"Then to which kind do we say that the body will be more similar and more
5   akin?"

"That's clear to anyone: obviously to the seen."

"And what about the soul? Is it seen or invisible?"

"It's not seen by human beings, at any rate, Socrates."

"But we meant, surely, things seen and not seen with reference to human
10   nature; or do you think we meant any other?"

"We meant human nature."

"What do we say about soul, then? Is it seen or unseen?"

"It's not seen."

"Then it's invisible?"

15   "Yes."

"Then soul is more similar than body to the invisible, whereas body is more similar to that which is seen."

"That must be so, Socrates."   c

"Now weren't we saying a while ago that whenever the soul uses the body
as a means to study anything, either by seeing or hearing or any other sense—
because to use the body as a means is to study a thing through sense-percep- 5
tion—then it is dragged by the body towards objects that are never constant;
and it wanders about itself, and is confused and dizzy, as if drunk, by virtue of
contact with things of a similar kind?"

"Certainly."

"Whereas whenever it studies alone by itself, it departs yonder towards that d
which is pure and always existent and immortal and unvarying, and by virtue
of its kinship with it, enters always into its company, whenever it has come to
be alone by itself, and whenever it may do so; then it has ceased from its wan- 5
dering and, when it is about those objects, it is always constant and unvarying,
because of its contact with things of a similar kind; and this condition of it is
called 'wisdom,' is it not?"

"That's very well said and perfectly true, Socrates."

"Once again, then, in the light of our earlier and present arguments, to
which kind do you think that soul is more similar and more akin?"   e

"Everyone, I think, Socrates, even the slowest learner, following this line of
inquiry, would agree that soul is totally and altogether more similar to what is 5
unvarying than to what is not."

"And what about the body?"

"That is more like the latter."

Symposium 209e–212a
PLATO

"'Now, it's not impossible, Socrates, that you too could be initiated into the
ways of love I've spoken of so far. But I don't know whether you're ready for the 210ª
final grade of Watcher, which is where even the mysteries I've spoken of lead if
you go about them properly. All I can do,' she said, 'is tell you about them,
which I'm perfectly willing to do; you must try to follow as best you can.

"'The proper way to go about this business,' she said, 'is for someone to
start as a young man by focusing on physical beauty and initially—this depends
on whether his guide is giving him proper guidance—to love just one person's
body and to give birth in that medium to beautiful reasoning. He should realize
next that the beauty of any one body hardly differs from that of any other body, b
and that if it's physical beauty he's after, it's very foolish of him not to regard the
beauty of all bodies as absolutely identical. Once he's realized this and so
become capable of loving every single beautiful body in the world, his obsession

From Plato, *Symposium*, translated by Robin Waterfield (Oxford: Oxford University
Press, 1998). Reprinted with the permission of Oxford University Press.

with just one body grows less intense and strikes him as ridiculous and petty. The next stage is for him to value mental beauty so much more than physical beauty that even if someone is almost entirely lacking the bloom of youth, but still has an attractive mind, that's enough to kindle his love and affection, and

c that's all he needs to give birth to and enquire after the kinds of reasoning which help young men's moral progress. And this in turn leaves him no choice but to look at what makes people's activities and institutions attractive and to see that here too any form of beauty is much the same as any other, so that he comes to regard physical beauty as unimportant. Then, after activities, he must press on towards the things people know, until he can see the beauty there too. Now he

d has beauty before his eyes in abundance, no longer a single instance of it; now the slavish love of isolated cases of youthful beauty or human beauty of any kind is a thing of the past, as is his love of some single activity. No longer a paltry and small-minded slave, he faces instead the vast sea of beauty, and in gazing upon it his boundless love of knowledge becomes the medium in which he gives birth to plenty of beautiful, expansive reasoning and thinking, until he gains enough energy and bulk there to catch sight of a unique kind of knowledge whose natural object is the kind of beauty I will now describe.

e   "'Try as hard as you can to pay attention now,' she said, 'because anyone who has been guided and trained in the ways of love up to this point, who has viewed things of beauty in the proper order and manner will now approach the culmination of love's ways and will suddenly catch sight of something of unbelievable beauty—something, Socrates, which in fact gives meaning to all his pre-

211a vious efforts. What he'll see is, in the first place, eternal; it doesn't come to be or cease to be, and it doesn't increase or diminish. In the second place, it isn't attractive in one respect and repulsive in another, or attractive at one time but not at another, or attractive in one setting but repulsive in another, or attractive here and repulsive elsewhere, depending on how people find it. Then again, he won't perceive beauty as a face or hands or any other physical feature, or as a piece of reasoning or knowledge, and he won't perceive it as being anywhere else either—in something like a creature or the earth or the heavens. No, he'll

b perceive it in itself and by itself, constant and eternal, and he'll see that every other beautiful object somehow partakes of it, but in such a way that their coming to be and ceasing to be don't increase or diminish it at all, and it remains entirely unaffected

        "'So the right kind of love for a boy can help you ascend from the things of this world until you begin to catch sight of *that* beauty, and then you're almost

c within striking distance of the goal. The proper way to go about or be guided through the ways of love is to start with beautiful things in this world and always make the beauty I've been talking about the reason for your ascent. You should use the things of this world as rungs in a ladder. You start by loving one attractive body and step up to two; from there you move on to physical beauty in general, from there to the beauty of people's activities, from there to the beauty of intellectual endeavours, and from there you ascend to that final intellectual endeavour, which is no more and no less than the study of *that* beauty, so that you finally recognize true beauty.

"'What else could make life worth living, my dear Socrates,' the woman d
from Mantinea said, 'than seeing true beauty? If you ever do catch sight of it,
gold and clothing and good-looking boys and youths will pale into insignifi-
cance beside it. At the moment, however, you get so excited by seeing an attractive boy that you want to keep him in your sight and by your side for ever, and
you'd be ready—you're far from being the only one, of course—to go without
food and drink, if that were possible, and to try to survive only on the sight and
presence of your beloved. How do you think someone would react, then, to the
sight of beauty itself, in its perfect, immaculate purity—not beauty tainted by e
human flesh and colouring and all that mortal rubbish, but absolute beauty,
divine and constant? Do you think someone with his gaze fixed there has a miserable life? Is that what you think about someone who uses the appropriate fac- 212a
ulty to see beauty and enjoy its presence? I mean, don't you appreciate that
there's no other medium in which someone who uses the appropriate faculty to
see beauty can give birth to true goodness instead of phantom goodness,
because it is truth rather than illusion whose company he is in? And don't you
realize that the gods smile on a person who bears and nurtures true goodness
and that, to the extent that any human being does, it is he who has the potential
for immortality?'

"So there you are, Phaedrus—not forgetting the rest of you. That's what b
Diotima told me, and I believe her."

Republic 596d–597e
PLATO

"All right. Shall we get the enquiry going by drawing on familiar ideas? Our
usual position is, as you know, that any given plurality of things which have a
single name constitutes a single specific type. Is that clear to you?"

"Yes."

"So now let's take any plurality you want. Would it be all right with you if
we said that there were, for instance, lots of beds and tables?"   b

"Of course."

"But these items of furniture comprise only two types—the type of bed and
the type of table."

"Yes."

"Now, we also invariably claim that the manufacture of either of these items
of furniture involves the craftsman looking to the type and then making the
beds or tables (or whatever) which we use. The point is that the type itself is not
manufactured by any craftsman. How could it be?"

"It couldn't."

"There's another kind of craftsman too. I wonder what you think of him."

From Plato, *Republic*, translation by Robin Waterfield (Oxford: Oxford University Press,
1993). Reprinted with the permission of Oxford University Press.

c   "What kind?"

"He makes everything—all the items which every single manufacturer makes."

"He must be extraordinarily gifted."

"Wait: you haven't heard the half of it yet. It's not just a case of his being able to manufacture all the artefacts there are: every plant too, every creature (himself included), the earth, the heavens, gods, and everything in the heavens and in Hades under the earth—all these are made and created by this one man!"

d   "He really must be extraordinarily clever," he said.

"Don't you believe me?" I asked. "Tell me, do you doubt that this kind of craftsman could exist under any circumstances, or do you admit the possibility that a person could—in one sense, at least—create all these things? I mean, don't you realize that you yourself could, under certain circumstances, create all these things?"

"What circumstances?" he asked.

"I'm not talking about anything complicated or rare," I said. "It doesn't take long to create the circumstances. The quickest method, I suppose, is to get hold

e   of a mirror and carry it around with you everywhere. You'll soon be creating everything I mentioned a moment ago—the sun and the heavenly bodies, the earth, yourself, and all other creatures, plants, and so on."

"Yes, but I'd be creating appearances, not actual real things," he said.

"That's a good point," I said. "You've arrived just in time to save the argument. I mean, that's presumably the kind of craftsman a painter is. Yes?"

"Of course."

"His creations aren't real, according to you; but do you agree that all the same there's a sense in which even a painter creates a bed?"

"Yes," he said, "he's another one who creates an apparent bed."

597a   "What about a joiner who specializes in making beds? Weren't we saying a short while ago that what he makes is a particular bed, not the type, which is (on our view) the real bed?"

"Yes, we were."

"So if there's no reality to his creation, then it isn't real; it's similar to something real, but it isn't actually real. It looks as though it's wrong to attribute full reality to a joiner's or any artisan's product, doesn't it?"

"Yes," he said, "any serious student of this kind of argument would agree with you."

"It shouldn't surprise us, then, if we find that even these products are obscure when compared with the truth."

b   "No, it shouldn't."

"Now, what about this representer we're trying to understand? Shall we see if these examples help us?" I asked.

"That's fine by me," he said.

"Well, we've got these three beds. First, there's the real one, and we'd say, I imagine, that it is the product of divine craftsmanship. I mean, who else could have made it?"

"No one, surely."

"Then there's the one the joiner makes."

"Yes," he said.

"And then there's the one the painter makes. Yes?"

"Yes, agreed."

"These three, then—painter, joiner, God—are responsible for three different kinds of bed."

"Yes, that's right."

"Now, God has produced only that one real bed. The restriction to only one c might have been his own choice, or it might just be impossible for him to make more than one. But God never has, and never could, create two or more such beds."

"Why not?" he asked.

"Even if he were to make only two such beds," I said, "an extra one would emerge, and both the other two would be of that one's type. It, and not the two beds, would be the real bed."

"Right," he said.

"God realized this, I'm sure. He didn't want to be a kind of joiner, making a d particular bed: he wanted to be a genuine creator and make a genuine bed. That's why he created a single real one."

"I suppose that's right."

"Shall we call him its progenitor, then, or something like that?"

"Yes, he deserves the name," he said, "since he's the maker of this and every other reality."

"What about a joiner? Shall we call him a manufacturer of beds?"

"Yes."

"And shall we also call a painter a manufacturer and maker of beds and so on?"

"No, definitely not."

"What do you think he does with beds, then?"

"I think the most suitable thing to call him would be a representer of the oth- e ers' creations," he said.

"Well, in that case," I said, "you're using the term 'representer' for someone who deals with things which are, in fact, two generations away from reality, aren't you?"

"Yes," he said.

COMMENTS

Plato does not give a great deal of space to Forms; these are the major passages in which Forms are discussed, along with the passages from *Phaedo* 96a–101e in section 4.C and the *Republic* 475b–484a and 523a–525b in section 3.D. Nonetheless, the idea is important to him in a number of ways. Forms are, in some of his works, the objects of the highest kind of philosophical knowledge; they are also, as you can see from the *Symposium* passage, the object of the highest kind of love that humans can experience, one that leads to aspiration to intellectual understanding; and in many of his works they function as ideals that humans should try to emulate. Plato often talks about Forms in imaginative ways that convey a general picture, but it is actually difficult to say exactly what Forms are. Here are some questions that are useful for you to think about.

Prominent in these passages are terms like *beautiful* and *just,* and *equal* and *double.* Why do you think Plato focuses on these two groups of terms? Notice the way that the arguments bring out the fact that these are terms that have opposites, and the relevant Form, say in the case of *beautiful,* is beautiful and never, in any of a variety of ways, the opposite of beautiful. Would Plato's arguments in these passages work for terms without opposites?

One passage, from the end of the *Republic,* contains such terms—*bed* and *table.* Do these terms fit well in the other passages?

Would the argument that produces a Form for *beautiful* also produce a Form for *ugly?* If not, why not?

Do these passages imply that the Form for *beautiful* is itself something beautiful? But it is something grasped only by the mind through argument—how can it be beautiful like the beautiful things we see? Is it beautiful in some other way? What could that be?

What do you think that Forms are: Universals? Concepts? Notice that whatever Forms are, Plato always associates them with thinking and using your mind, as opposed to relying passively on sense-experience. The existence of Forms is something that becomes clear only to someone who does a lot of hard thinking.

Parmenides 128e–135c
PLATO

"I accept that," said Socrates. "But tell me: do you not believe that there exists, 129a alone by itself, a certain character of likeness, and again, another character opposite to it, what it is to be unlike; and that you and I and the other things we call many get a share of these two things? Things that get a share of likeness become like in the respect and to the degree that they get a share; things that get a share of unlikeness become unlike; and things that get a share of both become both. Even if all things get a share of both, opposite as they are, and by reason of having a share of both it is possible for them to be both like and unlike themselves, what is surprising in that? If someone were to show that things that are b *just* like become unlike, or *just* unlike like, no doubt that would be a portent. But I find nothing strange, Zeno, if he shows that things which get a share of both undergo both qualifications, nor if he shows that all things are one by reason of having a share of the one, and that those very same things are also in turn many

From *Plato: Parmenides*, by R. E. Allen (New Haven, Conn.: Yale University Press, 1998). Reprinted with the permission of Yale University Press.

by reason of having a share of multitude. But if he shows that what it is to be one is many, and the many in turn one, that *will* surprise me. The same is true in like manner of all other things. If someone should show that the kinds and characters in themselves undergo these opposite qualifications, there is reason for surprise. But what is surprising if someone shows that I am one and many? When he wishes to show that I am many, he says that my right side is one thing and my left another, that my front is different from my back, and my upper body in like manner different from my lower; for I suppose I have a share of multitude. To show that I am one, he says I am one man among the seven of us, since I also have a share of the one. The result is that he shows that both are true. Now, if someone should undertake to show that sticks and stones and things like that are many, and the same things one, we shall grant that he has proved that something is many and one, but not that the one is many or the many one; he has said nothing out of the ordinary, but a thing on which we all agree. But I should be filled with admiration, Zeno," said Socrates, "if someone were first to distinguish separately alone by themselves the characters I just mentioned—likeness and unlikeness, for example, multitude and the one, rest and motion, and all such similar things—and then show that these things in themselves can be combined and distinguished. You have do doubt dealt manfully with the former issue. But as I say, I should admire it much more if someone should show that this same perplexity is interwoven in all kinds of ways in the characters themselves—that just as you and Parmenides have explained in the things we see, so it proves too in what we apprehend by reflection."

As Socrates was speaking, Pythodorus said he expected Parmenides and Zeno to be annoyed at every word. Instead, they paid close attention, and from time to time glanced at each other and smiled as if in admiration. When Socrates finished, Parmenides expressed this. "Socrates," he said, "your impulse toward argument is admirable. Now tell me: do you yourself thus distinguish, as you say, certain characters themselves separately, and separately in turn the things that have a share of them? And do you think that likeness itself is something separate from the likeness that we have, and one and many, and all the others you just heard Zeno mention?"

"Yes, I do," said Socrates.

"And characters of this sort too?" said Parmenides. "For example, a certain character of just, alone by itself, and of beautiful and good, and all such as those in turn?"

"Yes," he said.

"Well, is there a character of man separate from us and all such as we are, a certain character of man itself, or fire, or even water?"

"I have often been in perplexity, Parmenides," he said, "about whether one should speak about them as about the others, or not."

"And what about these, Socrates—they would really seem ridiculous: hair and mud and dirt, for example, or anything else which is utterly worthless and trivial. Are you perplexed whether one should say that there is a separate character for each of them too, a character that again is other than the sorts of things we handle?"

"Not at all," said Socrates. "Surely those things actually are just what we see them to be, and it would be quite absurd to suppose that something is a character of them. Still, I sometimes worry lest what holds in one case may not hold in all; but when I take that stand, I retreat, for fear of tumbling undone into depths of nonsense. So I go back to the things we just said have characters, and spend my time dealing with them."

e   "You are still young, Socrates," said Parmenides, "and philosophy has not yet taken hold of you as I think it one day will. You will despise none of these things then. But as it is, because of your youth, you still pay attention to what people think. Now tell me this: do you think, as you say, that there are certain characters, and that these others here, by reason of having a share of them, get their names from them? As for example, things that get a share of likeness
131a become like, of largeness large, of beauty and justice beautiful and just?"

"Yes, certainly," said Socrates.

"Then does each thing that gets a share get a share of the whole character, or of a part? Or could there be any kind of sharing separate from these?"

"Surely not," Socrates replied.

"Well, does it seem to you that the whole character, being one, is in each of the many?"

"What prevents it, Parmenides?" said Socrates.

b   "Therefore, being one and the same, it will be present at once and as a whole in things that are many and separate, and thus it would be separate from itself."

"No, it would not," he said, "at least if it were like one and the same day, which is in many different places at once and nonetheless not separate from itself. If it were in fact that way, each of the characters could be in everything at once as one and the same."

"Very neat, Socrates," he said. "You make one and the same thing be in many different places at once, as if you'd spread a sail over a number of men and then claimed that one thing as a whole was over many. Or isn't that the sort of thing you mean to say?"

c   "Perhaps," he said.

"Now, would the whole sail be over each man, or part of it over one and part over another?"

"Part."

"Therefore, Socrates," he said, "the characters themselves are divisible, and things that have a share of them have a share of parts of them; whole would no longer be in each, but part of each in each."

"Yes, so it appears."

"Well, Socrates, are you willing to say that the one character is in truth divided for us, and yet that it will still be one?"

"Not at all," he said.

"No, for consider," he said, "if you divide largeness itself, and each of the
d many large things is to be large by a part of largeness smaller than largeness itself, won't that appear unreasonable?"

"Of course," he said.

"Well then, suppose something has a given small part of the equal. Will the possessor be equal to anything by what is smaller than the equal itself?"

"Impossible."

"But suppose that one of us is to have a part of the small. The small will be larger than this part of itself, because it is part of it, and thus the small itself will be larger. But that to which the part subtracted is added will be smaller, not e larger, than before."

"Surely that could not happen," he said.

"Then in what way, Socrates, will the others get a share of characters for you, since they cannot get a share part by part or whole by whole?"

"Such a thing, it seems to me, is difficult, emphatically difficult, to determine," he said.

"Really! Then how do you deal with this?"

"What is that?"

"I suppose you think that each character is one for some such reason as this: 132a when some plurality of things seem to you to be large, there perhaps seems to be some one characteristic that is the same when you look over them all, whence you believe that the large is one."

"True," he said.

"What about the large itself and the other larges? If with your mind you should look over them all in like manner, will not some one large again appear, by which they all appear to be large?"

"It seems so."

"Therefore, another character of largeness will have made its appearance alongside largeness itself and the things that have a share of it; and over and above all those, again, a different one, by which they will all be large. And each of the characters will no longer be one for you, but unlimited in multitude." b

"But Parmenides," said Socrates, "may it not be that each of these characters is a thought, and that it pertains to it to come to be nowhere else except in minds? For in that way, each would still be one, and no longer undergo what was just now said."

"Well," he said, "is each of the thoughts one, but a thought of nothing?"

"No, that is impossible," he said.

"A thought of something, then?"

"Yes."

"Of something that is, or is not?" c

"Of something that is."

"Of some one thing which that thought thinks as being over all, that is, of some one characteristic?"

"Yes."

"Then that which is thought to be one will be a character, ever the same over all?"

"Again, it appears it must."

"Really! Then what about this," said Parmenides, "in virtue of the necessity by which you say that the others have a share of characters, does it not seem to you that either each is composed of thoughts and all think, or that being thoughts they are unthought?"

"But that," he said, "is hardly reasonable."

"Still, Parmenides," he said, "this much is quite clear to me: these characters
d stand, as it were, as paradigms fixed in the nature of things, and the others resemble them and are likenesses of them; this sharing that the others come to have of characters is nothing other than being a resemblance of them."

"Well," Parmenides said, "if something resembles a character, is it possible for that character not to be like what has come to resemble it, insofar as it has become like it? Is there any way in which what is like is not like what is like it?"

"There is not."

"Rather, what is like must have a share of one and the same character as
e what it is like?"

"True."

"But will not that of which like things have a share so as to be like be the character itself?"

"Certainly."

"Then it is not possible for anything to be like the character, or the character like anything else. For otherwise, another character will always appear along-side it, and should that character be like something, a different one again. Con-
133a tinual generation of a new character will never stop, if the character comes to be like what has a share of it."

"You are quite right."

"Then the others do not get a share of characters by likeness. It is necessary to look for something else by which they get a share."

"So it seems."

"Do you see, then, Socrates, how great the perplexity is, if someone should distinguish as characters things that are alone by themselves?"

"Yes indeed."

"Rest assured," he said, "that you hardly even have yet begun to grasp how
b great the perplexity is, if you are going to assume that each character of things that are is one, ever marking it off as something."

"How so?" he said.

"There are many other difficulties," he said, "but the greatest is this. If some-one said that it does not even pertain to the characters to be known if they are such as we say they must be, one could not show him that he was mistaken unless the disputant happened to be a man of wide experience and natural abil-ity, willing to follow many a remote and laborious demonstration. Otherwise,
c the man who compels them to be unknowable would be left unconvinced."

"Why is that, Parmenides?" said Socrates.

"Because, Socrates, I suppose that you and anyone else who assumes that the nature and reality of each thing exists as something alone by itself would agree, first of all, that none of them is in us."

"No, for how would it still be alone by itself?" said Socrates.

"You are right," he said. "And further, as many of the characteristics as are what they are relative to each other have their nature and reality relative to themselves, but not relative to things among us—likenesses, or whatever one assumes they are—of which we have a share and in each case are called by their d names. But things among us, in turn, though they are of the same name as those, are relative to themselves but not to the characters, and it is to themselves but not to those that as many as are so named refer."

"How do you mean?" said Socrates.

"Take an example," said Parmenides. "If one of us is master or slave *of* someone, he is surely not a slave of master itself, what it is to be master, nor is a master the master of slave itself, what it is to be slave. Being a man, we are either of the two of another man. But mastership itself is what it is *of* slavery itself, and e slavery in like manner slavery *of* mastership. Things in us do not have their power and significance relative to things there, nor things there relative to us. Rather, as I say, things there are themselves of and relative to themselves, and in like manner things among us are relative to themselves. Or don't you see what 134a I mean?"

"Of course I do," said Socrates.

"And furthermore," he said, "knowledge itself, what it is to be knowledge, would be knowledge of what is there, namely, what it is to be real and true?"

"Of course."

"And each of the branches of knowledge in turn would be knowledge of what it is to be each of the things that are. Not so?"

"Yes."

"But knowledge among us would be knowledge of the truth and reality among us? And does it not in turn follow that each branch of knowledge among us is knowledge of each of the things that are among us?"   b

"Necessarily."

"Moreover, as you agree, we surely do not have the characters themselves, nor can they be among us."

"No."

"But the kinds themselves, what it is to be each thing, are known, I take it, by the character of knowledge?"

"Yes."

"Which we do not have."

"No."

"Then none of the characters is known by us, since we have no share of knowledge itself."

"It seems not."

"Therefore, what it is to be beautiful itself, and the good, and everything we at this point accept as characteristics themselves, is for us unknowable."   c

"Very likely."

"Consider then whether the following is not still more remarkable."

"What is it?"

"You would say, I take it, that if there is a certain kind of knowledge itself, it is much more exact than knowledge among us. So too of beauty, and all the rest."

"Yes."

"Now, if anything has a share of knowledge itself, would you say that no one but god has the most exact knowledge?"

"Necessarily."

d   "Then will it be possible for the god, having knowledge itself, to know things among us?"

"Why shouldn't it be?"

"Because, Socrates," said Parmenides, "we agreed that those characters do not have the power they have relative to things among us, nor things among us relative to those, but each relative to themselves."

"Yes, we agreed to that."

"Now, if the most exact mastership and most exact knowledge is in the god's realm, mastership there would never master us here, nor knowledge there
e know us or anything where we are. In like manner, we do not rule there by our authority here, and know nothing divine by our knowledge. By the same account again, those there are not our masters, and have no knowledge of human things, being gods."

"But surely," said Socrates, "it would be too strange an account, if one were to deprive the gods of knowing."

"And yet, Socrates," said Parmenides, "these difficulties and many more in
135a addition necessarily hold of the characters, if these characteristics of things that are exist, and one is to distinguish each character as something by itself. The result is that the hearer is perplexed, and contends that they do not exist, and that even if their existence is conceded, they are necessarily unknowable by human nature. In saying this, he thinks he is saying something significant, and as we just remarked, it is astonishingly hard to convince him to the contrary. Only a man of considerable natural gifts will be able to understand that there is
b a certain kind of each thing, a nature and reality alone by itself, and it will take a man more remarkable still to discover it and be able to instruct someone else who has examined all these difficulties with sufficient care."

"I agree with you, Parmenides," said Socrates. "You are saying very much what I think too."

"Nevertheless," said Parmenides, "if, in light of all the present difficulties and others like them, one will not allow that there are characters of things that are, and refuses to distinguish as something a character of each single thing, he will not even have anything to which to turn his mind, since he will not allow that there is a characteristic, ever the same, of each of the things that are; and so
c he will utterly destroy the power and significance of thought and discourse. I think you are even more aware of that sort of consequence."

"True," he replied.

"What will you do about philosophy, then? Which way will you turn while these things are unknown?"

"For the moment, at least, I am not really sure I see."

COMMENTS

These six arguments against Forms (here translated as "characters") are by Plato himself, who provides no answers to them. Are any of them objections that had already occurred to you when you were reading the other passages about Forms?

The first problem raised is the scope of the theory of Forms; what are there Forms for? Facing this question forces us to ask what the arguments are for Forms and which Forms they produce. Note that Socrates here appears to be more confident that there are Forms for terms with opposites than for others. How does this relate to arguments in the *Phaedo* and *Republic* that use terms with opposites and to the argument in the *Republic* book 10?

The second argument focuses on the relation of Forms to things which "have a share" of them. It forces a dilemma in terms of wholes and parts. Note that for this argument to go through, it has to be the case that the Form or character of largeness, for example, must be itself something that can be said to be large (and, similarly, for other cases). Is this a fair assumption to make about Forms as they have figured in Plato's arguments for them?

The third argument is the most famous, since its conclusion is so spectacular; if there is even one Form of large, there are infinitely many. Why, we may ask, is this an objection (as it clearly seems to be)? This argument is commonly known as the Third Man Argument, because that is how Aristotle refers to it, but Plato's own example is Large, rather than Man. Does this make a difference? Think of the first argument and the different arguments for Forms; there is an opposite to being large, but not to being a man.

The fourth argument focuses again on the relation between Forms and the things that "have a share in" them. A thought is not divided or made many by the fact that many people can have the same thought; perhaps the same is true of Forms (which would provide an answer to the second argument). How strong are the arguments against this conception?

The fifth argument, like the third, claims that if we get to even one Form by a certain form of argument, we thereby get to infinitely many (showing us that the argument will not do). Is it just a variant on the third? We might suspect that *likeness* would be a different kind of term from *largeness*. If so, the argument is different, but the conclusion is equally problematic.

The sixth argument focuses on our knowledge of Forms or characters and the things whose Forms they are, drawing some uncomfortable consequences. What does Plato have in mind when he says that some things are "relative to" other things? Does his example of master being relative to slave pick out the same kind of relation as that of knowledge being relative to its object? Plato seems to think that the sixth argument is the strongest; do you agree?

Notice that Plato does not conclude that the theory should be rejected because of these arguments; rather, these difficulties are taken to show that we need to think harder about Forms before we are entitled *either* to accept *or* to reject the theory. Can you think how these arguments might be answered?

DIOGENES OF SINOPE (THE CYNIC)

Diogenes, from Sinope on the Black Sea (c. 412/403–324/321 B.C.), was regarded as the founder of Cynicism, a practical and anti-intellectual philosophy. (Antisthenes, one of Socrates' disciples, is sometimes also regarded as a founding figure.) Diogenes lived most of his life in Athens, where he aggressively rejected social conventions and notions of shame—hence the name "Cynic," from the Greek for a dog, the model of shamelessness. In living a life of self-sufficient poverty alienated from society's values and claiming wisdom for his often-rough pronouncements, he was a forerunner of wise or holy men living on the margins of society. He may have written a *Republic* (possibly in response to Plato), but his "philosophy" was practical and left a legacy of stories, anecdotes, and jokes.

Lives of the Philosophers VI, 53
DIOGENES OF SINOPE

Once Plato was discussing Forms and using the words *tableness* and *cupness*. Diogenes the Cynic said, "I can see a table and a cup, Plato, but tableness and cupness—no way." "That's to be expected," replied Plato, "since you have eyes, by which tables and cups are seen, but the understanding by which tableness and cupness are discerned is something you don't have."

COMMENTS

Who do you think really wins this exchange? Is Diogenes just being crass? Why does he use examples like *table* and *cup*? What if he had used examples like *just* or *good*?

The Stoics on Plato's Forms

1. Zeno thinks the following. The Stoics say that concepts are neither *somethings* nor *qualified things*, but are quasi-*somethings* and quasi-*qualified things*. They are apparitions to the soul. These are what were called Forms by past philosophers. For there are Forms for things that fall under concepts, e.g., for men, horses, and more generally for all living things and as many other things as they say there are Forms of. These, however, the Stoics say do not exist. There are concepts, which we participate in, and cases, which they call common nouns, that we bear. (John Stobaeus, *Eclogae* 1, 136.21–137.6)

2. Chrysippus compared such theorems to Forms. For just as Forms include the coming into being of unlimited objects within defined limits, so too in these theorems the inclusion of unlimited figures comes to be within defined loci. (Proclus, Commentary on Euclid, 395-13-18)

COMMENTS

The Stoics, unlike Diogenes, have philosophical reasons for rejecting Plato's Forms. Like many modern critics of Plato, they think that Forms are supposed to do the work of concepts, but that Plato makes the mistake of thinking of Forms as though they were nonmaterial, individual objects of a special and wonderful kind, whereas in fact there are only individual humans using concepts to classify things.

Is it reasonable to think that the point of Forms is to do the work of concepts? Is it the only point?

On Forms

ARISTOTLE

The argument that tries to establish Ideas from relatives is as follows. In those cases where some same thing is predicated of several things not homonymously but as revealing some single nature, it is true of them either by their strictly 83.1 being what is indicated by what is predicated, as when we say Socrates is a man and Plato is; or by their being likenesses of the genuine things, as when we predicate man of painted men (for in the case of these latter we reveal the likenesses of men by indicating the same particular nature in all of them); or on the 5 grounds of one of them being the pattern, while the rest are likenesses, as if we were to call both Socrates and likenesses of him men. And we predicate the equal itself of things here, although it is predicated of them only homonymously; for neither does the same account fit all of them, nor do we indicate things that are truly equal; for among perceptibles quantity changes and shifts continuously and is not determinate. Nor moreover do any of the things here 10 accurately receive the account of the equal. And no more indeed on the grounds of one of them being pattern, the other likeness; for one is no more pattern or likeness than the other. And even if someone were to accept that the likeness is not homonymous with its pattern, it still follows that these equal things are equal as likenesses of that which is strictly and truly equal. And if this is the case, there is some equal itself quite strictly, relative to which things here, as like- 15 nesses, are both produced and called equal, and this is an Idea, a pattern for those things which are produced relative to it.

Plato, Vatican Museums,
Vatican State. Alinari/Art
Resource, New York

Philosophy in the ancient world was perceived in different ways, depending on its relation to established society. Here we have sculptures of Plato, Aristotle, and another philosopher. The busts of Plato and Aristotle do not attempt to portray individual features, as we would expect from a portrait; instead, they show us the philosophers as types of respected figures within society. Plato and Aristotle are depicted with carefully groomed hair and beards (beards were normal for all adult males at the time) and are presented in the same way as other outstanding members of society. Plato was the first philosopher to found a teaching institution, the Academy, and Aristotle, who was a member of the Academy for twenty years, later founded his own school, the Lyceum. Philosophy, from the fourth century B.C. onward, formed part of an ordinary education for young men, and most educated people would know something about it. These are the philosophers whose works have (more or less) come down to us.

Aristotle, Kunsthistorische Museum,
Vienna. © Photograph by Erich Lessing

Statue of a Cynic, Capitoline Museum,
Rome. Alinari/Art Resource, New York

On the other hand, in the third sculpture we see a philosopher as a figure who challenges the accepted order. Scruffy and unwashed, with tangled hair and a casually draped and tattered garment, this is probably a "Cynic," a philosopher who rejected social mores, often in a confrontational way. Cynics took their name from the Greek word for dogs, since dogs in the ancient world were seen not as faithful pets but as symbols of shamelessness. Cynics were not the only philosophers who rejected connections with institutions. Dio Chrysostom, a famous orator of the first century A.D., after being exiled by the emperor, took to traveling around "in humble attire. Some of the people I met called me a tramp, some a beggar, and some called me a philosopher. . . . Many came up and asked me my view on good and evil."

This argument, Aristotle says, establishes Ideas even of relative terms. At any rate the present proof has been advanced in the case of the equal, which is a relative; but they used to say that there were no Ideas of relatives because
25 while Ideas, being for them kinds of substances, existed in their own right, relatives had their being in their relationship to one another. And again, if the equal is equal to an equal, there will be more than one Idea of the equal; for the equal-itself is equal to an equal-itself; for if it were not equal to something, it would not be equal at all. Again, by the same argument there will have to be Ideas of unequals too; for opposites are in a similar case—there will or will not be Ideas
30 of both; and the unequal is admitted by them too to involve more things than one.

The argument which introduces the third man is as follows. They say that what are commonly predicated of substances both are strictly such things and
84.1 are Ideas. And again, things that are like each other are like each other by sharing in the same certain thing, which is strictly the thing in question; and this is the Idea. But if this is the case, and what is commonly predicated of certain things, if it is not the same as any one of those things of which it is predicated, is some other thing apart from it (for that is why man-himself is a genus—because while being predicated of the particulars it is not the same man as any
5 of them), then there will be some third man apart both from the particular, e.g. Socrates and Plato, and from the Idea; and this too will be itself one in number.

The third man is proved also in the following way. If what is predicated truly of several particulars is also something other apart from the things of which it is predicated, separated from them (for it is this that those who posit
25 the Ideas think to prove; for in their opinion man-himself is something because man is predicated truly of particular men, who are more than one in number, and is different from these particular men)—but if this is so, there will be some third man. For if the man that is predicated is different from those of whom he is predicated, and exists on his own, and man is predicated both of the particular men and of the Idea, then there will be some third man apart both from the
85.1 particular and from the Idea. On this basis there will be also a fourth man, predicated of the third man, of the Idea, and of the particulars; and similarly also a fifth, and so on ad infinitum.

COMMENTS

Aristotle was Plato's pupil in his philosophical school, the Academy, for twenty years; like any pupil, he disagreed with many of his teacher's ideas, and one of his works consists entirely of arguments against Plato's Forms. Here we have two. One is the "argument from relatives" and what Aristotle thinks it shows. Compare it with Plato's treatment of "the Equal" in the first *Phaedo* argument. The other is the "Third Man" argument. Compare it with the two infinite regress arguments in the *Parmenides* (note that there, Plato is not sure that there is a Form for Man, and the regress concerns the Form Large). Does Aristotle pick on weak points in the theory? Could Plato avoid these arguments?

Aristotle himself doesn't reject the notion of Form; you'll find in section 4.C that Form is one of his four types of explanation. What he objects to is Plato's particular way of thinking of Forms, so that he thinks that the theory needs to be modified, rather than rejected outright.

C. Cause and Explanation

Understanding the world around us and exploring what we would call scientific questions led the ancients to seek more clarity about causes, reasons, and generally what we mean when we try to explain why things are the way they are.

HIPPOCRATIC WRITINGS

About sixty medical writings have come down to us from the ancient world under the name of Hippocrates, a shadowy figure from the island of Cos who came to stand for the ideal of the physician. Individual medical writers ascribed their work to Hippocrates by way of identifying themselves with medical tradition. Most of the Hippocratic writings date from between 430 and 330 B.C., although some are later. As we would expect from a developing tradition, they differ widely in style, method, and degree of excellence.

The author of *The Sacred Disease* is generally thought to be the same as, or a pupil or teacher of, the author of another work in the corpus, *Airs, Waters, Places,* which gives an account of the effect of climate on human health. These works, written in the fifth century, take a naturalistic view of health and disease, refusing to allow that humans are under threat from capricious divine forces. In particular, they hold that no disease is particularly the result of divine intervention. "The sacred disease" was the term for epilepsy, which, because the patient suffers seizures, was thought of as an arbitrary attack by some divine force.

The Sacred Disease SELECTIONS
HIPPOCRATIC WRITINGS

I do not believe that the "Sacred Disease" is any more divine or sacred than any other disease but, on the contrary, has specific characteristics and a definite

---

Translated by John Chadwick and W. N. Mann.

cause. Nevertheless, because it is completely different from other diseases, it has been regarded as a divine visitation by those who, being only human, view it with ignorance and astonishment. This theory of divine origin, though supported by the difficulty of understanding the malady, is weakened by the simplicity of the cure, consisting merely of ritual purification and incantation. If remarkable features in a malady were evidence of divine visitation, then there would be many "sacred diseases," as I shall show. Quotidian, tertian and quartan fevers are among other diseases no less remarkable and portentous and yet no one regards them as having a divine origin. I do not believe that these diseases have any less claim to be caused by a god than the so-called "sacred" disease but they are not the objects of popular wonder. Again, no less remarkably, I have seen men go mad and become delirious for no obvious reason and do many strange things. I have seen many cases of people groaning and shouting in their sleep, some who choke; others jump from their bed and run outside and remain out of their mind till they wake, when they are as healthy and sane as they were before, although perhaps rather pale and weak. These things are not isolated events but frequent occurrences. There are many other remarkable afflictions of various sorts, but it would take too long to describe them in detail.

It is my opinion that those who first called this disease "sacred" were the sort of people we now call witch-doctors, faith-healers, quacks and charlatans. These are exactly the people who pretend to be very pious and to be particularly wise. By invoking a divine element they were able to screen their own failure to give suitable treatment and so called this a "sacred" malady to conceal their ignorance of its nature. By picking their phrases carefully, prescribing purifications and incantations along with abstinence from baths and from many foods unsuitable for the sick, they ensured that their therapeutic measures were safe for themselves. The following fish were forbidden as being the most harmful: mullet, black-tail, hammer and eel. Goat, venison, pork and dog were considered most likely among meats to upset the stomach. Of fowls: cock, turtle-dove and buzzard and those which are considered very rich were forbidden; white mint, garlic and onion were excluded from the diet because over-flavoured food is not good for a sick man. Further, their patients were forbidden to wear black because it is a sign of death, to use goat skin blankets or to wear goat skins, nor were they allowed to put one foot on the other or one hand on the other; and all these things were regarded as preventative measures against the disease. These prohibitions are added on account of the divine element in the malady, suggesting that these practitioners had special knowledge. They also employ other pretexts so that, if the patient be cured, their reputation for cleverness is enhanced while, if he dies, they can excuse themselves by explaining that the gods are to blame while they themselves did nothing wrong; that they did not prescribe the taking of any medicine whether liquid or solid, nor any baths which might have been responsible.

I suppose none of the inhabitants of the interior of Libya can possibly be healthy seeing that they sleep on goat skins and eat goat meat. In fact, they possess neither blanket, garment nor shoe that is not made of goat skin, because goats are the only animals they keep. If contact with or eating of this animal causes and exacerbates the disease while abstinence from it cures the disease, then diet is alone the factor which decides the onset of the disease and its cure. No god can be blamed and the purifications are useless and the idea of divine intervention comes to nought.

It seems, then, that those who attempt to cure disease by this sort of treatment do not really consider the maladies thus treated of sacred or of divine origin. If the disease can be cured by purification and similar treatment then what is to prevent its being brought on by like devices? The man who can get rid of a disease by his magic could equally well bring it on; again there is nothing divine about this but a human element is involved. By such claims and trickery, these practitioners pretend a deeper knowledge than is given to others; with their prescriptions of "sanctifications" and "purifications," their patter about divine visitation and possession by devils, they seek to deceive. And yet I believe that all these professions of piety are really more like impiety and a denial of the existence of the gods, and all their religion and talk of divine visitation is an impious fraud which I shall proceed to expose.

If these people claim to know how to draw down the moon, cause an eclipse of the sun, make storms and fine weather, rain and drought, to make the sea too rough for sailing or the land infertile, and all the rest of their nonsense, then, whether they claim to be able to do it by magic or by some other method, they seem to be impious rogues. Either they do not believe in the existence of the gods or they believe that the gods are powerless or would not refrain from the most dastardly acts. Surely conduct such as this must render them hateful to the gods. If a man were to draw down the moon or cause an eclipse of the sun, or make storms or fine weather by magic and sacrifices, I should not call any of these things a divine visitation but a human one, because the divine power has been overcome and forced into subjection by the human will. But perhaps these claims are not true and it is men in search of a living who invent all these fancy tales about this particular disease and all the others too.

In using purifications and spells they perform what I consider a most irreligious and impious act, for, in treating sufferers from this disease by purification with blood and like things, they behave as if the sufferers were ritually unclean, the victims of divine vengeance or of human magic or had done something sacrilegious. It would have been better if they had done the opposite and taken the sick into the temples, there, by sacrifice and prayer, to make supplication to the gods; instead they simply purify them and do none of these things. Charms are buried in the ground, thrown into the sea or carried off into the mountains where no one may touch them or tread on them. If a god really be responsible, surely these things should be taken into the temples as offerings.

Personally I believe that human bodies cannot be polluted by a god; the basest object by the most pure. But if the human body is polluted by some other agency or is harmed in some way, then the presence of a god would be more likely to purify and sanctify it than pollute it. It is the deity who purifies, sanctifies and cleanses us from the greatest and most unholy of our sins. We ourselves mark out the precincts of the temples of the gods so that no one should enter without purifying himself; as we go in, we sprinkle ourselves with holy water, not because we are thereby polluted, but to rid ourselves of any stain we may have contracted previously. This then is my opinion of the purifications.

I believe that this disease is not in the least more divine than any other but has the same nature as other diseases and a similar cause. Moreover, it can be cured no less than other diseases so long as it has not become inveterate and too powerful for the drugs which are given.

Like other diseases it is hereditary. If a phlegmatic child is born of a phlegmatic parent, a bilious child of a bilious parent, a consumptive child of a consumptive parent and a splenetic child of a splenetic parent, why should the children of a father or mother who is afflicted with this disease not suffer similarly? The seed comes from all parts of the body; it is healthy when it comes from healthy parts, diseased when it comes from diseased parts. Another important proof that this disease is no more divine than any other lies in the fact that the phlegmatic are constitutionally liable to it while the bilious escape. If its origin were divine, all types would be affected alike without this particular distinction.

So far from this being the case, the brain is the seat of this disease, as it is of other very violent diseases. I shall explain clearly the manner in which it comes about and the reason for it.

The brain may be attacked both by phlegm and by bile and the two types of disorder which result may be distinguished thus: those whose madness results from phlegm are quiet and neither shout nor make a disturbance; those whose madness results from bile shout, play tricks and will not keep still but are always up to some mischief. Such are the causes of continued madness, but fears and frights may be caused by changes in the brain. Such a change occurs when it is warmed and that is the effect bile has when, flowing from the rest of the body, it courses to the brain along the blood-vessels. Fright continues until the bile runs away again into the blood-vessels and into the body. Feelings of pain and nausea result from inopportune cooling and abnormal consolidation of the brain and this is the effect of phlegm. The same condition is responsible for loss of memory. Those of a bilious constitution are liable to shout and to cry out during the night when the brain is suddenly heated; those of phlegmatic constitution do not suffer in this way. Warming of the brain also takes place when a plethora of blood finds its way to the brain and boils. It courses along the blood-vessels I have described in great quantity when a man is having a nightmare and is in a state of terror. He reacts in sleep in the same way that he would if he were awake; his face burns, his eyes are bloodshot as they are when scared or when the mind is intent upon the commission of a crime. All this ceases as soon as the man wakes and the blood is dispersed again into the blood-vessels.

For these reasons I believe the brain to be the most potent organ in the body. So long as it is healthy, it is the interpreter of what is derived from the air. Consciousness is caused by air. The eyes, ears, tongue, hands and feet perform actions which are planned by the brain, for there is a measure of conscious thought throughout the body proportionate to the amount of air which it receives. The brain is also the organ of comprehension, for when a man draws in a breath it reaches the brain first, and thence is dispersed into the rest of the body, having left behind in the brain its vigour and whatever pertains to consciousness and intelligence. If the air went first to the body and subsequently to the brain, the power of understanding would be left to the flesh and to the blood-vessels; it would only reach the brain hot and when it was no longer pure owing to admixture with fluid from the flesh and from the blood and this would blunt its keenness.

This so-called "sacred disease" is due to the same causes as all other diseases, to the things we see come and go, the cold and the sun too, the changing and inconstant winds. These things are divine so that there is no need to regard this disease as more divine than any other; all are alike divine and all human. Each has its own nature and character and there is nothing in any disease which is unintelligible or which is insusceptible to treatment. The majority of maladies may be cured by the same things as caused them. One thing nourishes one thing, another another and sometimes destroys it too. The physician must know of these things in order to be able to recognize the opportune moment to nourish and increase one thing while robbing another of its sustenance and so destroying it.

In this disease as in all others, it should be your aim not to make the disease worse, but to wear it down by applying the remedies most hostile to the disease and those things to which it is unaccustomed. A malady flourishes and grows in its accustomed circumstances but is blunted and declines when attacked by a hostile substance. A man with the knowledge of how to produce by means of a regimen dryness and moisture, cold and heat in the human body, could cure this disease too provided that he could distinguish the right moment for the application of the remedies. He would not need to resort to purifications and magic spells.

COMMENTS

The disease we call epilepsy was called in ancient Greece the "sacred disease" because the patient suffers seizures that cannot be explained by normal circumstances, and so the seizures were thought of as literal seizures by some external divine force. This author, although he has to refer to the disease by its usual name, rejects the idea that a disease can be either explained or cured by reference to divine powers that intervene in human life in arbitrary and irregular ways; hence, he says, the disease is no more sacred than any other. It has an explanation that is the same in kind as for any other disease—the conditions of the body and the environment.

The author's explanation is, by our standards, crude and wrong—he appeals to a theory about bodily secretions like phlegm, coupled with the impact of climate, and his anatomy is wildly incorrect. But he has a strikingly modern view of the natural world, including humans and their diseases, as totally open to explanation in scientific terms. Unlike many modern scientists, however, he does not try to debunk religion. He thinks of the natural world that the physician studies as divine as well as human—that is, explanations of it need to go beyond humans and what they can do; it would be foolish and presumptuous to think that there are no gods, since that would be to claim that humans are the highest and most important things in the world. What he attacks is only the idea that the gods act in arbitrary and unintelligible ways and can be propiated or bought off in similarly arbitrary ways by humans.

It is interesting to compare this author's attitude with modern medical attitudes to disease and to religion. Is it possible for us to think of all diseases as being not only human but also divine? If not, what does this say about our concept of the divine?

ANAXAGORAS

Anaxagoras of Clazomenae (c. 500–c. 428 B.C.) came from Asia Minor to the intellectual center of Athens, where he lived for about thirty years, though eventually he was forced out by anti-intellectual pressures and was perhaps prosecuted for impiety on the grounds of his belief that the sun was a fiery stone (thus undermining the belief that it was a god). He then went to Lampsacus, near his hometown. He held a complex theory of the principles of which things were made, but is remembered more for his idea that the universe was formed from its constituents by a force he calls Mind. Plato complains that Anaxagoras' Mind was a mechanical force that worked without bringing things about for the best, and the fragments of his work that survive suggest an attitude to the world that is naturalistic and unmysterious; Anaxagoras looks for the principles he needs to produce an adequate theory of the way the world is without regarding it as being made for a good purpose.

Phaedo 96a–101e
PLATO

"Then listen to my story. When I was young, Cebes, I was remarkably keen on the kind of wisdom known as natural science; it seemed to me splendid to know
10 the reasons for each thing, why each thing comes to be, why it perishes, and
b why it exists. And I was always shifting back and forth, examining, for a start, questions like these: is it, as some said, whenever the hot and the cold give rise
5 to putrefaction, that living creatures develop? And is it blood that we think with, or air, or fire? Or is it none of those, but the brain that provides the senses of hearing and seeing and smelling, from which memory and judgement come to

---

From Plato, *Phaedo*, translated by David Gallop (Oxford: Oxford University Press, 1993). Reprinted with the permission of Oxford University Press.

be; and is it from memory and judgement, when they've acquired stability, that knowledge comes to be accordingly? Next, when I went on to examine the c destruction of those things, and what happens in the heavens and the earth, I finally judged myself to have absolutely no gift for that kind of inquiry. I'll tell you a good enough sign of this: there had been things that I previously did know for sure, at least as I myself and others thought; yet I was then so utterly 5 blinded by this inquiry, that I unlearned even those things I formerly supposed I knew, including, amongst many other things, why it is that a human being grows. That, I used earlier to suppose, was obvious to everyone: it was because d of eating and drinking; whenever, from food, flesh came to accrue to flesh, and bone to bone, and similarly on the same principle the appropriate matter came to accrue to each of the other parts, it was then that the little bulk later came to be big; and in this way the small human being comes to be large. That was what 5 I supposed then: reasonably enough, don't you think?"

"I do," said Cebes.

"Well, consider these further cases: I used to suppose it was an adequate view, whenever a large person standing beside a small one appeared to be larger just by a head; similarly with two horses. And, to take cases even clearer than e these, it seemed to me that ten was greater than eight because of the accruing of two to the latter, and that two cubits were larger than one cubit, because of their exceeding the latter by half."

"Well, what do you think about them now?" said Cebes.   5

"I can assure you that I'm far from supposing I know the reason for any of those things, when I don't even accept from myself that when you add one to one, it's either the one to which the addition is made that's come to be two, or the one that's been added and the one to which it's been added, that have come 97 to be two, because of the addition of one to the other. Because I wonder if, when they were apart from each other, each was one and they weren't two then; whereas when they came close to each other, this then became a reason for their 5 coming to be two—the union in which they were juxtaposed. Nor again can I any longer be persuaded, if you divide one, that this has now become a reason for its coming to be two, namely division; because if so, we have a reason oppo- b site to the previous one for its coming to be two; then it was their being brought close to each other and added, one to the other; whereas now it's their being drawn apart, and separated each from the other. Why, I can't even persuade myself any longer that I know why it is that one comes to be; nor, in short, why 5 anything else comes to be, or perishes, or exists, following that method of inquiry. Instead I rashly adopt a different method, a jumble of my own, and in no way incline towards the other.

"One day, however, I heard someone reading from a book he said was by Anaxagoras, according to which it is, in fact, intelligence that orders and is the c reason for everything. Now this was a reason that pleased me; it seemed to me, somehow, to be a good thing that intelligence should be the reason for every- thing. And I thought that, if that's the case, then intelligence in ordering all 5 things must order them and place each individual thing in the best way possi-

ble; so if anyone wanted to find out the reason why each thing comes to be or
d perishes or exists, this is what he must find out about it: how is it best for that
thing to exist, or to act or be acted upon in any way? On this theory, then, a person should consider nothing else, whether in regard to himself or anything else,
but the best, the highest good; though the same person must also know the
5 worse, as they are objects of the same knowledge. Reckoning thus, I was pleased
to think I'd found, in Anaxagoras, an instructor in the reason for things to suit
my own intelligence. And I thought he'd inform me, first, whether the earth is
e flat or round, and when he'd informed me, he'd go on to expound the reason
why it must be so, telling me what was better—better, that is, that it should be
like this; and if he said it was in the centre, he'd go on to expound the view that
98 a central position for it was better. If he could make those things clear to me, I
was prepared to hanker no more after any other kind of reason. What's more, I
was prepared to find out in just the same way about the sun, the moon, and the
stars, about their relative velocity and turnings and the other things that happen
5 to them, and how it's better for each of them to act and be acted upon just as they
are. Because I never supposed that, having said they were ordered by intelligence, he'd bring in any reason for them other than its being best for them to be
b just the way they are; and I supposed that in assigning the reason for each individual thing, and for things in general, he'd go on to expound what was best for
the individual, and what was the common good for all; nor would I have sold
those hopes for a large sum, but I made all haste to get hold of the books and
5 read them as quickly as I could, so that I might know as quickly as possible what
was best and what was worse.
"Well, my friend, those marvellous hopes of mine were dashed; because, as
I went on with my reading, I beheld a man making no use of his intelligence at
c all, nor finding in it any reasons for the ordering of things, but imputing them
to such things as air and ether and water and many other absurdities. In fact, he
seemed to me to be in exactly the position of someone who said that all Socrates'
5 actions were performed with his intelligence, and who then tried to give the reasons for each of my actions by saying, first, that the reason why I'm now sitting
here is that my body consists of bones and sinews, and the bones are hard and
separated from each other by joints, whereas the sinews, which can be tightened
d and relaxed, surround the bones, together with the flesh and the skin that holds
them together; so that when the bones are turned in their sockets, the sinews by
stretching and tensing enable me somehow to bend my limbs at this moment,
5 and that's the reason why I'm sitting here bent in this way; or again, by mentioning other reasons of the same kind for my talking with you, imputing it to
vocal sounds, air currents, auditory sensations, and countless other such things,
98e yet neglecting to mention the true reasons: that Athenians judged it better to
condemn me, and therefore I in my turn have judged it better to sit here, and
5 thought it more just to stay behind and submit to such penalty as they may
99 ordain. Because, I dare swear, these sinews and bones would long since have
been off in Megara or Boeotia, impelled by their judgement of what was best,
had I not thought it more just and honourable not to escape and run away, but
5 to submit to whatever penalty the city might impose. But to call such things 'rea-

sons' is quite absurd. It would be quite true to say that without possessing such things as bones and sinews, and whatever else I possess, I shouldn't be able to do what I judged best; but to call those things the reasons for my actions, rather b than my choice of what is best, and that too though I act with intelligence, would be a thoroughly loose way of talking. Fancy being unable to distinguish two different things: the reason proper, and that without which the reason could never be a reason! Yet it's this latter that most people call a reason, appearing to me to 5 be feeling it over blindfold, as it were, and applying a wrong name to it. That's why one man makes the earth stay in position by means of the heaven, putting a whirl around it; while another presses down the air as a base, as if with a flat kneading-trough. Yet the power by which they're now situated in the best way c that they could be placed, this they neither look for nor credit with any supernatural strength; but they think they'll one day discover an Atlas stronger and more immortal than that, who does more to hold everything together. That it's the good or binding, that genuinely does bind and hold things together, they 5 don't believe at all. Now I should most gladly have become anyone's pupil, to learn the truth about a reason of that sort; but since I was deprived of that, proving unable either to find it for myself or to learn it from anyone else, would you d like me, Cebes, to give you a display of how I've conducted my second voyage in quest of the reason?"

"Yes, I'd like that immensely," he said.

"Well then, it seemed to me next, since I'd been wearing myself out studying things, that I must take care not to incur what happens to people who 5 observe and examine the sun during an eclipse; some of them, you know, ruin their eyes, unless they examine its image in water or something of that sort. I e had a similar thought: I was afraid I might be completely blinded in my soul, by looking at objects with my eyes and trying to lay hold of them with each of my senses. So I thought I should take refuge in theories, and study the truth of mat- 5 ters in them. Perhaps my comparison is, in a certain way, inept; as I don't at all 100 admit that one who examines things in theories is any more studying them in images than one who examines them in concrete. But anyhow, this was how I proceeded: positing on each occasion the theory I judge strongest, I put down as 5 true whatever things seem to me to accord with it, both about a reason and about everything else; and whatever do not, I put down as not true. But I'd like to explain my meaning more clearly; because I don't imagine you understand it as yet."

"Not entirely, I must say!" said Cebes.

"Well, this is what I mean: it's nothing new, but what I've spoken of inces- b santly in our earlier discussion as well as at other times. I'm going to set about displaying to you the kind of reason I've been dealing with; and I'll go back to 5 those much harped-on entities, and start from them, positing the existence of a beautiful, itself by itself, and of a good and a large and all the rest. If you grant me that and agree that those things exist, I hope that from them I shall display to you the reason, and find out that soul is immortal."

"Well, you may certainly take that for granted," said Cebes, "so you c couldn't be too quick to conclude."

"Then consider the next point, and see if you think as I do. It seems to me
5 that if anything else is beautiful besides the beautiful itself, it is beautiful for no
reason at all other than that it participates in that beautiful; and the same goes
for all of them. Do you assent to a reason of that kind?"

"I do."

10   "Then I no longer understand nor can I recognize those other clever reasons;
d but if anyone gives me as the reason why a given thing is beautiful either its having a blooming colour, or its shape, or something else like that, I dismiss those
other things—because all those others confuse me—but in a plain, artless, and
5 possibly simple-minded way, I hold this close to myself: nothing else makes it
beautiful except that beautiful itself, whether by its presence or communion or
whatever the manner and nature of the relation may be; as I don't go so far as to
affirm that, but only that it is by the beautiful that all beautiful things are beautiful. Because that seems to be the safest answer to give both to myself and to
e another, and if I hang on to that, I believe I'll never fall: it's safe to answer both
to myself and to anyone else that it is by the beautiful that beautiful things are
beautiful; or don't you agree?"

"I do."

5   "Similarly it's by largeness that large things are large, and larger things
larger, and by smallness that smaller things are smaller?"

"Yes."

"Then you too wouldn't accept anyone's saying that one person was larger
101 than another by a head, and that the smaller was smaller by the same thing; but
you'd protest that you for your part will say only that everything larger than
something else is larger by nothing but largeness, and largeness is the reason for
its being larger; and that the smaller is smaller by nothing but smallness, and
5 smallness is the reason for its being smaller. You'd be afraid, I imagine, of meeting the following contradiction: if you say that someone is larger and smaller by
a head, then, first, the larger will be larger and the smaller smaller by the same
b thing; and secondly, the head, by which the larger person is larger, is itself a
small thing; and it's surely monstrous that anyone should be large by something
small; or wouldn't you be afraid of that?"

"Yes, I should," said Cebes laughing.

5   "Then wouldn't you be afraid to say that ten is greater than eight by two,
and that that is the reason for its exceeding, rather than that it's by numerousness, and because of numerousness? Or that two cubits are larger than one cubit
by half, rather than by largeness? Because, of course, there'd be the same fear."

"Certainly," he said.

"And again, wouldn't you beware of saying that when one is added to one,
c the addition is the reason for their coming to be two, or when one is divided,
that division is the reason? You'd shout loudly that you know no other way in
which each thing comes to be, except by participating in the particular reality of
5 any given thing in which it does participate; and in those cases you own no
other reason for their coming to be two, save participation in twoness: things
that are going to be two must participate in that, and whatever is going to be one
must participate in oneness. You'd dismiss those divisions and additions and

other such subtleties, leaving them as answers to be given by people wiser than yourself; but you, scared of your own shadow, as the saying is, and of your inex- d perience, would cling to the safety of the hypothesis, and answer accordingly. But if anyone fastened upon the hypothesis itself, you would dismiss him, and you wouldn't answer till you should have examined its consequences, to see if, in your view, they are in accord or discord with each other; and when you had 5 to give an account of the hypothesis itself, you would give it in the same way, once again positing another hypothesis, whichever should seem best of those e above, till you came to something adequate; but you wouldn't jumble things as the contradiction-mongers do, by discussing the starting-point and its conse- quences at the same time, if, that is, you wanted to discover any realities."

COMMENTS

In this passage, Plato makes Socrates give an "intellectual autobiography" in which he moves from enthusiasm for explanations in terms of physical causes to explana- tions in terms of Platonic Forms. Few scholars nowadays think that this is a faithful account of what the historical Socrates thought. Plato presents Socrates (in a dia- logue that depicts him just before his death) as the true philosopher, who is driven by a desire to seek the truth from an unsatisfactory kind of theory to a more satis- factory one (regardless of the views of the historical Socrates).

Socrates never says that he turned to explanations in terms of Platonic Forms because merely physical causes as such are inadequate. Rather, he develops two lines of argument. One comes out in the complaints about Anaxagoras—that expla- nations in terms of physical causes, even if they cite items like Mind, make no appeal to things being for the better or to their aiming at some good outcome. The other comes out in the way that Socrates marshals examples in which one item explains not only one result, but its opposite, or when one result can be explained equally well by the supposed explaining item and its opposite. (This line of thought bears a strong resemblance to other passages introducing Forms; see section 4.B.)

How do Plato's two complaints go together? How do they relate to the opening complaint that *physical* causes are inadequate? How does Plato think that Forms can be causes? Obviously, he is not talking about causes in the sense in which we think— that a cause is something that begins a change. What does he have in mind?

On Coming-to-Be and Passing-Away II, 9

ARISTOTLE

Now cause, in the sense of matter, for the things which are such as to come-to- be is that which can be and not be; and this is identical with that which can come

---

to be and pass away, since the latter, while it *is* at one time, at another time *is not*. (For whereas some things *are* of necessity, viz. the eternal things, others of neces-
335ª1 sity *are not*. And of these two sets of things, since they cannot diverge from the necessity of their nature, it is impossible for the first *not to be* and impossible for the second *to be*. Other things, however, can both *be* and *not be*.) Hence coming-to-be and passing-away must occur within the field of that which can be and not
5 be. This, therefore, is cause in the sense of matter for the things which are such as to come-to-be; while cause, in the sense of their end, is their figure or form— and that is the formula expressing the substance of each of them.

But the third principle must be present as well—the cause vaguely dreamed of by all our predecessors, definitely stated by none of them. On the contrary some amongst them thought the nature of the Forms was adequate to account
10 for coming-to-be. Thus Socrates in the *Phaedo* first blames everybody else for having given no explanation; and then lays it down that some things are Forms, others participants in the Forms, and that while a thing is said to be in virtue of the Form, it is said to come-to-be qua sharing in, to pass-away qua losing, the
15 Form. Hence he thinks that assuming the truth of these theses, the Forms *must* be causes both of coming-to-be and of passing-away. On the other hand there were others who thought the matter was adequate by itself to account for com- ing-to-be, since the movement originates from the matter.

Neither of these theories, however, is sound. For if the Forms are causes, why is their generating activity intermittent instead of perpetual and continu-
20 ous—since there always *are* participants as well as Forms? Besides, in some instances we *see* that the cause is other than the Form. For it is the doctor who implants health and the man of science who implants science, although Health itself and Science itself *are* as well as the participants; and the same principle applies to everything else that is produced in accordance with a capacity.

Physics II, 3, 7–9
ARISTOTLE

3. Now that we have established these distinctions, we must proceed to consider causes, their character and number. Knowledge is the object of our inquiry, and men do not think they know a thing till they have grasped the
20 "why" of it (which is to grasp its primary cause). So clearly we too must do this as regards both coming to be and passing away and every kind of natural change, in order that, knowing their principles, we may try to refer to these prin- ciples each of our problems.

In one way, then, that out of which a thing comes to be and which persists, is called a cause, e.g. the bronze of the statue, the silver of the bowl, and the gen- 25 era of which the bronze and the silver are species.

In another way, the form or the archetype, i.e. the definition of the essence, and its genera, are called causes (e.g. of the octave the relation of 2:1, and generally number), and the parts in the definition.

Again, the primary source of the change or rest: e.g. the man who deliber- 30 ated is a cause, the father is cause of the child, and generally what makes of what is made and what changes of what is changed.

Again, in the sense of end or that for the sake of which a thing is done, e.g. health is the cause of walking about. ("Why is he walking about?" We say: "To be healthy," and, having said that, we think we have assigned the cause.) The 35 same is true also of all the intermediate steps which are brought about through the action of something else as means towards the end, e.g. reduction of flesh, purging, drugs, or surgical instruments are means towards health. All these 195ª1 things are for the sake of the end, though they differ from one another in that some are activities, others instruments.

This then perhaps exhausts the number of ways in which the term "cause" is used.

As things are called causes in many ways, it follows that there are several causes of the same thing (not merely accidentally), e.g. both the art of the sculp- 5 tor and the bronze are causes of the statue. These are causes of the statue qua statue, not in virtue of anything else that it may be—only not in the same way, the one being the material cause, the other the cause whence the motion comes. Some things cause each other reciprocally, e.g. hard work causes fitness and vice versa, but again not in the same way, but the one as end, the other as the princi- 10 ple of motion. Further the same thing is the cause of contrary results. For that which by its presence brings about one result is sometimes blamed for bringing about the contrary by its absence. Thus we ascribe the wreck of a ship to the absence of the pilot whose presence was the cause of its safety.

All the causes now mentioned fall into four familiar divisions. The letters 15 are the causes of syllables, the material of artificial products, fire and the like of bodies, the parts of the whole, and the premisses of the conclusion, in the sense of "that from which." Of these pairs the one set are causes in the sense of what underlies, e.g. the parts, the other set in the sense of essence—the whole and the 20 combination and the form. But the seed and the doctor and the deliberator, and generally the maker, are all sources whence the change or stationariness originates, which the others are causes in the sense of the end or the good of the rest; for that for the sake of which tends to be what is best and the end of the things that lead up to it. (Whether we call it good or apparently good makes no 25 difference.)

Such then is the number and nature of the kinds of cause.

Similar distinctions can be made in the things of which the causes are causes, e.g. of this statue or of a statue or of an image generally, of this bronze or of bronze or of material generally. So too with the accidental attributes. Again 10 we may use a complex expression for either and say, e.g., neither "Polyclitus" nor a "sculptor" but "Polyclitus, the sculptor."

All these various uses, however, come to six in number, under each of which again the usage is twofold. It is either what is particular or a genus, or an acci-
15 dental attribute or a genus of that, and these either as a complex or each by itself; and all either as actual or as potential. The difference is this much, that causes which are actually at work and particular exist and cease to exist simultaneously with their effect, e.g. this healing person with this being-healed person
20 and that housebuilding man with that being-built house; but this is not always true of potential causes—the house and the housebuilder do not pass away simultaneously.

In investigating the cause of each thing it is always necessary to seek what is most precise (as also in other things): thus a man builds because he is a builder, and a builder builds in virtue of his art of building. This last cause then
25 is prior; and so generally.

Further, generic effects should be assigned to generic causes, particular effects to particular causes, e.g. statue to sculptor, this statue to this sculptor; and powers are relative to possible effects, actually operating causes to things which are actually being effected.

This must suffice for our account of the number of causes and the modes of
30 causation.

Now the modes of causation are many, though when brought under heads they too can be reduced in number. For things are called causes in many ways
30 and even within the same kind one may be prior to another: e.g. the doctor and the expert are causes of health, the relation 2:1 and number of the octave, and always what is inclusive to what is particular. Another mode of causation is the accidental and its genera, e.g. in one way Polyclitus, in another a sculptor is the
35 cause of a statue, because being Polyclitus and a sculptor are accidentally conjoined. Also the classes in which the accidental attribute is included; thus a man
195a1 could be said to be the cause of a statue or, generally, a living creature. An accidental attribute too may be more or less remote, e.g. suppose that a pale man or a musical man were said to be the cause of the statue.

All causes, both proper and accidental, may be spoken of either as potential
5 or as actual; e.g. the cause of a house being built is either a house-builder or a house-builder building.

7. It is clear then that there are causes, and that the number of them is what
15 we have stated. The number is the same as that of the things comprehended under the question "why." The "why" is referred ultimately either, in things which do not involve motion, e.g. in mathematics, to the "what" (to the definition of straight line or commensurable or the like); or to what initiated a motion, e.g. "why did they go to war?—because there had been a raid"; or we are inquir-
20 ing "for the sake of what?"—"that they may rule"; or in the case of things that come into being, we are looking for the matter. The causes, therefore, are these and so many in number.

Now, the causes being four, it is the business of the student of nature to know about them all, and if he refers his problems back to all of them, he will assign the "why" in the way proper to his science—the matter, the form, the mover, that for the sake of which. The last three often coincide; for the what and 25 that for the sake of which are one, while the primary source of motion is the same in species as these. For man generates man—and so too, in general, with all things which cause movement by being themselves moved; and such as are not of this kind are no longer inside the province of natural science, for they cause motion not by possessing motion or a source of motion in themselves, but being themselves incapable of motion. Hence there are three branches of study, 30 one of things which are incapable of motion, the second of things in motion, but indestructible, the third of destructible things.

The question "why," then, is answered by reference to the matter, to the form, and to the primary moving cause. For in respect of coming to be it is mostly in this last way that causes are investigated—"what comes to be after what? what was the primary agent or patient?" and so at each step of the series. 35

Now the principles which cause motion in a natural way are two, of which one is not natural, as it has no principle of motion in itself. Of this kind is what- 98ᵇ1 ever causes movement, not being itself moved, such as that which is completely unchangeable, the primary reality, and the essence of a thing, i.e. the form; for this is the end or that for the sake of which. Hence since nature is for the sake of something, we must know this cause also. We must explain the "why" in all the 5 senses of the term, namely, that from this that will necessarily result ("from this" either without qualification or for the most part); that this must be so if that is to be so (as the conclusion presupposes the premises); that this was the essence of the thing; and because it is better thus (not without qualification, but with ref- erence to the substance in each case).

8. We must explain then first why nature belongs to the class of causes 10 which act for the sake of something; and then about the necessary and its place in nature, for all writers ascribe things to this cause, arguing that since the hot and the cold and the like are of such and such a kind, therefore certain things *necessarily* are and come to be—and if they mention any other cause (one friend- 15 ship and strife, another mind), it is only to touch on it, and then good-bye to it.

A difficulty presents itself: why should not nature work, not for the sake of something, nor because it is better so, but just as the sky rains, not in order to make the corn grow, but of necessity? (What is drawn up must cool, and what has been cooled must become water and descend, the result of this being that 20 the corn grows.) Similarly if a man's crop is spoiled on the threshing-floor, the rain did not fall for the sake of this—in order that the crop might be spoiled— but that result just followed. Why then should it not be the same with the parts in nature, e.g. that our teeth should come up of necessity—the front teeth sharp, 25 fitted for tearing, the molars broad and useful for grinding down the food— since they did not arise for this end, but it was merely a coincident result; and so with all other parts in which we suppose that there is purpose? Wherever

then all the parts came about just what they would have been if they had come
30 to be for an end, such things survived, being organized spontaneously in a fitting way; whereas those which grew otherwise perished and continue to perish,
as Empedocles says his "man-faced ox-progeny" did.

Such are the arguments (and others of the kind) which may cause difficulty
on this point. Yet it is impossible that this should be the true view. For teeth and
all other natural things either invariably or for the most part come about in a
199ª1 given way; but of not one of the results of chance or spontaneity is this true. We
do not ascribe to chance or mere coincidence the frequency of rain in winter, but
frequent rain in summer we do; nor heat in summer but only if we have it in
winter. If then, it is agreed that things are either the result of coincidence or for
5 the sake of something, and these cannot be the result of coincidence or spontaneity, it follows that they must be for the sake of something; and that such
things are all due to nature even the champions of the theory which is before us
would agree. Therefore action for an end is present in things which come to be
and are by nature.

Further, where there is an end, all the preceding steps are for the sake of
10 that. Now surely as in action, so in nature; and as in nature, so it is in each action,
if nothing interferes. Now action is for the sake of an end; therefore the nature
of things also is so. Thus if a house, e.g., had been a thing made by nature, it
would have been made in the same way as it is now by art; and if things made
by nature were made not only by nature but also by art, they would come to be
15 in the same way as by nature. The one, then, is for the sake of the other; and generally art in some cases completes what nature cannot bring to a finish, and in
others imitates nature. If, therefore, artificial products are for the sake of an end,
so clearly also are natural products. The relation of the later to the earlier items
is the same in both.

20   This is most obvious in the animals other than man: they make things neither by art nor after inquiry or deliberation. That is why people wonder whether
it is by intelligence or by some other faculty that these creatures work,—spiders,
ants, and the like. By gradual advance in this direction we come to see clearly
25 that in plants too that is produced which is conducive to the end—leaves, e.g.
grow to provide shade for the fruit. If then it is both by nature and for an end
that the swallow makes its nest and the spider its web, and plants grow leaves
for the sake of the fruit and send their roots down (not up) for the sake of nourishment, it is plain that this kind of cause is operative in things which come to
30 be and are by nature. And since nature is twofold, the matter and the form, of
which the latter is the end, and since all the rest is for the sake of the end, the
form must be the cause in the sense of that for the sake of which.

Now mistakes occur even in the operations of art: the literate man makes a
mistake in writing and the doctor pours out the wrong dose. Hence clearly mis-
199b1 takes are possible in the operations of nature also. If then in art there are cases
in which what is rightly produced serves a purpose, and if where mistakes
occur there was a purpose in what was attempted, only it was not attained, so
must it be also in natural products, and monstrosities will be failures in the pur-

posive effort. Thus in the original combinations the "ox-progeny" if they failed 5
to reach a determinate end must have arisen through the corruption of some
principle, as happens now when the seed is defective.

Further, seed must have come into being first, and not straightway the animals: what was "undifferentiated first" was seed.

Again, in plants too we find that for the sake of which, though the degree of 10
organization is less. Were there then in plants also olive-headed vine-progeny,
like the "man-headed ox-progeny," or not? An absurd suggestion; yet there
must have been, if there were such things among animals.

Moreover, among the seeds anything must come to be at random. But the
person who asserts this entirely does away with nature and what exists by
nature. For those things are natural which, by a continuous movement origi- 15
nated from an internal principle, arrive at some end: the same end is not reached
from every principle; nor any chance end, but always the tendency in each is
towards the same end, if there is no impediment.

The end and the means towards it may come about by chance. We say, for
instance, that a stranger has come by chance, paid the ransom, and gone away, 20
when he does so as if he had come for that purpose, though it was not for that
that he came. This is accidental, for chance is an accidental cause, as I remarked
before. But when an event takes place always or for the most part, it is not acci- 25
dental or by chance. In natural products the sequence is invariable, if there is no
impediment.

It is absurd to suppose that purpose is not present because we do not
observe the agent deliberating. Art does not deliberate. If the ship-building art
were in the wood, it would produce the same results by nature. If, therefore,
purpose is present in art, it is present also in nature. The best illustration is a doc- 30
tor doctoring himself: nature is like that.

It is plain then that nature is a cause, a cause that operates for a purpose.

9. As regards what is of necessity, we must ask whether the necessity is
hypothetical, or simple as well. The current view places what is of necessity in
the process of production, just as if one were to suppose that the wall of a house 200^{a}1
necessarily comes to be because what is heavy is naturally carried downwards
and what is light to the top, so that the stones and foundations take the lowest
place, with earth above because it is lighter, and wood at the top of all as being
the lightest. Whereas, though the wall does not come to be *without* these, it is not 5
due to these, except as its material cause: it comes to be for the sake of sheltering
and guarding certain things. Similarly in all other things which involve that for
the sake of which: the product cannot come to be without things which have a
necessary nature, but it is not due to these (except as its material); it comes to be
for an end. For instance, why is a saw such as it is? To effect so-and-so and for 10
the sake of so-and-so. This end, however, cannot be realized unless the saw is
made of iron. It is, therefore, necessary for it to be of iron, if we are to have a saw
and perform the operation of sawing. What is necessary then, is necessary on a
hypothesis, not as an end. Necessity is in the matter, while that for the sake of
which is in the definition.

15   Necessity in mathematics is in a way similar to necessity in things which
come to be through the operation of nature. Since a straight line is what it is, it
is necessary that the angles of a triangle should equal two right angles. But not
conversely; though if the angles are *not* equal to two right angles, then the
straight line is not what it is either. But in things which come to be for an end,
20 the reverse is true. If the end is to exist or does exist, that also which precedes it
will exist or does exist; otherwise just as there, if the conclusion is not true, the
principle will not be true, so here the end or that for the sake of which will not
exist. For this too is itself a principle, but of the reasoning, not of the action. (In
mathematics the principle is the principle of the reasoning only, as there is no
25 action.) If then there is to be a house, such-and-such things must be made or be
there already or exist, or generally the matter relative to the end, bricks and
stones if it is a house. But the end is not due to these except as the matter, nor
will it come to exist because of them. Yet if they do not exist at all, neither will
the house, or the saw—the former in the absence of stones, the latter in the
absence of iron—just as in the other case the principles will not be true, if the
30 angles of the triangle are not equal to two right angles.
      The necessary in nature, then, is plainly what we call by the name of matter
and the changes in it. Both causes must be stated by the student of nature, but
especially the end; for that is the cause of the matter, not vice versa, and the end
is that for the sake of which, and the principle starts from the definition or
200^{b}1 essence: as in artificial products, since a house is of such-and-such a kind, certain things must *necessarily* come to be or be there already, or since health is this,
these things must necessarily come to be or be there already, so too if man is this,
then these; if these then those. Perhaps the necessary is present also in the definition. For if one defines the operation of sawing as being a certain kind of
5 dividing, then this cannot come about unless the saw has teeth of a certain kind;
and these cannot be unless it is of iron. For in the definition too there are some
parts that stand as matter.

COMMENTS

Aristotle is criticizing the *Phaedo* passage you have just read. Are these good objections? Is Aristotle a fair critic of Plato here?

      Aristotle's own account of "the four causes," as it is often called, distinguishes
four types of factors that we point to when we give explanations of a thing. Clearly,
he thinks that philosophers like Plato have gone wrong by failing to see that different kinds of factors explain in different ways, which need not compete with one
another.

      Only Aristotle's moving or efficient cause is at all like what we would call a
cause—something that gets things moving, makes a difference. (Later Greek philosophers tended to think that this was the basic or proper notion of cause.) The material from which a thing is made and a thing's form or defining nature are factors that
are important for Aristotle in his discussions of change in the natural world. Also

important for him is the "final cause"; he defends what is called teleology, the view that in nature things work toward goals and that some changes are end directed. He thinks that if we do not regard some things as being the way they are for the sake of larger systems of which they form parts, we shall be hopelessly unable to explain what we find in nature. This claim has generally been rejected by modern science, but sometimes for the wrong reason. Aristotle thinks that what we observe about animals shows us that the way they are made up serves the good of the species and is there for that purpose. Animals, including ourselves, are not there for the sake of some larger purpose. In the medieval period, Aristotle's ideas were made part of systems of thought in which we and everything in nature are seen as having a part in God's purpose, but this is no part of Aristotle's thought.

PLUTARCH

Plutarch of Chaironea (c. A.D. 50–120) lived in a small town all his life, but was a widely respected Platonic philosopher and had a philosophical school. He wrote extensively on philosophy and religion (he was a priest at Delphi), but many of his more philosophical works have been lost. He is best known for his series of "Parallel Lives," in which famous Romans are paired with famous Greeks. Like many Greeks living under the Roman empire, Plutarch had a view of the Greek past that was highly inflated and romanticized and presented the Greeks as the equals of and culturally superior to the Romans. The "Parallel Lives" were popular when they were translated in the Renaissance (they are the major source of some of Shakespeare's plays, for example) and greatly influenced educated people's perspectives on the ancient world until the start of more scholarly studies in the nineteenth century.

Life of Pericles 6

PLUTARCH

Pericles, the Athenian politician, gained advantages from his association with Anaxagoras, including that of being above superstition, which is produced by amazement about heavenly phenomena in people who are ignorant of the causes of these things, terrified out of their wits where the gods are concerned, and confused through their inexperience of them. Theories about the natural world rid us of fearful and morbid superstition and produce piety that is secure and brings good hopes with it.

There is a story that once Pericles was sent from his country estate the head of a one-horned ram. Lampon the prophet saw that the horn grew strong and

solid from the middle of the forehead and said that although there were two
political factions in the city, that of Thucydides and that of Pericles, power
would come to only one—and it would be the one to whom this sign had been
given. Anaxagoras, however, had the skull cut open and showed that the brain
had not filled its receptacle, but had contracted to a point like an egg at the place
in the cavity from which the root of the horn took its origin. At the time, it was
Anaxagoras whom the audience admired, but later it was Lampon, since
Thucydides was overthrown, and the people's affairs were run entirely by
Pericles.

In my view there was nothing to prevent both of them being right, the natural philosopher and the prophet. One of them discovered the cause and the
other the purpose. It was Anaxagoras' business to observe what a thing comes
from and how it does so, and Lampon's to foretell what the point of it was and
what it was a sign of. People who say that discovering the cause of a thing gets
rid of it as a sign fail to notice that along with divine matters they are abolishing
indicators that have been contrived by human skill, such as the ringing of
gongs. the lighting of fire-beacons, and shadows on sundials. Each of these has
been made, by means of some cause and contrivance, to be the sign for something. But this is doubtless the subject of another essay.

COMMENTS

Plutarch, who is a Platonist, is more open-minded than Plato himself about the compatibility of types of explanation; possibly he is influenced by Aristotle's idea that different kinds of explanations need not compete. The kind of purpose in this story,
however, is not Aristotle's kind of natural goal, but particular divine intervention.
What do you think Aristotle would have said about this case?

The Epicureans against Teleology

1. Even if I were ignorant of what the elements of the world in fact are, I
would still dare to assert on the basis of the ways of heaven themselves, and to
prove from many other things, that in no way is the nature of things brought
about for us by divine power; so great are the faults with which it is endowed.

First, of all, that is covered by the huge expanse of the heaven; mountains
and forests full of wild beasts have taken possession of a greedy share, while
part is held by rocks and broad marshes and the sea that keeps the shores of
lands wide apart. Of these about two thirds are robbed from humans by burning heat and constantly falling frost. Even the farmland that remains would be
covered with briars by nature's own force, if force by humans did not resist—a
force used to groaning over stout hoes in order to survive and to part the earth
by the pressure of the plough. If we did not, by turning the fruitful soils with the

ploughshare and furrowing the earth, bring about their growth, crops would not of their own accord spring up into the soft breezes. And sometimes even then, when they have been produced with great labor, and are already all spreading leaves and flowers over the earth, they are dried up by too great heat from the heavenly sun or perish because of sudden rains or cold frosts or are battered by the blasts of winds in a violent storm.

Besides, why does nature nourish and increase on land and sea the fearsome tribe of wild beasts, hostile to humans? Why do the yearly seasons bring on diseases? Why does premature death walk abroad?

A baby lies naked on the ground when once nature has spilt him forth with throes from his mother's womb, like a sailor cast ashore by the cruel waves, without speech, lacking every vital support; he fills the place with unhappy wailings—as is right, considering how many evils it remains for him to go through in life. But the various herds of domestic and wild animals grow up without need of rattles or for any of them to have the smiling and broken baby talk of a nurse and without seeking different clothes for different seasons of the year. They need no weapons, besides, or high walls to protect what they have, since the earth itself and nature the maker of things provides everything for all of them in plenty. (Lucretius, *The Nature of Things* V, 194–234)

2. Here is a fault in these matters that I strongly wish you to avoid, a mistake to shun with precaution—taking the clear lights of the eyes to have been created so that we might see, the ends of the calves and thighs to be jointed and based upon the feet precisely so that we could take long strides forward, the forearms fitted to the strong upper arms and fitted with hands on both sides so that we might be able to do what would be of use for life. All other explanations of this kind get things backward because of twisted reasoning, since nothing is brought about in our body in order that we may be able to use it—rather, what has been brought about gives rise to its use. The lights of the eyes were not brought about before there was seeing, nor was there using of words to plead before the tongue was made. Rather, the origins of the tongue came far before there was speech; ears were made long before sounds were heard; and all our limbs, in my view, existed long before there could be a use for them.

To the contrary, fighting hand to hand, tearing limbs apart, and fouling bodies with blood existed long before flashing weapons flew through the air, and nature compelled humans to avoid wounds before the left arm could hold up the protection of a shield made by skill. Doubtless, giving the tired body to repose is also much more ancient than the soft sheets of a bed, and quenching our thirst came before drinking cups. It can be believed, therefore, that these things, which were discovered from their use and from living, were invented for the sake of being used. But it is entirely different with all those things that were brought about first and only afterward gave rise to a preconception of their usefulness. Foremost among these we see to be the senses and the limbs; so, to repeat, it is completely incredible that they could have been brought about for the function of usefulness. (Lucretius, *The Nature of Things* IV, 823–857)

COMMENTS

Epicurus is the only major ancient philosopher to reject teleology and hence to claim that our philosophical and scientific accounts of the world we live in should make no appeal to goals or ends in nature. The Epicurean theory of the universe is very economical: all there ultimately is are atoms and void, and our world is the product of random, non-goal-directed collisions of atoms in the void. Moreover, we have no reason to think that our world is the only one that there is; atomic collisions are likely to have produced other worlds, too—in fact, infinitely many. This is a worldview that is designed to stress to would-be Epicureans that the world was not created for their benefit and hence to get them to realize that they should take responsibility for their own lives and happiness.

How good are the arguments, however? Lucretius stresses that we do not have good reason to think that the world was created by the gods for our benefit. Aristotle's teleology, however, does not include such a view. Lucretius also gives us arguments against the idea that animal parts or behavior were designed to fulfill a function. Again, though, this is not what Aristotle is arguing. Are the Epicurean arguments here effective against Aristotle's arguments, in *Physics* II, 8–9, for teleology in nature?

D. Time

Ancient philosophy contains many fascinating discussions of metaphysical questions about problems, such as time, place, the infinite, motion, and the question of what the basic entities in our universe are. This selection gives you an idea of the richness and variety to be found.

Physics IV, 10–11, 14

ARISTOTLE

10. Next for discussion after the subjects mentioned is time. The best plan
30 will be to begin by working out the difficulties connected with it, making use of the current arguments. First, does it belong to the class of things that exist or to that of things that do not exist? Then secondly, what is its nature? To start, then:
218ᵉ1 the following considerations would make one suspect that it either does not exist at all or barely, and in the obscure way. One part of it has been and is not, while the other is going to be and is not yet. Yet time—both infinite time and any time you like to take—is made up of these. One would naturally suppose that what is made up of things which do not exist could have no share in reality.

Further, if a divisible thing is to exist, it is necessary that, when it exists, all or some of its parts must exist. But of time some parts have been, while others 5 are going to be, and no part of it *is*, though it is divisible. For the "now" is not a part: a part is a measure of the whole, which must be made up of parts. Time, on the other hand, is not held to be made up of "nows."

Again, the "now" which seems to bound the past and the future—does it always remain one and the same or is it always other and other? It is hard to say. 10

If it is always different and different, and if none of the *parts* in time which are other and other are simultaneous (unless the one contains and the other is contained, as the shorter time is by the longer), and if the "now" which is not, but formerly was, must have ceased to be at some time, the *"nows"* too cannot 15 be simultaneous with one another, but the prior "now" must always have ceased to be. But the prior "now" cannot have ceased to be in itself (since it then existed); yet it cannot have ceased to be in another "now." For we may lay it down that one "now" cannot be next to another, any more than a point to a point. If then it did not cease to be in the next "now" but in another, it would 20 exist simultaneously with the innumerable "nows" between the two—which is impossible.

Yes, but neither is it possible for the "now" to remain always the same. No determinate divisible thing has a single termination, whether it is continuously extended in one or in more than one dimension; but the "now" is a termination, and it is possible to cut off a determinate time. Further, if coincidence in time (i.e. 25 being neither prior nor posterior) means to be in one and the same "now," then, if both what is before and what is after are in this same "now," things which happened ten thousand years ago would be simultaneous with what has happened to-day, and nothing would be before or after anything else.

This may serve as a statement of the difficulties about the attributes of time. 30

As to what time is or what is its nature, the traditional accounts give us as little light as the preliminary problems which we have worked through.

Some assert that it is the movement of the whole, others that it is the sphere itself.   218ᵇ1

Yet part, too, of the revolution is a time, but it certainly is not a revolution; for what is taken is part of a revolution, not a revolution. Besides, if there were more heavens than one, the movement of any of them equally would be time, so that there would be many times at the same time.   5

Those who said that time is the sphere of the whole thought so, no doubt, on the ground that all things are in time and all things are in the sphere of the whole. The view is too naive for it to be worth while to consider the impossibilities implied in it.

But as time is most usually supposed to be motion and a kind of change, we 10 must consider this view.

Now the change or movement of each thing is only *in* the thing which changes or *where* the thing itself which moves or change may chance to be. But time is present equally everywhere and with all things.

Again, change is always faster or slower, whereas time is not; for fast and 15 slow are defined by time—fast is what moves much in a short time, slow what moves little in a long time; but time is not defined by time, by being either a certain amount or a certain kind of it.

Clearly then it is not movement. (We need not distinguish at present
20 between movement and change.)

11. But neither does time exist without change; for when the state of our minds does not change at all, or we have not noticed its changing, we do not think that time has elapsed, any more than those who are fabled to sleep among
25 the heroes in Sardinia do when they are awakened; for they connect the earlier "now" with the later and make them one, cutting out the interval because of their failure to notice it. So, just as, if the "now" were not different but one and the same, there would not have been time, so too when its difference escapes our notice the interval does not seem to be time. If, then, the non-realization of the
30 existence of time happens to us when we do not distinguish any change, but the mind seems to stay in one indivisible state, and when we perceive and distinguish we say time has elapsed, evidently time is not independent of movement
219ª1 and change. It is evident, then, that time is neither movement nor independent of movement.

We must take this as our starting-point and try to discover—since we wish to know what time is—what exactly it has to do with movement.

Now we perceive movement and time together; for even when it is dark and
5 we are not being affected through the body, if any movement takes place in the mind we at once suppose that some time has indeed elapsed; and not only that but also, when some time is thought to have passed, some movement also along with it seems to have taken place. Hence time is either movement or something that belongs to movement. Since then it is not movement, it must be the other.
10 But what is moved is moved from something to something, and all magnitude is continuous. Therefore the movement goes with the magnitude. Because the magnitude is continuous, the movement too is continuous, and if the movement, then the time; for the time that has passed is always thought to be as great as the movement.
15 The distinction of before and after holds primarily, then, in place; and there in virtue of relative position. Since then before and after hold in magnitude, they must hold also in movement, these corresponding to those. But also in time the distinction of before and after must hold; for time and movement always corre-
20 spond with each other. The before and after in motion identical in substratum with motion yet differs from it in being, and is not identical with motion.

But we apprehend time only when we have marked motion, marking it by before and after; and it is only when we have perceived before and after in
25 motion that we say that time has elapsed. Now we mark them by judging that one thing is different from another, and that some third thing is intermediate to them. When we think of the extremes as different from the middle and the mind pronounces that the "nows" are two, one before and one after, it is then that we say that there is time, and this that we say is time. For what is bounded by the "now" is thought to be time—we may assume this.

When, therefore, we perceive the "now" as one, and neither as before and 30
after in a motion nor as the same element but in relation to a "before" and an
"after," no time is thought to have elapsed, because there has been no motion
either. On the other hand, when we do perceive a "before" and an "after," then
we say that there is time. For time is just this—number of motion in respect of 219ᵇ1
"before" and "after."

Hence time is not movement, but only movement in so far as it admits of
enumeration. An indication of this: we discriminate the more or the less by
number, but more or less movement by time. Time then is a kind of number. 5
(Number, we must note, is used in two ways—both of what is counted or countable and also of that with which we count. Time, then, is what is counted, not
that with which we count: these are different kinds of thing.)

Just as motion is a perpetual succession, so also is time. But every simulta- 10
neous time is the same; for the "now" is the same in substratum—though its
being is different—and the "now" determines time, in so far as time involves the
before and after.

The "now" in one sense is the same, in another it is not the same. In so far
as it is in succession, it is different (which is just what its being now was supposed to mean), but its substratum is the same; for motion, as was said, goes 15
with magnitude, and time, as we maintain, with motion. Similarly, then, there
corresponds to the point the body which is carried along, and by which we are
aware of the motion and of the before and after involved in it. This is an identical *substratum* (whether a point or a stone or something else of the kind), but it
is different in definition—as the sophists assume that Coriscus' being in the
Lyceum is a different thing from Coriscus' being in the market-place. And the 20
body which is carried along is different, in so far as it is at one time here and at
another there. But the "now" corresponds to the body that is carried along, as
time corresponds to the mention. For it is by means of the body that is carried
along that we become aware of the before and after in the motion, and if we 25
regard these as countable we get the "now." Hence in these also the "now" as
substratum remains the same (for it is what is before and after in movement),
but its being is different; for it is in so far as the before and after is that we get
the "now." This is what is most knowable; for motion is known because of that
which is moved, locomotion because of that which is carried. For what is carried 30
is a "this," the movement is not. Thus the "now" in one sense is always the
same, in another it is not the same; for this is true also of what is carried.

Clearly, too, if there were no time, there would be no "now," and vice versa. 220ᵃ1
Just as the moving body and its locomotion involve each other mutually, so too
do the number of the moving body and the number of its locomotion. For the
number of the locomotion is time, while the " now" corresponds to the moving
body, and is like the unit of number.

Time, then, also is both made continuous by the "now" and divided at it. For 5
here too there is a correspondence with the locomotion and the moving body.
For the motion or locomotion is made one by the thing which is moved, because
it is one—not because it is one in substratum (for there might be pauses in the

movement of such a thing)—but because it is one in definition; for this determines the movement as "before" and "after." Here, too, there is a correspon-
10 dence with the point; for the point also both connects and terminates the
length—it is the beginning of one and the end of another. But when you take it
in this way, using the one point as two, a pause is necessary, if the same point is
to be the beginning and the end. The "now" on the other hand, since the body
carried is moving, is always different.
15   Hence time is not number in the sense in which there is number of the same
point because it is beginning and end, but rather as the extremities of a line form
a number, and not as the parts of the line do so, both for the reason given (for
we can use the middle point as two, so that on that analogy time might stand
still), and further because obviously the "now" is no *part* of time nor the section
20 any part of the movement, any more than the points are parts of the line—for it
is two *lines* that are *parts* of one line.
          In so far then as the "now" is a boundary, it is not time, but an attribute of
it; in so far as it numbers, it is number; for boundaries being only to that which
they bound, but number (e.g. ten) is the number of these horses, and belongs
also elsewhere.
25   It is clear, then, that time is number of movement in respect of the before and
after, and is continuous since it is an attribute of what is continuous.

          14. It is also worth considering how time can be related to the soul; and why
time is thought to be in everything, both in earth and in sea and in heaven. It is
because it is an attribute, or state, of movement (since it is the number of move-
20 ment) and all these things are movable (for they are all in place), and time and
movement are together, both in respect of potentiality and in respect of actuality?
          Whether if soul did not exist time would exist or not, is a question that may
fairly be asked; for if there cannot be some one to count there cannot be anything
that can be counted either, so that evidently there cannot be number; for num-
25 ber is either what has been, or what can be, counted. But if nothing but soul, or
in soul reason, is qualified to count, it is impossible for there to be time unless
there is soul, but only that of which time is an attribute, i.e. if *movement* can exist
without soul. The before and after are attributes of movement, and time is these
qua countable.

COMMENTS

Aristotle begins his discussion of time, as he often does in introducing philosophical
problems, by bringing together difficulties that arise from our ordinary view of time
and use of temporal expressions. His own solution is supposed to solve these problems and to be helpful in showing why they arise.
          For Aristotle, difficulties about the nature of time involve the question of whether
time exists, or is real, and this question is connected with problems about the past
and future, as opposed to the present. Intuitively, the present seems to be real in a

way that the past and future are not. But the past, present, and future are all "parts" of time, so we are faced with the problem that if time exists, its parts do not.

Aristotle's own solution, though difficult in detail, stresses two main points. One is that "now," which we use to pick out the present, does not mark out a period of time. Rather, "now" divides past from future at an instant, which is a boundary, rather than a period. The other point is that time is dependent on change; it is, in fact, the number or measure of change. Hence (this connects with Aristotle's views about the "now") time is continuous, since it is dependent on change, which is continuous, and change is, in turn, dependent on magnitude, which is continuous.

Aristotle does not doubt that time is a feature of the natural world that we study, He also considers the issue that time seems to be dependent on the existence of human beings to count or measure times. For Aristotle, this is not deeply problematic, since we humans are part of the natural world and subject to study like the rest of it. Later Augustine will draw a radically different kind of conclusion from the relation of time and the human mind.

The Stoics on Time

1. Chrysippus most clearly says this—that no time is wholly present. Since continuous things are infinitely divisible, every time is also infinitely divisible in accordance with this division, so that no time is present exactly, but is broadly said to be present. Only the present, he says, obtains, while the past and the future subsist, but in no way obtain, just as only those predicates are said to obtain that actually belong—e.g., walking around obtains in my case when I am walking around, but does not obtain when I am lying down or sitting down. (Stobaeus, *Eclogae* I, 106, 13–22)

2. It is contrary to our common [intuitive] conception to hold that future and past time exist while no present time exists, to hold that *just now* and *the other day* subsist while *now* is in no way at all. But this is what happens to the Stoics, who do not allow that there is a minimal time and don't want *now* to be partless, but assert that whatever you think you have grasped as present in your thought is partly future and partly past, so that nothing is left corresponding to *now* and no part of the present time is left, if whatever time is said to be present is distributed into parts that are future and parts that are past.

Hence one of two things follows for them. Either in positing "time was" and "time will be" they destroy "time is." Or if they keep "there is present time," of which part was present and part will be present, they also have to say that of what obtains part is future and part is past and that there is a part of *now* that is earlier and a part that is later—and hence that what is not yet *now* and what is no longer *now* both *are now*, since the past is no longer *now* and the future is not yet *now*. If they divide things this way, it follows that they have to say that today is partly yesterday and partly tomorrow, this year is partly last year and partly next year, and simultaneously is partly earlier and partly later. They muddle things and can produce nothing more reasonable, once they identify *not yet* and *already* and *no longer* and *now* and *not now*. All other people assume that *recently* and *soon* are parts [of time] distinct from *now*—the former before *now*, the latter after it. That's what they think. That's how they usually proceed.

But among the Stoics, Archedemus says that *now* is a kind of joining and connection of the past and of what is coming. He fails to notice that he has destroyed all of time. For if *now* is not time but a limit of time and if every part of time is like *now*, then it appears that there is no part that the whole of time has; it is completely dissolved into limits and connections and joinings.

But Chrysippus, wanting to make a good job of the division [of time into parts] says in *On the Void* and some other books that the part of time that is past and the part that is future do not obtain, but subsist, while only the present obtains. However, in *On Parts*, books 3, 4, and 5, he posits that of present time part is future and part past. So it turns out that he divides the part of time that obtains into parts of what obtains that don't obtain! Or, rather, he leaves nothing at all obtaining of time if the present has no part that is not future or past. (Plutarch, *On Common Conceptions* 1081c–1082a)

COMMENTS

We learn of the Stoic view of time partly through a later account and partly through hostile criticism of it. Plutarch, who was a Platonist, finds the Stoics dislikable and fundamentally misguided. This passage is from a work in which he tries to show that Stoic theories are grossly counterintuitive, although they claim support from our intuitions. Rather than just read the Stoic view from these passages, the reader has to do some work and come to a conclusion as to whether Plutarch is right or whether the Stoics can say all the things he ascribes to them without conflicting with our ordinary views about time.

Chrysippus, an influential early Stoic, held two views about time. One is that only the present exists (or "obtains") while past and future do not exist (though for the Stoics they can still "subsist" as conditions for the existence of things that do exist). The other is that the present is what has been called "retrenchable." If we say that something is happening now, the extent of time that we indicate by "now" may vary a great deal, depending on what exactly it is that we focus on. By "now," we may indicate today—or a smaller part of today, such as the present minute, or a larger span than today—this month, this year, even this century. Plutarch complains that Chrysippus, in holding both these positions, is trapped into holding that there is no such time as the present, a conclusion that is grossly counterintuitive. Another Stoic, Archedemus, seems to have concluded that Aristotle was right and that "now" picks out a boundary of time, not a period. But is Chrysippus' position in fact viable? Plutarch says nothing of the point we find in the first passage, that no time is present *exactly*, but is said to be present "broadly." What difference is made by paying attention to this distinction?

AUGUSTINE

Aurelius Augustinus (A.D. 354–430), from Thagaste in North Africa, is the first major ancient philosopher to write in Latin without knowledge of Greek, and his work forms in many ways a transition from ancient to early medieval ways of thinking. Trained in oratory, Augustine restlessly went through a series of intellectual conversions to philosophy and forms of religion, until in 386 he was finally converted to orthodox catholic Christianity, the subject of his well-known *Confessions*. Augustine spent many years as bishop of Hippo in northern Africa and produced a vast range of works, ranging from philosophy to pastoral concerns. The *Confessions* is an unusually personal work for the time, giving us insights into his individual personality, but it is also a work of religious philosophy. In the section on time, we can see that Augustine finds intense and inward meaning in a philosophical problem in a way that makes it quite unlike Aristotle's more detached treatment of the issue.

Confessions IX, SELECTIONS

AUGUSTINE

xiv (17) There was therefore no time when you had not made something, because you made time itself. No times are coeternal with you since you are permanent. If they were permanent, they would not be times.

What is time? Who can explain this easily and briefly? Who can comprehend this even in thought so as to articulate the answer in words? Yet what do we speak of, in our familiar everyday conversation, more than of time? We surely know what we mean when we speak of it. We also know what is meant when we hear someone else talking about it. What then is time? Provided that no one asks me, I know. If I want to explain it to an inquirer, I do not know. But I confidently affirm myself to know that if nothing passes away, there is no past time, and if nothing arrives, there is no future time, and if nothing existed there would be no present time. Take the two tenses, past and future. How can they "be" when the past is not now present and the future is not yet present? Yet if the present were always present, it would not pass into the past: it would not be time but eternity. If then, in order to be time at all, the present is so made that it passes into the past, how can we say that this present also "is"? The cause of its being is that it will cease to be. So indeed we cannot truly say that time exists except in the sense that it tends towards non-existence.

From Augustine, *Confessions*, translated by H. Chadwick (Oxford: Oxford University Press, 1991). Reprinted with the permission of Oxford University Press.

xv (18) Nevertheless we speak of "a long time" and "a short time," and it is only of the past or the future that we say this. Of the past we speak of "a long time," when, for example, it is more than a hundred years ago. "A long time" in the future may mean a hundred years ahead. By "a short time ago" we would mean, say, ten days back, and "a short time ahead" might mean "in ten days' time." But how can something be long or short which does not exist? For the past now has no existence and the future is not yet. So we ought not to say of the past "It is long," but "it was long," and of the future "it will be long." My Lord, my light, does not your truth mock humanity at this point? This time past which was long, was it long when it was past or when it was still present? It could be long only when it existed to be long. Once past, it no longer was. Therefore it could not be long if it had entirely ceased to exist.

Therefore let us not say "The time past was long." For we cannot discover anything to be long when, after it has become past, it has ceased to be. But let us say "That time once present was long" because it was long at the time when it was present. For it had not yet passed away into non-existence. It existed so as to be able to be long. But after it had passed away, it simultaneously ceased to be long because it ceased to be.

(19) Human soul, let us see whether present time can be long. To you the power is granted to be aware of intervals of time, and to measure them. What answer will you give me? Are a hundred years in the present a long time? Consider first whether a hundred years can be present. For if the first year of the series is current, it is present, but ninety-nine are future, and so do not yet exist. If the second year is current, one is already past, the second is present, the remainder lie in the future. And so between the extremes, whatever year of this century we assume to be present, there will be some years before it which lie in the past, some in the future to come after it. It follows that a century could never be present.

Consider then whether if a single year is current, that can be present. If in this year the first month is current, the others lie in the future; if the second, then the first lies in the past and the rest do not yet exist. Therefore even a current year is not entirely present; and if it is not entirely present, it is not a year which is present. A year is twelve months, of which any month which is current is present; the others are either past or future. Moreover, not even a month which is current is present, but one day. If the first day, the others are future; if the last day, the others are past; any intermediary day falls between past and future.

(20) See—present time, which alone we find capable of being called long, is contracted to the space of hardly a single day. But let us examine that also; for not even one day is entirely present. All the hours of night and day add up to twenty-four. The first of them has the others in the future, the last has them in the past. Any hour between these has past hours before it, future hours after it. One hour is itself constituted of fugitive moments. Whatever part of it has flown away is past. What remains to it is future. If we can think of some bit of time which cannot be divided into even the smallest instantaneous moments, that alone is what we can call "present." And this time flies so quickly from future

into past that it is an interval with no duration. If it has duration, it is divisible into past and future. But the present occupies no space.

Where then is the time which we call long? Is it future? We do not really mean "It is long," since it does not yet exist to be long, but we mean it will be long. When will it be long? If it will then still lie in the future, it will not be long, since it will not yet exist to be long. But if it will be long at the time when, out of the future which does not yet exist, it begins to have being and will become present fact, so that it has the potentiality to be long, the present cries out in words already used that it cannot be long.

xvi (21) Nevertheless, Lord, we are conscious of intervals of time, and compare them with each other, and call some longer, others shorter. We also measure how much longer or shorter one period is than another, and answer that the one is twice or three times as much as the other, or that the two periods are equal. Moreover, we are measuring times which are past when our perception is the basis of measurement. But who can measure the past which does not now exist or the future which does not yet exist, unless perhaps someone dares to assert that he can measure what has no existence? At the moment when time is passing, it can be perceived and measured. But when it has passed and is not present, it cannot be.

xviii (23) Allow me, Lord, to take my investigation further. My hope, let not my attention be distracted. If future and past events exist, I want to know where they are. If I have not the strength to discover the answer, at least I know that wherever they are, they are not there as future or past, but as present. For if there also they are future, they will not yet be there. If there also they are past, they are no longer there. Therefore, wherever they are, whatever they are, they do not exist except in the present. When a true narrative of the past is related, the memory produces not the actual events which have passed away but words conceived from images of them, which they fixed in the mind like imprints as they passed through the senses. Thus my boyhood, which is no longer, lies in past time which is no longer. But when I am recollecting and telling my story, I am looking on its image in present time, since it is still in my memory. Whether a similar cause is operative in predictions of the future, in the sense that images of realities which do not yet exist are presented as already in existence, I confess, my God, I do not know. At least I know this much: we frequently think out in advance our future actions, and that premeditation is in the present; but the action which we premeditate is not yet in being because it lies in the future. But when we have embarked on the action and what we were premeditating begins to be put into effect, then that action will have existence, since then it will be not future but present.

(24) Whatever may be the way in which the hidden presentiment of the future is known, nothing can be seen if it does not exist. Now that which already exists is not future but present. When therefore people speak of knowing the future, what is seen is not events which do not yet exist (that is, they really are future), but perhaps their causes or signs which already exist. In this way, to those

who see them they are not future but present, and that is the basis on which the future can be conceived in the mind and made the subject of prediction.

Again, these concepts already exist, and those who predict the future see these concepts as if already present to their minds.

Among a great mass of examples, let me mention one instance. I look at the dawn. I forecast that the sun will rise. What I am looking at is present, what I am forecasting is future. It is not the sun which lies in the future (it already exists) but its rise, which has not yet arrived. Yet unless I were mentally imagining its rise, as now when I am speaking about it, I could not predict it. But the dawn glow which I see in the sky is not sunrise, which it precedes, nor is the imagining of sunrise in my mind the actuality. These are both discerned as present so that the coming sunrise may be foretold.

So future events do not yet exist, and if they are not yet present, they do not exist; and if they have no being, they cannot be seen at all. But they can be predicted from present events which are already present and can be seen.

xx (26) What is by now evident and clear is that neither future nor past exists, and it is inexact language to speak of three times—past, present, and future. Perhaps it would be exact to say: there are three times, a present of things past, a present of things present, a present of things to come. In the soul there are these three aspects of time, and I do not see them anywhere else. The present considering the past is the memory, the present considering the present is immediate awareness, the present considering the future is expectation. If we are allowed to use such language, I see three times, and I admit they are three. Moreover, we may say, There are three times, past, present, and future. This customary way of speaking is incorrect, but it is common usage. Let us accept the usage. I do not object and offer no opposition or criticism, as long as what is said is being understood, namely that neither the future nor the past is now present. There are few usages of everyday speech which are exact, and most of our language is inexact. Yet what we mean is communicated.

xxi (27) A little earlier I observed that we measure past periods of time so that we can say that one period is twice as long as another or equal to it, and likewise of other periods of time which we are capable of measuring and reporting. Therefore, as I was saying, we measure periods of time as they are passing, and if anyone says to me "How do you know?" I reply: I know it because we do measure time and cannot measure what has no being; and past and future have none. But how do we measure present time when it has no extension? It is measured when it passes, but not when it has passed, because then there will be nothing there to measure.

When time is measured, where does it come from, by what route does it pass, and where does it go? It must come out of the future, pass by the present, and go into the past; so it comes from what as yet does not exist, passes through that which lacks extension, and goes into that which is now non-existent. Yet what do we measure but time over some extension? When we speak of lengths of time as single, duple, triple, and equal, or any other temporal relation of this kind, we must be speaking of periods of time possessing extension. In what extension then do we measure time as it is passing? Is it in the future out of which it comes to pass by? No, for we do not measure what does not yet exist. Is it in the present through which it passes? No, for we cannot measure that which has no extension. Is it in the past into which it is moving? No, for we cannot measure what now does not exist.

xxvi (33) My confession to you is surely truthful when my soul declares that times are measured by me. So my God, I measure, and do not know what I am measuring. I measure the motion of a body by time. Then am I not measuring time itself? I could not measure the movement of a body, its period of transit and how long it takes to go from A to B, unless I were measuring the time in which this movement occurs. How then do I measure time itself? Or do we use a shorter time to measure a longer time, as when, for example, we measure a transom by using a cubit length? So we can be seen to use the length of a short syllable as a measure when we say that a long syllable is twice its length. By this method we measure poems by the number of lines, lines by the number of feet, feet by the number of syllables, and long vowels by short, not by the number of pages (for that would give us a measure of space, not of time). The criterion is the time words occupy in recitation, so that we say "That is a long poem, for it consists of so many lines. The lines are long, for they consist of so many feet. The feet are long for they extend over so many syllables. The syllable is long, for it is double the length of a short one."

Nevertheless, even so we have not reached a reliable measure of time. It may happen that a short line, if pronounced slowly, takes longer to read aloud than a longer line taken faster. The same principle applies to a poem or a foot or a syllable. That is why I have come to think that time is simply a distension. But of what is it a distension? I do not know, but it would be surprising if it is not that of the mind itself. What do I measure, I beg you, my God, when I say without precision "This period is longer than that," or with precision "This is twice as long as that"? That I am measuring time I know. But I am not measuring the future which does not yet exist, nor the present which has no extension, nor the past which is no longer in being. What then am I measuring? Time as it passes but not time past? That is what I affirmed earlier.

xxvii (34) Stand firm, my mind, concentrate with resolution. "God is our help, he has made us and not we ourselves" (Ps. 61: 9; 99: 3). Concentrate on the point where truth is beginning to dawn. For example, a physical voice begins to sound. It sounds. It continues to sound, and then ceases. Silence has now come, and the voice is past. There is now no sound. Before it sounded it lay in the future. It could not be measured because it did not exist; and now it cannot be measured because it has ceased to be. At the time when it was sounding, it was possible because at that time it existed to be measured. Yet even then it had no permanence. It came and went. Did this make it more possible to measure? In process of passing away it was extended through a certain space of time by which it could be measured, since the present occupies no length of time. Therefore during that transient process it could be measured. But take, for example, another voice. It begins to sound and continues to do so unflaggingly without any interruption. Let us measure it while it is sounding; when it has ceased to sound, it will be past and will not exist to be measurable. Evidently we may at that stage measure it by saying how long it lasted. But if it is still sounding, it cannot be measured except from the starting moment when it began to sound to the finish when it ceased. What we measure is the actual interval from the beginning to the end. That is why a sound which has not yet ended cannot be measured: one cannot say how long or how short it is, nor that it is equal to some other length of time or that in relation to another it is single or double or any such proportion. But when it has come to an end, then it will already have ceased to be. By what method then can it be measured?

Nevertheless we do measure periods of time. And yet the times we measure are not those which do not yet exist, nor those which already have no existence, nor those which extend over no interval of time, nor those which reach no conclusions. So the times we measure are not future nor past nor present nor those in process of passing away. Yet we measure periods of time.

(35) "God, Creator of all things"—*Deus Creator omnium*—the line consists of eight syllables, in which short and long syllables alternate. So the four which are short (the first, third, fifth, and seventh) are single in relation to the four long syllables (the second, fourth, sixth and eighth). Each of the long syllables has twice the time of the short. As I recite the words, I also observe that this is so, for it is evident to sense-perception. To the degree that the sense-perception is unambiguous, I measure the long syllable by the short one, and perceive it to be twice the length. But when one syllable sounds after another, the short first, the long after it, how shall I keep my hold on the short, and how use it to apply a measure to the long, so as to verify that the long is twice as much? The long does not begin to sound unless the short has ceased to sound. I can hardly measure the long during the presence of its sound, as measuring becomes possible only after it has ended. When it is finished, it has gone into the past. What then is it which I measure? Where is the short syllable with which I am making my measurement? Where is the long which I am measuring? Both have sounded; they have flown away; they belong to the past. They now do not exist. And I offer my measurement and declare as confidently as a practised sense-perception will allow, that the short is single, the long double—I mean in the time they occupy. I can do this only because they are past and gone. Therefore it is not the syllables which I am measuring, but something in my memory which stays fixed there.

(36) So it is in you, my mind, that I measure periods of time. Do not distract me; that is, do not allow yourself to be distracted by the hubbub of the impressions being made upon you. In you, I affirm, I measure periods of time. The impression which passing events make upon you abides when they are gone. That present consciousness is what I am measuring, not the stream of past events which have caused it. When I measure periods of time, that is what I am

actually measuring. Therefore, either this is what time is, or time is not what I am measuring.

What happens when we measure silences and say that a given period of silence lasted as long as a given sound? Do we direct our attention to measuring it as if a sound occurred, so that we are enabled to judge the intervals of the silences within the space of time concerned? For without any sound or utterance we mentally recite poems and lines and speeches, and we assess the lengths of their movements and the relative amounts of time they occupy, no differently from the way we would speak if we were actually making sounds. Suppose someone wished to utter a sound lasting a long time, and decided in advance how long that was going to be. He would have planned that space of time in silence. Entrusting that to his memory he would begin to utter the sound which continues until it has reached the intended end. It would be more accurate to say the utterance has sounded and will sound. For the part of it which is complete has sounded, but what remains will sound, and so the action is being accomplished as present attention transfers the future into the past. The future diminishes as the past grows, until the future has completely gone and everything is in the past.

xxviii (37) But how does this future, which does not yet exist, diminish or become consumed? Or how does the past, which now has no being, grow, unless there are three processes in the mind which in this is the active agent? For the mind expects and attends and remembers, so that what it expects passes through what has its attention to what it remembers. Who therefore can deny that the future does not yet exist? Yet already in the mind there is an expectation of the future. Who can deny that the past does not now exist? Yet there is still in the mind a memory of the past. None can deny that present time lacks any extension because it passes in a flash. Yet attention is continuous, and it is through this that what will be present progresses towards being absent. So the future, which does not exist, is not a long period of time. A long future is a long expectation of the future. And the past, which has no existence, is not a long period of time. A long past is a long memory of the past.

COMMENTS

The tone of Augustine's *Confessions* is deliberately different from that of previous discussions of time; for Augustine, the discussion is part of an intensely personal account of his intellectual and spiritual life, and he is writing for God, rather than for participants in a philosophical debate. Nonetheless, he is concerned about working through problems about time and coming to a satisfactory conclusion.

Augustine takes up more seriously than Aristotle the connection between time and the human mind. He also presses the importance of the point that we found in the Stoics, that the present is retrenchable. Augustine draws the conclusion that time is radically subjective; the different parts of time are simply mental states that can coexist in a human mind, although no coherent account can be given of how they can exist outside it.

Why does Augustine draw such a different conclusion from Aristotle from the dependence of time, as a measure of change, on human minds to do the measuring? Augustine and Aristotle differ not only in their accounts of time, but in their more general views of the place of humans in nature.

Does Augustine's account of time make sense of our ordinary views about time, as those of Aristotle and the Stoics are intended to do? If not, is this a problem for Augustine or for our ordinary views about time?

SECTION FIVE

HOW SHOULD YOU LIVE?

A. The Starting Point for Ethical Reflection

In the ancient world, the starting point for thinking ethically is the point at which you start thinking about your life as a whole. This will not happen until you have reached a stage of life at which you are mature enough to think about your life in the long term, and by that point you will already have an ethical context: You have grown up in a certain society, have a family and a position, and have taken in the major beliefs of your society about ethics. Ancient ethical theories do not try to get you to throw away all these beliefs or to pretend that ethically you are a blank sheet of paper. They get you to do what you are already doing—thinking about your life as a whole—but to do it more clearly and rigorously

Rhetoric I, 5 (EXTRACT)
ARISTOTLE

Nearly everyone has a kind of target, both privately for each person and in common, in aiming at which they make their choices and avoidances, and this is, in brief, happiness and its parts. So let us, by way of illustration, grasp what it is that happiness is, generally speaking, and what its parts consist of. All attempts to persuade and dissuade concern this and the things that conduce toward it and those opposed to it. For one should do the things that provide happiness or one of its parts or provide more, rather than less, and not do the things that destroy it or prevent it or produce the opposite.

Let happiness, then, be said to be doing well together with virtue or self-sufficiency of life or the most pleasant life together with security or affluence in possessions . . . together with the power to protect and make use of them. For virtually all agree that happiness is one or more of these things. If happiness is something like this, then its parts must necessarily be good birth, having many friends, having good friends, wealth, having good children, having many children, a good old age; further, the bodily virtues, such as health, beauty, strength, size, competitive power; and reputation, honor, good luck, and virtue. For a person would be most self-sufficient if he possessed the goods internal to him and external, since there are no others. Internal are those of the soul and in the body, and external are good birth, friends, money, and honor. Further, we think that there should be powers and luck, for this is how one's life would be most secure.

COMMENTS

Aristotle is giving an outline sketch of what ordinary people think about happiness. He points out that most people think in terms of their lives as a whole and try consciously to organize their lives each as a unity, rather than blundering from one decision to another. Aristotle finds this a natural and widespread way of thinking that can be taken for granted. He also takes it for granted that people think of this overall goal as happiness.

These two points are important for the form that ancient ethics takes. The assumption is that most people already think, more or less intelligently, in terms of seeking happiness in their life as a whole. Philosophers begin from these basic beliefs and work within this framework, accepting that we all seek happiness, that thoughtful people seek it consciously and reflectively, and that ethical philosophy tries to improve our ordinary beliefs about it. The Greek for happiness is *eudaimonia,* and Greek ethics are often called *eudaimonist* because of this framework.

What is wrong with ordinary people's views of happiness? As presented here, they appear commonsensical. People want to be healthy, rich, and good-looking, and they want to be popular and have a happy family life. They also want to be good people, who have the virtues. This is not very surprising and probably not different from the idea of happiness that many people have now. Questions and problems seem near the surface, however.

First, a view of your life as a whole demands that you set some priorities. If you want to be a virtuous person, for example, this will set bounds on the extent to which you can devote yourself to making money. If you regard all these things as "parts" of happiness, then a sensible view of your life as a whole is going to force some decisions about what kinds of parts they are and which are the most important.

Second, people seem to want "self-sufficiency"; they want not just to have riches, say, but to feel secure in their possession of riches. Yet many of the good things listed here as "parts" of happiness are such that either getting or keeping them is not, or not entirely, under your control. You may lose all your money if the stock market crashes, regardless of what you do. So people want things like health and wealth, but also want something more long term that their pursuit of health and wealth cannot guarantee.

It doesn't take much thought, then, to see that when reflecting on how best to live, people should ask whether happiness is really a matter of money and good looks or has more to do with what you make of your own life.

HERODOTUS

Herodotus of Halicarnassus (in Asia Minor) lived from the 480s to the 420s B.C. His *Histories,* the earliest historical narrative we possess, focuses on the earlier Persian Wars, together with much social and geographic background material. Herodotus' interests are narrative and discursive, but the word *historie,* from which we derive *history,* means inquiry, and Herodotus' stories are often shaped by a desire to raise or explore points of theoretical interest. The story of Solon and Croesus is unlikely to rest on an actual event, although both were real people. Solon, an Athenian politician, figures here as the stock Wise Man, and Croesus, a ruler of the Asia Minor kingdom of Lydia, figures as the Rich and Powerful King. The audience knew that Croesus had extended his prosperous kingdom and made it powerful, but eventually provoked the Persians, who conquered Lydia and deposed Croesus. This story is a Greek reflection on what happened to someone who trusted in the power of riches.

Histories I, 29–34

HERODOTUS

When these peoples had been subdued and while Croesus was increasing the Lydian empire, Sardis was at the height of its prosperity and was visited on occasion by every learned Greek who was alive at the time, including Solon of Athens. Two or three days after his arrival, Croesus had some attendants give Solon a thorough tour of his treasuries and show him how magnificent and valuable everything was. Once Solon had seen and examined everything, Croesus found an opportunity to put a question to him. "My dear guest from Athens," he said, "we have often heard about you in Sardis: you are famous for your learning and your travels. We hear that you love knowledge and have journeyed far and wide, to see the world. So I really want to ask you whether you have ever come across anyone who is happier than everyone else?"

In asking the question, he was expecting to be named as the happiest of all men, but Solon preferred truth to flattery and said, "Yes, my lord: Tellus of Athens."

Croesus was surprised at the answer and asked urgently: "What makes you think that Tellus is the happiest man?"

"In the first place," Solon replied, "while living in a prosperous state, Tellus had sons who were fine, upstanding men and he lived to see them all have children, all of whom survived. In the second place, his death came at a time when

From Herodotus, *Histories,* translated by Robin Waterfield (Oxford: Oxford University Press, 1998). Reprinted with the permission of Oxford University Press.

he had a good income, by our standards, and it was a glorious death. You see, in a battle at Eleusis between Athens and her neighbours he stepped into the breach and made the enemy turn tail and flee; he died, but his death was splendid, and the Athenians awarded him a public funeral on the spot where he fell, and greatly honoured him."

Croesus' attention was engaged by Solon's ideas about all the ways in which Tellus was well off, so he asked who was the second happiest person Solon knew; he had absolutely no doubt that he would carry off the second prize, at least. But Solon replied, "Cleobis and Biton, because these Argives made an adequate living and were also blessed with amazing physical strength. It's not just that the pair of them were both prize-winning athletes; there's also the following story about them. During a festival of Hera at Argos, their mother urgently needed to be taken to the sanctuary on her cart, but the oxen failed to turn up from the field in time. There was no time to waste, so the young men harnessed themselves to the yoke and pulled the cart with their mother riding on it. The distance to the temple was forty-five stades, and they took her all the way there. After this achievement of theirs, which was witnessed by the people assembled for the festival, they died in the best possible way; in fact, the god used them to show that it is better for a person to be dead than to be alive. What happened was that while the Argive men were standing around congratulating the young men on their strength, the women were telling their mother how lucky she was in her children. Their mother was overcome with joy at what her sons had done and the fame it would bring, and she went right up to the statue of the goddess, stood there and prayed that in return for the great honour her children Cleobis and Biton had done her, the goddess would give them whatever it is best for a human being to have. After she had finished her prayer, they participated in the rites and the feast, and then the young men lay down inside the actual temple for a rest. They never got to their feet again; they met their end there. The Argives had statues made of them and dedicated them at Delphi, on the grounds that they had been the best of men."

Croesus was angry with Solon for awarding the second prize for happiness to these young men, and he said, "My dear guest from Athens, do you hold our happiness in utter contempt? Is that why you are ranking us lower than even ordinary citizens?"

"Croesus," Solon replied, "when you asked me about men and their affairs, you were putting your question to someone who is well aware of how utterly jealous the divine is, and how it is likely to confound us. Anyone who lives for a long time is bound to see and endure many things he would rather avoid. I place the limit of a man's life at seventy years. Seventy years make 25,200 days, not counting the intercalary months; but if you increase the length of every other year by a month, so that the seasons happen when they should, there will be thirty-five such intercalary months in the seventy years, and these extra months will give us 1,050 days. So the sum total of all the days in seventy years is 26,250, but no two days bring events which are exactly the same. It follows, Croesus, that human life is entirely a matter of chance.

"Now, I can see that you are extremely rich and that you rule over large numbers of people, but I won't be in a position to say what you're asking me to say about you until I find out that you died well. You see, someone with vast wealth is no better off than someone who lives from day to day, unless good fortune attends him and sees to it that, when he dies, he dies well and with all his advantages intact. After all, plenty of extremely wealthy people are unfortunate, while plenty of people with moderate means are lucky; and someone with great wealth but bad fortune is better off than a lucky man in only two ways, whereas there are many ways in which a lucky man is better off than someone who is rich and unlucky. An unlucky rich man is more capable of satisfying his desires and of riding out disaster when it strikes, but a lucky man is better off than him in the following respects. Even though he is not as capable of coping with disaster and his desires, his good luck protects him, and he also avoids disfigurement and disease, has no experience of catastrophe, and is blessed with fine children and good looks. If, in addition to all this, he dies a heroic death, then he is the one you are after—he is the one who deserves to be described as happy. But until he is dead, you had better refrain from calling him happy, and just call him fortunate.

"Now, it is impossible for a mere mortal to have all these blessings at the same time, just as no country is entirely self-sufficient; any given country has some things, but lacks others, and the best country is the one which has the most. By the same token, no one person is self-sufficient: he has some things, but lacks others. The person who has and retains more of these advantages than others, and then dies well, my lord, is the one who, in my opinion, deserves the description in question. It is necessary to consider the end of anything, however, and to see how it will turn out, because the god often offers prosperity to men, but then destroys them utterly and completely."

These sentiments did not endear Solon to Croesus at all, and Croesus dismissed him as of no account. He was sure that anyone who ignored present benefits and told him to look to the end of everything was an ignoramus.

After Solon's departure, the weight of divine anger descended on Croesus, in all likelihood for thinking that he was the happiest man in the world.

COMMENTS

Croesus, a king of legendary riches, is here presented as someone who thinks that external goods are what matter for happiness, so that the more riches and power you have, the happier you will be. But Herodotus' audience already knew that Croesus eventually lost his kingdom.

Solon stresses that happiness cannot just lie in having riches and power; it depends on how your life as a whole turns out. His examples, however, show that he does not mean that the happy person will be the careful planner who saves for her later years. Tellus lived a conventionally good and happy life, leaving children to carry on the family, but he died prematurely in battle. Cleobis and Biton, at the height of their achievement, died young. The happy life is not the life devoted to achieving security, but may involve risk and aspiration. The point is that whether you are happy depends on what you make of your life. If you have made your life a noble one, then it is happy even if cut short. But Croesus' loss of riches and power will make his life unhappy because he sees his happiness as depending on them. Solon's point is not just that riches can always be lost, but that Croesus' priorities are wrong.

B. The First Theories: Virtue and Happiness

It is remarkable that the first ethical theories that we have—those of Democritus and Plato—are both very bold in the way that they try to reform ordinary people's thoughts about happiness. Both of them think that we should think about our lives more rationally and reflectively than we do and that the results of doing so would make us happy. Plato, in particular, stresses the importance of being a virtuous, moral person, implying (though he does not work it out rigorously) that this is all that is needed to be happy. Neither philosopher, however, makes his assumptions and framework explicit. Both simply take over the assumption that everyone seeks to be happy and give us a surprising account of how to achieve happiness.

DEMOCRITUS

Democritus of Abdera (c. 460–350s B.C.) wrote extensively on a wide number of topics, but apart from some fragments and later reports, his works are lost. His ideas were influential on later philosophers, however. Both his theory of atomism and his ethical view that our final end is a pleasant and tranquil state were taken up and developed later by Epicurus.

The actual inventor of atomism seems to have been an obscure figure called Leucippus, but it was Democritus who developed the theory and was associated with it. Atomism is the most influential of the pre-Socratic theories that attempted to account for the nature of the observable world by positing a small number of unobservable theoretical entities and a small number of mechanisms to get from them to the world we experience. Democritus posits only atoms, with differences of shape, and void and is notable among ancient theorists for having no use for teleology. The comments we have from him about knowledge are puzzling and have been thought both to support and to undermine skepticism about knowledge. We have a large number of fragments on ethical matters, enough to see how they might have fitted into the framework that later writers tell us he employed—that of criticizing our conception of the happiness that we all seek and of trying to replace it with a better one.

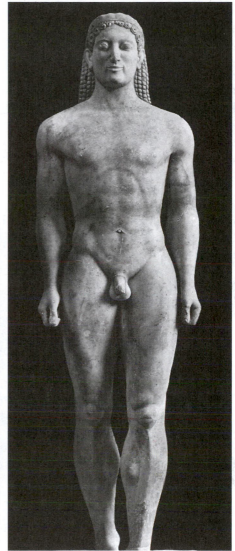

The Greeks were fascinated by the rich Eastern kingdom of Lydia. This is the sixth-century B.C. monument to a young man named after its king, Croesus. The inscription reads: "Stop and grieve at the tomb of dead Croesus, killed by wild Ares [the god of war] in the front rank of battle." The naked youth is not a portrait of Croesus; ideal types of young men and women were a common dedication, and the aim was to produce a beautiful statue, not a portrait of an individual. (Marble kouros [statue of a young man] from Anavysos, Attica, c. 540 B.C. National Museum, Athens. Foto Marburg/Art Resource, New York.)

Fragments on Ethics

DEMOCRITUS

Democritus and Plato unite in placing happiness in the soul. Democritus writes like this: "Happiness and unhappiness belong to the soul" [B 170] and, "Happiness does not dwell in flocks or in gold; it is the soul that is the home of a person's *daimon* (guardian spirit)" [B 171]. He also calls it cheerfulness, well-being, concord, symmetry, and tranquillity. He says that it consists in distinguishing and discriminating pleasures and that this is the finest and most advantageous thing for humans [A 166].

Democritus says that the end is cheerfulness, which is not the same as pleasure, as some people mistakenly interpret it, but a state in which the soul lives calmly and stably, disturbed by no fear or superstition or any other passion [A 1, 45].

People are happy not because of their bodies or possessions, but because of rightness and breadth of understanding [B 40].

The cause of going wrong is ignorance of the better [B 45].

Things turn from good to bad for people, if one does not know how to guide and keep them resourcefully. It is not right to judge these things to be bad; they are good. But it is possible to make use of good things, if one wishes, to ward off bad [B 173].

People fashioned an image of chance as an excuse for their own lack of counsel. For chance seldom fights with practical wisdom, and intelligent sharp-sightedness sets straight most things in life [B 119].

A cheerful person who is led to deeds that are just and lawful rejoices day and night and is strengthened and without care. But whoever disregards justice and does not do what he ought finds all such things unenjoyable when he remembers any of them and is afraid and reproaches himself [B 174].

The person who chooses the goods of the soul chooses what is more divine; one who chooses those of the body chooses what is human [B 37].

The wrongdoer is unhappier than the person wronged [B 45].

COMMENTS

Democritus is the first Greek philosopher to write systematically on ethics, but unfortunately his continuous works are lost, and we have to rely on accounts of his ideas by other people (the A passages) and "fragments" or isolated sayings or opinions that were found memorable and handed down (the B passages). (The A and B numbers come from the standard edition of "Presocratic" philosophers, Diels-Kranz.)

In the case of many early philosophers, we are in the position of relying only on secondhand accounts and fragments. Democritus has been particularly unfortunate, since his contemporary, Socrates, is generally regarded as the first Greek ethical philosopher, and this may be doing an injustice to Democritus.

As with all philosophy that we can read only in the form of isolated sayings, Democritus' ethics poses a problem of seeing it in a general framework. Clearly, he thinks that we all seek happiness and is offering a philosophical account of what happiness is. It is, he thinks, a positive and cheerful life, which requires a reflective and rational attitude toward getting pleasure. It also requires the person to have the virtues—that is to be wise, just, courageous, and self-controlled. In fact, Democritus clearly regards the virtues as far more important than everyday possessions, as far as being happy is concerned.

Is it surprising that someone who thinks that happiness consists of being cheerful and tranquil puts so much emphasis on being virtuous? Why might we think that happiness is mostly up to us and not much threatened by chance?

Gorgias 468E–479E

PLATO

SOCRATES   I was right, then, when I said that someone might do what he thinks it's best for him to do in his community, but still fail to have a great deal of power and fail to do what he wants.

POLUS   As if you wouldn't prefer to be able to do whatever you felt like doing in your community rather than the opposite, Socrates! You make it sound as though the sight of someone executing people when he thinks it's best, or confiscating their property, or throwing them into prison, doesn't make you envious.

SOCRATES   Do you mean when these actions of his are justified or when they're unjustified?

POLUS   It doesn't make any difference. Isn't it enviable anyway?   469a

SOCRATES   That's a terrible thing to say, Polus.

POLUS   Why?

SOCRATES   Because pity, not envy, is the appropriate response to people who are either unenviable or unhappy.

POLUS   Do you really think these descriptions fit the people I've been talking about?

SOCRATES   Of course they do.

POLUS   Well, if a person decides to execute someone, and does so, and is *right* to have done so, is he unhappy or in a pitiful state, do you think?

SOCRATES   No, I don't, but he's certainly not in an enviable position.

POLUS   But didn't you just claim that he was unhappy?

SOCRATES   No, Polus, I meant that anyone who executes a person *un*justly is in b an unhappy state, and deserves our pity as well; to do so justly is merely unenviable.

From Plato, *Gorgias*, translated by Robin Waterfield (Oxford: Oxford University Press, 1994). Reprinted with the permission of Oxford University Press.

POLUS   Well, at least it's certain that the person who's being wrongly executed is in a pitiful and unhappy state!

SOCRATES   But less so than his executioner, Polus, and less so than a person whose execution is just.

POLUS   What do you mean, Socrates?

SOCRATES   I mean that in actual fact there's nothing worse than doing wrong.

POLUS   Really? *Nothing* worse? Isn't it worse to suffer wrong?

SOCRATES   No, not at all.

POLUS   So you'd rather have wrong done to you than do wrong?

c   SOCRATES   I'd rather avoid them both, but if I had to choose between doing wrong and having wrong done to me, I'd prefer the latter to the former.

POLUS   So you wouldn't opt for being a dictator?

SOCRATES   No, if dictatorship means the same to you as it does to me.

POLUS   What I mean by it is what I said a moment ago, the licence to do whatever you think it's best for you to do in your community—the licence to execute people and banish them, and to go to any lengths to see your personal predilections fulfilled.

d   SOCRATES   Well, Polus, here are some thoughts of *mine* for you to criticize. Imagine I'm in the agora when it's chock-full, and I've got a dagger tucked in my armpit. I tell you, "Polus, I've recently gained an incredible amount of power, as much as any dictator. Look at all these people. If I decide one of them has to die, he's dead, just like that; if I decide one of them should have his head split open, it'll be split open on the spot; if I decide someone's

e   cloak needs shredding, shredded it is. So you can see that I have a great deal of power in this community." And suppose you don't believe me, so I show you my dagger. I bet you'd say, "Socrates, in that case everyone has a great deal of power, since by the same token you could also burn down any houses you decide to burn down—and then there are Athens' dockyards and warships and the whole merchant fleet in public and private ownership." So the ability to do what you feel like doing isn't a sign of a great deal of power. What do you think?

POLUS   I agree, it isn't. Not that kind of power, anyway.

470a   SOCRATES   Can you tell us what's wrong with that sort of power, to your mind?

POLUS   Yes.

SOCRATES   What is it? Do please tell us.

POLUS   It's that anyone who does the kinds of things you were describing is bound to be punished.

SOCRATES   By which you mean that punishment is bad?

POLUS   Yes.

SOCRATES   So you've again come round to the view, my friend, that doing what it seems best to do is a good thing if it turns out to be in one's interest to do it. That, I suppose, is what it is to have a great deal of power. If it isn't in one's interest, however, it's a bad thing, and signifies little power. And

b   here's another point for us to consider. Are we agreed that the actions we were talking about a while back (the execution and banishment of people and the confiscation of property) may be better or worse, depending on the circumstances?

POLUS   Yes.

SOCRATES   Here's something we apparently both agree on, then!

POLUS   Yes.

SOCRATES   Well, what are the circumstances under which they become better, do you think? Can you tell me what makes the difference, in your opinion?

POLUS   I'd like to hear your response to that question, Socrates.

SOCRATES   You'd rather hear what I have to say? All right, Polus. My view is   c
that if they're morally right, they're better, but if they're wrong, they're worse.

POLUS   Do you want to know how unassailable a position you're in, Socrates? Even a child could prove this idea of yours wrong.

SOCRATES   Then I'd be very grateful to the child. But I'll be no less grateful to you if you prove me wrong and free me from the snares of absurdity. You should never tire of doing friends favours, so go on: prove me wrong.

POLUS   Well, I don't need ancient history to help me prove you wrong, Socrates: there's enough counter-evidence from the very recent past for me to show   d
that happiness and wrongdoing do commonly go together.

SOCRATES   What is this evidence?

POLUS   You know that man Archelaus, Perdiccas' son, the one who rules Macedonia?

SOCRATES   Not exactly, but I've heard of him.

POLUS   Does he strike you as being happy or unhappy?

SOCRATES   I don't know, Polus. I've never met the man.

POLUS   Would you really have to meet him before appreciating how happy he   e
is? Can't you tell already?

SOCRATES   No, I certainly can't.

POLUS   It goes without saying that you won't admit that the king of Persia is happy either, Socrates.

SOCRATES   No, and I'm right not to, since I don't know whether or not he's an educated, moral person.

POLUS   Does happiness really depend entirely on that?

SOCRATES   Yes, I think so, Polus. In my opinion, it takes true goodness to make a man or a woman happy, and an immoral, wicked person is unhappy.

POLUS   My man Archelaus is unhappy, then, according to you.   471a

SOCRATES   Yes, if he does wrong, Polus.

POLUS   But of course he does. He didn't have the slightest claim to the throne he currently occupies. His mother was a slave of Perdiccas' brother Alcetas, so by rights he should have been Alcetas' slave too. If he'd wanted to behave morally, he'd have been Alcetas' slave and that would have made him happy, according to you. As it is, though, he's become incredibly unhappy as a result of the awful crimes he's committed! In the first place, he sent a message to Alcetas, who was his uncle as well as his master, in which he   b
invited him to stay on the grounds that he would restore the kingdom

which Perdiccas had stolen from him. So he welcomed Alcetas and his son Alexander, his own cousin (who was more or less the same age as him), into his house; then he got them drunk, bundled them into a cart, took them away under cover of darkness, murdered them both, and disposed of the bodies. He didn't realize how terribly unhappy these crimes had made him and he showed no sign of regret either, but a little later made his next vic-

c tim his brother, a lad aged about seven, who was Perdiccas' legitimate son and the rightful heir to the throne. Instead of choosing happiness by fol- lowing the moral course of looking after the lad until he had grown up and then handing the kingdom over to him, he threw him into a well and drowned him—and then told the boy's mother Cleopatra that he'd fallen in and died while chasing a goose. There's no one in Macedonia, then, who has committed worse crimes than him, and that's why he's the most miserable Macedonian alive today, not the happiest. And that also explains why everyone in Athens would presumably follow your lead: Archelaus would

d be the last Macedonian they'd swap places with!

SOCRATES I want to repeat a point I made early in our conversation, Polus, when I complimented you on what I'm sure is an excellent training in rhet- oric—but was disappointed to find that you've taken no interest in how to carry on a rational argument. Is the argument you've just come up with the one by means of which "even a child" would expose my errors? Do you really think that with this argument you've disproved my claim that a crim- inal isn't happy? How on earth could you think that, my friend? I have to tell you that I disagree with absolutely everything you're saying.

e POLUS You mean you're not prepared to admit it; you do actually agree with me.

SOCRATES The trouble is, Polus, that you're trying to use on me the kind of rhetorical refutation which people in lawcourts think is successful. There too, you see, people think they're proving the other side wrong if they pro- duce a large number of eminent witnesses in support of the points they're making, but their opponent comes up with only a single witness or none at all. This kind of refutation, however, is completely worthless in the context

472a of the truth, since it's perfectly possible for someone to be defeated in court by a horde of witnesses with no more than apparent respectability who all testify falsely against him. In the present dispute, if you feel like calling wit- nesses to claim that what I'm saying is wrong, you can count on your posi- tion being supported by almost everyone in Athens, whether they were born and bred here or elsewhere . . .

Nevertheless, there's still a dissenting voice, albeit a single one—mine. You're producing no compelling reason why I should agree with you; all you're doing is calling up a horde of false witnesses against me to support your attempt to dislodge me from my inheritance, the truth. To my mind, however, I won't have accomplished anything important with regard to the issues we've been discussing, unless I get you yourself to act as my wit-

c ness—albeit a single one!—to testify to the truth of my position; and I'm sure you won't think you've accomplished anything important either unless I testify for your position. It doesn't matter that there's only one of me; you'd let all the others go if you could get me as your witness.

So although there's the kind of refutation whose validity you take for granted (and you're far from being alone), there's also another kind, the kind I have in mind. Let's compare them and see how they differ. You see, the issues we're disagreeing about are in fact hardly trivial: I'd almost go so far as to say that in their case there's nothing more admirable than knowledge and nothing more contemptible than ignorance, since that would amount to knowledge or ignorance about what it is to be happy and what it is to be unhappy.

SOCRATES   Let's start with the question facing us, which is the crux of our pres- d
ent discussion. You think it's possible for someone to be happy in spite of the fact that he does wrong and is an immoral person, and you cite the case of Archelaus who is, in your opinion, an immoral, but happy, person. Is that a fair representation of your view?

POLUS   Yes.

SOCRATES   On the other hand, I claim that this is impossible. So here's one point on which we disagree. Now then, this happy criminal . . . will he be happy if he pays the penalty for his actions and is punished?

POLUS   Definitely not. That would make his condition very unhappy.

SOCRATES   So is it your view that a criminal is happy as long as he doesn't get e
punished?

POLUS   Yes.

SOCRATES   My view, however, Polus, is that although an unjust person, a criminal, is in a thoroughly wretched state, he's worse off if he doesn't pay the penalty and continues to do wrong without getting punished than if he does pay the penalty and has punishment meted out to him by gods and men.

POLUS   That's an extraordinary position to take, Socrates.   473a

SOCRATES   And it's exactly the one I'm going to try to convert you to as well, my friend—I do count you as a friend, you see. Now, as things stand at the moment, the difference between us is this. Please see whether I've got this right. I maintained earlier that doing wrong was worse than suffering wrong.

POLUS   Yes.

SOCRATES   While you claimed that suffering wrong was worse.

POLUS   Yes.

SOCRATES   And then my claim about the unhappiness of criminals was refuted by you . . .

POLUS   It certainly was.

SOCRATES   Or so you think, Polus.   b

POLUS   And I'm right.

SOCRATES   Maybe, maybe not. Anyway, you then said that criminals were happy as long as they avoided punishment.

POLUS   That's right.

SOCRATES   Whereas my position is that this makes their condition completely wretched, and that punishment alleviates their condition somewhat. Do you want to refute this as well?

POLUS   It's going to be really hard to disprove this claim, Socrates—even harder than it was to refute the earlier one.

SOCRATES   It's not just hard, Polus—it's impossible. The truth can never be proved wrong.

POLUS   What do you mean? Imagine someone who's been caught in a criminal
c   conspiracy against a dictatorship. After having been captured, he's stretched on the rack, bits of his body are cut off, his eyes are burned out, and he's terribly mutilated in a great many and a wide variety of other ways; in addition to being mutilated himself, he watches his wife and children being tortured as well; finally he's crucified or covered with boiling pitch. Is this a happier state for him to be in than if he'd avoided being caught, had become dictator, and had spent the rest of his life ruling over his community and doing whatever he wanted, with everyone from home and
d   abroad regarding him with envy and congratulating him for his happiness? Is this your "irrefutable" position?

SOCRATES   My dear Polus, first it was witnesses, now it's scare tactics. You're not doing anything to prove me wrong. Still, please refresh my memory a bit. The man in your scenario was involved in a criminal conspiracy against a dictatorship?

POLUS   Yes.

SOCRATES   Well then, neither situation will make him happier—whether he succeeds in making himself dictator by criminal means or pays the penalty— because you can't compare any two miserable people and say that one is hap-
e   pier than the other. Nevertheless, if he avoids being caught and becomes dictator, his stock of misery will increase. What's this, Polus? You're laughing? Is this yet another kind of refutation, which has you laughing at ideas rather than proving them wrong?

POLUS   Don't you think the sheer eccentricity of what you're saying is enough of a refutation, Socrates? Why don't you ask anyone here whether they agree with you?

SOCRATES   I'm no politician, Polus. In fact, last year I was on the Council, thanks to the lottery, and when it was the turn of my tribe to form the exec-
474a   utive committee and I had to put an issue to the vote, I made a fool of myself by not knowing the procedure for this. So please don't tell me to ask the present company to vote now either. No, if this is your best shot at a refutation, why don't you do what I suggested a short while ago and let me have a go at one? Then you'll see what I think a refutation should be like. My expertise is restricted to producing just a single witness in support of my ideas—the person with whom I'm carrying on the discussion—and I pay no attention to large numbers of people; I only know how to ask for a single

person's vote, and I can't even begin to address people in large groups. What I'm wondering, then, is whether you'll be prepared to submit to an attempt at refutation by answering questions. You see, I think that both of us—and everyone else as well, in fact—believe that doing wrong is worse than suffering wrong, and that for a wrongdoer not paying the penalty is worse than doing so. b

POLUS   And I say that no one—not me, and not anyone else either—believes that. Would *you* prefer to have wrong done to you than to do wrong?

SOCRATES   Yes, and so would you and everyone else.

POLUS   You're quite wrong. I wouldn't, you wouldn't, and nobody else would either.

SOCRATES   Why don't you answer my questions, then? c

POLUS   All right. I'm certainly longing to hear what you're going to say.

SOCRATES   You'll find out; you only have to answer my questions. I'll pretend that we're starting afresh. Which do you think is worse, Polus, doing wrong or having wrong done to you?

POLUS   Having wrong done to you, I'd say.

SOCRATES   And which is more contemptible, doing wrong or having wrong done to you? Can you tell me what you think?

POLUS   Doing wrong.

SOCRATES   Well, isn't it also worse, given that it's more contemptible?

POLUS   Certainly not.

SOCRATES   I see. You don't identify "admirable" with "good," and "contempt- d ible" with "bad," apparently.

POLUS   No, I don't.

SOCRATES   But what about this? Isn't there always a standard to which you refer before calling things admirable? It doesn't matter what the object is; it could be a body, a colour, a figure, a sound or an activity. Take an admirable physique, for instance. Don't you call it admirable either on account of its utility (by considering the particular purpose it is useful for), or on account of a certain kind of pleasure (if it gives people pleasure to look at it)? Can you think of anything else which might make one admire a person's physique?

POLUS   No, I can't. e

SOCRATES   And doesn't the same go for everything else as well? Don't you call figures and colours admirable either because they give a certain kind of pleasure, or because they're beneficial, or for both reasons at once?

POLUS   Yes.

SOCRATES   And isn't that also the case with sounds and all musical phenomena?

POLUS   Yes.

SOCRATES   And these criteria are surely relevant to the whole sphere of people's customs and activities as well. I mean, provided they're admirable, they're either beneficial or pleasant or both.

POLUS   I agree. 475a

SOCRATES   And does the same go for admirable fields of study too?

POLUS   Yes. In fact, Socrates, in defining what is admirable in terms of pleasure and goodness, as you are at the moment, you've come up with an admirable definition!

SOCRATES   And also if I define what is contemptible in the opposite way, in terms of unpleasantness and harmfulness?

POLUS   Yes, of course.

SOCRATES   So when one of a pair of admirable things is more admirable than the other, this is because it exceeds the other in one of these two respects or in both—either in pleasantness or in benefit or in both at once.

POLUS   Yes.

SOCRATES   And when one of a pair of contemptible things is more contemptible
b   than the other, this is because it exceeds the other either in unpleasantness or in harmfulness. Isn't that bound to be so?

POLUS   Yes.

SOCRATES   Now, what was the position we reached a moment ago as regards doing and suffering wrong? Didn't you maintain that although suffering wrong was worse, doing it was more contemptible?

POLUS   Yes, I did.

SOCRATES   So if doing wrong is more contemptible than suffering wrong, then either it's more unpleasant and it's more contemptible because it exceeds the alternative in unpleasantness, or it's more contemptible because it exceeds the alternative in harmfulness or in both qualities at once. Isn't that bound to be the case?

POLUS   Of course.

c SOCRATES   So the first point for us to consider is whether doing wrong is more unpleasant than suffering wrong, and whether people who do wrong are more distressed than those who have it done to them.

POLUS   No, of course that's not the case, Socrates.

SOCRATES   So it doesn't exceed the alternative in unpleasantness.

POLUS   No.

SOCRATES   And if that's the case, it doesn't exceed the alternative in *both* respects either.

POLUS   That seems right.

SOCRATES   The only remaining possibility, then, is that it exceeds the alternative in the other respect.

POLUS   Yes.

SOCRATES   In harmfulness.

POLUS   I suppose so.

SOCRATES   Well, if doing wrong exceeds suffering wrong in harmfulness, it must be worse than suffering wrong.

POLUS   Obviously.

d SOCRATES   Now, isn't it invariably accepted, and wasn't it admitted by you earlier, that doing wrong is more contemptible than suffering wrong?

POLUS   Yes.

SOCRATES   And now we've found that it's worse as well.

POLUS   So it seems.

SOCRATES   Well, if you were faced with a choice between two things, and one of them was worse and more contemptible than the other, would you prefer it to the alternative? ... Don't you feel like answering? You needn't worry: you won't come to any harm. Imagine that the argument is a doctor who demands sincerity from you, and tell us what you think. Do you say yes or no to my question?

POLUS   No, I wouldn't prefer it, Socrates.   e

SOCRATES   Would anyone?

POLUS   I don't think so: the argument doesn't make it seem possible.

SOCRATES   I was right, then, when I suggested that doing wrong is held by everyone, including you and me, to be less preferable than suffering wrong, and the reason I was right is that doing wrong is in fact worse than having it done to you.

POLUS   I suppose so.

SOCRATES   Now that we've compared our techniques of refutation, Polus, you can see how completely different they are. You rely on the fact that everyone in the world agrees with you except for me, while I'm satisfied if I gain the assent of just one person—you. I'm content if *you* testify to the validity   476a of my argument, and I canvass only for your vote, without caring about what everyone else thinks.

SOCRATES   So much for that issue. Next we need to look into the second point of disagreement between us. You claim that nothing could be worse for a criminal than paying the penalty for his crimes, whereas I claim that he's worse off if he doesn't pay the penalty. Which of us if right? Here's a way into the question: would you agree that there's no difference between a criminal paying the penalty for his crimes and being justly punished for them?

POLUS   Yes.

SOCRATES   Now, wouldn't you describe any instance of justice as admirable, in   b so far as it is just? Think about it. What's your view?

POLUS   I think it has to be admirable, Socrates.

SOCRATES   What about this, then? If a person does something, doesn't there also have to be something which undergoes what that person is doing?

POLUS   I think so.

SOCRATES   And isn't the object which is undergoing the action also bound to be affected by the *way* the agent acts? For instance, if a person hits, there must be something which is hit.

POLUS   Of course there must.

SOCRATES   And if the hitter hits hard or fast, it also follows that the object which is hit is hit in that way.   c

POLUS   Yes.

SOCRATES   The effect on the object which is hit, then, is qualified by the way in which the hitter performs the action.

POLUS   Agreed.

SOCRATES   Then again, if a person cauterizes, there must be something which
    is cauterized, mustn't there?

POLUS   Of course.

SOCRATES   And if the process of cautery is intense or painful, the cauterized
    object is inevitably cauterized in the way in which the cautery is performed.
    Yes?

POLUS   Yes.

SOCRATES   And the same goes for when someone makes a cut, doesn't it? That
    is, something is cut.

POLUS   Yes.

d SOCRATES   And if the incision is large or deep or painful, then isn't the cut
    object cut in a way which reflects the kind of cut the cutter is making?

POLUS   Obviously.

SOCRATES   To sum up, then, do you agree with what I said a moment ago—that
    in all cases the affected object is affected in a way which reflects the way in
    which the agent acts?

POLUS   Yes, I agree.

SOCRATES   Please bear these conclusions in mind. I want to ask next whether to
    be punished is to do something or to have something done to you.

POLUS   It's to have something done to you, of course, Socrates.

SOCRATES   And this something is done by an agent, presumably.

POLUS   Naturally. By the person who implements the punishment.

SOCRATES   And when a person is right to carry out a punishment, is he justified
    in doing so?

e POLUS   Yes.

SOCRATES   Is he acting justly, then, or not?

POLUS   He is.

SOCRATES   So to be punished by paying a fair penalty for your crimes is to have
    justice done to you?

POLUS   Obviously.

SOCRATES   But we've agreed that anything just is admirable, haven't we?

POLUS   Yes.

SOCRATES   So the agent is carrying out an admirable deed, while the one who's
    being punished is having an admirable deed done to him.

POLUS   Yes.

477a SOCRATES   Now, if he's having an admirable deed done to him, he must be hav-
    ing a good deed done to him, in the sense that it's either pleasant or benefi-
    cial.

POLUS   Yes, he must be.

SOCRATES   Anyone who pays a fair penalty for his crimes, then, is having good
    done to him. Agreed?

POLUS   I suppose so.

SOCRATES   He's being benefited, then, isn't he?

POLUS   Yes.

SOCRATES   I imagine that the kind of benefit he receives if his punishment is just is that his mind is made better. Do you think I'm right?

POLUS   It sounds plausible.

SOCRATES   If so, then a person who pays a fair penalty for his crimes is escaping a bad psychological state, isn't he?

POLUS   Yes.

SOCRATES   In which case, he's escaping the worst state there is, isn't he? Look   b at it this way: can you think of anything other than poverty which constitutes a bad state for one's financial condition?

POLUS   No, that's it.

SOCRATES   What about a person's physical condition? Wouldn't you say that in this case it's weakness, sickliness, ugliness, and so on which constitute badness?

POLUS   Yes.

SOCRATES   Well, do you think there's also such a thing as psychological badness?

POLUS   Of course.

SOCRATES   Which consists, wouldn't you say, in injustice, ignorance, cowardice and so on?

POLUS   Yes.

SOCRATES   So it's your opinion that there's a pernicious state for each of the   c three—for property, body, and mind—and that these are respectively poverty, sickliness, and immorality. Yes?

POLUS   Yes.

SOCRATES   Well, which of these three kinds of iniquity is the most contemptible? Isn't it immorality and psychological iniquity in general?

POLUS   Yes, that's by far the most contemptible.

SOCRATES   And if it's the most contemptible, it's the worst too, isn't it?

POLUS   Why should you think that, Socrates?

SOCRATES   Because it follows from our earlier conclusions that in any situation it's the thing which causes the maximum amount of unpleasantness or harm or both that is the most contemptible.

POLUS   That's very true.

SOCRATES   And didn't we just agree that immorality—that is, psychological iniquity in general—is particularly contemptible?

POLUS   Yes, we did.   d

SOCRATES   Either it's exceptionally unpleasant, then, and it's particularly contemptible because it exceeds the others in its unpleasantness, or it's particularly contemptible because it exceeds the others in harmfulness or in both qualities at once. Yes?

POLUS   Of course.

SOCRATES   Well, are injustice, lack of self-discipline, cowardice, and ignorance more unpleasant than hunger and exhaustion?

POLUS   I don't think we've found any reason to say that, Socrates.

SOCRATES   Why, then, is psychological iniquity more contemptible than anything else? If, as you say, it isn't because it causes more distress than other
kinds of badness, it must be because it exceeds the alternatives in harmful-
e   ness. In some sense, then, it causes an incredible amount of harm and is
unbelievably bad.

POLUS   I suppose so.

SOCRATES   Well, if something causes more harm than anything else, isn't it the
worst thing in the world?

POLUS   Yes.

SOCRATES   Doesn't it follow that psychological iniquity—injustice, self-indulgence, and so on—is the worst thing in the world?

POLUS   It does seem to.

SOCRATES   Now, which is the branch of expertise that rescues people from
poverty? Isn't it commercial business?

POLUS   Yes.

SOCRATES   And which one relieves us of illness? Isn't it medicine?

478a POLUS   Of course.

SOCRATES   And which one saves us from iniquity and injustice? Is that too hard
a question for you? Look at it this way. When people have a physical ail-
ment, where do we take them? Whom do we take them to?

POLUS   Doctors, Socrates.

SOCRATES   And where do we take people who do wrong and lack self-
discipline?

POLUS   To appear before judges. Is that what you're getting at?

SOCRATES   And don't we take them there so that they can pay a fair penalty for
their crimes?

POLUS   Yes.

SOCRATES   Now, it takes justice to punish and discipline someone correctly,
doesn't it?

POLUS   Obviously.

b SOCRATES   So commerce relieves us of poverty, medicine relieves us of illness,
and the administration of justice relieves us of self-indulgence and injustice.

POLUS   That seems to make sense.

SOCRATES   Well, which of them is the most admirable?

POLUS   Which of what?

SOCRATES   Of commerce, medicine, and the administration of justice.

POLUS   The administration of justice, Socrates, by a long way.

SOCRATES   In that case, it must confer either more pleasure than the others, or
more benefit, or both. Otherwise it wouldn't be the most admirable of these
three areas of expertise. Do you agree?

POLUS   Yes.

SOCRATES   Well, is medical treatment pleasant? Do patients enjoy themselves?

POLUS   I don't think so.

SOCRATES   But it is beneficial, isn't it?

POLUS   Yes.

SOCRATES   The point is that medical treatment saves us from a terrible state, and so it is worth our while to put up with the pain and get well.

POLUS   Of course.

SOCRATES   Now, which is the happier state to be in, as far as one's body is concerned—to receive medical treatment, or actually to avoid being ill in the first place?

POLUS   To avoid being ill, obviously.

SOCRATES   Yes, it does seem to be true that happiness consists not in losing any badness you have, but in not having it in the first place.

POLUS   Exactly.

SOCRATES   Now, imagine two people both of whom are physically or psychologically in a bad state. One of them is receiving treatment and is being freed from his badness, while the other isn't, and so still has it. Which of these two people is worse off?   d

POLUS   I should say it's the one who isn't being treated.

SOCRATES   Well, we found that paying the penalty for one's crimes saves one from the worst kind of badness—iniquity.

POLUS   We did.

SOCRATES   The reason being, I suppose, that the administration of justice makes people self-controlled, increases their morality, and cures them of iniquity.

POLUS   Yes.

SOCRATES   Since psychological badness is the worst kind there is, it follows that the height of happiness is not to have it at all . . .

POLUS   Obviously.   e

SOCRATES   . . . and the next best thing is to be saved from it, I suppose.

POLUS   That makes sense.

SOCRATES   Which we found to be a result of censure, criticism, and punishment.

POLUS   Yes.

SOCRATES   The worst state of all, then, is to have it and not to be saved from it.

POLUS   I suppose so.

SOCRATES   And isn't this precisely the state of an arch-criminal, with his utter immorality, who successfully avoids being criticized and disciplined and punished—in other words, exactly what, according to you, Archelaus and   479a
his fellow dictators, rhetoricians, and political leaders have managed to do?

POLUS   I suppose so.

SOCRATES   Their achievement, then, Polus, is not so very different from that of someone in the grip of an extremely severe illness who successfully avoids having the doctors exact the penalty for his body's crimes—that is, who avoids medical treatment—because he's childishly frightened of the pain of cautery and surgery. Don't you agree?   b

POLUS   Yes, I do.

SOCRATES   And he's afraid, I suppose, because he doesn't understand health and doesn't know what a good physical state is like. I mean, the position we've reached in our discussion makes it seem likely that this is what peoc

ple who evade punishment are up to as well, Polus. They can see that punishment is painful, but they have a blind spot about how beneficial it is, and
they fail to appreciate that life with an unhealthy mind—a mind which is
unsound, immoral, and unjust—is infinitely more wretched than life with
an unhealthy body. This also explains why they go to such lengths to avoid
being punished—that is, to avoid being saved from the worst kind of badness. Instead they equip themselves with money and friends, and make
sure that they're as persuasive as they can be at speaking. Now, if this position of ours is right, Polus, are you aware of the consequences, or shall we
summarize them?

POLUS   Summarize them by all means, if you feel like it.

SOCRATES   Well, one consequence is that there's nothing worse than injustice
and wrongdoing.

d POLUS   So it seems.

SOCRATES   Didn't we also find that punishment saves one from this bad state?

POLUS   I suppose so.

SOCRATES   Whereas to escape punishment is to perpetuate the bad state?

POLUS   Yes.

SOCRATES   It follows that wrongdoing is the second worst thing that can happen; the worst thing in the world, the supreme curse, is to do wrong and not
pay the penalty for it.

POLUS   I suppose so.

SOCRATES   Well, wasn't that the point at issue between us, Polus? You were calling Archelaus happy for getting away with terrible crimes without being

e

punished for them, whereas I was upholding the contrary view. I was claiming that Archelaus or anyone else who does wrong without paying the
penalty is likely to be far worse off than others; that doing wrong always
makes people more miserable than suffering wrong does; and that evading
punishment always makes people more miserable than paying the penalty
does. Wasn't that what I was saying?

polus   Yes.

socrates   And have I been proved right?

POLUS   Apparently.

COMMENTS

In the *Gorgias,* Socrates defends, against a wordly-wise public speaker, the view that
the only thing relevant for happiness is being a good, moral person, someone with
the virtues. Plato stresses how weird and unworldly this appears to people who have
never stopped to consider whether money, success, and other conventional goods
may not be what matters for happiness.

Why does Plato hold that the person who reflects in the right kind of way about
conventional goods will be moral? Could she not be happy using her reason and
intelligence to achieve selfish goals? Polus certainly claims to think so. Here, Socrates

subjects him to arguments to show that his views are internally incoherent. Note that Socrates thinks that when it comes to the happiness of each one of us, the views of others are not to the point—all that matters is what the person thinks when his or her views are subject to rational scrutiny.

In this passage Socrates' arguments show that Polus' opposition to Socrates' apparently strange views is based on confusion. Are Socrates' arguments, in fact, good ones? They have to be if he is entitled to claim that Polus really does believe conclusions that he began by claiming not to believe.

If virtue is really more important than conventional goods and vice far worse than conventional evils like poverty and punishment, then it follows, as Socrates brings home at the end, that the wrongdoer is unhappier than the person wronged (as Democritus also held; see p. 304). All one needs for happiness is to be a virtuous person, regardless of what conventional evils befall one.

Are Plato's views on virtue and happiness too demanding and uncompromising? His greatest pupil Aristotle thought so.

C. The Major Theories

The most famous ancient ethical theories, which are well worked out and make their framework explicit, are those of Aristotle, the Stoics, and Epicurus. Aristotle argues that happiness requires virtue, but also some measure of "external goods" like health and wealth. The Stoics disagree with this view, starting what became the major ethical debate in the ancient world. Epicurus offers a different idea: Happiness is a life of pleasure. He takes care to avoid obvious objections to this idea and, like Aristotle and the Stoics, presents his theory as a theory of happiness, our ultimate end.

Nicomachean Ethics I, 1, 2, 4, 5, 7–10

ARISTOTLE

1. Every art and every inquiry, and similarly every action and pursuit, is thought to aim at some good; and for this reason the good has rightly been declared to be that at which all things aim. But a certain difference is found among ends; some are activities, others are products apart from the activities that produce them. Where there are ends apart from the actions, it is the nature of the products to be better than the activities. Now, as there are many actions, arts, and sciences, their ends also are many; the end of the medical art is health,

From Aristotle, *Nicomachean Ethics*, translated by W. D. Ross, revised by J. L. Ackrill and J. O. Urmson (Oxford: Oxford University Press, 1980). Reprinted with the permission of Oxford University Press.

that of shipbuilding a vessel, that of strategy victory, that of economics wealth. But where such arts fall under a single capacity—as bridle-making and the other arts concerned with the equipment of horses fall under the art of riding, and this and every military action under strategy, in the same way other arts fall under yet others—in all of these the ends of the master arts are to be preferred to all the subordinate ends; for it is for the sake of the former that the latter are pursued. It makes no difference whether the activities themselves are the ends of the actions, or something else apart from the activities, as in the case of the sciences just mentioned.

2. If, then, there is some end of the things we do, which we desire for its own sake (everything else being desired for the sake of this), and if we do not choose everything for the sake of something else (for at that rate the process would go on to infinity, so that our desire would be empty and vain), clearly this must be the good and the chief good. Will not the knowledge of it, then, have a great influence on life? Shall we not, like archers who have a mark to aim at, be more likely to hit upon what is right? If so, we must try, in outline at least, to determine what it is, and of which of the sciences or capacities it is the object. It would seem to belong to the most authoritative art and that which is most truly the master art. And politics appears to be of this nature; for it is this that ordains which of the sciences should be studied in a state, and which each class of citizens should learn and up to what point they should learn them; and we see even the most highly esteemed of capacities to fall under this, e.g. strategy, economics, rhetoric; now, since politics uses the rest of the sciences, and since, again, it legislates as to what we are to do and what we are to abstain from, the end of this science must include those of the others, so that this end must be the good for man. For even if the end is the same for a single man and for a state, that of the state seems at all events something greater and more complete whether to attain or to preserve; though it is worth while to attain the end merely for one man, it is finer and more godlike to attain it for a nation or for city-states. These, then, are the ends at which our inquiry aims, since it is political science, in one sense of that term.

4. Let us resume our inquiry and state, in view of the fact that all knowledge and every pursuit aims at some good, what it is that we say political science aims at and what is the highest of all goods achievable by action. Verbally there is very general agreement; for both the general run of men and people of superior refinement say that it is happiness, and identify living well and faring well with being happy; but with regard to what happiness is they differ, and the many do not give the same account as the wise. For the former think it is some plain and obvious thing, like pleasure, wealth, or honour; they differ, however, from one another—and often even the same man identifies it with different things, with health when he is ill, with wealth when he is poor; but, conscious of their ignorance, they admire those who proclaim some great thing that is above their comprehension. Now some thought that apart from these many goods there is another which is good in itself and causes the goodness of all these as well. To examine all the opinions that have been held were perhaps somewhat fruitless; enough to examine those that are most prevalent or that seem to be arguable.

5. Let us, however, resume our discussion from the point at which we digressed. To judge from the lives that men lead, most men, and men of the most vulgar type, seem (not without some ground) to identify the good, or happiness, with pleasure; which is the reason why they love the life of enjoyment. For there are, we may say, three prominent types of life—that just mentioned, the political, and thirdly the contemplative life. Now the mass of mankind are evidently quite slavish in their tastes, preferring a life suitable to beasts, but they get some ground for their view from the fact that many of those in high places share the tastes of Sardanapallus. A consideration of the prominent types of life shows that people of superior refinement and of active disposition identify happiness with honour; for this is, roughly speaking, the end of the political life. But it seems too superficial to be what we are looking for, since it is thought to depend on those who bestow honour rather than on him who receives it, but the good we divine to be something of one's own and not easily taken from one. Further, men seem to pursue honour in order that they may be assured of their merit; at least it is by men of practical wisdom that they seek to be honoured, and among those who know them, and on the ground of their virtue; clearly, then, according to them, at any rate, virtue is better. And perhaps one might even suppose this to be, rather than honour, the end of the political life. But even this appears somewhat incomplete; for possession of virtue seems actually compatible with being asleep, or with lifelong inactivity, and, further, with the greatest sufferings and misfortunes; but a man who was living so no one would call happy, unless he were maintaining a thesis at all costs. But enough of this; for the subject has been sufficiently treated even in the popular discussions. Third comes the contemplative life, which we shall consider later.

The life of money-making is one undertaken under compulsion, and wealth is evidently not the good we are seeking; for it is merely useful and for the sake of something else. And so one might rather take the aforenamed objects to be ends; for they are loved for themselves. But it is evident that not even these are ends; yet many arguments have been wasted on the support of them. Let us leave this subject, then.

7. Let us again return to the good we are seeking, and ask what it can be. It seems different in different actions and arts; it is different in medicine, in strategy, and in the other arts likewise. What then is the good of each? Surely that for whose sake everything else is done. In medicine this is health, in strategy victory, in architecture a house, in any other sphere something else, and in every action and pursuit the end; for it is for the sake of this that all men do whatever else they do. Therefore, if there is an end for all that we do, this will be the good achievable by action, and if there are more than one, these will be the goods achievable by action.

So the argument has by a different course reached the same point; but we must try to state this even more clearly. Since there are evidently more than one end, and we choose some of these (e.g. wealth, flutes, and in general instruments) for the sake of something else, clearly not all ends are final ends; but the chief good is evidently something final. Therefore, if there is only one final end, this will be what we are seeking, and if there are more than one, the most final of these will be what we are seeking. Now we call that which is in itself worthy of pursuit more final than that which is worthy of pursuit for the sake of something else, and that which is never desirable for the sake of something else more final than the things that are desirable both in themselves and for the sake of that other thing, and therefore we call final without qualification that which is always desirable in itself and never for the sake of something else.

Now such a thing happiness, above all else, is held to be; for this we choose always for itself and never for the sake of something else, but honour, pleasure, reason, and every virtue we choose indeed for themselves (for if nothing resulted from them we should still choose each of them), but we choose them also for the sake of happiness, judging that through them we shall be happy. Happiness, on the other hand, no one chooses for the sake of these, nor, in general, for anything other than itself.

From the point of view of self-sufficiency the same result seems to follow; for the final good is thought to be self-sufficient. Now by self-sufficient we do not mean that which is sufficient for a man by himself, for one who lives a solitary life, but also for parents, children, wife, and in general for his friends and fellow citizens, since man is born for citizenship. But some limit must be set to this; for if we extend our requirement to ancestors and descendants and friends' friends we are in for an infinite series. Let us examine this question, however, on another occasion, the self-sufficient we now define as that which when isolated makes life desirable and lacking in nothing; and such we think happiness to be; and further we think it most desirable of all things, not a thing counted as one good thing among others—if it were so counted it would clearly be made more desirable by the addition of even the least of goods; for that which is added becomes an excess of goods, and of goods the greater is always more desirable. Happiness, then, is something final and self-sufficient, and is the end of action.

Presumably, however, to say that happiness is the chief good seems a platitude, and a clearer account of what it is is still desired. This might perhaps be given, if we could first ascertain the function of man. For just as for a flute-player, a sculptor, or any artist, and, in general, for all things that have a function or activity, the good and the "well" is thought to reside in the function, so would it seem to be for man, if he has a function. Have the carpenter, then, and the tanner certain functions or activities, and has man none? Is he born without a function? Or as eye, hand, foot, and in general each of the parts evidently has a function, may one lay it down that man similarly has a function apart from all these? What then can this be? Life seems to belong even to plants, but we are seeking what is peculiar to man. Let us exclude, therefore, the life of nutrition and growth. Next there would be a life of perception, but it also seems to be shared even by the horse, the ox, and every animal. There remains, then, an active life of the element that has a rational principle; of this, one part has such a principle in the sense of being obedient to one, the other in the sense of possessing one and exercising thought. And, as "life of the rational element" also has two meanings, we must state that life in the sense of activity is what we mean; for this seems to be the more proper sense of the term. Now if the function of man is an activity of soul which follows or implies a rational principle, and if we say "a so-and-so" and "a good so-and-so" have a function which is the same in kind, e.g. a lyre-player and a good lyre-player, and so without qualification in all cases, eminence in respect of goodness being added to the name of the function (for the function of a lyre-player is to play the lyre, and that of a good lyre-player is to do so well): if this is the case [and we state the function of man to be a certain kind of life, and this to be an activity or actions of the soul implying a rational principle, and the function of a good man to be the good and noble performance of these, and if any action is well performed when it is performed in accordance with the appropriate excellence: if this is the case], human good turns out to be activity of soul exhibiting excellence, and if there are more than one excellence, in accordance with the best and most complete.

But we must add "in a complete life." For one swallow does not make a summer, nor does one day; and so too one day, or a short time, does not make a man blessed and happy.

Let this serve as an outline of the good; for we must presumably first sketch it roughly, and then later fill in the details. But it would seem that any one is capable of carrying on and articulating what has once been well outlined, and that time is a good discoverer or partner in such a work; to which facts the advances of the arts are due; for any one can add what is lacking. And we must also remember what has been said before, and not look for precision in all things alike, but in each class of things such precision as accords with the subject-matter, and so much as is appropriate to the inquiry. For a carpenter and a geometer investigate the right angle in different ways; the former does so in so far as the right angle is useful for his work, while the latter inquires what it is or what sort of thing it is; for he is a spectator of the truth. We must act in the same way, then, in all other matters as well, that our main task may not be subordinated to minor questions. Nor must we demand the cause in all matters alike; it is enough in some cases that the *fact* be well established, as in the case of the first principles; the fact is a primary thing and first principle. Now of first principles we see some by induction, some by perception, some by a certain habituation, and others too in other ways. But each set of principles we must try to investigate in the natural way, and we must take pains to determine them correctly, since they have a great influence on what follows. For the beginning is thought to be more than half of the whole, and many of the questions we ask are cleared up by it.

8. But we must consider happiness in the light not only of our conclusion and our premises, but also of what is commonly said about it; for with a true view all the data harmonize, but with a false one the facts soon clash. Now goods have been divided into three classes, and some are described as external, others as relating to soul or to body; we call those that relate to soul most properly and truly goods, and psychical actions and activities we class as relating to soul. Therefore our account must be sound, at least according to this view, which is an old one and agreed on by philosophers. It is correct also in that we identify the end with certain actions and activities; for thus it falls among goods

of the soul and not among external goods. Another belief which harmonizes with our account is that the happy man lives well and fares well; for we have practically defined happiness as a sort of living and faring well. The characteristics that are looked for in happiness seem also, all of them, to belong to what we have defined happiness as being. For some identify happiness with virtue, some with practical wisdom, others with a kind of philosophic wisdom, others with these, or one of these, accompanied by pleasure or not without pleasure; while others include also external prosperity. Now some of these views have been held by many men and men of old, others by a few eminent persons; and it is not probable that either of these should be entirely mistaken, but rather that they should be right in at least some one respect, or even in most respects.

With those who identify happiness with virtue or some one virtue our account is in harmony; for to virtue belongs virtuous activity. But it makes, perhaps, no small difference whether we place the chief good in possession or in use, in state of mind or in activity. For the state of mind may exist without producing any good result, as in a man who is asleep or in some other way quite inactive, but the activity cannot; for one who has the activity will of necessity be acting, and acting well. And as in the Olympic Games it is not the most beautiful and the strongest that are crowned but those who compete (for it is some of these that are victorious), so those who act win, and rightly win, the noble and good things in life.

Their life is also in itself pleasant. For pleasure is a state of *soul*, and to each man that which he is said to be a lover of is pleasant; e.g. not only is a horse pleasant to the lover of horses, and a spectacle to the lover of sights, but also in the same way just acts are pleasant to the lover of justice and in general virtuous acts to the lover of virtue. Now for most men their pleasures are in conflict with one another because these are not by nature pleasant, but the lovers of what is noble find pleasant the things that are by nature pleasant; and virtuous actions are such, so that these are pleasant for such men as well as in their own nature. Their life, therefore, has no further need of pleasure as a sort of adventitious charm, but has its pleasure in itself. For, besides what we have said, the man who does not rejoice in noble actions is not even good; since no one would call a man just who did not enjoy acting justly, nor any man liberal who did not enjoy liberal actions; and similarly in all other cases. If this is so, virtuous actions must be in themselves pleasant. But they are also *good* and *noble*, and have each of these attributes in the highest degree, since the good man judges well about these attributes; his judgement is such as we have described. Happiness then is the best, noblest, and most pleasant thing in the world, and these attributes are not severed as in the inscription at Delos—

Most noble is that which is justest, and best is health;
But most pleasant it is to win what we love.

For all these properties belong to the best activities; and these, or one—the best—of these, we identify with happiness.

Yet evidently, as we said, it needs the external goods as well; for it is impossible, or not easy, to do noble acts without the proper equipment. In many actions we use friends and riches and political power as instruments; and there are some things the lack of which takes the lustre from happiness—good birth, goodly children, beauty; for the man who is very ugly in appearance or ill-born or solitary and childless is not very likely to be happy, and perhaps a man would be still less likely if he had thoroughly bad children or friends or had lost good children or friends by death. As we said, then, happiness seems to need this sort of prosperity in addition; for which reason some identify happiness with good fortune, though others identify it with virtue.

9. For this reason also the question is asked, whether happiness is to be acquired by learning or by habituation or some other sort of training, or comes in virtue of some divine providence or again by chance. Now if there is *any* gift of the gods to men, it is reasonable that happiness should be god-given, and most surely god-given of all human things inasmuch as it is the best. But this question would perhaps be more appropriate to another inquiry; happiness seems, however, even if it is not god-sent but comes as a result of virtue and some process of learning or training, to be among the most godlike things; for that which is the prize and end of virtue seems to be the best thing in the world, and something godlike and blessed.

It will also on this view be very generally shared; for all who are not maimed as regards their potentiality for virtue may win it by a certain kind of study and care. But if it is better to be happy thus than by chance, it is reasonable that the facts should be so, since everything that depends on the action of nature is by nature as good as it can be, and similarly everything that depends on art or any rational cause, and especially if it depends on the best of all causes. To entrust to chance what is greatest and most noble would be a very defective arrangement.

The answer to the question we are asking is plain also from the definition of happiness; for it has been said to be a virtuous activity of soul, of a certain kind. Of the remaining goods, some must necessarily preexist as conditions of happiness, and others are naturally co-operative and useful as instruments. And this will be found to agree with what we said at the outset; for we stated the end of political science to be the best end, and political science spends most of its pains on making the citizens to be of a certain character, viz. good and capable of noble acts.

It is natural, then, that we call neither ox nor horse nor any other of the animals happy; for none of them is capable of sharing in such activity. For this reason also a boy is not happy; for he is not yet capable of such acts, owing to his age; and boys who are called happy are being congratulated by reason of the hopes we have for them. For there is required, as we said, not only complete virtue but also a complete life, since many changes occur in life, and all manner of chances, and the most prosperous may fall into great misfortunes in old age, as is told of Priam in the Trojan Cycle; and one who has experienced such chances and has ended wretchedly no one calls happy.

10. Must no one at all, then, be called happy while he lives; must we, as Solon says, see the end? Even if we are to lay down this doctrine, is it also the case that a man *is* happy when he is *dead?* Or is not this quite absurd, especially for us who say that happiness is an activity? But if we do not call the dead man happy, and if Solon does not mean this, but that one can then safely *call* a man blessed, as being at last beyond evils and misfortunes, this also affords matter for discussion; for both evil and good are thought to exist for a dead man, as much as for one who is alive but not aware of them; e.g. honours and dishonours and the good or bad fortunes of children, and in general of descendants. And this also presents a problem; for though a man has lived blessedly until old age and has had a death worthy of his life, many reverses may befall his descendants—some of them may be good and attain the life they deserve, while with others the opposite may be the case; and clearly too the degrees of relationship between them and their ancestors may vary indefinitely. It would be odd, then, if the dead man were to share in these changes and become at one time happy, at another wretched; while it would also be odd if the fortunes of the descendants did not for *some* time have *some* effect on the happiness of their ancestors.

But we must return to our first difficulty, for perhaps by a consideration of it our present problem might be solved. Now if we must see the end and only then call a man blessed, not as being blessed but as having been so before, surely this is a paradox, that when he is happy the attribute that belongs to him is not to be truly predicated of him because we do not wish to call living men happy, on account of the changes that may befall them, and because we have assumed happiness to be something permanent and by no means easily changed, while a single man may suffer many turns of fortune's wheel. For clearly if we were to follow his fortunes, we should often call the same man happy and again wretched, making the happy man out to be "a chameleon, and insecurely based." Or is this following his fortunes quite wrong? Success or failure in life does not depend on these, but human life, as we said, needs these as well, while virtuous activities or their opposites are what determine happiness or the reverse.

The question we have now discussed confirms our definition. For no function of man has so much permanence as virtuous activities (these are thought to be more durable even than knowledge of the sciences), and of these themselves the most valuable are more durable because those who are blessed spend their life most readily and most continuously in these; for this seems to be the reason why we do not forget them. The attribute in question, then, will belong to the happy man, and he will be happy throughout his life; for always, or by preference to everything else, he will do and contemplate what is excellent, and he will bear the chances of life most nobly and altogether decorously, if he is "truly good" and "foursquare beyond reproach."

Now many events happen by chance, and events differing in importance; small pieces of good fortune or of its opposite clearly do not weigh down the scales of life one way or the other, but a multitude of great events if they turn out well will make life more blessed (for not only are they themselves such as to add beauty to life, but the way a man deals with them may be noble and good), while if they turn out ill they crush and maim blessedness; for they both bring pain with them and hinder many activities. Yet even in these nobility shines through, when a man bears with resignation many great misfortunes, not through insensibility to pain but through nobility and greatness of soul.

If activities are, as we said, what determines the character of life, no blessed man can become miserable; for he will never do the acts that are hateful and mean. For the man who is truly good and wise, we think, bears all the chances of life becomingly and always makes the best of circumstances, as a good general makes the best military use of the army at his command, and a good shoemaker makes the best shoes out of the hides that are given him; and so with all other craftsmen. And if this is the case, the happy man can never become miserable— though he will not reach *blessedness*, if he meet with fortunes like those of Priam.

Nor, again, is he many-coloured and changeable; for neither will he be moved from his happy state easily or by any ordinary misadventures, but only by many great ones, nor, if he has had many great misadventures, will he recover his happiness in a short time, but if at all, only in a long and complete one in which he has attained many splendid successes.

Why then should we not say that he is happy who is active in accordance with complete virtue and is sufficiently equipped with external goods, not for some chance period but throughout a complete life? Or must we add "and who is destined to live thus and die as befits his life"? Certainly the future is obscure to us, while happiness, we claim, is an end and something in every way final. If so, we shall call blessed those among living men in whom these conditions are, and are to be, fulfilled—but blessed *men*. So much for these questions.

COMMENTS

Unlike Plato, Aristotle's ethical thought builds outward from common sense. His view of happiness requires that we alter our views, but not as much as Plato's does, and he finds it important that his account fit a number of our intuitions.

Aristotle's work is famous partly because he is the first who explicitly lays out the framework for ethical theory. Each of us, he says, has an overall final end within which each of our actions fits and makes sense. He brings out a formal implication of this view: A proper account of happiness must show that it is complete and self-sufficient. It is complete if all we do is ultimately done to achieve it, while it is not sought for the sake of anything further. It is self-sufficient if it leaves out none of our concerns.

We all agree that our overall end is happiness, but this does not settle matters, for there is a dispute as to what happiness is. Aristotle finds it obvious that the overall end for the sake of which all our actions are performed can't be pleasure, for that would be to take too low a view of human nature. Epicurus will challenge him on this point. He also thinks it cannot be virtue, as this would imply that the virtuous person would be happy even in misfortunes, such as torture, and this he finds absurd. The Stoics will challenge him on this idea.

Aristotle's own view is that happiness requires a life of activity in accordance with virtue, with an adequate supply of external goods. He disagrees with common sense (as he reported it in the *Rhetoric*) in that he holds that virtue is not just one thing you need to be happy, along with material things. It is the most important aspect of happiness, since it is necessary; riches, power, and other external goods can't make you happy if you are not virtuous. But virtue alone will not make you happy. First, you need external goods to be able to perform virtuous actions. And second, external goods add something in their own right, which Aristotle describes as beautifying life. He finds it hard to divorce the idea of a happy life from conventional success; nobody, he says, would call someone happy who, like Priam in the stories, lost family, city, and everything in old age. Yet if virtue matters so much more than these other things that it enables you to make the best of what you have (like the cobbler who uses bad leather when he has to), then the loss of external goods should not make you unhappy: You still have what matters, since you are still the kind of person who can make the best of what you have. It is thus awkward for Aristotle to say that the virtuous person who loses external goods is either happy or unhappy. His argument toward the end of this passage brings out, in typically honest fashion, some difficulties in the position he has established.

The Stoics
On Final Ends III, 16–17, 20–26, 32–39, 42–71
Cicero

16 "Those whose theory I accept," said Cato, "have the following view. Every animal, as soon as it is born (this is where one should start), is concerned with itself, and takes care to preserve itself. Its constitution, and whatever preserves its constitution, it favours; whereas it recoils from its destruction and whatever appears to promote its destruction. In support of this thesis, the Stoics point out that babies seek what is good for them and avoid the opposite before they ever feel pleasure or pain. This would not happen unless they valued their own constitution and feared destruction. But neither could it happen that they would seek anything at all unless they had self-awareness and thereby self-love. So one must realize that it is self-love which provides the primary motivation.

17   "Most Stoics do not believe that pleasure should be ranked among the natural principles—I passionately agree. If it were otherwise, if nature were thought to have included pleasure amongst the primary objects of desire, then a host of loathsome consequences would follow. As to why we love those objects which by nature we first take up, the following is sufficient explanation: anyone, given the choice, would prefer all the parts of their body to be well-adapted and sound rather than of equal utility but impaired and twisted.

20   "We begin with a classification: the Stoics call 'valuable' (this is, I think, the

From Julia Annas (ed.) and Raphael Woolf (trans.), *Cicero: On Moral Ends* (New York: Cambridge University Press). Reprinted with the permission of Cambridge University Press.

term we should use) whatever is either itself in accordance with nature, or brings about something that is. Worthy of selection, therefore, is whatever has sufficient importance to be worthy of value (value the Stoics call *axia*). On the other hand, they call 'non-valuable' what is contrary to the above. The starting point, therefore, is that things in accordance with nature are to be obtained for their own sake, and their contraries are likewise to be rejected.

"With this established, the initial 'appropriate action' (this is what I call the Greek *kathekon*) is to preserve oneself in one's natural constitution. The next is to take what is in accordance with nature and reject its opposite. Once this method of selection (and likewise rejection) has been discovered, selection then goes hand in hand with appropriate action. Then such selection becomes continuous, and, finally, stable and in agreement with nature. At this point that which can truly be said to be good first appears and is recognized for what it is.

"A human being's earliest concern is for what is in accordance with nature. 21 But as soon as one has gained some understanding, or rather 'conception' (what the Stoics call *ennoia*) and sees an order and as it were concordance in the things which one ought to do, one then values that concordance much more highly than those first objects of affection. Hence through learning and reason one concludes that this is the place to find the highest human good, that good which is to be praised and sought on its own account. This good lies in what the Stoics call *homologia*. Let us use the term 'consistency,' if you approve. Herein lies that good, namely moral action and morality itself, at which everything else ought to be directed. Though it is a later development, it is nonetheless the only thing to be sought in virtue of its own power and worth, whereas none of the primary objects of nature is to be sought on its own account.

"What I have called 'appropriate actions' originate from nature's starting- 22 points, and so the former must be directed towards the latter. Thus it may rightly be said that all appropriate actions are aimed at our attaining the natural principles. It does not mean, however, that this is our ultimate good, since moral action does not inhere in our original natural attachments. Rather, such action is a consequence and a later development, as I said. But it too is in accordance with nature and, to a far greater extent than all the earlier objects stimulates us to seek it.

"Here, though, one must immediately avoid the error of thinking that the theory is commited to there being two ultimate goods. Take the case of one whose task is to shoot a spear or arrow straight at some target. One's ultimate aim is to do all in one's power to shoot straight, and the same applies with our ultimate good. In this kind of example, it is to shoot straight that one must do all one can; nonetheless, it is to do all one can to accomplish the task that is really the ultimate aim. It is just the same with what we call the supreme good in life; to actually hit the target is, as we say, to be selected but not sought.

"Since all appropriate actions originate from the natural principles, so too 23 must wisdom itself. Now it often happens that when one is introduced to someone, one comes to value that person more highly than one does the person who made the introduction. Similarly it is the starting-points of nature which first introduce us to wisdom, but it is no surprise that we then come to cherish wis-

dom itself far more than we do those objects by which we came to her. The bodily parts which we are given are evidently given to us for some particular way
of life. So too our mind's desire—termed *hormē* in Greek—seems given not for
24 any kind of life but for a particular form of living. The same goes for reason and
complete reason. Just as actors and dancers are not assigned arbitrary roles or
steps but certain fixed ones, so too life is to be led in a certain fixed way, not however one pleases.

   "This is the way we refer to as consistent and concordant. We do not think
that wisdom is like navigation or medicine. Rather it is like the acting or dancing which I just mentioned. Here the end, namely the performance of the art, is
contained within the art itself, not sought outside it. Yet even these latter arts are
in another way different from wisdom. In their case, when something is rightly
done it does not include every aspect of which the art consists. But what we
might call—if you approve—either 'right actions' or 'rightly performed actions'
(the Stoics call them *katorthōmata*) contain all the measures of virtue. Only wisdom is directed at itself in its entirety; this is not the case with other arts.

25   "Now it is foolish to compare the goal of wisdom with that of medicine or
navigation. Wisdom embraces magnanimity and justice, and judges itself superior to anything which might befall a person. This is not a feature of the other
arts. Indeed no-one could attain those very virtues which I just mentioned without determining that all things are indifferent and indistinguishable from one
another except for virtue and vice.

26   "Let us now see how evidently the following points flow from what I have
just laid down. The final aim (I think you realize it is the Greek word *telos* I have
long been translating, sometimes as what is 'final,' sometimes 'ultimate' and
sometimes 'supreme,' though one may also use 'end' for what is final or ultimate)—the final aim, then is to live consistently and harmoniously with nature.
This being so, all who are wise necessarily live happy, perfect and blessed lives,
with no impediment or obstacle, lacking nothing. The controlling idea behind
not only the philosophical system I am discussing but our lives and destinies too
is the belief that what is moral is the only good. This idea can be elaborated and
dressed up in rhetorical style, with an abundant outpouring of every choice
phrase and weighty sentiment. I however prefer the brief and pointed way in
which the Stoics express their 'consequences.'

32   "Now in the case of the other arts, the term 'artistic' should in a sense be
considered applicable only subsequent to and as a result of the activity in question—what the Stoics call *epigennēmatikon*. The term 'wise,' on the other hand, is
quite properly applied at the outset of a wise act. Every act which the wise person initiates must be immediately complete in all its parts, since we say that the
desirable end is located within the act. Some things are judged wrong by reference to their outcomes—betraying one's country, assaulting one's parents, robbing temples; but fear, grief and lust are wrong without reference to outcome.
These latter, then, are wrong not so much in their subsequent effects as in their
original and immediate nature. So too an act motivated by virtue should be
judged as right at its inception, not its completion.

"The term 'good,' used so much in this discussion, may also be clarified by 33
the definition. The Stoics define it in a number of slightly different ways, which
nonetheless point in the same direction. . . . Conceptions of things are formed in
our minds by various cognitive processes: experience, association of ideas, analogy, rational inference. Our notion of the good is given by the fourth and last of
these. By the process of rational inference our mind ascends from those things
which are in accordance with nature to a conception of the good.

"It is not by addition or extension or comparison with other objects that we 34
have awareness of this good in itself, and call it good, but by reference to its own
proper quality. Honey is the sweetest thing; but it is perceived as sweet through
its own particular kind of flavour, and not by comparison with other foods. In
the same way the good we are discussing is supremely valuable, but its value is
a matter of kind not quantity. Value (the Greek word *axia*) is not counted
amongst goods nor again amongst evils, so however much you add to it it will
remain in its own category. So the particular value of virtue is distinct; a matter
of kind, not degree.

"The view that anything moral is to be sought for its own sake is one we 36
share with many other philosophers. With the exception of the three schools
which do not include virtue in their highest good, this is the position universally
maintained, in particular of course by those who held that nothing else counts
as a good except morality. This position has a simple and ready defence. However burning one's greed, however unbridled one's desires, there is no one
today, nor was there ever, who would even dream of attaining some goal by an
act of wickedness, when the same goal was achievable without such means,
even if complete impunity was offered in the former case.

"Moreover, it is surely no utilitarian calculation of advantage that motivates 37
our desire to discover the secrets of the universe, and the nature and causes
of the movements of the heavenly bodies. Whatever barbarian standards one
lives by, however absolutely one might be set against scientific pursuits, no one
could find such worthy objects of study repugnant in themselves and seek them
only as a means to some pleasure or advantage, and otherwise value them at
nought. . . .

"On the other hand, no one raised in a good family and brought up with 38
decency can fail to be sickened by immoral behaviour in its own right, regardless of whether such behaviour causes oneself harm. It is impossible to regard
with equanimity one who lives a sordid and profligate life; impossible to
approve of squalid, empty-headed, fickle or untrustworthy people. One must
declare that immorality is to be shunned on its own account; otherwise there is
nothing to be said against those who act disreputably but do so alone or under
cover of darkness. The only deterrent here is that immoral behaviour is hideous
in itself. I could go on endlessly in support of this view, but there is no need.
Nothing is more certain than that morality is to be sought for its own sake, and
immorality likewise avoided.

"Now we earlier established the point that what is moral is the only good. 39
From this it cannot but be understood that morality has a higher value than

those intermediate objects which it procures. We also say that foolishness, cowardice, injustice and intemperance are to be avoided because of what results from them. But this is not a statement which should give the impression of conflicting with the proposition that what is immoral is the only evil. The results we are talking about are not bodily damage but the immoral acts which flow from the vices. . . .

42   "The theory which regards pain as an evil has this certain consequence: the wise person cannot be happy when being tortured on the rack. The theory which does not consider pain an evil carries the equally inevitable conclusion that the wise person's life remains happy whatever the torments. The same pain is borne more easily when endured for the sake of one's country than for some less worthy cause. This shows that it is one's attitude, not its own nature, which makes pain more or less intense.

43   "The Peripatetic view [i.e., Aristotle's] is that there are three kinds of goods, and that the richer one is in bodily or external goods, the happier. But it is hardly consistent for us Stoics to agree that possession of what is greatly valued with regard to the body makes one happier. The Peripatetics think that no life is completely happy without bodily well-being. We Stoics could not agree less. In our opinion not even an abundance of those goods which we really do call good makes a difference to the happiness, desirability or value of one's life. So when it comes to a happy life, the amount of bodily advantages has no relevance at all.

44   "If wisdom and health are both worth seeking, then the two together are more worth seeking than wisdom alone. But if each commands some value, it does not follow that the two together are worth more than wisdom on its own. In judging that health deserves a certain value, but not deeming it a good, we thereby consider that there is no value great enough to take precedence over virtue. This is not the Peripatetic position. They have to say that an act which is both virtuous and painless is more desirable than a virtuous act accompanied by pain. We think differently. Whether rightly or wrongly is a question to be considered later. But there could hardly be a greater difference between the two views.

45   "It is like the light of a lamp eclipsed and obliterated by the rays of the sun; like a drop of honey lost in the vastness of the Aegean sea; a penny added to the riches of Croesus, or a single step on the road from here to India. Such is the value of bodily goods that it is unavoidably eclipsed, overwhelmed and destroyed by the splendour and grandeur of virtue as the Stoic candidate for the highest good.

          "Ripeness (this is how I translate *eukairia*) does not increase with length of time, in that what is called 'ripe' has reached its full measure. In the same way right conduct (this is how I translate *katorthōsis, katorthōma* being an individual right act)—right conduct, as I say, consistency likewise, and goodness itself, which is found in one's being in harmony with nature, do not admit of cumula-
46 tive enlargement. Like ripeness, these features which I am speaking of do not become greater over time. That is why, for the Stoics, a happy life is no more desirable or worth seeking if long than if short. They use the following compar-

ison: a shoe is judged by how well it fits the foot. Many shoes are no better than few, larger no better than smaller. So too where goods are determined solely by their consistency and ripeness, more of them are no better than less, nor the long-lasting better than the brief.

"The following argument is less than incisive: good health is more valuable 47 the longer its duration; so the wisdom which is exercised over the longest period also has the highest value. This argument fails to grasp that, while the value of good health is judged by its duration, the value of virtue is judged by its ripeness. One might suppose that the proponents of the argument would go on to say that a long drawn out death or child-birth is better than a speedy one! They fail to see that some things are of value if brief, others if long-lasting.

"Consistent with the theory which states that the highest good (which we 48 call the 'final' or 'ultimate' good) is capable of increase is the view that one person may have more wisdom than another; and likewise that one person may act more wrongly or rightly than another. We cannot say this, since we rule out any increase in the highest good. When submerged in water one can no more breathe just below the surface and on the verge of getting out than one can in the depths. A puppy that has almost reached the point of opening its eyes can no more see than one newly born. In the same way one who has made some progress towards the acquisition of virtue is just as unhappy as one who has made no progress at all. I realize that all this seems strange. But our earlier conclusions are certainly secure and true, and the present theses follow logically from them. So their truth ought not to be doubted either. However, though the Stoics deny increase to virtue or vice, they do nonetheless hold that each in a sense may spread and expand.

"As for material wealth, Diogenes considers it a power not merely con- 49 ducive to achieving pleasure and good health, but essential. But he denies it has the same force when it comes to virtue or even the other arts. Money may be conducive to their attainment, but it is not essential. Hence, if pleasure or good health count as goods, wealth must also be so regarded, whereas if wisdom is a good, we are not committed to calling wealth a good. Nothing that is not a good can be essential for anything that is a good. Now thought and understanding are the basis of every art and stimulate our desire. But since wealth does not 50 count as a good, it cannot be essential for any art. Even if this point were conceded for the other arts, the case of virtue would still be different. Virtue requires a vast amount of study and experience, which the other arts do not. Moreover virtue demands life-long steadiness, firmness of purpose and consistency, which is evidently not so with the other arts.

"Next I shall expound our principle of ranking. If nothing ranked above anything else, the whole of life would be thrown into chaos. Wisdom would have no role or function, since there would be no difference whatsoever between any of the things that pertain to the conduct of life, and so no method of choosing could properly be applied. It has been well-established that what is moral is the only good and what is immoral the only evil, but as for those items which have no bearing on whether one lives happily or miserably, the Stoics then determined a certain ranking among them. Some have positive value, some the opposite, others are neutral.

51   "For some, though not all, of the items which are valuable, there is good reason to prefer them to other things, as is the case with health, well-functioning senses, freedom from pain, honour, wealth and so on. Likewise, with the items which are not deserving of value, some offer good reason to reject them—for example pain, loss of a sense, poverty, ignominy and so forth—while others do not. . . .

52   "At court, says Zeno, no one speaks of the king, with regard to rank, as being 'preferred.' . . . The term is applied to those who hold an office which, while lower in order, approaches nearest to the pre-eminence of a king. So too in life, it is not the items that occupy the first rank, but rather the second, which should be called 'preferred.' . . .

53   "Now everything that is good, we say, occupies the first rank. So what we call advantageous or superior must be what is neither good nor bad. Hence we define this as 'indifferent' . . . but with a moderate value. It had to be the case that there were some things left in the middle that would be either in accordance with nature or not. This being so, there were bound to be included among the former category items of some value. And given this, there had to be some things that were advantageous.

54   "Thus the distinction we are discussing is a correct one, and the Stoics offer the following analogy to facilitate comprehension: assume (they say) that our final end was to throw the knuckle-bone so that it stayed upright. A knuckle-bone thrown so as to *land* upright will have some advantage with regard to achieving this end; one thrown otherwise some disadvantage. But the 'advantage' of the knuckle-bone will not constitute the end I have mentioned. In the same way, the actual advantageous items are certainly relevant to achieving the end, but do not constitute its essence and nature.

58   "Now although we say that what is moral is the only good, it is still consistent to perform appropriate action despite the fact that we regard it as neither good nor evil. This is because reasonableness is found in this area, such that a rational explanation could be given of the action, and so of an action reasonably performed. Indeed an appropriate action is any action such that a reasonable explanation could be given of its performance. Hence one can see that appropriate action is something intermediate, falling into the category neither of goods nor their opposite. Since there may yet be something useful about what is neither a virtue nor a vice, it should not be rejected. Included in this category is also a certain kind of action, such that reason demands that one bring about or create one of the intermediates. What is done with reason we call an appropriate action. Hence appropriate action falls under the category of what is neither good nor the opposite.

59   ". . . Now it cannot be doubted that some of the intermediates should be adopted, and others rejected. So whatever one does or says in this fashion is included under appropriate action. This shows, since everyone by nature loves themselves, that the foolish no less than the wise will adopt what is in accor-

dance with nature and reject what is contrary. This is how a certain kind of
appropriate action is common to both wise and foolish, and it is here that its 60
involvement in what we call intermediates arises. From the latter all appropriate action proceeds; and so it is with good reason that all our deliberations are
said to be directed at them, including the question of our departing from life or
remaining alive.

"It is the appropriate action to live when most of what one has is in accordance with nature. When the opposite is the case, or is envisaged to be so, then
the appropriate action is to depart from life. This shows that it is sometimes the
appropriate action for the wise person to depart from life though happy, and the 61
fool to remain in it though miserable. Stoic good and evil, which I have now often
mentioned, is a subsequent development. But the primary objects of nature,
whether they are in accordance with it or against, fall under the judgement of the
wise person, and are as it were the subject and material of wisdom. . . .

"Now the Stoics consider it important to realize that parents' love for their 62
children arises naturally. From this starting-point we trace the development of
all human society. It should be immediately obvious from the shape and the
parts of the human body that procreation is part of nature's plan. And it would
hardly be consistent for nature to wish us to procreate yet be indifferent as to
whether we love our offspring. Even among non-human animals the power of
nature is evident. When we observe the effort they devote to breeding and rearing, it is as if we hear nature's very own voice. Thus our impulse to love what
we have generated is given by nature herself as manifestly as our aversion to
pain.

"This is also the source of the mutual and natural sympathy between 63
humans, so that the very fact of being human requires that no human be considered a stranger to any other. Some of our bodily parts—for example our eyes
and ears—are as it were created just for themselves. Others—for example legs
and hands—also enhance the utility of the other parts. In the same way, certain
animals of great size are created merely for themselves. But take the so-called
'sea-pine,' with its broad shell, and the creature known as the 'pine-guard,'
because it watches over the sea-pine, swimming out of the latter's shell and
being shut up inside it when it retreats as if apparently having warned the sea-
pine to beware. Or take ants, bees and storks—they too act altruistically. Yet the
ties between human beings are far closer. Hence we are fitted by nature to form
associations, assemblies and states.

"The Stoics hold that the universe is ruled by divine will, and that it is vir- 64
tually a single city and state shared by humans and gods. Each one of us is a part
of this universe. It follows naturally from this that we value the common good
more than our own. Laws value the welfare of all above the welfare of individuals. In the same way one who is good and wise, law-abiding and mindful of
civic duty, considers the good of all more than that of any particular person
including oneself. Even to betray one's country is no more despicable than to
neglect common advantage and welfare for the sake of one's own. That is why
a preparedness to die for one's country is so laudable—it is right and proper that

we love our homeland more than our very selves. It is thought wicked and inhuman to profess indifference about whether the world will go up in flames once one is dead. . . . And so it is undoubtedly true that we must consider on their own account the interests of those who will one day come after us.

65   "This human affection is the reason why people make wills and appoint guardians for their children when dying. And the fact that no one would choose to live in splendid isolation, however well-supplied with pleasures, shows that we are born to join together and associate with one another and form natural communities. Indeed we are naturally driven to want to help as many people as

66 possible, especially by teaching and handing on the principles of prudence. It is hard to find anyone who does not pass on what they know to someone else. Thus we have a propensity for teaching as much as for learning. Nature has given bulls the instinct to defend their calves against lions with maximum passion and force. In the same way, those with great talent and the capacity to achieve, as is said of Hercules and Liber, have a natural inclination to help the human race. . . .

67   "But although they hold that there is a code of law which binds humans together, the Stoics do not consider that any such code exists between humans and other animals. Chrysippus made the famous remark that all other things were created for the sake of humans and gods, but that humans and gods were created for the sake of their own community and society; and so humans can use animals for their own benefit with impunity. He added that human nature is such that a kind of civil code mediates the individual and the human race: whoever abides by this code will be just, whoever breaches it unjust.

"Now although a theatre is communal, it can still rightly be said that the seat which one occupies is one's own. So too, in city or universe, though these

68 are communal, there is no breach of law in an individual owning property. Also, since we observe that humans are born to protect and defend one another, it is consistent with human nature for the wise person to want to take part in the business of government, and, in living by nature, to take a spouse and to wish to have children. Not even sexual passion, so long as it is pure, is considered to be incompatible with being wise. Some Stoics say that the Cynics' philosophy and way of life is suitable for the wise person, should circumstances arise conducive to its practice. But others rule this out altogether.

70   "Stoics consider that friendship should be cultivated, since it falls under the category of what is helpful. Some say that in a friendship the interest of one's friend will be as precious to the wise person as one's own, though others claim that one's own will be more precious. But even these latter declare that it is incompatible with justice, to which we seem to be born, to take something from another for the purpose of enriching oneself. Indeed the school which I am discussing rejects absolutely the adoption or approbation of justice or friendship for utility's sake, since the same utility might ruin or corrupt these. There can be

71 no justice or friendship at all except where sought for their own sake. Now whatever can be spoken of or called a 'law' is so by nature; and it is foreign to

the wise person not only to wrong, but even to harm, another. Nor can one conspire or collude in a wrong with one's friends or benefactors. Indeed it is maintained with utter severity and truth that fairness and utility necessarily go hand in hand. Whatever is fair and just is also good, and again whatever is good is also just and fair."

COMMENTS

The Stoics' most famous claim is that virtue is sufficient for happiness: All you need to be happy is to be a moral person. Aristotle finds this position ridiculous: How can you be happy, even if virtuous, in great misfortunes or on the rack?

The Stoics think that it is Aristotle who is making the mistake and that he does so by following ordinary belief in thinking that virtue has the same kind of value as external goods like health and wealth, so that to be happy you need to add these goods to the virtuous life. The Stoics think that this is an immature attitude, which has not fully realized what matters about being a rational human.

Our human nature equips us with instincts to go for things that are naturally good for us and to avoid things that are naturally bad for us. As we develop, we become ever better at reasoning and value our reasoning for the way it enables us to get these things reliably. However, it is also natural, they claim, for humans to develop further and to realize that our reason directs us to a further point of view, from which we see that morality has a different kind of value, one that overrides the value of things like health and wealth. (We find out later that this development also makes it clear to us that we have a moral relation to every other human being purely as a rational being, regardless of the particular ties we have to him or her.

The Stoics mark this radical difference of value in many ways, some of which sound artificial. Only virtue is good, they say; other things are all "indifferent," although those, like health and wealth, that are natural for us to go for are "preferred indifferents." The point of the artificial terminology is to stress that virtue does not have the same kind of value as health and wealth; they cannot make virtue better or be added on to it to produce a better life. The person who truly achieves a life of virtue has everything that matters for happiness, since other things that we think advantages are not the right kinds of things to improve it.

The Stoics seem to be left saying that a human life will involve our trying to achieve two kinds of value, though only one of them is relevant for happiness. Most of this passage is devoted to showing that there is nothing incoherent about the Stoic picture of happiness as the final end of our life. Happiness is to be found in a life in which our overall end is living virtuously; we do so by living our ordinary lives as parents, teachers, workers, and so on and by trying to stay healthy, earn money, and so forth. The difference from Aristotle is that for the Stoics these things are only the "material of virtue"; they do not have a value that could compete with or add to that of virtue. The Stoic will value her job, for example, but would not hesitate to give it up were it to involve her acting immorally.

This passage brings out some aspects of looking at your life this way. For one thing, the Stoic will be emotionally detached from things that others care about. If you are clear that the value of money cannot compete with that of virtue, you will not think that losing all your money is the disaster that most of us would consider it. Another point is brought out by the analogy with the archer. What matters is living your life (doing your job and so on) virtuously, and if you do so, then you have succeeded in what matters, even if you do not succeed in worldly terms. The Stoics compare virtue to skills in that what matters is the exercise of the skill, not whether the normal results are produced.

The Stoics are often compared to Kant, because of their insistence that moral value is utterly different from nonmoral value. But they are also working within the same framework as Aristotle: What we all seek is happiness, and we need to find what happiness really is, not to aim at something different. Do they succeed in showing *both* that all we need to be happy is to be virtuous and that it is natural and reasonable for us to go for health, wealth, and other things that we normally think of as good?

The Epicureans
Letter to Menoeceus 121–135
EPICURUS

121 | From Epicurus. Dear Menoeceus,

122 | Let no one when young put off doing philosophy, nor when old get tired of the study. Nobody is too young or too old when it comes to the health of their soul. The person who says that the time for doing philosophy has not yet come or that the time for it has passed is like the person who says with respect to happiness that the time for it has not yet come or has passed. Hence we should do philosophy both when young and when old. The old person should do it so that even when aging, he may stay youthful in good things because of thankfulness for the past. The young person should do it so that although young, he may also be mature because of lack of fear of the future. We should therefore focus on the things that produce happiness, since when it is present we have everything, but when it is absent we do everything in order to have it.

123 | There are things that I constantly recommended to you—do these and focus on them, taking these to be the principles of living finely.

First, consider god to be an imperishable and happy living being, as is suggested by the common conception of god, and do not attach to this anything alien to his imperishability or inappropriate to his happiness. Believe of him everything that can maintain his happiness and imperishability. There *are* gods—for knowledge of them is clear—but they are *not* as they are thought to be by most people, who do not even stick to the way they think about them. As for impiety, this is found not in the person who rejects most people's gods, but

in the person who attaches to the gods most people's beliefs. | For most peo- 124
ple's statements about the gods are false suppositions, not basic conceptions.
Hence come the greatest harms from the gods to bad people and benefits to the
good; for the gods, finding their own virtues congenial, always welcome people
like themselves and consider whatever is not like this as alien.

Become used to thinking that death is nothing to us. All good and bad lie in
sense-experience, but death is the deprivation of sense-experience. Hence, a correct understanding of death's being nothing to us makes the mortality of our life
something to welcome; it does not add infinite time to it, but removes the crav-
ing for immortality. | There is nothing in living to be dreaded for the person 125
who has genuinely grasped that there is nothing to be dreaded in not living.
Hence it is foolish to say that you fear death not because it will be painful when
it comes, but because it is painful before it comes. If something is not a trouble
when it comes, it produces only an empty pain when anticipated. The most ter-
rifying bad thing, then, death, is nothing to us, since as long as we exist, death
is not there, and when death is there, then we do not exist. Death, therefore, is
nothing to the living or to the dead, since it does not exist for the former, and the
latter no longer exist. But as for most people and death—sometimes they flee it
as though it were the greatest of evils, but sometimes choose it as a respite from
the evils in life. | The wise person, however, neither rejects living nor fears not 126
living; living does not offend him, and he does not think that not living is something evil. Just as with food he does not in every case choose the biggest portion,
but rather the most pleasant, so with time it is not the longest time but the most
pleasant that he enjoys. The person who advises the young man to have a fine
life and the old man to make a fine death is naive, not just because of what there
is to like about life, but because it is the same thing to focus on living finely and
on dying finely. Much worse is the person who says that it is good not to be born
at all, and "once born to pass through the gates of Hades as quickly as possibly."
| If he says this because he is convinced by it, why doesn't he leave and stop liv- 127
ing? If he has resolved firmly, this is easy for him to do. But if he is joking, he is
wasting our time, and we don't welcome this.

We should remember that the future is not altogether ours nor altogether
not ours; this way we will not altogether expect it as though it will happen nor
despair of it as though altogether it will not happen.

We should consider that, among desires, some are natural, others empty;
among the natural ones, some are necessary and some merely natural; and
among the necessary ones, some are necessary for happiness, others for the
body's being free of trouble, and others for life itself. | Steady contemplation of 128
these points lets us refer every choice and avoidance to the body's health and
the soul's freedom from trouble, since this is the goal of living happily. It is on
account of this that we do everything—so as to have neither pain nor anguish.
Once we achieve this, all the soul's storm is dispelled, since a living being has
nowhere else to go as though to fill a need or to seek something else with which
to complete the good of the soul and of the body. The time we are in need of
pleasure is when we are in pain because of pleasure not being present. When we
are not in pain, we no longer have need of pleasure.

This is why we say that pleasure is the starting point and the end—that is,
129 the goal—of living happily. | This is what we have recognized as the good that
is first and innate; it is from this that we begin every choice and avoidance, and
we come back to this, since we judge every good by the criterion of this feeling.
Precisely because this is the first and innate good, we do not choose every pleasure, Sometimes we pass over many pleasures, when more discomfort follows
for us from them, and we consider many pains superior to pleasures, whenever
greater pleasure follows for us when we stand the pains for a long time. Every
pleasure, therefore, because of its having a congenial nature, is good, *but* not
every pleasure is to be chosen, just as every pain is bad, but not every pain is
130 such as always to be avoided. | However, we should judge all these matters by
comparative measuring and by examination of the advantages and disadvantages, since we treat the good at certain times as bad and the bad, conversely, as
good.

Self-sufficiency we consider a great good, not so that we may always make
do with little, but so that if we do not have a lot, we may make do with little,
being genuinely persuaded that it is those least in need of it who enjoy luxury
most; that everything natural is easy to provide, while it is the empty that is hard
to provide; and that simple flavors produce pleasure equal to that of a luxurious
131 diet, once all the pain of need is removed, | and bread and water produce the
highest pleasure, when it is someone in need taking them. Therefore, getting
used to a simple, inexpensive diet is productive of health; makes a person res-
olute in the face of the necessary activities of life; puts us in a better state for the
luxuries that come along at intervals; and renders us fearless in the face of
chance.

When, therefore, we say that pleasure is the final goal, it is not the pleasures
of extravagant people we mean or those that consist in consumption—as some
think, from ignorance or disagreement or taking it the wrong way. Rather, we
132 mean having no pain in the body or disturbance in the soul. | It is not drinking
and parties that give rise to the pleasant life nor the enjoyment of sex with boys
and women or consumption of gourmet fish and other products of a luxury
table. It is sober reasoning, which works out the causes of every choice and
avoidance and drives out the beliefs from which come the greatest turmoil that
grips the soul.

The starting point for all this, and the greatest good, is practical wisdom.
This is why practical wisdom is more valuable even than philosophy. From it
flow all the other virtues, since it teaches that it is not possible to live pleasantly
without living in accordance with practical wisdom, the fine, and the just nor
possible to live in accordance with practical wisdom, the fine, and the just without living pleasantly. For the virtues are part of the nature of living pleasantly,
and living pleasantly is inseparable from them.
133 | So, who do you think superior to the person whose beliefs about the gods
are pious, who is in all ways fearless about death and who has reasoned out the
goal of our nature and grasps that the limit of good things is easy to fulfil and
easy to provide, while the limit of bad things either lasts a short time or has troubles that are slight?

As to Fate, introduced by some as the ruler of all things, he holds [that some things happen by necessity], others from chance, and others depend on us, for he sees that necessity is not accountable and chance is unstable, but what depends on us has no ruler, and blame and its opposite follow naturally on this. | It would be better to follow the myths about the gods than to be a slave to the 134 Fate of the natural philosophers. The former at least suggests hope of placating the gods by honoring them, but the latter makes necessity inexorable. Chance, however, he does not suppose to be a god, as most people hold—for nothing is done by god in a disorderly way—nor a shifting cause, since he does not think that good and bad with regard to living happily is given to people by chance, although they are provided by it with the starting points for great goods and evils. | He considers it better, then, to fail in a well-reasoned way than to suc- 135 ceed in an unreasoned way, since in actions it is better for what is well judged [not to turn out well than what is not well judged] to turn out well because of chance.

Focus on these thoughts and ones akin to them day and night, by yourself and in company with those like you, and you will never be troubled, waking or sleeping. You will live like a god among humans, for a person who lives among immortal gods is in no way like a mortal living being.

On Final Ends I, 29–33, 37–70
CICERO

| "I shall begin," he said, "in the way that the author of this teaching himself 29 recommended. I shall establish what it is, and what sort of thing it is, that we are investigating. This is not because I think you don't know it, but in order that my exposition should proceed systematically and methodically. We are investigat- ing, then, what is the final and ultimate good. This, in the opinion of every philosopher, is such that everything is to be subordinate to it, while it is not itself to be subordinate to anything. Epicurus locates this quality in pleasure, which he maintains is the highest good, with pain as the highest evil. Here is how he sets about demonstrating this thesis:

| "Every animal as soon as it is born seeks pleasure and rejoices in it, while 30 shunning pain as the highest evil and avoiding it as much as possible. This is behaviour which has not yet been corrupted, and nature reigns pure and whole. Hence he denies that there is any need for justification or debate as to why pleas- ure should be sought, and pain shunned. He thinks that this truth is perceived by the senses, as fire is perceived to be hot, snow white, and honey sweet. In none of these examples is there any call for proof by sophisticated reasoning; it is enough simply to point them out. He maintains that there is a difference between

From Julia Annas (ed.) and Raphael Woolf (trans.), *Cicero: On Moral Ends* (New York, Cambridge University Press). Reprinted with the permission of Cambridge University Press.

reasoned argumentative proof and mere noticing or pointing out; the former is for the discovery of abstruse and complex truths, the latter for judging what is clear and straightforward.

"Now since nothing remains if a person is stripped of sense-perception, nature herself must judge what is in accordance with, or against, nature. What does she perceive and judge as the basis for pursuing or avoiding anything

31   except pleasure and pain? | Now some Epicureans wish to refine this doctrine: they deny that the senses can be an adequate judge of what is good and bad. Rather they claim that intellect and reason can also grasp that pleasure is to be sought for its own sake, and likewise pain to be avoided. Hence they say that there is as it were a natural and innate conception in our minds by which we are aware that the one is to be sought, the other shunned. Still others, with whom I agree myself, observing the multitude of arguments from a multitude of philosophers as to why pleasure is not to be counted a good, nor pain an evil, conclude that we ought not to be overconfident of our cause, and should therefore employ argument, rigorous debate and sophisticated reasoning in discussing pleasure and pain.

32 | "To help you see precisely how the mistaken attacks on pleasure and defences of pain arose, I shall make the whole subject clear and expound the very doctrines of that discoverer of truth, that builder of happiness. People who shun or loathe or avoid pleasure do not do so because it is pleasure, but because for those who do not know how to seek pleasure rationally great pains ensue. Nor again is there anyone who loves pain or pursues it or seeks to attain it because it is pain; rather, there are some occasions when effort and pain are the means to some great pleasure. To take a slight example, which of us would ever do hard bodily exercise except to obtain some agreeable state as a result? Who on the other hand could find fault with anyone who wished to enjoy a pleasure which had no harmful consequences—or indeed to avoid a pain which would not result in any pleasure?

33 | "Then again we criticize and consider wholly deserving of our odium those who are so seduced and corrupted by the blandishments of immediate pleasure that they fail to foresee in their blind passion the pain and harm to come. Equally blameworthy are those who abandon their duties through mental weakness—that is, through the avoidance of effort and pain. It is quite simple and straightforward to distinguish such cases. In our free time, when our choice is unconstrained and there is nothing to prevent us doing what most pleases us, every pleasure is to be tasted, every pain shunned. But in certain circumstances it will often happen that either the call of duty or some sort of crisis dictates that pleasures are to be repudiated and inconveniences accepted. And so the wise person will uphold the following method of selecting pleasures and pains: pleasures are rejected when this results in other greater pleasures; pains are selected when this avoids worse pains.

37 | "... For now I shall explain the nature and character of pleasure itself, with the aim of removing the misconceptions of the ignorant, and engendering an understanding of how serious, sober and severe is Epicurean philosophy, despite the view that it is sensual, spoilt and soft.

"We do not simply pursue the sort of pleasure which has a natural tendency to produce sweet and agreeable sensations in us: rather, the pleasure we deem greatest is that which is felt when all pain is removed. For when we are freed from pain, we take delight in that very liberation and release from all that is distressing. Now everything in which one takes delight is a pleasure (just as everything which distresses one is a pain). And so every release from pain is rightly termed a pleasure. When food and drink rid us of hunger and thirst, that very removal of the distress brings with it pleasure in consequence. In every other case too removal of pain causes a resultant pleasure. | Thus Epicurus did not 38 hold that there was some halfway state between pain and pleasure. Rather, that very state which some deem halfway, namely the absence of all pain, he held not only to be true pleasure, but the highest pleasure.

"Now whoever is to any degree conscious of how he is feeling must to that extent be either in pleasure or pain. But Epicurus considers that absence of pain constitutes the upper limit of pleasure. Beyond that limit pleasure can vary and be of different kinds, but it cannot be increased or expanded. | My father used 39 to mock the Stoics with wit and elegance by telling me how in the Ceramicus at Athens there is a statue of Chrysippus sitting with an outstretched hand, that hand symbolizing the delight Chrysippus took in the following little piece of argument: 'Does your hand, in its present condition, want anything?' 'Not at all.' 'But if pleasure were a good, it would be wanting it.' 'I suppose so.' 'Therefore pleasure is not a good.'

"My father remarked that not even a statue would produce such an argument, if it could speak. Though the reasoning has some force against a Cyrenaic position, it has none whatsoever against Epicurus. If pleasure were simply the kind of thing which, so to speak, titillated the senses and flooded them with a stream of sweetness, then neither the hand nor any other part of the body could be satisfied with mere absence of pain and no delightful surge of pleasure. But if, as Epicurus maintains, the highest pleasure is to feel no pain, well then, Chrysippus, the initial concession, that the hand in its present condition wants nothing, was correct; but the subsequent one, that if pleasure were a good the hand would have wanted it, is not. For the reason that it did not want it was that to have no pain is precisely to be in a state of pleasure.

| "That pleasure is the highest good can be seen most readily from the fol- 40 lowing example: let us imagine someone enjoying a large and continuous variety of pleasures, of both mind and body, with no pain intervening or threatening to. What more excellent and desirable state could one name but this one? To be in such a state one must have a strength of mind which fears neither death nor pain, in that in death there is no sensation, and pain is generally long-lasting but slight, or serious but brief. Thus intense pain is moderated by its short duration, and chronic pain by its lesser force. | Add to this an absence of terror 41 at divine power, and a retention of past pleasures which continual recollection allows one to enjoy, and what could be added to make things any better?

"Imagine on the other hand someone worn down by the greatest mental and physical pain that can befall a person, with no hope that the burden might one day be lifted, and with no present or prospective pleasure either. What condition can one say or imagine to be more miserable than that? But if a life filled with pain is to be above all avoided, then clearly the greatest evil is to live in pain. And from this thesis it follows that the highest good is a life of pleasure. Our mind has no other state where it reaches, so to speak, the final point. Every fear and every sorrow can be traced back to pain, and there is nothing other than pain which by its own nature has the power to trouble and distress us.

42 | "Furthermore, the impulse to seek and to avoid and to act in general derives either from pleasure or from pain. This being so, it is evident that a thing is rendered right and praiseworthy just to the extent that it is conducive to a life of pleasure. Now since the highest or greatest or ultimate good—what the Greeks call the *telos*—is that which is means to no other end, but rather is itself the end of all other things, then it must be admitted that the highest good is to live pleasantly.

"Those who locate the highest good in virtue alone, beguiled by the splendour of a name, fail to understand nature's requirements. Such people would be freed from egregious error if they listened to Epicurus. Those exquisitely beautiful virtues of yours—who would deem them praiseworthy or desirable if they did not result in pleasure? We value medical science not as an art in itself but because it brings us good health; helmsmanship too we praise for providing the techniques of navigation—for its utility, not as an art in is own right. In the same way wisdom, which is to be considered the art of living, would not be sought if it had no practical effect. As things are, it is sought because it has, so to speak,

43 mastered the art of locating and obtaining pleasure. | (What I mean by 'pleasure' you will have grasped by now, so my speech will not suffer from a pejorative reading of the term).

"The root cause of life's troubles is ignorance of what is good and bad. The mistakes that result often rob one of the greatest pleasures and lead to the harshest pains of mental torment. This is when wisdom must be brought to bear. It rids us of terror and desire and represents our surest guide to the goal of pleasure. For it is wisdom alone which drives misery from our hearts; wisdom alone which stops us trembling with fear. Under her tutelage one can live in peace, the flame of all our desires extinguished. Desire is insatiable: it destroys not only individuals but whole families; often it can even bring an entire nation to its

44 knees. | It is from desire that enmity, discord, dissension, sedition and war [are] born. Desire not only swaggers around on the outside and hurls itself blindly at others: even when desires are shut up inside the heart they quarrel and fight amongst themselves. A life of great bitterness is the inevitable result. So it is only the wise person, by pruning back all foolishness and error, who can live without misery and fear, happy with nature's own limits.

45 | "There is no more useful or suitable guide for good living than Epicurus' own classification of desires. One kind of desire he laid down as both natural and necessary; a second kind are natural but not necessary; and a third neither natural nor necessary. The basis for this classification is that necessary desires are satisfied without much effort or cost. Natural desires do not require much either, since the riches with which nature herself is content are readily available

and finite. But there is no measure or limit to be found in the other, worthless desires.

| "So we see that life becomes completely disordered when we err through 46 lack of knowledge, and that wisdom alone will free us from the onrush of appetite and the chill of fear. Wisdom teaches us to bear the slings of fortune lightly, and shows us all the paths that lead to tranquility and peace. Why then should we hesitate to declare that wisdom is to be sought for the sake of pleasure and ignorance to be avoided on account of distress?

| "By the same token we should say that not even temperance itself is to be 47 sought for its own sake, but rather because it brings our hearts peace and soothes and softens them with a kind of harmony. Temperance is what bids us follow reason in the things we seek and avoid. But it is not enough simply to decide what must or must not be done; we have also to stick to what we have decided. Very many people, unable to hold fast to their own decisions, become defeated and debilitated by whatever spectre of pleasure comes their way. So they put themselves at the mercy of their appetites, and fail to foresee the consequences; and thus for the sake of some slight and nonnecessary pleasure—which might have been obtained in a different way, or even neglected altogether without any ensuing pain—they incur serious illness, financial loss, a broken reputation, and often even legal and judicial punishment.

| "On the other hand, those who are minded to enjoy pleasures which do not 48 bring pain in their wake, and who are resolute in their decision not to be seduced by pleasure and act in ways in which they feel they ought not to, obtain the greatest pleasure by the foregoing of pleasure. They will also often endure pain, where not doing so would result in greater pain. This makes it clear that intemperance is not to be avoided for its own sake, and temperance is to be sought not because it banishes pleasures but because it brings about still greater ones.

| "The same rationale applies in the case of courage. Neither hard effort nor 49 the enduring of pain is intrinsically enticing; nor is patience, persistence, watchfulness, nor—for all that people praise it—determination; not even courage. We seek these virtues because they enable us to live without trouble or fear, and to free our minds and body as much as possible from distress. Fear of death can shake to the roots an otherwise tranquil life; and succumbing to pain, bearing it with a frail and feeble spirit, is pitiable. Such weak-mindedness has led many to betray their parents, their friends, in some cases even their country; and in most cases, deep down, their own selves. On the other side, a strong and soaring spirit frees one from trouble and concern. It disparages death, in which one is simply in the same state as before one was born; it faces pain with the thought that the most severe of it ends in death, slight pain has long intervals of respite, and moderate pain is under our governance. Thus if the pain is tolerable, we can endure it, and if not, if life no longer pleases us, we can leave the stage with equanimity. Hence it is clear that cowardice and faint-heartedness are not condemned in their own right, nor courage and endurance praised. We reject the former because they lead to pain, we choose the latter because they lead to pleasure.

50 | "Only justice remains, and then we will have discussed all the virtues. But here too there are pretty similar things to be said. I have demonstrated that wisdom, temperance and courage are so closely connected with pleasure that they cannot be severed or detached from it at all. The same judgement is to be made in the case of justice. Not only does justice never harm anyone, but on the contrary it also brings some benefit. Through its own power and nature it calms the spirits; and it also offers hope that none of the resources which an uncorrupted nature requires will be lacking. Foolhardiness, lust and cowardice unfailingly agitate and disturb the spirits, and cause trouble. In the same way, when dishonesty takes root in one's heart, its very presence is disturbing. And once it is activated, however secret the deed, there is never a guarantee that it will remain secret. Usually with dishonest acts there first arises suspicion, then gossip and rumour, then comes the accuser, and then the judge. Many wrongdoers even indict themselves.

51 | "But even those who appear to be well enough fortified and defended against discovery by their fellow humans still live in fear of the gods, and believe that the worry which eats away at their heart day and night has been sent by the immortal gods to punish them. What contribution can wicked deeds make to lessening the discomforts of life which is not outweighed by the bad conscience, the legal penalties, and the hatred of one's fellow-citizens which they generate? Yet some people put no limit on their greed, their love of honour or power, their lust, their gluttony, or any of their other desires. It is not as if ill-gotten gain dimin-

52 ishes these desires—rather it inflames them. | That is why true reason calls those of sound mind to justice, fairness and integrity. Wrongdoing is of no avail to one who lacks eloquence or resources, since one cannot then easily get what one is after, or keep hold of it even if one does get it. For those, on the other hand, who are well-endowed materially or intellectually, generosity is more appropriate. Those who are generous earn themselves the goodwill of others and also their affection, which is the greatest guarantor of a life of peace.

53 | "Above all there is never any reason to do wrong. Desires which arise from nature are easily satisfied without resort to wrongdoing, while the other, worthless desires are not to be indulged since they aim at nothing which is truly desirable. The loss inherent in any act of wrongdoing is greater than any profit which wrongdoing brings. Thus the right view is that not even justice is choice-worthy in its own right, but only insofar as it affords the greatest abundance of pleasure. To be valued and esteemed is agreeable just because one's life is thereby more secure and full of pleasure. Hence we consider that dishonesty is to be avoided not simply because of the troublesome turn of events which it leads to, but much rather because its presence in one's heart prevents one ever breathing freely or finding peace.

54 | "So if not even the virtues themselves, which other philosophers praise above all else, have a purpose unless directed towards pleasure, but it is pleasure above all which calls us and attracts us by its very own nature, then there can be no doubt that pleasure is the highest and greatest of all goods, and that to live happily consists entirely in living pleasantly.

| "Now that this thesis has been firmly and securely established, I shall 55 briefly expound some corollaries. There is no possibility of mistake as far as the highest goods and evils themselves—namely pleasure and pain—are concerned. Rather, error occurs when people are ignorant of the ways in which these are brought about. Pleasures and pains of the mind, we say, originate in bodily pleasures and pains—and so I concede your earlier point that any Epicurean who says otherwise cannot be defended. I am aware that there are many of this sort, albeit ignorant. In any event, although mental pleasure does bring one joy and mental pain distress, it remains the case that each of these originates in the body and is based upon the body.

"But this is no reason for denying that mental pleasure and pain may be much greater than physical pleasure and pain. For in the case of the body, all we can feel is what is actually now present. With the mind, both the past and future can affect us. To be sure, when we feel physical pain we still feel pain; but the pain can be hugely increased if we believe there is some eternal and infinite evil awaiting us. The same point applies to pleasure: it is all the greater if we fear no such evil. | It is already evident, then, that great mental pleasure or pain has 56 more influence on whether our life is happy or miserable than does an equal duration of physical pleasure or pain. But we do not hold that when pleasure is removed distress immediately follows, unless it is a pain that happens to take its place. Rather, we take delight in the removal of pain even if this is not followed by the kind of pleasure which arouses the sense. One can see from this the extent to which pleasure consists in the absence of pain.

| "Still, we are cheered by the prospect of future goods, and we enjoy the 57 memory of past ones. But only fools are troubled by recollected evils; the wise are pleased to welcome back past goods with renewed remembrance. We have within us the capacity to bury past misfortune in a kind of permanent oblivion, no less than to maintain sweet and pleasant memories of our successes. But when we contemplate our whole past with a keen and attentive eye, the bad times will cause us distress, though the good ones happiness.

"What a splendid path to the happy life this is—so open, simple and direct! There can certainly be nothing better for a person than to be free of all pain and distress, and to enjoy the greatest pleasures of body and mind. Do you see, then, how this philosophy leaves out nothing which could more readily assist us in attaining what has been set down as life's greatest good? Epicurus, the man whom you accuse of being excessively devoted to pleasure, in fact proclaims that one cannot live pleasantly unless one lives wisely, honourably and justly; and that one cannot live wisely, honourably and justly without living pleasantly. | For a state cannot be happy if it is engaged in civil strife, nor a household 58 where there is a fight over who should head it. Still less can a mind at odds and at war with itself taste any part of freely flowing pleasure. One who constantly entertains plans and projects which compete amongst themselves and pull in different directions can know nothing of peace or tranquility. | Yet if life's pleas- 59 ure is diminished by serious illness, how much more must it be diminished by a sickness of the mind! And sickness of mind is the excessive and hollow desire for wealth, glory, power and even sensual pleasure, as well as the discomfort, distress and sadness that arises to eat up and wear out with worry the hearts of those who fail to understand that there need be no mental pain except that which is connected to present or future physical pain.

60   "Yet there is no foolish person who does not suffer from one of these sicknesses; there is none therefore who is not miserable. | Consider also death, which hangs over such people like Tantalus' rock. Then there is superstition—no-one steeped in it can ever be at peace. Moreover foolish people are forgetful of past successes, and fail to enjoy present ones. They simply await success in the future, but because that is necessarily uncertain, they are consumed with anxiety and fear. They are especially tormented when they realize, too late, that they pursued wealth or power or possessions or honour to no avail, and have failed to obtain any of the pleasures whose prospect drove them to endure a variety of great suffering.

61 | "Look at them! Some are petty and narrow-minded, or in constant despair; others are spiteful or envious, surly or secretive, foul-mouthed or moody; there are still others who are dedicated to the frivolity of romances; there are the reckless, the wanton, the headstrong, lacking at the same time both self-control and courage, never sticking to their guns. This is why there is never any respite from trouble for such people. So no fool is happy, and no-one wise unhappy. We support this maxim in a much better and truer way than do the Stoics. For they deny that there is any good except for some sort of shadowy thing which they call being 'honourable,' a term of more splendor than substance. They also deny that virtue, which rests upon this being 'honourable,' has any need of pleasure. Rather, it is sufficient unto itself as far as a happy life is concerned.

62 | "But there is a way in which this theory can be stated which we would not only not repudiate, but actually approve. Epicurus represents the wise person who is always happy in the following way: he limits his desires: he is heedless of death; he knows the truth about the immortal gods, and has no fear; he will not hesitate to leave life behind if that is best. Equipped with these principles, he is in a constant state of pleasure, since there is no time in which he does not have more pleasure than pain. He recalls the past with affection; he has hopes for the future, but does not rely on it—he is enjoying the present. He is entirely lacking in the faults of character which I just now listed. A comparison of life with that of the foolish affords him great pleasure. If the wise person suffers any pain, the pain will never have sufficient force to prevent him having more pleas-

63   ure than distress. | Epicurus made the excellent remark that "the wise person is hardly affected by fortune; the really important and serious things are under the control of his own deliberation and reason. No more pleasure could be derived from a life of infinite span than from the life which we know to be finite." . . .

65   "There remains a topic that is absolutely essential to this discussion, and that is friendship. Your view is that if pleasure is the highest good then there is no room for friendship. But Epicurus' view is of all the things which wisdom procures to enable us to live happily, there is none greater, richer or sweeter than

friendship. This doctrine he confirmed not simply by the persuasiveness of his words but much more so by his life, his actions and his character. The mythical stories of old tell how great a thing is friendship. Yet, for all the quantity and range of these stories, from earliest antiquity onwards, you will scarcely find three pairs of friends among them, starting with Theseus and ending with Orestes. Epicurus, however, in a single household, and one of slender means at that, maintained a whole host of friends, united by a wonderful bond of affection. And this is still a feature of present-day Epicureanism.

"But to return to our theme, since there is no need to speak of individual cases: | I understand that friendship has been discussed by Epicureans in three 66 ways. Some deny that the pleasures which our friends experience are to be given the same intrinsic value as those we experience ourselves. This position has been thought to threaten the whole basis of friendship. But its proponents defend it, and acquit themselves comfortably, so it seems to me. As in the case of the virtues, which I discussed above, so too with friendship, they deny that it can be separated from pleasure. Solitude, and life without friends, is filled with fear and danger; so reason herself bids us to acquire friends. Having friends strengthens the spirit, and inevitably brings with it the hope of obtaining pleasure. | And just as hatred, jealousy and contempt are the enemies of pleasure, so 67 too is friendship not only its most faithful sponsor, but also the author of pleasure as much for our friends as for ourselves. Friends not only enjoy the pleasures of the moment, but are cheered with hope for the near and distant future. We cannot maintain a stable and lasting enjoyment of life without friendship; nor can we maintain friendship itself unless we love our friends no less than we do ourselves. Thus this attitude is created within friendship, while at the same time friendship is connected to pleasure. We delight in our friends' happiness, and suffer at their sorrow, as much as we do our own.

| "Hence the wise person will feel the same way about his friends as he 68 does about himself. He would undertake the same effort to secure his friends' pleasure as he would to secure his own. And what has been said about the inextricable link between the virtues and pleasure is equally applicable to friendship and pleasure. Epicurus famously put it in pretty much the following words: 'The same doctrine that gave our hearts the strength to have no fear of ever-lasting or long-lasting evil, also identified friendship as our firmest protector in the short span of our life.'

| "Now there are certain Epicureans who react a little more timidly to your 69 strictures, though still with some intelligence. They fear that if we hold that friendship is to be sought for the sake of our own pleasure, then the whole notion of friendship will look utterly lame. And so these people hold that the early rounds of meeting and socializing, and the initial inclination to establish some closeness, are to be accounted for by reference to our own pleasure, but that when the frequency of association has led to real intimacy, and produced a flowering of affection, then at this point friends love each other for their own sake, regardless of any utility to be derived from the friendship. After all, familiarity can make us fall in love with particular locations, temples and cities; gym-

nasia and playing-fields; horses and dogs; and displays of fighting and hunting. How much more readily and rightly, then, could familiarity with our fellow human beings have the same effect?

70 | "A third group of Epicureans holds that, among the wise, there is a kind of agreement to love one's friends as much as oneself. We certainly recognize that this can happen, and often even observe it happening. It is evident that nothing more conducive to a life of pleasure could be found than such an association.

"All of this goes to show not only that the theory of friendship is not threatened by the identification of the highest good with pleasure, but it even demonstrates that the whole institution of friendship has no basis without it."

COMMENTS

Aristotle found it obvious that pleasure could not be a good candidate for happiness. How could it be merely pleasure that we ultimately seek in everything that we do? Epicurus retorts that there are two kinds of pleasure, only one of which is subject to Aristotle's dismissal. In all we do, we seek the kind of pleasure that consists of the quiet state and lack of disturbance that comes from having our desires filled and lacking nothing. This is *ataraxia* or tranquillity. Cicero's Epicurean puts some effort into claiming that both this and the more familiar notion of pleasure (the welcome accompaniment of satisfying a desire) are both *pleasure* and, moreover, that tranquillity is the greatest possible pleasure. Epicurus is a hedonist; he thinks it obvious that pleasure is what motivates us in all we do. But he also thinks that we are largely mistaken about what pleasure really is and that once we realize that the greatest pleasure is really to be found in tranquillity and satisfaction, we will alter our beliefs so as to achieve them.

Note that Epicurus appeals to experience—babies are a good example of human motivation for him, since having no beliefs, they have no false beliefs. Adults who have grown up in corrupt societies have unhappy lives because they have false beliefs. They have false beliefs about pleasure that lead them to cultivate desires whose satisfaction will leave them further from tranquillity than ever. (They also have beliefs that Epicurus himself begins from: that the gods will reward and punish us and that death is an evil. Epicurus thinks that these beliefs, in particular, poison our lives in a number of unobvious ways, and his arguments, especially the ones about death, have an interest of their own. Do you think that his arguments against the fear of death are good ones?)

Epicurus (like John Stuart Mill) thinks that you cannot successfully achieve a pleasant life without being virtuous and without having friends. That is, although we all achieve happiness by aiming at pleasant tranquillity, this is not supposed to be a selfish or egoistic theory; Epicurus claims that it makes room for caring for other people and requires that the person be virtuous—that is, brave, just, and so on. Is Epicurus successful in this claim? Look at his account of the virtues. Is his account of them somewhat surprising? Similarly, does he successfully account for friendship in the happy life, or does an Epicurean think of a friend as merely a means to more of her own pleasure? Intuitively, we think that someone whose aim in life is pleasure cannot be counted on to act in the morally right way or to be a good friend. Is Epicurus successful in opposing this belief?

Epicurus thinks that we go for "greater," rather than "lesser," pleasures, but he does not have a mechanical calculus for maximizing pleasure, as the Utilitarians were to do. Rather, we get the greatest pleasure, tranquillity, by monitoring our desires and employing certain strategies. Are these good strategies for someone who is aiming at a tranquil life?

Is Epicurus' version of happiness appealing? Is it too passive and risk aversive to be our overall aim in life?

D. Different Directions

All the theories we have seen so far assume that happiness, and our way of seeking it, should be sought within a framework of what is suitable for human nature. There is another strand in ancient ethics, however, both in pagan writers and emerging in the Christian tradition, which locates happiness in our aspiration to transcend the boundaries of ordinary human expectations and rise above the everyday constraints of the human condition. It is not surprising that these ideas look very different from what we have seen so far.

Theaetetus 172b–177c
PLATO

SOCRATES   But we're being overtaken by a new argument. Theodorus, a bigger one than the last.

THEODORUS   Well, we've got plenty of time, haven't we, Socrates?   c

SOCRATES   Yes, we seem to have. It strikes me now—I've often thought of it before, too—how natural it is that people who have spent a lot of time in 5 philosophical pursuits should look ridiculous when they go into the lawcourts to make speeches.

THEODORUS   How do you mean?

SOCRATES   If you compare people who have been knocking about in lawcourts and such places since they were young with people who have been brought up in philosophy and other such pursuits, it's as if you were comparing the d upbringing of slaves with that of free men.

THEODORUS   In what way?

SOCRATES   In that the philosophers always have what you mentioned, plenty 5 of time; they carry on their discussions in peace and with time to spare. For instance, look at us now, taking up one argument after another: we're

From Plato, *Theaetetus*, translated and edited by J. McDowell (Oxford: Oxford University Press, 1973). Reprinted with the permission of Oxford University Press.

already on our third. That's what they'll do, too, if the next argument to
come up attracts them more than the one in front of them, which is what
happened to us. It doesn't matter at all whether they talk for a long time or
a short one, provided only that they hit on that which is.

e   The others, on the contrary, are always short of time when they speak,
because they're hurried on by the clock; and they aren't allowed to make
speeches about anything they please, but the opposing counsel stands over
them, equipped with compulsion in the shape of a document specifying the
points outside which they may not speak, which gets read out while they're
5   speaking. Their speeches are always about a fellow slave, and addressed to
a master, who sits there with some suit or other in his hand. And their contests are never for some indifferent prize, but always for one that concerns
173   themselves; often they're running a race for life itself. Because of all that,
they become tense and sharp, knowing how to flatter their master with
words and fawn on him with deeds, but small and crooked in their minds.
The reason is that they have been deprived of growth, straightness, and
5   freedom, by the slavery they have suffered since they were young. It forces
them to do crooked things, and imposes great dangers and fears on their
minds while they're still soft; and because they're unable to withstand them
with the help of justice and truthfulness, they turn at once to falsehood, and
b   to retaliating against injustice with injustice, and they get twisted and
stunted in many ways. The result is that they finally come from youth to
manhood with nothing healthy in their intellects; though what they think is
that they have become clever and wise.

So that's what those people are like. Theodorus. But what about the
5   members of our own chorus? Would you like us to describe them, or shall
we leave them and go back to our argument? We don't want to go too far in
exploiting that freedom to take up one argument after another which we
were talking about just now.

c THEODORUS   No, Socrates, let's describe them first. You were quite right when
you said that in this sort of discussion it isn't a matter of our dancing attendance on the arguments; on the contrary, the arguments are, so to speak,
slaves to us, and each of them has to wait about, to get finished off when it
5   suits us. We don't have a judge, or, like dramatists, a spectator, presiding
over us to issue criticisms and commands.

SOCRATES   Well then, let's talk about them, since that's what you think fit. And
let's talk about the leaders of the chorus, because there's no reason to talk
about those who practise philosophy in a commonplace way. Now since
d   their youth, to begin with, they haven't known the way to the market place,
or where to find a lawcourt or council chamber or any other public meeting-
place of the state. They don't hear laws or decrees being pronounced, or see
them written down. As for cliques, exerting themselves to win office, gath-
5   erings, dinners, banquets complete with flute-girls—even in dreams it
doesn't occur to them to take part. Such a person is quite oblivious of
whether someone in the state is well or ill born, or whether he has had some

evil handed down to him from his ancestors, male or female—more oblivious than he is of the proverbial number of drops in the sea. And with all e
those things, he doesn't even know that he doesn't know them. Because it
isn't for the sake of a good reputation that he keeps away from them. On the
contrary, the fact is that it's only his body that's in the state, here on a visit,
whereas his intellect has come to regard all those things as of little or no
account, and to despise them; it flies about everywhere, as Pindar says, "in 5
the depths of the earth" and on the surfaces when it does geometry, and
"above the heavens" when it does astronomy, searching in every way into 174
the total nature of each of the things which are, taken as a whole, but never
settling on any of the things near it.

THEODORUS   How do you mean that, Socrates?

SOCRATES   In the sense of the story they tell about Thales, Theodorus. The story
is that he was doing astronomy and looking upwards, when he fell into a pit; 5
and a Thracian servant, a girl of some wit and humour, made fun of him,
because, as she said, he was eager to know the contents of heaven, but didn't
notice what was in front of him, under his feet. That same gibe will do for b
everyone who spends his life in philosophy. Because such a person really
does fail to notice his next-door neighbour: he's oblivious not only of what
he's doing, but almost of whether he's a man or some other creature. But as
for the question what, exactly, a man is, and what it's distinctively charac- 5
teristic of such a nature to do or undergo, that's something he does ask and
take pains to inquire into. You do understand, don't you, Theodorus?

THEODORUS   Yes, and you're quite right.

SOCRATES   Hence what happens when a man of that sort comes into contact
with anyone else, either privately or in public. As I was saying when I c
began, whenever he's forced to engage in a discussion about what's at his
feet and before his eyes, in a lawcourt or anywhere else, he raises a laugh,
not just among Thracian girls but among the rabble in general, because his
inexperience makes him fall into pits and into every possible difficulty. His 5
gracelessness is terrible, giving him a reputation for stupidity. When it's a
matter of discrediting people, he has nothing specific to say to anyone's dis-
credit, because, as a result of not having practised it, he knows no evil of
anyone; so he finds himself in difficulties, and looks ridiculous. And when
it's a matter of praise and the boasting of others, he makes himself conspic- d
uous by laughing, not affectedly but genuinely, and is thought to be silly.
Because if he hears a dictator or a king being eulogized, he thinks he's hearing some livestock-keeper, for instance a pigman or shepherd or cowherd of
some sort, being congratulated on having got a high yield; except that he 5
believes the animal which they tend and milk is more ill-tempered and
prone to scheming than those which ordinary herdsmen deal with, and that
lack of leisure is bound to make a man of that kind no less boorish and uneducated than herdsmen, penned in, as he is, by fortifications, like the herds- e
man's fold in the mountains. When he hears of someone who owns ten
thousand acres of land, or still more, as if that's a marvellously large estate,

he thinks he's hearing of quite a tiny amount of land, accustomed as he is to looking at the earth as a whole. And when people wax lyrical about families, and talk about how noble someone is if he can point to seven rich forebears in a row, he believes that the praise is coming from people whose vision is entirely dim and short-sighted, unable, because of their lack of education, to look always at the whole, and work it out that everyone has had countless forebears and ancestors, including thousands and thousands of rich men and beggars, kings and slaves, foreigners and Greeks, in every case. When people give themselves airs over a list of twenty-five ancestors, and trace their descent back to Heracles, the son of Amphitryon, it seems extraordinary pettiness to him; he laughs at their inability to get rid of the vacancy of an unintelligent mind, and work it out that it was just a matter of chance what sort of person the twenty-fifth back from Amphitryon was, and what sort of person the fiftieth back from him was. In all those situations, then, a man of that kind gets laughed at by the masses, partly because he seems to be arrogant, and partly because he's ignorant of what's at his feet, and gets into difficulties in every one of those situations.

THEODORUS   Yes, that's exactly what happens, Socrates.

SOCRATES   But things are different when he drags someone upwards: when he finds someone prepared to give up asking "What injustice am I doing to you, or you to me?," in favour of the investigation of justice and injustice themselves—what each of them is, and in what respect they differ from each other and from everything else; or when he finds someone prepared to give up asking "Is a king happy?," or again "Is a man with money happy?," in favour of an investigation about kingship, and human happiness and unhappiness in general—what sort of thing each of the two is, and in what way it's fitting for human nature to obtain the one and avoid the other. When it's all those things that that man with the small, sharp, litigious mind has to give an account of, the tables are turned. He gets dizzy, suspended from a height and looking down from high up; because of his unfamiliarity with the situation, he feels dismay and difficulty, and with his stammering, he raises a laugh, not among Thracian girls or any other uneducated people, because they can't see him, but among people whose upbringing has been the opposite to that of slaves.

Well then, Theodorus, that's what each of them is like. The one, whom you call a philosopher, has really been brought up in freedom and leisure, and it's excusable if he seems simple-minded and worthless when he gets involved in slave-like tasks: for instance, when he doesn't know how to make up a roll of bedding, or how to sweeten a dish or an obsequious speech. The other can perform any task of that kind smartly and quickly, but he doesn't know how to wear his coat like a gentleman, or how to take up the harmony of discourse and rightly hymn the life of gods and happy men.

THEODORUS   Socrates, if you convinced everyone of what you're saying, the way you've convinced me, there'd be more peace and fewer evils among men.

SOCRATES But, Theodorus, it isn't possible that evils should be destroyed; 5
because there must always be something opposite to the good. And it isn't
possible for them to become established among the gods; of necessity, they
haunt our mortal nature, and this region here. That's why one ought to try
to escape from here to there as quickly as one can. Now the way to escape is b
to become as nearly as possible like a god; and to become like a god is to
become just and religious, with intelligence. But it's not at all easy to persuade people that it's not for the reasons which the masses give that one
ought to avoid wickedness and pursue virtue. The masses say that it's in 5
order not to seem to be bad and in order to seem to be good that one should
practise one and not the other. Now in my view that's what they call an old
wives' tale, and we can state the truth like this. A god is by no means and in c
no way unjust, but as just as it's possible to be, and there's nothing more like
a god than one of us who has become as just as possible. It's in relation to
this point that we find a man's true cleverness, or else his worthlessness and
unmanliness. Because knowledge of this point is true wisdom and virtue, 5
whereas ignorance of it is patent stupidity and vice. Anything else that
passes for cleverness and wisdom is cheap, if it occurs in the exercise of
political power, or mechanical, if it occurs in the exercise of skills. So if d
someone behaves unjustly, and says or does things not in conformity with
religion, it's far and away the best course not to concede to him that his
sticking at nothing makes him clever. People take pride in that reproach,
and think they're being told that they're not silly fools, useless burdens on
the earth, but real men, the sort one needs to be if one's to survive in a state. 5
So we should tell them the truth: they're just the sort of people they don't
think they are, and all the more for not thinking so; because they're ignorant
of the penalty for injustice, which is the last thing one should be ignorant of.
It isn't what they think, beatings and executions: people sometimes behave
unjustly and suffer none of those penalties. No, it's a penalty which it's e
impossible to escape.

THEODORUS What penalty do you mean?

SOCRATES There are patterns set up in that which is, one of them divine and
supremely happy, the other with nothing divine in it and supremely unhappy. Now, not seeing that that's so, they fail to notice, because of their fool- 5
ishness and utter lack of intelligence, that through their unjust actions 177
they're becoming like one of the patterns and unlike the other. For that they
pay the penalty of living the life which resembles the one they become like.
Now suppose we tell them that if they don't get rid of their "cleverness," that 5
region untainted by evils will not receive them even when they die, but here
on earth they'll for ever lead a life resembling themselves, evil men associated with evils. If we do, they'll simply take it as a speech addressed to men
who are clever and stick at nothing, by some people devoid of intelligence.

THEODORUS That's quite true, Socrates.

SOCRATES I know it is. But there's one thing that does happen with them. b
When they have to exchange arguments in private about the things they

find fault with, and when they're willing to endure it for some time, like
5   men, instead of showing unmanliness by running away, it's strange how, in
the end, they find themselves unsatisfactory on the subjects they're talking
about; that oratory of theirs dries up somehow, so that they seem no better
than children.

But let's stop talking about all this, since it's all really a digression
anyway.

COMMENTS

This passage begins with a contrast between the philosopher, who is portrayed in
extremely unworldly terms, and the sharp litigious type of person, who is always up
on the latest moves in politics and the law courts. (Plato does not always depict philosophy as such a detached intellectual pursuit of truth; in some other passages, he
shows philosophy to be a directing intelligent practical activity.) The passage goes on
to make a wider claim: We should all try to escape being bogged down in the mixture of good and evil that inevitably surrounds us in ordinary life and to become "like
a god." This claim is startling; in ordinary Greek thought, mortals should remember
that they are mortal and refrain from aspiring to the condition of the gods. But here,
Plato has a refined conception of god: Becoming like a god is achieved by becoming virtuous, "with intelligence"—that is, in a philosophical and reflective way. This
is nothing like the gods of Greek religion: Plato is insisting that the divine is only good
and in no way evil, so that becoming like a god is becoming, as far as we can, completely good and virtuous.

Two things are striking about this passage (which was famous in the ancient
world and thought to express Plato's view about our final end, happiness). First, it is
an even more uncompromising claim than we saw in the earlier Plato passage from
the *Gorgias* that virtue is all you need for happiness. The virtuous person here seems
not merely not to need external goods, but actually to distance himself from the ordinary world and to regard what is important as being above everyday concerns. Is this
really a viable conception of *virtue?* How is the virtuous person supposed to work
out how to act in the world?

Second, does it really make sense to think of virtue as becoming like a god, given
that a god or the gods, however conceived, are fundamentally different kinds of beings
from humans? If a god is just, it can hardly be in the way we are, by refraining from
selfishness and exploitation and giving others what is their due. Aristotle complains
that to praise the gods for being virtuous is "vulgar," since it drags them down to our
level by implying that, like us, they have bad desires to overcome. How can humans
become *like* the gods by becoming virtuous when virtue is so different for humans and
for beings who lack the constraints and problems of the human condition?

Does this passage strike you as giving a better picture of a religious ideal than an
ethical ideal? If so, why? What does the difference come to?

THE GOSPEL OF MATTHEW

The Gospel of Matthew is one of the four Gospels, accounts of the life and teachings of Jesus, which were recognized as canonical by the ancient Christian Church and have come down as part of the New Testament of Christian scriptures. It was probably written around the end of the first century A.D. Scholarly opinion generally holds that Matthew and Luke both draw on material in Mark, which was earlier, as well as another earlier common source. The Beatitudes passage is one of many in Matthew to which there is a parallel in Luke, but Luke's account is somewhat different.

The Gospel of Matthew 5, 2–20

2 Jesus opened his mouth and taught them, saying:

3 "Happy are the poor in spirit, because theirs is the kingdom of heaven.

4 "Happy are those who grieve, because they shall be comforted.

5 "Happy are the gentle, because they shall inherit the earth.

6 "Happy are those who hunger and thirst for righteousness, because they shall be satisfied.

7 "Happy are the merciful, because they shall receive mercy.

8 "Happy are the pure in heart, because they shall see God.

9 "Happy are the peacemakers, because they shall be called children of God.

10 "Happy are those who are persecuted because of righteousness, because theirs is the kingdom of heaven.

11 "Happy is what you are when people abuse you and persecute you and say every sort of wickedness about you on account of me.

12 "Rejoice and be glad, because your reward is great in heaven. This is how they persecuted the prophets before you.

13 "You are the salt of the earth; but if salt has lost its taste, how can it be made salty again? It is good for nothing but to be thrown out and trodden underfoot.

14 "You are the light of the world. A city set up on a hill cannot be hidden.

15 "People do not light a lamp and put it under a bushel-basket; they put it on the lampstand, and it gives light to everyone in the house.

16 "In the same way, let your light shine before people, so they may see your fine deeds and render glory to your Father in heaven.

17 "Do not consider that I have come to annul the Law or the prophets. I have come not to annul but to fulfill.

18 "Truly I say to you that until heaven and earth pass away, not one letter, or stroke of a letter, will pass from the Law until all comes about.

19 "Thus whoever annuls one of the least of these commandments, and teaches people likewise, shall be called least in the kingdom of heaven; but whoever does and teaches them shall be called great in the kingdom of heaven.

20 "For I say to you that unless your righteousness exceeds that of the scribes and Pharisees you will not enter the kingdom of heaven."

In this fifth-century A.D. carving, Christ is shown as a teacher, flanked by Saint Peter, Saint Paul, and the apostles. The elaborate throne on which he is seated emphasizes his authority. Here Christ is shown beardless, as a divine youth whose wisdom is different from that of philosophers, who are always shown bearded. Here the normal association of wisdom with age and experience is deliberately rejected. However, the image of Christ that overwhelmingly prevailed in Christian art shows him bearded (like a philosopher) and with long hair (like a holy man). Both types of images stress that Christ is a teacher, and in early Christian art both turn up together, since neither is adequate on its own. (Ivory pyxis, after A.D. 400, Berlin, Staatliche Museum.)

COMMENTS

This famous passage, the Beatitudes, is usually translated as "Blessed are the . . ." rather than "Happy are the . . ." The Greek word is *makarios*. Jesus' words were not originally in Greek, but whatever exactly he meant by them, educated Greek-speaking Jews and pagans would certainly think of happiness when they heard *makarios*, a synonym for *eudaimon*, the more common word for happiness.

Jesus is obviously not putting forward a theory of happiness, but he is making claims that are meant to be startling and to radicalize our views about happiness. (Aristotle, who thinks it is important to do justice to widespread views, would find it hard to take seriously the idea that it is the poor and unfortunate who are really the happy people.) Happiness, Jesus tells us, is not being conventionally well off. It lies in something that is internal to the person, and hence even the poor and persecuted can be happy. This internal achievement is partly a state of having, or at least aiming at, certain virtues, such as gentleness and mercy. (The word that is translated as "righteousness" in verses 6 and 10 is *dikaiosune*, which strictly means justice, but in philosophical contexts [such as Plato's *Republic*] can come to mean morality or righteousness more generally.) It also involves following established moral principles and committing yourself to Jesus himself and his claims.

The idea that happiness lies within you and not in external prosperity is familiar in ancient philosophy, but here it appears with a new idea of commitment to a particular religious teacher. Thus it is presented not as something that the individual can achieve for herself by rational reflection, but as something requiring commitment to authority. (Compare the adherence of the Jewish martyrs to observance of the Law as a way of life in the passage on pp. 118–128.)

PLOTINUS

Plotinus (A.D. 205–270), probably from Lycopolis in Egypt, studied Platonic philosophy in Alexandria and settled in Rome from the age of about forty, where he taught a small group of pupils and associates. Plotinus thought of himself as a Platonist, someone who studied and discussed the thoughts of Plato. However, he came to Plato's thought from a background of philosophical problems developed by subsequent philosophy, and his own work, though it develops from Platonic themes, is so original by comparison with previous rather pedestrian interpretations of Plato's thought that Plotinus is generally considered the founder of "Neo-Platonism," a distinct philosophy. These ideas were developed in a more academic form by later Neo-Platonists. Plotinus himself works through arguments and lines of thought, rather than laying out doctrines in a systematic form.

Enneads I, 4

PLOTINUS

1. Suppose we assume the good life and well-being to be one and the same; shall we then have to allow a share in them to other living things as well as ourselves? If they can live in the way natural to them without impediment, what prevents us from saying that they too are in a good state of life? For whether one considers the good life as consisting in satisfactory experience or accomplishing one's proper work, in either case it will belong to the other living things as well as us. For they can have satisfactory experiences and be engaged in their natural work; musical creatures, for instance, which are otherwise well off and sing in their natural way as well, and so have the life they want. Then again, suppose we make well-being an end, that is, the ultimate term of natural desire; we shall still have to allow other living things a share in well-being when they reach their final state, that where, when they come to it, the nature in them rests, since it has passed through their whole life and fulfilled it from beginning to end. But if anyone dislikes the idea of extending some degree of well-being down to the other living things—which would involve giving a share in it even to the meanest; one would have to give a share to plants, because they too are alive and have a life which unfolds to its end—first of all, why will it not seem absurd of him to deny that other living things live well just because he does not think them important? Then, one is not compelled to allow to plants what one allows to all other living beings; for plants have no sensations. But there might perhaps be someone who would allow well-being to plants just because they have life; one life can be good, another the opposite, as plants too can be well or badly off, and bear fruit or not bear fruit. If pleasure is the end and the good life is determined by pleasure, it is absurd of anyone to deny the good life to other living things; the same applies to tranquillity, and also if the life according to nature is stated to be the good life.

2. Those who deny it to plants because they have no sensation run the risk of denying it to all living things. For if they mean by sensation being aware of one's experiences, the experience must be good before one is aware of it; for example, to be in a natural state is good, even if one is not aware of it, and so is to be in one's own proper state, even if one does not yet know that it is one's own proper state, and that it is pleasant (as it must necessarily be). So if something is good and is there its possessor is already well off; so why should we bring sensation into it? Unless of course people attribute good not to the actual experience or condition but to the knowledge and perception of it. But in this way they will be saying that the good is really the sensation, the activity of the sense-life; so that it will be all the same whatever is sensed. But if they say that the good is

Reprinted by permission of the publishers and the Loeb Classical Library from *Plotinus: Enneads*, Volume I, translated by A. H. Armstrong, Cambridge, Mass.: Harvard University Press, 1966.

the product of the two, the sensation of an object of a particular kind, why, when each of the constituents is neutral, do they say that the product is good? But if it is the experience which is good, and the good life is the special state when someone knows that the good is present to him, we must ask them whether he lives well by knowing that this present thing is present or whether he must know not only that it gives him pleasure but that it is the good. But if he must know that it is the good, this is no longer the business of sensation but of another greater power than that of sense. So the good life will not belong to those who feel pleasure but to the man who is able to know that pleasure is the good. Then the cause of living well will not be pleasure, but the power of judging that pleasure is good. And that which judges is better than mere experience, for it is reason or intellect; but pleasure is an experience; and the irrational is never better than reason. How then can the reason set itself aside and assume that something else which has its place in the contrary kind is better than itself? It looks as if the people who deny well-being to plants, and those who place it in a particular kind of sensation, were unconsciously in search of a good life which is something higher, and were assuming that it is better the purer and clearer life is. Those who say that it is to be found in a rational life, not simply in life, even life accompanied by sensation, may very likely be right; but we ought to ask them why they posit well-being only in the case of rational living things. "Do you add the 'rational' because reason is more efficient and can easily find out and procure the primary natural needs, or would you require reason even if it was not able to find them out or obtain them? If you require it because it is better able to find them out, then irrational creatures too, if by their nature they can satisfy the primary natural needs without reason, will have well-being; and then reason would be a servant and not worth having for itself, and the same would apply to its perfection, which we say is virtue. But if you say that reason has not its place of honour because of the primary natural needs, but is welcome for its own sake, you must tell us what other work it has and what is its nature and what makes it perfect." For it cannot be the study of these primary natural needs which perfects reason; its perfection is something else, and its nature is different, and it is not itself one of these primary natural needs or of the sources from which the primary natural needs derive; it does not belong to this class of beings at all, but is better than all these; otherwise I do not think they would be able to explain its place of honour. But until these people find a better nature than the things at which they now stop, we must let them stay where they are, which is where they want to be, unable to answer the question how the good life is possible for the beings which are capable of it.

3. We, however, intend to state what we understand by well-being, beginning at the beginning. Suppose we assume that it is to be found in life; then if we make "life" a term which applies to all living things in exactly the same sense, we allow that all of them are capable of well-being, and that those of them actually live well who possess one and the same thing, something which all living beings are naturally capable of acquiring; we do not on this assumption grant the ability to live well to rational beings, but not to irrational. Life is com-

mon to both, and it is life which by the same acquisition [in both cases] tends towards well-being, if well-being is to be found in a kind of life. So I think that those who say that well-being is to be found in rational life are unaware that, since they do not place it in life in general, they are really assuming that it is not a life at all. They would have to say that the rational power on which well-being depends is a quality. But their starting-point is rational *life*. Well-being depends on this as a whole; that is, on another kind of life. I do not mean "another kind" in the sense of a logical distinction, but in the sense in which we Platonists speak of one thing as prior and another as posterior. The term "life" is used in many different senses, distinguished according to the rank of the things to which it is applied, first, second and so on; and "living" means different things in different contexts; it is used in one way of plants, in another of irrational animals, in various ways of things distinguished from each other by the clarity or dimness of their life; so obviously the same applies to "living well." And if one thing is an image of another, obviously its good life is the image of another good life. If then well-being belongs to that which has a superabundance of life, (this means that which is in no way deficient in life), it will belong only to the being which lives superabundantly: this will have the best, if the best among realities is being really alive, is perfect life. So its good will not be something brought in from outside, nor will the basis of its goodness come from somewhere else and bring it into a good state; for what could be added to the perfect life to make it into the best life? If anyone says "The Absolute Good," that is our own way of talking, but at present we are not looking for the cause, but for the immanent element.

We have often said that the perfect life, the true, real life, is in that transcendent intelligible reality, and that other lives are incomplete, traces of life, not perfect or pure and no more life than its opposite. Let us put it shortly; as long as all living things proceed from a single origin, but have not life to the same degree as it, the origin must be the first and most perfect life.

4. If then man can have the perfect life, the man who has this life is well off. If not, one would have to attribute well-being to the gods, if among them alone this kind of life is to be found. But since we maintain that this well-being is to be found among men we must consider how it is so. What I mean is this; it is obvious from what has been said elsewhere that man has perfect life by having not only sense-life but reasoning and true intelligence. But is he different from this when he has it? No, he is not a man at all unless he has this, either potentially or actually (and if he has it actually we say that he is in a state of well-being). But shall we say that he has this perfect kind of life in him as a part of himself? Other men, we maintain, who have it potentially, have it as a part, but the man who is well off, who actually is this and has passed over into identity with it, [does not have it but] *is* it. Everything else is just something he wears; you could not call it part of him because he wears it without wanting to; it would be his if he united it to him by an act of the will. What then is the good for him? He is what he has, his own good. The Transcendent Good is Cause of the good in him; the fact that It is good is different from the fact that It is present to him. There is evidence for

this in the fact that the man in this state does not seek for anything else; for what could he seek? Certainly not anything worse, and he has the best with him. The man who has a life like this has all he needs in life. If he is virtuous, he has all he needs for well-being and the acquisition of good; for there is no good that he has not got. What he seeks he seeks as a necessity, not for himself but for something that belongs to him; that is, he seeks it for the body which is joined to him; and even granting that this is a living body, it lives its own life and not the life which is that of the good man. He knows its needs, and gives it what he gives it without taking away anything from his own life. His well-being will not be reduced even when fortune goes against him; the good life is still there even so. When his friends and relations die he knows what death is—as those who die do also if they are virtuous. Even if the death of friends and relations causes grief, it does not grieve him but only that in him which has no intelligence, and he will not allow the distresses of this to move him.

5. But what about pain and sickness and everything that hinders activity? And suppose the good man is not even conscious? That could happen as the result of drugs and some kinds of illness. How could he in all these circumstances have a good life and well-being? We need not consider poverty and disgrace; though someone might raise an objection in regard of these too, and especially the "fate of Priam" that people are always talking about. For even if he bore them and bore them lightly, he would not want them; and the life of well-being must be something one wants. This good man, it might be objected, is not a good soul, without reckoning his bodily nature as part of his essential being. Our opponents might say that they willingly accept our point of view, as long as the bodily affections are referred to the man himself, and it is he himself who chooses and avoids for reasons connected with the body. But if pleasure is counted as part of the life of well-being, how can a man be well off when chance and pain bring distress, even if it is a good man that these things happen to? This kind of state of self-sufficient well-being belongs to the gods; since men have a supplement of lower nature one must look for well-being in the whole of what has come into existence, and not in a part; for if one part is in a bad state the other, higher, part must necessarily be hindered in its proper work if the affairs of the lower part are not going well. Otherwise one must cut off the body, and even perception of the body, from human nature, and in this way try to find self-sufficiency in the matter of well-being.

6. But [we should answer], if our argument made well-being consist in freedom from pain and sickness and ill-luck and falling into great misfortunes, it would be impossible for anyone to be well off when any of these circumstances opposed to well-being was present. But if well-being is to be found in possession of the true good, why should we disregard this and omit to use it as a standard to which to look in judging well-being, and look for other things which are not reckoned as a part of well-being? If it was a collection of goods and necessities, or things as well which are not necessities but even so are called goods, we should have to try and see that these were there too. But if the end at which we

aim must be one and not many—otherwise one would not be aiming at an end but at ends—one must gain that alone which is of ultimate and highest value, and which the soul seeks to clasp close within itself. This search and willing is not directed to not being in this condition. These things are not of our very nature, but only [incidentally] present, and it is our reasoning power that avoids and manages to get rid of them, or also sometimes seeks to acquire them. But the real drive of desire of our soul is towards that which is better than itself. When that is present within it, it is fulfilled and at rest, and this is the way of living it really wills. We cannot be said to "will" the presence of necessities, if "willing" is used in its proper sense and not misapplied to the occasions when we prefer the necessities also to be there: for we generally avoid evils, but this sort of avoidance is not, I suppose, a matter of willing, for we should will rather not to have occasion for this sort of avoidance. The necessities themselves provide evidence of this when we have them, health and freedom from pain, for instance. What attraction have they for us? We despise health when we have it, and freedom from pain as well. But these things, which have no attraction for us when they are there and do not contribute anything to our well-being, but which we seek in their absence because of the presence of things which distress us, can reasonably be called necessities, but not goods. So they must not be reckoned as part of the end we aim at; even when they are absent and their opposites are present, the end must be kept intact.

7. Why then does the man who is in a state of well-being want these necessities to be there and reject their opposites? We shall answer that it is not because they make any contribution to his well-being, but rather, to his existence: and he rejects their opposites either because they help towards nonexistence or because they get in the way of his aim by their presence, not by taking anything away from it but because he who has the best wants to have it alone, and not something else with it, something which when it is there has not made away with the best, but, still, exists alongside it. But even if something which the man who is well off does not want is there all the same, nothing at all of his well-being is taken away; otherwise he would change every day and fall from his well-being—if he lost a servant, for instance, or any one of his possessions: there are thousands of things which, if they do not turn out according to his mind, disturb in no way the final good which he has attained. But, people say, consider great disasters, not ordinary chances! What human circumstance is so great that a man will not think little of it who has climbed higher than all this and depends on nothing below? He does not think any piece of good fortune great, however important it may be, kingship, for instance, and rule over cities and peoples, or founding of colonies and states (even if he founds them himself). Why then should he think that falling from power and the ruin of his city are great matters? If he thought that they were great evils, or evils at all, he would deserve to be laughed at for his opinion; there would be no virtue left in him if he thought that wood and stones, and, (God help us!) the death of mortals, were important, this man who, we say, ought to think about death that it is better than life with

the body! If he himself is offered in sacrifice, will he think his death an evil, because he dies by the altars? If he is not buried, his body will rot anyhow, on the earth or under it. If he is distressed because he does not have an expensive funeral but is buried without a name and not thought worth a lofty monument—the pettiness of it! If he is taken away as a war-slave, "the way lies open" to depart, if it is not possible to live well. If his relatives are captured in war, "his daughters-in-law and daughters dragged off"—well, suppose he had died without seeing anything of the sort; would he then leave the world in the belief that it was impossible that it should happen? If so, he would be a fool. So will he not think that it is possible for his relatives to fall into such misfortune? And does his belief that this may happen prevent his well-being? Then neither does the fact of its happening. For he will think that the nature of this universe is of a kind to bring these sorts of misfortunes, and we must follow it obediently. Anyhow, many people will do better by becoming war-slaves; and it is in their own power to depart if they find the burden heavy. If they stay, either it is reasonable for them to stay and there is nothing terrible about it, or if they stay unreasonably, when they ought not to, it is their own fault. The good man will not be involved in evil because of the stupidity of others, even if they are his relatives; he will not be dependent on the good or bad fortune of other people.

8. As far as his own pains go, when they are very great, he will bear them as long as he can; when they are too much for him, they will bear him off. He is not to be pitied in his pain; his light burns within, like the light in a lantern when it is blowing hard outside with a great fury of wind and storm. But suppose the pain brings delirium, or goes on at such a height that, though it is extreme it does not kill? If it goes on, he will consider what he ought to do; the pain has not taken away his power of self-disposal. One must understand that things do not look to the good man as they look to others; none of his experiences penetrate to the inner self, pleasures and pains no more than any of the others. And when the pains concern others? [To sympathise with them] would be a weakness in our soul. There is evidence for this in the fact that we think it something gained if we do not know about other people's sufferings, and even regard it as a good thing if we die first, not considering it from their point of view but from our own, trying to avoid being grieved. This is just our weakness, which we must get rid of and not leave it there and then be afraid of its coming over us. If anyone says that it is our nature to feel pain at the misfortunes of our own people, he should know that this does not apply to everybody, and that it is the business of virtue to raise ordinary nature to a higher level, something better than most people are capable of; and it is better not to give in to what ordinary nature normally finds terrible. One must not behave like someone untrained, but stand up to the blows of fortune like a great trained fighter, and know that, though some natures may not like them, one's own can bear them, not as terrors but as children's bogeys. Does the good man, then, want misfortune? No, but when what he does not want comes he sets virtue against it, which makes his soul hard to disturb or distress.

9. But suppose he is unconscious, his mind swamped by sickness or magic arts? If they maintain that he is a good man when he is in this state, only fallen into a sort of sleep, what prevents him from being well off? After all, they do not remove him from well-being when he is asleep, or reckon the time he spends asleep so as to show that he is not well off for his whole life. But if they say that he is not good when he is in this state, then they are not any longer discussing the good man. But we are taking the good man as our starting-point, and enquiring if he is well off as long as he is good. "But," they say, "granted that he is good, if he is not conscious of it or engaged in virtuous activity, how can he be in a state of well-being?" But if he does not know that he is healthy, he is healthy just the same, and if he does not know that he is handsome, he is handsome just the same. So if he does not know that he is wise, will he be any the less wise? Perhaps someone might say that wisdom requires awareness and consciousness of its presence, because it is in actual and active wisdom that well-being is to be found. If intelligence and wisdom were something brought in from outside, this argument would perhaps make sense: but if wisdom essentially consists in a substance, or rather in *the* substance, and this substance does not cease to exist in someone who is asleep or what is called unconscious; if the real activity of the substance goes on in him, and this activity is unsleeping; then the good man, in that he is a good man, will be active even then. It will not be the whole of him that is unaware of this activity, but only a part of him. In the same way when our growth-activity is active no perception of it reaches the rest of the man through our sense-faculties; and, if that in us which grows were ourselves, it would be ourselves that would be active [irrespective of the fact that we were unconscious of it]. Actually, however, we are not it, but we *are* the activity of the intellect; so that when that is active, we are active.

10. Perhaps we do not notice it because it is not concerned with any object of sense; for our minds, by means of sense-perception—which is a kind of intermediary when dealing with sensible things—do appear to work on the level of sense and think about sense-objects. But why should not intellect itself be active [without perception], and also its attendant soul, which comes before sense-perception and any sort of awareness? There must be an activity prior to awareness if "thinking and being are the same." It seems as if awareness exists and is produced when intellectual activity is reflexive and when that in the life of the soul which is active in thinking is in a way projected back, as happens with a mirror-reflection when there is a smooth, bright, untroubled surface. In these circumstances when the mirror is there the mirror-image is produced, but when it is not there or is not in the right state the object of which the image would have been is [all the same] actually there. In the same way as regards the soul, when that kind of thing in us which mirrors the images of thought and intellect is undisturbed, we see them and know them in a way parallel to sense-perception, along with the prior knowledge that it is intellect and thought that are active. But when this is broken because the harmony of the body is upset, thought and intellect operate without an image, and then intellectual activity takes place without a mind-picture. So one might come to this sort of conclusion, that intel-

lectual activity is [normally] accompanied by a mind-picture but is not a mind-picture. One can find a great many valuable activities, theoretical and practical, which we carry on both in our contemplative and active life even when we are fully conscious, which do not make us aware of them. The reader is not necessarily aware that he is reading, least of all when he is really concentrating: nor the man who is being brave that he is being brave and that his action conforms to the virtue of courage; and there are thousands of similar cases. Conscious awareness, in fact, is likely to enfeeble the very activities of which there is consciousness; only when they are alone are they pure and more genuinely active and living; and when good men are in this state their life is increased, when it is not spilt out into perception, but gathered together in one in itself.

11. If some people were to say that a man in this state is not even alive, we shall maintain that he is alive, but they fail to observe his well-being just as they do his life. If they will not believe us, we shall ask them to take as their starting-point a living man and a good man and so to pursue the enquiry into his well-being, and not to minimise his life and then to enquire if he has a good life, or to take away his humanity and then enquire about human well-being, or to agree that the good man has his attention directed inward and then to look for him in external activities, still less to seek the object of his desire in outward things. There would not be any possibility of the existence of well-being if one said that outward things were to be desired and that the good man desired them. He would like all men to prosper and no one to be subject to any sort of evil; but if this does not happen, he is all the same well off. But if anyone maintains that it will make the good man absurd to suppose him wanting anything like this—for it is impossible that evils should not exist—then the person who maintains this will obviously agree with us in directing the good man's desire inwards.

12. When they demand to be shown what is pleasant in a life of this kind, they will not be requiring the presence of the pleasures of debauchees, or of bodily pleasures at all—these could not be there and would abolish well-being—or of violent emotions of pleasure—why should the good man have any?—but only those pleasures which accompany the presence of goods, pleasures not consisting in movements, which are not the results of any process: for the goods are there already, and the good man is present to himself; his pleasure and happiness are at rest. The good man is always happy; his state is tranquil, his disposition contented and undisturbed by any so-called evils—if he is really good. If anyone looks for another kind of pleasure in the life of virtue it is not the life of virtue he is looking for.

13. The good man's activities will not be hindered by changes of fortune, but will vary according to what change and chance brings; but they will all be equally fine, and, perhaps, finer for being adapted to circumstances. As for his speculative activities, some of them which are concerned with particular points will possibly be hindered by circumstances, those for instance which require research and investigation. But the "greatest study" is always ready to hand and always with him, all the more if he is in the so-called "bull of Phalaris"—which

it is silly to call pleasant, though people keep on saying that it is; for according to their philosophy that which says that its state is pleasant is the very same thing which is in pain; according to ours that which suffers pain is one thing, and there is another which, even while it is compelled to accompany that which suffers pain, remains in its own company and will not fall short of the vision of the universal good.

14. Man, and especially the good man, is not the composite of soul and body; separation from the body and despising of its so-called goods make this plain. It is absurd to maintain that well-being extends as far as the living body, since well-being is the good life, which is concerned with soul and is an activity of soul, and not of all of it—for it is not an activity of the growth-soul, which would bring it into connexion with body. This state of well-being is certainly not in the body's size or health, nor again does it consist in the excellence of the senses, for too much of these advantages is liable to weigh man down and bring him to their level. There must be a sort of counterpoise on the other side, towards the best, to reduce the body and make it worse, so that it may be made clear that the real man is other than his outward parts. The man who belongs to this world may be handsome and tall and rich and the ruler of all mankind (since he is essentially of this region), and we ought not to envy him for things like these, by which he is beguiled. The wise man will perhaps not have them at all, and if he has them will himself reduce them, if he cares for his true self. He will reduce and gradually extinguish his bodily advantages by neglect, and will put away authority and office. He will take care of his bodily health, but will not wish to be altogether without experience of illness, nor indeed also of pain. Rather, even if these do not come to him he will want to learn them when he is young, but when he is old he will not want either pains or pleasures to hinder him, or any earthly thing, pleasant or the reverse, so that he may not have to consider the body. When he finds himself in pain he will oppose to it the power which he has been given for the purpose; he will find no help to his well-being in pleasure and health and freedom from pain and trouble, nor will their opposites take it away or diminish it. For if one thing adds nothing to a state, how can its opposite take anything away?

15. But suppose there were two wise men, one of whom had all of what are called natural goods and the other their opposites, shall we say that they both have well-being equally? Yes, if they are equally wise. Even if one is good-looking and has all the other advantages which have nothing to do with wisdom, or in any way with virtue and the vision of the best, or with the best itself, what does that amount to? After all, even the man who has these advantages will not give himself airs about them as if he was better off than the one who has not got them; to have more of them than others would be no help even towards becoming a piper. But we bring our own weakness into it when we are considering whether a man is well off, and regard things as frightening and terrible which the man in a state of well-being would not so regard. He would not yet have attained to wisdom or well-being if he had not freed himself of all imaginations

about this sort of thing, and become in a way quite a different man, with confidence in himself that evil can never touch him. In this state of mind he will be without fear of anything. If he is afraid at all he is not perfect in virtue, but a kind of half-man. If sometimes when he is concerned with other things an involuntary fear comes upon him before he has time to reflect, the wise man [in him] will come and drive it away and quiet the child in him which is stirred to a sort of distress, by threatening or reasoning; the threatening will be unemotional, as if the child was shocked into quietness just by a severe look. A man of this sort will not be unfriendly or unsympathetic; he will be like this to himself and in dealing with his own affairs: but he will render to his friends all that he renders to himself, and so will be the best of friends as well as remaining intelligent.

16. If anyone does not set the good man up on high in this world of intellect, but brings him down to chance events and fears their happening to him, he is not keeping his mind on the good man as we consider he must be, but assuming an ordinary man, a mixture of good and bad, and assigning to him a life which is also a mixture of good and bad and of a kind which cannot easily occur. Even if a person of this sort did exist, he would not be worth calling well off; he would have no greatness in him, either of the dignity of wisdom or the purity of good. The common life of body and soul cannot possibly be the life of well-being. Plato was right in maintaining that the man who intends to be wise and in a state of well-being must take his good from There, from above, and look to that good and be made like it and live by it. He must hold on to this only as his goal, and change his other circumstances as he changes his dwelling-place, not because he derives any advantage in the point of well-being from one dwelling-place or another, but guessing, as it were, how his alien covering will be affected if he lodges here or there. He must give to this bodily life as much as it needs and he can, but he is himself other than it and free to abandon it, and he will abandon it in nature's good time, and, besides, has the right to decide about this for himself. So some of his activities will tend towards well-being; others will not be directed to the goal and will really not belong to him but to that which is joined to him, which he will care for and bear with as long as he can, like a musician with his lyre, as long as he can use it; if he cannot use it he will change to another, or give up using the lyre and abandon the activities directed to it. Then he will have something else to do which does not need the lyre, and will let it lie unregarded beside him while he sings without an instrument. Yet the instrument was not given him at the beginning without good reason. He has used it often up till now.

COMMENTS

In this essay on happiness (here translated "well-being"), Plotinus stresses one idea that we have about a happy life; it is one in which what goes well is something with which we identify. Plotinus uses this point to criticize other accounts and to develop his own. Theories, like those of Epicurus, that locate happiness in pleasure have us identify with the body, that is, take our real self to be our bodily self. However, people who think that they hold this view, Plotinus says, are often not really thinking of the bodily experience itself, but of its place in a rationally reflective life, so they are really thinking of the true self that matters for happiness as being the aspect of us that reflects. Still, theories like the Stoics', which propose that happiness is found in developing our reason, do not ask what is so valuable about reason that we should identify with it.

Plotinus takes over Plato's view that the life of our true self, the kind of living that we should identify with, is the life not of the body but of the soul, and particularly the rational soul. Plotinus, however, pushes further than does Plato the idea that the life to which we truly aspire and in which we find our true happiness lies not in reasoning, but in something beyond reasoning and on which reasoning depends. Following up hints in Plato he thinks of this something beyond reasoning as the Good or the One. It is something to which we can come only via rigorous argument and thinking, but itself is prior to and cannot be captured by discursive thought. Our grasp of it, insofar as we can achieve this, is immediate and something to be described in mystical and imaginative, rather than intellectual, terms.

If happiness lies in living the life that a human should aspire to, and if it turns out to be our life to the extent that we can pass beyond identification with the body, the soul, and even the reasoning mind to a unity with the Good, which is the reality grounding them, then happiness turns out to be not just very different from the ordinary view that it involves external goods, but also very different from every other ancient view so far, in that it involves detachment from everything that we normally identify with. Plotinus follows through some implications of this view: The person who achieves happiness by transcending the level of thinking and reasoning will not think of external goods, or even his own body, as affecting the real him.

So great a degree of detachment from everyday concerns leads to an attitude that may seem inhuman, as with Plotinus' attitude to the misfortunes of others, particularly others to whom we are attached as family members or friends. He also recognizes that there is a problem as to why the person who has achieved happiness in the way he describes should pay any attention to the needs of the body and everyday life, and faces and works through the point that in this view, being happy does not require being aware of being happy.

Plotinus' philosophy was congenial to the intellectual development of Christianity and encouraged an other-worldly and ascetic development of some ideas within it. However, detachment from worldly concerns is found in both pagans and Christians in the later ancient world and does not depend on a particular religious position.

A. IS NATURE OR CONVENTION THE BASIS OF SOCIETY AND THE STATE?

Plato *Protagoras* 320c–323c
Antiphon the Sophist *Fragment 7*
Plato *Gorgias* 482e–484c
Plato *Crito* 50a–54e
Plato *Republic* 358c–360d
Aristotle *Politics* I, 2
Aristotle *Politics* III, 9
Epicureans
Epicurus *Principal Doctrines* 31–38
Diogenes of Oenoanda *Epicurean Inscription* fragment 56
Cicero *On Duties* III, 37–39
Stoicism
Cicero *On Laws* I, 17–35, 42–45

B. POLITICAL RULE: EXPERTISE AND THE RULE OF LAW

Twofold Arguments 7
Plato *Republic* 488a–489c
Plato *Statesman* 291d–303b
Aristotle *Politics* I, 1; III, 4, 11

C. DEMOCRACY AND THE BEST FORM OF GOVERNMENT

Herodotus *Histories* III, 80–83
The Old Oligarch *Selections*
Aristotle *Politics* IV, 3, 4, 7–9, 11
Polybius *Histories*, VI, 2

A. Is Nature or Convention the Basis of Society and the State?

From the fifth century B.C. onward, both philosophers and ordinary people grappled with the idea that society and the state might not have their bases in human nature, but might be the product of agreements and compromises that might have been different and could be changed. This need not be a threatening idea, and the earlier discussion runs together ideas that became more clearly distinguished as the debate developed.

Protagoras 320c–323c
PLATO

"Once upon a time there were just the gods; mortal beings did not yet exist. And d when the appointed time came for them to come into being too, the gods moulded them within the earth, mixing together earth and fire and their compounds. And when they were about to bring them out into the light of day, they 5 appointed Prometheus and Epimetheus to equip each kind with the powers it required. Epimetheus asked Prometheus to let him assign the powers himself. 'Once I have assigned them,' he said, 'you can inspect them'; so Prometheus agreed, and Epimetheus assigned the powers. To some creatures he gave e strength, but not speed, while he equipped the weaker with speed. He gave some claws or horns, and for those without them he devised some other power for their preservation. To those whom he made of small size, he gave winged flight, or a 321a dwelling underground; to those that he made large, he gave their size itself as a protection. And in the same way he distributed all the other things, balancing one against another. This he did to make sure that no species should be wiped out; and when he had made them defences against mutual destruction, he devised for them protection against the elements, clothing them with thick hair and tough skins, so as to withstand cold and heat, and also to serve each kind as their 5 own natural bedding when they lay down to sleep. And he shod some with b hooves, and others with tough, bloodless skin. Then he assigned different kinds of food to the different species; some were to live on pasture, others on the fruits of trees, others on roots, and some he made to prey on other creatures for their food. These he made less prolific, but to those on whom they preyed he gave a large increase, as a means of preserving the species.

"Now Epimetheus, not being altogether wise, didn't notice that he had used c up all the powers on the nonrational creatures; so last of all he was left with human kind, quite unprovided for, and he was at a loss what to do. As he was

From Plato, *Protagoras*, translated by C. C. W. Taylor (Oxford: Oxford University Press, 1996). Reprinted with the permission of Oxford University Press.

racking his brains Prometheus came to inspect the distribution, and saw the
5   other creatures well provided for in every way, while man was naked and
unshod, without any covering for his bed or any fangs or claws; and already the
appointed day was at hand, on which man too had to come out of the earth to
the light of day. Prometheus was at his wits' end to find a means of preservation
d   for mankind, so he stole from Hephaestus and Athena their technical skill along
with the use of fire—for it was impossible for anyone to acquire or make use of
5   that skill without fire—and that was what he gave to man. That is how man
acquired his practical skill, but he did not yet have skill in running a city; Zeus
kept watch over that. Prometheus had no time to penetrate the citadel of Zeus—
moreover the guards of Zeus were terrible—but he made his way by stealth into
the workshop which Athena and Hephaestus shared for the practice of their
e   arts, and stole Hephaestus' art of working with fire, and the other art which
322a Athena possesses, and gave them to men. And as a result man was well provided with resources for his life, but afterwards, so it is said, thanks to Epimetheus, Prometheus paid the penalty for theft.

   "Since man thus shared in a divine gift, first of all through his kinship with
5   the gods he was the only creature to worship them, and he began to erect altars
and images of the gods. Then he soon developed the use of articulate speech and
of words, and discovered how to make houses and clothes and shoes and bed-
b   ding and how to get food from the earth. Thus equipped, men lived at the beginning in scattered units, and there were no cities; so they began to be destroyed
by the wild beasts, since they were altogether weaker. Their practical art was
sufficient to provide food, but insufficient for fighting against the beasts—for
5   they did not yet possess the art of running a city, of which the art of warfare is
part—and so they sought to come together and save themselves by founding
cities. Now when they came together, they treated each other with injustice, not
possessing the art of running a city, so they scattered and began to be destroyed
c   once again. So Zeus, fearing that our race would be wholly wiped out, sent Hermes bringing conscience and justice to mankind, to be the principles of organization of cities and the bonds of friendship. Now Hermes asked Zeus about the
5   manner in which he was to give conscience and justice to men: 'Shall I distribute these in the same way as the arts? These are distributed thus: one doctor is
sufficient for many laymen, and so with the other experts. Shall I give justice
and conscience to men in that way too, or distribute them to all?'
d   "'To all,' said Zeus, 'and let all share in them; for cities could not come into
being, if only a few shared in them as in the other arts. And lay down on my
5   authority a law that he who cannot share in conscience and justice is to be killed
as a plague on the city.' So that, Socrates, is why when there is a question about
how to do well in carpentry or any other expertise, everyone including the Athe-
e   nians thinks it right that only a few should give advice, and won't put up with
advice from anyone else, as you say—and quite right, too, in my view—but
323a when it comes to consideration of how to do well in running the city, which
must proceed entirely through justice and soundness of mind, they are right to
accept advice from anyone, since it is incumbent on everyone to share in that

sort of excellence, or else there can be no city at all. That is the reason for it, Socrates.

"Just in case you still have any doubts that in fact everyone thinks that every 5 man shares in justice and the rest of the excellence of a citizen, here's an extra bit of evidence. In the case of the other skills, as you say, if anyone says he's a good aulos-player or good at any other art when he isn't, they either laugh at him or b get angry at him, and his family come and treat him like a madman. But in the case of justice and the rest of the excellence of a citizen, even if they know someone to be unjust, if he himself admits it before everyone, they regard that sort of truthfulness as madness, though they called it sound sense before, and they say that everybody must say that he is just whether he is or not, and anyone who doesn't pretend to be just must be mad. For they think that everyone must possess it to some extent or other, or else not be among men at all.

ANTIPHON

Antiphon of Athens, the Sophist, is known to us mainly from fragmentary papyrus texts that turned up in the early twentieth century. Scholars are divided as to whether this Antiphon is the same as another Athenian Antiphon, who lived in the second half of the fifth century B.C. and wrote courtroom speeches for a variety of trials, many of which survive. This Antiphon was one of the people who carried out a coup against the democracy in 411 B.C. and replaced it with a more narrowly based form of government. When this new government collapsed after a few months, most of the leaders fled, but Antiphon stayed and defended himself in a trial for treason. His speech in his own defense was much admired in the ancient world, but nevertheless (and unsurprisingly in the circumstances) Antiphon was convicted and executed.

Fragment 7
ANTIPHON THE SOPHIST

7a. . . . <the laws (?) of nearby communities> we know and respect, but those of communities far away we neither know nor respect. We have thereby become barbarous toward each other, when by nature we are all at birth in all respects equally capable of being both barbarians [i.e., foreigners] and Greeks.

From *Early Greek Political Thought from Homer to the Sophists*, by Michael Gagarin and Paul Woodruff (eds.) (Cambridge University Press, 1995). Reprinted with the permission of Cambridge University Press.

We can examine those attributes of nature that are necessarily in all men and are provided to all to the same degree, and in these respects none of us is distinguished as foreign or Greek. For we all breathe the air through our mouth and through our nostrils, and we laugh when we are pleased in our mind or we weep when we are pained, and we take in sounds with our hearing, and we see by the light with our sight, and we work with our hands and we walk with our feet . . . They agreed . . . laws . . .

7b. . . . . Justice, therefore, is not violating the rules of the city in which one is a citizen. Thus a person would best use justice to his own advantage if he considered the laws important when witnesses are present, but the consequences of nature important in the absence of witnesses. For the requirements of the laws are supplemental but the requirements of nature are necessary; and the requirements of the laws are by agreement and not natural, whereas the requirements of nature are natural and not by agreement. Thus someone who violates the laws avoids shame and punishment if those who have joined in agreement do not notice him, but not if they do. But if someone tries to violate one of the inherent requirements of nature, which is impossible, the harm he suffers is no less if he is seen by no one, and no greater if all see him; for he is harmed not in reputation but in truth.

I inquire into these things for the following reason, that most things that are just according to law are inimical to nature. For rules have been made for the eyes, what they should and should not see, and for the ears, what they should and should not hear, and for the tongue, what it should and should not say, and for the hands, what they should and should not do, and for the feet, where they should and should not go, and for the mind, what it should and should not desire. Thus the things from which the laws dissuade us are in no way less congenial or akin to nature than the things toward which they urge us. For living and dying both belong to nature, and for humans living is the result of advantageous things, whereas dying is the result of disadvantageous things. The advantages laid down by the laws are bonds on nature, but those laid down by nature are free. Thus things that bring pain do not, according to a correct account (*orthos logos*), help nature more than things that bring joy. Nor would things that bring pain be more advantageous than things that bring pleasure; for things that are in truth advantageous ought not to harm but to benefit. Thus things that are advantageous to nature . . .

. . . and those who defend themselves when attacked and do not themselves begin the action, and those who treat their parents well even when they have been badly treated by them, and those who let their opponent swear an oath when they have not sworn one themselves. One would find many of the things I have mentioned inimical to nature; and they involve more pain when less is possible and less pleasure when more is possible, and ill treatment which could be avoided. Thus, if the laws provided some assistance for those who engaged in such behavior, and some penalty for those who did not but did the opposite, then the tow-rope of the laws would not be without benefit. But in fact it is apparent that the justice derived from law is not sufficient to assist those who engage in such behavior. First, it permits the victim to suffer and the agent to act, and at the time it did not try to prevent either the victim from suffering or the agent from acting; and when it is applied to the punishment, it does not favor either the victim or the agent; for he must persuade, the punishers that he suffered, or else be able to obtain justice by deception. But these means are also available to the agent, (if he wishes) to deny . . . the defendant has as long for his defense as the plaintiff for his accusation, and there is an equivalent opportunity for persuasion for the victim and for the agent.

7c. . . . to testify truthfully for one another is customarily thought to be just and to no lesser degree useful in human affairs. And yet one who does this will not be just if indeed it is just not to injure anyone if one is not injured oneself; for even if he tells the truth, someone who testifies must necessarily injure another somehow, and will then be injured himself, since he will be hated when the testimony he gives leads to the conviction of the person against whom he testifies, who then loses his property or his life because of this man whom he has not injured at all. In this way he wrongs the person against whom he testifies, because he injures someone who is not injuring him; and he in turn is injured by the one against whom he testified in that he is hated by him despite having told the truth. And it's not only that he is hated but also that for his whole life he must be on guard against the man against whom he testified. As a result he has an enemy who will do him whatever harm he can in word or deed.

Now, these are clearly no small wrongs, neither those he suffers nor those he inflicts. For it is impossible that these things are just and that the rule not to injure anyone nor to be injured oneself is also just; on the contrary, it is necessary either that only one of these be just or that they both be unjust. Further, it is clear that, whatever the result, the judicial process, verdicts, and arbitration proceedings are not just, since helping some people hurts others. In the process those who are helped are not injured, while those who are hurt are injured.

Gorgias 482e–484c
Plato

CALLICLES   You pretend that truth is your goal, Socrates, but in actual fact you steer discussions towards this kind of ethical idea—ideas which are unsophisticated enough to have popular appeal, and which depend entirely on convention, not on nature. They're invariably opposed to each other, you know—nature and convention, I mean—and consequently if someone is too embarrassed to go right ahead and voice his convictions, he's bound to con- 483a

From Plato, *Gorgias*, translated by Robin Waterfield (Oxford: Oxford University Press, 1994). Reprinted with the permission of Oxford University Press.

tradict himself. This in fact is the source of the clever, but unfair, argumentative trick you've devised: if a person is talking from a conventional standpoint, you slip in a question which presupposes a natural point of view, and if he's talking about nature, you substitute convention. On this matter of doing and suffering wrong, for instance—to take the case at hand—Polus was talking about what was more contemptible from a conventional standpoint, but you adopted the standpoint of nature in following up what he said, because in nature everything is more contemptible if it is also worse (as suffering wrong is), whereas convention ordains that doing wrong is more contemptible. In fact, this thing—being wronged—isn't within a real

b   man's experience; it's something which happens to slaves, who'd be better off dead, because they're incapable of defending themselves or anyone else they care for against unjust treatment and abuse.

In my opinion it's the weaklings who constitute the majority of the human race who make the rules. In making these rules, they look after themselves and their own interest, and that's also the criterion they use

c   when they dispense praise and criticism. They try to cow the stronger ones—which is to say, the ones who are capable of increasing their share of things—and to stop them getting an increased share, by saying that to do so is wrong and contemptible and by defining injustice in precisely those terms, as the attempt to have more than others. In my opinion, it's because they're second-rate that they're happy for things to be distributed equally. Anyway, that's why convention states that the attempt to have a larger share than most people is immoral and contemptible; that's why people call it doing wrong. But I think we only have to look at nature to find evidence

d   that it is *right* for better to have a greater share than worse, more capable than less capable. The evidence for this is widespread. Other creatures show, as do human communities and nations, that right has been determined as follows: the superior person shall dominate the inferior person and have more than him. By what right, for instance, did Xerxes make war on Greece or his father on Scythia, not to mention countless further cases of

e   the same kind of behaviour? These people act, surely, in conformity with the natural essence of right and, yes, I'd even go so far as to say that they act in conformity with natural *law,* even though they presumably contravene our man-made laws.

What do we do with the best and strongest among us? We capture them young, like lions, mould them, and turn them into slaves by chanting spells

484a and incantations over them which insist that they have to be equal to others and that equality is admirable and right. But I'm sure that if a man is born in whom nature is strong enough, he'll shake off all these limitations, shatter them to pieces, and win his freedom; he'll trample all our regulations, charms, spells, and unnatural laws into the dust; this slave will rise up and

b   reveal himself as our master; and then natural right will blaze forth. I think Pindar is making the same point as me in the poem where he says, "Law, lord of all, both gods and men ..." And law, he continues, "instigates extreme violence with a high hand and calls it right. Heracles' deeds are proof of this, since without paying for them . . ." Something like that—I don't know the actual words, but he says that Heracles drove off Geryon's cattle without paying for them and without Geryon giving them to him, presumably because it was natural justice for him to do so, in the sense that all the belongings of worse, inferior people—not just their cattle—are the property of a man who is better and superior.

c

Crito 50a–54e
PLATO

SOCRATES   Well, look at it this way. Suppose we were on the point of running away from here, or whatever else one should call it. Then the Laws, or the State of Athens, might come and confront us, and they might speak as follows:

"Please tell us, Socrates, what do you have in mind? With this action you are attempting, do you intend anything short of destroying us, the Laws and the city as a whole, to the best of your ability? Do you think that a city can still exist without being overturned, if the legal judgments rendered within it possess no force, but are nullified or invalidated by individuals?"

b

5

What shall we say, Crito, in answer to that and other such questions? Because somebody, particularly a legal advocate, might say a great deal on behalf of the law that is being invalidated here, the one requiring that judgments, once rendered, shall have authority. Shall we tell them: "Yes, that is our intention, because the city was treating us unjustly, by not judging our case correctly"? Is that to be our answer, or what?

c

CRITO   Indeed it is, Socrates.

SOCRATES   And what if the Laws say: "And was that also part of the agreement between you and us, Socrates? Or did you agree to abide by whatever judgments the city rendered?"

5

Then, if we were surprised by their words, perhaps they might say: "Don't be surprised at what we are saying, Socrates, but answer us, seeing that you like to use question-and-answer. What complaint, pray, do you have against the city and ourselves, that you should now attempt to destroy us? In the first place, was it not we who gave you birth? Did your father not marry your mother and beget you under our auspices? So will you inform those of us here who regulate marriages whether you have any criticism of them as poorly framed?"

10

d

"No, I have none," I should say.

5

From Plato, *Defence of Socrates, Euthyphro, Crito,* translated by David Gallop (Oxford: Oxford University Press, 1993). Reprinted with the permission of Oxford University Press.

"Well then, what of the laws dealing with children's upbringing and
education, under which you were educated yourself? Did those of us Laws

e   who are in charge of that area not give proper direction, when they required
your father to educate you in the arts and physical training?"

"They did," I should say.

"Very good. In view of your birth, upbringing, and education, can you
deny, first, that you belong to us as our offspring and slave, as your fore-

5   bears also did? And if so, do you imagine that you are on equal terms with
us in regard to what is just, and that whatever treatment we may accord to
you, it is just for you to do the same thing back to us? You weren't on equal
terms with your father, or your master (assuming you had one), making it
just for you to return the treatment you received—answering back when

51a   you were scolded, or striking back when you were struck, or doing many
other things of the same sort. Will you then have licence against your fatherland and its Laws, if we try to destroy you, in the belief that that is just? Will

5   you try to destroy us in return, to the best of your ability? And will you
claim that in doing so you are acting justly, you who are genuinely exercised
about goodness? Or are you, in your wisdom, unaware that, in comparison

b   with your mother and father and all your other forebears, your fatherland
is more precious and venerable, more sacred and held in higher esteem
among gods, as well as among human beings who have any sense; and that
you should revere your fatherland, deferring to it and appeasing it when it
is angry, more than your own father? You must either persuade it, or else do
whatever it commands, and if it ordains that you must submit to certain

5   treatment, then you must hold your peace and submit to it: whether that
means being beaten or put in bonds, or whether it leads you into war to be
wounded or killed, you must act accordingly, and that is what is just; you
must neither give way nor retreat, nor leave your position, rather, in war-

10   fare, in court, and everywhere else, you must do whatever your city or

c   fatherland commands, or else persuade it as to what is truly just; and if it is
sinful to use violence against your mother or father, it is far more so to use
it against your fatherland."

What shall we say to that, Crito? That the Laws are right or not?

5   CRITO   I think they are.

SOCRATES   "Consider then, Socrates," the Laws might go on, "whether the following is also true: in your present undertaking you are not proposing to
treat us justly. We gave you birth, upbringing, and education, and a share in

d   all the benefits we could provide for you along with all your fellow citizens.
Nevertheless, we proclaim, by the formal granting of permission, that any
Athenian who wishes, once he has been admitted to adult status, and has
observed the conduct of city business and ourselves, the Laws, may—if he

5   is dissatisfied with us—go wherever he pleases and take his property. Not
one of us Laws hinders or forbids that: whether any of you wishes to emi-

e   grate to a colony, or to go and live as an alien elsewhere, he may go wherever he pleases and keep his property, if we and the city fail to satisfy him.

"We do say, however, that if any of you remains here after he has observed the system by which we dispense justice and otherwise manage our city, then he has agreed with us by his conduct to obey whatever orders 5 we give him. And thus we claim that anyone who fails to obey is guilty on three counts: he disobeys us as his parents; he disobeys those who nurtured him; and after agreeing to obey us he neither obeys nor persuades us if we are doing anything amiss, even though we offer him a choice, and do not 52a harshly insist that he must do whatever we command. Instead, we give him two options: he must either persuade us or else do as we say; yet he does neither. Those are the charges, Socrates, to which we say you too will be liable if you carry out your intention; and among Athenians, you will be not 5 the least liable, but one of the most."

And if I were to say, "How so?" perhaps they could fairly reproach me, observing that I am actually among those Athenians who have made that agreement with them most emphatically.

"Socrates," they would say, "we have every indication that you were b content with us, as well as with our city, because you would never have stayed home here, more than is normal for all other Athenians, unless you were abnormally content. You never left our city for a festival—except once 5 to go to the Isthmus—nor did you go elsewhere for other purposes, apart from military service. You never travelled abroad, as other people do; nor were you eager for acquaintance with a different city or different laws: we c and our city sufficed for you. Thus, you emphatically opted for us, and agreed to be a citizen on our terms. In particular, you fathered children in our city, which would suggest that you were content with it.

"Moreover, during your actual trial it was open to you, had you wished, to propose exile as your penalty; thus, what you are now attempting to do 5 without the city's consent, you could then have done with it. On that occasion, you kept priding yourself that it would not trouble you if you had to die: you would choose death ahead of exile, so you said. Yet now you dishonour those words, and show no regard for us, the Laws, in your effort to destroy us. You are acting as the meanest slave would act, by trying to run d away in spite of those compacts and agreements you made with us, whereby you agreed to be a citizen on our terms.

"First, then, answer us this question: are we right in claiming that you agreed, by your conduct if not verbally, that you would be a citizen on our 5 terms? Or is that untrue?"

What shall we say in reply to that, Crito? Mustn't we agree?

CRITO   We must, Socrates.

SOCRATES   "Then what does your action amount to," they would say, "except e breaking the compacts and agreements you made with us? By your own admission, you were not coerced or tricked into making them, or forced to reach a decision in a short time: you had seventy years in which it was open to you to leave if you were not happy with us, or if you thought those 5 agreements unfair. Yet you preferred neither Lacedaemon nor Crete—

53a   places you often say are well governed—nor any other Greek or foreign
       city: in fact, you went abroad less often than the lame and the blind or other
       cripples. Obviously, then, amongst Athenians you were exceptionally con-
       tent with our city and with us, its Laws—because who would care for a city
5   apart from its laws? Won't you, then, abide by your agreements now? Yes
       you will, if you listen to us, Socrates; and then at least you won't make your-
       self an object of derision by leaving the city.
              "Just consider: if you break those agreements, and commit any of those
10   offences what good will you do yourself or those friends of yours? Your
b   friends, pretty obviously, will risk being exiled themselves, as well as being
       disenfranchised or losing their property. As for you, first of all, if you go to
5   one of the nearest cities, Thebes or Megara—they are both well governed—
       you will arrive as an enemy of their political systems, Socrates: all who are
       concerned for their own cities will look askance at you, regarding you as a
       subverter of laws. You will also confirm your jurors in their judgment, mak-
c   ing them think they decided your case correctly: any subverter of laws, pre-
       sumably, might well be thought to be a corrupter of young, unthinking
       people.
              "Will you, then, avoid the best-governed cities and the most respectable
5   of men? And if so, will your life be worth living? Or will you associate with
       those people, and be shameless enough to converse with them? And what
       will you say to them, Socrates? The things you used to say here, that good-
       ness and justice are most precious to mankind, along with institutions and
       laws? Don't you think that the predicament of Socrates will cut an ugly fig-
d   ure? Surely you must.
              "Or will you take leave of those spots, and go to stay with those friends
       of Crito's up in Thessaly? That, of course, is a region of the utmost disorder
       and licence; so perhaps they would enjoy hearing from you about your
5   comical escape from gaol, when you dressed up in some outfit, wore a
       leather jerkin or some other runaway's garb, and altered your appearance.
       Will no one observe that you, an old man with probably only a short time
e   left to live, had the nerve to cling so greedily to life by violating the most
       important laws? Perhaps not, so long as you don't trouble anyone. Other-
       wise, Socrates, you will hear a great deal to your own discredit. You will live
       as every person's toady and lackey; and what will you be doing—apart
5   from living it up in Thessaly, as if you had travelled all the way to Thessaly
54a   to have dinner? As for those principles of yours about justice and goodness
       in general—tell us, where will they be then?
              "Well then, is it for your children's sake that you wish to live, in order
       to bring them up and give them an education? How so? Will you bring them
       up and educate them by taking them off to Thessaly and making foreigners
5   of them, so that they may gain that advantage too? Or if, instead of that,
       they are brought up here, will they be better brought up and educated just
       because you are alive, if you are not with them? Yes, you may say, because

those friends of yours will take care of them. Then will they take care of
them if you travel to Thessaly, but not take care of them if you travel to   10
Hades? Surely if those professing to be your friends are of any use at all, you   b
must believe that they will.

"No, Socrates, listen to us, your own nurturers: do not place a higher
value upon children, upon life, or upon anything else, than upon what is
just, so that when you leave for Hades, this may be your whole defence   5
before the authorities there: to take that course seems neither better nor
more just or holy, for you or for any of your friends here in this world. Nor
will it be better for you when you reach the next. As things stand, you will   c
leave this world (if you do) as one who has been treated unjustly not by us
Laws, but by human beings; whereas if you go into exile, thereby shame-
fully returning injustice for injustice and ill-treatment for ill-treatment,
breaking the agreements and compacts you made with us, and inflicting
harm upon the people you should least harm—yourself, your friends, your   5
fatherland, and ourselves—then we shall be angry with you in your lifetime; and our brother Laws in Hades will not receive you kindly there,
knowing that you tried, to the best of your ability, to destroy us too. Come   d
then, do not let Crito persuade you to take his advice rather than ours."

That, Crito, my dear comrade, is what I seem to hear them saying, I do
assure you. I am like the Corybantic revellers who think they are still hearing the music of pipes: the sound of those arguments is ringing loudly in my   5
head, and makes me unable to hear the others. As far as these present
thoughts of mine go, then, you may be sure that if you object to them, you
will plead in vain. None the less, if you think you will do any good, speak up.

CRITO   No, Socrates, I've nothing to say.

SOCRATES   Then let it be, Crito, and let us act accordingly, because that is the   e
direction in which God is guiding us.

Republic 358c–360d

PLATO

"First, I'll explain the usual view of the nature and origin of morality; second,   c
I'll claim that it is only ever practised reluctantly, as something necessary, but
not good; third, I'll claim that this behaviour is reasonable, because people are
right to think that an immoral person's life is much better than a moral person's
life.

"Now, I don't agree with any of this, Socrates, but I don't know what to
think. My ears are ringing from listening to Thrasymachus and countless others,

From Plato, *Republic*, translated by Robin Waterfield (Oxford: Oxford University Press,
1993). Reprinted with the permission of Oxford University Press.

but I've never yet heard the kind of support for morality, as being preferable to
d immorality, that I'd like to hear, which is a hymn to the virtues it possesses in
and of itself. If I can get this from anyone, it'll be you, I think. That is why I'll
speak at some length in praise of the immoral life; by doing so, I'll be showing
you the kind of rejoinder I want you to develop when you criticize immorality
and commend morality. What do you think of this plan?"

"I thoroughly approve," I replied. "I mean, I can't think of another topic
which any thinking person would more gladly see cropping up again and again
in his conversations."

e   "That's wonderful," he said. "Well, I promised I'd talk first about the nature
and origin of morality, so here goes. The idea is that although it's a fact of nature
that doing wrong is good and having wrong done to one is bad, nevertheless the
disadvantages of having it done to one outweigh the benefits of doing it. Consequently, once people have experienced both committing wrong and being at
the receiving end of it, they see that the disadvantages are unavoidable and the
359a benefits are unattainable; so they decide that the most profitable course is for
them to enter into a contract with one another, guaranteeing that no wrong will
be committed or received. They then set about making laws and decrees, and
from then on they use the terms 'legal' and 'right' to describe anything which is
enjoined by their code. So that's the origin and nature of morality, on this view:
it is a compromise between the ideal of doing wrong without having to pay for
it, and the worst situation, which is having wrong done to one while lacking the
means of exacting compensation. Since morality is a compromise, it is endorsed
because, while it may not be good, it does gain value by preventing people from
b doing wrong. The point is that any real man with the ability to do wrong would
never enter into a contract to avoid both wronging and being wronged: he
wouldn't be so crazy. Anyway, Socrates, that is what this view has to say about
the nature and origin of morality and so on."

"As for the fact that morality is only ever practised reluctantly, by people
who lack the ability to do wrong—this would become particularly obvious if we
c performed the following thought-experiment. Suppose we grant both types of
people—moral and immoral—the scope to do whatever they want, and we then
keep an eye on them to see where their wishes lead them. We'll catch our moral
person red-handed: his desire for superiority will point him in the same direction as the immoral person, towards a destination which every creature naturally regards as good and aims for, except that people are compelled by convention to deviate from this path and respect equality.

"They'd have the scope I'm talking about especially if they acquired the
d kind of power which, we hear, an ancestor of Gyges of Lydia once acquired. He
was a shepherd in the service of the Lydian ruler of the time, when a heavy rain-
storm occurred and an earthquake cracked open the land to a certain extent, and
a chasm appeared in the region where he was pasturing his flocks. He was fascinated by the sight, and went down into the chasm and saw there, as the story
goes, among other artefacts, a bronze horse, which was hollow and had win-

dows set in it; he stooped and looked in through the windows and saw a corpse inside, which seemed to be that of a giant. The corpse was naked, but had a golden ring on one finger; he took the ring off the finger and left. Now, the shep- e herds used to meet once a month to keep the king informed about his flocks, and our protagonist came to the meeting wearing the ring. He was sitting down among the others, and happened to twist the ring's bezel in the direction of his body, towards the inner part of his hand. When he did this, he became invisible to his neighbours, and to his astonishment they talked about him as if he'd left. 360a While he was fiddling about with the ring again, he turned the bezel outwards, and became visible. He thought about this and experimented to see if it was the ring which had this power; in this way he eventually found that turning the bezel inwards made him invisible and turning it outwards made him visible. As soon as he realized this, he arranged to be one of the delegates to the king; once b he was inside the palace, he seduced the king's wife and with her help assaulted and killed the king, and so took possession of the throne.

"Suppose there were two such rings, then—one worn by our moral person, the other by the immoral person. There is no one, on this view, who is iron-willed enough to maintain his morality and find the strength of purpose to keep his hands off what doesn't belong to him, when he is able to take whatever he wants from the market-stalls without fear of being discovered, to enter houses c and sleep with whomever he chooses, to kill and to release from prison anyone he wants, and generally to act like a god among men. His behaviour would be identical to that of the other person: both of them would be heading in the same direction.

"Now this is substantial evidence, it would be claimed, that morality is never freely chosen. People do wrong whenever they think they can, so they act morally only if they're forced to, because they regard morality as something which isn't good for one personally. The point is that everyone thinks the rewards of immorality far outweigh those of morality—and they're right, d according to the proponent of this view. The sight of someone with that kind of scope refusing all those opportunities for wrongdoing and never laying a finger on things that didn't belong to him would lead people to think that he was in an extremely bad way, and was a first-class fool as well—even though their fear of being wronged might make them attempt to mislead others by singing his praises to them in public."

COMMENTS

In the fifth century B.C., the Greeks, as a result of increased awareness of differences in culture and society between Greek cities and between Greeks and other peoples, began to reflect on the nature of social and cultural life. Many of the sophists, or traveling intellectual teachers, such as Protagoras, brought into public discussion the idea that society was the product of human agreement and convention (*nomos*) and, as such, was radically different from the world of nature (*phusis*). The world of nature is the same everywhere, and humans have to learn to adjust to it, whereas society and culture happen to be the way they are only because of particular historical development and can be changed by humans. Society, unlike the natural world, does not have to be the way it is.

This general contrast between nature and convention does not imply that the products of convention should be regarded as inferior. Indeed, society can be seen as a highly successful answer to the question of how humans are to survive in a difficult environment. In Plato's *Protagoras*, society is presented as the product of human resourcefulness, which, in turn, is presented as the best humans have in the face of the superior powers of other animals. Society, by requiring a universal commitment to conscience and justice, makes civilized life possible.

But isn't convention arbitrary and ungrounded by comparison to what rests on nature? Antiphon, in fragment 7, contrasts the requirements of nature, which we are bound to follow whether we want to or not, and the requirements of law, which rest on agreement and convention. Antiphon's position is not easy to work out, especially since the papyrus text is damaged in several places. However, Antiphon seems to be exploring a viewpoint of self-interest, from which it is clear that you do not have the same reason to obey the laws as you do to obey the requirements of nature. Whether you have reason to disobey the laws depends on a number of factors—for example, whether you will get away with it.

In the *Gorgias*, Callicles (we do not know whether he was a real person or Plato's invention) vigorously defends the idea that what is natural is for strong individuals to dominate weaker ones and that laws are based merely on the agreement of the weak majority to run things in their own interest. Hence laws frustrate the self-interest of the strong, who would do better without them. Callicles can agree that in society as it is, even the would-be strong man has reason to obey the laws, since if he does not, he will not get away with it. Indeed, in the dialogue Callicles is an aspiring politician who, to get ahead in democratic Athens, must go along with democratic laws and values. Even so, he wants to establish that self-interest conflicts with respecting laws and conventional values. He sees society as a second-best alternative to the unrestrained pursuit of self-interest.

In the *Crito* passage, Plato presents Socrates, after his trial and condemnation by Athens, turning down the chance to escape execution. Socrates imagines the laws of Athens representing what he is doing as breaking the agreement he has made with them. He presents the life of an Athenian citizen, which he has led, as the result of agreements that he has made to obey the laws, by freely choosing to become a citizen, when of age, and to stay in Athens, when he could have chosen to go elsewhere. Plato is rethinking the idea of a social agreement or contract; here the laws do not rest on the agreement of the citizens; rather, the obligation to obey the laws is presented as the result of an individual citizen's accepting an agreement with the laws. Plato, however, complicates the idea by also insisting that the laws stand to individual citizens as parents to children—and this is an example of a relationship, with obligations, that is *not* chosen and not freely entered into.

In the *Republic* passage, we again find the more usual conception of a social agreement or contract: Society and laws are based on the mutual agreement of citizens to obey the laws and live in society together. The speakers here bring out a point that is like those made by Callicles and Antiphon. Justice, the virtue displayed in being a good member of society and obeying the laws, can conflict with my self-interest—for example, if I am strong and would do better by being unjust and immoral. Here, "morality" translates the Greek word *dikaiosune,* which can also be translated "justice." It looks, therefore, as though the social-contract account of society and law can never show that I have an unconditional reason to be just and moral. I have reason to *seem* to be just (a point also made by Antiphon) because otherwise people would not respect or trust me, but seeming to be just is different from a concern actually to *be* just. Moreover, the major reason for being just is that I am unlikely to get away with being unjust, but, then, if I *were* able to get away with it (if I had the ring of Gyges in the story), I would have no reason to be just.

Plato thinks that for this reason all social-contract accounts of justice and morality fail: They cannot show why I have reason to be just and moral even if I could get away with being unjust and immoral. He thinks that being a virtuous, moral person is sufficient for happiness (see the passages in section 5), so that it is not in your self-interest to be unjust and immoral. This view is defended in many of his dialogues (including the *Gorgias*), and in the *Republic* and *Laws*, Plato sketches ideal forms of society in which virtue would be socially encouraged and rewarded. Thinkers prior to Plato seem not to have taken seriously the point that a social-contract defense of justice does not account for the idea that I am properly virtuous only if I am virtuous even when I could get away with injustice. (Later, Epicurus defends the social-contract idea in a more sophisticated way.)

Which version of the social contract theory do you find the most convincing? Can it meet Plato's objection (in the *Republic*)? Should it?

Politics I, 2

ARISTOTLE

In this, as in other fields, we shall be able to study our subject best if we begin at the beginning and consider things in the process of their growth. First of all, there must necessarily be a union or pairing of those who cannot exist without one another. Male and female must unite for the reproduction of the species—not from deliberate intention, but from the natural impulse, which exists in animals generally as it also exists in plants, to leave behind them something of the same nature as themselves. Next, there must necessarily be a union of the natu-

rally ruling element with the element which is naturally ruled, for the preservation of both. The element which is able, by virtue of its intelligence, to exercise
forethought, is naturally a ruling and master element; the element which is able,
by virtue of its bodily power, to do the physical work, is a ruled element, which
is naturally in a state of slavery; and master and slave have accordingly a common interest.

The first result of these two elementary associations is the household or
family. Hesiod spoke truly in the verse,

First house, and wife, and ox to draw the plough,

for oxen serve the poor in lieu of household slaves. The first form of association
naturally instituted for the satisfaction of daily recurrent needs is thus the family; and the members of the family are accordingly termed by Charondas "associates of the breadchest," as they are also termed by Epimenides the Cretan
"associates of the manger."

The next form of association—which is also the first to be formed from more
households than one, and for the satisfaction of something more than daily
recurrent needs—is the village. The most natural form of the village appears to
be that of a colony [or offshoot] from a family; and some have thus called the
members of the village by the name of "sucklings of the same milk," or, again,
of "sons and the sons of sons." This, it may be noted, is the reason why cities
were originally ruled, as the peoples of the barbarian world still are, by kings.
They were formed of people who were already monarchically governed, for
every household is monarchically governed by the eldest of the kin, just as villages, when they are offshoots from the household, are similarly governed in
virtue of the kinship between their members. This is what Homer describes:

Each of them ruleth
Over his children and wives,

a passage which shows that they lived in scattered groups, as indeed men generally did in ancient times. The fact that men generally were governed by kings
in ancient times, and that some still continue to be governed in that way, is the
reason that leads everyone to say that the gods are also governed by a king. People make the lives of the gods in the likeness of their own—as they also make
their shapes.

When we come to the final and perfect association, formed from a number
of villages, we have already reached the city [or *polis*]. This may be said to have
reached the height of full self-sufficiency; or rather we may say that while it
comes into existence for the sake of mere life, it exists for the sake of a good life.
For this reason every city exists by nature, just as did the earlier associations
[from which it grew]. It is the end or consummation to which those associations
move, and the "nature" of things consists in their end or consummation; for
what each thing is when its growth is completed we call the nature of that thing,
whether it be a man or a horse or a family. Again the end, or final cause, is the
best and self-sufficiency is both the end, and the best.

From these considerations it is evident that the city belongs to the class of things that exist by nature, and that man is by nature a political animal. He who is without a city, by reason of his own nature and not of some accident, is either a poor sort of being, or a being higher than man: he is like the man of whom Homer wrote in denunciation:

Clanless and lawless and heartless is he.

The man who is such by nature at once plunges into a passion of war; he is in the position of a solitary advanced piece in a game of draughts.

It is thus clear that man is a political animal, in a higher degree than bees or other gregarious animals. Nature, according to our theory, makes nothing in vain; and man alone of the animals is furnished with the faculty of language. The mere making of sounds serves to indicate pleasure and pain, and is thus a faculty that belongs to animals in general: their nature enables them to attain the point at which they have perceptions of pleasure and pain, and can signify those perceptions to one another. But language serves to declare what is advantageous and what is the reverse, and it is the peculiarity of man, in comparison with other animals, that he alone possesses a perception of good and evil, of the just and the unjust, and other similar qualities; and it is association in these things which makes a family and a city.

We may now proceed to add that the city is prior in the order of nature to the family and the individual. The reason for this is that the whole is necessarily prior to the part. If the whole body is destroyed, there will not be a foot or a hand, except in that ambiguous sense in which one uses the same word to indicate a different thing, as when one speaks of a "hand" made of stone; for a hand, when destroyed [by the destruction of the whole body], will be no better than a stone "hand." All things derive their essential character from their function and their capacity; and it follows that if they are no longer fit to discharge their function, we ought not to say that they are still the same things, but only that, by an ambiguity, they still have the same names.

We thus see that the city exists by nature and that it is prior to the individual. For if the individual is not self-sufficient when he is isolated he will stand in the same relation to the whole as other parts do to their wholes. The man who is isolated, who is unable to share in the benefits of political association, or has no need to share because he is already self-sufficient, is no part of the city, and must therefore be either a beast or a god. There is therefore a natural impulse in all men towards an association of this sort. But the man who first constructed such an association was none the less the greatest of benefactors. Man, when perfected, is the best of animals; but if he be isolated from law and justice he is the worst of all. Injustice is all the graver when it is armed injustice; and man is furnished from birth with weapons which are intended to serve the purposes of wisdom and goodness, but which may be used in preference for opposite ends. That is why, if he be without goodness [of mind and character], he is a most unholy and savage being, and worse than all others in the indulgence of lust and gluttony. The virtue of justice belongs to the city; for justice is an ordering of the political association, and the virtue of justice consists in the determination of what is just.

Politics III, 9

ARISTOTLE

We must next ascertain what are said to be the distinctive principles of oligarchy and democracy, and what are the oligarchical and the democratic conceptions of justice. All parties have a hold on a sort of conception of justice; but they both fail to carry it far enough, and do not express the true conception of justice in the whole of its range. For example, justice is considered to mean equality. It does mean equality—but equality for those who are equal, and not for all. Again, inequality is considered to be just; and indeed it is—but only for those who are unequal, and not for all. These people fail to consider for whom there should be equality or inequality and thus make erroneous judgements. The reason is that they are judging in their own case; and most people, as a rule, are bad judges where their own interests are involved. Justice is concerned with people; and a just distribution is one in which there is proportion between the things distributed and those to whom they are distributed, a point which has already been made in the *Ethics*. There is general agreement about what constitutes equality in the thing, but disagreement about what constitutes it in people. The main reason for this is the reason just stated, they are judging, and judging erroneously, in their own case; but there is also another reason, they are misled by the fact that they are professing a sort of conception of justice, and professing it up to a point, into thinking that they profess one which is absolute and complete. Some think that if they are superior in one point, for example in wealth, they are superior in all: others believe that if they are equal in one respect, for instance in free birth, they are equal all round.

Both sides, however, fail to mention the really cardinal factor. If property is the end for which people come together and form an association, one's share of the city would be proportionate to one's share of the property; and in that case the argument of the oligarchical side would appear to be strong: they say that is not just for someone who has contributed one mina to share in a sum of a hundred minae on equal terms with one who has contributed all the rest and that this applies both to the original sum and to the interest accruing upon it. But the end of the city is not mere life; it is, rather, a good quality of life. Otherwise, there might be a city of slaves, or even a city of animals; but in the world as we know it any such city is impossible, because slaves and animals do not share in happiness nor in living according to their own choice. Similarly, it is not the end of the city to provide an alliance for mutual defence against all injury, nor does it exist for the purpose of exchange or [commercial] dealing. If that had been the end, the Etruscans and the Carthaginians would be in the position of belonging to a single city; and the same would be true to all peoples who have commercial treaties with one another. It is true that such peoples have agreements about imports; treaties to ensure just conduct; and written terms of alliance for mutual defence. On the other hand, they have no common offices to deal with these matters: each, on the contrary, has its own offices, confined to itself. Neither party concerns itself to ensure a proper quality of character among the members of the other; neither of them seeks to ensure that all who are included in the scope of the treaties are just and free from any form of vice; and they do not go beyond the aim of preventing their own members from committing injustice against one another. But it is the goodness or badness in the life of the city which engages the attention of those who are concerned to secure good government.

The conclusion which clearly follows is that any city which is truly so called, and is not merely one in name, must devote itself to the end of encouraging goodness. Otherwise, a political association sinks into a mere alliance, which only differs in space [i.e. in the contiguity of its members] from other forms of alliance where the members live at a distance from one another. Otherwise, too, law becomes a mere covenant—or (in the phrase of the sophist Lycophron) "a guarantor of just claims"—but lacks the capacity to make the citizens good and just.

That this is the case may be readily proved. If two different sites could be united in one, so that the city [i.e., the *polis*] of Megara and that of Corinth were embraced by a single wall, that would not make a single city. If the citizens of two cities intermarried with one another, that would not make a single city, even though intermarriage is one of the forms of social life which are characteristic of a city. Nor would it make a city if a number of people, living at a distance from one another, but not at so great a distance but they could still associate, had a common system of laws to prevent their injuring one another in the course of exchange. We can imagine, for instance, one being a carpenter, another a farmer, a third a shoemaker, and others producing other goods; and we can imagine a total number of as many as 10,000. But if these people were associated in nothing further than matters such as exchange and alliance, they would still have failed to reach the stage of a city. Why should this be the case? It cannot be ascribed to any lack of contiguity in such an association. The members of a group so constituted might come together on a single site; but if that were all— if each still treated his private house as if it were a city, and all of them still confined their mutual assistance to action against aggressors (as if it were only a question of a defensive alliance)—if, in a word, they associated with each other in the same fashion after coming together as they did when they were living apart—their association, even on its new basis, could not be deemed by any accurate thinker to be a city.

It is clear, therefore, that a city is not an association for residence on a common site, or for the sake of preventing mutual injustice and easing exchange. These are indeed conditions which must be present before a city can exist; but the presence of all these conditions is not enough, in itself, to constitute a city. What constitutes a city is an association of households and clans in a good life, for the sake of attaining a perfect and self-sufficing existence. This, however, will not come about unless the members inhabit one and the self-same place and practise intermarriage. It was for this reason that the various institutions of a common social life—marriage-connections, kin-groups, religious gatherings, and social pastimes generally—arose in cities. This sort of thing is the business of friendship, for the pursuit of a common social life is friendship. Thus the purpose of a city is the good life, and these institutions are means to that end. A city is constituted by the association of families and villages in a perfect and self-sufficing existence; and such an existence, on our definition, consists in living a happy and truly valuable life.

It is therefore for the sake of actions valuable in themselves, and not for the sake of social life, that political associations must be considered to exist. Those who contribute most to this association have a greater share in the city than those who are equal to them (or even greater) in free birth and descent, but unequal in civic excellence, or than those who surpass them in wealth but are surpassed by them in excellence. From what has been said it is plain that all sides in the dispute about constitutions profess only a partial conception of justice.

COMMENTS

For Aristotle, a contrast between nature and convention as the basis for political association is misleading because society and the state are natural for humans. It is part of our nature to have needs and aptitudes that can be fulfilled only within the life shared with others in a state. Aristotle has in mind the *polis,* or city-state, the form of political association that was normal in the Greek world.

In book I of his *Politics,* Aristotle presents a genetic account. Humans naturally form families and groups like villages and eventually city-states. Only at this point is society self-sufficient for a good life; that is, within the narrower confines of the home and the small village, something is lacking that is needed for a life to be a *good* life. Family life is fine as far as it goes, but a good life also requires some broadening of the horizons to take in concerns and goals that are shared with people to whom you relate as fellow-citizens.

There are (at least) three important points to consider:

Why is Aristotle so sure that the city-state is natural? For Aristotle, nature is a principle of change that excludes force. He sees the state as something that will happen, given the right conditions, without being forced on people. Nature is also, for Aristotle, what happens "always or for the most part." Institutions that we see everywhere, among different peoples, are therefore taken to be natural. This makes Aristotle sure that the city-state is natural: It happens everywhere and is not forced on people. (Unfortunately, the same considerations led Aristotle to accept the naturalness of slavery and of the view that women's role is a domestic one in the home. Since he knew of no society in which women had political rights or that lacked slavery, he concluded that these states of affairs are natural, overlooking the role of force in sustaining them.)

Why does Aristotle stop at the city-state? Why is it not natural for us to have political and social concerns for larger units? In Aristotle's world, larger units, like the Persian Empire, were imposed by force. Are modern political units, such as the nation-state, too large for us to have unforced concern for a shared life and goals?

When Aristotle says that humans are "political animals," does he mean that the good human life requires positive participation in political activity? Or does he mean something weaker—that the good life requires sharing the life of a city-state, without necessarily being politically active oneself? (In this view, the Greek might be better translated "social animal.") Both interpretations have been defended. The latter is nearer to modern views, since modern nation-states provide fewer opportunities for political involvement.

In III, 9, Aristotle rejects some inadequate views of the state. It is not like a company or commercial project, in which it is reasonable that reward should be proportionate to contribution. (Oligarchs, who think that the rich should have greater political rewards than the poor, think of the state in this way.) Nor is it like an alliance to ensure or forbid the performance of certain acts. A state must be concerned to produce and sustain certain virtues in its citizens, or it is not functioning to produce a genuinely shared life with shared goals; it is just facilitating the way individuals achieve their own individual aims.

Does Aristotle argue convincingly that the state is more than a guarantor of just claims and rights? Do you agree with him on the role of the state?

Epicureans
Principal Doctrines 31–38
EPICURUS

31. Natural justice is a pledge of advantage, toward not harming or being harmed by one another.

32. With those animals that were unable to make contracts about neither harming nor being harmed by one another, with these there is no justice or injustice. Similarly with those peoples who were unable or unwilling to make contracts about neither harming nor being harmed.

33. There is no such thing as justice in itself; in people's relations with one another in any place and at any time, it is a contract about not harming or being harmed.

34. Injustice is not a bad thing in itself, but because of the fear that comes with the suspicion that one will not evade those established as punishers of such things.

35. It is impossible for the person who secretly does one of the things about which people have contracted with one another about not harming or being harmed to be confident that he will evade detection, even if he evades it thousands of times for the present. For right up to death, it is not clear that he will evade it.

36. From a general point of view, justice is the same for all, for it is a kind of advantage in people's community with one another. But from the particular point of view of the place and of any other causes, it does not follow for all that the same thing is just.

37. Of the things deemed to be just by law, what is confirmed as advantageous in the needs of people's community with one another should have the status of being just, whether it is the same for all or not the same. But if someone only sets up a law, but there is no result that accords with advantage in community with one another, then this no longer contains the nature of the just. And even if the advantage according to the just changes, but for a while fits the preconception, it is none the less just for that time—to those who do not trouble themselves with empty sounds but look to the facts.

38. Where things considered to be just have been shown in actual fact not to fit our preconception [of justice] although circumstances have not changed, then those things were not just. And where circumstances have changed and the same things that were just are no longer advantageous, then in that case they were just before, when they were advantageous for the mutual community of fellow citizens, but later when they were not advantageous, they were no longer just.

DIOGENES OF OENOANDA

Diogenes of Oenoanda left no mark at all on the written tradition that has come down to us from the ancient world and is known to us from accidental discovery of stone fragments.

Oenoanda is a city in Lycia (modern Turkey). In the second century A.D., Diogenes, rich citizen of the town and a committed Epicurean, paid for a huge stone portico with a long inscription proclaiming Epicurus' message. Fragments of the stone inscription have been found, showing that it was a mixture of Epicurus' own words and Diogenes' own ideas. Like a modern billboard, the inscription was supposed to catch the attention of people going about their everyday business and to get them to think of their lives as inadequate and unhappy. The remedy is Epicurus' philosophy, chunks of which the inscription contains. Diogenes himself comes across as a down-home type of person, rather than a serious philosopher. He paid for the inscription when he was old and ill, wishing to spread Epicurus' message in an urgent way that would last after his death.

Epicurean Inscription FRAGMENT 56
DIOGENES OF OENOANDA

[We will not all have wisdom], since all people are not capable of it. But if we suppose it to be possible, then truly the life of the gods will pass over to humans. For everything will be full of justice and mutual love, and there will be no need for walls and laws and all the things that we contrive because of one another. Concerning the necessities from farming, since we shall have no [slaves] then—for we shall [plough] and dig ourselves, and look after the crops and divert rivers . . . and as is needful such things will break into our continuous philosophizing together, for the farming activities will provide what our nature needs.

On Duties III, 37–39
CICERO

Also, any hope or thought of concealment and covering up must be taken out of all our deliberations. If we have got anywhere in philosophy, we should be adequately convinced that we should not do anything greedy or unjust or anything intemperate or against our better judgment, even if we could escape the notice of all gods and humans.

This is the purpose of Plato's introduction of the famous Gyges. Once after a huge storm, the earth gaped open; Gyges went down the opening and noticed (so the stories go) a bronze horse with doors in its sides. When these doors were opened, he saw the body of a dead man of unusual size and with a gold ring on his finger. Gyges removed this ring and put it on himself and then went to a meeting of the shepherds (he was one of the king's shepherds). When he turned the ring's bezel round toward his palm, he became invisible to everyone there, although he continued to see everything, but when he turned the ring back to its original position, he became visible again. And so, making use of this opportunity of the ring, he seduced the queen and, with her help, killed the king, his master, and removed those he considered to be in his way without anyone's being able to see him in these wrongdoings. So by the help of the ring, he shortly rose to be the king of Lydia.

If a wise person were to have just this ring, he would not think himself any more at liberty to do wrong than if he lacked it; good men seek to do moral, not secret, actions.

On this point, certain philosophers [Epicureans], who are not by any means bad people, but are not very bright, say that Plato's story is a made-up and fictional one—as though he were defending it as having happened, or even as possible! Here is the force of the ring and of this example: If nobody were going to know—if nobody were even going to suspect—when you did something for the sake of riches, power, domination, or lust, and if it were always to be unknown to gods and humans, then would you do it? They say that it's not possible.

Right—in no way could it be possible. But what I'm asking is what they *would* do if what they say is not possible *were* possible. They persevere in a philistine way: They say that it's not possible and go on about that and don't see the force of the story. When we are asking what they *would* do, if they *were* able to get away with it, we are *not* asking whether they could get away with it! Rather, we are, so to speak, putting pressure, so that if they reply that they *would* do it, given that they had impunity, they are admitting that they are criminally minded, whereas if they deny it, they are conceding that all disgraceful acts should be avoided on their own account.

COMMENTS

Epicurus revives a social-contract account of justice, although he is aware of the kind of objection that Plato brought to it: It cannot give a convincing account of the virtue of justice. Epicurus thinks that given his account of our final end and of virtue, he can produce an account that withstands Plato's kind of objection.

According to Epicurus, what we all aim at is pleasure, understood as tranquillity and freedom from disturbance (see the readings in section 5). The virtues are necessary for us to achieve this. Justice is a virtue because the unjust person is always going to be afraid of detection and so always anxious and upset. Even if she is not afraid of being detected in her lifetime, she will be anxious about the gods' opinion of wrongdoing and will feel uneasy because she has a guilty conscience.

When the Epicurean inquires what justice actually is, the answer is given by looking at what is socially advantageous. Epicurus makes the point that what is socially advantageous will differ between different times and places, since different circumstances make different institutions and practices socially advantageous or not. Note that this is not a relativistic account of justice: The institutions that embody justice will vary, but justice itself will not vary; it is whatever is socially advantageous.

Does this fit with the idea that justice is a virtue that enables us to achieve tranquillity? One objection may be that if we are always working out what is socially advantageous, we will not be in the kind of stable state that produces tranquillity, since we will be chopping and changing. But if we are in a state such as to make us tranquil, will we be energetically tracking changes in what is socially advantageous?

The fragment here from the Epicurean inscription that was set up by Diogenes of Oenoanda shows that at least some Epicureans thought of justice as something forced on us by the un-ideal conditions of the actual world. If everyone were Epicurean, social conditions would be completely different, since people would no longer be motivated by greed and competition. Diogenes appears to realize that this would involve changing people's social expectations quite a bit; ordinary people would have to grow their own crops, for example, and not rely on there being workers to do it for them. (It is not certain, because of the state of the stone fragment, that Diogenes is saying that there would be no need for slaves, but he is certainly saying that there would be no need for some people to do the manual work for others.)

Cicero gives us a standard objection against Epicurean views of justice and society: They do not really avoid the objection Plato makes in his account of the ring of

Gyges. Epicureans argue that Plato is missing the point of an account of justice, since he argues that a theory should show that you have reason to be just even if you have the ring of Gyges. But this, they say, is a completely unrealistic thought-experiment, and a theory should have to account for realistic, not unrealistic examples. Hence they discount the ring of Gyges, rather than trying to show that an Epicurean would be just even if she had it. Is Cicero being unfair in insisting that the Epicureans answer Plato on his own terms? Is Epicurus missing the point in refusing to do so?

See also Cicero, *On Final Ends* p. 346 (the discussion of justice is part of the account of Epicurean ethics as a whole).

Stoicism

On Laws I, 17–35, 42–45
CICERO

MARCUS We must clarify the *nature* of justice, and that has to be deduced from the nature of man. Then we must consider the laws by which states ought to be governed, and finally deal with the laws and enactments which peoples have compiled and written down. There the so-called civil law of our own people too will not be overlooked.

QUINTUS You certainly *are* going far back, Marcus! Quite rightly, you are trac- 18 ing the object of our search back to its source. Those who present civil law in a different way are presenting modes of litigation rather than justice.

MARCUS Not so, Quintus. Ignorance rather than knowledge of the law leads to litigation. But that can wait till later; now let's inspect the first principles of justice.

Well then, the most learned men have chosen to take law as their starting point. I'm inclined to think they are right, if indeed (as they define it) law is the highest reason, inherent in nature, which enjoins what ought to be done and forbids the opposite. When that reason is fully formed and completed in the human mind, it, too, is law. So they think that law, whose function is to enjoin right action and to forbid wrong-doing, is wisdom. . . . 19 As they stress the element of fairness in law, we stress that of choice; but in fact each of these is an essential property of law. If this assertion is correct, as on the whole I think it is, the origin of justice must be derived from law. For law is a force of nature, the intelligence and reason of a wise man, and the criterion of justice and injustice. At the same time, as our whole discourse has to do with ordinary ways of thinking, we shall sometimes have to use ordinary language, applying the word "law" to that which lays down

From Cicero, *De Legibus*, translated by Niall Rudd (Oxford: Oxford University Press, 1998). Reprinted with the permission of Oxford University Press.

in writing what it wishes to enjoin or forbid. For that's what the man in the street calls law. But in establishing what justice is let us take as our point of departure that highest law which came into being countless centuries before any law was written down or any state was even founded.

20 QUINTUS   Yes, that's more fitting and sensible in view of the method we have chosen for our discussion.

MARCUS   Shall we, then, look for the origin of justice at its source? Once we have found that, we will have a reliable standard for testing our investigations.

QUINTUS   Yes, I think that's the way to proceed.

ATTICUS   Include me, too, in your brother's opinion.

MARCUS   It is our business, then, to maintain and preserve the constitution of that state which Scipio in those six books proved to be the best. All the laws must be framed to fit that kind of community. Patterns of behaviour are also to be implanted, and not everything is to be laid down in writing. For all these reasons I shall look to nature for the origins of justice. She must be our constant guide as our discussion unfolds.

ATTICUS   Absolutely right. With her as our guide there can be no danger of
21   going astray.

MARCUS   Well then, Pomponius, will you grant me this (for I already know Quintus' view) that the whole of nature is ruled by the immortal gods, with their force, impetus, plan, power, sway (or whatever other word may express my meaning more plainly)? If you don't accept that, our argument will have to start on that very point.

ATTICUS   I'll grant it if you insist. . . .

MARCUS   I'll be brief; this is the point. The creature of foresight, wisdom, variety, keenness, memory, endowed with reason and judgement, which we call man, was created by the supreme god to enjoy a remarkable status. Of all the types and species of living creatures he is the only one that participates in reason and reflection, whereas none of the others do. What is there, I will not say in man, but in the whole of heaven and earth, more divine than reason (a faculty which, when it has developed and become complete, is rightly called wisdom)?

23   Since, then, there is nothing better than reason, and reason is present in both man and God, there is a primordial partnership in reason between man and God. But those who share reason also share right reason; and since that is law, we men must also be thought of as partners with the gods in law. Furthermore, those who share law share justice. Now those who share all these things must be regarded as belonging to the same state; and much the more so if they obey the same powers and authorities. And they do in fact obey this celestial system, the divine mind, and the all-powerful god. Hence this whole universe must be thought of as a single community shared by gods and men. Now in communities there is a system (which I shall describe at the appropriate point) whereby differences of status within families are determined by blood-relationships. In the context of the cosmos the same

applies on a much vaster and more splendid scale, establishing ties of blood between men and gods.

In debates on the nature of man it is usually maintained, doubtless correctly, that in the course of the continuous circuits and revolutions of the heavens the right moment arrived for sowing the human race; that after being scattered and sown in the earth it was further endowed with the divine gift of mind; that whereas men derived the other elements in their make-up from their mortal nature—elements which are fragile and transitory—their mind was implanted in them by God. Hence we have what can truly be called a lineage, origin, or stock in common with the gods. That is why, out of so many species, no creature apart from man has any conception of God; and why, within mankind itself, there is no tribe so civilized or so savage as not to know that it should believe in a god, even if it is mistaken about the *kind* of god it should believe in. As a result, man recognizes God in as much as he, as it were, remembers his place of origin. Again, the same moral excellence resides in man and in God, and in no other species besides. And moral excellence is nothing other than the completion and perfection of nature.

There is, therefore, a similarity between man and God. Since that is so, what kinship, I ask you, can be closer or firmer? Nature has lavished such a wealth of things on men for their use and convenience that every growing thing seems to have been given to us on purpose; it does not come into existence by chance. And I don't mean just what shoots forth from the fertile earth, but also domestic animals; for they were obviously created for man's use or his enjoyment or his food. Again, countless skills have been discovered thanks to nature's teaching. By copying her, reason has cleverly acquired the necessities of life.

Nature, too, has not only equipped man with mental agility; she has provided him with senses which act as his servants and messengers. She has given him, as a preliminary outline, dim and not fully developed perceptions of very many things, which form a foundation, as it were, of knowledge. And she has blest him with a versatile physique in keeping with the human mind. For whereas nature made other animals stoop down to feed, she made man alone erect, encouraging him to gaze at the heavens as being, so to speak, akin to him and his original home. She also shaped his facial features so as to express his innermost character. Our eyes tell our emotional state very clearly; and what we call the expression, which cannot exist in any creature except in man, indicates our character. . . . I need not mention the faculties and abilities of the rest of the body, such as the control of the voice and the power of speech, which is above all else the promoter of human fellowship. For not everything is germane to our present discussion, and I think Scipio has dealt adequately with this topic in the books which you have read. Since, then, God has created and equipped man in this way, intending him to take precedence over everything else, this point should be clear (not to go into every detail) that nature on her own account

goes further. Without any teacher, starting from the sort of things she apprehended through that original rudimentary perception, she herself strength-
ens and completes human reason.

28 ATTICUS   Good Lord! You're certainly going a long way back in your search for
the basis of justice. For that reason I shan't hurry you on to the discussion of
civil law which I was hoping for. I would gladly have you spend the whole
day on this subject. For these points that you are bringing in, as ancillary
perhaps to other matters, are actually more important than the things which
they serve to introduce.

MARCUS   Yes, the points which I am now briefly touching on are important. But
of all the issues dealt with in philosophical debates surely nothing is more
vital than the clear realization that we are born for justice, and that what is
just is based, not on opinion, but on nature. This will at once become clear
if you examine the society of men and their relations to one another.

29   Now there is no single thing that is so similar to, so like, anything else
as all of us are like one another. If corrupt habits and foolish opinions did
not twist and turn aside our feeble minds from their original paths, no individual would be more like himself than everyone would be like everyone
30   else. Thus, however one defines man, the same definition applies to us all.
This is sufficient proof that there is no essential difference within mankind.
If there were, the same definition would not cover everyone. Reason in
fact—the one thing in which we are superior to the beasts, which enables us
to make valid deductions, to argue, refute our opponents, debate, solve
problems, draw conclusions—that certainly is common to us all. While it
may vary in what it teaches, it is constant in its ability to learn. For the same
things are grasped by the senses of all, and those things that act on the
senses act on the senses of all alike; and those rudimentary perceptions that
are impressed on the mind (the perceptions I mentioned above) are impressed alike on *all* minds. Speech, which interprets the mind, uses different languages but expresses the same ideas. Nor is there any member of any
nation who cannot attain moral excellence by using nature as his guide.

31   The similarity between human beings is evident in their vices as well as
their virtues. They are all beguiled by pleasure, which, though it leads on to
vice, bears some resemblance to what is naturally good; for it gives delight
by its lightness and charm, and so, through an error of judgement, is
accepted as something beneficial. Owing to a similar misconception death
is shunned as though it involved the extinction of our true nature, while life
is sought because it preserves us in the condition in which we were born.
Pain is counted as one of the greatest evils, because it is harsh in itself and
32   apparently leads to the dissolution of our nature. Again, because good character and good reputation look alike, those who receive public honours are
regarded as blessed, and the obscure are objects of pity. Troubles and joys,
desires and fears, haunt the minds of all alike; and if men differ in their
opinions it does not follow that those who worship a dog or a cat as divine
are not afflicted by the same superstition as other nations. What community
does not love friendliness, generosity, and an appreciative mind which

remembers acts of kindness? What community does not reject the arrogant, the wicked, the cruel, and the ungrateful—yes, and hate them too? So, since the whole human race is seen to be knit together, the final conclusion is that the principles of right living make everyone a better person. If you agree with this, let us move on to the rest of our discussion; but if you have any questions we should clear them up first.

ATTICUS   No, we have nothing to raise, if I may answer for us both.

MARCUS   The next point, then, is that we have been made by nature to share 33 justice amongst ourselves and to impart it to one another. I should add that in the whole of this discussion I want it to be understood that what I call "justice" comes from nature, but that the corruption brought by bad habits is so great that it extinguishes, so to speak, the sparks given by nature and allows the corresponding vices to spring up and flourish. If human beings believed in their hearts what is in fact the case, namely that, in the poet's words, "nothing human is alien to them," then justice would be respected equally by all. For those who have been endowed by nature with reason have also been endowed with right reason, and hence with law, which is right reason in commanding and forbidding; but if with law, then with justice too. But reason has been bestowed on everybody; therefore the same applies to justice. And Socrates was right to curse the man who first separated self-interest from justice; for that, he complained, was the source of 34 everything pernicious. Hence that famous saying of Pythagoras . . . [*There is a gap in the text here*]

It is clear, then, that when a wise man shows this goodwill, which ranges so far and wide, to someone endowed with equal moral excellence, an effect is produced which some people think incredible though it is actually inevitable, namely that he loves the other person as much as he loves himself. For what difference can there be when everything is equal? If there could be some distinction, however tiny, in a friendship, the name of friendship would already have gone; for the essential feature of friendship is that, the moment one partner prefers to have something for himself rather than for the other, it vanishes.

All these arguments provide a firm basis for the rest of our discussion and debate, for they help to show that justice is founded on nature. When I have said a little more about this point, I will come to civil law, the subject from which this whole discourse began.

QUINTUS   Yes, you need add very little. From what you've said it certainly 35 seems to me that justice is derived from nature. I don't know whether Atticus agrees.

ATTICUS   How could I fail to agree when you have proved first that we are, as it were, equipped and arrayed with the gifts of the gods, and secondly that men have a single way of living with one another which is shared equally by everyone, and finally that all are held together by a natural goodwill and kindliness and also by a fellowship in justice? Since we have agreed (rightly, I think) that these assertions are true, how can we now dissociate law and justice from nature?

42   Most foolish of all is the belief that everything decreed by the institutions or laws of a particular country is just. What if the laws are the laws of
tyrants? If the notorious Thirty had wished to impose their laws on Athens,
even if the entire population of Athens welcomed the tyrants' laws, should
those laws on that account be considered just? No more, in my opinion,
should that law be considered just which our interrex passed, allowing the
Dictator to execute with impunity any citizen he wished, even without trial.
There is one, single, justice. It binds together human society and has been
established by one, single, law. That law is right reason in commanding and
forbidding. A man who does not acknowledge this law is unjust, whether it
has been written down anywhere or not. If justice is a matter of obeying the
written laws and customs of particular communities, and if, as our opponents allege, everything is to be measured by self-interest, then a person will
ignore and break the laws when he can, if he thinks it will be to his own
advantage. That is why justice is completely non-existent if it is not derived
from nature, and if that kind of justice which is established to serve self-
43   interest is wrecked by that same self-interest. And that is why every virtue
is abolished if nature is not going to support justice.

What room will there be for liberality, patriotism, and devotion; or for
the wish to serve others or to show gratitude? These virtues are rooted in
the fact that we are inclined by nature to have a regard for others; and that
is the basis of justice. Moreover, not just our services to other men, but also
ceremonies and rituals in honour of the gods will be abolished—practices
which, in my view, should be retained, not out of fear, but in consequence
of the association between man and God. If on the other hand laws were
validated by the orders of peoples, the enactments of politicians, and the
verdicts of judges, then it would be just to rob, just to commit adultery, just
to introduce forged wills, provided those things were approved by the votes
or decrees of the populace.

44   If there is such power in the decisions and decrees of foolish people that
they can overturn the nature of things by their votes, why do they not enact
that things wicked and destructive should be deemed good and wholesome? And why is it that, if a law can make what is unjust just, it cannot turn
evil into good? But in fact we can distinguish a good law from a bad one
solely by the criterion of nature. And not only justice and injustice are differentiated by nature, but all things without exception that are honourable
and dishonourable. For nature has created perceptions which we have in
common, and has sketched them in our minds in such a way that we classify honourable things as virtues and dishonourable things as vices.

45   It is insane to suppose that these things are matters of opinion and not
grounded in nature. The so-called "virtue" of a tree or a horse (which is
actually a misuse of the word) does not depend on opinion but on nature. If
that is so, then honourable and dishonourable things too must be distinguished by nature. If moral excellence as a whole were certified by opinion,
the same would apply to its parts. In that case who would judge a wise and,
shall we say, shrewd man, not on the basis of his natural character but of

some external factor? No, moral excellence is reason fully developed, and that is certainly grounded in nature; the same goes for everything that is honourable.

COMMENTS

In this passage, Cicero is putting forth the Stoic view of justice, which in this work he supports. The argument first appeals to the fact that all humans are rational and that this is not just a casual fact about us, but one that determines what it is to be human. Notice that this point is developed in a way that is egalitarian as far as humans are concerned—the ways we differ in talents, wealth, and so on are unimportant by comparison with our fundamental sameness in being rational—but that excludes animals from sharing a moral community with us.

That we are all rational does not mean that we all always think and act rationally, in the sense of thinking and acting on good reasons. Still, Cicero thinks that it is enough to be able to point to the way that humans converge in their thinking; we agree on the basic principles of right and wrong when we are thinking rationally and are not being diverted by our feelings or misled into thinking that our own particular circumstances are ones that should hold universally. That we converge in this way is due to "nature"; it corresponds to something objective, since only nature could explain why all humans think alike on basic matters of ethics and justice. Much of Cicero's argument here is devoted to showing that alternative explanations of justice, which claim that justice is nothing more than what various states consider to be just, fail to account for the way we actually think of justice (and of other virtues). If this is right, then all humans have a robust notion of justice and injustice; we do not live up to it, but we are all equally capable of recognizing and acting on it, since we are all equally endowed with reason, which is what humans need to achieve such a notion.

The Stoics do not think of nature simply as what is objectively there; they think of it as having, where value is concerned, a special force like that of a command: To recognize what is natural is to recognize that it is demanded of you. Justice is not merely natural, it is a matter of natural *law*. The Stoics were the first to work out an idea of natural law as the demands of justice, which the just person recognizes, equally available to any human who uses his or her reason. This idea was influential in the ancient world, and it has been argued that it made an impact on Roman law. It was a central and important idea in the medieval period and is still alive as a theory of the justification of law.

B. Political Rule: Expertise and the Rule of Law

One issue that debate over forms of government pushed to the fore was that of expertise. Democracy established the idea that any citizen was competent to hold any (or nearly any) political office, an idea embodied in the practice of selecting people for office by lottery. This put in its sharpest form the idea that political rule does not require any special expertise, an idea that drew sharp criticism and some important discussion.

TWOFOLD ARGUMENTS

Twofold Arguments (*Dissoi Logoi*) is the title of a short anonymous collection of arguments, usually, as the name suggests (though not in this case), arguments for and arguments against a given position. It has come down to us as an appendix to the works of Sextus Empiricus, and we know nothing about its author, place, or date. It is generally dated about 400 B.C., on the basis of references to events, but it could be considerably later. Since the arguments are uneven—some are interesting, others are terrible, and they are laid out in a rather naive way—the author is often taken to be feeble as a philosopher. However, this view is not justified; although the author sometimes indicates approval of some lines of thought, he does not put forward any of the arguments as his own. Rather, like the later Skeptics, he just puts forward the arguments, and it is up to the reader to make what she can of them.

Twofold Arguments 7

1 7. | Some of the popular orators say that public offices should be assigned by
2 lot, but this opinion is not the best. | What if you should ask him, "Why do you
not assign your servants their jobs by lot, so that if the ox-leader drew the job of
cook, he would cook, and the cook would lead the oxen, and similarly with the
3 other jobs? | And how come we didn't assemble the smiths and the cobblers
and the carpenters and the jewelers and draw lots and compel them each to
4 practice the craft he was assigned by lot and not the one he knew?" | In the
same way we could also draw lots for competitors in music contests, and each
person would compete in whatever contest he was assigned by lot, a flute-
player perchance competing on the lyre and a lyre-player on the flute. And in
war an archer and an infantryman will ride in the cavalry and the cavalryman
will shoot a bow. Thus all will be doing jobs for which they have neither knowl-
5 edge nor competence. | They say that this method is both a good thing and very

---

From Gagarin, Michael and Woodruff, Paul (eds.) *Early Greek Political Thought from Homer to the Sophists* (Cambridge: Cambridge University Press, 1995). Reprinted with the permission of Cambridge University Press.

democratic, but I don't think it is democratic at all. For in these cities there are those who hate the common people (*dēmos*), and if their lot happens to be selected, they will destroy the people. | The people themselves, however, 6 should watch closely and in all cases choose those who are sympathetic toward their interests, and choose as generals those suited for commanding troops, others suited to be guardians of the law, and so forth.

COMMENTS

The author here objects to the democratic practice (which we know about from Athens, but was practiced elsewhere) of selecting officials by lottery. Assignment by lottery played a large part in democratic political activity; some of the stone "allotment machines" have been found in excavations in the Athenian Agora. Whereas we tend to think of elections as an indication of democracy, the ancients thought of elections as oligarchic, indeed antidemocratic. The elections distinguish between those who are elected and do the job and those who are merely voters (voting is not seen as an exercise of a worthwhile political capacity), and they embody the principle that some should be chosen for office rather than others because they are better fitted for it. The lottery embodies the democratic principle that everybody is equally fitted for political rule (rather than just being ruled), so that it does not matter who does it.

The author points out that the lottery principle flouts our recognition of expertise and makes for avoidable inefficiency. He also points out that it does not select those who favor democracy, which he takes to be an objection because he assumes that democracy is rule by the majority in its own interests.

Republic 488a–489c
PLATO

"Imagine the following situation on a fleet of ships, or on a single ship. The owner has the edge over everyone else on board by virtue of his size and b strength, but he's rather deaf and short-sighted, and his knowledge of naval matters is just as limited. The sailors are wrangling with one another because each of them thinks that he ought to be the captain, despite the fact that he's never learnt how, and can't name his teacher or specify the period of his apprenticeship. In any case, they all maintain that it isn't something that can be taught, and are ready to butcher anyone who says it is. They're for ever crowding closely around the owner, pleading with him and stopping at nothing to get him c to entrust the rudder to them. Sometimes, if their pleas are unsuccessful, but

From Plato, *Republic*, translated by Robin Waterfield (Oxford: Oxford University Press, 1993). Reprinted with the permission of Oxford University Press.

others get the job, they kill those others or throw them off the ship, subdue their
worthy owner by drugging him or getting him drunk or something, take control of the ship, help themselves to its cargo, and have the kind of drunken and
indulgent voyage you'd expect from people like that. And that's not all: they
think highly of anyone who contributes towards their gaining power by showing skill at winning over or subduing the owner, and describe him as an accom-
d plished seaman, a true captain, a naval expert; but they criticize anyone different as useless. They completely fail to understand that any genuine sea-captain
has to study the yearly cycle, the seasons, the heavens, the stars and winds, and
everything relevant to the job, if he's to be properly equipped to hold a position
of authority in a ship. In fact, they think it's impossible to study and acquire
e expertise at how to steer a ship (leaving aside the question of whether or not
people want you to) and at the same time be a good captain. When this is what's
happening on board ships, don't you think that the crew of ships in this state
would think of any true captain as nothing but a windbag with his head in the
489a clouds, of no use to them at all?"

"They definitely would," Adeimantus replied.

"I'm sure you don't need an analysis of the analogy to see that it's a
metaphor for the attitude of society towards true philosophers," I said. "I'm
sure you take my point."

"I certainly do," he said.

"You'd better use it, then, in the first instance, to clarify things for that person who expressed surprise at the disrespect shown to philosophers by society,
and try to show him how much more astonishing it would be if they were
b respected."

"All right, I will," he said.

"And that you're right to say that the best practitioners of philosophy are
incapable of performing any public service. But you'd better tell him to blame
their uselessness on the others' failure to make use of them, rather than on the
fact that they are accomplished philosophers. I mean, it's unnatural for the captain to ask the sailors to accept his authority and it's unnatural for wise men to
dance attendance on rich men; this story is misleading. The truth of the matter
is that it makes no difference whether you're rich or poor: if you feel ill, you're
c bound to dance attendance on a doctor, and if you need to accept authority, you
must dance attendance on someone in authority who is capable of providing it.
If he is really to serve any useful purpose, it's not up to him to ask those under
him to accept his authority. And you won't be mistaken if you compare present-
day political leaders to the sailors in our recent tale, and the ones they call useless airheads to the genuine captain."

Statesman 291d–303b

PLATO

VISITOR   There's a form of government which is monarchy, isn't there?   d
YOUNG SOCRATES   Yes.
VISITOR   And I suppose one could say that the next form of government is when power is in the hands of the few.
YOUNG SOCRATES   Of course.
VISITOR   A third type of political system is the rule of the many, which is known as democracy. Yes?
YOUNG SOCRATES   Certainly.
VISITOR   Now aren't these three systems of government in a sense five? Don't two of them give rise to other systems as well, with different names?
YOUNG SOCRATES   Which other systems are you thinking of?
VISITOR   If we now take into consideration whether they involve constraint or   e
consent, poverty or wealth, and regard or disregard for law, we have a criterion for dividing each of the two systems into two parts. Let's take monarchy first. Since it appears in two different guises, there are two terms for it—dictatorship and kingship.
YOUNG SOCRATES   Naturally.
VISITOR   And a state which is controlled by a few of its members may be called either an aristocracy or an oligarchy.
YOUNG SOCRATES   Yes.
VISITOR   As for democracy, it doesn't make any difference whether the general   292a
populace rules over the propertied class by constraint or by consent: people still invariably tend to use the same term for it.
YOUNG SOCRATES   True.
VISITOR   Now, the principles which distinguish each of these political systems are, for instance, whether power is in the hands of one person or a few people or many people, whether the ruling class is rich or poor, whether rule is by constraint or consent, and whether or not the system happens to involve a written legal code. Doesn't this exclude them from being perfect systems?
YOUNG SOCRATES   Why should it?
VISITOR   You need to consider the matter more carefully. Try to follow my line   b
of reasoning.
YOUNG SOCRATES   Go on.
VISITOR   There's something we said right at the beginning of our discussion. Shall we continue to affirm it, or do we disagree with it now?
YOUNG SOCRATES   What are you referring to?

From Plato, *Statesman*, translated by Robin Waterfield with notes by Julia Annas (New York: Cambridge University Press, 1995). Reprinted with the permission of Cambridge University Press.

VISITOR   We said that government by a king was a branch of knowledge, didn't we?

YOUNG SOCRATES   Yes.

VISITOR   And we were more precise than that. We narrowed the branches of knowledge that interested us down to an evaluative kind and an instructional kind.

YOUNG SOCRATES   Yes.

VISITOR   And we broke the instructional kind down into a branch that is responsible for inanimate things and a branch that is responsible for living creatures. The process of continually making these kinds of divisions has brought us to where we are now, but we've borne in mind throughout that kingship is a sort of knowledge—even if we haven't been able to specify with enough precision exactly what sort.

c

YOUNG SOCRATES   That's an accurate summary.

VISITOR   What I want us to appreciate, then, is that if we're to be consistent with these early stages of the argument, the standard by which we assess constitutions should not be the number of its rulers, consent and constraint, poverty and wealth; it should be a branch of knowledge.

d YOUNG SOCRATES   But we must of course be consistent.

VISITOR   It inevitably follows, then, that what we have to try to find out is which of these systems of government in fact possesses knowledge of what is probably the most difficult, and the most important, kind of rulership to master—ruling over human beings. As long as we fail to understand what this knowledge is, we'll never be able to distinguish a king with his wisdom from those who merely pretend to be statesmen, but in fact aren't in the slightest, however widely their claim may be believed.

YOUNG SOCRATES   Yes, we already know from earlier stages of the discussion how important this distinction is.

e VISITOR   Now, can a large body of people within a state master this branch of knowledge, do you think?

YOUNG SOCRATES   Of course not.

VISITOR   Suppose a state has a population of a thousand. Could a hundred or even fifty of them become competent statesmen?

YOUNG SOCRATES   If they could, mastering statesmanship would be easier than mastering any other branch of knowledge, because we'd obviously never find that many top-notch *backgammon* players in a population of a thousand people—I mean, people who could match other Greek players—let alone *kings*. I use the plural because, as we've already argued, a person is to be described as a king whether or not he's actually a ruler, as long as he has

293a   mastered the branch of knowledge which is kingship.

VISITOR   That's a useful reminder. But it follows from what we're saying, surely, that in looking for the phenomenon of perfect rulership, we should be considering a single individual, or two or a very limited number of people, anyway.

YOUNG SOCRATES   Of course.

VISITOR   And it doesn't matter whether they rule by consent or constraint, whether they use or lack a written code, whether they're rich or poor—we still have to regard them as rulers, just as the presence of expertise is the criterion we currently employ to distinguish those who are in charge of any sphere whatsoever. We certainly don't apply or withhold the label "doctor" depending on whether or not his patients have consented to the treatment, b which might involve surgery or cautery or some other painful procedure, or depending on whether or not he has a written code, or is rich or poor. None of these factors makes the slightest bit of difference: we still call him a doctor, as long as the instructions he issues are guided by expertise, whether he is purging us or otherwise reducing or even increasing our bulk. The only factor we take into consideration is whether the treatment is good for our bodies. We ask only that in tending to our bodies, he is always concerned to c preserve them and improve their condition. Surely it is this factor, and this factor alone, which will make us claim that expertise is the only true criterion for being a doctor and for wielding any other kind of authority.

YOUNG SOCRATES   Absolutely.

VISITOR   The same necessarily goes for political systems too, then, I suppose. The only true system—the political system par excellence—is one where it can be shown that the rulers are genuinely and not merely apparently knowledgeable. And by any standard of what constitutes correctness, there's absolutely no need for us to take into consideration whether they rule with or without a legal code, whether or not their subjects have consented to their rule, or whether they are rich or poor.   d

YOUNG SOCRATES   Right.

VISITOR   And suppose they purge the state, for its own good, by killing or banishing some of its members; suppose they reduce its size by sending out a bee-swarm of colonists, or increase its size by bringing outsiders in from elsewhere and granting them citizenship. Provided that in doing so they are drawing on their knowledge and their moral sense and are doing their best to preserve the state and improve its condition, then the state still conforms to the factors and the criteria which compel us to identify it as having the e one and only perfect political system. And we have to say that any other so-called political systems are unreal impostors which merely reflect the one true system and are more or less commendable, depending on how well regulated they are.

YOUNG SOCRATES   On the whole, I find what you've been saying perfectly reasonable, but the idea that one should rule without a legal code strikes a discordant note.

VISITOR   I was just about to ask *you* a question, Socrates; you got yours in first. 294a I was going to ask whether you were happy with everything I'd been saying, or whether there was anything you objected to. But now I see that you'd like us to discuss the matter of how rulers can be true rulers if they lack a legal code.

YOUNG SOCRATES   Of course I do.

VISITOR   Although from one point of view legislation and kingship do certainly go together, the ideal is for authority to be invested not in a legal code but in an individual who combines kingship with wisdom. I wonder if you can see why.

YOUNG SOCRATES   No, why?

b   VISITOR   Because legislation can never issue perfect instructions which precisely encompass everyone's best interests and guarantee fair play for everyone at once. People and situations differ, and human affairs are characterized by an almost permanent state of instability. It is therefore impossible to devise, for any given situation, a simple rule which will apply to everyone for ever. I'm sure you agree.

YOUNG SOCRATES   Of course.

VISITOR   But that is obviously exactly what the law aims for. It is like a stub-
c   born, stupid person who refuses to allow the slightest deviation from or questioning of his own rules, even if the situation has in fact changed and it turns out to be better for someone to contravene these rules.

YOUNG SOCRATES   You're right. That's an accurate description of how the law treats us.

VISITOR   Well, it's impossible for something which is unremittingly simple to cope well with things which are never simple, isn't it?

YOUNG SOCRATES   I suppose so.

VISITOR   So why do we feel compelled to make laws, since they can never be
d   entirely successful? We'd better try to discover why.

YOUNG SOCRATES   Of course.

VISITOR   Now, here in Athens, as in other states, you have ways of training groups of people to excel at running or some other sport, don't you?

YOUNG SOCRATES   Yes, there are a great many methods for that.

VISITOR   Well, let's try to remember the instructions professional trainers give when they're in charge of these groups.

YOUNG SOCRATES   What are you getting at?

VISITOR   They don't find it possible to deal with people selectively, one by one,
e   and to prescribe an appropriate regimen for each individual. Instead, they find they have to prescribe a collective regimen, one which *usually* benefits *most* people's bodies.

YOUNG SOCRATES   That's right.

VISITOR   And that's also why they assign to all the members of the group the same amount of exercise. Whatever form of physical exercise is involved— running or wrestling or whatever—they start them all off at the same time, and make them all finish at the same time.

YOUNG SOCRATES   True.

VISITOR   I don't think we should ever expect a legislator either to make his
295a   injunctions to his flock in the sphere of morality and human interaction perfectly appropriate to every individual, since he too is issuing instructions for the group as a whole.

YOUNG SOCRATES   Yes, it seems unlikely that he could.

VISITOR   Instead, whether he's issuing written edicts or whether his legislation relies on the unwritten law which consists of time-honoured traditions, his regulations for each community will be rather imprecise and will be concerned, I think, with the majority of the population, with the most common situations, and with being broadly right.

YOUNG SOCRATES   True.

VISITOR   Of course it is, Socrates, because it's impossible to imagine anyone b ever being capable of spending his whole life in close proximity to a given individual, prescribing in minute detail what is appropriate for him. I mean, in my opinion, if anyone with a genuine grasp of kingship were capable of that, he'd hardly complicate things for himself by creating one of these written legal codes we're talking about.

YOUNG SOCRATES   Yes, that certainly follows from what we've been saying.

VISITOR   And it fits even better with the next point, Socrates.

YOUNG SOCRATES   Which is . . . ?

VISITOR   I'll tell you. Let's imagine a doctor or a trainer who is planning a trip c abroad and expects to be away from his charges for quite a long time. If he thought that his trainees or his patients would forget his instructions, he'd want to leave written reminders for them, don't you think?

YOUNG SOCRATES   Yes.

VISITOR   But what if his trip didn't last as long as he'd expected? On his return, wouldn't he go about substituting alternative instructions—ones which went against his original instructions—if an alternative course turned out to be better for his patients because some heaven-sent phenomenon or other d which he hadn't anticipated (the wind, for example) had behaved in an unusual fashion? Would he obstinately insist on adherence to his original regulations, and forbid himself from making any new recommendations and any of his patients from daring to act in any way which went against what he'd written down, on the grounds that his original instructions were medically sound and promoted health, whereas if they were changed they'd promote ill health and wouldn't be based on medical expertise? Isn't it rather the case that when such persistent inflexibility is encountered in a man of knowledge, a true professional, it makes the whole enterprise of rule-making look extremely absurd?   e

YOUNG SOCRATES   Yes, absolutely.

VISITOR   Now consider the founder of one of the written and unwritten codes which ordain norms of justice and injustice, right and wrong, and good and bad for human beings—or at least for those who are herded together in their various states and are subject to their legislators' codes—and suppose this expert legislator or his double were to return. Is he really not to be allowed to make new regulations which contravene the original code? Isn't the truth of the matter that this prohibition would be just as absurd as the one we 296a mentioned before?

YOUNG SOCRATES   Of course.

VISITOR   You know what the usual position is on this, don't you?

YOUNG SOCRATES   I can't recall it just at the moment.

VISITOR   It's the view—which is certainly plausible—that if a person knows of laws which improve on those of his predecessors, he should get them established, but only once he has persuaded his state to approve them, and not otherwise.

YOUNG SOCRATES   Well, that's right, isn't it?

b VISITOR   It may be, but what if force rather than persuasion is used to improve the constitution? What should we call that kind of force, do you think? Actually, no, don't answer that question yet. Let's start with the case we were looking at earlier.

YOUNG SOCRATES   Which one?

VISITOR   Suppose that, for all his expertise, a doctor fails to persuade someone he's treating, and forces this patient of his (who may not be a child, but an adult man or woman) to follow a better course of action which goes against the instructions he had written out before. What shall we call this kind of force? We're hardly going to call it an unprofessional defect which will promote ill health, are we? That's the very last thing we'd say. And a patient who has been at the receiving end of this kind of constraint is entitled to say

c anything he likes about it, except that the doctors who forced the treatment on him dealt with him in an unprofessional manner which was liable to promote ill health.

YOUNG SOCRATES   You're absolutely right.

VISITOR   Now, what do we call a defect in statesmanship? Don't we call it an offence, a wrong, a miscarriage of justice?

YOUNG SOCRATES   Exactly.

VISITOR   What about when people have been forced to go against their written code and their traditions, then, and to follow a course of action which is

d more just, moral and honourable than what they were doing before? How is one to react when these people express dissatisfaction with the constraint they've been subjected to? Wouldn't it be the height of absurdity to say that those who applied the pressure treated those who were at the receiving end of it wrongly, unjustly and badly? Wouldn't that be the last thing one should say?

YOUNG SOCRATES   I couldn't agree more.

VISITOR   And is what they're forced to do right if the pressure comes from a rich person and wrong if it comes from a poor person? Isn't it rather the case that whether or not a person gains approval for his measures, whether he is

e rich or poor, whether he adheres to or contravenes the written code, he can still act in their best interests? This is surely where we must find the truest criterion by which to judge whether or not a state is correctly governed; this is the standard a wise and good ruler uses in his management of his subjects' affairs. Here's an analogy. A ship's captain is constantly trying to

297a ensure the best interests of his ship and crew; the way he keeps everyone on board safe is not by giving them written rules to follow, but by making his expertise available to them—his expertise is their law. It's exactly the same, no different at all, in a state. It is those who are capable of governing in an

equivalent way who are the authors of sound systems of government; they make their expertise available, and their expertise is more effective than a legal code. As long as these wise rulers have the single overriding concern of always using their intelligence and expertise to maximize the justice they b dispense to the state's inhabitants, there's no defect in what they do, is there? After all, they're not only capable of keeping their subjects safe, but they're also doing all they can to make them better people than they were before.

YOUNG SOCRATES   These ideas of yours are undeniable.

VISITOR   And there's a point that was raised earlier which should also be allowed to stand.

YOUNG SOCRATES   Which one are you talking about?

VISITOR   That it's quite out of the question for a large number of people—never mind who they are—to acquire this knowledge and so govern a state with intelligence. No, if we're to discover the one and only perfect political sys- tem we've been talking about, we have to think in terms of scarceness, rar- c ity—uniqueness, even. And we have to count all other systems as more or less commendable reflections of the true set-up, as we said a short while ago.

YOUNG SOCRATES   Actually, I didn't understand what you meant when you talked about reflection before, so could you explain now?

VISITOR   Of course. It would do no good just to raise the idea and leave it there, without a convincing explanation of where current systems go wrong.   d

YOUNG SOCRATES   And where do they go wrong?

VISITOR   Yes, we're going to have to look into this, but it's unfamiliar territory, which makes it hard to investigate. Still, we must try to make sense of it. So . . . on the assumption that the political system we've been talking about is the only perfect one, do you appreciate that other systems have to rely on its written regulations in order to survive? That the course of action they therefore follow is the one which people currently think highly of, although it is not the ideal?

YOUNG SOCRATES   What course of action do you mean?

VISITOR   Forbidding any member of the state to show the slightest inclination e to infringe the laws, and imposing the maximum penalties, up to and including death, on anyone who does dare to do so. Now, there's nothing wrong with this, and it's a perfectly acceptable second-best course of action to fall back on when the ideal we've been discussing has been modified. But do you think we should try to describe how this second-best course, as we called it, starts?

YOUNG SOCRATES   Yes, please.

VISITOR   I think we'd better make further use of the analogies we constantly have to rely on to illustrate the nature of kingship.

YOUNG SOCRATES   What analogies?

VISITOR   Our excellent ship's captain and our doctor "whose worth is that of many others." Let's make them the players in an imaginary scenario and see what we discover.

YOUNG SOCRATES   What scenario?

298a VISITOR   I'll tell you. Suppose it was universally believed that they treat people
terribly—that although, when they want to, members of both professions
keep a person safe and sound, they sometimes choose to injure him. Doctors
use surgery and cautery to injure a patient; then they make him pay them a
fee (which is their equivalent of taxation) and spend next to nothing on him,
but use the bulk of it on themselves and their families; and to cap it all they
b   end up by being bribed by their patient's family, or by an enemy of his, and
killing him. Then there are sea-captains, with a wide variety of alternative
measures at their disposal, whose effect is just the same. Here are just two
of their crimes: they enter into conspiracies against people and leave them
behind in some deserted spot just as they're about to embark, and they
arrange for accidents on the high seas and tip people overboard. So suppose, since this is our impression of them, that we were to make it a matter
of policy that members of these professions are no longer to be allowed
c   unchecked authority over anyone, not even a slave, let alone a free man. We
decide to convene ourselves into an assembly which might either be open
to the whole citizen body or be restricted to the wealthier citizens. We make
it possible for anyone to voice an opinion about sailing and sickness,
whether or not he has any professional knowledge of these or any other
occupations. He can suggest how we are to use drugs and medical equipment in treating the sick, and he can also suggest not only what to do with
d   the actual ships, but also how to make use of nautical equipment to cope
with seafaring and its risks—some of which arise just from the fact of being
out at sea, subject to wind and water, while others arise from encountering
pirates—and whether it is advisable to pit our warships in a naval engage-
ment against other warships.

Once the assembly has heard all this advice, whether it has come from
doctors and captains or else from laymen, the majority decision about these
matters is written up on the official notice-boards and inscribed on stelae
(and also included within the unwritten code consisting of our time-
e   honoured traditions), and from then on it dictates the ways in which sailing
and the treatment of the sick are practised.

YOUNG SOCRATES   You've certainly thought up a strange scenario.

VISITOR   Yes, and it is also our policy, let us suppose, to hold an annual lottery
as a means of appointing people (either from among the wealthier citizens
or the whole citizen body) to rule over the general populace. Once these
rulers have been appointed, they let the written code guide how they direct
shipping and heal the sick.

YOUNG SOCRATES   This is even more difficult to take seriously.

VISITOR   But there's a consequence of all this that you also have to consider.
Once the rulers' year of office is over, we'll have to set up a court and
empanel jurors (who can either be selected from among the wealthier citi-
299a   zens or alternatively be chosen by lot from the whole citizen body), and
bring the rulers before this court for a review. Anyone who wants to can

prosecute any of the rulers for having failed during his year of office to direct shipping in accordance with either our written code or our time-honoured traditions. And the same also goes for those who were responsible for healing the sick. In the case of a guilty verdict, the court decides on the appropriate punishment or fine.

YOUNG SOCRATES   Anyone who voluntarily and of his own free will holds office in circumstances like these deserves any punishment and fine he gets!   b

VISITOR   But we haven't finished yet; there's another decree we'll have to enact in addition to all the regulations we've already made. Anyone who is caught looking into how to direct shipping and thinking about seamanship in general, or enquiring into health and trying to discover the true medical position on the effect of climatic factors such as winds and the temperature—whoever develops theories about these matters which go beyond what has been written down in the legal code—is, first, not to be called an expert in medical or naval matters, but a sophist, talking hot air and drivel; second, anyone who is entitled to may, if he wants, bring an indictment against this person and take him to court on the grounds that he is corrupt-   c ing the young people around him and persuading them to engage illegally in naval and medical matters. And if it is decided that he does influence people of any age to behave illegally and in contravention of the written code, then we shall impose the maximum penalty on him, because no one should presume to know more than the law, seeing that anyone who isn't a medical expert with an understanding of health, or a naval expert with an understanding of commanding ships, can remedy this defect by consulting the established written code and traditions.   d

So, Socrates, suppose this scenario of ours really happened. What would the effect be? Suppose this approach was not restricted to these two branches of knowledge, but was extended to military command and hunting in all its forms, painting and other kinds of representation, carpentry and manufacture of all kinds, and farming and agriculture in general as well. Suppose horse-farming and stock-farming in general were evidently being regulated by a written code, or divination or any other form of service, or backgammon or all the mathematical sciences from straightforward arithmetic to plane e geometry, solid geometry and the study of bodies in motion. If this was how all these branches of knowledge were practised—by reference to a written code and not to expertise—what do you think would happen?

YOUNG SOCRATES   Obviously it would completely obliterate expertise in all its forms, and the ban on research means that there'd be no chance of it ever recurring again either. Life is hard enough as it is, but the effect of all this would be to make life absolutely unbearable in the future.

VISITOR   But here's something else to think about. Suppose all the professions 300a we've mentioned had to conform to written regulations, and we elected (or let a lottery choose) an official to supervise the regulations, but he didn't care about them in the slightest and set about infringing them, not because he knew what he was doing, but perhaps because he'd been bribed, or

because he owed someone a personal favour. This would be an even worse
state of affairs, wouldn't it, though the previous scenario was bad enough?

YOUNG SOCRATES   You're quite right.

b   VISITOR   Yes, he'd be infringing the results of a great deal of experience, I think,
and a great deal of clever advice and persuasive argument. That's what it
took for the laws to become established, and to go about infringing them
would be to commit a far worse error and would undermine all kinds of
activities far more effectively than a written legal code.

YOUNG SOCRATES   Of course it would.

c   VISITOR   And that is why, when laws and statutes *have* been established (whatever situation they may apply to), the second-best course is to prevent any
individual or any body of people from ever infringing them in the slightest.

YOUNG SOCRATES   Right.

VISITOR   Now, these regulations will reflect the truth in their various ways,
since they transcribe as accurately as possible what men of knowledge have
said.

YOUNG SOCRATES   Of course.

VISITOR   And do you remember what we said before about a man of knowledge, a true statesman? We said that if he saw a course of action which
improved on the one he had put into writing and told people to follow
d   while he couldn't be with them, he would throw away the rule-book and
rely on his expertise to guide what he did.

YOUNG SOCRATES   Yes, we did.

VISITOR   So whenever a person or a body of people who do in fact have a code
attempt to do something different, something which contravenes this code,
they're doing their best to behave just as our true statesman would, aren't
they?

YOUNG SOCRATES   Yes.

VISITOR   Doesn't it follow that infringement of law by people who lack knowledge is an attempt—albeit an atrocious attempt—to behave in a way which
reflects something authentic, whereas infringement of law by experts is the
e   absolutely authentic real thing, not a reflection of it?

YOUNG SOCRATES   Definitely.

VISITOR   But we've already established that no large body of people can master any branch of expertise.

YOUNG SOCRATES   Yes, we have.

VISITOR   So—assuming that there is such a thing as expertise at kingship—it
cannot be wealthy people collectively or the general populace as a whole
who have this branch of knowledge, statesmanship, at their command.

YOUNG SOCRATES   Of course not.

VISITOR   States which are governed by these bodies of people apparently have
no choice, then; their only chance of being true reflections of the authentic
301a   political system we've been talking about, which is government by a single
person with expertise, lies in their never allowing the slightest infringement

of their written laws and their time-honoured traditions, once these have been established.

YOUNG SOCRATES   You're quite right.

VISITOR   Now, the term for a political system which reflects the one in question and involves government by wealthy people is "aristocracy," unless they take no notice of the laws, in which case it is called "oligarchy."

YOUNG SOCRATES   That sounds right.

VISITOR   On the other hand, when a single individual who merely reflects the behavior of a man of knowledge and never infringes the legal code is in power, we call him a "king," since we don't have different terms for law-abiding government by a single person, depending on whether he relies on knowledge or belief.

YOUNG SOCRATES   No, I suppose we don't.

VISITOR   There's no different term, then, even if the single ruler is a genuinely knowledgeable person: we still use the word and call him a "king." And that's why there are no more than five terms in all for the systems of government we mentioned earlier.

YOUNG SOCRATES   Yes, I suppose that's why.

VISITOR   What about when a single ruler contravenes both law and tradition, while making the same claim that our man of knowledge makes—that he has to infringe written law in order to get the best result—when in fact his reflection of the man of knowledge is being prompted by mere ignorant desire? These are the circumstances which make us call a single ruler a "dictator," aren't they?

YOUNG SOCRATES   Naturally.

VISITOR   So there we have the provenance of dictators, kings, oligarchy, aristocracy and democracy. These systems are a result of discomfort with the kind of government by a single individual that we've been talking about. People doubt that anyone could ever live up to this ideal rulership; they doubt the possibility of a moral and knowledgeable ruler who would dispense justice and deal fairly with everyone in the matter of their rights; and if such a ruler were possible, they doubt that he would be prepared to rule in that way, rather than injuring and killing and harming any of us whenever he felt like it. And yet, if they were faced with the kind of ruler we're describing, people would feel perfectly comfortable; he'd take sole command of the only system of government which, if we were speaking strictly, we would call authentic, and he'd govern in a way which guaranteed their happiness.

YOUNG SOCRATES   He certainly would.

VISITOR   But what we're saying is that in real life countries aren't like hives of bees: they don't simply grow a king—an individual whose physical and mental attributes make him stand out from the rest. The only way people can follow the scent of the true political system is apparently by forming assemblies and drawing up written codes.

YOUNG SOCRATES   I suppose so.

VISITOR   So does it come as any surprise, Socrates, to find that these systems are and will continue to be thoroughly rotten, given that they are based on the inadequate foundation of relying on statutes and traditions to guide their actions, when anyone can see that every other branch of knowledge finds that this way of going about things produces disastrous results? Isn't it more surprising to see the inherent strength which states exhibit? I mean, they've been suffering under these systems from time immemorial, but some of them still manage to remain stable and avoid catastrophe. Nevertheless, states do from time to time founder like ships—they often have in the past, and they will continue to do so in the future—as a result of having bad commanders and crew, the extent of whose ignorance is matched only by the importance of the matters they are ignorant about. Despite their total ignorance of statesmanship, they believe that there's no subject which they have mastered more surely and more thoroughly.

YOUNG SOCRATES   This is all too true.

VISITOR   Now, although these flawed political systems all make life difficult, I wonder whether we ought to decide where they stand on a scale from least disagreeable to most oppressive. It may not be strictly relevant to the matter at hand, but it remains the case, generally speaking, that in virtually everything we do we bear this kind of thing in mind.

YOUNG SOCRATES   Yes, I'm sure we ought to decide about this.

c VISITOR   On a threefold division of the systems, you'll find that one of them makes life particularly difficult *and* particularly easy at the same time.

YOUNG SOCRATES   What do you mean?

VISITOR   Just that the three systems we mentioned at the beginning of this argument (which has now burst its banks) were government by a single person, by a limited number of people and by a large number of people.

YOUNG SOCRATES   Yes, that's right.

VISITOR   Well, if we split each of them in two, then we have six, not counting the authentic system which is the seventh.

YOUNG SOCRATES   Can you explain?

d VISITOR   Government by a single person generates kingship and dictatorship; government by a limited number generates the creditable version, aristocracy, and oligarchy; and government by a large number of people generates something which we earlier counted as single and called "democracy," but now we'd better divide this kind of government as well into two categories.

YOUNG SOCRATES   But how? What criterion do we use?

VISITOR   The same one as usual. The fact that a single term is involved here doesn't make any difference. It's just as possible for there to be law-abiding and law-breaking versions of it as of the others.

YOUNG SOCRATES   True.

VISITOR   We didn't need to divide it before, when we were trying to discover what the perfect system of government was, because (as we explained at the time) it wouldn't have helped us then. But now we're not taking the perfect system into consideration, and we've found that the others are what we're forced to live with. And the issue of legality and illegality is what divides each of these others into two.

YOUNG SOCRATES   I find this argument of yours quite convincing.

VISITOR   Now when government by a single person is harnessed by adherence to a sound set of stipulations, which we call a legal code, it is the best of the six. When it has no regard for law, however, it is oppressive and makes life difficult.

YOUNG SOCRATES   It looks as though you're right.   303a

VISITOR   And I think we should regard government by a limited number of people as occupying the middle position in both the law-abiding and the law-breaking tables, as is suggested by the fact that "few" falls between "one" and "many." Government by a large number of people is thoroughly feeble, however; compared with the other systems, it is incapable of being an effective force for either good or ill, because under this system authority is broken up into tiny portions and distributed to so many people. That's why it's the worst of all the law-abiding systems, and the best of all the law-breaking ones. If no political system restrained its subjects, life in a democ-   b racy would take the first prize; if they all did, democracy would be the last one to live in, and the one which would stand out as by far the best is the first one on the list. All this is not counting the seventh system, which we should keep as far apart from all the rest as God is from humankind.

YOUNG SOCRATES   Your conclusions seem to be inescapable.

COMMENTS

Plato vigorously opposes the idea that everybody is equally equipped to exercise political rule. One of the constant themes of his political thought is that there is such a thing as expertise in politics, just as there is in other areas of practical life. In many of his dialogues, Plato develops the idea of political expertise, but he does not provide much argument that there is such a thing. Like the author of *Twofold Arguments*, he takes the existence of skill in other areas to be so obvious that it is perverse to deny it in politics. In the *Republic* extract, he relies on analogies with experts like physicians and navigators to make his point. In the *Statesman* passage, we find arguments to support the analogies.

For Plato, political experts would be not practical politicians, but people who have knowledge of politics, and for him this requires abstract reflection and thought. In the *Republic,* he takes these people to be philosophers, but in the *Statesman,* he calls them kings; either way, they are ideal, knowledgeable rulers. Note that in both passages Plato is openly indifferent to the consent of the people being ruled. Does the analogy of expertise justify this view?

The *Statesman* makes the point that an expert can deal with individual cases properly; however, laws are inevitably stated in general terms that apply imperfectly to the complexities of individual cases. Moreover, political institutions tend to serve as clogs in the functioning of expertise. The main speaker, the Visitor from Elea, satirizes the workings of Athenian institutions. Anybody is supposed to be as expert on any political topic as anyone else, so the real expert gets no recognition. Moreover, he has to cope with committees before he starts and committees when he finishes and must always exactly follow the letter of the law. Plato's argument appeals to efficiency; where political expertise is not recognized, everyone, not just the expert, suffers.

This whole argument is hypothetical, and the *Statesman* brings this point out. *If* political rule were in the hands of experts, then laws and committees would be nothing but a nuisance. But if we do not actually have experts, then laws serve as protection against the abuse of power, and it is better to have them than not. Democratic laws fragment power as much as they can, so if there were ideal expert rulers, these laws would be the worst to live under. But in the actual world, there are no experts, so these laws, which protect against individual bribery and abuse of power, are the best to live under.

Is Plato overemphasizing the importance of efficiency in government? Are there other important factors in democratic government that he neglects to consider? If democracy is the best form of government in the actual world, does it matter that it would not be the best in an ideal world?

Politics I, 1; III, 4, 11
ARISTOTLE

I.1

Observation shows us, first, that every city [*polis*] is a species of association, and, secondly, that all associations come into being for the sake of some good—for all men do all their acts with a view to achieving something which is, in their view, a good. It is clear therefore that all associations aim at some good, and that the particular association which is the most sovereign of all, and includes all the rest, will pursue this aim most, and will thus be directed to the most sovereign of all goods. This most sovereign and inclusive association is the city [or *polis*], as it is called, or the political association.

It is a mistake to believe that the statesman is the same as the monarch of a kingdom, or the manager of a household, or the master of a number of slaves. Those who hold this view consider that each one of these differs from the others not with a difference of kind, but according to the number, large or small, of those with whom he deals. On this view someone who is concerned with few people is a master, someone who is concerned with more is the manager of a household, and someone who is concerned with still more is a statesman, or a monarch. This view abolishes any real difference between a large household and a small city; and it also reduces the difference between the "statesman" and the monarch to the one fact that the latter has an uncontrolled and sole authority, while the former exercises his authority in conformity with the rules imposed by the art of statesmanship and as one who rules and is ruled in turn. But this is a view which cannot be accepted as correct.

Our point will be made clear if we proceed to consider the matter according to our normal method of analysis. Just as, in all other fields, a compound should be analysed until we reach its simple elements (or, in other words, the smallest parts of the whole which it constitutes), so we must also consider analytically the elements of which a city is composed. We shall then gain a better insight into the way in which these differ from one another; and we shall also be in a position to discover whether there is any kind of expertise to be acquired in connection with the matters under discussion.

III, 4

A question connected with those which have just been discussed is the question whether the excellence of a good man and that of a good citizen are identical or different. If this question is to be investigated, we must first describe the excellence of the citizen in some sort of outline. Just as a sailor is a member of an association, so too is a citizen. Sailors differ from one another in virtue of the different capacities in which they act: one is a rower, another a steersman, another a look-out man; and others will have still other such titles. It is, nevertheless, clear that, while the most accurate definition of the excellence of each sailor will be special to the man concerned, a common definition of excellence will apply to all, inasmuch as safety in navigation is the common task of all and the object at which each of the sailors aims. The same is also true of citizens. Though they differ, the end which they all serve is the safety of their association; and this association consists in the constitution. The conclusion to which we are thus led is that the excellence of the citizen must be an excellence relative to the constitution. It follows that if there are several different kinds of constitution there cannot be a single absolute excellence of the good citizen. But the good man is a man so called in virtue of a single absolute excellence.

It is thus clear that it is possible to be a good citizen without possessing the excellence by which one is a good man. But we may reach the same conclusion in another way, by discussing the question with particular reference to the best constitution. Although it is impossible for a city to be composed entirely of good men, each citizen must, none the less, perform well his particular function and this requires [the appropriate kind of] excellence. But, since it is impossible for all the citizens to be alike, the excellence of a citizen cannot be identical with that of a good man. The excellence of a good citizen must belong to all citizens, because that is the condition necessary for the city being the best city; but the excellence of a good man cannot possibly belong to all—unless, indeed, we hold that every citizen of a good city must also be a good man. Furthermore, the city is composed of unlike elements. Just as a living being is composed of soul and body, or the soul of the different elements of reason and appetite, or the household of man and wife, or property of master and slave, so the city too is composed of different and unlike elements, among them not only the various elements already mentioned, but also others in addition. It follows that there cannot be a single excellence common to all the citizens, any more than there can be a single excellence common to the leader of a dramatic chorus and his assistants.

Although it is clear from these considerations why they are not in all cases identical, the question may still be raised whether there are not some cases in which the excellence of the good man and that of the good citizen are the same. We say that a good ruler is a good man and possesses practical wisdom, while the citizen does not need to have practical wisdom. Indeed there are some who hold that the very training of the ruler should be, from the first, of a different kind; and it is a matter of observation that the sons of kings are specially trained in riding and the art of war. Thus Euripides says

No subtleties for me,
But what the city most needs.

which implies a special training for the ruler. We may thus assume that the excellence of the good ruler is identical with that of the good man. But subjects too are citizens. It follows that the excellence of the good citizen cannot be identical with that of the good man in all cases, though it may be so in a particular case. The excellence of the ordinary citizen is different from that of the ruler; and this may well be the reason why Jason [the tyrant of Pherae] said that he was "a hungry man except when he was tyrant," meaning that he did not know how to live as an ordinary person.

On the other hand, people hold in esteem the capacity both to rule and to obey, and they regard the excellence of a good citizen as being a matter of ruling and obeying well. Now if the excellence of the good man is in ruling, while that of the good citizen is in both ruling and obeying, these two excellences cannot be held in the same esteem.

Since it thus seems that ruler and ruled should acquire different kinds of knowledge, rather than the same kind, while the citizen should have both sorts of knowledge, and share in both, we can now see the next step which our argument has to take. There is rule of the sort which is exercised by a master; and by this we mean the sort of rule connected with the necessary functions of life. Here it is not necessary for the ruler to know how to do the task himself, but only to know how to use those who do: indeed the former kind of knowledge (by which we mean an ability to do menial services personally) has a servile character. There are a number of kinds of servant, because there are a number of kinds of menial service which have to be rendered. One of these forms of service is that which is rendered by manual labourers. These, as their very name signifies, are those who live by the work of their hands; and the menial craftsman [or mechanic] belongs to this class. This is the reason why in some cities the manual workers were once upon a time excluded from office, in the days before the institution of the extreme form of democracy. The occupations pursued by those who are subject to rule of the sort just mentioned need never be studied by the good man, or by the statesman, or by the good citizen—except occasionally and in order to satisfy some personal need, in which case there ceases to be any question of the relation of master and slave.

But there is also rule of the sort which is exercised over those who are similar in birth to the ruler, and are similarly free. Rule of this sort is what we call political rule; and this is the sort of rule which the ruler must begin to learn by being ruled—just as one learns to be a commander of cavalry by serving under another commander, or to be a general of infantry by serving under another general and by acting first as colonel and, even before that, as captain. This is why it is a good saying that "you cannot be ruler unless you have first been ruled." Ruler and ruled have indeed different excellences; but the fact remains that the good citizen must possess the knowledge and the capacity requisite for ruling as well as for being ruled, and the excellence of a citizen may be defined as consisting in "a knowledge of rule over free men from both points of view."

III, 11

The other alternatives may be reserved for later inquiry; but the suggestion that the people at large should be sovereign rather than the few best men would [seem to present problems which] need resolution, and while it presents some difficulty it perhaps also contains some truth. There is this to be said for the many: each of them by himself may not be of a good quality; but when they all come together it is possible that they may surpass—collectively and as a body, although not individually—the quality of the few best, in much the same way that feasts to which many contribute may excel those provided at one person's expense. For when there are many, each has his share of goodness and practical wisdom; and, when all meet together, the people may thus become something like a single person, who, as he has many feet, many hands, and many senses, may also have many qualities of character and intelligence. This is the reason why the many are also better judges of music and the writings of poets: some appreciate one part, some another, and all together appreciate all. The thing which makes a good man differ from a unit in the crowd—as it is also the thing which is generally said to make a beautiful person differ from one who is not beautiful, or an artistic representation differ from ordinary reality—is that elements which are elsewhere scattered and separate are here combined in a unity. If the elements are taken separately, one may say of an artistic representation that it is surpassed by the eye of this person and by some other feature of that.

It is not clear, however, that this contrast between the many, on the one hand, and the few good men, on the other, can apply to every people and to every large group. Perhaps, by heaven, there are some of which it clearly cannot be true; for otherwise the same argument would apply to the beasts. Yet what difference, one may ask, is there between some men and the beasts? All the same, there is nothing to prevent the view we have stated from being true of a particular group.

It would thus seem possible to solve, by the considerations we have advanced, both the problem raised in the previous chapter ["Which people should be sovereign?"] and the further problem which follows upon it, "What are the matters over which freemen, or the general body of citizens—the sort of people who neither have wealth nor can make any claim on the ground of goodness—should properly exercise sovereignty?" Of course there is a danger in people of this sort sharing in the highest offices, as injustice may lead them into wrongdoing, and thoughtlessness into error. But there is also a serious risk in not letting them have some share of power; for a city with a body of disfranchised citizens who are numerous and poor must necessarily be a city which is full of enemies. The alternative left is to let them share in the deliberative and judicial functions. This is why Solon, and some of the other legislators, allow the people to elect officials and to call them to account at the end of their tenure of office, but not to hold office themselves in their individual capacity. When they all meet together, the people display a good enough gift of perception, and combined with the better class they are of service to the city (just as impure food, when it is mixed with pure, makes the whole concoction more nutritious than a small amount of the pure would be); but each of them is imperfect in the judgements he forms by himself.

But this arrangement of the constitution presents some difficulties. The first difficulty is that it may well be held that the function of judging when medical attendance has been properly given should belong to those whose profession it is to attend patients and cure the complaints from which they suffer—in a word, to members of the medical profession. The same may be held to be true of all other professions and arts; and just as medical men should have their conduct examined before a body of medics, so, too, should those who follow other professions have theirs examined before a body of members of their own profession. But the term "medic" is applied to the ordinary practitioner, to the specialist who directs the course of treatment, and to someone who has some general knowledge of the art of medicine. (There are people of this last type to be found in connection with nearly all the arts.) We credit those who have a general knowledge with the power of judging as much as we do the experts. When we turn to consider the matter of election, the same principles would appear to apply. To make a proper election is equally the work of experts. It is the work of those who are versed in geometry to choose a geometrician, or again, of those who are acquainted with steering to choose a steersman; and even if, in some occupations and arts, there are some non-experts who also share in the ability to choose, they do not share in a higher degree than the experts. It would thus appear, on this line of argument, that the people should not be made sovereign, either in the matter of election of magistrates or in that of their examination.

It may be, however, that these arguments are not altogether well founded for the reason given above—provided, that is to say, that the people are not too debased in character. Each individual may indeed be a worse judge than the experts; but all, when they meet together, are either better than experts or at any rate no worse. In the second place, there are a number of arts in which the craftsman is not the only, or even the best, judge. These are the arts whose products can be understood even by those who do not possess any skill in the art. A house, for instance, is something which can be understood by others besides the builder: indeed the user of a house, or in other words the householder, will judge it even better than he does. In the same way a steersman will judge a rudder better than a shipwright does; and the diner, not the cook, will be the best judge of a feast.

The first difficulty would appear to be answered sufficiently by these considerations. But there is a second difficulty still to be faced, which is connected with the first. It would seem to be absurd that people of poor character should be sovereign on issues which are more important than those assigned to the better sort of citizens. The election of officials, and their examination at the end of their tenure, are the most important of issues; and yet there are constitutions, as we have seen, under which these issues are assigned to the people, since the assembly is sovereign in all such matters. To add to the difficulty, membership of the assembly, which carries deliberative and judicial functions, is vested in people of little property and of any age; but a high property qualification is demanded from those who serve as treasurers or generals, or hold any of the highest offices.

This difficulty too may, however, be met in the same way as the first; and the practice followed in these constitutions is perhaps, after all, correct. It is not the individual juryman, councillor, or assemblyman, who is vested with office, but the court, the council, or the popular assembly; and in these bodies each member, whether he be a councillor, an assemblyman, or a juryman, is simply a part of the whole. It is therefore just that the people should be sovereign on the more important issues, since the assembly, the council, and the court consist of many people. Moreover, the property owned by all these people is greater than that of those who either as individuals or as members of small bodies hold the highest offices.

This may serve as a settlement of the difficulties which have been discussed. But the discussion of the first of these difficulties leads to one conclusion above all others. Rightly constituted laws should be [the final] sovereign; but rulers, whether one or many, should be sovereign in those matters on which law is unable, owing to the difficulty of framing general rules for all contingencies, to make an exact pronouncement. But what rightly constituted laws ought to be is a matter that is not yet clear; and here we are still confronted by the difficulty stated at the end of the previous chapter. Laws must be good or bad, just or unjust in the same way as the constitutions to which they belong. The one clear fact is that laws must be laid down in accordance with constitutions; and if this is the case, it follows that laws which are in accordance with right constitutions must necessarily be just, and laws which are in accordance with perverted constitutions must be unjust.

COMMENTS

Aristotle often thinks that a question under discussion has been considered in too simple a way—in this case, whether political rule should be entrusted to experts. More thought should go into the preliminary work of establishing what political rule is and what it is not. In the opening chapter of book I of the *Politics,* he starts an investigation of what political rule is by examining the nature of the state; we need to know what makes a state different from other forms of association before we can characterize the kind of rule exercised in it. In the process, he explicitly criticizes Plato's *Statesman* (in a passage different from the previous one, the main speaker claims that size is the only thing that distinguishes a small city from a large household).

In book III, chapter 4, Aristotle is trying to answer the puzzle of whether the virtue of a good person is the same as or different from the virtue of a good citizen. His answer to this question is tangled and difficult to follow, but in the process he says a good deal about political rule. Rule in a state is rule over fellow-citizens and, therefore, has to take account of the fact that you are exercising authority over people who are your political equals. This makes it fundamentally different from other forms of authority that are not exercised over political equals; Aristotle thinks that the authority of a head of a household is of this sort. Even though we reject the idea that there are legitimate forms of authority that are rule over unequals (the nearest we come to this is a parent's authority over a child), we can still recognize the distinction Aristotle is concerned to draw. In his insistence that political authority is constrained by its being exercised over people with political rights equal to those of the person in authority, he contrasts strongly with Plato.

In book III, chapter 11, Aristotle strongly criticizes the idea that political rule is at all like expertise. In fields in which we recognize experts, we take their judgment as authoritative, whereas in politics this is not the case; the final judgment on policies is made by the people affected, not the experts. He also produces arguments in support of collective decision making that defend it against the kind of criticism produced by Plato.

It is clear from these passages that Aristotle knew the *Statesman* well and thought it important to show how and why Plato's ideas were fundamentally mistaken.

C. Democracy and the Best Form of Government

Debates about the best form of government in the ancient world begin by assuming that the relevant choice is between the rule of one (monarchy), the rule of a few (oligarchy), and the rule of the many (democracy). Later this simple framework is modified in more subtle ways.

Histories III, 80–83

HERODOTUS

Five days later, when things had settled down, the conspirators against the Magi met to discuss the general state of things. There are those in Greece who are not convinced of the authenticity of the speeches that were delivered there, but they did take place. Otanes recommended entrusting the management of the country to the Persian people. "It is my view," he said, "that we should put an end to the system whereby one of us is the sole ruler. Monarchy is neither an attractive nor a noble institution. You have seen how vicious Cambyses became and you have also experienced similar behaviour from the Magus. How can monarchy be an orderly affair, when a monarch has the licence to do whatever he wants, without being accountable to anyone? Make a man a monarch, and even if he is the most moral person in the world, he will leave his customary ways of thinking. All the advantages of his position breed arrogant abusiveness in him, and envy is ingrained in human nature anyway. With these two qualities he has in himself every evil: all his atrocities can be attributed to an excess of abusiveness or envy. Now, you might think that an absolute ruler is bound to be free from envy, since there is nothing good that he lacks, but in fact his natural attitude towards his people is the opposite of what you would expect. He resents the existence of the best men, while the worst of them make him happy. There is no one better than him at welcoming slander, and there is no one more erratic in his behaviour. I mean, if your admiration for him is moderate, he is offended at your lack of total subservience, and if you are totally subservient, he is angry at you as a flatterer. And now I come to the most important problems with monarchy. A monarch subverts a country's ancestral customs, takes women against their will, and kills men without trial. What about majority rule, on the other hand? In the first place, it has the best of all names to describe it—equality before the law. In the second place, it is entirely free of the vices of monarchy. It is government by lot, it is accountable government, and it refers all decisions to

---

Herodotus, *Histories*, translated by Robin Waterfield (Oxford: Oxford University Press, 1998). Reprinted with the permission of Oxford University Press.

the common people. So I propose that we abandon monarchy and increase the power of the people, because everything depends on their numbers." These were Otanes' thoughts.

Next Megabyzus spoke in favour of oligarchy. "Otanes' arguments for abolishing monarchy," he said, "represent my own views too. However, in so far as he was recommending the transference of power to the general populace, his argument is flawed. A mob is ineffective, and there is nothing more stupid or more given to brutality. People are hardly going to tolerate escaping from the brutality of a despot only to fall into the brutal clutches of the unruly masses, when any action taken by a despot is the action of someone who knows what he is doing, but knowledge and the masses are incompatible. How could anyone know what is right without either having been taught it or having innate awareness of it? No, the approach of the general populace is that of a river swollen with winter rain: they rush blindly forward and sweep things before them. Let us leave democracy to Persia's enemies, while we choose a number of the best men and put power in their hands. After all, we will be members of such a company, and it is reasonable to assume that the best men make the best decisions." This was Megabyzus' proposal.

The third person to express his opinion was Darius, and he said, "I think Megabyzus was right in what he said about the masses, but wrong about oligarchy. There are three choices before us, and let us suppose that each of them is the best of its kind—the best democracy, the best oligarchy, and the best monarchy. In my opinion, the best monarchy far outstrips the others. I mean, if you have a single person, and he is the best person in the world, how could you hope to improve on that? His views are the best there are, he can govern the people blamelessly, and he is particularly good at keeping to himself his plans against hostile opponents. In an oligarchy, however, a number of people are trying to benefit the community, and in this situation violent personal feuds tend to arise, because every one of them wants to come out on top and have his own views prevail. This leads them to become violently antagonistic towards one another, so that factions arise, which lead to bloodshed, which leads ultimately to monarchy—which just goes to show that it is by far the best system. Then again, corruption is inevitable in a democracy. So, in the context of corruption in the political sphere, the corrupt ones become firm friends, rather than opponents, because corrupt practitioners of politics act by forming alliances. This kind of thing goes on until someone emerges as a champion of the people and puts an end to these corrupt politicians. But by doing this he wins the admiration of the people, and then he turns out to be a monarch. So he again is proof that monarchy is the best system. One point sums the whole thing up—where did we get our independence from and who gave it to us? Was it the people or an oligarchy or a monarch? My view, then, is that since we gained our freedom thanks to a single individual, we should keep to this way of doing things. And I would add that we should not abolish our ancestral customs, which serve us well. That is not the way to improve matters."

These were the three views that were put forward for consideration. Four out of the seven endorsed Darius' view. Finding that his proposal recommending for Persia the idea of equality before the law had been defeated, Otanes spoke openly to all of them. "My fellow conspirators," he said, "whether we choose by lot, or give the Persian people the chance to elect their preferred candidate, or use some other method, it will obviously be one of us who is to become king. Under these circumstances, I am not going to stand against you as a candidate; I have as little desire to be a ruler as I have to be ruled. However, I renounce my claim to the kingdom on one condition—that I and my descendants should never be ruled by any of you." The other six agreed to his idea, so he stood down and did not compete against them for the kingdom. And to this day the house of Otanes is the only house in Persia which remains free and, while obeying the laws of the Persians, is subject to the king only to the extent that it wishes to be.

COMMENTS

Herodotus inserts this discussion of the relative merits of the rule of one, a few, and many at the point in his account of the rise of the Persian empire when Darius successfully seizes power. Although he insists that the debate occurred, and may even have believed that it did, the discussion obviously illustrates Greek attitudes to the matter more than Persian ones. One point of the story is to insist that the Persians chose to be ruled by a monarch, even when they were aware of alternatives (which, it is implied, that Greeks would never do). In contrast, Otanes, the supporter of democracy, is given a defense of it that would appeal to Greeks, and the particularly unlikely sequel stresses the point that for Greeks, the individual self-assertion that requires that democracy is the only form of government it will tolerate does not exclude obedience to laws—only to rule by another individual.

Although Herodotus is intellectually naive, his posing of the alternatives here captures what was for some time seen as the basic choice—rule by one person, by a few, or by the many. Democracy here is rule by the majority; it does not include a necessary connection to considering the interests of everybody, including members of the minority. It is worth thinking about some differences between this view of democracy and modern ones.

THE OLD OLIGARCH

A short work has come down among the writings of Xenophon, an Athenian politician and one of the followers of Socrates, but scholars have shown that it is not by Xenophon. The author is writing about fifth-century Athens, and from the fact that he refers to the Athenians as both "they" and "we," scholars have inferred that he was a voluntary or involuntary exile. It is easy to see why he has been named the Old Oligarch; he makes a strikingly frank presentation of his antidemocratic views.

Selections

THE OLD OLIGARCH

My subject is the constitution (*politeia*) of the Athenians. I do not approve their choice of this type of constitution, for in making their choice they preferred the well-being of the inferior class (*poñeroi*) at the expense of the better class. For this reason, then, I do not approve of it. But since they think these policies best, I will show how they successfully preserve their constitution and manage their other affairs in ways that seem mistaken to the rest of the Greeks.

My first point is this: It is just for the poor and the common people (*dēmos*) there to have more than the well-born and wealthy because it is the common people who man the ships and confer power on the city—helmsmen, signal-men, captains, look-out men, and shipwrights—these are the ones who confer power on the city much more than the hoplites, the well-born and the better class. Since this is the case, it seems just to allow everyone access to the political offices, whether assigned by lot or election, and to allow any citizen to speak if he wishes. Second, the people do not ask that the offices that bring safety to the people if managed well, and danger to all if managed poorly, be open to every-one: they don't think they should be given access by lot to positions of general or cavalry commander. For the people know that it is more beneficial for them not to hold these offices, but to let the most capable men hold them. They them-selves seek to hold only the offices that carry a salary and bring personal gain.

Now it surprises some that everywhere they distribute more to the inferior class, the poor, and the common people than to the better class, but it is clear that in precisely this way they preserve democracy. For when the poor, the common people, and the worst citizens are well off and their kind is many, they increase the power of the democracy, but when the wealthy and the better class are well

From Gagarin, Michael and Woodruff, Paul (eds.), *Early Greek Political Thought from Homer to the Sophists* (Cambridge: Cambridge University Press, 1995). Reprinted with the permission of Cambridge University Press.

off, the common people are making their opposition stronger. Everywhere on earth the best element is opposed to democracy. For in the best citizens there is the least injustice and lack of restraint and the greatest concern for good things, but in the common people there is the greatest ignorance, unruliness, and wickedness. For poverty drives them more to shameful acts, and some men go without culture and education for lack of money.

Someone might say that they should not allow everyone equal opportunity to speak and to deliberate, but only the most skillful and the best men. Yet here too in allowing even the lower class to speak they show excellent judgment. For if the better class alone spoke and deliberated, the results would be good for those like themselves but not good for those belonging to the common class. But as it is, any inferior man who wishes rises up and speaks and tries to obtain what is good for himself and those like himself. Someone might ask how a man of this sort would know what is good for himself and the common people, but they know that the ignorance, baseness, and good will of this man is more advantageous than the excellence, wisdom, and ill will of a better man. A city would not be the best as a result of such practices, but in this way democracy would be most effectively preserved. For the common people do not want to be slaves in a city with good government, but to be free and hold power. Bad government is of little concern to them. And what you regard as a government of bad laws is, in fact, the source of the common people's strength and freedom. If you seek good government, you will first see the most skillful men establishing the laws. Then the better class will restrain the inferior class, and the better class will make decisions about the city's affairs and not allow madmen to deliberate or speak or form an assembly. Through these good practices, however, the common people would very quickly fall into slavery. In Athens, on the other hand, the slaves and the *metics* [resident aliens] show the greatest lack of restraint. There, one is not permitted to strike them, and a slave will not step aside for you. I will explain why this is their custom. If it were lawful for a free man to strike a slave or a *metic* or a freedman, one would often strike an Athenian, thinking he was a slave! For the common people there dress no better than the slaves and *metics*, nor is their physical appearance any better. And if anyone is also surprised that they allow slaves there to live luxuriously and some of them magnificently, clearly they do this too by design. For where there is a naval power, it is necessary to be slaves to one's slaves in order to pay for their services, and eventually to set them free. And where there are wealthy slaves, it is no longer advantageous for my slave to be afraid of you. In Sparta, my slave is afraid of you, and if your slave fears me, he will risk giving up even his own money so that he can avoid any risk of bodily harm. So, for this reason we gave slaves the same freedom to speak as free men and *metics* the same freedom to speak as citizens, because the city needs *metics* for many businesses and for the fleet. And so, for this reason, it was reasonable for us to give the *metics* equal freedom to speak.

But then again, they do not tolerate any satire or censure of the people as a whole, so that they will not hear themselves being maligned, but they encourage anyone who wishes to satirize an individual; for they are well aware that the person satirized is usually wealthy, or well born, or powerful, rather than from the people or the masses. Only a few of the poor or the common people are satirized, and these only if they are meddlesome or have sought to raise themselves above the people. They don't mind seeing such people satirized also.

So I say that the common people at Athens recognize which citizens are better and which are inferior. With full knowledge of this, they favor those who are useful to them and serve their interests, even if they are inferior; and they tend to be hostile toward good men. For they do not believe that the excellence of these men by nature favors the good of the people but rather their harm. And yet in contrast to this, some are truly on the people's side, but they are not democratic by nature. I can understand democracy for the common people. It is understandable when anyone pursues his own well-being. But if someone who is not from the common people has chosen, nonetheless, to live in a democratic instead of an oligarchic city, he is prepared to commit injustice and has recognized that a bad man is better able to go unnoticed in a democratic city than in an oligarchic one.

Still, I notice that some people also criticize the Athenians because sometimes a man there cannot transact his business with the Council or the Assembly, even if he sits waiting all year. The only reason this happens at Athens is the size of their agenda: they cannot send everyone on his way with his business fully transacted. Indeed, how could they? First, they need to celebrate more festivals than any other Greek city and on these occasions they are less able to conduct any of the city's business. Then, they have to decide more civil and criminal cases and conduct more examinations into the conduct of their officials than all other people combined. And the Council has to make many decisions about the war, about raising revenues and making laws, about local city matters that arise constantly, and about matters concerning the allies. It must also see to the receipt of tribute and the supervision of dockyards and shrines. Is it any wonder then that they are unable to transact business with everyone when so many other matters concern them? Some say: "If a man approaches the Council or the Assembly with money in his hands, he transacts his business." And I would agree with them that much is accomplished in Athens with money, and even more would get done if more people brought money. I am quite certain, however, that the city lacks the resources to accomplish everyone's business, no matter how much gold and silver one might offer it!

COMMENTS

The Old Oligarch is one of the more unpleasant people whose words we can read from the ancient world, but he is intelligent. His position about democracy is straightforward: It is the rule of the people, the *dēmos*, the poor majority, in their own interest. Since he is not one of the people, democracy is against his interest, so he is against it. Nonetheless, he is quite dispassionate in his account of how the people do act in their own interest.

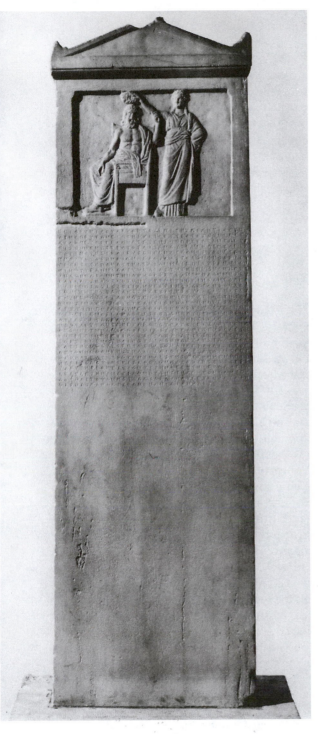

Here *Dēmokratia* (Democracy) is shown crowning *Dēmos* (the People) in an inscription from the Athenian Agora (marketplace). The inscription dates from 336 B.C., well after the heyday of Athenian democracy, and reflects anxiety about the status of democracy in the period after the king of Macedonia, Philip II, father of Alexander the Great, had defeated an alliance of Greek cities. The decree provides that if anyone subverts the democracy with a view to tyranny or tries to overthrow the rule of the people, anyone who kills him shall be free from penalty. (It also provides for the expense of carving and setting up two inscriptions recording the decree.) (Inscription from 336 B.C., from the Athenian Agora. American School of Classical Studies at Athens. Copyright © Agora Excavations 19 American Studies at Athens. Photograph by Craig A. Mauzy.)

We may wonder if the Old Oligarch is right in being so definite that democracy is the rule of the majority in their own interest. Still, here we have some interesting reactions to the understanding of democracy as majority rule. Some of the Old Oligarch's reactions are simply hateful, such as his comments about slaves and the poor. But he makes some perceptive points—such as that a democracy is self-protective in not allowing democratic ideas to be satirized and allowing mockery only of "enemies of the people." Also, it is interesting that he complains that in a democracy the amount of official business greatly increases. Democracy, he holds, is inefficient because there are large number of officials who make work for themselves and each other. The complaint that democracy creates this kind of bureaucratic inefficiency is one that Plato also stresses.

Politics IV, 3, 4, 7–9, 11
ARISTOTLE

3. The reason why there are many different constitutions is to be found in the fact that every city has many different parts. In the first place, every city is obviously composed of households. Secondly, in this number there are bound to be some rich, some poor, and some in the middle, with the rich possessing and the poor being without the equipment of the heavy-armed soldier. Thirdly, the common people [or *dēmos*] are engaged partly in agriculture, partly in trade, and partly in menial jobs. Fourthly, there are also differences among the notables— differences based on their wealth and the amount of their property; and these differences appear, for example, in the matter of keeping horses. This can only be done by the very wealthy, which is the reason why cities whose strength lay in cavalry were in former times the homes of oligarchies. These oligarchies used their cavalry in wars with adjoining cities: we may cite the examples of Eretria and Chalcis [in the island of Euboea] and of Magnesia on the Maeander and many other cities in Asia Minor. Besides differences of wealth, there is also difference of birth, and difference of merit; and there are differences based on other factors of the same order—factors already described as being parts of a city in our discussion of aristocracy, where we distinguished and enumerated the essential parts from which every city is composed.

Sometimes all these parts share in the control of the constitution; sometimes only a few of them share; sometimes a number of them share. It thus follows clearly that there must be a number of constitutions, which differ from one another in kind. This is because the parts differ in kind from one another. A constitution is an arrangement in regard to the offices of the city. By this arrangement the citizen body distributes office, either on the basis of the power of those who participate in it, or on the basis of some sort of general equality (i.e. the equality of the poor, or of the rich, or an equality existing among both rich and poor). There must therefore be as many constitutions as there are modes of arranging the distribution of office according to the superiorities and the differences of the parts of the city.

There is indeed a prevalent opinion that there are only two constitutions. Just as winds, in ordinary speech, are simply described as north or south, and all other winds are treated as deviations from these, so constitutions are also described as democratic or oligarchical. On this basis aristocracy is classified as being a sort of oligarchy, under the heading of oligarchical, and similarly the so-called "constitutional government" [polity] is classified under the heading of democracy—just as westerly winds are classified under the head of northerly, and easterly winds under that of southerly. The situation is much the same, so some people think, with the modes in music. In their case also two modes (the Dorian and the Phrygian) are treated as basic and other arrangements are called by one or other of these two names. But though this is the prevalent view about constitutions in current opinion, we shall do better, and we shall come nearer the truth, if we classify them on a different basis, as has already been suggested. On that basis we shall have one or two constitutions which are properly formed; all the others will be perversions of the best constitution (just as in music we may have perversions of the properly tempered modes); and these perversions will be oligarchical when they are too severe and dominant, and democratic when they are soft and relaxed.

4. It ought not to be assumed, as some people are nowadays in the habit of doing, that democracy can be defined, without any qualification, as a form of constitution in which the greater number are sovereign. Even in oligarchies, and indeed in all constitutions, the majority is sovereign. Similarly, oligarchy cannot be simply defined as a form [of government] in which a few people have sovereignty over the constitution. Suppose that the total population is 1,300, that 1,000 of the 1,300 are wealthy, and that these 1,000 assign no share in office to the remaining 300 poor, although they are men of free birth and like them in other respects. Nobody will say that these people are democratically governed. Or suppose, again, that there are only a few poor men, but that they are stronger than the rich men who form the majority. Nobody would term such a constitution an oligarchy, if no share in official honours is given to the group that is rich. It is better, therefore, to say that democracy exists wherever the free-born are sovereign, and that oligarchy exists wherever the rich are sovereign, though it so happens that the former are many and the latter few—there are many who are free-born, but few who are rich. Otherwise we should have an oligarchy if offices were distributed on the basis of height (as they are said to be in Ethiopia), or on the basis of looks; for the number of tall or good-looking men must always be small.

Yet even this criterion [of poverty and wealth] is not sufficient to distinguish the constitutions in question. We have to remember that the democratic and the oligarchical city both contain a number of parts. We cannot, therefore, apply the term "democracy" to a constitution under which those who are free-born rule a majority who are not freeborn. (A system of this sort once existed at Apollonia, on the Ionian Gulf, and at Thera. In both of these cities honours and offices were reserved for those who were of the best birth—in the sense of being the descendants of the original settlers—though they were only a handful of the whole population.) Nor can we apply the term democracy to a constitution under which the rich are sovereign simply because they are more numerous than the poor. An example of such a constitution formerly existed at Colophon, where before the war with Lydia a majority of the citizens were the owners of large properties. There is a democracy when the free-born and poor control the government, being at the same time a majority; and similarly there is an oligarchy when the rich and better-born control the government, being at the same time a minority.

The fact that there are a number of constitutions, and the cause of that fact, have been established. We must now explain why there are more constitutions than the two just mentioned [i.e. democracy and oligarchy], indicate what they are, and suggest the reasons for their existence. In doing so we may start from the principle which was previously stated, and which we can now take as agreed, that every city consists, not of one, but of many parts.

7. There are still two forms of constitution left, besides democracy and oligarchy. One of these is usually reckoned, and has indeed already been mentioned; as one of the four main forms of constitution, which are counted as being kingship, oligarchy, democracy, and the form called aristocracy. There is, however, a fifth form, which is called by the generic name common to all the forms—for people call it a "constitutional government" [or polity]—but being of rare occurrence it has not been noticed by the writers who attempt to classify the different forms of constitution—in their [accounts of] constitutions they usually limit themselves, like Plato, to an enumeration of only four forms. The name "aristocracy" should properly be applied to the form of constitution which has already been treated in our first part. The only constitution which can with strict justice be called an aristocracy is one where the members are not merely "good" in relation to some standard or other, but are absolutely the "best" [*aristoi*] so far as excellence [of mind and character] is concerned. Only in such a constitution can the good man and the good citizen be absolutely identified; in all others the "good" are only so relatively to the particular constitution. Nevertheless there are some further forms of constitution, which differ both from oligarchies and from the so-called "constitutional government" and are also called aristocracies. This is the case when elections to office are based not only on wealth but also on excellence. This type of constitution differs from both of the forms [just mentioned]; and is called aristocracy. [This usage is just, because] even in cities which do not make the encouragement of excellence a matter of public policy, there may still be found individuals who have a good reputation and are seen as respectable people. Accordingly, a constitution which pays regard to wealth,

goodness, and [the will of] the people, as the Carthaginian does, may be called an aristocratic constitution; and the same may also be said of constitutions such as the Spartan, which pay regard to excellence and to [the will of] the people, and where there is thus a mixture of the two factors, democracy and excellence. There are thus these two forms of aristocracy in addition to the first or best form of that constitution; and there is also a third form presented by those varieties of the so-called "constitutional government" which incline particularly to oligarchy.

8. It remains for us to speak of the so-called "constitutional government" [polity] and of tyranny. Here we are associating "constitutional government" with a perverted constitution, although it is not in itself a perversion, any more than are the forms of aristocracy which we have just mentioned. But, to tell the truth, all these constitutions really fall short of the best form of right constitution, and are therefore to be reckoned among perversions; and we may add that, as has already been mentioned in our first part, the perversions among which they are reckoned are those to which they themselves give rise. It is reasonable to mention tyranny last, because we are engaged in an inquiry into constitutions; and tyranny, of all others, has least the character of a constitution. We have thus explained the reason for the order we propose to follow; and we must now proceed to treat of "constitutional government." Its character will emerge the more clearly now that we have already defined the nature of oligarchy and democracy.

"Constitutional government" may be described, in general terms, as a mixture of oligarchy and democracy; but in common usage the name is confined to those mixtures which incline to democracy, while those which incline more to oligarchy are called aristocracies, the reason being that culture and breeding are more associated with the wealthier classes. Furthermore, the wealthy are generally supposed to possess already the advantages for want of which wrongdoers fall into crime; and this is the reason why they are called "gentlemen" or "notables." Now as aristocracy aims at giving preeminence to the best, people tend to describe oligarchies too as cities governed by gentlemen.

It seems impossible that there should be good government in a city which is ruled by the poorer sort, and not by the best of its citizens; and, conversely, it is equally impossible for a city which is not well governed to be an aristocracy. But good government does not consist in having a good set of laws which are not actually obeyed. We have to distinguish two senses of good government—one which means obedience to such laws as have been enacted and another which means that the laws obeyed have also been well enacted. (Obedience can also be paid to laws which have been enacted badly.) The latter sense admits, in its turn, of two subdivisions: people may render obedience to laws which are the best that are possible for them, or to ones which are absolutely the best.

Aristocracy is thought to consist primarily in the distribution of office according to merit: merit is the criterion of aristocracy, as wealth is the criterion of oligarchy, and free birth of democracy. The principle of the rule of majority-decision is present in all constitutions. Alike in oligarchies, in aristocracies, and

in democracies, the decision of the majority of those who share in the constitution is final and sovereign. In most cities the form of government is called "constitutional government," since the mixture attempted in it seeks only to blend
the rich and the poor, or wealth and free birth, and the rich are regarded by common opinion as holding the position of gentlemen. But in reality there are three
elements which may claim an equal share in the mixed form of constitution: free
birth, wealth, and merit. (So-called "nobility" of birth, which is sometimes reckoned a fourth, is only a corollary of the two latter, and simply consists in inherited wealth and merit.) Obviously, therefore, we ought always to use the term
"constitutional government" for a mixture of only two elements, where these
elements are the rich and the poor; and we ought to confine the name "aristocracy" to a mixture of three, which is really more of an aristocracy than any other
form so called, except the first and true form. We have now shown that there are
other forms of constitution besides monarchy, democracy, and oligarchy; what
the nature of these other forms is; how aristocracies differ from one another, and
"constitutional governments" differ from aristocracy; and, finally, that these are
not far removed from one another.

9. We may now discuss, in continuation of our argument, how what is
called "constitutional government" [polity] comes into existence by the side of
democracy and oligarchy and in what way it ought to be organized. In the
course of that discussion it will also be evident what are the distinguishing
marks of democracy and oligarchy; for we have first to ascertain the difference
between these two forms, and then to form a combination between them by taking, as it were, a token from each. There are three different principles on which
such a combination or mixture may be based. The first is to take and use simultaneously both democratic and oligarchical laws. We may take as an example
those about jury service. In oligarchies the rich are fined if they do not serve on
juries, and the poor receive no pay for serving. In democracies, on the other
hand, the poor are given pay [for jury service] while the rich are not fined [if
they fail to serve on juries]. To follow both of these practices is to adopt a common or middle term between them; and for that reason such a method is characteristic of a "constitutional government," which is a mixture of the two constitutions. This is, accordingly, one of the possible ways of combination. A
second is to take the mean, between the two different systems. Some cities, for
example, require no property qualification at all, or only a very low qualification, for membership of the assembly: others require a high qualification. Here
we cannot use both practices to provide a common term; we have, rather, to take
the mean between the two. The third way is to combine elements from both, and
to mix elements of the oligarchical rule with elements of the democratic. In the
appointment of magistrates, for example, the use of the lot is regarded as democratic, and the use of the vote as oligarchical. Again, it is considered to be democratic that a property qualification should not be required, and oligarchical that
it should be. Here, accordingly, the method appropriate to an aristocracy or a
"constitutional government" [polity] is to take one element from one form of
constitution and another from the other—that is to say, to take from oligarchy

the practice of choosing office-holders by voting, and from democracy the practice of requiring no property qualification.

This is the general method of mixture. The sign that a good mixture of democracy and oligarchy has been achieved is that the same constitution is described both as a democracy and as an oligarchy. Obviously the feelings of those who speak in this way are due to the excellence of the mixture. This happens in the case of the mean because each of the two extremes can be traced within it. The constitution of Sparta is an example. There are many who wish to describe it as a democracy, on the ground that its organization has a number of democratic features. The first such feature concerns the way in which the young are brought up: the children of the rich have the same upbringing as those of the poor, and the type of education they receive is one which the children of the poor could afford. The same policy is followed in the next stage of their lives and when they become adults. No difference is made between the rich and the poor: the provision of food at the common mess is the same for all, and the dress of the rich is such as any of the poor could also provide for themselves. Another such feature is the fact that, of the two most important offices, one is elected by the people and the other is open to them (that is, they elect the Council of Elders and are eligible for the Ephorate). On the other hand, some people describe the Spartan constitution as an oligarchy, on the ground that it has many oligarchical features. For example, office-holders are all appointed by vote, and none by lot, the power of inflicting the penalty of death or banishment rests in the hands of a few people, and there are many other similar features. A properly mixed constitution should look as if it contained both democratic and oligarchical elements—and as if it contained neither. It should owe its stability to its own intrinsic strength, and not to external support; and its intrinsic strength should be derived from the fact, not that a majority are in favour of its continuance (that might well be the case even with a poor constitution), but rather that no section at all in the city would favour a change to a different constitution.

We have now described the way in which a "constitutional government," and what are called aristocracies, ought to be organized.

11. We have now to consider what is the best constitution and the best way of life for the majority of cities and the majority of mankind. In doing so, we shall not employ a standard of excellence above the reach of ordinary people, or a standard of education requiring exceptional natural endowments and equipment, or the standard of a constitution which attains an ideal level. We shall be concerned only with the sort of life which most people are able to share and the sort of constitution which it is possible for most cities to enjoy. The "aristocracies," so called, of which we have just been treating, either lie at one extreme, beyond the reach of most cities, or they approach so closely to what is called "constitutional government" [polity] that the two can be considered as a single form.

The issues we have just raised can all be decided in the light of one body of fundamental principles. If we were right when, in the *Ethics*, we stated that the truly happy life is one of goodness lived in freedom from impediments and that goodness consists in a mean, it follows that the best way of life is one which consists in a mean, and a mean of the kind attainable by each individual. Further, the same criteria should determine the goodness or badness of the city and that of the constitution; for a constitution is the way in which a city lives. In all cities there are three parts: the very rich, the very poor, and the third class which forms the mean between these two. Now, since it is admitted that moderation and the mean are always best it is clear that in the ownership of all gifts of fortune a middle condition will be the best. Those who are in this condition are the most ready to listen to reason. Those who are over-handsome, over-strong, over-noble, or over-wealthy, and, at the opposite extreme, those who are over-poor, over-weak, or utterly ignoble, find it hard to follow the lead of reason. Those in the first class tend more to arrogance and serious offences: those in the second tend too much to criminality and petty offences; and most wrong-doing arises either from arrogance or criminality. [It is a further characteristic of those in the middle that] they are least prone either to refuse office or to seek it, both of which tendencies are dangerous to cities.

It must also be added that those who enjoy too many advantages—strength, wealth, friends, and so forth—are both unwilling to obey and ignorant how to obey. This [defect] appears in them from the first, during childhood and in home-life: nurtured in luxury, they never acquire a habit of obedience, even in school. But those who suffer from a lack of such things are far too mean and poor-spirited. Thus there are those who are ignorant how to rule and only know how to obey, as if they were slaves, and, on the other hand, there are those who are ignorant how to obey any sort of authority and only know how to rule as if they were masters [of slaves]. The result is a city, not of freemen, but only of slaves and masters: a state of envy on the one side and of contempt on the other. Nothing could be further removed from the spirit of friendship or of a political association. An association depends on friendship—after all, people will not even take a journey in common with their enemies. A city aims at being, as far as possible, composed of equals and peers, which is the condition of those in the middle, more than any group. It follows that this kind of city is bound to have the best constitution since it is composed of the elements which, on our view, naturally go to make up a city. The middle classes enjoy a greater security themselves than any other class. They do not, like the poor, desire the goods of others; nor do others desire their possessions, as the poor desire those of the rich, and since they neither plot against others, nor are plotted against themselves, they live free from danger. Phocylides was therefore right when he prayed:

Many things are best for those in the middle;
I want to be at the middle of the city.

It is clear from our argument, first, that the best form of political association is one where power is vested in the middle class, and, secondly, that good government is attainable in those cities where there is a large middle class—large enough, if possible, to be stronger than both of the other classes, but at any rate large enough to be stronger than either of them singly; for in that case its addition to either will suffice to turn the scale, and will prevent either of the opposing extremes from becoming dominant. It is therefore the greatest of blessings for a city that its members should possess a moderate and adequate property. Where some have great possessions, and others have nothing at all, the result is either an extreme democracy or an unmixed oligarchy; or it may even be, as a result of the excesses of both sides, a tyranny. Tyranny grows out of the most immature type of democracy, or out of oligarchy, but much less frequently out of constitutions of the middle order, or those which approximate to them. We shall explain the reason for this later, when we come to treat of the ways in which constitutions change.

Meanwhile, it is clear that the middle type of constitution is best. It is the one type free from faction; where the middle class is large, there is less likelihood of faction and dissension than in any other constitution. Large cities are generally more free from faction just because they have a large middle class. In small cities, on the other hand, it is easy for the whole population to be divided into only two classes; nothing is left in the middle, and all, or almost all, are either poor or rich. Democracies are generally more secure and more permanent than oligarchies because of their middle class. This is more numerous, and has a larger share of [offices and] honours, than it does in oligarchies. Where democracies have no middle class, and the poor are greatly superior in number, trouble ensues, and they are speedily ruined. It must also be considered a proof of its value that the best legislators have come from the middle class. Solon was one, as he makes clear in his poems: Lycurgus was another (after all he was not a king); and the same is true of Charondas and most of the other legislators.

What has just been said also serves to explain why most constitutions are either democratic or oligarchical. The middle class in these cities is often small; and the result is that as happens whenever one class—be it the owners of property or the masses—gains the advantage, it oversteps the mean, and draws the constitution in its own direction so that either a democracy or an oligarchy comes into being. In addition, factious disputes and struggles readily arise between the masses and the rich; and the side, whichever it is, that wins the day, instead of establishing a constitution based on the common interest and the principle of equality, exacts as the prize of victory a greater share in the constitution. It then institutes either a democracy or an oligarchy. Furthermore, those who have gained ascendancy in Greece have paid an exclusive regard to their own types of constitution; one has instituted democracies in the cities [under its control], while the other has set up oligarchies: each has looked to its own advantage, and neither to that of the cities it controlled. These reasons explain why a middle or mixed type of constitution has never been established—or, at the most, has only been established on a few occasions and in a few cities. One man, and one only, of all who have hitherto been in a position of ascendancy, has allowed himself to be persuaded to allow this sort of system to be established. And now it has also become the habit for cities not even to want a system of equality. Instead they seek to dominate or, if beaten, to submit.

It is clear, from these arguments, which is the best constitution, and what are the reasons why it is so and it is easy to see which of the others (given that we distinguish several varieties of democracy and several varieties of oligarchy) should be placed first, which second, and so on in turn, according as their quality is better or worse. The nearest to the best must always be better, and the one farthest removed from the mean must always be worse, unless we are judging on the basis of a particular assumption. I use the words "on the basis of a particular assumption" because it often turns out that, although one sort of constitution may be preferable, there is nothing to prevent another sort from being better suited to certain peoples.

COMMENTS

Aristotle thinks that the choice among the rule of one, of few, and of many is far too simple to work with; it fails to take account of important facts about political life. Here, it is more obvious than usual that these are Aristotle's notes that were not worked into their final form; the passage stops and starts, and there are different attempts to discuss the same problem. However, the unfinished state of this part of the *Politics* enables us to see Aristotle at work and illuminates his approach to a problem.

Although in some places he is tempted by the idea of an ideal ruler, Aristotle does not consider actual monarchy a good political solution. In the conditions of the Greek city-state, there had been political struggle for years been between democracy and oligarchy. Instead of choosing one of these two, Aristotle points out many complicating factors.

For a start, there are many different kinds of democracy and oligarchy. Aristotle takes many different shots at listing them, and he tries to bring out the importance of a number of factors. We shouldn't just speak of "the rule of the many"; a constitution or form of government is defined by the ways in which political office is organized, and since there are many ways of doing so, there are many ways in which a constitution can be democratic or oligarchic. Also important are economic factors: Democracy is the rule of the poor, not just the majority (even if it is generally true that the poor form the majority).

For Aristotle, democracy and oligarchy are most usefully thought of as ideal types that can both been seen as "mixed" in a single actual form of government. Thus the best form of government turns out not to be simply democracy or oligarchy, but a form that combines elements from each. In this section of the *Politics*, Aristotle makes two attempts to characterize such a form of government.

First, he introduces, as the best form of government, "polity" (*politeia*, the word for constitution or form of government), which he thinks of as a "mixture" or combination of democracy and oligarchy, specifying a variety of ways in which the mixture can be understood. Second, he describes a form of government in which power lies with the "middle class." This notion has nothing to do with modern socially defined notions of class; it simply means people who are neither rich nor poor. Aristotle explains how such a state would avoid most causes of civil strife and confrontation. It is obvious that for Aristotle, excellence in a form of government requires stable functioning, not excellence by some theoretical standard.

Is the form of government that results from a mixture of oligarchy and democracy the same as the form of government dominated by the "middle" people? You may find, reading the passage, reasons both for and against identifying those forms of government. Is Aristotle right to think of oligarchy and democracy as extremes? How would he classify modern democracies in which elections are determined by majority vote and stress individuals' rights, which safeguard the position of those in the minority?

POLYBIUS

Polybius of Megalopolis (c. 200–c. 118 B.C.) was a Greek politician in the period when the rising power of Rome was conquering the city-states of Greece. He was among a thousand citizens of the area of Achaea who were deported to Rome in 168, where he stayed for seventeen years. He became friendly with leading Romans and wrote a long history designed to explain to fellow Greeks the course of events that had made Rome a world power in the space of fifty years. Polybius is aware that Greeks had not taken Rome or its culture very seriously and lacked the intellectual framework to make sense of Roman domination. He explains that it is Rome's "mixed" constitution that enabled it to avoid the continuing cycle of political change that exhausted and weakened the Greek city-states and gave it the internal strength to conquer them and other Mediterranean peoples. Polybius is explaining Roman success to other Greeks, but he is also conceptualizing for the unintellectual Romans something that they had not hitherto thought much about.

Polybius' theory of the mixed constitution was important in the ancient world, as well as in the modern period. It influenced the English constitutional idea of checks and balances among different parts of government and the idea of separation of the powers of different functions of government, defended by Montesquieu and the Federalist Papers.

Histories VI, 2
POLYBIUS

In the case of those Greek states which have often risen to greatness and have often experienced a complete change of fortune, it is an easy matter both to

Reprinted by permission of the publishers and the Loeb Classical Library from *Polybius: Histories*, Volume III, translated by W. R. Patton, Cambridge, Mass.: Harvard University Press, 1915.

describe their past and to pronounce as to their future. For there is no difficulty in reporting the known facts, and it is not hard to foretell the future by inference from the past. But about the Roman state it is neither at all easy to explain the present situation owing to the complicated character of the constitution, nor to foretell the future owing to our ignorance of the peculiar features of public and private life at Rome in the past. Particular attention and study are therefore required if one wishes to attain a clear general view of the distinctive qualities of their constitution.

Most of those whose object it has been to instruct us methodically concerning such matters, distinguish three kinds of constitutions, which they call kingship, aristocracy, and democracy. Now we should, I think, be quite justified in asking them to enlighten us as to whether they represent these three to be the sole varieties or rather to be the best; for in either case my opinion is that they are wrong. For it is evident that we must regard as the best constitution a combination of all these three varieties, since we have had proof of this not only theoretically but by actual experience, Lycurgus having been the first to draw up a constitution—that of Sparta—on this principle. Nor on the other hand can we admit that these are the only three varieties; for we have witnessed monarchical and tyrannical governments, which while they differ very widely from kingship, yet bear a certain resemblance to it, this being the reason why monarchs in general falsely assume and use, as far as they can, the regal title. There have also been several oligarchical constitutions which seem to bear some likeness to aristocratic ones, though the divergence is, generally, as wide as possible. The same holds good about democracies. The truth of what I say is evident from the following considerations. It is by no means every monarchy which we can call straight off a kingship, but only that which is voluntarily accepted by the subjects and where they are governed rather by an appeal to their reason than by fear and force. Nor again can we style every oligarchy an aristocracy, but only that where the government is in the hands of a selected body of the justest and wisest men. Similarly that is no true democracy in which the whole crowd of citizens is free to do whatever they wish or purpose, but when, in a community where it is traditional and customary to reverence the gods, to honour our parents, to respect our elders, and to obey the laws, the will of the greater number prevails, this is to be called a democracy. We should therefore assert that there are six kinds of governments, the three above mentioned which are in everyone's mouth and the three which are naturally allied to them, I mean monarchy, oligarchy, and mob-rule. Now the first of these to come into being is monarchy, its growth being natural and unaided; and next arises kingship derived from monarchy by the aid of art and by the correction of defects. Monarchy first changes into its vicious allied form, tyranny; and next, the abolishment of both gives birth to aristocracy. Aristocracy by its very nature degenerates into oligarchy; and when the commons inflamed by anger take vengeance on this government for its unjust rule, democracy comes into being; and in due course the licence and lawlessness of this form of government produces mob-rule to complete the series. The truth of what I have just said will be quite clear to anyone who pays due attention to such beginnings, origins, and changes as are in each case natural. For he alone who has seen how each form naturally arises and develops, will be able to see when, how, and where the growth, perfection, change, and end of each are likely to occur again. And it is to the Roman constitution above all that this method, I think, may be successfully applied, since from the outset its formation and growth have been due to natural causes.

Perhaps this theory of the natural transformations into each other of the different forms of government is more elaborately set forth by Plato and certain other philosophers; but as the arguments are subtle and are stated at great length, they are beyond the reach of all but a few. I therefore will attempt to give a short summary of the theory, as far as I consider it to apply to the actual history of facts and to appeal to the common intelligence of mankind. For if there appear to be certain omissions in my general exposition of it, the detailed discussion which follows will afford the reader ample compensation for any difficulties now left unsolved.

What then are the beginnings I speak of and what is the first origin of political societies? When owing to floods, famines, failure of crops or other such causes there occurs such a destruction of the human race as tradition tells us has more than once happened, and as we must believe will often happen again, all arts and crafts perishing at the same time, then in the course of time, when springing from the survivors as from seeds men have again increased in numbers and just like other animals form herds—it being a matter of course that they too should herd together with those of their kind owing to their natural weakness—it is a necessary consequence that the man who excels in bodily strength and in courage will lead and rule over the rest. We observe and should regard as a most genuine work of nature this very phenomenon in the case of the other animals which act purely by instinct and among whom the strongest are always indisputably the masters—I speak of bulls, boars, cocks, and the like. It is probable then that at the beginning men lived thus, herding together like animals and following the lead of the strongest and bravest, the ruler's strength being here the sole limit to his power and the name we should give his rule being monarchy.

But when in time feelings of sociability and companionship begin to grow in such gatherings of men, then kingship has struck root; and the notions of goodness, justice, and their opposites begin to arise in men. The manner in which these notions come into being is as follows. Men being all naturally inclined to sexual intercourse, and the consequence of this being the birth of children, whenever one of those who have been reared does not on growing up show gratitude to those who reared him or defend them, but on the contrary takes to speaking ill of them or ill treating them, it is evident that he will displease and offend those who have been familiar with his parents and have witnessed the care and pains they spent on attending to and feeding their children. For seeing that men are distinguished from the other animals by possessing the faculty of reason, it is obviously improbable that such a difference of conduct should escape them, as it escapes the other animals: they will notice the thing and be displeased at what is going on, looking to the future and reflecting that they may all meet with the same treatment. Again when a man who has been helped or succoured when in danger by another does not show gratitude to his preserver, but even goes to the length of attempting to do him injury, it is clear that those who become aware of it will naturally be displeased and offended by such conduct, sharing the resentment of their injured neighbour and imagining themselves in the same situation. From all this there arises in everyone a notion of the meaning and theory of duty, which is the beginning and end of justice. Similarly, again, when any man is foremost in defending his fellows from danger, and braves and awaits the onslaught of the most powerful beasts, it is natural that he should receive marks of favour and honour from the people, while the man who acts in the opposite manner will meet with reprobation and dislike. From this again some idea of what is base and what is noble and of what constitutes the difference is likely to arise among the people; and noble conduct will be admired and imitated because it is advantageous, while base conduct will be avoided. Now when the leading and most powerful man among the people always throws the weight of his authority on the side of the notions on such matters which generally prevail, and when in the opinion of his subjects he apportions rewards and penalties according to desert, they yield obedience to him no longer because they fear his force, but rather because their judgement approves him; and they join in maintaining his rule even if he is quite enfeebled by age, defending him with one consent and battling against those who conspire to overthrow his rule. Thus by insensible degrees the monarch becomes a king, ferocity and force having yielded the supremacy to reason.

Thus is formed naturally among men the first notion of goodness and justice, and their opposites; this is the beginning and birth of true kingship. For the people maintain the supreme power not only in the hands of these men themselves, but in those of their descendants, from the conviction that those born from and reared by such men will also have principles like to theirs. And if they ever are displeased with the descendants, they now choose their kings and rulers no longer for their bodily strength and brute courage, but for the excellency of their judgement and reasoning powers, as they have gained experience from actual facts of the difference between the one class of qualities and the other. In old times, then, those who had once been chosen to the royal office continued to hold it until they grew old, fortifying and enclosing fine strongholds with walls and acquiring lands, in the one case for the sake of the security of their subjects and in the other to provide them with abundance of the necessities of life. And while pursuing these aims, they were exempt from all vituperation or jealousy, as neither in their dress nor in their food and drink did they make any great distinction, but lived very much like everyone else, not keeping apart from the people. But when they received the office by hereditary succession and found their safety now provided for, and more than sufficient provision of food, they gave way to their appetites owing to this superabundance, and came to think that the rulers must be distinguished from their subjects by a peculiar dress, that there should be a peculiar luxury and variety in the dressing and serving of their viands, and that they should meet with no denial in the pursuit of their amours, however lawless. These habits having given rise in the one case to envy and offence and in the other to an outburst of hatred and passionate resentment, the kingship changed into a tyranny; the first steps towards its overthrow were taken by the subjects, and conspiracies began to be formed. These conspiracies were not the work of the worst men, but of the noblest, most high-spirited, and most courageous, because such men are least able to brook the insolence of princes. The people now having got leaders, would combine with them against the ruling powers for the reasons I stated above; kingship and monarchy would be utterly abolished, and in their place aristocracy would begin to grow. For the commons, as if bound to pay at once their debt of gratitude to the abolishers of monarchy, would make them their leaders and entrust their destinies to them. At first these chiefs gladly assumed this charge and regarded nothing as of greater importance than the common interest, administering the private and public affairs of the people with paternal solicitude. But here again when children inherited this position of authority from their fathers, having no experience of misfortune and none at all of civil equality and liberty of speech, and having been brought up from the cradle amid the evidences of the power and high position of their fathers, they abandoned themselves some to greed of gain and unscrupulous money-making, others to indulgence in wine and the convivial excess which accompanies it, and others again to the violation of women and the rape of boys; and thus converting the aristocracy into an oligarchy aroused in the people feelings similar to those of which I just spoke, and in consequence met with the same disastrous end as the tyrant. For whenever anyone who has noticed the jealousy and hatred with which they are regarded by the citizens, has the courage to speak or act against the chiefs of the state he has the whole mass of the people ready to back him. Next, when they have either killed or banished the oligarchs, they no longer venture to set a king over them, as they still remember with terror the injustice they suffered from the former ones, nor can they entrust the government with confidence to a select few, with the evidence before them of their recent error in doing so. Thus the only hope still surviving unimpaired is in themselves, and to this they resort, making the state a democracy instead of an oligarchy and assuming the responsibility for the conduct of affairs. Then as long as some of those survive who experienced the evils of oligarchical dominion, they are well pleased with the present form of government, and set a high value on equality and freedom of speech. But when a new generation arises and the democracy falls into the hands of the grandchildren of its founders, they have become so accustomed to freedom and equality that they no longer value them, and begin to aim at pre-eminence; and it is chiefly those of ample fortune who fall into this error. So when they begin to lust for power and cannot attain it through themselves or their own good qualities, they ruin their estates, tempting and corrupting the people in every possible way. And hence when by their foolish thirst for reputation they have created among the masses an appetite for gifts and the habit of receiving them, democracy in its turn is abolished and changes into a rule of force and violence. For the people, having grown accustomed to feed at the expense of others and to depend for their livelihood on the property of others, as soon as they find a leader who is enterprising but is excluded from the honours of office by his penury, institute the rule of violence; and now uniting their forces massacre, banish, and plunder, until they degenerate again into perfect savages and find once more a master and monarch.

Such is the cycle of political revolution, the course appointed by nature in which constitutions change, disappear, and finally return to the point from which they started. Anyone who clearly perceives this may indeed in speaking of the future of any state be wrong in his estimate of the time the process will take, but if his judgement is not tainted by animosity or jealousy, he will very seldom be mistaken as to the stage of growth or decline it has reached, and as to the form into which it will change. And especially in the case of the Roman state will this method enable us to arrive at a knowledge of its formation, growth, and greatest perfection, and likewise of the change for the worse which is sure to follow some day. For, as I said, this state, more than any other, has been formed and has grown naturally, and will undergo a natural decline and change to its contrary. The reader will be able to judge of the truth of this from the subsequent parts of this work.

The three kinds of government that I spoke of above all shared in the control of the Roman state. And such fairness and propriety in all respects was shown in the use of these three elements for drawing up the constitution and in its subsequent administration that it was impossible even for a native to pronounce with certainty whether the whole system was aristocratic, democratic, or monarchical. This was indeed only natural. For if one fixed one's eyes on the power of the consuls, the constitution seemed completely monarchical and royal; if on that of the senate it seemed again to be aristocratic; and when one looked at the power of the masses, it seemed clearly to be a democracy. The parts of the state falling under the control of each element were and with a few modifications still are as follows.

The consuls, previous to leading out their legions, exercise authority in Rome over all public affairs, since all the other magistrates except the tribunes are under them and bound to obey them, and it is they who introduce embassies to the senate. Besides this it is they who consult the senate on matters of urgency, they who carry out in detail the provisions of its decrees. Again as concerns all affairs of state administered by the people it is their duty to take these under their charge, to summon assemblies, to introduce measures, and to preside over the execution of the popular decrees. As for preparation for war and the general conduct of operations in the field, here their power is almost uncontrolled; for they are empowered to make what demands they choose on the allies, to appoint military tribunes, to levy soldiers and select those who are fittest for service. They also have the right of inflicting, when on active service, punishment on anyone under their command; and they are authorized to spend any sum they decide upon from the public funds, being accompanied by a quaestor who faithfully executes their instructions. So that if one looks at this part of the administration alone, one may reasonably pronounce the constitution to be a pure monarchy or kingship. I may remark that any changes in these matters or in others of which I am about to speak that may be made in present or future times do not in any way affect the truth of the views I here state.

To pass to the senate. In the first place it has the control of the treasury, all revenue and expenditure being regulated by it. For with the exception of payments made to the consuls, the quaestors are not allowed to disburse for any particular object without a decree of the senate. And even the item of expenditure which is far heavier and more important than any other—the outlay every five years by the censors on public works, whether constructions or repairs—is under the control of the senate, which makes a grant to the censors for the purpose. Similarly crimes committed in Italy which require a public investigation, such as treason, conspiracy, poisoning, and assassination, are under the jurisdiction of the senate. Also if any private person or community in Italy is in need of arbitration or indeed claims damages or requires succour or protection, the senate attends to all such matters. It also occupies itself with the dispatch of all embassies sent to countries outside of Italy for the purpose either of settling differences, or of offering friendly advice, or indeed of imposing demands, or of receiving submission, or of declaring war; and in like manner with respect to embassies arriving in Rome it decides what reception and what answer should be given to them. All these matters are in the hands of the senate, nor have the people anything whatever to do with them. So that again to one residing in Rome during the absence of the consuls the constitution appears to be entirely aristocratic; and this is the conviction of many Greek states and many of the kings, as the senate manages all business connected with them.

After this we are naturally inclined to ask what part in the constitution is left for the people, considering that the senate controls all the particular matters I mentioned, and, what is most important, manages all matters of revenue and expenditure, and considering that the consuls again have uncontrolled authority as regards armaments and operations in the field. But nevertheless there is a part and a very important part left for the people. For it is the people which alone has the right to confer honours and inflict punishment, the only bonds by which kingdoms and states and in a word human society in general are held together. For where the distinction between these is overlooked or is observed but ill applied, no affairs can be properly administered. How indeed is this possible when good and evil men are held in equal estimation? It is by the people, then, in many cases that offences punishable by a fine are tried when the accused have held the highest office; and they are the only court which may try on capital charges. As regards the latter they have a practice which is praiseworthy and should be mentioned. Their usage allows those on trial for their lives when found guilty liberty to depart openly, thus inflicting voluntary exile on themselves, if even only one of the tribes that pronounce the verdict has not yet voted. Such exiles enjoy safety in the territories of Naples, Praeneste, Tibur, and other *civitates foederatae*. Again it is the people who bestow office on the deserving, the noblest reward of virtue in a state; the people have the power of approving or rejecting laws, and what is most important of all, they deliberate on the question of war and peace. Further in the case of alliances, terms of peace, and treaties, it is the people who ratify all these or the reverse. Thus here again one might plausibly say that the people's share in the government is the greatest, and that the constitution is a democratic one.

Having stated how political power is distributed among the different parts of the state, I will now explain how each of the three parts is enabled, if they wish, to counteract or co-operate with the others. The consul, when he leaves with his army invested with the powers I mentioned, appears indeed to have absolute authority in all matters necessary for carrying out his purpose; but in fact he requires the support of the people and the senate, and is not able to bring his operations to a conclusion without them. For it is obvious that the legions require constant supplies, and without the consent of the senate, neither corn, clothing, nor pay can be provided; so that the commander's plans come to nothing, if the senate chooses to be deliberately negligent and obstructive. It also depends on the senate whether or not a general can carry out completely his conceptions and designs, since it has the right of either superseding him when his year's term of office has expired or of retaining him in command. Again it is in its power to celebrate with pomp and to magnify the successes of a general or on the other hand to obscure and belittle them. For the processions they call triumphs, in which the generals bring the actual spectacle of their achievements before the eyes of their fellow-citizens, cannot be properly organized and sometimes even cannot be held at all, unless the senate consents and provides the requisite funds. As for the people it is most indispensable for the consuls to conciliate them, however far away from home they may be; for, as I said, it is the people which ratifies or annuls terms of peace and treaties, and what is most important, on laying down office the consuls are obliged to account for their actions to the people. So that in no respect is it safe for the consuls to neglect keeping in favour with both the senate and the people.

The senate again, which possesses such great power, is obliged in the first place to pay attention to the commons in public affairs and respect the wishes of the people, and it cannot carry out inquiries into the most grave and important offences against the state, punishable with death, and their correction, unless the *senates consultum* is confirmed by the people. The same is the case in matters which directly affect the senate itself. For if anyone introduces a law meant to deprive the senate of some of its traditional authority, or to abolish the precedence and other distinctions of the senators or even to curtail them of their private fortunes, it is the people alone which has the power of passing or rejecting any such measure. And what is most important is that if a single one of the tribunes interposes, the senate is unable to decide finally about any matter, and cannot even meet and hold sittings; and here it is to be observed that the tribunes are always obliged to act as the people decree and to pay every attention to their wishes. Therefore for all these reasons the senate is afraid of the masses and must pay due attention to the popular will.

Similarly, again, the people must be submissive to the senate and respect its members both in public and in private. Through the whole of Italy a vast number of contracts, which it would not be easy to enumerate, are given out by the censors for the construction and repair of public buildings, and besides this there are many things which are farmed, such as navigable rivers, harbours, gardens, mines, lands, in fact everything that forms part of the Roman dominion. Now all these matters are undertaken by the people, and one may almost say that everyone is interested in these contracts and the work they involve. For certain people are the actual purchasers from the censors of the contracts, others are the partners of these first, others stand surety for them, others pledge their own fortunes to the state for this purpose. Now in all these matters the senate is supreme. It can grant extension of time; it can relieve the contractor if any accident occurs; and if the work proves to be absolutely impossible to carry out it can liberate him from his contract. There are in fact many ways in which the senate can either benefit or injure those who manage public property, as all these matters are referred to it. What is even more important is that the judges in most civil trials, whether public or private, are appointed from its members, where the action involves large interests. So that all citizens being at the mercy of the senate, and looking forward with alarm to the uncertainty of litigation, are very shy of obstructing or resisting its decisions. Similarly everyone is reluctant to oppose the projects of the consuls as all are generally and individually under their authority when in the field.

Such being the power that each part has of hampering the others or co-operating with them, their union is adequate to all emergencies, so that it is impossible to find a better political system than this. For whenever the menace of some common danger from abroad compels them to act in concord and support each other, so great does the strength of the state become, that nothing which is requisite can be neglected, as all are zealously competing in devising means of meeting the need of the hour, nor can any decision arrived at fail to be executed promptly, as all are co-operating both in public and in private to the accomplishment of the task they have set themselves; and consequently this peculiar form of constitution possesses an irresistible power of attaining every object upon which it is resolved. When again they are freed from external menace, and reap the harvest of good fortune and affluence which is the result of their success, and in the enjoyment of this prosperity are corrupted by flattery and idleness and wax insolent and overbearing, as indeed happens often enough, it is then especially that we see the state providing itself a remedy for the evil from which it suffers. For when one part having grown out of proportion to the others aims at supremacy and tends to become too predominant, it is evident that, as for the reasons above given none of the three is absolute, but the purpose of the one can be counterworked and thwarted by the others, none of them will excessively outgrow the others or treat them with contempt. All in fact remains *in statu quo*, on the one hand, because any aggressive impulse is sure to be checked and from the outset each estate stands in dread of being interfered with by the others. . . .

COMMENTS

Polybius' approach is very much that of a politician; he is careful to specify the economic and social factors that are relevant for the functioning of political institutions, and he is interested in the results of different systems. Still, he does have a bold philosophical theory: Political institutions of the Greek form, variants on the rule of one person, few or many, are doomed to rise and fall in a cycle, while the Roman form of "mixed" constitution, within which there are all three types of rule that keep a check on one another, has a chance of escaping this cycle and dominating states that are still stuck in it. Compare Polybius' notion of "mixture" here to the types that Aristotle discusses in the previous reading.

Polybius stresses that the cycle of constitutions is "natural"; it happens inevitably because of the kind of thing these constitutions are, not because of deliberate policy. How, then, can states escape the cycle? We may think that they may do so by coming to understand the process and modifying their institutions to avoid it. Although it would be possible for them to do so in theory, Polybius stresses that the Roman state came into being in an equally "natural" way; the Romans were staunchly traditionalist and unreflective about politics, the last people who could work out a constitution theoretically and then impose it on themselves. What, then, is the crucial difference that enabled the Romans to develop a more successful state than the Greeks? Were the Romans just lucky that their political development turned out the way it did?

Compare Polybius' account of the "mixed" constitution to a description of a modern constitution that relies on separating the powers of different branches so that they form checks and balances on one another. Is Polybius right in finding this a source of strength?

Further Reading

Many collections of texts of ancient philosophy are available, and there is a huge amount of "secondary literature" discussing it. Here I have included only a few books that are accessible to a beginner and will lead you to more specialized discussions if you become interested.

Pre-Socratics

A convenient collection of the fragments of the Pre-Socratic thinkers can be found in *Early Greek Philosophy*, ed. Jonathan Barnes (New York: Penguin, 1987). Texts with more discussion are in Richard McKirahan, *Philosophy before Socrates* (Indianapolis: Hackett, 1994). A more detailed and scholarly treatment can be found in Malcolm Schofield, Geoffrey S. Kirk, and John E. Raven, *The Presocratic Philosophers*, 2nd ed. (New York: Cambridge University Press, 1983). A lengthy but accessible treatment of the main ideas is Jonathan Barnes, *The Presocratic Philosophers* (New York: Routledge, 1979).

Socrates and Plato

All of Plato's dialogues, in good new translations, can be found in Plato, *Complete Works*, ed. John Cooper (Indianapolis: Hackett, 1997). Individual dialogues can be read in recent and inexpensive translations published in the World's Classics series by Oxford University Press, as well as those published by Penguin and by Hackett.

A good introduction to many facets of Plato's thought is *The Cambridge Companion to Plato*, ed. Richard Kraut (New York: Cambridge University Press, 1992), which has an extensive and well-organized bibliography.

The idea that there is a distinct "Socratic" phase to Plato's thinking is defended in Gregory Vlastos, *Socrates, Ironist and Moral Philosopher* (Ithaca, N.Y.: Cornell University Press, 1991), and opposed in Charles H. Kahn, *Plato and the Socratic Dialogue* (New York: Cambridge University Press, 1996).

There are many short introductions to Plato; among the best is C. J. Rowe, *Plato* (Sussex, England: Harvester Press, 1984). Most modern studies are specialized, but a broad survey of Plato's ideas can be found in Ian Crombie, *An Examination of Plato's Doctrines,* 2 vols. (London and New York: Routledge and Kegan Paul, 1962).

Aristotle

Aristotle should be read in the recent revised version of his complete works, *The Complete Works of Aristotle,* ed. Jonathan Barnes, 2 vols. (Princeton, N.J.: Princeton University Press, 1984). Selections can be found in *A New Aristotle Reader,* ed. J. L. Ackrill (Princeton, N.J.: Princeton University Press, 1987), and *Aristotle: Selections,* ed. Terence Irwin and Gail Fine (Indianapolis: Hackett, 1995).

Most work on Aristotle is rather specialized. A good introduction is *The Cambridge Companion to Aristotle,* ed. Jonathan Barnes (New York: Cambridge University Press, 1995). Recent good short introductions to Aristotle's thought are Jonathan Barnes, *Aristotle* (New York: Oxford University Press, 1982), and J. L. Ackrill, *Aristotle the Philosopher* (New York: Oxford University Press, 1981).

Philosophy after Aristotle

The texts for studying Epicureans, Stoics, and Skeptics can be found in Brad Inwood and L. P. Gerson, *Hellenistic Philosophy,* 2nd ed. (Indianapolis: Hackett, 1997), and A. A. Long and D. N. Sedley, *The Hellenistic Philosophers,* 2 vols. (New York: Cambridge University Press, 1987) (volume 1 contains translations of the sources; volume 2 contains the original texts). Good introductions to Hellenistic philosophy are A. A. Long, *Hellenistic Philosophy,* 2nd ed. (London: Duckworth, 1986), and R. Sharples, *Stoics, Epicureans, and Sceptics* (New York: Routledge, 1996). All of these works contain bibliographies that can lead you to further, more specialized reading.

For other movements in later philosophy see John M. Dillon, *The Middle Platonists,* rev. ed. (Ithaca, N.Y.: Cornell University Press, 1996), Richard T. Wallis, *Neoplatonism* (London: Duckworth, 1995), and, on classical Christian philosophy, Christopher Stead, *Philosophy in Christian Antiquity* (New York: Cambridge University Press, 1994).

If you want to pursue ancient philosophy in a way that is centered on issues, rather than philosophers or schools, you will want to read Terence Irwin's *Classical Philosophy* (New York: Oxford University Press, 1999) (in the series of Oxford Readers). Irwin's book is more comprehensive and less introductory than this one.